THE WAKES OF
NORTHAMPTONSHIRE

VIGILA ET ORA

The Wakes of Northamptonshire

A family history

PETER GORDON

**Northamptonshire
County Council**
Libraries and Information Service

Published by Northamptonshire
Libraries and Information Service
27 Guildhall Road, Northampton NN1 1EF

© 1992 Text Copyright Northamptonshire
Libraries and Information Service and Peter Gordon
The author asserts the moral right to be identified
as the author of this work in accordance
with the Copyright, Designs and Patents Act, 1988

ISBN: 0 905391 15 2

Designed by Bernard Crossland

Typeset in Bembo and printed in Great Britain by
Stanley L. Hunt (Printers) Ltd, Midland Road
Rushden, Northamptonshire NN10 9UA

Bound by Woolnough Bookbinding Ltd
Express Works, Church Street, Irthlingborough
Northamptonshire NN9 5SE

Contents

Foreword

OUR FAMILY HAVE RECORDS THAT GO BACK AN unusually long way. We started in Normandy and thence to Lincolnshire and Northamptonshire and spread to other counties, including Cumberland, Yorkshire, Somerset, Suffolk and Essex. Thus the research for this book has necessitated extensive travelling in order to unravel our story.

My grandfather died in 1916 the year in which I was born. I was blessed with a wonderful father who died when I was forty seven. I feared that my children might grow up knowing as little about their grandfather as I knew about mine. So I asked Professor Peter Gordon to record their lives; and that is how this book started – it all grew from that.

The Northamptonshire County Council then asked me if they too might be involved, believing that the book could be of interest not just to the Wakes but to a wider public, particularly in Northamptonshire. Consequently the scope of this book has grown considerably. My thanks go to the staff of the Education and Libraries Department of the County Council for their help in producing this handsome volume.

Finally, I and my family are greatly indebted to Professor Peter Gordon for recording our family's history in such a scholarly and readable way.

Hereward Wake

Sir Hereward Wake, Bart.
Courteenhall
April 1992

Acknowledgments

DURING THE COURSE OF WRITING THIS BOOK, I HAVE received much assistance from a large number of individuals and institutions. I should first of all like to thank the owners of houses with Wake connections for their kindness and hospitality on the occasion of my visits, particularly Mr and Mrs C. Cottrell-Dorner, Rousham House, Oxfordshire; Lady Elton, Clevedon Court, Somerset; Mr and Mrs William Proby, Elton Hall, near Peterborough; Sir Reresby and Lady Sitwell, Renishaw Hall, Derbyshire; and Mr Simon Wingfield Digby, Sherborne Castle, Dorset. The Mother Superior of Lanherne Carmelite Convent, St. Mawgan, Cornwall, readily granted access to view their fine seventeenth-century portrait of Mother Mary Margaret Wake.

Amongst the many people who answered numerous queries and provided much useful information where Mrs Helen Braham, Curator of the Princess Gate Collection, Courtauld Institute Galleries; George Freeston, Blisworth; John Harris, Royal Institute of British Architects; Rieke van Leeuwen, Curator, Mauritshuis, The Hague; Paul Quarrie, Librarian, Eton College; Dr A. A. Stamp, Cottingham, East Yorkshire; Christopher Tongue, Archivist, Northamptonshire Record Office; and Susan Youngs, Department of Medieval and later Antiquities, British Museum. I am grateful to Lord Deedes for his reminiscences of Sir Hereward Wake, thirteenth baronet, and to Jehanne Wake for her help in unravelling the Benson family history. Mrs Elsie Lewis, Joan Wake's former assistant, and Patrick King, previously County Archivist, Northamptonshire Record Office, were able to add much to my knowledge of the life and work of Joan Wake.

The bulk of the remaining Wake family papers are at the Northamptonshire Record Office. During the years when I consulted the documents at Delapre Abbey, my heavy demands were cheerfully coped with by Miss Rachel Watson, County Archivist, and her excellent staff. Leslie Skelton, Secretary of the Northamptonshire Record Society, very kindly allowed me access to the Society's papers. I am also grateful to the national and local record offices where relevant manuscript collections are held. These are listed in full elsewhere in the book. The librarians and staff of the British Library, the Institute of Historical Research and the London Library were most helpful in tracing many obscure references for me.

When the book was in draft, I benefited greatly from the detailed knowledge of Dr

ACKNOWLEDGMENTS

Ken Bascombe, President Waltham Abbey Historical Society, Professor Edmund King, University of Sheffield, and James Collet-White, Senior Records Officer, Bedfordshire County Record Office, all of whom read sections of the book. The late Victor Hatley, with typical generosity, provided much invaluable information relating to Northamptonshire history. The responsibility for the final version, is of course, mine. Maurice Ottman kindly helped me with the translation of Dutch and German texts and Louise Hampton with medieval and other documents.

The task of transforming the manuscript into the finished book has been undertaken with great expertise and efficiency by members of the Northamptonshire County Council Education and Libraries Department. I have enjoyed working with Mrs Verna Taylor, County Librarian, and Eric Wright, Principal Assistant County Librarian, who provided much encouragement since the County Council became involved in the project. Similarly, I am grateful to John Stafford, Senior Assistant County Librarian, for making available his expertise and long experience during the past few years. My sincere thanks, too, to Christopher Phillips, Senior Librarian Resources, for undertaking the day-to-day supervision of the book at its earliest stages and for explaining to me the various technical processes involved in producing a book. I would also like to thank Heather Hammond and Barbara Leigh, Publications Assistants, and my son David Gordon, for reading my text with such care, thus helping to eliminate many errors and inconsistencies. I am pleased, too, to acknowledge the splendid efforts of Bernard Crossland, who has been responsible for designing this book, John Parish, Northamptonshire County Council, Print and Design Centre, for his work on the maps and David Hunt, Stanley L. Hunt (Printers) Ltd., for his expertise and guidance. Pam Golden and Patricia Thomas very efficiently undertook the typing of the first draft, transcribing my difficult handwriting with great skill and patience.

Finally, I wish to thank the many organizations who have provided and given permission to reproduce the colour and black and white illustrations for the book. These are separately acknowledged on page 461.

Introduction

IN 1959, TOWARDS THE END OF HIS LIFE, THE THIRTEENTH baronet Sir Hereward Wake wrote to his sister Joan, the historian, 'We are worth a proper Family History if only because we have carried on for nearly eight centuries in unbroken, undisputed, legitimate male descent from a Norman baron – which I suppose is unique'.[1] Joan Wake had during her long lifetime accumulated masses of material relating to the family and possessed an unrivalled knowledge of its history up to the present day. It was typical of her that she declined her brother's request to undertake the writing of such a history, stating, 'There is no such boring thing in the world as ancestor worship to other people, and I was determined not to become that particular kind of bore'.[2]

It is the present author's view that Miss Wake's modesty on behalf of her family was perhaps misplaced. The intriguing history of the Wakes has over the centuries attracted many writers. One notable member of the family, Archbishop William Wake, in 1694 wrote a manuscript account entitled *A Brief Enquiry into the Antiquity, Honour and Estate of the Name and Family of Wake*, which started with the twelfth century Wakes and continued until his own time.[3] Before this, in the 1620s, Robert Sanderson, a Lincolnshire country clergyman at Boothby Pagnell who became Bishop of Lincoln, began collecting material on the history of families, including the Wakes.[4]

Although we find the eighth baronet, Sir William Wake, over a century later making enquiries to the College of Heralds in 1782 about his ancestors,[5] it was not until Sir Walter Scott began to publish his historical novels in the first three decades of the nineteenth century that there was a revival of interest in the early history of families and their traditions.[6] It is significant that the Wake connection with the Saxon Hereward was first acknowledged when the tenth baronet, Sir Charles, named his fourth son Herwald Craufurd Wake in 1828. The publication of Charles Kingsley's novel *Hereward the Wake* in 1866 led to much wider public interest in the family.

The most ambitious attempt to set down the family's history was that of the twelfth baronet, Sir Herewald Wake. He wrote on 10 December 1883, 'These notes are compiled with a view to completing an autotype MSS, containing a full account of the Wakes from the foundation of their family up to the present date, with the arms of the different families to which they became allied; with illustrations of all places, monuments and other matters of interest, with which the family have been connected;

also an account of the great personages and noble families from whom they have descended or who have descended from them'.[7] Unfortunately, constant ill-health prevented Sir Herewald from undertaking the project. The thirteenth baronet began collecting material for a history of the early Wakes, but this too never materialised.

When I was asked by Sir Hereward Wake, the fourteenth baronet, to write for the family an account of his forebears, it was considered that, with the loss or destruction of papers and documents over the centuries, it would be possible to follow the fortunes of only the later Wakes. However, the existence of records in many national and county archives as well as in private ownership, supplemented by accounts of the Wakes by writers such as Matthew Paris, a monk at St. Albans in the thirteenth century,[8] has enabled me to build up a reasonably clear picture of the lives and activities of successive generations of the family from much earlier times. Although the Wakes have produced many individuals who played an important part in national affairs, such as Joan of Kent, mother of Richard II, an Archbishop of Canterbury, Members of Parliament, an ambassador at Venice and at Paris and several military and naval leaders, the focus of the family's life has been, for much of the time, Northamptonshire, first from about 1200 at Blisworth and from the seventeenth century, the adjoining parish of Courteenhall. London was never an attraction for this essentially 'landed family'; and none entered into trade or commerce.[9] This continuity of residence within the county over such a long period of time, combined with activities on a much wider stage, makes the history of the Wakes a particularly interesting one.

The list of individuals and institutions who kindly assisted me in my enquiries and provided documents and photographs is acknowledged separately. My wife, Tessa, has been closely involved with the book from the very beginning and it would have been impossible to have carried out the project without her help. To her, my sincere thanks. I am also particularly grateful to Mr. John Munro, formerly County Leisure and Libraries Officer, Northamptonshire County Council, for persuading Sir Hereward and myself that the book would be of interest to a wider audience than was originally envisaged. My greatest debt, however, is to Sir Hereward Wake, the fourteenth baronet, who has encouraged me at every stage in the writing and put at my disposal both his own documentary resources as well as his considerable knowledge of the Wake family. The many hours spent at Courteenhall in discussing various aspects of the project were most fruitful. Sir Hereward was reluctant that he personally should figure in the last chapter; but the story of the Wake family would be incomplete without an account of what has happened in the last half century. Finally, I would like to acknowledge the warm hospitality I have received from Sir Hereward and Lady Wake during the last six years which has helped to make the writing of the book a very enjoyable experience.

1
Beginnings:
Hereward the Wake

THE NAME HEREWARD THE WAKE IS FAMILIAR TO MOST people. The story of Hereward, 'the last of the English', appears in many primary school history books and though the events of his life can be recalled by few, he has remained a popular figure in the public memory. A ten-part television serial of Hereward's adventures was shown in 1965 and the name is commemorated in five generations of the Wakes of Courteenhall.

Not surprisingly, the exact details of the historical Hereward are difficult to elucidate. Within a few decades of his death, Hereward's exploits were being recorded and embroidered by chroniclers, a tradition which was carried on into subsequent centuries. Certainly he was the only Saxon whose stories survive in such quantity and detail. We know from Domesday Book, a survey carried out by William the Conqueror, that there was a certain Hereward who held land in Warwickshire and Lincolnshire, including some belonging to Crowland Abbey,[1] close to Bourne where Wakes later became Lords of the Manor.

His parents, according to legend, were Leofric, Earl of Chester and Mercia, and his better known wife, Lady Godiva. A self-willed and rebellious youth, Hereward became involved in serious feuds as well as acts of insubordination towards his parents. Leofric eventually obtained an order from King Edward the Confessor to banish Hereward from the country. At the age of eighteen and accompanied by a single retainer, Hereward travelled widely in Northumberland, Cornwall, Ireland and Flanders.

One twelfth-century chronicler, Thomas of Ely, recorded some of Hereward's subsequent exploits in his *De Gestis Herewardi Saxonis*.[2] In Northumberland, his first stopping place, Hereward was received into the household of a powerful nobleman who kept wild beasts which, at Easter, Whitsuntide and Christmas, were let out to test the strength and courage of youths who were candidates for knighthood. One day a large and fierce Norwegian bear, normally kept chained up in a cell, escaped by accident, killing all who were in its path. As it approached the ladies' apartment, Hereward confronted it and, after a desperate struggle, slayed the beast. This action made him a hero in the eyes of the ladies though he incurred the hatred and envy of his companions. Hereward narrowly escaped a plot to assassinate him and proceeded to Cornwall.

Notes and references begin on page 391

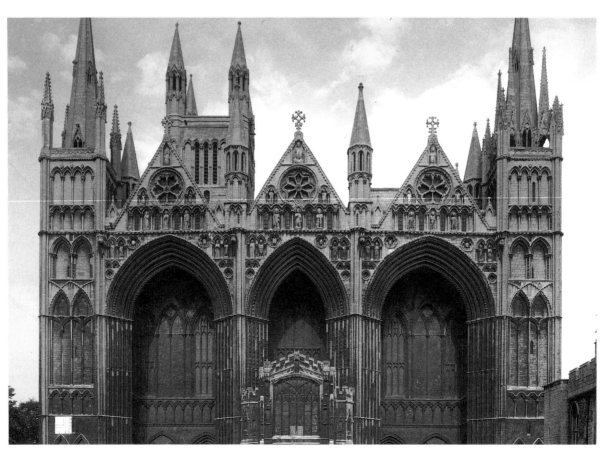

LD1. Extract from the Anglo-Saxon Chronicle for the year 1071, describing the gathering of William the Conqueror's forces at Ely and Hereward the Wake's valiant opposition to them

1. Peterborough Cathedral, west front

There a Cornish chief, Alef, welcomed him to his court. His beautiful daughter had been promised by her father to a tyrannical Cornishman of immense strength and skill in fighting. Hereward taunted the suitor in the presence of the princess. A duel followed in which Hereward was the victor. The dead man's friends called for revenge but Alef protected Hereward by the pretence of throwing him into prison whilst awaiting trial. Then his daughter helped him to escape, with tokens of remembrance, to Ireland and to safety though not without further bloodthirsty adventures first befalling him.

Arriving in Flanders, he was arrested as a spy but when his identity was known, he was received by the Count of Flanders. Hereward happily assisted him in the wars in which he was engaged. It was then that Hereward met Turfrida, a Flemish princess, a scholarly and romantic lady who, in Kingsley's novel, *Hereward the Wake*, immediately fell in love with him and they were soon married.

Much of what the chronicler of the *De Gestis* recounted has no historical basis, but there is stronger evidence for the events which followed. In 1069, some three years after William's invasion of England, Hereward returned from exile. He immediately headed for his father's estates at Bourne in Lincolnshire which had remained unoccupied by the Normans. Here he gathered round him a band of Saxons who would await his signal for further action.

In the spring of 1070, the opportunity presented itself when the Danish fleet, under a treaty signed by William, proceeded to the Humber and the Ouse. According to the *Anglo-Saxon Chronicle*, when a contingent which included Christian the Danish bishop, Earl Osbeorn and the Danish housecarls arrived at Ely 'the English people from all the Fenlands came to them and expected that they were going to conquer all the country'.[3] Hereward, now joined by the Danes, led a force to Peterborough where a despotic Norman abbot, Turold, had displaced the abbot Brand, reputed to be Hereward's uncle. The motley army, called by the chronicler 'Hereward and his gang', landed by boat at Peterborough and set fire to the town. They then burst into the minster, climbed up the great rood and took away the gold ornaments and the gold and silver pastoral staff hidden in the steeple. They also took two golden shrines, nine silver shrines and fifteen great crosses. Turold and his soldiers arrived too late to prevent the force reaching their ships and sailing back to Ely. There, the spoils were divided between them after which the Danes left the country.

Nothing more is heard or recorded of Hereward's whereabouts during the following year, but it is likely that he remained in the Isle of Ely, which formed a natural and safe defensive position. At this time, which was well before the large-scale fenland drainage schemes had been carried out, approaches to the encampment would have been hazardous and difficult to find. The site was also strategically placed for forays against the enemy. Akeman Street, the old Roman road, led directly to Cambridge and another to Huntingdon; at both of these places William had erected castles. Access to the camp itself was from a bridge across a causeway. The island now became a stronghold and rallying point for those opposing Norman rule. Morcar and Siward Bearn, two important English nobles, threw in their lot with Hereward as did many monks who had been dispossessed or disillusioned with the new regime.

William himself was now determined to lead an expedition against the outlaws,

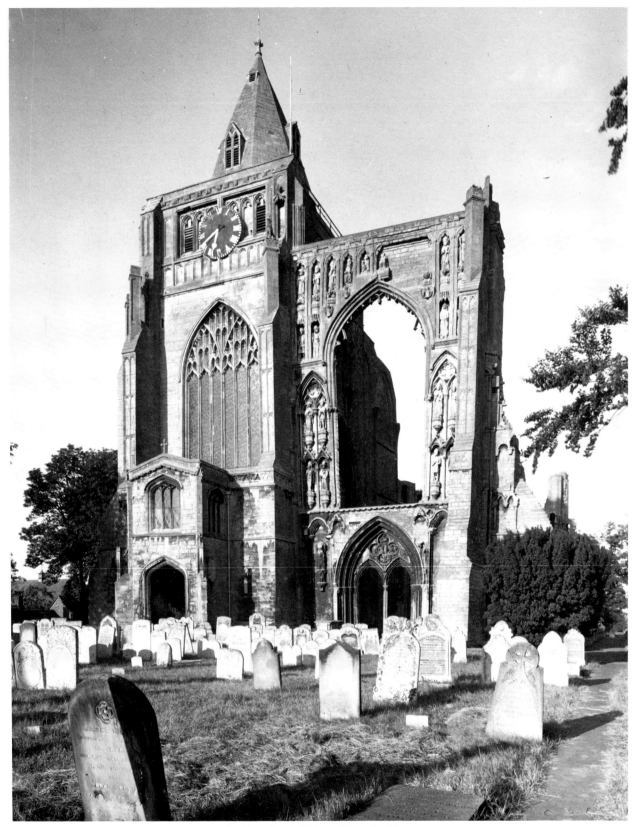

2. Crowland Abbey, Lincolnshire

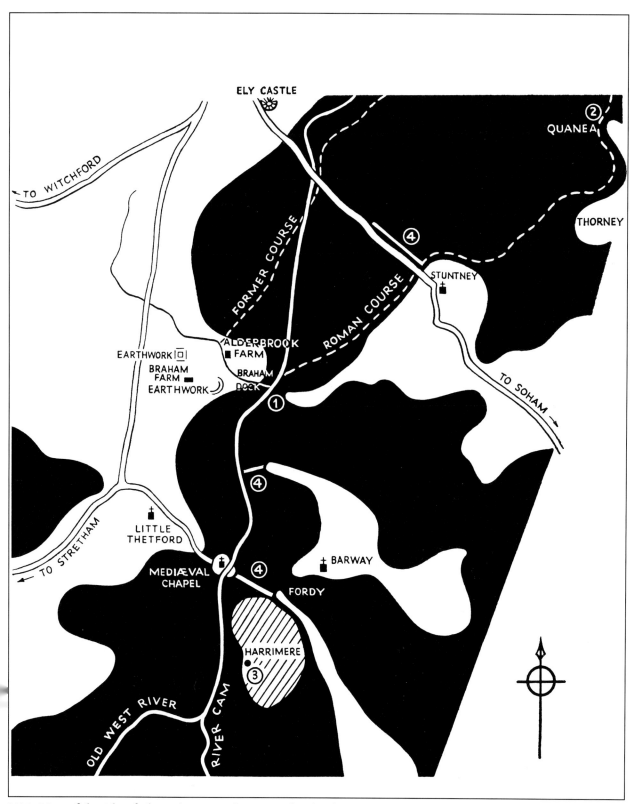

LD2. Map of the Isle of Ely at the time of Hereward. It has been claimed that the earthwork at Braham Farm was Hereward's fort. Eleventh century weapons have been found at (1), similar weapons, pottery and a dam at (2), late Saxon pottery at (3) and a late Bronze Age causeway at (4)

making his base at Cambridge. As rumours of this move reached the island, it was decided to send out a spy to discover the enemy's plans. One of the best-known legends of Hereward attaches to this incident. Disguised as a potter, Hereward took with him his mare Swallow and reached the Norman camp, crying his wares. On the way he had lodged at a house where he heard two women discussing the plans being laid to attack the English. The reeve, on seeing the potter, remarked on his striking likeness to Hereward. One man asked if he knew the outlaw. 'Know him?' replied Hereward, 'Alas! I know him too well. It was but the other day that he robbed me of a cow and four sheep which were all I had in the world, except my mare and these pots, to support myself and two children'.

The cooks then invited Hereward to their quarters and celebrated the potter's appearance by drinking large quantities of wine and ale. As they became more uproarious, the cooks attempted to shave his beard and his head like a monk and make him dance blindfold. In anger, Hereward killed and wounded several of the servants before being shut up in a room. However, he snatched the guard's sword, slew many soldiers, mounted Swallow and escaped from the encampment. He was pursued by a horseman who was dealt with mercifully by Hereward, who took away his sword and sent the Norman back to William with the news of the potter's real identity.

By 1072, the Isle of Ely had held out for more than two years against the invaders and the defenders were becoming weary. William, from his camp at Cambridge, attacked the island by land and water. A bridge was thrown across from the mainland and the soldiers poured in. Charles Kingsley graphically describes one of the assaults:

> And now advanced along the causeway, and along the bridge, a dark column of men, surmounted by glittering steel; knights in complete mail; footmen in leather coats and jerkins; at first orderly enough, each under the banner of his lord: but more and more mingled and crowded, as each hurried forward, eager for his selfish share of the inestimable treasures of Ely. They pushed along the bridge. The mass became more and more crowded; men stumbled over each other, and fell off into the mire and water, calling vainly for help . . . The bridge, strained more and more by its living burden, and by the falling tide, had parted – not at the Ely end, where the sliding of the sow [a structure for protecting men advancing on the walls of a besieged fort] took off the pressure, but at the end nearest the camp. One sideway roll it gave, and then, turning over, engulfed in that foul stream the flower of Norman chivalry; leaving a line – a full quarter of a mile in length – of wretches drowning in the dark water, or, more hideous still, in the bottomless slime of peat and mud.[4]

Despite these calamities, the Normans were successful in capturing the island, though Hereward is supposed to have escaped with six of his companions through the connivance of a friendly fisherman. There are few details surviving of what happened next. Chroniclers told of his daring exploits against the Normans after raising an army of some seven hundred Saxons based at *Bruneswald*, a densely forested area on the borders of Huntingdonshire and Northamptonshire. In one of the skirmishes, Hereward outwitted a party led by Ivo Taillebois, a leading Norman soldier, and Turold, the unpopular abbot of Peterborough. Turold was taken prisoner and only released after a ransom had been paid. One stratagem which the outlaws were said to have used was to turn the shoes of their horses backwards so that any pursuing Normans would take the wrong direction. Hereward also marched against the town of Stamford, which he took by surprise, but magnanimously liberated and pardoned the soldiers captured there.

Accounts differ on subsequent events. One version states that Hereward, tired after many years of adventure, was reconciled with William, pardoned and died in peace. It is also claimed that Hereward joined the King in his campaign following the revolt of the earls in 1072. Another version goes further and tells of Hereward's desertion of his wife, Turfrida and that he married a widow, Elfrida. However, his many enemies had not forgiven him and aware of possible dangers, Hereward ensured that his house at Bourne was heavily guarded. One day his chaplain, Ailward, who was acting as sentinel whilst Hereward was at dinner, fell asleep. A large party of soldiers stormed the house, seized Hereward, who was unarmed, and after a heroic struggle he was killed. Yet another version states that his death occurred in a quarrel with his son-in-law, Hugh de Envermeu.

*   *   *   *   *

Why did the stories of Hereward, both historical and legendary, fascinate so many writers in the following centuries? It has to be remembered that the Norman Conquest was a traumatic experience for the English. Harsh laws were imposed by the Normans, freedom was restricted and any opposition was dealt with ruthlessly. At times such as these, stories of an heroic figure who had outwitted and triumphed over the invaders were especially welcome. As one historian has pointed out, 'The popularity of outlaws and their reputation did not rest, as in the case of their later counterparts, the "gentlemen of the road" like Dick Turpin, upon the mere glamour of courteous thieving. Their stories were popular because they were part of a literature of popular protest. They were not just defying accepted authority, they were fighting against it because it was unjust, and it was this that made them heroes for the common people who were the victims of this same injustice'.[5] This was to be seen in later centuries with the somewhat similar adventures shared by another popular figure, Robin Hood.

Whilst little is known of other Saxon heroes, there is evidence that songs of Hereward's exploits continued to be sung in taverns for many hundreds of years and the stories, with variations, passed from generation to generation. That Hereward was an outlaw was praiseworthy, for this simply meant that he was outside the law of the land because of his defiance of a foreign ruler. In the earlier accounts, Hereward is described as 'the Exile' and it is not until the *Peterborough Chronicle*, which was completed in 1368, that the better-known nomenclature 'Hereward the Wake' is used. It is not difficult to understand why one of the thirteenth century Wakes, Baldwin Wake, whose family held Bourne, considered himself a descendant of Hereward.[6] He had joined with other barons in rebellion against Henry III, taking part in raids and battles throughout the country.

By this time, though, the hardships caused by the Norman Conquest had been ameliorated. Richard I was a popular King, not least because of his prowess as a soldier in the Crusades, and the commingling of Norman and English blood lessened the differences between the two peoples. The deeds of Hereward perhaps lived on in the memories of the common people, but faded as new heroes took his place. Remarkably, it was not until the last century that a great revival of interest in the Hereward story was to take place.

*   *   *   *   *

In 1846, the learned but inaccurate antiquary, Thomas Wright, published two volumes entitled *Essays on Subjects Connected with the Literature, Popular Superstitions and History of England in the Middle Ages*. The second volume contained a long chapter, 'Adventures of Hereward the Saxon',[7] based entirely on the *De Gestis Herewardi Saxonis*. The essay had recently appeared in *Ainsworth's Magazine* and its reappearance in book form was well received. Kingsley greatly admired Wright and later submitted the proofs of his novel to him for historical accuracy:[8]

> My dear Wright,
> Thus does Hereward, the hero of your youth, reappear at last in a guise fitted for a modern drawing-room. To you is due whatever new renown he may win for himself in that new field. You first disinterred him long ago, when scarcely a hand or foot of him was left standing out from beneath dust of ages. You taught me, since then, how to furbish his rusty harness, botch his bursten saddle, and send him forth once more, upon the ghost of his gallant mare. Truly he should feel obliged to you; and though we cannot believe that the last infirmity of noble minds endures beyond the grave, or that any touch of his old vanity still stains the spirit of the mighty Wake; yet we will please ourselves – why should we not? – with the fancy that he is as grateful to you as I am this day.[9]

Kingsley's own fascination with the Hereward story stemmed from the formative years of his life which were spent in the Soke of Peterborough, then part of the shire of Northampton. His father, the Reverend Charles Kingsley, was offered the rectorship of Barnack, near Stamford, in 1823 when the young Charles was five years of age. The large Gothic rectory was to be the family home for the next eight years.[10] As soon as he was able to ride, Charles would accompany his father on shooting expeditions where he became familiar with Northamptonshire and the Lincolnshire Fen country which were close at hand. These journeys made a powerful impression on the imaginative child. Kingsley describes the scenery at the beginning of *Hereward the Wake* thus:

> They have a beauty of their own, these great fens even now, when they are dyked and drained, tilled and fenced – beauty as of the sea, of boundless expanse and freedom. Much more had they that beauty eight hundred years ago, when they were still, for the most part, as God had made them, or rather was making them even then. The low rolling uplands were clothed in primeval forest; oak and ash, beech and elm, with here and there, perhaps, a group of ancient pines,

ragged and decayed, and fast dying out in England even then; though lingering still in the forests of the Scotch highlands.

Between the forests were open wolds, dotted with white sheep and golden gorse; rolling plains of rich though ragged turf, whether cleared by the hand of man or by the wild fires which often swept over the hills . . . Here and there, too, upon the far horizon, rose a tall line of ashen trees, marking some island of firm rich soil. In some of them, as at Ramsey and Crowland, the huge ashes had disappeared before the axes of the monks; and a minster tower rose over the fen, amid orchards, cornfields, pastures, with here and there a tree left standing for shade.[11]

Kingsley's father left Barnack for the balmier climate of Devonshire in 1830 but his son's affection for the region remained. In 1848, Kingsley made an expedition with his friend, F.D. Maurice, to Crowland Abbey and Peterborough which, his wife later stated, gave him the inspiration for the story of Hereward.[12] According to the twelfth baronet, Sir Herewald Wake, Kingsley's interest in the topic was also stimulated by a paper on the subject entitled 'Hereward, the Saxon Patriot', given before the Architectural Society of Lincoln by the Reverend Edward Trollope, MA, FSA, at Bourne on 5 June 1861.[13] In the previous year, Kingsley had become Regius Professor of Modern History at Cambridge University, a post for which many historians considered him ill-equipped. He was a cleric of firm views, though with a genuine social conscience.[14] He was a supporter of Imperialism as was made clear in his inaugural lecture. Kingsley expounded his view of the study of history, namely that 'instead of saying that the history of mankind is the history of the masses, it would be much more true to say, that the history of mankind is the history of its great men'. This view, coupled with his belief as a Christian Socialist that 'God inspires the poor with the desire for liberty, that He helps them to their rights', made the subject of Hereward an attractive one for him.

The novel had a moral message aimed not only at his adult audience but also at youths. 'Hard knocks in good humour, strict rules, fair play and equal justice for high and low, this was the old outlaw spirit, which has descended to their inlawed descendants; and makes, to this day, the life and marrow of an English public school.' The vivid descriptions of the battles in the Fens reflected Kingsley's Muscular Christianity, although this was a phrase which he disliked. On the other hand, the book has many strengths. It deals with the complex character of Hereward, half-savage, half-heroic, and the relationship with his wife, Turfrida, is handled in a sensitive manner. Historically, Kingsley attempted to keep to the known early documents in telling the story. The narrative is lively and we can obtain a good impression of English life at the time of the Conquest. Above all, Kingsley presents us with a rounded picture of Hereward which has not been superseded.

Like Kingsley's previous novel *The Water Babies*, *Hereward the Wake* was published in instalments, in a magazine *Good Words* (1865) and in book form the following year. The romanticism, the lurid narration and the patriotic sentiments expressed appealed to the mid-Victorian reader. Charlotte Yonge, the novelist, made the tale more accessible for children by including it in *Cameos From English History* first published in 1869.[15]

It is not surprising that the Wake family should have found the novel to be of immediate interest. Sir Charles Wake, who succeeded as tenth baronet in 1846, had commissioned a genealogist, Thomas Close of Nottingham, to research into the Wake pedigree; it was printed before Kingsley's novel was written. The family were not acquainted with Kingsley but Sir Charles and his wife Charlotte met the author after the book's publication.[16] Their opinion of it is not recorded.

The twelfth baronet, Sir Herewald, on the other hand, was determined to attempt to trace the origins of the family name. He claimed that original Anglo-Saxon charters which would have been conclusive evidence of the Wake descent were seized and destroyed by Cromwell's troops when they plundered Clevedon Court, Somerset, during the Civil War. Sir Herewald entered into a detailed correspondence with W.W. Skeat, Professor of Anglo-Saxon at Cambridge, who was a great authority on the language. Skeat pointed out that there were no surnames before the Conquest, only Christian names; very few nicknames occur. In any event, as regular surnames are not found before 1200, it would be impossible to trace Hereward's descendants by nickname only. Skeat stated that Wake was a proper name in 1271, but he did not know what 'the Wake' or the Norman 'le Wake' meant exactly. The word *Wake*, Anglo-Saxon *wacu*, means a watching or a funeral feast, like the German *wache*. The epithet would be Anglo-Saxon *wacor*. Skeat concluded, 'I suppose *Wake* is a Norman error for *wacor*, which they would spell *waker*, and then might drop the *r*.' He then added, 'The whole of the story is highly suspicious'.[17]

Sir Herewald refused to accept this verdict, accusing the historian, E.A. Freeman, of dismissing the Wake connection on the grounds of a violent disagreement with Kingsley.[18] Sir Herewald, who had read all the major sources for the Hereward story, both historical and legendary, demonstrated in a detailed memorandum that the historians and genealogists were incorrect and that the Wake line began with Hereward.[19] But there were also other claimants to the descent outside the family. In 1896 there appeared a book by Lieutenant-General T.N. Harward entitled *Hereward the Saxon Patriot: A History of his life and character, with a record of his ancestors and descendants, A.D. 445 to A.D. 1896.* Containing elaborate family trees, Harward claimed that he was the undoubted next of kin now living.[20] Responding to the appearance of a review of Harward's book in a journal, Sir Herewald simply pointed out that a few years previously more than two thousand people had written to the editor of *The Times* claiming that honour. In another letter to Skeat, Sir Herewald mentioned as proof of Saxon ancestry that to the present day the Wakes possessed Saxon features – 'light coloured hair and eyes and *nez retroussé*'. In addition, he noted, 'we seem to have inherited Hereward's spirit as every generation has proved whenever an occasion offered'.[21]

Whilst modern historians and genealogists are agreed on the Norman origins of the Wakes,[22] the legends and such facts as are known about the first Hereward provide a fascinating backcloth to English history and to the Wake family during the next eight hundred years.

2
The Early Wakes:
From Normandy to Northamptonshire

IT IS A REMARKABLE FACT THAT THOUGH, AS WE HAVE seen, there is no known link between the legendary Hereward and the family of Wakes which followed after the Norman Conquest, both are firmly rooted geographically, in the first instance, in Lincolnshire.

The founder of the line was Geoffrey Wac, a Norman, born during the eleventh century and who probably died about 1150. He held land in Guernsey and probably in Contentin, Brittany and was witness to a Bayeux charter early in the reign of King Stephen (1135–54). It may well be through Geoffrey's standing that his first son and heir, Hugh Wac, appeared with Stephen at Stamford in 1142 and, like many subsequent Wakes during the Middle Ages, married well. His bride, Emma, was the daughter of Baldwin fitzGilbert, a son of the great house of Clare and founder of Bourne Abbey in 1138[1] and Deeping Priory in the following year. Baldwin gave the barony of Bourne to them during his lifetime and Hugh held property in other parts of Lincolnshire and in Hertfordshire and Leicestershire, as well as at Thrapston in Northamptonshire. After the Norman Conquest, there were many opportunities for Normans to establish themselves in England. Hugh gained his opportunity as one of the chief lieutenants of Earl Ranulf of Chester.[2] Hugh seems to have managed his estates, both in England and in Normandy efficiently,[3] and accumulated much wealth. He retained his strong links with his native country, founding a Benedictine abbey at Longues, near Bayeux in 1168, four years before his death. However, it is significant that Hugh began a connection with Bourne which is carried on by the family to the present day. Although the lordship of the manor was sold to William Cecil, Lord Burghley, along with Deeping in 1574, the town and district still bear the Wake coat of arms.

The consolidation of the family's position a few miles north of the Northamptonshire border continued with succeeding generations. Hugh's son, Baldwin, the first of the line to use the Anglicized spelling, Wake, died before he was thirty. He had married Agnes de Hommet, daughter of the Constable of Normandy, and increased grants to the religious houses at Bourne and Deeping. Baldwin attended Richard I's coronation at Westminster in 1189 and was one of the hostages for the

See Appendix A – Family Tree I. Notes and References pages 392–394

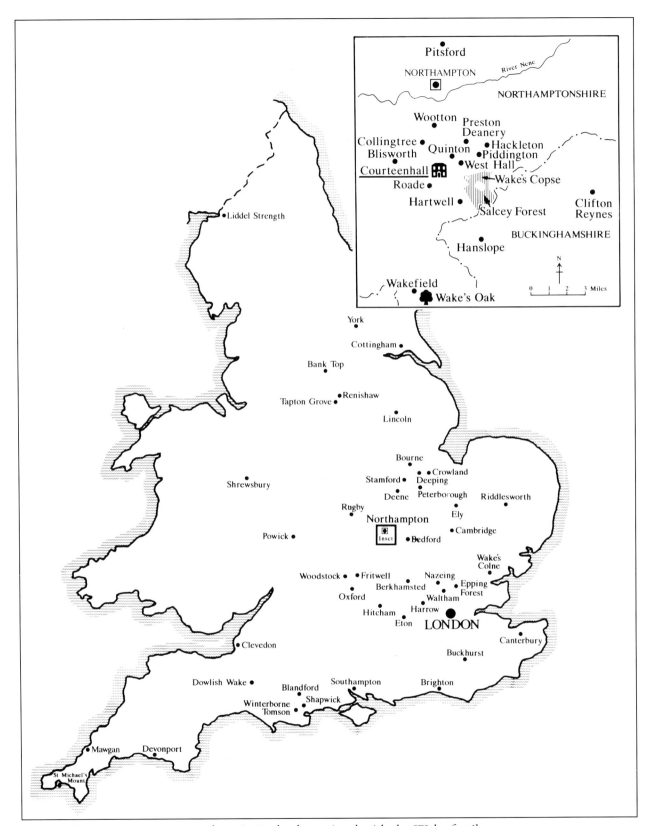

LD3. Places in England associated with the Wake family
Inset The Wakes in Northamptonshire

12

payment of the King's ransom of 150,000 marks in February 1194 after Richard had been taken prisoner by the Duke of Austria. Shortly after his father's death Baldwin had granted the village of Thrapston to his aunt, Margaret, on her marriage to Robert de Vere of Great Addington, which lies four miles south-west of Thrapston.[4]

His son, also called Baldwin Wake of Bourne, died equally young but he had a colourful life. In 1201, together with his grandfather, William de Hommet, Baldwin gave King John a thousand marks for his lands in England and Normandy, promising not to marry without the King's consent. Baldwin came into conflict with the King: his lands were seized in 1206 and he was ordered to leave the realm but he was later restored to favour. He is believed to have been killed by a crossbow bolt at the siege of a castle in Gascony some time before 1213. Baldwin's marriage to Isabel, daughter of William Briwere, was to be significant later in establishing for many generations the Wake connection with Blisworth, a few miles south of Northampton.

Baldwin's son, Hugh, a minor at the time of his father's death (the family was uniquely unfortunate with minorities in the thirteenth and early fourteenth centuries), displayed the Wakes' military prowess to good effect. He served with Henry III, accompanying him to Brittany in April 1230 and after selling off the Wake estates in Guernsey, he set out for the Holy Land, joining the Crusade of Richard of Cornwall, the King's brother, in 1240.[5] Travelling with Simon de Montfort, Hugh made his way through Lombardy and Apulia, boarding a ship at Brindisi, and landing at Acre in October. Unfortunately, within two years he had died,[6] possibly from one of the many diseases which had caused havoc amongst the Christian armies, and was buried in the Church of the Holy Sepulchre at Jerusalem. Hugh was the first bearer of the Wake arms, which consist of or, two bars gules, with three roundels gules in the chief. More land was accumulated during his short lifetime. In 1233, he inherited the estates of his uncle, William Briwere, at Chesterfield, Derbyshire,[7] an estate at Clifton Reynes, Buckinghamshire, known as Wakes Manor[8] and elsewhere. His marriage to Joan, daughter of Nicholas de Stuteville of Liddel in Cumberland brought further wealth. After her sister's death, she was sole heir to the Liddel barony and the family territory extended as far as Yorkshire.[9]

Liddel Strength, which now became a Wake property, has been called 'the most remarkable defensive earthwork in Cumberland'. The castle itself was a fortified medieval private house, consisting of a motte, on which stood a tower measuring not more than 25 feet each side, a large inner bailey and an even larger outer bailey. The inner bailey was surrounded by an earth rampart 35 feet high, with a large ditch facing south whilst to the north, there are sheer cliffs, some 160 feet in height, overlooking the River Liddel.[10] The castle had originally been occupied by the Scots, as King Stephen had given the district to King David I of Scotland in 1136 as a reward for supporting his claim to the English throne. In 1217, Henry III demanded the surrender of these lands and Liddel was once more an English fortress. In 1242, when the King of Scotland renounced all claim to Cumberland, it became *de jure* as well as *de facto* a part of England.[11]

A good description of Liddel is to be found in an inquisition of 18 March 1281, which contains some curious unexplained terms:

3. Liddel Strength, Cumberland, motte and ditch

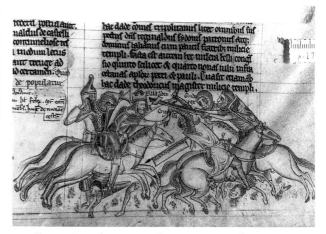

4. Seal of Haltemprice Priory, East Yorkshire, 1332. Obverse: a representation of the Priory with two roof banners bearing the arms of Thomas Wake. On the right is his shield and on the left a shield possibly of the Stutevilles of Liddel. Reverse: a building beneath which the Prior kneels between St. Peter and St. Paul, with five canons at prayer beneath. On the extreme left is the founder, Thomas Wake, and on the extreme right his wife, Blanche. Above each of them is a banner of Wake, and his shield at the foot of the seal

5. Illustration from Matthew Paris's *Chronica Majora* showing the defeat of the Crusaders by Saladin at the Battle of Hattin and the capture of the relic of the True Cross, 3 July 1187

There is at Lydel the site of a castle containing these domiciles, namely, a wooden hall with two solars and cellars, a chapel, a kitchen, a byre, a grange, and a wooden granary, which threaten ruin; but might now be repaired for 5 marks: not extended, as they need more yearly keeping up than they can be let for. There are 65^1/$_2$ acres and one rood of land in demesne, by the perch of eighteen feet, rendering yearly 32 skeps and 12^1/$_2$ wyndells of oat meal, namely each one half a skep, each skep worth, one year with another, 6s.8d. Note that each skep contains 16 windells, and sixteen windells make the quarter of a lond and a half. Total £10 18s 6d. There are 2^1/$_2$ acres of meadow in demesne, the acres worth 10d. and the half acre 12d.[12]

Liddel continued to be a Wake stronghold until the middle of the fourteenth century, the last of the Liddel Wakes, Thomas, building the first stone tower there.

Joan de Stuteville outlived her husband and married Hugh Bigod, Chief Justiciar of England, who predeceased her. There were two sons of her marriage to Hugh, namely Baldwin and Hugh. Like his father, Baldwin was a warrior, though he used his energies in some dangerous causes. He joined with the rebellious barons against Henry III at the Battle of Northampton on 5 April 1264; before the battle there had been a siege of the town where the townspeople fought alongside the rebels. Baldwin was captured and his lands in Lincolnshire were given in custody to Hugh Bigod, his stepfather, during his imprisonment in Nottingham Castle.[13] The next two years saw further action. After his release he was twice more taken prisoner in 1265, at Kenilworth and at Evesham, escaped from Brunesfield Castle and joined the younger Simon de Montfort, becoming one of the barons who ravaged the country. It was at this point that Blisworth became part of the Wake estates. The manor had belonged since 1199 to William Briwere, whose daughter Isabel, as we have seen, had married a Wake; on William's death in 1227, the property passed to his son, William, who died five years later and then to his widow, Joan. On her death without issue in 1265 Blisworth was inherited by Baldwin.[14]

He was twice married, first, to Ela, daughter of William de Beauchamp, Baron of Bedford, and secondly, to Hawise, daughter of Robert de Quency, youngest brother of the second Earl of Winchester. We last hear of him in May 1276 paying homage to Edward I and fighting in his service in Wales. Baldwin died in 1281 at the age of forty one. After Baldwin's death, the King ordered the delivery of four oaks to Hawise from Salcey Forest, a royal medieval hunting preserve, which Edward had given to Baldwin for building his hall at Stevington, Bedfordshire. At the same time, the King took Baldwin's stud of horses on account of debts. Hawise brought into the family the manor of Colne Quency, Essex, which has since been known as Wakes Colne.[15]

There were no sons of the first marriage but two from the second, John and Hugh, who settled at Winterbourne Stoke, Wiltshire. John was made a ward of King Edward I during his minority and later served with the King in Gascony and in Scotland. To commemorate his service to the King in the Scottish wars, the Wake shield and heraldic glass were placed, amongst those of other nobles in the early fourteenth century, in the great nave of York Minster, where they can be seen today.[16] He was summoned to

Parliament as a baron by writs from 24 June 1295 to 29 December 1299, and was now known as Lord Wake of Liddel in Cumberland.

Although the family lived mainly in the north-western part of England, the Wakes kept a close watch on their interests elsewhere. This is shown in a charter of 1294 which concerned the distribution of fines levied in a local court at Deeping and it laid down the respective rights of the Lords Wake and Thorney Abbey, of which Deeping was a dependency. John Wake allowed the Priory to continue with the custom which had grown up in the previous 150 years of receiving fines for minor offences committed by the Priory's tenants, but 'saving to ourselves punishments of life and limb and corporal sentences.'

John's death at the age of thirty two in 1300 meant that his heir, Thomas the second Lord Wake, succeeded him when he was three years old. Like many of his contemporaries, Thomas steered a delicate path between retaining the King's favour and seizing opportunities for self-advancement. He supported Queen Isabella and Mortimer in their rebellion against Edward II in 1326. Something of a showman, Thomas publicly declared 'that as far as he was concerned the old King should never again rule'. In January 1327 in London at a meeting to confirm Edward III as King, he raised his arms and shook his fists, asking theatrically whether the people would wish for this change.[17] He was forced to flee the country when his brother-in-law, the Earl of Kent, was arrested and executed in 1330 (see Chapter 3), but he was restored to favour, together with his lands, later the same year. Of all the Wakes up to this time, Thomas received most royal appointments, though he constantly had trouble with his finances.[18] He was Keeper of the Tower of London, 1326–8, Keeper of the Channel Islands, 1331–3, and an ambassador who treated with the King of France to consider the possibility of a Crusade to the Holy Land. In April 1340 he was one of the Council formed to assist Edward, Duke of Cornwall, during Edward III's long absence. He was also summoned to Parliament as a baron from 20 November 1317 to 20 November 1348.

From his youth Thomas assumed control of his estates. He involved himself in local affairs, as at Cottingham, in East Yorkshire, which he had inherited through his grandmother. He was concerned in the rebuilding of Cottingham church from 1317, received a charter for a weekly market and an annual fair two years later. In 1322 he founded an Augustinian priory there, bringing some canons from Bourne, and in 1327 Thomas was given a licence to fortify his manor house; this was built on the site of his forebears' castle, the mound of which is still visible.[19] He also raised troops there to fight the Scots. (When a dispute arose in 1324 between himself and the prior of Spalding, Lincolnshire, concerning the Fen between Deeping and Spalding, Thomas gathered a company of armed men and rode to Spalding, wounding many people there.)[20]

Thomas's stronghold at Liddel became increasingly threatened following the outbreak of war with Scotland in 1296 and which continued intermittently until the second half of the fourteenth century. After withstanding an earlier siege, the castle was captured by King David II in 1346. The defence was staunchly conducted by Sir Walter Selby and his garrison of 200. On the fourth night of the siege the Scots filled up the

6. Funeral stone of Blanche Wake, wife of Thomas, the second Lord Wake, 1380. It was rediscovered during demolition in Stamford in 1968.

The inscription in full reads:

Vous que ceste mesoun entrez
pur blanche femme al seignur Wake priez
file al counte de lancastre Henri
as quex dieu face vraye merci

[All you who enter this house pray for Blanche wife of Lord Wake daughter of Earl of Lancaster on whom God have true mercy]

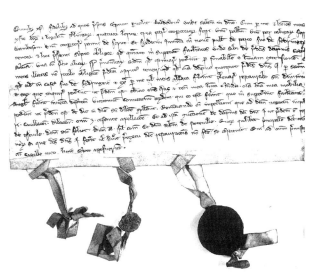

8. Deed of 1266 stating 'Baldwin Wake owes John de Balliol 100 marks'

7. List of tenants holding land belonging to Peterborough Abbey, 13th–14th century forming part of *The Chronicle of Peterborough Abbey* from its foundation to 1338-9, partly compiled by Walter de Whittlesey, a monk. 'Baldwin Wake holds land in Deeping and other places in Lincolnshire and Northamptonshire'

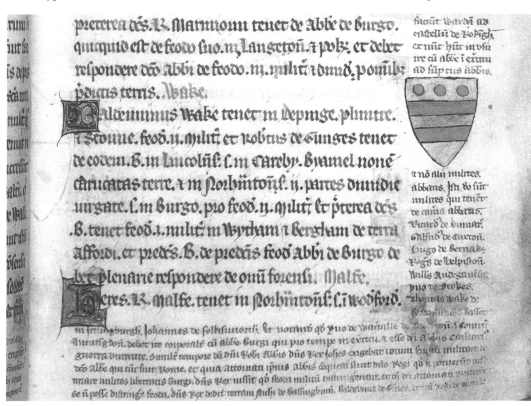

ditch, attacked at daybreak and overpowered the soldiers. By the rules of chivalry, Sir Walter could have been honourably treated as a prisoner of war; but vexed by the delay caused by the defenders, the Scots seized Sir Walter's two sons and strangled them in his presence. He himself was then beheaded in chains under the eyes of King David.

Thomas, the second Lord Wake, had married Blanche, daughter of Henry, Earl of Lancaster, but when he died in 1349, there were no children. Upon the death of John of Gaunt's first wife, Blanche of Lancaster, in 1369, Blanche Wake was put in charge of their only surviving son, Henry, later to be Henry IV. He was then three years old. Blanche, who was his great-aunt, was paid a hundred marks or £66 13s. 4d. by John of Gaunt for looking after Henry and his servants.[21] She outlived her husband by thirty years and at her request was buried in the church of the Friars Minor at Stamford in 1380.[22] In this way, the Liddel branch of the Wakes came to an end after a little more than a century. Thomas's brother, John, predeceased him and his only sister, Margaret Wake, inherited. It was her daughter, Joan, who became wife of Edward, the Black Prince.

The arrival of the Wakes in Northamptonshire at Blisworth in the sixth decade of the thirteenth century heralded a new chapter in the family's history. It has been mentioned earlier that after the death of Baldwin Wake in 1281, Blisworth became the property of his widow, Hawise. It then passed to her second son, Hugh, who in turn enfeoffed his uncle, Sir Hugh Wake of Deeping. Little is known of his life, except that as knight of the shire, he represented the county of Northampton in seven Parliaments between 1299 and 1313.[23] He received a pardon from Edward II in the latter year as a follower of Thomas, Earl of Lancaster, after the death of Piers Gaveston, the King's favourite.[24] Hugh died in 1315.

*   *   *   *   *

It may be of interest to note that the Wake coat of arms lapsed with the last baron and that Sir Hugh was granted a similar coat, or on argent field instead of or; some later members of the family used a rouge field with bars argent. It was not until 1621 that the original coat with or field was readopted by Sir Baldwin Wake, the first baronet.[25]

Coats of arms date from about the middle of the twelfth century. The earliest ones were mostly very simple, being painted fittings on shields. Crests were used on the top of helmets long before coats of arms were authorized by the monarch. Much controversy and speculation surrounds the origins and adoption of the Wake Knot as a crest. It may be described as a cordon of four continuous Stafford Knots. There appears to be a link between the two: Joan of Kent's grandson, Sir Thomas Holand, third Earl of Kent, married Joan, daughter of the second Earl of Stafford. The latter was the first Stafford to use a modified version of the Wake Knot. It was the opinion of a former Bluemantle Pursuivant of Arms that the Wake Knot is a badge rather than a crest and that the crest should be a lion statant sable ducally gorged or.[26] In the British Museum's Collection of Seals (No.14206), there is a seal showing a shield of arms with two bars and in chief three roundels, crest on helmet and short mantling, a lion statant with extended queue. This belonged to Thomas Wake V of Blisworth, of whom more hereafter, and is dated 1429. In the *Heralds' Visitation of Northamptonshire* in 1564, there is a Wake pedigree showing the usual arms and over the top a Wake Knot but without a wreath underneath it; all the other coats of arms and crests in the book have such a wreath.[27] The only place in the records of the College of Arms where the knot is given as a crest rather than a badge is in the *Visitation of Wiltshire* in 1677. This happened possibly because reference was made to the 1564 Northamptonshire Visitation and it was assumed that the wreath had been omitted by mistake. Whatever the speculation and hypotheses which may be put forward, the origins are very difficult to trace. Since early times, the family have been proud to use the Wake Knot as its crest.

*   *   *   *   *

Sir Hugh's manor house at Blisworth, where successive Wakes lived for over two centuries, has long disappeared. All that is known is that it lay to the north-west of the existing parish church; according to Bridges, the eighteenth century Northamptonshire historian, there was a park and a warren.[28] After Sir Hugh's death, he was succeeded by his son, Thomas, the first of six successive Wakes who bore this name. He was among the knights of the county of Northampton that were returned in Chancery in 1343, the same year as he was appointed Chief Falconer to the King, and he was Sheriff of the county, 1329–30 and 1335–6. By his marriage to Elizabeth Cransley he inherited the Manor of Cransley, which lies immediately south-east of Kettering. Sir Hugh was a distinguished soldier, being among those who chose 200 archers to go to France in 1345. He fought with the Black Prince at Crécy and probably died during the siege of Calais in 1346.

Thomas, as Sheriff, was the chief officer of the Crown in the county at a very interesting time. The justices in eyre, (itinerant judges who rode the counties), were given powers by the king to try a whole range of law cases and to review local administration. The justices made a circuit round the country every seven years. By the beginning of the fourteenth century, it had ceased to operate on a regular basis: in 1329, Edward III was determined to revive it as a regular form of judicial administration. Two commissions were arranged, one in Nottinghamshire and the other in Northamptonshire. The last eyre of the county had been in 1285 and a detailed review of events spanning the forty five years had to be undertaken. The eyre of Northampton lasted from November 1329 to June 1330. It was held in Northampton Castle, in the great hall and other buildings there, which were especially repaired for the occasion.[29] A few days before proceedings began, the incumbent Sheriff was removed and Thomas Wake, who had never served in the office before, was appointed.

The work was very onerous. Whilst they were in session, the justices held court six days a week, resting on Sunday, but with recessions for holy days and festivals. After completing their business at Northampton in June, the justices immediately moved on to Bedfordshire. The range of cases which were heard was enormous. We read of a murder at Haselbech on 27 July 1328 and of Thomas le Corour who broke into the Earl of Lancaster's pound at Higham Ferrers on 14 May 1329 and stole a steer and two cows.[30] The details of the eyre were carefully recorded by the law reporters who were present. One man who was arraigned for felony refused all three juries which were offered to him. As a result, he was condemned to suffer the *peine forte et dure* in this form. He was to be stripped of all his clothing except the linen, placed in a clean-swept house and loaded with as many irons as could be placed on him. He was to have a piece of bread on one day and the next day a drink of whatever stagnant water was found nearby. This was to continue until he died.[31]

All of the criminals were remanded in prison in the custody of Thomas Wake, who was responsible for making the necessary arrangements arising from the sentences. Besides sitting in judgment on cases of murder, theft and riot, Thomas was also involved in civil matters, concerning for example, debts and disputes over inheritance.[32]

Sir Thomas II, his son, led a less eventful life. He married Alice, daughter of Sir John Patishall[33] and had one son and four daughters. He was summoned to Parliament as a baron in 1341. Exactly twenty years later, it was decreed by Act of Parliament that every county in England should appoint a Commission of the Peace, consisting of leading men 'to restrain the offendors, rioters, and all other barators and to pursue, arrest, take and chastise them according to their trespass or offence, and cause them to be imprisoned and duly punished according to the law and customs of the realm'. Thomas was one of the eleven Justices of the Peace to be appointed to the first Commission of the Peace for Northamptonshire.[34]

Sir Thomas III died four years after his father, in 1383, leaving a wife Maude, and a son, Thomas IV, to succeed. Like his son and grandson, Thomas was an esquire, though he was appointed Sheriff of Northamptonshire in 1413 and 1418. His wife, Margaret, was sister to Sir John Philpot, a leading London citizen, who led the opposition to John of Gaunt and assisted Richard II during the Peasants' Revolt.

Thomas V, a Gentleman of the Privy Chamber, sometimes described in pedigrees as the 'Great Wake', inherited in 1425. By his marriage to Agnes, daughter of Thomas Lovell of Clevedon in Somerset, he became possessed of the manor of Clevedon in 1432. He was now a great landowner. Besides the Lincolnshire estates, Thomas held the manors of Blisworth, Collingtree and Milton Malsor in Northamptonshire, Crawley in Buckinghamshire, Bromham and Cardington in Bedfordshire, and in right of his wife, Clevedon and Milton Clevedon in Somerset with property at Yatton and Wanstrow, as well as land in Kent. He was very active in county affairs, being Sheriff of Northamptonshire in 1434, 1446 and 1450, Commissioner for the Peace of Northamptonshire, 1439–43 and 1452–6, for Somerset, 1449–57 and for Kesteven, 1456–8; he was also called to attend the Winchester Parliament of 1449.

Thomas VI was twenty three on his father's death in 1458. He was Sheriff of Northamptonshire in 1461 and 1463, and married twice. The name of his first wife is unknown, but the second was Elizabeth Beauchamp, daughter of Thomas Beauchamp, Earl of Warwick; she was some twenty years older than her husband. By his first wife, Thomas had three sons and a daughter, the eldest son Roger succeeding him in 1476, at one of the most turbulent moments in English history.

*   *   *   *   *

The Wars of the Roses, a civil war between the Yorkists and the Lancastrians, had been raging since three years after Roger's birth in 1452. Battles between the rival factions were bitterly fought, including that at Northampton on 10 July 1460, where the Yorkists defeated the Royal army. The bloody battle lasted for only half an hour; Henry

CP1. Illustration by Monro S Orr for the 1910 children's edition of Kingsley's *Hereward the Wake*

CP3. The tomb of Roger Wake and his wife Elizabeth in Blisworth Church, 1503

CP4. The Wake coat of arms and knot as drawn by the College of Arms, 1989

VIGILA·ET·ORA

CP2. Shield in York Minster of Lord Thomas Wake of Liddel Castle, Cumberland, fourteenth century. The arms are also depicted in the stained glass window above

VI was taken prisoner and eleven years later murdered.[35] Matters came to a head with the death of Edward IV in April 1483. Richard, Duke of York, who was born at Fotheringhay Castle, now saw his opportunity to claim the throne. His nephews, the twelve year old Edward V and his brother Richard, the main obstacles to his succession, were put to death in the Tower under still unexplained circumstances.[36] On 6 July 1483, he was crowned Richard III. The following year was an uneasy one, with rumours of an invasion from France where Henry Tudor, the true heir to the House of Lancaster, had been in exile since 1471. Henry landed at Milford Haven in South Wales on 7 August 1485 and fifteen days later the final battle took place near Market Bosworth. Richard was slain, his naked body being taken on a pack horse to Leicester for burial. With the victory at Bosworth Field, Henry, now Henry VII, began the Tudor dynasty. But revenge was sought against those who had supported Richard. The consequences for the Wakes were to be serious.

Few details can be discovered of Roger's life. We know that he founded a free school at Blisworth and was Sheriff of Northamptonshire, 1483–4. He married Elizabeth, daughter of William Catesby of Ashby St. Ledgers, who survived him and married Sir John Grey, fourth son of the Marquess of Dorset. Roger had been a follower of Richard and fought at Bosworth. As a result, he was imprisoned and forfeited his manors and lands in 1485: these were restored to him by Act of Parliament in 1487. Roger was more fortunate than his father-in-law. Catesby was a close adviser of Richard III, being given the post of Chancellor of the Exchequer in 1483 and Speaker of Richard's only Parliament in the following year. He fought at Bosworth where he was captured and beheaded at Leicester three days later, 25 August 1485.[37] The treasonable rhyme pinned up on the door of St. Paul's Cathedral during Richard's reign contains a reference to Catesby as well as others who advised the King:

> The Rat, the Cat and Lovell our Dog
> Rule all England under a Hog

(The Rat was Sir Richard Ratcliffe, the Cat William Catesby, Lovell our Dog was Francis Viscount Lovell and the Hog, Richard III).

In his will dated 12 March 1503, Roger gave land at Crawley and Chicheley in Buckinghamshire in order to endow a priest to say prayers for him, for Elizabeth and for his ancestors, in the Lady Chapel of Blisworth Church.

The fine table tomb of freestone commemorating Roger and his wife has survived the centuries and was restored in 1988 to its original position. So far as it is known, there are no earlier Wake memorials. On the Purbeck marble top are brass figures of the couple together with their ten children. Roger is bareheaded, with long hair, and wears plain plate armour with an apron of mail. A long sword hangs from his left side. Elizabeth is dressed in a tight-bodiced gown with an ornamental girdle round her waist, fur cuffs and pedimental cap with a veil on her head. The seven boys wear short, loose gowns and their shoes are visible. The three girls have very long hair and wear gowns similar to that of their mother. The marginal inscription, which is partly mutilated, around the figures reads:

9. Blisworth Church by George Clark(e) of Scaldwell, c.1835

10. Brasses of Roger and Elizabeth Wake, Blisworth Church, 1503

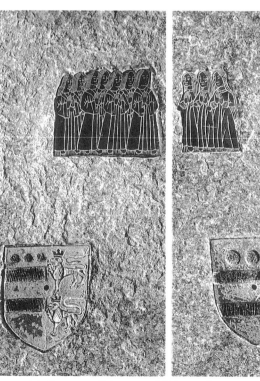

11. Brasses of the ten children of Roger and Elizabeth Wake

> Here lyeth Roger Wake Esquyer lord of Blysworthe in the counte of [Northampton and Elizabeth] his [wife] which Roger decessyed the XVI day of Marche the yere of our Lord God MCCCCCIII on whose soule ihs have mercy.[38]

On the sides of the tomb, there are three shields in ornamental surrounds with three Wake Knots in between. One of the shields is different from the others with Wake impaling three chevrons, de Clare. The significance of the inclusion of this shield is not obvious. Was Roger possibly proudly recalling his earliest ancestor, Emma de Clare, who married Hugh Wac?

*   *   *   *   *

The Wake fortunes in Northamptonshire now declined. Roger's son, Thomas, who married Isabel Sapcoates of Burley, Rutland, hardly improved matters. Shortly after his father's death, Thomas, 'by reason of a certain trespass he had done', was sent to the Tower and his life was in peril. His mother, Elizabeth, who continued to live at Blisworth after her second marriage, pleaded for him with Edmund Dudley, who with Sir Richard Empsom, acted as a sub-committee of the Privy Council and wielded great power. They were notorious for indicting guiltless persons and extorting large fines as a condition of discontinuing proceedings. Dudley heard her petition and passed her on to Empsom, who incidentally was born at Towcester and held extensive estates in the county. By means of bribery, Thomas was released from captivity and received a general pardon, but there are indications that he was thriftless. He had sold Collingtree by 1515; eight years later, he disposed of Blisworth to Sir Richard Knightley of Fawsley, Northamptonshire thus ending the Wake association with that place. His grandson, another Thomas, sold the Wakes' manors of Market Deeping and Bourne to William Cecil, Lord Burghley, in 1574.

Because of Thomas' disgrace, the position of chief member of the family fell to his younger brother, Richard Wake of Hartwell, as he is called in the 1564 *Visitation of Northamptonshire*, though he also held the manors of Clevedon and Wanstrow. He married first Dorothy, daughter of Sir John Dyve of Bromham, Bedfordshire and secondly, Margaret, daughter of Thomas Grey, Marquess of Dorset, the niece of his stepfather. Richard and his two wives were buried at Roade near Blisworth. By Dorothy, he had no fewer than eighteen children, twelve sons and six daughters, none of whom were distinguished. Indeed, the youngest son, Francis, was reported in December 1564 to be among the 'capital thieves apprehended' for robberies and felonies in West Yorkshire.[39]

The Wakes now had their principal residence in Northamptonshire at Piddington. John, heir to Richard Hartwell's estate, from 1558 is described as of Piddington, Salcey Forest and Clevedon. He was the first of a succession of Wakes to hold the post of Lieutenant of Salcey Forest during the sixteenth and seventeenth centuries.[40] John was Lieutenant to William Parr, the Marquess of Northampton, Master of Game in Salcey Forest in 1564 and as a perquisite received one 'booty' tree for each of the four walks, forty loads of lopped wood and one acre of underwood each year.[41] In 1571 the year before he died he was paid £4 salary as Lieutenant. At the same time, he complained that the 'livings' of the keepers under him were too small – they received £2 8s. per annum – necessitating them taking other employment in addition to their main post.[42] Both he and his wife, Elizabeth Gorges, were buried in Piddington Church, as were his heirs. Of the five sons and five daughters, a number had interesting careers. Two sons, Arthur and William, became Masters of St. John's Hospital, Northampton, whilst Magdalen married Richard Ouseley of Courteenhall. More details of these and their descendants will be found in later chapters.

On John's death in 1572, he was succeeded by his eldest son who bore the same name. One of the most remarkable facts of the latter's life was that he lived until 1621, when he was eighty years of age, a considerable achievement in Elizabethan times. He lived at Salcey Lawn in the middle of Salcey Forest[43] and was employed by the Earl of Leicester as a surveyor of Whittlewood and Salcey Forests. John contributed £25 to the defence of the country at the time of the Armada and was a Justice of the Peace. In 1615 he petitioned for a supplementary allowance for hay for the deer. In previous years, he had bought hay worth £10 for winter, as 'none grows in Salcey Forest', but the extreme weather that winter cost him £20 a month. A warrant was granted for the extra amount.[44]

We are fortunate that the details have survived, in the Privy Council Register at the Public Record Office, of an interesting incident in his life. At the Michaelmas Quarter Sessions in 1592, the justices of the county met at Northampton Castle; they included amongst their number Sir Edward Montagu, Sir John Spencer of Althorp, John Wake and Sir George Fermor of Easton Neston. Apparently, Fermor had brought with him a servant, George Beekly, whilst Wake was accompanied by a nephew, Robert Osborne, who was to appear before the magistrates for some unknown offence at the Sessions. Osborne was attacked by Beekly when approaching the Castle, following which John Wake spoke heated words to Fermor. Later, as the justices were dining together, a fresh quarrel broke out and Wake and Fermor, though both described as 'gentlemen of good credit and account', actually fell to blows at the dinner table.

As a result, the two offenders were bound over to keep the peace; the matter was reported to the Privy Council and an inquiry was held by the justices. The Privy Council urged the two men to effect a reconciliation at the next Assizes. This failed and Wake and Fermor appeared before the Council in March 1593. They were told to shake hands 'and to be good friends hereafter' which they did, and resumed their offices as Justices of the Peace once more.[45]

John's wife was Margaret, daughter of Robert Goodwin of Portbury, Somerset. They had one son and two daughters, Mary and Sybil; to the latter, John left in his will a legacy of £40 'wch. is to much'. The son, Baldwin, was to start the line of Wake baronets which continues to the present day.

*   *   *   *   *

From the time of the arrival of Hugh Wac at Bourne to the Elizabethan Wakes mentioned at the end of this chapter is almost 450 years. The boundary between the counties of Lincolnshire and Northamptonshire, formed by the River Welland, presents the only geographical barrier and the early Wakes would have been familiar with the area where the family eventually settled. With the ending of the Liddel Strength branch, Blisworth became their main base for the next three and a half centuries. Between the time of Sir Hugh's settlement there in the second half of the thirteenth century to that of the first baronet, Sir Baldwin, there had been eleven generations of Northamptonshire squires. For the most part, the Wakes were content to tend their estates and become involved in aspects of county administration and law and order. Some held royal appointments, though political events following the Tudor succession had dramatic consequences for Roger and his successors. In several generations, too, a younger Wake went into the Church. William Wake was Rector of Fotheringhay, 1322–38, Richard Wake was Rector of Blisworth, 1462–75 and John Wake was Rector of Woburn, Bedfordshire, 1491–3.

Among the prudent marriages contracted are the names of Cransley, Catesby, Dyve, Gorges, Patishall, Philpot, Pigot, Lovell and Sapcotes, what J.H. Round, the historian, called 'armorial families', several of whom added their considerable dowries to the Wake possessions. But with the decline in their fortunes from the beginning of the sixteenth century, the Wakes looked more to their Somerset estates, whilst remaining in Northamptonshire at Piddington, Salcey Forest and Hartwell. The process by which Courteenhall eventually became the family home is a complex one and will be described in a subsequent chapter.

3

Joan,
The Fair Maid of Kent

THERE CAN BE FEW WOMEN IN THE MIDDLE AGES WHOSE
lives were as colourful as that of one of the most notable Wakes, Joan, known as the Fair
Maid of Kent. Her story contains all the elements which we associate with that
turbulent period – violence, bloodshed and intrigue, as well as romance and chivalry.

Joan was born in 1328, probably in Gascony, and was a Plantagenet of royal descent.
She was the third of four children; Margaret, an elder sister, Edmund, a year older than
Joan and who died at five, herself, and John, born after the death of his father in 1330,[1]
but who died without issue aged twenty two. Her father, Edmund of Woodstock, was
the youngest son of Edward I by his second wife Margaret. He was half brother of
Edward II though some seventeen years younger. In 1321 Edmund was created Earl of
Kent and some few years later he married Margaret, daughter of John, Lord Wake of
Liddel. She was the widow of Sir John Comyn of Badenock who was killed at the Battle
of Bannockburn in 1314. Margaret was only sixteen when she married for a second
time. Edmund loyally supported his half-brother, the King, against the rebellious
barons. He was made Constable of Dover Castle and Warden of the Cinque Ports and
later took part in the war in Scotland. In 1324, Edmund was sent to France to safeguard
the King's interests in Gascony. Queen Isabella of France, Edward II's wife, who had
been harshly treated by her husband, left England for her native country to negotiate
over the war which had broken out between the two countries. There she formed an
alliance with Roger Mortimer, one of the great Marcher lords. Mortimer, an
unscrupulous and ambitious adventurer, had defied the King with his army. He was
defeated by Edward in 1322 and sentenced to perpetual imprisonment, but within two
years he had escaped to France from the Tower of London. Now Isabella's lover,
Mortimer, planned with her an invasion of England with the aim of overthrowing her
husband.

Edmund joined the plotters and landed in Suffolk with Isabella and Mortimer in
September 1326. The King fled to Wales but was taken prisoner in November. In
January 1327 he was declared deposed by Parliament and his fourteen year old son
succeeded him as Edward III. For the next four years, Mortimer virtually ruled the
country. Edmund was a member of the Council appointed to govern for the young King

See Appendix A – Family Tree II. Notes and References pages 394, 395

Edward and received grants of lands and castles which were confirmed by Parliament. Meanwhile, Edward II had been moved from place to place and in September 1327, in the greatest secrecy, he was brutally murdered at Berkeley Castle.

The growing influence of Isabella and Mortimer was now openly opposed by Edmund; but the latter's presence constituted a threat to the couple's ultimate ambitions, and it was important that he should be dealt with. A plot was hatched by Mortimer and the Queen in order to achieve this. Through their spies and agents, they spread information that Edward II was still alive and that he was imprisoned in Corfe Castle. Mortimer contrived to send, under an apparent cloak of secrecy, two men who assured Edmund that there were many people willing to join him in a plan to release King Edward. Convinced of the truth of this information, Edmund visited Pope John XXII at Avignon and consulted with him about the steps which he should take to release his half-brother. The Pope ordered him to do his utmost to obtain the monarch's release; thus, on his return to England, Edmund set about his task. He obtained, amongst others, the support of the Archbishop of York and the Bishop of London. He also went to Corfe and sent a friar to the castle to make enquiries. The governor, who was one of Mortimer's supporters, pretended to show the King to the friar who in turn gave the news to Edmund. The latter now visited the governor himself and, though not allowed to see the prisoner, left an incriminating letter which he had written to his half-brother. The governor sent it on to Mortimer and Edmund's fate was sealed.

On 11 March 1330 he was brought before Parliament at Winchester and charged with treason. Two days later he was arrested and confessed to writing many letters and making inflammatory speeches. Dressed only in a shirt with a rope around his neck, Edmund pleaded for mercy. His two ecclesiastical co-plotters were pardoned but Mortimer and the Queen were determined to destroy their dangerous prisoner. Edmund was condemned to death after a hurried trial.

Fearing that there might be an attempt to release Edmund, Mortimer ordered that the execution should take place without delay. However, on the appointed day, 19 March, no one could be found who was willing to carry out the order. For the whole of the day, Edmund was kept waiting in suspense until a condemned criminal from the Marshalsea, whose own life would be spared if he consented to be the executioner, volunteered for the grim task. The sentence was carried out outside the gates of Winchester Castle in the evening.[2] His body was later removed to Westminster Abbey for burial. Edmund's death, at the age of twenty nine, was widely criticized though he was unpopular in his lifetime because of his ruthlessness and opportunism.

*   *   *   *   *

Before the execution had taken place, Margaret and her children were removed from Arundel to Salisbury Castle into the custody of the Sheriff of Wiltshire; Joan was barely two at the time. However, the downfall and execution of Mortimer eight months later considerably changed the situation. On her petition to Parliament in December 1330, Margaret was allowed to have her dower, and her husband's goods were restored to his executors in February of the following year. The young Queen Philippa adopted Joan, and Edward III, who was Margaret's nephew, treated her kindly. It is possible that

Emma. Alienora. Margareta. Alienora. Margareta. Isabella. Philippa. obtulit unū pannum aureum preciosum. Domina Johanna principissa magnis oblationibz sepius martirem honorauit. inter quas nobile monile aureū ei dedit. 7 p caritate conuentui centum solidos assignauit.

12. Joan, the Fair Maid of Kent, 1328-85

13. The Battle of Crécy, 1346, from Froissart's *Chronicles*

14. The Black Prince (1330-76) arriving at Bordeaux after the Battle of Poitiers, 1356

Margaret may have taken her other children to Deeping Priory, where she had long-standing family connections.

Little is known of Joan's childhood. Later, according to a contemporary French chronicler, Froissart, she grew up to be *en son temps la plus belle de tout la roiaulme d'Engleterre et la plus amoureuse* ('in her time the most beautiful and attractive woman in all the Kingdom of England'). Her great beauty attracted many suitors; at the age of eleven or even earlier, Joan was drawn to a former squire of her father and an outstanding warrior, Sir Thomas Holand, and they lived together as man and wife.[3]

Holand was some eight years older than Joan[4] and wore a distinctive white silk patch over one eye, which he vowed to retain until he had carried out some heroic deed in France. He accompanied Edward III on his invasion of France in 1346 and showed great gallantry at the siege of Caen by saving the lives of the two French commanders, the Counts of Eu and Tancarville, who were isolated on the city's battlements. Later that year, on 28 August 1346, Holand fought in the Black Prince's division at Crécy and after the battle helped in the gruesome work of identifying the dead.

In 1341, Joan, to the surprise of many of her contemporaries, married a younger man, William Montagu, later second Earl of Salisbury who had taken advantage of Holand's absence abroad. Holand, who was steward to Salisbury, on his return to England began proceedings to have the marriage nullified. He petitioned Pope Clement VI and the matter was investigated at great length by Cardinal Adhemar. On 13 November 1349, Clement pronounced in Holand's favour and the marriage with Salisbury was declared void. The path was now open for Joan and Holand to marry. Subsequently there were three sons of the marriage, Thomas, born 1351, who became Earl of Kent and was a notable soldier, Edmund, born in 1352 and John, born in 1353 and later Earl of Huntingdon and Duke of Exeter.

Holand's high standing with his monarch was marked in a memorable way. King Edward, harking back to the days of Arthur and his knights, wished to recreate the pomp and ceremony of that age. The means by which this was accomplished was the founding of the Order of the Garter.

Recent research favours another explanation for its establishment. A ball was held at Calais to celebrate the fall of the town at which Joan and the King, who was in love with her, were present. As she was dancing, Joan dropped her garter and Edward stopped and bound it round his own knee. He rebuked the jests of bystanders with the words which became the motto of the Order, *Honi soi qui mal y pense.*[5]

On St. George's Day, 1348, a year's celebration reached its climax at Windsor with the inauguration of the Brotherhood of the Blue Garter of St. George, the highest honour in the land. Membership was (and still is) restricted to twenty six members, Knight Companions, with the monarch, as Sovereign of the Order, and the Prince of Wales as *ex-officio* members. At the first ceremony, the Black Prince led one of the two cohorts of twelve knights, many of whom had fought alongside him in France. One of these was Thomas Holand. The wives and daughters of the Knights were also later admitted as Dames of the Order. Wearing a scarlet mantle covered with garters in blue taffeta, Joan became the third woman member of the Order in 1378.

Holand's military career abroad continued to flourish. He was appointed Lieutenant of Brittany in 1354 and Governor of the Channel Islands in 1356, and, jointly with Philip of Navarre, Lieutenant and Captain-General of all the English possessions in France and Normandy. In this last post, he was charged with supervising the withdrawal of English troops from Normandy, Anjou and Maine. Many of the commanders, however, refused to give up their strongholds and often jeered at him from the battlements.[6] Thomas's work abroad was recognized in 1357 when the King created him Lord Holand. In the following year, Joan briefly joined her husband in France, creating a great impression at Vannes, Creuilly and St. Sauveur. But the exhausting task with which Holand was entrusted proved too much and he died in Rouen on 28 December 1360; he was buried at the Grey Friars Church in Stamford.

* * * * *

Joan, now a widow of thirty two with three children, was still famed for her beauty and a further marriage seemed likely. Besides being granted Holand's estates by the King, she had earlier, in 1352, inherited from her brother John, who died childless, the titles of the Countess of Kent, Baroness Woodstock and Baroness Wake, together with the large possessions belonging to these baronies. In addition to the properties which she had inherited from her father, Edmund of Woodstock, and also from her mother, she now possessed the greater part of the estates which the elder branch of the Wakes had accumulated in seven generations of alliances with the fitzGilberts, de Humets, de Bruyères, de Stutevilles, de Quinceys and the Plantagenets of Lancaster. She had, in fact, become the wealthiest heiress in the Kingdom. It was from her assumption of the title of the Countess of Kent that she became known as the Fair Maid of Kent, but there is no contemporary evidence to show that she was known by this soubriquet during her lifetime. Joan's great beauty was enhanced by the splendour of her clothes. She had a love of fineries and she possessed hundreds of dresses, many of them of the most costly fabrics. These were complemented by jewelled belts, furs (she is reputed to have introduced the custom of decorating bodices with ermine) and silks and she wore the rarest jewels.[7]

  After Holand's death, Joan was at Waltham and it was there that King Edward III's eldest son, Edward, Prince of Wales, later known as the Black Prince, came to offer his condolences. Various explanations have been put forward to account for this appellation and none of them is conclusive. There is no support for the story that he wore black armour and it was not until nearly two hundred years after his death that the nickname was first used in Leland's history, written in 1540, and taken up by Shakespeare a few years later.

  Edward was outstandingly popular with his fellow countrymen throughout his life and even his enemies acknowledged his noble spirit and fairness. As a soldier he was fearless and a fine leader but these qualities were matched with gentleness and courteousness. Froissart described him as 'the flower of chivalry of all the world'. His religious feelings ran deep and were reflected in the message to his troops after the victory at Poitiers in 1356: 'This is the work of God, not mine: we should thank Him and pray to Him with all our heart that He may give us His grace and pardon us this victory'.

  Edward was born at Woodstock, Oxfordshire on 15 June 1330 and shortly after

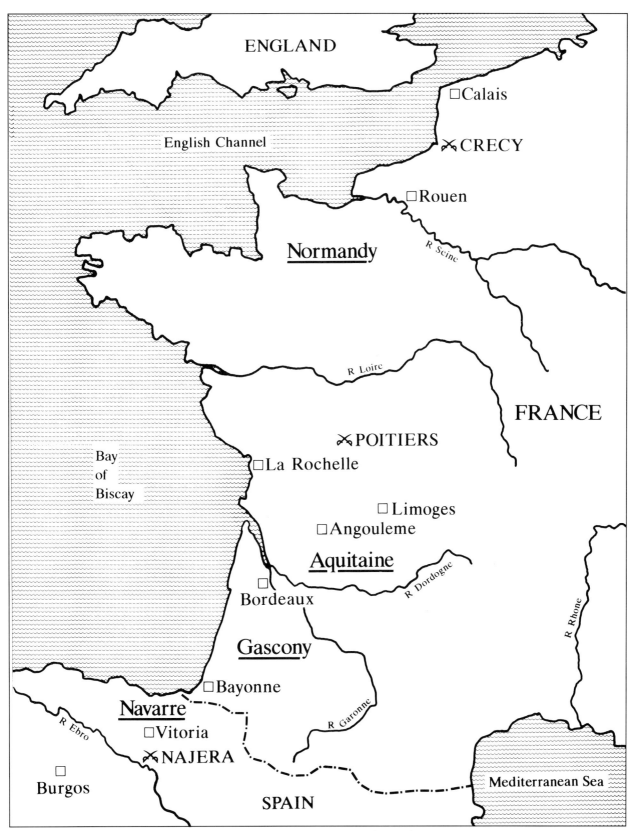

LD4. France and Spain at the time of the Black Prince

31

being invested by his father with the Duchy of Cornwall was appointed Guardian of the Realm during Edward III's expedition to Antwerp to support his claim to the throne of France. The Black Prince was then only seven years of age. The so-called 'Hundred Years War' (1337 to 1453) which involved intermittent conflict between England and France, followed the occupation of English possessions in Normandy by Philip VI of France. These wars were to dominate the whole of the Black Prince's life. At the age of sixteen he laid the foundations of his military reputation by a display of bravery and leadership at the battle of Crécy which took place on 26 August 1346. The story has been told many times of how, at one point in the engagement, the smaller English force who were pursuing the enemy were charged in the flank, and the whole of the first line, which involved the Prince of Wales, became engaged in a desperate fight. The Earl of Warwick sent a message to King Edward asking for assistance. 'Let the boy win his spurs', was the reply. The Prince rallied his troops and led the attack against the French; he was joined by his father with the last English reserves. The enemy finally broke and retired in panic. Amongst those killed on the French side was the blind King of Bohemia. In honour of a gallant foe, the Prince of Wales adopted his motto and badge *Ich dien* (I serve) and the three ostrich feathers.

Edward's greatest triumph in the French campaigns was achieved at Poitiers on 19 September 1356. Once more the English were greatly outnumbered by the French King, John II, who was determined to destroy his enemy. The Black Prince, employing skilful manoeuvres, defeated the French and inflicted heavy casualties. Amongst the 2,000 nobles and knights taken prisoner was King John. Six months later, the Prince returned to England with his principal captives and made a triumphal entry into the City of London with John at his side. The event was cleverly stage-managed: the streets were decorated, the populace rapturously greeted their hero and King Edward received his son amidst great acclaim at Westminster Abbey. The King was determined now to complete the conquest of France. In 1359, he assembled an army of 100,000 and marched on Rheims, himself leading one of the two divisions of which the army was composed, the Prince leading the other. The French, however, declined battle and the campaign developed into a series of sieges which continued into the following year. In 1360, the Treaty of Brétigny brought the war with France to a temporary halt and the Prince was able to turn his attention to more domestic matters.

*   *   *   *   *

It was shortly after Edward's return that Thomas Holand, Joan's husband, had died. At the age of thirty one, the Prince was still unmarried[8] and his father, with an eye to the political advantages which might follow, settled upon Marguerite of Flanders, the young widow of the Duke of Burgundy, as a suitable wife for his son. But this plan did not take account of the Prince's own wishes; he had fallen deeply in love with Joan.

The young couple were by no means strangers. They were second cousins and the Prince was already a godfather to two of Joan's sons. Even earlier, as a child, Joan, as we have seen, was taken into the care of Queen Philippa, the Prince's mother, at Woodstock after her own father's execution. She would have been well acquainted with Edward during her stay there.[9]

There exists a fourteenth century French account of the wooing of Joan, the *Chronique des Quatres Premiers Valois*, which, whilst largely a literary *tour de force*, affords some insight into Joan's personality. The chronicler records how, after Holand's death, many nobles approached the Prince to speak on their behalf to Joan. One of them, Sir Bernard Brocas, who had fought alongside the Prince at Poitiers, urged Edward to arrange a match with the Countess on his behalf. According to the chronicler, the Prince agreed to do so. When Edward put this proposal to Joan, she refused to listen to Brocas's suit, maintaining that she would never marry again. Then, to quote from the chronicle:

> She showed herself a lady of great subtilty and wisdom. For the Prince was enchanted with her and said to her, 'Ah, my dear cousin, is it the case that you refuse to marry any of my friends in spite of your great beauty? Although you and I are of the same lineage, there is no lady under heaven that I hold so dear as you.' Thereon the Prince became greatly enamoured of the Countess and the Countess commenced to weep like a subtle and far-seeing woman. And then the Prince began to comfort her and kiss her passionately, grievously distressed at her tears, and said to her, 'I have spoken to you on behalf of one of the most chivalrous Knights of England and one of the most honourable of men.' Madame the Countess replied in tears to the Prince, 'Ah, Sir, before God do you not talk to me thus. For I have given myself to the most chivalrous Knight under heaven, and for love of him it is, that before God I will never marry again for as long as I live. For it is impossible that I should have to my husband and my love for him parts me from all men: it is my intention never to marry'. The Prince was extremely curious to know who was the most chivalrous Knight in the world, and pressed the Countess to tell him. But the Countess the more she saw him aflame, the more she begged him to make no further enquiry and said to him. 'Before God, my very dear Lord, by His agony, by the sweet Virgin Mother, suffer it to be so'. To make a long story short, the Prince told her that if she did not tell him who was the most chivalrous Knight in the world, he would make him his deadly enemy. Then the Countess said to him, 'My dear and indomitable lord it is you, and for love of you that I will never have any other Knight by my side'. The Prince, greatly amazed by the love of the Countess, replied, 'My Lady, I also vow to God that as long as you live never will I have any other woman save you to my wife'.

On hearing of the proposed marriage, the King was displeased but did not take any action to forbid it. Early in the summer of 1361, the Prince sent his esquire to Avignon in order to obtain dispensations from Pope Innocent VI. This arose from the fact that Joan and the Prince were related in the second and third degree (besides being second cousins, they had a common great-grandfather, Edward I). The Pope's agreement to the marriage, sent on 8 September to the Archbishop of Canterbury, set out the complex story of Joan's previous 'marriages', that to Holand and the annulled contract with Salisbury. Dispensation was also necessary on two further matters, the first, because of the Prince's spiritual relationship to Joan's children as godparent and second because Joan and the Prince had made a marriage contract before the dispensation was issued. In return for the dispensations, the Prince surrendered his manor at Vauxhall to the monks of Christ Church, Canterbury, in order to pay for the building of a chantry chapel in the crypt of the Cathedral.[10] All the obstacles to the marriage had now been overcome.

A formal wedding ceremony took place at Lambeth on 6 October 1361 and a public ceremony at Windsor four days later. Among those attending were the King and Queen Philippa, Joan, Queen of Scotland, the Bishops of Winchester, Salisbury, Lincoln and Worcester and John Islip, Archbishop of Canterbury, who officiated. Joan was thirty three years of age, two years older than her husband.

*   *   *   *   *

There seems little doubt that the marriage was a successful one. Their devotion to each other during the next fifteen years was remarked upon by several chroniclers of the time. Edward and Joan were well-matched in many ways, not least in their love of extravagance. After the ceremonies, the Prince and his bride resided at his two manors, at Berkhamsted and Kennington, though making two short visits to Peterborough. Edward had incurred much expense in building, decorating and furnishing the hall at Kennington. He allotted Joan a sum of £1,000 a year for expenses and bought her many beautiful clothes and jewels. For his own part, the Prince participated in tournaments: there were two at Smithfield in 1362 and one, proposed at Cheapside, was to have the opponents dressed as the seven deadly sins.[11]

But these pastimes were soon to come to an end. On 19 July 1362, the King invested his son as Prince of Aquitaine and sent him to Bordeaux. One feature which was new in Gascony, the south-western region of France, was that so far the territory had been held by force; now it was proposed to bring peace and prosperity to the area and at the same time to relieve the Exchequer of a heavy financial burden. Joan and Edward, newly entitled the Prince and Princess of Wales, Aquitaine and Gascony,[12] left Plymouth for La Rochelle in June 1363, having earlier received a visit from the King and Queen at Berkhamsted. France was to be their home for the next seven years.

Much of their early stay was occupied with receiving homages from the leading men in Aquitaine, the first to their new sovereign the King of England and the second to the Prince himself. In the first eight months Edward had taken homages from some 1,047 counts, viscounts, barons, knights, prelates and gentlemen. Joan and Edward had their court at Bordeaux in Gascony and sometimes at Angoulême in Aquitaine. One chronicler painted a tranquil picture of the early years, commenting that 'since the birth of God such fair state was never kept as his, nor more honourable, for ever he had at his table more than fourscore knights and full four times as many squires . . . there abode all nobleness, all joy and jollity, largesse, gentleness and honour, and all his subjects and all his men loved him right dearly, for he dealt liberally with them'.

Their first son, Edward, was born at Angoulême in March 1365. The event was celebrated with a tournament paid for by the Prince, on such a scale that it involved the stabling of 18,000 horses, and forty eight nobles were attached to the Prince's retinue for the ten days of festivities. Meanwhile, there were several problems confronting the Prince. A growing number of unemployed mercenaries, both English and French, created by the Peace of Brétigny, were causing much damage in the country with their burning and looting. National sentiment was manifesting itself once again and was threatening to undermine the fragile peace which existed. More seriously, the French King John died in London, still a hostage, in April 1364. His son, Charles V, resolved to reconquer France from the English, using the strategic skills of Bertrand du Guesclin, his brilliant soldier. Bertrand du Guesclin took many of his troops into Spain where Charles intended to attack the English from the rear.

In Castile, the ruler, Don Pedro, often known as Peter the Cruel, was deposed in 1366 by du Guesclin aided by an English mercenary Sir Hugh Calveley, and Pedro's bastard brother, Henry, became King in his stead. Pedro, an ally of Edward III, sent word to the Prince, urging assistance in restoring him to the throne. The Black Prince's political judgement was not always trustworthy, particularly in this instance. He welcomed Pedro to Bordeaux, promising support and was no doubt delighted at the prospect of war. Many of his English and Gascon lords were at first reluctant to advance Don Pedro's cause. However at a three-day Parliament held at Bordeaux, the Prince persuaded his followers to seek the opinion of his father on the matter. Edward III enthusiastically gave his approval for the campaign.

Amongst the doubters of the wisdom of a Castilian war was Joan. According to Froissart,[13] she was not dazzled by the gold and jewelled imitation of the Round Table which Don Pedro presented to the Prince on his arrival, saying, 'I fear lest ill come of it. The present is beautiful, but it will cost us dear', a prophecy which proved to be correct. Although impatient to start the invasion, the Prince was obliged to wait for reinforcements and he remained at Bordeaux over Christmas. Joan, who was shortly to give birth to her second child, was distraught at the Prince's imminent departure. A contemporary account of the event was recorded by the Herald of Sir John Chandos, the Black Prince's able commander and close companion for some thirty years:

> According to what I heard, the Prince set out from Bordeaux fifteen days after Christmas. And then the Princess had right bitter grief at heart, and then she reproached the goddess of love who had brought her to such great majesty, for she had the most puissant Prince in this world. Often she said: 'Alas! what should I do, God and Love, if I were to lose the very flower of Nobleness, the flower of loftiest grandeur, him who has no peer in the world in valour? Death! thou wouldst be at hand. Now have I neither heart nor blood nor vein, but every member fails me, when I call to mind his departure; for all the world says this, that never did any man adventure himself on so perilous an expedition. O very sweet and glorious Father, comfort me of your pity'. Then did the Prince hearken to his gentle lady's words; he gave her right noble comfort and said to her: 'Lady, let be your weeping, be not dismayed, for God has power to do all'. The noble Prince gently comforts the lady, and then sweetly takes leave of her, saying lovingly: 'Lady, we shall meet again in such wise that we shall have joy, we and all our friends, for my heart tells me so'. Very sweetly did they embrace and take farewell with kisses. Then might you see ladies weep and damsels lament; one bewailing her lover and another her husband. The Princess sorrowed so much that, being then big with child, she through grief delivered and brought

forth a very fair son, the which was called Richard. Great rejoicings did all make, and the Prince also was right glad at heart, and all say with one accord: 'Behold a right fair beginning'.[14]

The baby, born on 6 January 1367, was later to be the King of England as Richard II. The Black Prince left Bordeaux early in February to meet the army assembling at Dax. His younger brother, John of Gaunt, Duke of Lancaster, joined him there a few days later with his army. The Prince crossed the Pyrenees in the middle of winter at the head of 30,000 mounted men in three columns, each of 10,000, a day's march between columns. The army arrived at Vitoria, later to be the scene of Wellington's victory over the French in 1813, and by the beginning of March had crossed the Ebro. His opponent, Don Henry, had assembled an army of over 90,000 men, of whom 30,000 were cavalry; on 2 April at Nájera the Spanish King awaited the attack. Next morning the Prince reconnoitred the enemy's position from a hill and then issued orders: Lancaster was to dismount and charge the enemy from the right whilst he himself led the assault on their left. The Spanish left flank eventually broke and fled, whereupon the Prince, with remarkable control over his troops, left the King of Majorca to follow up the pursuit; Edward now fell upon their main body under Don Henry and led three charges in person. The arrival of Lancaster's force on the Spanish right was decisive. The enemy took flight but at a bridge at Nájera some 5,000 Spaniards were slaughtered and 2,000 French and Spanish knights were taken prisoner. The victory was complete.

Two days after the battle Edward wrote to Joan, 'My dearest sweetheart and much loved companion, All of us send you our warmest good wishes'. After describing the details of the combat, he concluded, 'And now, Monday, the day I am writing this, we left and started for Burgos. Thank God we are well on our way. You will be glad to know, my darling companion, that my brother of Lancaster and all the gentlemen of our army are in good fettle, except only John Ferrers – he fought well. Very dear companion'.[15]

The Black Prince's military strategy had been successful but once more his political judgement proved to be faulty. He ignored Don Pedro's demand for vengeance on the prisoners taken at Nájera and allowed them to go free: a few months later, they were plotting against Don Pedro. Further, once more restored to the Castilian throne, Pedro refused to give Edward the huge sum of money, calculated at 2,720,000 gold florins, which he had promised in order to pay the English troops. In the summer of 1367, Pedro announced from Seville, much to the Prince's anger, that he would never honour the debt whilst a foreign army remained on Spanish soil. The outstanding sum was never repaid though Pedro gave the Prince some jewels. These the Prince distributed among his commanders, retaining only one fine ruby which is now set in the State Crown. Two years later Don Pedro was killed by his half-brother.[16]

It was becoming increasingly urgent for the Prince and his army to abandon their expedition. Don Henry had gathered an army of mercenaries in France which presented a potential threat to the Prince when he returned. Joan ordered a force under Sir James Audley to head off Henry's troops, at the same time reproaching Charles V for supporting Henry. Meanwhile, provisions were running low and the long, hot Spanish

CP5. Panel portrait of Richard II at his Coronation, 1377.
He was the younger son of Joan of Kent and the Black Prince

CP6. Sir Dru Drury, 2nd baronet of Riddlesworth (1531–1617), whose daughter and heiress Diana married Sir William Wake, 3rd baronet

CP7. Watercolour of the Elizabethan Manor at Courteenhall with Courteenhall Church in the background, painted before 1790

summer had taken its toll in death and disease among the English and Gascon soldiers, including the Prince himself. Towards the end of June, he became ill with amoebic dysentery which left him an invalid for the remaining nine years of his life.

In late August 1367, in poor health, the Prince began to retrace his steps through Navarre; nevertheless, he officially marked the closing of the campaign with five days of feasting at Bayonne. Edward reached Bordeaux in early September, where he was received at the cathedral by the priests and his knights. The Princess Joan with her three year old son, Edward, greeted him warmly. 'Very sweetly they embraced when they met together. The gentle Prince kissed his wife and son. They went to their lodgings on foot, holding each other by the hand'.

The Prince now found himself in serious financial difficulties. He was determined to pay the Gascons and the mercenaries who had fought for him in Spain and within a fortnight of his return summoned his Council for this purpose. In January 1368, a *fouage* (chimney tax) of ten sous a hearth was imposed. Though this was paid without objection in Aquitaine, the Gascon lords, furious at the financial failure of the Spanish expedition, looked elsewhere for redress. Charles V had embarked on a diplomatic campaign to undermine English authority in Aquitaine and Gascony. The Gascon magnates also entered into secret intrigues with Charles.

England and France were again at war by 1369. Edward III resumed the title of the King of France, and Charles V declared that all English possessions were forfeit; before the end of the year Aquitaine was in full revolt. The Prince's health was rapidly deteriorating and by the summer of 1370 he was bedridden at Angoulême. On hearing that the dukes of Berry and Anjou had reached Limoges and that the Bishop, du Cros, godfather of the Prince's eldest son, had opened the town gates to them, Edward swore to exact revenge for this treachery. The Prince's engineers spent a month undermining the ramparts and timbers were laid. When these were lit a section of the wall collapsed. The troops swarmed in and after fierce fighting and heavy loss of life, the garrison surrendered and the whole population was put to the sword. Edward was by this time too ill to lead his army and watched the attack from a litter. It is typical of the Prince's code of honour that the person responsible for allowing the French to occupy the city, du Cros, was allowed to go free. The Prince's mother, Philippa of Hainault, had died at the end of 1369: now an even heavier blow was to fall with the death of his elder and favourite son, Edward, at the age of six in January 1371. Unable to bear to stay in Bordeaux for the funeral, Joan and the Prince left the arrangements in the hands of his younger brother, John of Gaunt, Duke of Lancaster, and, with their four year old son Richard of Bordeaux, sailed for England. They were never to return to France.

During the next seven years they remained at Berkhamsted, making journeys only when matters of State were pressing. In August 1372, an expedition to La Rochelle was assembled by Lancaster and which included the King and the Prince. The inclement weather completely upset the plan; after nine weeks, when the fleet had got no further than Winchelsea, the force returned to England.[17] One result of the venture was that the Prince's health further deteriorated and he was obliged to give up his post in Aquitaine. Documentary references to their movements during this period are few, but it is known that Joan attended Queen Philippa's annual memorial service at

15. The Black Prince wearing his coat of arms

16. The Old Stone House, Wickhambreaux, near Canterbury, Kent, once the home of Joan, the Fair Maid of Kent

17. Effigy of the Black Prince, 1376, Trinity Chapel, Canterbury Cathedral

Marlborough in August 1371 without her husband.[18] The loss of Aquitaine following Lancaster's campaign of 1373–4 must have been a bitter blow to the ailing Prince. His father Edward III was also now frail and Lancaster's position had become more powerful.

The Prince was anxious that his son Richard should, on the hereditary principle, eventually succeed to the throne. When the so-called 'Good Parliament' assembled in London on 28 April 1376, the Prince was carried there from Berkhamsted and openly showed his sympathies with the Commons, who wished to remove the evil advisers surrounding the King.[19] A few weeks later it was obvious that the Prince was dying, and at the beginning of June he was moved to Westminster. He made his will on 7 June listing his bequests and setting out details of his funeral.[20] The next day he died. Chandos, who was a witness to the final scene, described it in the following terms:

> Then he called the King, his father, and the Duke of Lancaster, his brother; he commended to them his wife and his son, whom he greatly loved, and besought them right then that each one should help him. Each one swore it on the book and promised him without reserve to support his child and maintain him in his right; all the princes and all the barons standing round swore it; and the noble and renowned Prince gave them a hundred thousand thanks. But never, so God help me, was such sore grief beheld as there was at his departing. The lovely and noble Princess felt such grief at heart that her heart was nigh breaking. Of lamentation and sighing, of crying aloud and sorrowing, there was so great a noise that there was no man living in the world, if he had beheld the grief, but would have had pity at heart.[21]

The Prince's body lay in State in Westminster Hall for four months. In his will, he had stipulated that he should be buried at Canterbury Cathedral rather than, as was customary since Henry III's time, among the royal tombs in Westminster Abbey. The Prince's preference for Canterbury was closely linked with Joan, for, as mentioned earlier, one of the conditions of the Pope's sanctioning their marriage was the endowment of a chantry with two altars to be served by two chaplains in the cathedral. Accordingly in 1363, in the south transept of the crypt immediately below the high altar, the Norman work had been encased in the Decorated style to form the chantries of the Black Prince. It is here that he was buried, in the presence of Joan, at an elaborate ceremony on 5 October 1376. Among the roof bosses which would have looked down on the fine bronze effigy of the Prince is one which is a portrait of Joan. However, it was later considered that a grander and more prominent resting place was appropriate and the Prince was placed beside Thomas à Becket's tomb in the Trinity Chapel on the south side of the choir. As a mark of respect, his enemy, Charles V attended a requiem mass in Paris for the Prince.

Joan was now forty eight and widowed for a second time; she was never to marry again. Had the Black Prince lived one more year, she would have been Queen of England, for in June 1377, Edward III, the Black Prince's father died. The final year of the King's reign had been a troubled one. On Christmas Day 1376, King Edward had announced to his sons that on his death, his grandson, Richard was to succeed him.

Because of incapacity through the illness of the monarch his fourth son, John of Gaunt, the Duke of Lancaster, had become one of the most powerful figures in the land and had controlled the business at the meeting of Parliament in February 1377. His unpopularity with the citizens of London was increased by his threat to appoint a soldier in place of the Lord Mayor. The receipt of this news led to rioting. The Duke, together with Henry Percy, Earl of Northumberland, had hurried across the river to Kennington where they were given refuge by Joan. She dispatched three knights, skilled at diplomacy, to bring about a conciliation between the two sides which resulted in a temporary, but uneasy, peace.[22]

Joan's surviving son, Richard, was crowned King in Westminster Abbey on 16 July 1377 at the age of ten. Richard was unlike his father both in physique and in temperament. He was of a sensitive and artistic disposition and physically too slight in build to be a soldier. Nevertheless, Richard had greatly admired his father and did not lack courage when needed. He was too young to take an active part in politics for the first four years of his reign and Lancaster was the virtual ruler. Joan acted as his informal guardian and the centre of his Court: the day-to-day matters of State were handled by a Council of twelve. Quite early in his reign Richard adopted his mother's badge of the white hart.[23]

Joan held a remarkable position in the affection and respect of the people which enabled her to guide and shield Richard during her lifetime. The fact that he was the Black Prince's son also gave him an advantage over his ambitious uncles, Lancaster and Gloucester.

A true test of the new King's abilities was presented with the outbreak of the Peasants' Revolt in 1381.[24] The immediate cause was the imposition of a new poll tax but there were many other deeper and more complex reasons, not least the changes in the social structure of the country following the Black Death some thirty years earlier. In Kent, one of the leaders, a priest, John Ball, preached egalitarian sermons which were directed against their local lords and the King's ministers though not at Richard himself. A rebel army, led by Wat Tyler, left Canterbury on Monday 10 June and had reached the gates of London by Wednesday. Chroniclers have recorded that Joan was at this time on a pilgrimage to the shrines of Kent. On hearing of the uprising, she hurried back to London only to be caught up by the rebels marching on London. As they recognised the Princess Joan as their Fair Maid of Kent they did not harm her, and she was allowed to proceed to London.

In the meantime, a mob from Essex and Hertfordshire, under their leader Jack Straw, had reached the capital and had halted at Mile End. Tyler's men arrived on 13 June at Southwark and proceeded to wreak their revenge by releasing prisoners from the Fleet, burning down John of Gaunt's palace at the Savoy and murdering several clergy, lawyers and financiers. Whilst this turmoil was happening, the King together with Joan, the Earls of Buckingham, Oxford, Kent and Derby, and Sudbury, Archbishop of Canterbury, took refuge in the Tower of London.

On Friday 14 June, the young Richard rode out with a party to Mile End to meet Tyler[25] and his supporters who numbered, according to Froissart, some 60,000. Three of the King's escort are reputed to have turned back on the way, two of whom, the Earl of

Kent and Sir John Holand, were Joan's children. Richard showed considerable personal courage in confronting the rebels and promised to meet their demands. Many of the men now returned home, but about half, including Tyler, remained in London. The leader quickly led the rebels to the Tower, where Joan and the other refugees were still hiding. Tyler persuaded the garrison to allow them entry and, dividing into two parties, the men searched and ransacked the building room by room, killing, amongst others, the prelate Sudbury.

Joan, who was in her bedroom at the time, was subjected to insults by the mob. Her bed was torn to pieces and she fainted with fright. Fortunately, she was allowed to leave: her servants carried her down to the Thames, where a boat took her to the safety of the royal apartments which were near Blackfriars. Richard returned from Mile End and spent the Friday night with his mother. There Joan exclaimed upon his arrival, 'Ah, fair son, what pain and great sorrow I have suffered for you this day'. Richard replied, 'Certainly, madam, I know it well; but now rejoice and thank God, I have this day recovered my heritage and the realm of England, the which I had nearly lost'.

On the following morning, after first hearing mass, the King and his party left Westminster to meet Tyler once more, this time at Smithfield. One of Richard's followers, William Walworth, Lord Mayor of London, angered by Tyler's insolence towards the King, struck him down with his sword. At this, Richard rode forward, telling him that he was their natural leader and commanded them to return to their homes. The dispirited rebels obeyed their King and the revolt was over. Some of the leading figures, such as John Ball, were executed but on 13 December that year, a general pardon was granted, largely through Joan's persuasive powers.

The last few years of Joan's life saw no diminution in the range of her activities. In January 1382, Richard's marriage to Anne of Bohemia took place in Westminster Abbey; they were both fifteen. Joan's influence on her son in matters of State was probably considerable. She once more acted as mediator in 1385 between Richard and the Duke of Lancaster when it seemed likely that the country would erupt into civil war. A few months later, she pleaded with Richard to spare her son and the King's half brother, John Holand, from punishment for the murder of Ralph, Earl of Stafford. Richard's refusal of her request, the chroniclers claim, made her broken-hearted and proved to be fatal. In fact, Joan was suffering from dropsy and had grown corpulent. She made her will at Wallingford Castle, Berkshire, her home, on 7 August 1385 and died there the same day; she was fifty seven. Curiously enough, she stipulated that she should be buried in Grey Friars Church, Stamford, beside her first husband, Sir Thomas Holand, and her brother, John, Earl of Kent.[26] The funeral was delayed until Richard, who was in Scotland at the time, was able to attend.

*   *   *   *   *

Such was Joan's fame that many details of her life were recorded by contemporary chroniclers; it is therefore not difficult to obtain a fairly clear picture of her character and career. She witnessed much tragedy. Her uncle, Edward II, was betrayed by his Queen and murdered, and her father was beheaded before she was two. Her mother died when she was twenty and her only brother when she was twenty four. One son, Prince

Edward, who would have become King, died in childhood and she outlived both of her husbands. Fortunately she was spared the grief of knowing of the execution in 1400 of her son, John Holand, Duke of Exeter, for treason or of the foul murder of another son, Richard II, in the same year.[27]

Joan was renowned for her great beauty and was, in her youth, slim and elegant. According to Chaucer, who knew Joan personally, she was described as peace-loving, forthright in speech and capable, even in middle age, of blushing when praised. She was endowed with much common sense and courage and showed compassion for the poor and the unfortunate in any rank of society. Nor was she afraid to espouse causes which were not popular.

As the Princess of Wales, she proved to be a faithful and loving wife to Edward, the Black Prince. Her extravagances, which were matched by those of her husband, were commensurate with her extensive fortune. On the question of religion, she supported John Wyclif,[28] who favoured radical Church reform, though she died a good Catholic.[29] She was a shrewd politician and her interventions at times of crisis were often crucial. Joan's popularity both at court and with the people lasted throughout her life; she, like Edward, had few enemies. It is interesting to speculate on the course of Plantagenet history if Edward and Joan had become, as they so nearly did, King and Queen of England.

4
Mixed Fortunes

COURTEENHALL HAS BEEN IN THE POSSESSION OF THE Wakes for over three hundred years, though much is known of its previous history, which goes back at least to the time of the Norman Conquest. Odo, Bishop of Bayeux, had a great under-tenant, William Peverel, whose name is familiar from Scott's novel, *Peveril of the Peak*. Peverel possessed much land, his Northamptonshire estates alone covering more than a page of the Domesday survey. He founded St. James' Augustinian Abbey, Northampton and the Cluniac Priory of Lenton, Nottingham at the beginning of the twelfth century, endowing the latter from his holding at Courteenhall.[1] In 1086, in the hundred of Collingtree, William held three and a half hides in Blisworth and three and a half hides in Courteenhall. On the latter, Domesday states:

> Of this land 2 hides, less one virgate, are in demesne. There is land for 9 ploughs. In demesne there are 2 ploughs with 1 serf; and 12 villeins, with 1 bordar and the priest, have 7 ploughs. There is a mill rendering 12 pence, and 4 acres of meadow. Woodland 2 furlongs in length, and 2 furlongs in breadth. It was worth 4 pounds; now it is worth 5 pounds.

William's heir was less fortunate and on his downfall at the beginning of the reign of Henry II, the Northamptonshire estates reverted to the King. Henry gave eighty acres of assarts (forest converted into arable) in Courteenhall in exchange for some other lands. The Prior of Lenton had rights of pasturage in Salcey Forest in right of his manor at Courteenhall in 1236, valued at £32 18s. 7d. by 1291. The manor was usually let on lease by the Priory.[2]

How the name Courteenhall originated is not definitely known. The English Place-Name Society suggested that it was likely to have been a person's name, Corta or Curta, the whole meaning 'Corta's nook of land'.[3] Domesday, in 1086, records it as Cortenhale, and twelfth century documents as Curtehala. Later variations were: Kortinhale, Corinhall and Cortenhalle (thirteenth century); Cortnall, Cawtnall (sixteenth century); and Cotenhall, Coffenall and Courtinhall (seventeenth century). The last recorded change seems to be that in 1702, when it was called Courtnall.[4]

See Appendix A — Family Trees II, III and IV. Notes and References pages 396, 397

Normanni ten de Ro. ii. hid in BLARESWICHE. Tra e. vi.
car. hugo 7 Wills ten de eo. In dnio st. ii. car. 7 xii. uilli
7 v. bord hnt. iiii. car. Ibi molin de. xxx. den. 7 vi. ac
pa. Silua. i. leuu lg. 7 iii. qrent lat. Valet. xviii. sol.

Hugo ten dim hid in BADEBROC de Ro. In RODEWEL hd.
Tra e. i. car. Valuit 7 ual. xvi. den. Norman tenuit.

Ide h. ten de Ro. tcia parte uni hide in ead uilla.
Tra e dim car. Ibi e tam. i. car cu. i. bord.
Valuit. xii. den. Modo. iii. solid. Ulchet tenuit.

Wills ten de Ro. dim hid in RISTONE. Tra e. i.
car. Vna tam 7 dim car est ibi cu. i. uillis. ii. bord.
Ibi dim molin de. xii. den. 7 vi. ac silue. Ulchet tenuit.
Valuit. xii. den. Modo. vi. sol. Soca e in WILEDONE.

In ead uilla he dim v dre uasta. In SPERETHOU hd.
Ide W. ten de Ro. ii. hid 7 una v dre 7 dimid. in
MOLTONE. Tra e. v. car. In dnio sunt. iii. car cu. i. seruo.
7 vii. uilli 7 iiii. bord hnt. ii. car. Ibi molin de. vii.
denar. Valuit. xx. solid. Modo. l. sol. Thori tenuit.

Robt ten de Ro. iii. v dre una bouata min in BO...

hnt. iii. car. Ibi. viii. ac pa. Valuit. xx. sol. Modo. ix. sol.

Ide W. ten. ii. hid 7 dim in CORTESHALE. In COLESTREU hd.
De hac tra st. ii. hide in dnio una v min. Tra e. x. car.
In dnio sunt. ii. car cu. i. seruo. 7 xii. uilli cu. i. bord 7 pbro
hnt. vii. car. Ibi molin de. xii. den. 7 iiii. ac pa. Silua. ii.
qrent lg. 7 ii. qc lat. Valuit. iii. lib. Modo. v. lib.

Willelm Pevrel ten de rege HECHAM. Ibi sunt.
vi. hide. Tra e. xii. car 7 dim. In dnio st. ii. hide de hac tra.
7 ibi. iiii. car. 7 iiii. serui. 7 xvi. uilli 7 xx. bord cu pbro
hnt. viii. car 7 dim. Ibi e mercat redd. xx. sol p ann.
7 molin de. xx. sol. 7 x. ac pa. Silua. i. qc lg. 7 alia lat.
Ad hoc cn pan h mebra.

In RISDENE. vi. hide. Tra e. xii. car. has hnt ibi xxx.
sochi. 7 molin de. x. sol. 7 xxx. ac pa.

In Celuestone 7 Caldecote. i. hida 7 iii. v qc tra e. iii. car.
has hnt ibi. vi. sochi. 7 iii. ac pa.

In Enutestone. i. hida 7 una v qc dim. Tra e. i. car.
has hnt ibi. v. sochi 7 molin de. xx. sol. 7 vi. ac pa.

In Irencestre. i. hida 7 iii. v qc de soca. Tra e. ii. car.
has hnt ibi. iiii. sochi 7 x. ac pa. Ibi sun francig cu. i. car.
7 molin ibi de. xvi. sol. calumiosu ut rege 7 Willm.

In Furnedis. iii. v qc de soca. Tra e. i. car. hanc hnt ibi

In Pointone dim hida de soca. Ibi sunt iii. sochi.
iiii. uilli cu. i. car.

In Estone. una v qc 7 dimid. Vasta. e

In Rande. vii. hide 7 dim. 7 dim v qc de soca. cu append.
xx. uilli cu. xv. car. 7 xx. ac pa.
v. lib. qdo recep. Modo. xviii. lib.

...re 7 Rande fuer hoel burred
...matione eor. In Clipestone
...qrta parte uni v de soca ha
...un miles cu. i. car. 7 xix. sochi
...i. car. Valuit. xl. sol. modo. xx. sol.
...a 7 dim v qc. Tra e. iii. car.
...iiii. uilli 7 ii. bord hnt. i. car.
...e silue.
... parte. i. hide 7 s uirgat. Soca

In BRININTONE he id. W. una hid 7 dim. Tra e. ii. car.
has hnt ibi. vi. sochi cu pbro. q ten dim hid est ibi.

In HEROLVESTONE. e una hida 7 dim. Tra e. iii. car. has
hnt ibi. iii. sochi cu pbro.

In CLICHESTORP. e dim hida. Tra e. i. car. hanc ht ibi

In FLORE. e dim hida. Tra e. i. car. hanc hnt ibi. iiii. sochi.
Quando Wills has jas recep. ualb. iiii. lib. Modo. vii. lib.

Idem W. ten. iiii. hid in RISTONE. In dnio st. ii. 7 ii. serui. 7 xii. uilli 7 ii. bord
cu. iii. sochis hnt. vi. car. Ibi molin de. xx. sol. 7 xxx. ac
pa. 7 xi. ac silue. Valuit. xl. sol. modo. c. solid.

Idem W. ten. vii. hid in NAVESBERIE. Tra e. xiiii. car.
In dnio sunt. ii. 7 vii. uilli cu pbro 7 ii. sochis 7 xi. bord
hnt. iiii. car. Ibi. viii. ac pa. Valuit. xx. sol. Modo. ix. sol.

Ide W. ten. ii. hid 7 dim in CORTESHALE. In COLESTREU hd.
De hac tra st. ii. hide in dnio una v min. Tra e. x. car.
In dnio sunt. ii. car cu. i. seruo. 7 xii. uilli cu. i. bord 7 pbro
hnt. vii. car. Ibi molin de. xii. den. 7 iiii. ac pa. Silua. ii.

Radulfus pagenel ten de rege. ii. hid. In STOC hd.
7 Roger de eo. Tra e. iiii. car. In dnio e una. 7 iiii. uilli
7 iii. bord hnt. i. car 7 dimid. Ibi. ii. serui. Valuit. v. sol.
Modo. x. solid. Turchil libe tenuit.

Radulfus de Limesi ten de rege. ii. hid in WESTONE.
7 herluin de eo. Tra e. vi. car. In dnio sunt. ii 7 i. serui.
7 xvi. uilli 7 iii. bord hnt. v. car. Ibi molin de. xx. sol.
7 xii. ac pa. Silua. iii. qrent lg. 7 ii. qc lat. Valuit. c.
solid. modo. vi. lib. Comes Moritan tenuit.

Rotbertus alb. ten de rege. iii. hid in GRASTONE.
7 Roger de eo. Tra e. vii. car. In dnio e una. cu. i. seruo.
7 xii. uilli cu pbro 7 vi. bord hnt. v. car. Ibi. ii. ac pa.
Silua. i. leuu lg. 7 iii. qrent lat. Valuit 7 ual. xl. sol.
Achi libe tenuit. T.R.E.

LD5. Domesday Survey of 1086 giving details of William Peverel's holdings at Courteenhall
[for translation, see chapter 4. p. 43]

LD6. Early 12th century charter of Henry I confirming the manor of Courteenhall and other gifts made to Lenton Priory, Nottingham, by William Peverel

We know little about the earliest settlement, though there is still much visible evidence of ridge-and-furrow on the estate. There was a windmill on the highest point on the north side of the drive to the present House where stone was quarried; it was probably a wooden structure which could be turned round to catch the wind. The site of a watermill has also been located in the north-west corner of Courteenhall Park, now planted with a small wood called Watermill Spinney; within it there are three rectangular ponds bounded by a low stone-rubble dam.[5]

To the south-east remains the only building of this time, the parish church. Dedicated to St. Peter and St. Paul, it was probably originally a Norman twelfth-century structure as can be seen from the south doorway, the east pier of the three-bay north arcade and the font. In the thirteenth century the building was largely reconstructed; the fine south arcade and the arch from the chancel into the north chapel are from this time.[6] The chancel was rebuilt in the fourteenth century and the south porch was added. From the same period are the wall paintings on the west pier of the south arcade, probably depicting a king, the Virgin and a saint which are of unusual quality and interest.[7] There is evidence that there was a tower as early as the twelfth century. The present square three-stage structure dates from the fifteenth century and looks across the Park to the House.

The village of Courteenhall is mentioned in Domesday but the population is not recorded. An estate map of 1766 shows the village to be made up of three distinctive parts. The main part lay to the north-west of the church, running from north to the south; another group was to the west of the present House. To the east of the church was a single row of buildings on the north side of the street; this is now all that remains of the original village of Courteenhall.

Some account of the inhabitants of Courteenhall can be found in medieval records. On the 'Saturday before St. Peter ad Vincula in the second year of the reign of Edward I' (1273), a list of those who paid homage in one form or another under the entry for Courteenhall include William de Hays of Quinton, rendering 6d. yearly, John Abraham of Coluntre (Collingtree) who gave a pound of pepper yearly, and a fee from the land held there by the Master of the Hospital of St. John, Northampton.[8] At Easter 1316, there was a complaint by Philip de Hastang that the escheater (an officer of the Crown who enforced the reversion of land to the King) had taken into the King's hands a parcel of 'land in Cortenhale called Tenacres', then part of the manor of Quinton, which had been held by Theobald de Gayton. Chancery later awarded the properties to Scolistica, aged twenty four, and Juliana, aged twenty six, both sisters of Theobald and his heirs.[9] In 1346, Adam de Cortenhale held at Aldryngton (Alderton, near Roade) five and a half acres of meadow and five acres of pastures, paying four shillings annual rent. Five years later, Adam and his wife Margery were granted the rents of the manor of Wolverton.[10] Finally, in September 1504, following the death of Sir William Hertwell, Kt., the manor of Preston by Pidyngton was given to his widow for her lifetime, together with the rents from many places in Northamptonshire, including Courteenhall.[11]

*   *   *   *   *

The break with Rome by Henry VIII and the creation of a national church with the King as its head had important consequences for Courteenhall. At the Dissolution of the Monasteries, Lenton Priory and all its possessions, including Courteenhall, passed into the King's hands in 1538. The latter was incorporated into the newly-created honor of Grafton. In 1550, it was leased to Reynold Conyers for twenty one years. At the expiry of the lease in 1571, Queen Elizabeth leased Courteenhall to Richard Ouseley, a Clerk of the Privy Seal, also for a period of twenty one years, at a rent of £30 per annum. The manor was described at the time as 'all tillage, little or no pasture and no wood', and its yearly value was calculated at £90. Courteenhall's tenants enjoyed the privileges of the delightful-sounding hedgebote, ploughbote, cartbote and firebote.

Richard Ouseley, who according to his tomb in Courteenhall Church came from Shropshire, was an enterprising and ambitious man. Before his death, he had also obtained the post of Clerk of the Court of Requests and with the profits of his office, he was able to buy the lease of the manor. His first wife, Jane, the widow of Sir Miles Partridge, was already dead by this time. For his second wife, he married Magdalen, daughter of John Wake and Elizabeth Gorges of Hartwell. If Richard had married Magdalen before taking the lease on Courteenhall, this might explain his interest in that part of Northamptonshire, as Hartwell lies three miles south-east of Courteenhall. On the other hand, he may have consolidated his new position after acquiring the manor by marrying a neighbouring squire's daughter.

Although Richard's interest initially was in a twenty one year lease, there is evidence that he expected to extend or convert it into a grant of the freehold in due course. The year after settling at Courteenhall, he began to put the estate in order and started building. The first priority was to build a manor house. Situated between the present House and the church, it had, according to one early nineteenth century account, a very spacious hall, decorated with a cornice of solid oak, carved with Wake Knots and the initials R.O. placed within the bows of the Knots. The Hall also contained the royal coat of arms of Elizabeth.[12] At one time there was a barn with his initials and the date 1572 on it. On the 1766 estate map it can be seen that the Hall was a long straight range with six stacks of chimneys. To the south-west was a garden; in a dry summer, the outline of the old foundations is visible. Joan Wake, writing in 1940, stated that in the rabbit burrows around the old House, fragments of bottles and oyster shells, relics of ancestral feasts, could be found.[13]

Richard Ouseley devoted much of his energy to farming and building on the estate. We know that he constantly grumbled about the expense involved in keeping Courteenhall in good condition and complained especially at the cost of repairing his manor house, some £700, before rebuilding it in 1580. In his will, he wrote that the manor 'with so great chardges and small benefitt as I had bin happie yf I had never knowne it for I have spent uppon it and about it in buildinge and otherwise more than twise the purchase of yt in fee simple, but I never had this worldlie luck in aniethinge'.[14] Perhaps these complaints were calculated to help him obtain an extension of his lease, in which he was successful. In 1576 he was granted a thirty one year lease, followed in 1577 by a lease of the reversion for a further twenty one years; two more extensions followed in 1582 and 1583.

18. The Ouseley Tomb, Courteenhall Church, 1599

19. Monument to Sir Samuel Jones and his wife Mary, Courteenhall Church, 1672, attributed to William Stanton

20. Clevedon Court, Somerset, 1838, which passed into the Wake family with the marriage of Agnes Lovell to Thomas Wake of Blisworth in 1450

21. Interior of Clevedon Court before the fire of 1882. This fireplace is decorated with the Wake knot frieze and the arms and initials of John Wake (d.1621)

Richard died on 10 February 1599, Magdalen surviving him until December 1607. Their monument, in the former chapel on the north side of the chancel of Courteenhall, is the earliest surviving one in the church. It is a table-tomb, freestone, covered with a slab of black marble. On it are the indents of Richard and his two wives and two groups of children.[15] The monument is 4 feet high and 5 feet 6 inches long and there is an inscription in Gothic letters which runs round it and reads:

> A Sallop's Oseley I,
> A ruen Partrige woonne,
> No birds I had her by:
> Such work with her was doone.
> She dead I turtle sought,
> A Wake in Salsie bred:
> Twice six birds shee me brought,
> She lyvs, but I am dead.
> But when ninth yeare was come,
> I sleapt that was a-*Wake*:
> So yielding to Death's doome,
> Did here my lodging take.

The word 'dead' ends the speech of Richard Ouseley, after which are carved the holly leaf of the Ouseley arms and the Wake Knot. The last four lines are supposed to be spoken by Magdalen, his second wife, who died nine years after him. 'A ruen Partrige' in the second line referred, according to the researches of the twelfth baronet, to the red hair of Jane Partridge, Richard's first wife.[16] The 'twice six birds', of course, were the twelve children born during the marriage of Richard and Magdalen. His eldest son, Jasper Ouseley, who lived at Hartwell, married his cousin Sibil, daughter of John Wake of Salcey Forest.[17] In 1599, Jasper was examined in connection with a false rumour which was being spread, alleging that the Queen had died. He himself died in 1625; the second son, William, was buried at Courteenhall in 1616.

John Ouseley, the third son, born in 1568 and who succeeded his father at Courteenhall in 1599, was at that time in Ireland, serving under the ill-fated Earl of Essex. Knighted by James I in 1603, he was worried by his financial position. As John was away at the time of Richard's death, his mother was given the whole of her husband's Courteenhall estate for her lifetime, instead of merely the dower out of it. After Magdalen's own death in 1607, he obtained a grant of probate of his father's estate, but he must have returned to Courteenhall between 1602 and 1606, for at Christmas 1606, he sent Lord Salisbury 'a country New Year gift' from Courteenhall. A survey carried out in 1607 gives a clear picture of Courteenhall at this time. The manor house was of six bays: there was a barn of eight bays and two more of six bays each, a dovecote, orchard and garden, but only eight acres of enclosed land.

Sir John had married Martha, daughter of Bartholomew Tate of Delapre, in December 1588 when he was twenty years old, but much of their lives were spent apart because of his soldiering. Before the Irish expedition, he had acted as envoy from Lisbon to the Emperor of Morocco in 1589 and later became ambassador to that country. Sir John in his letters did not consider that his military service had been sufficiently rewarded and he aspired to the dignity of a baronet. His son Richard was promised this distinction by the government after Sir John had died in 1624 at the siege of Breda, but it was never implemented. Sir John was buried at Williamstadt in Holland. With the conclusion of the Irish and Spanish wars, many of the soldiers found themselves unemployed; this was probably the reason why, in about 1625, members of the Ouseley family settled in Ireland.

Soon after, in 1626, Richard made an agreement with the Rector of Courteenhall, William Castell,[18] to exchange some pieces of land so that he was able to extend his enclosed lands by about 300 acres, most of the parish having formerly been open field. By a stroke of good fortune, Richard obtained the freehold of the manor in 1628 from Charles I, who was desperate for money after he had prorogued Parliament that year. Richard now enlarged the estate; his grandfather had already bought forty acres in the adjoining parish of Wootton in 1576 and to this was added in 1630 forty more acres in Quinton and Ashton, to the east and south, and a long lease on some woods in the following year. To buy them, Richard obtained a loan of £500 from his father-in-law, Mark Parker of Olney.

The causes of the decline of the Ouseley family's fortunes can only be guessed at. England was in a state of unrest as the differences between Charles and his Parliaments worsened, leading to the Civil War. Whatever the reasons, Richard Ouseley, who later served as a major under the King,[19] found it necessary to raise the large sum of £3,300 in November 1640 and finally, in January 1647, to sell Courteenhall to a London merchant and businessman, Samuel Jones, for £8,819 18s. 8d.[20]

*　　　*　　　*　　　*　　　*

The Jones family were, like the Ouseleys, of Shropshire origin, owning in that county the manor of Sandford.[21] Samuel's father, Isaac, was a Merchant Taylor, who operated from Broad Street, London, and in due course Samuel joined him. Isaac acquired considerable property in Shropshire and in Surrey.

At the outbreak of the Civil War, in 1642, Samuel supported the parliamentary cause against King Charles. He commanded a regiment as Colonel of Foot, 1643–5, but his services were not required by the New Model Army. He held a number of local offices under the Commonwealth and was Sheriff of Northamptonshire in 1652; in that year, on the death of his father, Samuel inherited many estates. In the 1656 elections, Samuel Jones was one of the two MPs returned for Shrewsbury, the other being Colonel Humphrey Mackworth, governor of the city. At the instigation of Cromwell's major-generals, the Council of State scrutinized the list of Members and physically refused entry to the House of Commons of about 100 MPs of whom they did not approve. A spirited protest against this move in the form of a petition was made by many Members, including Samuel Jones.[22] It was during the following Session that Cromwell was offered, but did not accept, the Crown. On the Restoration of the monarchy two years later, Shrewsbury, with its Presbyterian Corporation, was less loyal than the rest of the county,[23] returning Samuel Jones and his cousin, Thomas Jones, the town clerk. Samuel had earlier begun to work his way back into favour by offering a loan to the exiled Court. On 24 May he was one of five MPs sent into the City to raise £2,000 'for the present service of his Majesty' (Charles II). As the response was lukewarm, the five Members agreed to advance the whole amount themselves. During his year in the House, Samuel revealed himself as an ultra-Royalist.[24] On 2 September 1660, shortly before the House rose for the autumn recess, Samuel was rewarded with a knighthood.

Sir Samuel married first, Mary, daughter of Timothy Myddelton of Stansted Mountfichet, Essex, and on her death, Mary, daughter of Peter Tryon of Bulwick, Northamptonshire. She remarried after Sir Samuel's death, he leaving her 'Jewells and all my stock of Cattle at Courteenhall . . . with her owne Picture made by Lillye', and a sum of £1,000 to buy a pearl necklace. There were no children of either of Sir Samuel's two marriages. Mary Myddelton came from a distinguished and wealthy family. Her grandfather was Sir Thomas Myddelton, Lord Mayor of London, 1613–14, a founder of the East India Company and owner of Chirk Castle, Denbighshire since 1595. His extensive properties in Wales and Shropshire were inherited by his son, also called Sir Thomas Myddelton, in 1631. Sir Thomas, Mary's step-uncle, fought on Cromwell's side during the Civil War. As a major-general, he played a prominent and successful part in campaigns in North Wales and Cheshire. From 1651, however, his sympathies were with the exiled Prince, the future Charles II, and at the Restoration was presented by the King with a cabinet said to have been worth £10,000.[25] Sir Thomas died in 1666 at the age of eighty. A brief view of life at Courteenhall at this time is afforded through the accounts of Sir Thomas Myddelton, following a visit there in 1653. Returning to Chirk Castle from London, Sir Thomas travelled via Courteenhall, staying there for five days, 24–29 March. He incurred the following expenses:

March	At Courtinghall in Northamptonshire paid for 6 Bushells of oates for one horse at xxxd p bushell	0 15 0
March	24th Paid at Northampton for our horses iiiid & for a flagon of drinke iid	0 0 6
	At Cortinghall, to the Butler iis vid, to the Cooke iis vid, to the Chambmaide iis vid, to the Groome iis vid, to the maide that made the fires there iis, to the maide of the Kitchin iis, to the boy of the Buttery is, to the boy of the stable is, to the ffalconer iis vid, to the workmen about the new stable iis	1 0 6
	To the man that brought us in our way from Cortinghall to Coventry	0 2 0

[26]

Sir Samuel was a man of strong views and did not hesitate to resort to law to establish his rights. On 2 December 1665, a letter was written from Courteenhall on his behalf, complaining of the behaviour of a Blisworth neighbour, Williamson, and his servants. 'The offenders', he wrote, 'are base clowns, enemies to His Majesty, and the gentry of the country desire their exemplary punishment.' Their offence was that they had taken away two low bells (contraptions for catching birds) after threatening Sir Samuel's servants. He continued:

> On their returning, Richard Plowman, owner of one of the bells, with ten or eleven others, assaulted and severely wounded them, recovered the bells, and said he would low bell in despite of Sir S. Jones at his very door, and the bells have been rung ever since.

Five days later, Lord O'Brien pleaded on behalf of Williamson, 'a man of good repute in the country, and prosecuted by one that is very abusive'. The case went to the Privy Council and was dismissed; an attempt by Sir Samuel to have a rehearing of the case at Northampton Assizes was also unsuccessful. To add insult to Sir Samuel's injury, Williamson accused him of slander and the jury awarded the petitioner £100. Almost two years later, Sir Samuel was still requesting a rehearing before the Council.[27]

Thanks to another law suit brought by Sir Samuel we can obtain some picture of landholding in the parish at this time. Extensive enclosure had taken place in Northamptonshire by the early seventeenth century and it continued to spread. At Courteenhall, the common fields of the parish were probably inclosed in 1631[28] and thus escaped the enclosure upheavals experienced from the eighteenth century onwards in many places. In parishes such as Courteenhall where there was a major landowner, i.e. the lord of the manor, it was often easier to reach agreement amongst the parishioners and others as to the exact siting of hedges. But even so, the issue of enclosure could lead to difficulties when a lord of the manor attempted to consolidate his holdings.[29]

In 1626, as we have seen, Richard Ouseley, Samuel Jones's predecessor, and the Rector, William Castell, agreed that the former should enclose eight acres of land near the Parsonage; in return, Castell was recompensed by 'certaine lands and meadows lying dispersed in the Common fields', which were also to be inclosed. In addition, Ouseley was to pay the Rector £20 a year in lieu of tithes. Twenty years later in 1646, on Castell's death, William Ponder, a Cromwellian nominee, was 'intruded' as Rector by Parliament. On 10 January 1650, Samuel Jones, now Lord of the Manor, continued Ouseley's endeavours to consolidate his holdings by reaching an agreement with Ponder whereby the Rector was to give up all the glebe land belonging to the Parsonage; in exchange, Ponder received a portion of land or field called Rode Dike (adjoining Hungry Hill on the south west side of the Park). This glebe land consisted of thirty six acres with a hedge and ditch round it. Ponder was also to have eight acres of the uppermost end of a meadow called Mickle-meade (the Great Meadow, one of the best portions of land in the parish). Sir Samuel was to pay Ponder £50 annually in lieu of tithes in addition to the £20 arising from the previous exchange.[30]

Ponder died in December 1660 and, much to Jones' annoyance, the new Rector, Francis Goodyear, refused to be bound by either of the previous agreements 'pretending', in Jones' words, 'that the Church was disadvantaged thereby'. (In fact, Jones claimed that the Parsonage was now worth £115 a year whereas before enclosure it was not worth more than £90).

Jones and four of his tenants brought the case to Chancery on 27 January 1661 after Goodyear threatened 'to throw downe the hedges and fences of the said ancient inclosures and to Common thereupon and to enter upon said Gleab Lands and plow up the same'. In addition, the petitioners alleged, Goodyear had 'caused severall suites to be commenced against your orators at Law for their tythes of the said inclosed Lands for the last yeare and hath caused them to be arrested severall times'.

In order to placate Goodyear and to end the dispute 'which might begette suites endlesse', Jones offered to increase the compensation for tithes to £70.[31] Goodyear, in his defence, dated 15 May 1662, claimed that Samuel Jones's contract with Ponder was invalid, as the latter, a Cromwellian preferment, was never the lawful incumbent of Courteenhall. Perhaps Goodyear's real reason for his attitude towards Ponder was revealed when he stated that 'he [Goodyear] was wrongly kept out by him [Ponder] during his life' from the Courteenhall rector- ship.[32] Unfortunately, as with many other Chancery law suits of this time, the outcome is not known.

Because of its geographical location, near to Watling Street, Courteenhall was a convenient base for Samuel Jones's travels to the City to supervise his business and to attend Parliament. He could also keep in contact fairly readily with his native county, and was Sheriff of Shropshire in 1663. By the time of his death in 1672, Sir Samuel held estates in many places, including Fritwell in Oxfordshire, Berwick in Shropshire, Holt in Denbighshire, and 'Lambethwick and elsewhere' in Surrey.

A different side of his character is seen in his philanthropic activities. Towards the end of his life, in 1670, he made provision for building sixteen almshouses at Berwick with gardens at the cost of £1,000; a further £300 was given for repairing the chapel there, with £60 per annum for the chaplain. The chapel and almshouses, built within the grounds of Berwick house in the 1670s, still retain many of their original fittings.[33]

A charming and tangible reminder of Sir Samuel at Courteenhall is the school which he provided for in his will. There had been a school at Courteenhall in 1593, but it had long since ceased to exist. Sir Samuel left a sum of £500 in order to convert a farmhouse for the master's and usher's dwelling and for the erection of a Free School. It stands to the west of the present House, a handsome two-storied building of limestone, with local ironstone dressing and a tiled roof. The school room itself occupies the west wing, with six squared-headed windows and the original panelling and desks. Pupils were to be taught, at Sir Samuel's directions, 'English, Lattin, Greeke, Writtinge, Casting of Account or such other qualityes as are usually taught in Free Schools'. Over the entrance door is proudly displayed a Latin inscription, translated as:

> Henry Edmunds Esq., and Francis Crane Esq., have completed, in accordance with the intention of the will, this little dwelling of the Muses, intended for the free teaching of youth living within four miles, which was begun and endowed at the charges of Sir Samuel Jones, Knight, a very generous patron of letters, A.D. 1680.

He also left money for repairing or building on to the church and increasing the number of bells. Against the east wall of the north chapel is a large monument to Sir

22. The Salcey Oak, which stood in the Park at Salcey Lawn, drawn by Major Rook, late 19th century. At that time the tree was supposed to be 'at least 1,500 years old'. The 12th baronet, Sir Herewald Wake, added the owl and child at the top. Little now remains standing

23. The Master's House, St John's Hospital, Northampton. In 1871, when the property was sold to the Midland Railway Company, the Master's House was demolished to make way for the Midland Station

Samuel and his first wife, for which he left £300. It has been attributed to William Stanton, the London sculptor,[34] and is of black and white marble, with Ionic columns and a large, open, segmental pediment. Above it is the Jones' coat of arms, argent, a lion vert, wounded gules in the breast. The figures are kneeling, a rather outdated convention for its time, and are almost facing each other. As there were no children, a large panegyric is instead inscribed on the tomb beneath. Inheritance was to cause some problems.

*   *   *   *   *

Although two generations of Ouseleys married Wakes, in both instances the latter were female; thus there was as yet only an indirect Wake link with Courteenhall. As was shown in Chapter 2, during the period of the Ouseley occupation of Courteenhall, the Wakes were settled at nearby Piddington, Hartwell and Salcey Forest, but these were not their only homes.

From the late twelfth century, the manor of East Dowlish or Dowlish Wake as it is called, some two miles south-east of Ilminster, Somerset, was held by the Wakes, together with West Dowlish. Dowlish Wake is now one of the largest villages in the area, with its curving main street, manor house and church, nestling under Wake Hill. The earliest Wake, Ralph, can be traced back there to the twelfth century, and he granted the church to Wells Cathedral before 1189.[35] His son, also called Ralph, succeeded in 1216. Andrew Wake, Ralph II's eldest son, was Sheriff of Somerset and Dorset, June 1267 to October 1269, and he appears frequently in the plea rolls between 1246–80. One intriguing entry records that he was 'in mercy for his great transgression and was fined ten marcs'.[36] He was summoned as one of the four representatives of Somerset and Dorset to the Parliament which met on 16 February 1275. Andrew died between 1280–4, and was succeeded by his son, Ralph, the third and last of this name.

According to an eighteenth century Somerset historian, the Reverend John Collinson, Ralph III was 'a person of great account in these parts, and one of those who in 25 Ed.I. [i.e. 1297] was summoned to be at London with horse and arms the next Lord's day after the octaves of St. John the Baptist, thence to attend the King beyond the seas'.[37] Besides possessing East and West Dowlish and Compton Martin in his native county, Ralph held manors in Dorset and Hampshire. The last of these Wakes was his son John (d.1348), who left three daughters. Today, the only surviving link with the Wakes' occupation of the manor between the twelfth and fourteenth centuries is the recumbent effigy of Isabel Wake, John's eldest daughter, (who died in 1359), in the chapel of St. Andrew's Church, Dowlish Wake.

Though Dowlish Wake now passed into other hands, this did not signal the end of the Wakes' interest in the county. It was noted in Chapter 2 that Thomas Wake of Blisworth (1402–58), known as the 'Great Wake', married Agnes, only daughter of Thomas Lovell of Clevedon, Somerset. In 1448, exactly a hundred years after the death of the last John Wake at Dowlish Wake, Thomas Lovell parted with his property by deed of gift on his daughter's marriage to Thomas Wake.[38]

The original manor house of Clevedon Court, built about 1320 by Sir John de Clevedon, is one of the very few of its time that have survived. It overlooks the Severn estuary and is wedged into the hillside which rises steeply behind it. Clevedon Court stands at the end of a long ridge of high ground running back ten miles eastwards to the Avon Gorge at Bristol. It has been suggested that when the Court was built, there was a tidal inlet flowing along the course of the River Yeo, now a small stream passing in front of the house. This would have afforded some protection from Welsh raiders.[39] There was also easy access to Bristol along the high ground behind the house; until the middle of the eighteenth century most goods were brought to Clevedon by packhorse. Normally, manor house and church are found fairly close together. Here, the parish church, St. Andrew, is two miles to the west, giving the house a feeling of isolation from the village.

Sir John de Clevedon's building was of an H plan, with short limbs lying north and south.[40] We can get some idea of the layout of the buildings from a topographical painting of the early eighteenth century. In front of the house on the left is a medieval barn and cow byres; in the foreground are the carp ponds where a constant supply of fresh fish was available. The gardens and walls were added later by Sir Abraham Elton, second baronet (1679–1742), who also made extensive alterations to the house. In the painting, on Court Hill can be seen Wake's Tower, an Elizabethan structure built as a look-out post during the time of the Spanish Armada. It was demolished before 1738.

The central portion of the house contains the Great Hall, with an entrance porch on the south side. Owing to the distance from the parish church, Sir John de Clevedon incorporated a chapel on the first floor with a remarkable fourteenth century window whilst the ante-room beneath it is an extension of the Great Hall.[41] The window gable to the east of the present porch has above it one of the so-called Wake bears which decorate the outside of the house and supports a shield.[42]

When the Wakes arrived at Clevedon in 1448, the house was probably cold and uncomfortable. Improvements were made by Roger Wake to the Great Hall. A new square-hooded fireplace was put in with flues dividing on each side of the window immediately above it. Such an innovation, compared with the open fires formerly found burning in the middle of a hall, would have been welcomed by its inhabitants.[43] Roger placed the transomed and mullioned windows in the south wall which would have given the room more light, and he probably inserted the stone and plaster doorway.

Roger's grandson, John, carried on the improvements, building two sets of rooms on the north side of the house, one on each side of its porch. His main achievement however was to build a new west wing, which was integrated into the rest of the structure. A fire in 1882 completely destroyed this wing which was rebuilt later. In what is now the Library, formerly the Parlour, was a magnificent Renaissance mantelpiece, with the Wake Knot circles along the frieze and above, the arms and initials of John Wake. A sketch drawn about 1850 gives some idea of its richness of detail. In the Elizabethan window, in the two centre panes, there were two lozenge-shaped insertions, one with the family motto 'Wake and Pray', the other with the Wake Knot, and underneath, the date 1570; these, too, perished in the fire.[44]

It is obvious from the interest taken by the Wakes in adding to Clevedon that successive generations undertook the long journey between Northamptonshire and Somerset, probably spending fairly lengthy periods of time at both places. The Somerset link was strengthened with the marriage of John Wake to Margaret Goodwin, probably in the 1560s. Portbury Priory, some eight miles north-east of Clevedon, an Augustinian house, was dissolved in 1536. The estate, with thirty five acres of woodland, was bought by Robert Goodwin for £64 19s. 0d. and passed to his daughter and John Wake after their wedding.[45] At the time of John's death in 1621, he possessed in Somerset, besides Clevedon and Portbury, Tickenham, Kenn, Walton-in-Gordano, Nailsea and Wraxall, all within a few miles of Clevedon. The only remaining evidence today of the Wakes at Clevedon is the tomb in the church of St.Andrew, Clevedon of Philippa Ethelreda Wake, who was born in 1626 and died in 1633.

John called his only son Baldwin, the first member of the family to be given this name since his illustrious forebear the warrior, Baldwin Wake in the early thirteenth century. He was baptized at Piddington on 6 October 1574 and was forty years old when he succeeded John. He had married first Abigail, who died childless and second, Elizabeth, only daughter of Sir George Digby of Coleshill, Warwickshire, at St. Margaret's, Westminster, in November 1600.

Few details of Baldwin's life are known, but there was one event which is documented and had significance for his descendants. On 5 December 1621, shortly before his father's death, he was granted the dignity of a baronet by James I, who had created this new class of hereditary aristocracy in 1611 to raise money for the colonization of Ulster. He was the first and only member of the family to place the Somerset property in his title before that of others, stating that he was of 'Clevedon and Piddington'. Now Sir Baldwin Wake, first baronet, he was on good terms with his brother-in-law, Sir John Digby, fourth and youngest son of Sir George. Digby had three spells as ambassador at Madrid between 1610 and 1618. In 1611, he was sent to Spain with instructions to obtain a settlement of claims of English merchants in the Spanish law courts and to negotiate a match between Prince Henry, eldest son of James I, and the Infanta Anne. Baldwin accompanied him on this task.[46] The mission was unsuccessful, as was a similar attempt in 1623 to cement an Anglo-Spanish alliance by a proposed marriage of the future Charles I to the Infanta.[47]

Baldwin's death early in 1628 was followed shortly afterwards by the sale of Clevedon and Portbury manors on 10 August 1630. John Wake, the eldest of Baldwin's four sons, now second baronet, was twenty six years of age and badly needed money. He had already petitioned the King in 1629 for royal protection for himself and others against his father's debts and this had been granted for one year. Now in 1630 he pleaded for an extension until 'the sale of such quantity of land lying in remote parts' could be effected.[48] Described in 1637 as Lieutenant and Forester of Salcey Forest, Sir John was fined on several occasions for committing a variety of offences, including keeping cattle in enclosed coppices, cutting wood without warrant, and keeping goats and kids in the Forest. In 1635 he was fined £20 for felling thirty oaks, and for building a kitchen and repairing his house without seeking authorization.[49] A further probable cause of Sir John's insolvency was his friendship with Digby, whose expensive life style he emulated. Digby was highly regarded by James I; he was made Baron Digby of Sherborne, having acquired in 1618 the estate there formerly belonging to Sir Walter Raleigh and was created the first Earl of Bristol in 1622. Following his attempts to impeach the King's favourite, the Duke of Buckingham, Bristol was sent to the Tower in 1626, but was released two years later.[50] It was ironic that the purchaser of Clevedon, for a sum of £17,000 10s. 0d., was Bristol himself.

A detailed survey of the manor of Clevedon, signed by Elizabeth Wake, was taken on 12 May 1629 and it still survives. The property consisted of 2,077 acres apart from the Commons: within the Park was a warren, orchards, mill houses and mills and a number of tenements. The yearly value of these tenements was £1,588 16s. 8d. and the demesnes, besides the manor house and woods, £326 3s. 4d.[51]

The Earl of Bristol's fortunes during the Civil War followed the pattern of many other noblemen. He sided at first with Parliament, then with Charles I, and fought at Edgehill. The House of Commons on 14 March 1648 ordered that he and his son should be put to death, but two years earlier he had left England for Paris, where he died in 1653 aged sixty six. Clevedon was completely sequestrated. As a result of a law case in 1650 brought by Colonel Owen Rowe, a Commissioner for Relief under Cromwell, Rowe was offered back a plot of land at Clevedon, held by his wife for thirty years, at a cost of 50s. a year for seven years. This was refused by Rowe, who complained that, 'considering that he had well served his party, he might have been better treated'.[52] At the Restoration, Clevedon was returned to the Digby family.

John, along with his three brothers, Baldwin, who died when two days old, George and another Baldwin and two sisters, Abigail and Elizabeth, was christened at Piddington. After selling Clevedon, John settled in Northamptonshire, as his title, Sir John Wake of Hartwell, suggests. Unlike the Earl of Bristol, Sir John was a loyal Royalist throughout Charles' struggles with Parliament. This was to lead to a severe decline in the fortunes of the family for the next century.

George Wake, John's younger brother, born in 1608, was more of an onlooker than a participator in the events of his time. He was a Fellow of Magdalen College, Oxford, 1630–48, but was ejected from his fellowship under the Commonwealth and his estates were sequestrated. Whilst he was studying for the clergy at the College, his mother had left him £150 in her will, 'hoping hee will followe his booke and continue at Oxford untill he shall be capeable and able to obteine some better preferment'.[53] In 1638 he was the third successive Wake to be Master of St. John's Hospital, Northampton following his great uncle William, (see Chapter 6). George must have been a very likeable person. As an adherent to the King's party however, he was in great danger of losing his post. In March 1647, the Mayor and citizens of the town, together with the co-brothers, almspeople and tenants of the Hospital, delivered a petition to the Committee for 'compounding with delinquents', begging that he might be allowed to continue.[54] George was readmitted to the mastership in November 1647 on payment of a £14 fine and he held that office until his death in 1682. After the Restoration, he was also made Chancellor of the Peterborough diocese.

Baldwin Wake, John's youngest brother, born in 1611, had a much more colourful life. The first known Wake to be a career sailor, Baldwin, called in documents Captain Wake, soon found himself caught up in the conflict between Charles and his Parliament. In 1641, a Grand Remonstrance, a list of grievances drawn up by leading Parliamentarians, demanded that only ministers and ambassadors who were acceptable

24. The interior of the Chapel, St John's Hospital

to both Houses should be appointed and that a synod of divines should be called to recommend church reform.[55] This important constitutional document was sent to the King, together with a petition, on 1 December. The Royalist advisers had already begun to make plans for the King's departure from London. One of them, Sidney Beere, wrote to Sir John Pennington on the day that the Grand Remonstrance was presented, 'Captain Wake is in the river here since Friday last, but being charged with the King's goods and plate he took the nearest way without passing by you, having orders to discharge in the river'.[56]

In the uneasy manoeuvring of the two sides during the first seven months of 1642, Baldwin Wake was in command of the *Expedition*, a ship of some 300 tons. He now became involved in a critical incident. Charles I had decided to take the Admiralty into his own hands after the Earl of Northumberland had delivered the Fleet to the Earl of Warwick, who supported Parliament. The King therefore ordered that a letter should be sent to each of the sea captains, upon receipt of which they were to weigh anchor and sail to Burlington Bay on the Yorkshire coast and there wait for further orders.

Warwick, who had been appointed Admiral of the Fleet by the Commons, also sent out a letter, summoning all the captains to attend him on his ship,

> the which, [wrote Clarendon] all but two did (Captain Slingsby and Captain Wake) who, being by His Majesties Letters, as the rest were, expressly charged to give no further obedience to the Earl of Warwick, refused to repair to him, making them ready to resist by violence and putting their ships in order to go out to sea that they might be at liberty to attend His Majesties Commands . . . but they were surrounded . . . seized and taken and carried by their own men to the Earl.[57]

Taken into custody, Slingsby and Wake decided to appeal to the Earl of Warwick for justice. On 3 July 1642, Slingsby, with Wake's approval, requested that 'those who serve in the ship and whose conscience will not permit them to serve contrary to His Majesties commands may be discharged and paid at their departure according to ancient custom for the time they have served'.[58] This plea was ignored and on 18 July, the Earl of Warwick communicated with the House of Lords, and Captains Slingsby and Wake were imprisoned. On 30 July, two crewmen submitted affidavits mentioning 'scandalous words' spoken by their captains; subsequently, requests for bail were refused. They were still in prison in October, according to their petition, but were later released.[59]

This was not the end of Baldwin Wake's exploits. In 1643, he arrived in Dublin with a small fleet of ships, where an attack on Liverpool was contemplated. He commanded the frigate *Proud Black Eagle* which took the Prince of Wales (later Charles II) to Jersey from Cornwall in April 1646 and he was knighted there. Sir Baldwin was made governor of Castle Cornet in Guernsey, which he defended against the parliamentary forces in 1648. It was in the following year, on his way to visit the Prince of Wales, then in exile in Holland, that he died at sea.

The second baronet fared little better than his brother Baldwin. Sir John had married Bridget, daughter of Henry Sandys, a squire of Plumpton, Northamptonshire, and there were two sons and three daughters of the marriage. After her death, he married Anne Brokesby of Frisby and Burstall, Leicestershire, a widow with one son, but there were no children of this marriage. John's financial position continued to deteriorate, despite the sale of the Somerset property. He gave a bond for £600 in 1637, for which he was sued. In 1639, he, along with others, was bailed for £2,600 which became forfeited and he mortgaged properties for £1,000 that same year.

The outbreak of hostilities in 1642 hardly helped his precarious situation. John raised a troop of horse for the King. Although the Royalists virtually lost the North after Prince Rupert's defeat at Marston Moor on 2 July 1644, Charles's armies were much more successful in the south and south-west. Sir John, who would have known the latter region well, was engaged in combat there. He is mentioned in an order dated 13 August 1644 from the King to Lord George Goring, General of Horse, following the escape of parliamentary forces into Devon after a confrontation. The King's order was to 'overtake and destroy the rebels'. It went on:

> Our further pleasure is that you command and send for, as occasion shall be, all the horse and foot under the command of Sir John Berkeley, Sir Francis Doddington, Sir John Wake, the governor of Dartmouth, the governor of Bridgewater, the governor of Dunster or any other who command any of our forces in Somerset, Devon, or any of those parts.[60]

There followed a pursuit into Cornwall and the Parliamentarians under their commander, the Earl of Essex, were soon hemmed in on all sides at Lostwithiel. On 31 August, Essex's cavalry broke out of the trap but the demoralized foot soldiers surrendered the following day, together with all their cannon and small arms.[61]

With the defeat of the Royalist forces at Naseby on 14 June 1645 and the surrender of the King to the Scots, the war was virtually over. Sir John was at Truro in March 1645 when Lord Hopton conceded victory to his opponents.[62] However he obtained a pass and marched away with his troop through Hampshire, but further bad luck was in store. They were set upon by some 'unruly and strong parties' who took from him £2,000. Sir John thought it advisable to take the Covenant, but as his properties had been sequestrated, this did not save him. He was fined £1,130 in April 1647, which represented one half of his estate. In 1654, in an appeal to reduce the fine, John set out his debts as £2,600, stating that 'he had been a long time a prisoner' in the King's Bench, that he had already lost his personal estate and that with a wife and six children,[63] there 'remained not to him or his a bed to lie upon'. According to his son's petition in 1660, Sir John's contribution of a troop of horse to the King was at a personal cost of £4,000 and he died £5,000 in debt.[64] In one of Sir John's last surviving notes he wrote, 'Fine at a moiety of £1,130 – paid nothing'. After his death in prison in 1658 his body was transported to Northamptonshire to be buried in the chancel of Piddington Church.

*   *   *   *   *

By the end of the Civil War, the Wake fortunes had reached one of its lowest points. This contrasted dramatically with the period in the middle of the fifteenth century, when the Somerset estates were acquired through marriage, and properties were held in many counties. The decline, following the death of the first baronet, was due to a combination of circumstances: particularly the thriftlessness of his son, Sir John, and the family's loyalty to the Royalist cause during the reign of Charles I. After generations of Wakes, between 1448 and 1630, Clevedon had been lost. But a quite unexpected series of events was to take place in Northamptonshire which more than compensated for the setbacks which had been suffered.

5

How the Wakes came to Courteenhall

JUDICIOUS MARRIAGES HAVE ALWAYS BEEN OF VALUE IN enhancing the fortunes of a family, and perhaps none was more propitious for the Wakes than that of Sir John's eldest son, William, the third baronet. He was born in 1632 and on his father's death in 1658 still described himself as 'of Piddington'. As Sir William Wake, he immediately petitioned for his restoration to the office of Lieutenant-Ranger of Salcey Forest, a post which his predecessors had held for more than a century. Surprisingly, in view of the sacrifices which William's father and uncle had made for the King during the Civil War, the bid was not successful. It was also at this time that he married Diana, daughter of Sir Dru Drury, second baronet of Riddlesworth in Norfolk. It is most likely that they had met at Courteenhall, for her mother, Susan, was the daughter of Isaac Jones; thus Diana was the niece of Sir Samuel Jones. This established a link between the two families which was to grow stronger.

Diana's great grandfather, Sir Dru Drury, had during the reign of Elizabeth built a hall at Riddlesworth, where the Roman Peddars Way enters the county. Branches of the Drurys existed elsewhere in Norfolk and Suffolk; many were distinguished in the field of statesmanship, such as Sir Robert Drury of Hawstead (d. 1536), Speaker of the House of Commons during Henry VII's reign,[1] and there was the colourful Sir Robert Drury (1575–1615), friend of John Donne, the divine and poet. His house in the middle of his London property lent its name to the immediate vicinity, Drury Lane.[2]

Sir Dru Drury, born in 1531, played a full part in national events during his long life. By 1559, he was Usher at Elizabeth's Court. His first wife Elizabeth Calthorpe was a Boleyn, a fact which may have influenced the Queen to favour him, and she brought half the manor of Riddlesworth to the Drurys some time before 1569. On her death, there were no children and he married Catherine Finch of Linstead, Kent.

Dru was a Justice of the Peace and was ordered by the Privy Council on 5 June 1570 to reside at Norwich to help in the government of the city. The outbreaks of disorder in Norfolk which had started in 1569 had a number of causes: local resentment at the Huguenot settlers, the closing of Continental markets for English cloth because of wars in the Netherlands and the unrest following the sending of the Duke of Norfolk to the Tower in October. An uprising in the county in December was quelled but the

See Appendix A – Family Trees V, VI and VII. Notes and References pages 398, 399 following May saw Norwich threatened by the insurgents. A plot by them to take charge of the city was betrayed to Drury, and stern action followed.[3]

Dru was knighted at Wanstead, Essex in 1579 and was MP for Mitchell, 1559, Camelford, 1563 and for Norfolk in 1584. Two years later, he witnessed the execution of the Babington conspirators – 'these horrebull traytores' – as he called them. Writing two years later to Lord Willoughby de Eresby on 23 September 1586, Drury told him of his new task: 'I beseche you let me tell you it is resoulved that 33 of the nobyllete and prevy council shall goe to the Queen of Skottes to Fotheryngam Castell to senser her accordyng to the law made the last session of Parlament'. As a result of this mission in November, he was sent to Fotheringhay to help Sir Amias Paulet in the wardership of Mary. On Wednesday 8 February 1587, Drury was present at the dramatic execution of the Queen.[4]

Since 1577, Drury had been one of the Commissioners appointed to determine disputes which had arisen respecting the right of poor fishermen to set nets in the River Yare, Norfolk, without the consent of the adjacent landowners. In 1593, he signed a letter to the Privy Council in his capacity as a Justice, 'in furtherance of the suit before-made about some relief for the Town of Yarmouth and the Haven thereof'.[5]

Informed of a dispute over a lease between his friend Sir Henry Hobart and the Lord of Horsford, Drury, now eighty one, wrote:

> Though the handmaydes of age hathe tacken hold of manie partes of my synfull boddy, and this vj weekes by part of one of my fyngers of my right hand, so it is as I feare you wyll hardly reade my hande, yet can I not, my old good worshipfull frend, but lete you know that it greves me no a lyttell to understand you are entered into lawe with so potent an adversary, and that you are so resolute that you wyll undergoe flecying than yeld to it.[6]

He was Lieutenant of the Tower of London, 1595–6, after which he spent more of his time at Riddlesworth.[7] Camden described him as 'a sincere honest man, and a Puritan in his religion'. Sir Dru died in 1617 and was buried at Riddlesworth Church. His fine monument on the north chancel wall depicts a kneeling knight at a desk, with two angels in long garments holding back the curtains. It was stated by earlier local historians, such as Blomfield, that Sir Dru lived until he was ninety nine, but he was in fact about eighty six.[8]

Sir Dru and his second wife Catherine had four children: a son, also called Dru, and three daughters, Elizabeth, Ann and Frances. In contrast to his father, Sir Dru II added little to the family's achievements. He was MP for Thetford, 1624, Commissioner for Subsidies, 1625–6 and was created a baronet in 1627. By his marriage to Ann, eldest daughter of Edward Waldegrave of Lawford, Essex, the other half of Riddlesworth came to the Drurys. Five of their children died in infancy, Dru III, the eldest son, succeeding as second baronet on the death of his father in 1632.

This Dru, who was born in January 1612, married Susan, Isaac Jones' daughter. They had a son, Robert, born 1634, and a daughter, Diana. Like his Wake contemporaries, Sir Dru fought for King Charles and was with Sir John Wake at the surrender of Truro in

March 1646. Dru took advantage of the system of compounding, introduced during the later stages of the war, whereby the estates of Royalists could be saved from sequestration by the payment of a single fine. This course was accepted by many as the hopelessness of the struggle became apparent. Sir Dru was fined £957, at the rate of one sixth of his estate, but under the scheme this was reduced to £639 10s. 0d.[9] His wife, Susan, had probably already died by this time and Sir Dru married secondly, Mary, in 1647.

On Sir Dru's death in 1651, his son, now Sir Robert, the third baronet, was under age and in the guardianship of his uncle, Sir Samuel Jones. In 1658, he was still a scholar at Eton. Sir Robert seems to have had more than his fair share of misfortune. On 27 March 1669, he was convicted of manslaughter of one John Powell; an inquiry into the circumstances of Powell's death, held at Bury St. Edmunds on 26 February 1668, described the incident as follows:

> Robert Drury late of Knettishall co. Suffolk baronet, not having the fear of God before his eyes, but by the instigation of the devil, 5 February 20 Chas. II (1668/9), at Knettishall upon a certain John Powell then and there being in the peace of God and of the King, feloniously, wilfully and of malice aforethought, made an assault, and the said Robert Drury with a certain sword, in English called 'a Tucke' of the value of 20s., held in his right hand, struck the said John Powell upon the left side of his body between his ribs, giving him a mortal wound, half an inch long and two inches deep, of which same mortal wound the said John Powell then and there instantly died, and thus the said Robert Drury the aforesaid John Powell in manner and form aforesaid then and there feloniously, wilfully and of his malice aforethought killed and murdered, against the peace of the said lord King and the dignity of the Crown.[10]

Though found not guilty of murder by the jury, Sir Robert was charged with felony and homicide. Fortunately for him, he escaped the ordinary course of law by seeking benefit of clergy, but he was sentenced 'to be cauterized [branded] "felo" as in such case is provided'.

He married three times: first Elizabeth, who died when young, then Eleanor who was killed in the Great Storm of 1703, and Diana, who outlived him and was buried at Riddlesworth in 1744. There were no children of these marriages and the baronetage ended with Sir Robert's death in 1712.

* * * * *

We must now turn our attention to what had befallen the Wakes during the period just described. Sir William, the third baronet, died in 1698 but his wife Diana, Sir Robert Drury's sister, predeceased him in 1675. Sir William had earlier sold Piddington, the home of six generations of Wakes, and built a house at West Hall in Preston Deanery, two miles south-west of Piddington. Sir William's only brother, Charles, who died as a prisoner for debt in Northampton Gaol,[11] was buried at All Saints, Northampton on 20 May 1709. There were also three sisters, Abigail, Elizabeth and Bridget, the first two of whom married.

25. Sir Robert Drury (d.1536), Speaker of the House of Commons, 1495-6, during the reign of Henry VII

26. Sir John Wake of Piddington, 4th baronet (1661–1714)

28. Piddington Church by E. F. Law, 1846 or 1848. From 1572 to the middle of the eighteenth century 18 Wakes were buried here

27. Fritwell Manor, Oxfordshire. The sixteenth century building was bought by Sir Baldwin Wake, 5th baronet, after 1683. It was sold in 1770 by the 8th baronet

HOW THE WAKES CAME TO COURTEENHALL

Sir William Wake and Diana had a large family, consisting of eight sons and four daughters. Of these, little is known of Isaac, the sixth son, and George, the eighth. Drury, the seventh, was, according to Barron, a captain, hanged for killing an innkeeper at Reigate, Surrey.[12] Robert, the fourth son, was the only one to enter the Church. Thanks to the good offices of his cousin, Archbishop William Wake, he held a number of clerical posts. Robert, born on 23 June 1666 at Piddington, gained an MA at Brasenose College, Oxford, in 1684 and was presented to Fritwell Vicarage, Oxfordshire, in 1691. Twelve years later, he moved to Ogbourne St. Andrew, Wiltshire and on 30 October 1714 became Rector of Farthingstone, Northamptonshire. After serving at Buxted with Cuckfield in Sussex from 1719 to 1723, Robert was appointed Dean and Rector of Bocking in Essex. The parish of Bocking is an archiepiscopal Peculiar, that is, the parish is not under the jurisdiction of the diocese in which it is situated: all matters are dealt with by the Archbishop of Canterbury or his commissary.[13] Robert's appointment to Bocking therefore presented no problems.

Robert's life was a tragic one. Married to Elizabeth Greenfield of Marlborough, they had three sons and two daughters. One son, Thomas, born 17 July 1706, died whilst still a pupil at Westminster School. Shortly after this, early in 1725 his eldest boy, Robert, who had graduated from Merton College, Oxford, four years previously and was about to follow his father into the Church, suddenly died. The third son, William, was to become the seventh baronet. To add to his troubles, the Dean was now heavily in debt. Much alarmed, Archbishop Wake wrote to his cousin:

April 9: 1725

Good Sr.
Being hindered from writing to you the last post, I desired Dr Wilkins [Dr David Wilkins, the Archbishop's domestic chaplain] to acquaint you how truly concern'd I am at the losse of your Son, whom I much liked when He came to me for Orders, and was resolved to have disposed of the very first Opportunity I had of making any tolerable provision for Him. But it has thanked God to take Him to Himselfe, and to provide better for Him than could have been done by any preferment upon Earth.

    Another most grievous Report was brought to me, wch I hope is not so bad as represented to me, of your own Circumstances: That you are so deeply plunged in debt, as to have been obliged as to confesse a judgment upon all your Goods; and those very goods yet unpay'd for to the poor widow of your predecessor. This may harm, if not timely prevented, not only to your Ruine, but to the Scandal of your ministry; and upon both those accounts should if possible be forthwith taken care of. I have heard that your Aunt Drury is willing to receive both yourself and your family. If you called in your debts, and agreed with yr Creditors to take all that comes in of yr benefice, the Curate payd, till yr debts were satisfied, you might retire with what you have of your own and in two or three years be clear in the world, with justice to others, and reputation to your selfe. This if you neglect, I doubt in a little time a writ will be taken out to sequester your living; that will be a new Charge; It will then be put into hands wch probably will not make the best of it; and what may happen to your person I cannot tell. These things reflect somewhat upon my selfe; who placed you in that good benefice; and you must give me leave on all these accounts to desire you to put yr affairs into some such way as I propose; the only remedy under your present Circumstances, if they are such as I have been informed. Your speedy answer to this will much oblige,

Reverend Sr.

Your loving friend,

W. Cant.[14]

It is unlikely that the Dean's personal affairs were ever put in order, for he died five months later, on 11 October 1725.

William, Sir William's second son, born in 1663, is said to have been murdered by his brother Baldwin, but the date of his death is not recorded. Few details are available also of the life of the eldest son, John, who was born in 1661 and became fourth baronet in 1698, except that he left Merton College, Oxford, in July 1679 and was admitted as a student of Gray's Inn on 27 October; he died in 1714, leaving no issue. The title now passed to his brother, Baldwin, third son of Sir William Wake, the third baronet, who was born at Piddington in June 1665.

Like his brother, Sir Baldwin was a lawyer and practised in London. He became the fifth baronet in 1714. It was probably in the 1680s[15] that Baldwin bought the manor of Fritwell, close to the Northamptonshire border, from Sir Pope Danvers, having already held the advowson. As was mentioned in Chapter 4, the fine manor house, situated at the west end of the village, remained the family home until 1770 when it was sold with the rest of the manor by Sir William Wake, the seventh baronet, to John Freke Willes of Astrop, Northamptonshire.[16] By his first wife, Anne Dereham, Sir Baldwin had one son, also called Baldwin. Anne died in 1696 and in the following year he married Mary Hart of Burford, Oxfordshire, by whom he had a son, Charles and two daughters, Diana and Mary. The significance of Charles in the history of Courteenhall will be shown below. In his will of May 1745, Sir Baldwin asked to be buried in Piddington chancel with his father, grandfather and many of his ancestors; but his wish was disregarded and he was interred at Fritwell on 29 July 1747. Thus ended the long line of Wake christenings, marriages and burials at Piddington, starting in 1572, of eighteen members of the family.[17]

*   *   *   *   *

Whilst the Wake baronets were seemingly weakening their links with Northamptonshire, a younger member of the family had been in possession of Courteenhall for some years. This had come about partly as an act of sentiment and partly as a deliberate calculation on the part of Samuel Jones. In his will dated 10 March 1671, Jones set out the proposed dispositions of his estates in Northamptonshire, Oxfordshire, Shropshire, Denbigh and Surrey. As he had no heirs, Jones bequeathed all his properties to his nephew, Samuel Pierrepoint, on condition that he changed his

CP8. Robert Wake, Dean of Bocking (1666–1725), father of William, the 7th baronet, who succeeded to Courteenhall, and Waltham and Nazeing in Essex

CP9. Sir Baldwin Wake, Kt (1611–1649), youngest son of the 1st baronet who, in the Civil War, took the Prince of Wales to safety in the Channel Islands in 1646

CP10. Sir John Wake, 2nd baronet, aged 26, a loyal supporter of Charles I; born 1600, died a prisoner of Cromwell in 1658

CP11. Sir Baldwin Wake, 5th baronet (1665–1745), the third son of the 3rd baronet, who lived at Fritwell Manor, Oxfordshire

CP12. Charles II when Prince of Wales, painted by Van Dyck in 1641, when the Prince was 11 years old. The portrait of his sister Mary painted at the same time also hangs at Courteenhall

surname to Jones. Should his nephew fail to have sons, then the estate was to pass to Samuel Wake, the fifth son of his niece, Diana Wake. He was probably chosen mainly because he bore the name Samuel, but also as he was unlikely to inherit the Wake estates, this would be a way of preserving the Jones' properties intact as an entity.[18] Two conditions which Jones imposed were that Samuel should 'call himself and be called and write himself Samuell Jones. And that hee the said Samuell Wake nor his Issue descending from him shall no more use the name of Wake for his or their sirname but the name of Jones only'.

A year later, a codicil of 16 September 1672 was added, partly because of the death of one of his nephews, 'But most of all by the Idle and unprofitable life of my indiscrete nephew Samuell Pierrepoint'. So incensed was Samuel Jones at this unspecified misbehaviour that Pierrepoint was deleted from the will: the estates were now left to Samuel Wake for his life and his sons after him. Jones mentioned that 'my said Cousin Samuel Wake is very young' – he was just two years old – and that the estate was to be in the hands of executors until Samuel had attained the age of twenty one. The condition of changing the name from Wake to Jones was reiterated.

Samuel Jones lay great store by the value of good education, as we saw in the previous chapter in his provision for Courteenhall Free School. He now set out how this was to be achieved for the young Samuel. A sum of £100 a year was earmarked for this purpose, the school to be chosen by his executor 'and not as Sir William Wake [Samuel's father] or such other person after him . . . shall think fitt'. Samuel Wake and his successors were abjured to 'avoid the sinns of Drunkennesse and Debauchery now so much in fashion and that they betake themselves during their younger yeares to the studdy of the Law and that they be industrious to imitate the examples of the best men and be deterred from the commitment of evill by the consequences which they observe doe attend the committers of it'.[19]

*   *   *   *   *

Since drawing up his original will, Sir Samuel Jones had, in January 1672, acquired a mortgage of the estate of Waltham in Essex, close to Epping Forest. It was there, probably in the early 1050s, that Harold Godwinson, Edward the Confessor's brother-in-law, was granted the estate by the King. A church at Waltham had about twenty five years previously received from Tovi, one of Canute's chief ministers, the Holy Cross of Waltham, a stone crucifix from Somerset reputed to have miraculous powers.[20] It was claimed that Harold recovered from an attack of paralysis through its agency and for this reason he raised a new church at Waltham in place of the old. The dedication took place in the presence of the King on 3 May 1060 and the church became a centre of pilgrimage in medieval times for those seeking healing. After the Battle of Hastings in 1066, Harold's body is considered to have been brought back to Waltham for burial. The chancel was destroyed at the Reformation and the site of the tomb is now marked in the churchyard, to the east of the present building. Harold's church was largely replaced at the end of the eleventh century and early in the twelfth and much enlarged after 1177 by Augustinian Canons introduced by Henry II. The spacious nave is Norman work at its grandest, the piers being strongly reminiscent of Durham Cathedral.[21]

29. The Abbey House, Waltham, Essex, 1735. Built during the reign of Henry VIII from the Abbey ruins, it was remodelled c.1690 for Samuel Wake Jones and later by his nephew Charles Wake Jones, c.1730

30-31. Panelling from the Abbey House, Waltham, c.1540.

HOW THE WAKES CAME TO COURTEENHALL

Waltham Abbey was the last religious house to be dissolved by Henry VIII, in 1540. One of the King's officials, Anthony Denny, Groom of the Stole and a Privy Councillor, had purchased a number of properties at this time, including Cheshunt Nunnery, Hertford Priory and several of the St. Albans estates. In April 1541, Denny was granted a lease of Waltham Grange, the home farm of the Abbey which lay to the south of it, and other lands in Waltham and Nazeing.[22] He was knighted by the King at Boulogne in 1544. After his death in 1549, little more is known about the Abbey site until the marriage of his grandson, Sir Edward Denny, in 1590 to Lord Burghley's granddaughter, Mary. Burghley himself owned the nearby and impressive house of Theobalds. This may have proved the incentive for Sir Edward to move from the family seat at Dallance, one mile from Waltham, to a more splendid home.[23]

During the 1590s, building began on a house to the north-east of the cloisters, adjoining the site of the Chapter House. It was typically an E-shaped building running north to south, containing much medieval masonry, with doors in the west and north walls of the main block. The design may have been based on Burghley's own Wimbledon House. Whether the house was a new structure or adapted at least in part from an existing building is not clear. Thomas Fuller, the church historian and author of *Worthies of England*, was a curate at Waltham Abbey from 1648 to 1658. He quotes from Master Thomas Smith, who worked for Sir Edward Denny before the turn of the seventeenth century, that the house 'at that time lay in ruinous heaps and then Sir Edward began slowly now and then to make even and re-edify some of this chaos.' The only known surviving fixtures from the old house are the 110 wooden panels from the time of either John Malyn, abbot of Waltham 1514 to 1526 or his successor, Robert Fuller, the last abbot. They are of very high quality and contain male and female profiles or medallions, framed by enriched moulding, and leaves. Parts of the decoration include the Tudor rose, the Beaufort portcullis (both badges of Henry VIII) and the pomegranate, the badge of Catherine of Aragon, as well as coats of arms. No two panels are alike. The panelling or wainscoting could have been placed in three tiers to a height of over seven feet. Alternatively, it has been suggested that these panels would have been arranged in one tier only, with plainer panels forming the other two tiers: in this way, the whole of the hall could have been panelled. The panels were removed to a house in Waltham in 1770 when the Abbey House became ruinous, and were moved again in 1898 to the Victoria and Albert Museum, forming for some time a complete Tudor room there.[24] In 1981 they were transferred on long loan to the Epping District Forest Museum in Sun Street, Waltham Abbey. The Abbey House would probably have incorporated the existing vaulted slype and part of the cloisters.[25]

Denny, who became Lord Denny of Waltham in 1604 and was created Earl of Norwich in 1626, left Waltham to his grandson, James Hay, second Earl of Carlisle. A staunch Royalist, Carlisle entertained Charles I at Waltham in 1641 and after being wounded at the Battle of Newbury two years later, went into exile. He died in 1660 without issue. It was a few years after this that Sir Samuel Jones acquired a mortgage on the estate, for which Carlisle's widow was lady of the manor; she died in 1676 and her co-heiresses were bought out by Jones' executors. In 1688, the estate was reunited in the residential ownership of the now-named Samuel Wake Jones, Sir Samuel Jones' great nephew.[26]

Samuel settled at Waltham, becoming Sheriff of Essex in 1699 and Deputy-Lieutenant of the county in 1711. Besides assuming the name of Jones, he also adopted the arms of that family. He married Elizabeth, daughter of Sir George Champion, alderman of London, but there were no legitimate offspring. At his death in 1713, Samuel's will shows that he owned the manor of Waltham Holy Cross with the site of Waltham Abbey monastery, Courteenhall, Preston, Wootton, Roade, Quinton, Ashton, Collingtree and Fritwell. Since 1672, he was also Lord of the Manor of Nazeing, which lies some four miles north of Waltham Abbey. Nazeing, or Nazeingbury had been part of the hundred of Waltham and was held by the canons of the Abbey until the Dissolution. In 1541, the King leased the manor and rectory of Nazeing to Anthony Denny and it subsequently descended with the manor of Waltham Abbey to the Wakes. Samuel Jones had also bought the romantically-named manor of Harold's Park, which included a great wood and park, and which lay between Waltham and Nazeing. It was sold about 1700. Nevertheless, the Wakes were the largest landowners in the area until well into the nineteenth century. In 1842, Sir William Wake owned 841 acres of titheable land in addition to a large area tithe-free in Waltham Abbey. Six years later, Sir Charles Wake possessed 802 acres of titheable land in Nazeing, including Nazeingbury Farm, which comprised 298 acres and 34 tithe-free strips in Nazeing Mead, totalling 50 acres.[27] The Wake baronets are still Lords of the Manor of Waltham Abbey and Nazeing. They also owned up to the time of the twelfth baronet part of Epping Forest. When the Corporation of the City of London began a movement to secure the Forest 'for purposes of health and recreation' to the public, Sir Herewald opposed the Corporation. The case was heard in the House of Lords and the baronet was unsuccessful.[28] The Forest was formally declared open in March 1882. The cost of the case was more than the compensation eventually paid to him. However, the Corporation agreed to continue sending Sir Herewald one buck in summer and one doe in winter each year. This custom continued until the death of his son, the thirteenth baronet, in 1963.

*   *   *   *   *

Samuel Wake Jones took care during his lifetime to ensure that he would have a successor at Waltham. He adopted the younger of his two nephews, Charles Wake, second son of Baldwin, the fifth baronet, and in his will of 1712, made shortly before his death, Samuel stated that he had the care and education of Charles. Born in January 1701 and christened at Preston Deanery, Northamptonshire, Charles was sent to a private boarding school at Enfield, Middlesex, very near to his uncle at Waltham.

The school was owned by Dr Robert Uvedale, a remarkable man better remembered as a horticulturalist than as a schoolmaster. Uvedale's ancestors included a peer of the realm in the reign of Edward III and another, Nicholas, was the first benefactor of William of Wykeham, having obtained a place for him at Winchester School in 1334. Robert Uvedale was born in 1642 and elected Fellow of Trinity College, Cambridge in 1664 first in divinity and later in law. About this time, he became

32. Waltham Abbey, dedicated to St. Lawrence and the Holy Cross, 1791. The Abbey House adjoined the north-east side of the cloisters

33. Waltham Abbey with the River Lea

Master of Enfield Grammar School, in the grounds of which he planted a cedar brought back from Mount Lebanon by one of his pupils. A century later it had a girth of twelve feet.[29] By 1676, Uvedale was accused of neglecting the school, having opened his own private establishment in Enfield Manor House.[30]

He gained a reputation for cultivating exotic plants and flowers, and was one of the earliest users of hothouses in England. An observer of London gardens visited Uvedale in 1691 and announced that he had 'become master of the greatest and choicest collection of exotic green that is perhaps anywhere in this land. His greens take up six or seven houses or roomsteads. His orange trees and largest myrtles fill up his biggest house, and … those more nice and curious plants that need closer keeping are in warmer rooms'. After Uvedale's death in 1722, Sir Robert Walpole bought most of his growing plants for Houghton Hall, Norfolk; his herbarium, in fourteen large volumes, is in the British Museum. Considered as one of Europe's first botanists, Uvedale conducted a correspondence with many people. On 29 May 1701, he advised one writer to direct his letters to The Bull in Bishopsgate rather than to Enfield post office, as they 'frequently stay three or four days and sometimes longer before we receive them, which yet the gentlemen of the neighbourhood can get no redress for'.[31]

This very unusual setting for a school no doubt impressed the pupils, who carried away with them some knowledge of the art of gardening. Charles Wake, who since 1718 had added Jones to his surname, certainly followed in the footsteps of Uvedale when he laid out the grounds at Waltham after coming of age. In 1735, one of Jones' tenants, John Farmer, a local attorney and amateur historian, dedicated a book to him on the history of Waltham. He also describes the improvements which Charles Wake Jones was making to the 'House's spacious fine Garden', covering twelve acres, which was surrounded by a canal, with all kinds of fish and an old red brick wall:

> There are the most curious ever green Hedges, Walks, Groves; and for Variety of Fruit, 'tis scarce to be equall'd by any private Gentleman's: Theyre are also fine Kitchen-Gardens, Vineyards, a Bowling-Green; nay, in short, every thing else that is commendable and praiseworthy. But above all I must not forget the Tulip-Tree, the largest and biggest that ever was seen; there being but one more in Great Britain (as I am informed) and that at the Lord Peterborough's. It blooms with innumerable Flowers in the Months of June and July.
>
> Here a Person may walk, and all his Senses be employ'd with every thing that is agreeable and delightful; so that it may be said, while you are in these Gardens of Paradise, (if I may so call them) that the Eye is not satisfied with seeing, nor the Ear with hearing, by reason of the sweet melodious Songs of the little inchanting Birds.[32]

By the time Charles moved into the Abbey House in 1724, there was a need to embark on a programme of refurbishing the house in a manner more in accord with the status of a wealthy eighteenth century country gentleman. We can only surmise at the appearance of the house at this time[33] but from Farmer's drawing of 1735, it seems probable that improvement rather than much rebuilding had taken place during the 1690s when Samuel Wake Jones was in occupation. The original plan of a central block with projecting wings was retained, Farmer giving the length of its 'sumptuous hall' as 49 feet 6 inches, its height 28 feet and its breadth 25 feet 6 inches.[34] About 1730, the facade was refaced with stone by Charles and a pediment with four Ionic pillars made an imposing entrance. Whilst the odd distribution of the Elizabethan chimneys was not disturbed, they were modernised, and the window casements on the ground and upper floors were renewed. Dormer windows giving more light were placed in the hipped roof.[35]

Inside the house, some fireplaces and stone casements in the rooms at the rear of the house were also kept. Farmer considered the Hall 'exceeding handsome, by reason of the Wainscotting and extraordinary Painting.' The floor of the Hall was of black and white marble squares and there was a marble chimney piece surmounted by the coats of arms of the Jones family and those of Charles' wife's, Elizabeth, daughter of Sir Samuel Vanacker Sambrooke, of Bush Hill, Enfield. Some of the paintings were of sea scenes, such as a Sea-calm with Men-of-War, Fishermen in the Boats, Storm with the Wreck of Ships, and Seafaring Men on the Shore, the latter two by Monamy. At the upper end of the Hall was a hunting scene by Ross representing Charles on horseback with his sister (Mary, who had married a Henry Jones and died in 1729) in riding habit and a huntsman with a dead hare in his hand, surrounded by twenty four hounds.[36] The improvements to the property can be seen from the rateable value, which increased from £40 in 1722 to £160 in 1727.[37]

Farmer claimed that Sir Edward Denny, in building his new house in the late sixteenth century, had, through his gardener, uncovered the marble tomb of King Harold. 'It is without Dispute', he wrote, 'that he was buried in the Garden under a leaden Fountain where there is now a Bowling-Green, which formerly belonged to the Earl of Carlisle, and which was by all Probability the End of the Choir, or rather some Eastern Chapel or consecrated Ground'. He describes the tomb as being of rich grey marble with a cross fleury inscribed, supported by small pillars. Farmer mentioned that he had in his own house 'a curious Face or Busto', traditionally part of Harold's tomb, and reproduces it in his book.[38] The piece, which still survives, has Renaissance or slightly later characteristics and was most likely to have been part of the fountain erected by Denny. However, Charles Wake Jones obviously regarded the tomb highly, for an anonymous author of an article on Waltham, writing about 1770, corrected Farmer stating, 'The slightest enquiry about Harold's Tomb at Waltham would have informed him that Mr. Jones fixt the fragment in question at the further end of his cellar (a large souterrain [in] which, if we believe Farmer, says his brothers Girth and Leoffen [Leofwin] were buried)'.[39]

A rather different light is cast on Charles' attitude to the relic if an anecdote, told to a traveller by a local curate in 1820 after partaking of a duck and a bottle of port, is to be believed:

> Between thirty and forty years ago, the manor-house of Waltham Abbey was inhabited by the famous Bumper-Squire Jones. In digging to enlarge his cellar, the body of King Harold was found, as evidently appeared from *Haroldus Rex* inscribed on the lid of the coffin. Jones thought he could not do greater honour

to the corpse than by placing it at the head of the cellar where it had been interred; and whenever any of his friends were led by curiosity to see it, he made them offer libations to the memory of the deceased, till they could not see it.[40]

The splendour of the Abbey House did not attract Charles Wake Jones's successors. After his death in 1739, it was only occupied from time to time and the house fell into ruin. It is generally stated that it was demolished in 1770,[41] though the Waltham Abbey rating books in the Essex Record Office for the 1770s and 1780s do not make clear the fate of the house. It is likely that the stables were converted into a dwelling house which retained the name Abbey House and was occupied by a tenant called Chapman.[42] The site was used for market gardening for the next two hundred years,[43] until in 1970 the Lee Valley Regional Park Authority took responsibility for the area which is now a public open space; the slype and the site of the chapter house are in the care of English Heritage. A visitor to the site today will be able to recognize the south wall of the house and the southern part of the west wall, with evidence of two chimney pieces of the 'sumptuous hall'.

Charles' elder brother was Baldwin, named after his father, the fifth baronet. Born five years before Charles, in 1696, he died in 1735, predeceasing his father by twelve years and Charles by four. He was buried at Fritwell. There is a family legend that the son Baldwin was killed in a quarrel during a game of cards by a blow from his father and that his younger brother Charles took the blame and hid abroad until Sir Baldwin confessed on his deathbed.[44] The story is patently untrue, for Charles died seven years before his father and had lived prosperously at Waltham since the 1720s. Baldwin had married Mary, daughter and coheir of Edward Lane of Tathall End, one mile from Hanslope, Buckinghamshire, close to the south-eastern border of Northamptonshire. Mary's share of the manor remained in the family until the younger brother of the ninth baronet the Reverend Richard Wake sold it to Edward Watts of Hanslope Park in 1802.[45]

In contrast to his own parents, who produced twelve children, Baldwin had as issue only one son, Charles. It was his uncle, Charles Wake Jones, who left to Charles Waltham Holy Cross and Nazeing, Fritwell and the Northamptonshire properties, which included Courteenhall. On the death of the third wife of Sir Robert Drury in 1744, Riddlesworth also came into the possession of the Wakes. Charles was born in 1725 and although he was married at Chingford, Essex on 16 June 1753, there is strong circumstantial evidence to show that he was the first Wake to reside at Courteenhall. His wife, Mary Jackson, was of Quinton and she was buried at Courteenhall Church in 1757, leaving no children. On succeeding to the baronetcy on the death of his grandfather in 1747, Charles took the name and arms of Jones. Thus the sixth baronet, Sir Charles Wake Jones of Courteenhall, settled there for the remaining eight years of his life; he was only thirty when he died. His is the earliest male Wake monument in the Church; it takes the form of a large white marble wall tablet, placed in the north aisle in 1769 by his kinsman, William, the eighth baronet and above the inscription a skull surmounted by a baldacchino with draperies.[46] There is also a simple contemporary memorial to him, largely hidden beneath the organ.

HOW THE WAKES CAME TO COURTEENHALL

The seven decades between the death of Sir Samuel Jones in 1672 and the succession of Charles Wake Jones to the baronetcy in 1739 saw the strengthening of connections with families which proved to be beneficial. One remarkable feature is the pattern of marriages between the Jones, the Drurys and the Wakes, which, through lack of direct descendants in the former two families, strengthened the Wake descent. A second feature is the manner in which Sir Samuel Jones made provision for the continuance of his name through his Wake successors, though perhaps not envisaging that a future Wake baronet would inherit his estates. Equally remarkable is the tortuous and fortuitous process by which the Jones property passed from one Wake generation to another – first, through Jones' great-nephew, Samuel, the fifth son of the third baronet, second, through Samuel's nephew, Charles, and finally through to his only nephew, Charles, the sixth baronet, and grandson of the fifth baronet.

The marriage of Diana Drury, also a niece of Samuel Jones, to a Wake brought Riddlesworth into the family, and the acquisiton of the lordship of the manor at Waltham re-established earlier Wake links with Essex. Within Northamptonshire, Piddington and the adjacent Salcey Forest ceased after many generations to be the focus of their activities, which shifted for several decades to Fritwell beyond the county boundary. It was almost exactly a century after Samuel Jones had purchased Courteenhall from the Ouseleys that the Wakes finally settled there. The years of wandering were over.

6

Sir Isaac Wake,
Diplomat

THE WAKES HAVE BEEN WELL REPRESENTED IN MANY OF
the professions since early times, but there has been only one ambassador, a seventeenth
century member of the family, Sir Isaac Wake, who influenced the course of events in
Europe.

Isaac was born about 1580 and his father, Arthur, was the third son of John Wake of
Piddington. It was Arthur's eldest brother, also called John, who carried out the
improvements at Clevedon (see Chapter 4). John's only son, Baldwin, who became the
first Wake baronet, was therefore Isaac's first cousin. Isaac was brought up in
Northamptonshire, for his father was Rector of Great Billing from 1565. Arthur, a
graduate of Christ Church, Oxford, was appointed canon two years later. Because of his
Nonconformist views, he was deprived of his living in 1573[1] and went to live in Jersey.
He had been appointed Master of St. John's Hospital, Northampton which provided for
the infirm poor, in 1569 and continued to hold the office though out of the country. The
main reason for this was that Queen Elizabeth's favourite, the Earl of Leicester, was one
of his supporters. When attempts were made to eject Arthur because of his non-
residence and Nonconformity, Leicester wrote to the Bishop of Lincoln in 1575 stoutly
defending Arthur Wake's 'gret honesty'. Further efforts to deprive him of this office
were equally unsuccessful. He died on 11 July 1596 and was buried on the north side of
the choir in Oxford Cathedral. Arthur was succeeded as Master, shortly before his death,
by his brother, William. William had also been a student at Christ Church, Oxford,
gaining an MA degree in 1577. He was Master for over forty years and shortly before his
resignation, he made his Will, dated 1 June 1637, leaving 'to the two Co-bretheren of St.
John's Hospitall in Northampton twentie shillinges apiece, and to each of the Poore of
the same Hospitall five shillings'.

Isaac's mother was Christian Wigston, daughter of Sir William Wigston of
Wolston, Warwickshire, and there were three children: Abraham, who also attended
Christ Church and became a barrister, Isaac, and Sarah, later wife of Henry Wilkinson,
Rector of Waddesdon, Buckinghamshire. Isaac inherited his love of learning from his
father.[2] At the early age of twelve, Isaac entered Christ Church, gaining his BA in July
1597 when he was seventeen.[3] In the following year he was elected Fellow of Merton

See Appendix A – Family Trees I and VIII. Notes and References pages 400–402

College, Oxford, and trained as a barrister at Middle Temple from 1604. On 14 December of that year, when only twenty three, Isaac received the great honour from the University of becoming its Public Orator. A man of formidable intellect, his achievements were recalled later in the seventeenth century by an historian of Oxford University, Anthony Wood:

> I have been informed by some of the ancients of Merton College that this our author Wake had his pen more at command in the Latin, English and French tongue than any of his time in the university. Also that his speaking was majestic, that he was better for oration than disputing, and that he employed his time more in reading political and civil matters than philosophy or the great faculties. Further also, that he was a genteel man in his behaviour, well spoken, and therefore put upon speeches at all receptions and funerals. There is no doubt but that he was a man of exquisite learning, strong parts of nature, and of a most refined wit.[4]

A few months after becoming Public Orator, in August 1605, Isaac Wake was present on the occasion of the Royal visit of James I to the University. On 27 August, the King entered the city, riding on horseback with his Queen, Anne of Denmark on his left and Prince Charles in front of them, attended by a large force of richly attired noblemen. After being greeted by the Chancellor and the Mayor, the Doctors of Philosophy and Heads of Colleges, the procession passed through the town, the streets of which were lined on one side with over 2,000 students, and on the other with Bachelors and Masters of Arts. At Carfax, the Professor of Greek made an oration in that langauge. A contemporary noted that 'the King heard him willingly, and the Queen much more, because she sayd she never had heard Greek'.[5]

The party then went to Christ Church, where at the foot of the Hall's stairs, Isaac delivered 'a good oration', which was followed by a service in the Cathedral. The only recorded reaction of the King to the address was set down by Wood in a note dated 9 July 1611; although typical of the bluntness of many of the King's utterances, the passage looks suspiciously dependent on the possibility of making a double pun:

> Anthony Sleepe, Master of Arts, of Cambridge. This person who was a member of Trinity College, was so excellent an Orator, that he gave King James I occasion several times to say that 'Isaac Wake, Orator of the University of Oxford, had a good Ciceronian style, but his utterance and manner was so grave, that when he spake before him he was apt to <u>sleep</u>, but <u>Sleepe</u>, the Deputy Orator of Cambridge, was quite contrary, for he never spake but kept him a<u>wake</u>, and made him apt to laugh'.[6]

One event which took place during the visit was of more than passing interest. When the Royal procession reached the gateway of St. John's College, it was met by three youths dressed as sibyls (i.e. witches who uttered prophecies) who opened the proceedings.[7] This was followed by a performance setting out in a laudatory fashion the ancient history of Scotland, as an acknowledgment of the King's own ancestry. Both

Macbeth and Banquo appeared in it. The play was performed in Latin and in English. In a lengthy account of the visit published in 1607 by Isaac Wake and entitled *Rex Platonicus*, he describes the plot of the play, which bears a strong resemblance to Shakespeare's *Macbeth*. It is a well-known fact that James I held the playwright in great esteem. Shakespeare for his part wished to acknowledge the accession of the new King and wrote *Macbeth* in 1606, based on that part of Holinshed's *Chronicles* which described the history of Scotland. As a member of the King's company of players in London at the time, it is possible that Shakespeare was stimulated to write the play following reports of the Oxford performance in the previous year. Whatever the facts, it is clear that *Rex Platonicus* presents us with a superb account of the King's visit by a participant observer of the proceedings.

One of the tasks which fell to the Public Orator was to attend the funerals of University men and extol their virtues at their burial services. A notable instance was that of Sir Thomas Bodley, whose activities as a diplomat are now less well known than his achievement in founding the Library at Oxford which since 1604 has borne his name. Like Isaac Wake, he was a Fellow of Merton and on his death on 28 January 1613, he was buried in the choir of the College. Isaac's speech *Oratio Funebris* extolling Bodley's accomplishments, was published later that year.[8]

*   *   *   *   *

Isaac's ambitions for advancement were not confined to an academic career at Oxford. The need for greater knowledge of the world outside led him in 1609 to travel to France and Italy; in the following year, he became secretary to Sir Dudley Carleton, the ambassador at Venice. Carleton, a competent, moody and self-seeking man, provided a sound apprenticeship for his younger colleague. Fortunately, we are able to follow many aspects of Isaac's future career through the correspondence which Carleton conducted with John Chamberlain, a London gentleman of independent means. Chamberlain called himself 'a Paul's walker', one of the group of men who frequented St. Paul's Cathedral, talking to people and pumping them for information.[9] His delightful style and sense of humour help to bring the early seventeenth century vividly to light, and as a friend of Isaac he was able from time to time to transmit 'two shillings worth of newes from Master Wake'.

Isaac acted as a carrier of documents between Carleton in Venice and officials in London, and also took the opportunity to see friends in the capital. Chamberlain was often on hand to give advice: the latter wrote to Carleton at the end of 1612, explaining 'some busines he [Wake] hath that belike finds slowe dispatch, so that he cannot make that haste backe that at first he pretended but sure I am deceved yf he do not, or may do you as goode service here (the times standing as they do) as yf he were with you, and therfor I perswade him to tarrie some time and take leysure'.[10] Wake's visit to England followed the death of the Earl of Salisbury. Carleton, anticipating the appointment of a new Secretary of State, charged Wake with delivering letters to the King and contacting other great men at court for their support. The mission proved to be a difficult one. Isaac complained to Carleton:

Some to whom I should goe are out of Towne, and have been since my comming hither in which case there is no remedye. Some others I heare of, that they are seen about the Citty many times but they have no certain rendevous, so yt I can learne no way to them, their dwelling being out of the towne in adjoining parkes. Lastly, many whose howses are well enough knowen are gone abroad so early and come home so late, yt is hard finding them within, and when they are found then are either so busy or so private that no accession be had.[11]

Isaac returned to England in the following year to report on the wedding of King James' daughter to Frederick, the Elector Palatine on 14 February 1613. Not all of Isaac's missions were strictly connected with his diplomatic work. He carried messages to Carleton's sister, Bridget, and sometimes brought money to her. Chamberlain later acknowledged the receipt of a 'boxe of seeds and plomstones from Italy':

We will set the plomstones at all adventures, though we have no great hope of them that they will grow, neither yf they shold have I any opinion of the goodnes of Italian plummes: they may bragge of theyre melons and grapes, for the rest of theyre fruit is not worth the talking of. We have set the vine-plants that came from Master Wake as carefully as we could, and I am not out of hope but they may prove, though they be very drie and promise litle by theyre lookes. I have not yet geven Master Wake thancks for them, but will not be long behind with him.[12]

Carleton was an experienced and successful diplomat and Isaac learnt the art of statescraft at first hand. A war had broken out between Charles Duke of Savoy and the Spanish Duchy of Milan; this event alarmed the republic of Venice which feared that Spain might use it as an excuse to increase its influence in Italy. In June 1615, Carleton accomplished the delicate task of concluding a treaty at Asti which brought the war to an end; the negotiations, establishing peace in Europe, involved Venice, Rome, England and France.[13] A month later, Carleton left Venice for England before becoming ambassador at The Hague and Isaac Wake was appointed in July 1615 as representative of the court of Savoy at Turin; he was to hold this post for the following nine years.

Since James had become King in 1603, an English ambassador had been appointed to Venice. The rest of Italy was kept under surveillence by English representatives: it was for this purpose that Isaac Wake was appointed as agent at Turin. Carleton's successor was Sir Henry Wotton who had already served at Venice between 1604 and 1609. Unlike Carleton, he was an obsequious if amiable dilettante, who only reluctantly accepted the ambassadorial post in the absence of a better one being offered. He had earlier offended the King by defining an ambassador, using the pun 'to lie' which meant 'to reside', as 'an honest man sent to lie abroad for the good of his country'.

Within a short space of time Isaac was witness to new developments in the region. On 7 September 1617, he expressed great alarm to Sir Thomas Edmondes, ambassador at Paris, at the action of Don Pedro di Toledo in invading the state of Venice, and sacking and pillaging villages. 'It is much feared here', he wrote, 'that the Ministers of State who do govern the affairs of France have a great part in this business and that Herod and Pilate have conspired together to betray the public liberty'.[14] In the same year, he was able to mediate an alliance between Savoy and the Swiss states. But life was not all work. Isaac arranged for his books to be sent from Venice and the Duke of Savoy lent him his hounds and hawks for hunting.[15] And towards the end of 1618, Chamberlain reported to Carleton that Wake had arrived in London, having recently 'found goode entertainment at Paris, and though he kept himselfe private yet he was visited in great troupes both by Monsieur Betunes with the other ambassador that was his colleague and others'.[16]

The high regard in which Isaac was held both in England and abroad naturally pleased him. 'Master Wake is very joviall', wrote Chamberlain in January 1619, 'and not without cause (yf all be as he sayes) for I have not heard of a man so generally applauded both by King and counsaile, but sure yf goode words could make a man druncke with joy, I shold ymagine when I saw him last that he was transported'.[17] The proof of his popularity with the King was displayed on 9 April, when James, who was ill in bed at his hunting lodge at Royston, bestowed a knighthood on Isaac. They also discussed the position in Germany, where the King was becoming involved through his son-in-law, Frederick, the Elector Palatine. Eight days later, Sir Isaac Wake left on his mission.

At Heidelberg, he met the Elector Palatine. The task was not to Isaac's liking. That same day he reported to James Hay, Earl of Carlisle, recounting 'as much as I have been able to learn in passing through the country *tamquam canis ad nilum*, [like a dog to no purpose], and I am sure you will not think the proverb ill applied when you shall see so many crocodiles as I have met withall'.[18] On his return to Italy, he also carried a message to the Duke of Savoy, promising James' support in the Duke's candidature for the Imperial Crown in return for the support of the Elector Palatine: the offer was not accepted.[19]

The increasing influence of George Villiers, the King's favourite, in both home and foreign affairs was not ignored by Isaac. He reported at length on the negotiations with the Elector Palatine and the Duke of Savoy to Villiers, who had recently been created the Earl of Buckingham. An opportunity for advancement arose in June 1619 which was too good to miss. Isaac ended his dispatch to Villiers accordingly:

> For my owne particuler, I do humbly beseech your Lordship that you will vouchsafe to cast an eye sometimes uppon one that is your onely creature, and that you will be pleased to perfect the worke of your owne hands, when in your wisdom you shall think it fit. Sir Henry Wotton is departed from Venice, without any purpose, as I understand, to returne thither any more. If he continue in the same minde, I do in all humility desire your Lordship to remember the gratious promise you were pleased to make mee, of procuring mee that employment, when it should be voide.[20]

In fact Isaac's hopes of promotion were premature. Wotton had been dispatched on a mission to Vienna and returned to Venice in 1621, resuming as ambassador there.

*   *   *   *   *

Isaac's scholarly interests did not diminish. Starting with his first travels to the Continent in 1609, he had been granted leave of absence from Oxford for three years which was then extended for a further three. In 1618, when the King ordered that his own writings should be translated into Latin, Sir Thomas Lake, Secretary of State and Latin Secretary, had fallen into disgrace. Wake was strongly recommended for the second of these posts but in his absence abroad, it was given to the man on the spot, Thomas Read. On the death in 1621 of Sir Henry Savile, the learned Warden of Merton, Wake was one of the candidates for the headship of his old college. George Abbot, then Archbishop of Canterbury and former Master of University College, Oxford, was a powerful figure in the choosing of a new Warden. The post was offered to Nathaniel Brent, but Prince Charles, happening to meet the Archbishop, told him that he was 'not well pleased' that Sir Isaac Wake had not been elected. The Prince ordered that no further action should follow until he was satisfied.[21] Wake's friends also made representations to the Lord Chamberlain questioning the validity of the election, but to no avail.[22]

In February 1623, at the age of forty three, Sir Isaac planned to return to England to marry. He was delayed for several months 'to the great griefe of his sweet hart Mistres Bray, my auncient Valentine', as Chamberlain quaintly called her: this was because of Prince Charles' arrival in Spain to woo the Spanish Infanta. Anna Bray was a stepdaughter of Sir Edward Conway, one of the Secretaries of State, who was created Viscount Conway in 1628. On 20 December 1623, 'the wooing that hath ben long adooing' came to a conclusion with the marriage of Sir Isaac and Anna at St. Bartholomew's Church, Smithfield.

Anna did not enjoy good health. Four months after their marriage, Isaac left for Venice on his own. Chamberlain informed Carleton:

> He meanes not to carrie his Lady along with him by reason of her weake constitution and many daungers that may happen in passing the mountaines, but she is to follow him in August: and he is very angrie with any that argue of the conveniencie of her going now as well in regard of his companie as of the charge, and season of the yeare, as yf they mistrusted his judgement or affection or that he knew not what were fitting for her, protesting withall that he will geve any man £1,500 that wold undertake to bring her safe after him to Venice.[23]

We are afforded a glimpse of Anna's fondness for Conway, her stepfather, in a letter she wrote on 11 November 1627 after learning of 'the phisitians sentance of her approaching end' she wrote of her 'humble acknowlagementes and unfained thankes for your extreordinary fatherly goodnes and mersie which ye have exersised upon me ever scence my infansie'.[24]

After their marriage, Isaac and Anna took up residence in Hampstead, then a very small settlement, some distance from the City. It was not until the end of the seventeenth century that the discovery of mineral waters there led to its expansion.[25] The house, built on the west side of Haverstock Hill, stood back from the road and was screened off by a grove. According to John Aubrey, Sir Isaac made walks of pines and firs, the first of their kind to be planted in England,[26] and the house overlooked London.

In 1664 it was the largest house in the parish, being assessed at seventeen hearths.[27] After Sir Isaac's death, it was bought by John Wilde, Chief Baron of the Exchequer, who remained there until his own death in 1669.[28]

Isaac's career was closely bound up with the tortuous and shifting foreign policy pursued by James I. Although his eldest daughter Elizabeth had married Frederick V, the Elector Palatine in February 1613, James wished to remain friendly with the most powerful country in Europe, Spain. Frederick had accepted the Bohemian throne in 1619, just after the Thirty Years War in Germany had broken out, in which Ferdinand, the Holy Roman Emperor fought the Elector; the Spaniards sided with the Emperor. On 8 November 1620, Frederick's forces were defeated at the battle of the White Mountain. Together with his wife Elizabeth he fled from Prague; Bohemia now became part of the Habsburg Empire. James hoped that if a marriage alliance could be achieved between his son, Charles, and the Spanish Infanta, England's entry into the war might be avoided. Villiers, now Duke of Buckingham, accompanied Charles to Spain early in 1623. After fruitless negotiations, the plan failed. Both Charles and Buckingham returned to England, seeking revenge against Spain and in December, James reluctantly agreed to summon Parliament.

There had been much resentment in the Commons during the King's reign at his exalted views on the monarchy. This was exacerbated by the numerous devices sought by the Crown to raise revenue, especially at a time of economic depression in the period 1614 to 1629. From the time of the dissolution of the stormy 1614 Parliament, James existed without summoning that body for another seven years. When the Parliament which opened in January 1621 condemned the proposed Spanish marriage, the King considered the proceedings as a challenge to the royal prerogative and dissolved Parliament in January 1622. Now, after the Spanish marriage fiasco and the ascendancy of Buckingham to power and influence over Prince Charles in foreign matters, James played a lesser role in proceedings. A new Parliament was called for early in 1624. To achieve a favourable hearing, both the Prince and Buckingham had to ensure that the Commons contained many of their supporters. Secretary Conway, who was closely associated with Buckingham and himself an MP, was probably instrumental in securing Sir Isaac's nomination as a Member of Parliament for the University of Oxford.[29]

The first election of university representatives of Oxford and Cambridge had taken place in 1604.[30] Initially, the elected burgesses of the universities were charged with the defence of their institutions; increasingly, nominations by the Crown were made for these seats. Between 1621 and 1640, of the fifteen university burgesses in the Commons, seven were members of the Privy Council.[31] At the 1624 Oxford election, two candidates were presented for the two seats, Sir George Calvert, Secretary of State since 1617, and Sir Isaac Wake. Both were elected. Calvert attended Parliament irregularly, but Sir Isaac played a much more conspicuous part, especially in promoting the Crown's new foreign policy towards the recovery of the Palatinate.

The Commons met on 12 February 1624. On 24th, Buckingham informed a committee of both Houses of his negotiations on the Prince's marriage and the underhand dealings of the Spanish. By 2 March, the Commons and the Lords unanimously agreed to recommend the King not to continue the negotiations. On the

CP13. *Mercury instructing Cupid before Venus* (The School of Love) by Correggio. Acquired from the Gonzagas with the assistance of Sir Isaac Wake for Charles I in 1628, and now in the National Gallery

CP14. One of the nine panels of *The Triumphs of Caesar* by Mantegna, also acquired from the Gonzagas by Sir Isaac Wake for the King. It is now at Hampton Court Palace

CP15. Anna Wake painted by Van Dyck in 1628 before her marriage to Pieter Stevens. The original is in the Mauritshuis, The Hague, a copy being at Courteenhall

CP16. Pieter Stevens' Picture Gallery in Antwerp, by Frans Francken the Younger and David Teniers the Younger, Courtauld Institute Galleries, Somerset House

following day, Buckingham arranged a further conference at which Sir Robert Cotton, the celebrated antiquary who took a leading part in creating baronets, and Sir Isaac Wake, gave the history of the negotiations since 1615,[32] the latter recounting the tale of Spanish treachery towards the Duke of Savoy. Wake's standing amongst his contemporaries was enhanced by 'his excellent elocution' in the Commons in advancing reasons for breaking the Spanish marriage treaty. Chamberlain, who was a close observer of the parliamentary scene, wrote to Carleton that Sir Isaac:

> who doth so plie the parlement that he is hard to be found, and yt stands him upon, for his employment is at the stake to stand or fall as matters passe there, though he have received his letters and instructions, and lords yt handsomly aldredy.[33]

It was common knowledge at the time that Isaac had, in December 1623, been offered the ambassadorship at Venice with responsibility for resident English agents in Savoy and Switzerland. Chamberlain describes him as 'a kind of ambassador paramount, or like an archbishop with so many suffragans'.[34] Six days before Parliament rose, Wake left England for Turin on the King's orders, to gain the support of Continental Catholic powers against Spain. After a good journey he arrived there in June. He was joined by Anna in September and by late December 1624 they proceeded to Venice to take up residence. The outgoing ambassador, Wotton, after his third spell at Venice, had protested to Buckingham at the prospect of being left 'utterly destitute' after seventeen years of foreign service.[35]

*   *   *   *   *

There were many duties to be performed by a resident ambassador. Perhaps the most important one was to act as a gatherer of information for his country. This could be achieved in several ways: by negotiation, through diplomatic channels, by the use of his agents and by employing spies. It was not uncommon too for ambassadors to receive pensions from foreign countries in return for retailing State secrets. He was the chief representative of his government and sent dispatches by couriers to England; this operation was often fraught with personal danger, as the bearers were frequently robbed, thrown into prison or even murdered. The ambassador also supervised the trading interests of compatriots who were resident in the country and encouraged the exchange of goods.[36] It was not unusual for him to act also as the natural guardian of English travelling youths. Sir Isaac was described in 1628 as being 'in place of a father' to Lord Doncaster, son of James Hay, Earl of Carlisle, and directed his travels to Alessandria, Genoa and Florence.[37]

Ambassadorial activities were accompanied by great pomp and ceremony which compensated for the onerous nature of the work. For example, ambassadors were each provided with a service of silver plate and in public were accompanied by a retinue of attendants. Sir Isaac Wake on his entry into Venice made a fine show 'as well in liveries, flaunting feathers and the like, as in number of followers, among whom are six footmen, three or four pages, and gentlemen not a few'.[38] On their departure, ambassadors received a gift of a gold chain worth a thousand crowns from their hosts.[39] The embassy itself was tastefully furnished in the modern style, with halberds, bucklers and arms, as well as pictures on the walls. The furniture was hired locally. No doubt Sir Isaac took with him his escutcheon which he had had made after he was knighted and which he hung in all public places where he went.[40] Wotton had diverted himself within the house with an ape on a chain, and sent the King cuttings from his garden.[41] In the summer, the ambassador and his family would retire to a villa on the nearby River Brenta.

Shortly after Sir Isaac's arrival in Venice, James I, who had long been in decline, died at Theobalds on 27 March 1625. The funeral at Westminster Abbey was conducted on an impressive scale. 'Blacks' were distributed to more than 9,000 people and the hearse was designed by Inigo Jones, the King's Surveyor. The Lord Keeper, John Williams, Bishop of Lincoln, preached a sermon of more than two hours' duration. The cost of the ceremony was in excess of £50,000, according to Chamberlain.[42] Sir Isaac was not able to attend the funeral, but he submitted, in his own hand, an epitaph on the King which has survived:

> Question:
> Can a king die and we no Comet see?
> Tell me, astrologers, how can this bee?
> Answer:
> Heaven's beacons burn not but to give alarm
> Unto a state of some ensuing harm.
> The angels carrying up our blessed king
> Did with still music his sweet requiem sing.
> No innovation being to be heard,
> Why should Heaven summon men unto his guard?
> His spirit was redoubled on his son:
> And that was seen on his assumption.

These flattering remarks were addressed to James' son, Charles. His accession to the throne created new problems. Within two months, he had married Henrietta Maria, the sister of King Louis XIII of France, and a Catholic. Henrietta had brought her French advisers to the Court. The unpopularity of this move led to their eventual expulsion. Buckingham now sought a way of leading the French and Spanish into war in Italy. He looked to Savoy where Charles Emmanuel I, the ruler, had hopes of invading Genoa or Milan, both Spanish interests. If Spain could be provoked, France, it was argued, could hardly remain neutral. Sir Isaac was instructed to persuade Venice to finance the Savoy enterprise and also gain the support of the Protestant Swiss cantons.[43]

To help King Charles gain some understanding of the situation at the beginning of his reign, Wake composed for him *A Discourse of the State of Italie as it stood about the year 1625 or Somewhat After*. Praising the Duke of Savoy, he wrote:

> This part of the world doth owe unto Charles Emmanuel Duke of Savoy the discovery of one great secret, which is, that the Spaniards are resistible in Italy;

for he did make his party good against them when not a sword in all Europe was drawn against them but his.[44]

Wake also extolled the constancy of Venice, and noted that 'Upon *terra firma* they have all their cities well furnished, and for the defensive, they are in good state. How they stand in matter of treasure is a secret, but certainly *omnes vias pecuniae norunt* [they know all ways of dealing with money], and they do spend as if they did not fear want'.[45]

His final words to the King contained some shrewd advice, as well as displaying an element of self-interest:

> Singular use may be made of their friendship, without any cost or trouble: for the Venetians will never desire more than to have their Ambassadors kindly used, and that the world may see, and take notice, that your majestie dothe respect them, and if upon fit occasions your Majestie will be pleased to favour the Duke of Savoy and the Prince of Piedmont with some horses and dogs, they will be proud of such a token of your love, and be ready to deserve it.[46]

In his quest for cementing alliances against Spain, Sir Isaac employed great persuasive powers. Urging the Duke of Savoy to forge a Venetian link with Denmark, he described its monarch as 'this great king of the North, who like a second Atlas holds up the Arctick pole, rich in treasure, numerous in men, dreadful, for his invincible generosity and courage'. In conclusion, Wake suggested, 'The only thing here sought for is to go with a common pace, that those that now are too heavily laden, may be supported by their friends, either by way of diversion or by way of assistance'.[47]

One of the major worries which constantly plagued Sir Isaac was the question of money. In common with other ambassadors, he was expected to maintain a household of some splendour commensurate with his position as the King's representative. He was also responsible for the payment of his household and officials, including secretaries and cipherers. Throughout the period whilst Sir Isaac served abroad, the Crown faced difficulties in raising sufficient finance. The position was exacerbated by the extravagance of James and Charles and their followers: the dowry for the proposed match between Charles and the Infanta was supposed to be some £600,000. But the main problem was the increasing cost of implementing foreign policy. The expenditure on ambassadors between 1619 and 1622 increased fivefold. Five times more was spent on jewels, a favourite form of bribe, than three years earlier and secret service expenditure soared. Worst of all, Lord Digby, ambassador to Spain and a notorious spender, disbursed £145,763 on special missions between 1619 and 1629, a half of the total cost of foreign policy in these years contributed by the Crown.[48]

Sir Isaac's own allowance consisted of £4 a day for ordinary entertainment plus £400 a year for 'extraordinary entertainment'. Within two years of his appointment as agent at Turin, Isaac was unable to meet his expenses. On 12 December 1617, he remarked that 'it will be some dishonour to have a public minister starve in a foreign country'. Three months later, 'I am now enforced to sell the poor stuff that was in my house to buy bread'. By June 1618, Isaac wrote, in desperation, 'It is now sixteen months since I have received one penny out of the Exchequer . . . I have lived many months upon my own poor stock, and have sold and pawned all that little which I had. I do not know how to subsist any longer'.[49] There had been occasional settling of debts. After Sir Isaac wrote to the Lord Treasurer, Cranfield, in December 1622 describing his 'deplorable condition' being £2,000 in arrears of pay, this sum was settled in the following February, thus allowing him to marry.[50] However, the position became worse over the years. On 28 September 1630, Anna Wake requested her husband's petition, following the exhaustion of their credit, to be presented to the King. In it, Anna claimed, 'They do not spend one penny on which they do not pay use upon use. Of £6,000 behind, they can only get £2,000, which is not be paid until Christ-tide come twelve months'.[51]

Apart from financial considerations, there were other difficulties facing the diplomat abroad. Albertus Morton, after serving less than a year as agent at Turin, wrote to the Duke of Somerset, commenting that Isaac Wake, who was then in the city as Carleton's secretary, should be appointed in his place. In a private conversation on 27 March 1615, Morton told Carleton that he 'suffered much by his absence out of England chiefly by being put out of the way of a good fortune by his mistress which he was in danger to lose'. Eight days later, Isaac became agent and Morton returned to England.[52] News from home was received often after long delay and could affect policies which ambassadors had been instructed to pursue. Exile for long periods on the Continent was naturally conducive to homesickness. Carleton, then serving at The Hague, writing to William Trumbull, ambassador at Brussels about a friend, remarked, 'I shall envy him that shall be nearer the air of England and that he shall have God's dear earth under his feet'.[53] Absence from London and the Court might also lessen the chances of promotion, though a number of ambassadors were rewarded for their efforts; Carleton was created Viscount Dorchester and Digby became Earl of Bristol, and there were prospects of an appointment as a Secretary of State or of a post in the Royal Household.

*   *   *   *   *

Issac's services were also called upon in quite a different sphere. Thomas, Earl of Arundel, was one of the greatest patrons of the arts in England at this time. He had travelled in Europe 1612–13 with Inigo Jones, studying works of art and buying pictures and ancient marbles. Arundel was responsible for bringing the collection of Leonardo drawings, now at Windsor, to England and admitted to a 'foolish curiosity' for Holbein's works.[54] Arundel House, with its sculpture and picture galleries, was greatly admired by connoisseurs and collectors of the day.[55] Arundel's wife, Aletheia Talbot, granddaughter of Bess of Hardwick, was an equally avid collector and foreign traveller. It was as a consequence of her sitting for Rubens in Antwerp that Van Dyck had been persuaded to come to England in 1620 and enter the services of James I.[56] Buckingham, too, was a collector with a preference for sixteenth century Venetian paintings. Before he ascended the throne, Charles was already influenced by the artistic tastes of his elder brother, Henry Prince of Wales, and of Arundel. On Henry's death at the early age of sixteen in 1612, Charles inherited his collection. Increasingly, ambassadors were the recipients of urgent requests from the King to assist in the purchase of works of art: these included Sir Dudley Carleton, himself a keen collector, at The Hague, Sir Balthazar Gerbier at Brussels, Sir Thomas Roe at Constantinople and Sir Isaac Wake.

A direct Wake family link with this period of acquisition of European masterpieces in Royal and private collections can be established. Lionel Wake was an English merchant and a wealthy financier trading at Antwerp. He was the eldest son of Robert, the eleventh son of Richard Wake of Hartwell, thus Lionel's father and Isaac's father were cousins. Lionel, born in London in October 1577, was a middleman for the flourishing art trade. He frequently acted as agent for Rubens, who lived at Antwerp, handling, amongst other commissions, the negotiations for the nine large paintings which in 1635 were placed in the ceiling of the Banqueting House in Whitehall.[57] Rubens was also a personal friend of Lionel Wake, whom he sometimes called in his correspondence 'Mr. Lionello'.[58]

Rubens' pupil, Van Dyck, returned to his native Antwerp in 1627 and in that year painted Pieter Stevens, almoner of the town and a wealthy collector. This portrait led to a commission by Lionel to paint the portrait of his eldest daughter, Anna Wake, who was married to Stevens at the age of twenty two in the church of St. Walburgis, Antwerp, on 12 March 1628. The date 1628 appears on Van Dyck's portrait of Anna, which, together with that of her husband, now hangs in the Mauritshuis, The Hague.[59] It is probable that Lionel Wake and the rest of his family were also among the painter's sitters.[60] During his many journeys between England and Italy, Isaac may well have visited Lionel.

Isaac found himself involved in the arrangements for Lady Arundel's visit to Italy during her adventurous two year stay there, 1621–3. One of her calls was at Turin. On 21 March 1623, a relieved Isaac reported to Cranfield that she had left for Genoa, attended at the departure by the Duke of Savoy, the Prince of Piedmont, all the nobility of the court and the horse and footguard. Before this, she had been presented with 'some fair pieces of cristal and a litter of crimson velvet', with three mules suitably fitted.[61]

Later as ambassador to Venice, Isaac was more directly concerned in the purchase of works of art, particularly for the new King, Charles. In June 1625, Nicholas Lanier, Master of the King's Music and a connoisseur, was sent by Charles to Italy to 'provide him with some choice Pictures'. In Venice, he contacted Nicholas Nys, a French merchant and art dealer of dubious reputation. Nys informed Lanier that he was already negotiating with the decaying Gonzaga dynasty in Mantua. After the death of Duke Ferdinand of Mantua in 1626, Nys was successful in persuading the new Duke, Vincenzo II, to sell the greater part of his collection, which consisted of sculptures as well as paintings. In 1627, Nys wrote to Endymion Porter, Charles' personal representative responsible for purchases, enthusiastically describing the paintings which were to be sent to England. There was Raphael's Madonna della Perla for which Vincenzo I was reputed to have given a marquisate, and works by Caravaggio, Correggio, Titian, Michaelangelo, Guido Reni and the nine large pictures of the *Triumphs of Caesar* by Mantegna. Lanier, returned to Italy to 'repair and trim up' some of the pictures and arrange their packing for the journey. Two water colours, which were too delicate for a sea voyage, were to be brought back overland by Lanier.[62]

Sir Isaac was, as ambassador, an important figure in the transaction. Informing his son-in-law of the plan at an early stage, 2 June 1625, Lord Conway warned him not to make known the cause of Lanier's coming 'because that would much enhance the prices'. Isaac, who had recently been asked to purchase a picture for Conway, expressed his opinion to his father-in-law on the vogue for collecting paintings at this time: 'Some in England who have taken unto themselves a monopolye of passing their verdict upon all things of this nature, so that if a man do not baptise his picture or his statue at the font of their censure he cannot be admitted into the Church'.[63] He obtained from the Prince a licence to export the pictures 'without paying of custome, which would have come to a round summe'. Isaac then boarded the ship, the *Margaret*, carrying the first consignment, and supervised the loading of the cases. Before the vessel left harbour, he gave the captain a document, exempting the crew of thirty seven from being employed in duties other than ensuring that the cargo was safely delivered.[64]

Three days out from Venice, on 1 May 1628, the ship encountered a heavy storm. Unfortunately, the cases had been packed next to jars filled with mercury which broke in the rough seas. Many of the pictures were 'utterly spoiled and defaced by quicksilver'. Nevertheless, the bulk of the magnificent collection, which cost the King £15,000, was soon displayed in the royal palaces. It almost rivalled the assembly of great Venetian masters which had been accumulated in Madrid.[65] The careful arrangement of pictures and sculptures was disrupted after Charles's execution in 1649 when the collection was sold off, much of it abroad. Cromwell admired Mantegna's *Triumphs of Caesar* and ordered it to be retained; it is still on display at Hampton Court Palace. For his efforts in the matter, Sir Isaac received £2,000 from Nys on the King's behalf for the maintenance of his house, and it also enabled Anna to return to England.[66] Over 350 years later, many of the Gonzaga works of art were temporarily brought together for an exhibition at the Victoria and Albert Museum, London which gave some notion of the treasures which Sir Isaac had once helped to assemble.[67]

*   *   *   *   *

Anna was conspicious in advancing the claims of kinsmen and friends to higher office,[68] and none more so than on behalf of her husband. Her stepfather, Conway, now Lord President of the Council, wrote to Isaac in December 1629, 'This day I have received from my daughter Wake a letter and notices to be presented to the King to stir up His gracious consideration of your services and for payment. I will not fail to procure the King to read them'. He assured his son-in-law that Charles held Isaac 'in good estimation' as did Dorchester. Conway ended his letter, 'I profess ingenuously that I take as much comfort in the nurture and goodness of my daughter, your lady, as in any daughter I have. I will endeavour all the duties of love and affection to become worthy to be accounted your lordship's loving father, faithful friend and humble servant'.[69] Conway's efforts were successful. In December 1630 Isaac was recalled from Venice to take up the ambassadorship at Paris.

It was not until 13 April 1631 that he arrived there to take up his new post.[70] In January, a serious outbreak of plague in Venice had resulted in the death of no fewer than thirteen of Sir Isaac's household, including three of his immediate servants. Anna, whose stepfather had died on 3 January, ordered thanksgiving to be made in London churches as well as prayers for her husband's safe return. The King granted Isaac £600 as a mark of his appreciation.[71] Exhausted after his experiences, Isaac rested for a month in Paris before actively participating in diplomatic work once more.

It was rumoured that Isaac was not acceptable to the King of France, Louis XIII[72] but he was soon granted a lengthy audience with the monarch in May 1631. Louis was dominated by Cardinal Richelieu, who directed both domestic and foreign policy in France. Richelieu intended to defeat the Habsburgs in the Thirty Years' War and to this end had subsidized Gustavus Adolphus of Sweden to fight the Emperor. Sir Isaac sent back to London detailed information on the tactics of the French. Gustavus' triumphs in Germany were greatly welcomed in England. Charles wished now to draw nearer to Richelieu and on 10 March 1632, a treaty was arranged which ended commercial disputes with France. Four days later, Isaac presented King Louis with a letter from Charles proposing joint action in Germany.[73]

In February, Viscount Dorchester, formerly Sir Dudley Carleton, had died. Dorchester had been Chief Secretary of State and the minister responsible for foreign affairs since December 1629. Isaac now wrote to the Earl of Carlisle, 'having understood from good friends how passionately your Lordship doth endeavour to promote your poore servant in this time of vacancy';[74] the prospect of filling Dorchester's position was a welcome one. However, Sir Isaac had an attack of fever which proved fatal. On 10 June 1632, Secretary Coke received a message from Paris, 'We have prepared you for those worser news we are now to send you of his Lordship's departure between 11 and 12 of the clock this morning'. King Charles, who greatly admired Isaac, ordered that the body should be transported to England 'in a manner befittinge his quality and yet without pompe or immoderate expences'. The funeral passed through Calais Roads on 6 July, when the governor of Boulogne 'pretending a great desire to do the body honour', caused all the French vessels in the Roads to take in their colours.[75] Sir Isaac was buried with due ceremony in the chapel of Dover Castle on the morning of 7 July. He was fifty two years old.

Isaac Wake was praised by his contemporaries for his intellectual abilities and for his devotion in serving for many years as ambassador abroad where, in Fuller's words, 'he neglected his own commodity to attend to His Majesty's employment'.[76] The rewards were not great. Anna later petitioned the King 'to relieve a poor widow' in order to sustain herself, and requested payment of £1,400 which was due to Sir Isaac as money spent on entertainment in Charles's service.[77] She lived on until 1642. There were no children of the marriage. In her will, Anna left all her pictures to a London merchant in consideration of a debt due to him from Sir Isaac, who had borrowed money 'to eat when in Venice'.[78]

Though of a serious disposition, he was not without a dry sense of humour. Attending a reception given in Turin by Cardinal Ludovisio, the Pope's envoy, he wrote to Carleton that 'his entertainment proved as lean as himself is fat'.[79] A biographical sketch, written some thirty years after his death, affords some insight into Isaac's character. 'Intelligence: he could afford (he said) a golden key for the pope's cabinet.

Books: his study was his estate. Entertaining knowing men often: applauding the emperour's maxim, that he had rather go fifty miles to hear a wise man, than five to see a fair city ... [he] was industrious to observe any useful invention that might improve the publick good'.[80] He was himself the author of *An Essay on Friendship* in which he praised friendship as 'the most excellent and perfectest end of Society'. Isaac wrote at the end of the book, 'I shall esteeme myself as happy as the World can make mee if ... I shall conclude my life, enjoying and being enjoyed of a constant Perfect friend, in the Noble entercourses of mutuall amity'.[81] Sir Isaac was a man of remarkable distinction. His comparatively early death cut short his highly successful career.

7

Mother Mary Margaret Wake, An English Carmelite

OVER THE CENTURIES, MANY WAKES HAVE BECOME clergymen of the Established Church. It may be surprising therefore to find one member of the family who rose to eminence in the Roman Catholic Church, Margaret Wake.

Her father was Lionel Wake, who, as explained in the previous chapter, was the eldest son of Robert Wake, the eleventh son of Richard Wake of Hartwell. Lionel, as a bachelor, had settled in Antwerp in order to seek his fortune. Whilst there, he was converted to Catholicism and shortly afterwards returned to England in April 1605 to marry Mary Thorne, the daughter of a Cambridge gentleman. It was not until almost the end of her life that she agreed also to become a Catholic. Of their ten children, five devoted themselves to the religious life. Richard, the eldest, was admitted to the English College of the Society of Jesus at Rome on 4 November 1628 when he was twenty one years of age and ordained a priest in 1634; two daughters became Canonesses Regular and another became a *devoté*, living in virginity under the direction of a spiritual father, without vows; and Margaret Wake, who was the fourth daughter.

Margaret was baptized in the parish church of St. Walburgis, Antwerp, on 12 November 1617. From an early age she was devoted to the Church and before she was fourteen, pleaded with her father to be allowed to become a Carmelite. Lionel sent her away to school promising Margaret that if after another year she was of the same mind, her wish would be granted. This promise was kept and the ceremony of clothing took place on 10 June 1633. An account of the proceedings was recorded by Father Percy Plowden, a Carmelite, who wrote his *Life of Margaret Wake* in 1726:

> She was led into the Monastery of the English Teresians by one of the principal ladies of the town, as the manner is upon these occasions, accompanied by all the friends and relations, and as many of the most considerable people of Antwerp as could crowd into their little church, to be spectators of that religious ceremony, more of devotion than of pomp, though even in this nothing was wanting that could contribute to the better honouring the joyful solemnity of that day.[1]

See Appendix A — Family Tree VIII. Notes and References page 402

During the ceremony, Margaret exchanged her bridal attire for the simple habit of the Blessed Mary of Mount Carmel, made up of dark brown material, with a black veil. The young novice now became known as Sister Mary Margaret of the Angels.

The Order of Our Lady of Mount Carmel had been founded in Palestine in about 1154 by St. Berthold during the Crusades, but it was traditionally believed to have been begun by the hermits living on Mount Carmel in early times who were direct descendants of Elijah.[2] The Order was established in the twelfth century as a response to the heretical beliefs which were being propagated in Southern France, Northern Italy, the Balkans, the Rhineland and the Low Countries.[3] It was one of a number of the new mendicant orders, such as the Dominicans and the Franciscans, all of whom had a strong missionary function; the Carmelites, for example, sent their brethren to Asia, Africa and the West Indies.

In 1452, an Order of Carmelite Sisters was founded in the Low Countries, but it was the mystic St. Teresa of Avila, born in that city in Spain in 1515, who provided the inspiration for the Antwerp and many other communities. In her book *The Way of Perfection*, St. Teresa emphasized the need for strict discipline among the nuns and unswerving obedience to the Order. A life of contemplation was to be one of the ideals. The Teresian reforms led to the setting up of houses of so-called Discalced Carmelites. In 1619, the Convent of English Carmelite nuns, under the protection of St. Joseph and St. Anne, had been founded in Antwerp at Hopland, in the northern part of the city, by Lady Mary Lovel, daughter of Lord Roper, Baron Teynham.[4]

It began in a very modest way with a Mother Superior, Anne Worsley, and five English nuns. By 1644, the number had risen to fifty.[5] The daily routine of Carmelites consists of rising at 6.00 a.m., then Lauds followed by Meditiation for an hour. At 8.00 a.m, Holy Mass is followed by morning reflection. After Terce at 11.00 a.m, there is dinner and the time between 1.00 p.m and 2.00 p.m is set aside for recreation. From 2.00 p.m to 3.00 p.m, there is spiritual reading, then Vespers and Meditation. At 6.00 p.m, there is a smaller meal Collation (Supper in summer) followed by recreation until 7.40 p.m. Compline at 8.00 p.m is followed by Matins at 9.30 p.m after which the nuns retire for the night.[6]

On 11 June 1634, the Feast of St. Barnaby, Margaret completed her year of probation and made the solemn vows. From the later testimony of her sister nuns, she was outstanding in her commitment to the Order. One, Sister Winifred, stated that:

> Of seven or eight-and-twenty religious whom she knew, and who had lived with Mother Mary Margaret, some for the whole forty-five years of her religious life, others for a very considerable part of it, she could never hear any of them say that they had ever seen her failing in the least point of their Constitutions, but on the contrary often heard them speak of her with the greatest veneration, as of a saint, and of her whole comportment and behaviour as of an exact model of all Christian and religious perfection.

Further, from observation Sister Mary Margaret 'could never accuse herself above twice of having cast up her eyes in the refectory'. Sister Winifred vouched for the fact

34. Sister Margaret Wake, Carmelite nun, seen here in the wedding dress she wore when she was admitted into the Order, aged 15, on 10 June 1633

35. A Carmelite nun

36. Wake's Oak, in Whittlewood Forest, from Baker's *History and Antiquities of the County of Northampton*. Burnt down by schoolboys on Shrove Tuesday, 1867. The circumference at its base was 46 feet 3 inches

that 'she never heard her raise her voice, never saw her lean upon anything, nor eye anything curiously, even in the time of the common hours of recreation'.[7] Within the convent, she was employed for some thirteen years in the more menial household tasks, such as serving in the kitchen and waiting on the sick. Margaret's training of the novices was a model of commonsense and understanding. It came as no surprise, therefore, that in 1665 she was chosen by the nuns to be prioress, and subseqently re-elected, serving until 1671. Still humble and self-effacing, she would speak to the community often at recreation time when they sat in a ring at her feet, moving them almost to tears by her addresses on spiritual topics.

Margaret was elected once again as prioress in 1677, and was soon busy making preparations for establishing an English Carmel at Hoogstraet in the Netherlands; but she was taken ill at Michaelmas and was subsequently often confined to her bed. Still carrying out her duties, she died on 21 June 1678 aged sixty one, having devoted forty five years of her life to the Order. Margaret was buried in the cellar where deceased Carmelites were laid to rest. In 1716, as the vault was then full, the Bishop of Antwerp ordered that the cellar should be enlarged. During this operation, the nuns were curious to see the state of Margaret's body. They found it in perfect condition. A deposition by doctors and surgeons of the city attested to this and the Bishop, who was 'struck with admiration and reverence' on seeing Margaret, ordered a second set of investigations; the doctors confirmed the findings of their colleagues.

The news of this apparent miracle quickly spread and many notable people, including Prince d'Escula, the governor of Antwerp, flocked to the monastery to see the body, which lay in state in the nuns' choir. Large crowds of people came to venerate the holy Carmelite and there were several reports of cures which occurred as a result of visits to the tomb. Finally, the nuns were obliged to close the gates to the public, so great was the disturbance, and soldiers were posted outside the building. The clamour did not subside. For several months, quantities of beads, medals, pictures, linen and other objects were sent to the convent to be touched by the holy body.

A century later the French Revolution broke out and in 1794, the Republicans overran Belgium. Because of their nationality, the English Carmelites were particularly vulnerable, so they made plans to leave. The nuns were unable to take the remains of Margaret Wake with them, so they were placed in the Bishop's vault in a cemetery. In 1843, Cardinal Stercx, the Archbishop of Mecklin, ordered that a rich coffin should be made for Margaret. It was subsequently deposited in the episcopal vault under the high altar of Antwerp Cathedral, where it still rests.

After departing from Antwerp, the Carmelites boarded a ship for England. The remaining sixteen nuns settled at Lanherne House, formerly the home of the Arundell family, at Mawgan-in-Pyder in Cornwall. The building dates from Elizabethan times and there is a plain chapel situated in the older part of the mansion.[8] In the walled garden is one of the most elaborate of the early Cornish crosses, bearing a portrait of Christ crucified.[9] To the present day, Lanherne is still a Carmelite convent. It is appropriate that the Cornish saint, Mawgan, from which the spot takes its name, should have been a missionary who travelled widely in the sixth century.[10]

The Convent has preserved several objects associated with Margaret. There is, for instance, the eighteenth century manuscript *Life of Margaret Wake* written by Father Percy Plowden, a copy of the entry in the baptismal register and a coloured drawing of the coats of arms of her father and mother; that of Lionel Wake is identical with the present day Wake arms. But perhaps the most precious survival is a large portrait of Margaret dressed in her bridal gown in June 1633 on the day when she entered the Order. Margaret's happy countenance gazes out at the viewer, for as her biographer related, when after the ceremony the nuns came round her with their welcome and congratulations 'she felt that she was almost in heaven since she was now to live in the company of as many angels as there were nuns in the community'.[11]

8
William Wake,
Archbishop of Canterbury

ONE OF THE MOST DISTINGUISHED CLERICS OF HIS generation was William Wake, who became Archbishop of Canterbury. William Wake was born in Blandford, Dorset, on 26 January 1657. This Dorset branch of the family descended from a younger brother of Roger Wake of Blisworth, John,[1] in early Tudor times.

William's great-grandfather had married Margaret Hooper near the beginning of Elizabeth's reign. They had two children, a daughter Joan, who never married, and William, the future Archbishop's grandfather, who was born on 14 August 1598. After attending Westminster School and taking his degree at Cambridge, William was ordained priest by the Bishop of Peterborough in 1622. By special Archbishop's dispensation, he held the rectorship of Holy Trinity and of St. Michael's, both in Wareham from 1626. When the Civil War broke out sixteen years later, William unhesitatingly gave his support to the King. In drawing up a 'list of Clergy, Outed, Sequestered or Silenced', Cromwell's Dorset Standing Committee, which was charged with this task, described Mr Wake as 'a turbulent person',[2] and with good reason.

He played a leading part in rallying the Royalists in Dorset and narrowly escaped with his life on several occasions. When the Parliamentary Commissioners set about fortifying Wareham, he urged the inhabitants to resist them. As a result, William was shot in the head several times by a pistol and received cuts with a sword. He was carried home in a basket and there recovered. Magdalene, his wife and the daughter of a Worcestershire gentleman, bravely supported him, even though she and her three children were turned out of their house and all their possessions sequestrated. Altogether, Wake was imprisoned nineteen times, including a period in Sherborne Castle in 1645, after being one of the defenders there. The prisoners were stripped naked and paraded through the town by their captives.[3] A visitor to Wareham in 1635 described him thus:

> Before I parted, I had a free and generous entertainment from the honest, merry and true-hearted parson there, both at his own house and in the town, and enjoyed much mirth with him . . . He was both a good scholar and a good soldier, an excellent drum-beating parson.[4]

See Appendix A – Family Tree IX. Notes and References pages 402–404

After the return of Charles II, his living was restored to him, but ill and exhausted, he died in 1661. Magdalene survived him for another thirty two years.

William left four children, three boys, William, Edward and Charles, and one girl, Magdalene. William, the eldest of the family and the Archbishop's father, was to play an even more prominent part in the Civil War than his father. He was born on 28 April 1628 and at an early age entered the King's Army, rising to the rank of Captain. William was imprisoned on twenty occasions and at Exeter Castle on 18 April 1655 was condemned to death for high treason, and sentenced to be hanged, drawn and quartered. He had been concerned in Colonel Penruddock's abortive uprising in the West Country. Penruddock and some of the other leaders were executed, but Wake's life was spared after he had protested by letter to Cromwell on the terms under which he had surrendered.[5] In the early eighteenth century, *The Spectator* circulated a story that the reprieve was due to the fact that the judge hearing the case had been a fellow pupil at Westminster School, when Dr Richard Busby was headmaster, but this has since been discounted.[6] However, he was still in prison when on 26 January 1657, his wife Amie, gave birth to William, the subject of this chapter.

Amie was a woman of great determination and resolve. The daughter of Edward Cutler, a rich Dorset farmer, she brought considerable wealth on her marriage. With this, the couple purchased what is now called Bishops Court in the village of Shapwick, four miles from Blandford. The house is an L-shaped building with a late sixteenth century wing,[7] and was the birthplace of the future Archbishop. It was largely due to her initiative that after the War, her husband established a clothing business based on Shapwick, with the wool from Dorset sheep. Becoming wealthy from this enterprise, he joined forces with Robert Pitt of Blandford, and rented from the Duke of Richmond the aulnage (i.e. the responsibility for examining and attesting the quality of woollen goods) for the five Western Counties.[8] After eighteen years in this trade, he retired. In 1675, William was re-appointed to the Army as Colonel of the Eastern regiment and was four times selected to be Bailiff of Blandford.

Three of their four children survived childhood, Magdalene, born 24 February 1655, Edward, born 17 December 1670 and his elder brother, William. At the age of six, William was sent first to the Free School at Blandford, and then to a private school at Iwerne, where he stayed until he was fifteen. In later years, as Archbishop, William demonstrated his affection for the Blandford School and its 'excellent Masters' by leaving in his will a sum of £1,000 for the maintenance and support of a Charity School in the town for the education of twelve poor boys, and to train them up in the principles of the Church of England. The School never had exclusive buildings of its own, but instruction was given by masters in private houses.[9] A direct link with this beneficence was celebrated in 1974, when the Blandford Primary School was officially renamed the Archbishop Wake Junior School.

*   *   *   *   *

In the year before young William left the school, 1671, his mother died of consumption whilst still in her thirties. He matriculated at Christ Church, Oxford in 1673 and was admitted as a student in July 1675. This was due partly to his outstanding ability as a scholar and partly to the patronage of Dr John Fell, Dean of the College and Bishop of Oxford and the subject of the well-known contemporary epigram:

> I do not like you, Dr Fell
> The reason why I cannot tell;
> But this I know and know full well;
> I do not like you, Dr Fell

William gained his Bachelor of Arts degree in 1676 and shortly afterwards fell dangerously ill; he was to be plagued by poor health for the rest of his life.

He enjoyed his time at Oxford, starting to read logic and philosophy, especially the works of Descartes. He determined to take Holy Orders but his father had other plans for him. In 1680, William senior rode over to Oxford to persuade his son to take over his trading and farming interests. The latter was deaf to all entreaties and his father left for London in a passion. Writing of this in later life the Archbishop reflected, 'The loss of this was at a moderate computation, £20,000: so much I paid for my profession'.[10] But his chosen career soon began to flourish. William was appointed Deacon in Christ Church Cathedral in September 1681 when he was almost twenty four and was ordained priest on 12 March in the following year; on the latter occasion, he was chosen as one of the four preachers at Carfax in the city.

A dramatic event in May 1683 changed the direction of his fortunes. At one day's notice, Dr Fell ordered him to accompany a fellow Christ Church man, Lord Preston, then ambassador at Paris and envoy extraordinary to the Court of Louis XIV, as chaplain. He was to stay there until Preston was recalled in 1685. Although William had to live in France at his own expense, he found the experience particularly valuable as he met a large number of eminent people, particularly churchmen, and men of many different political persuasions from various countries. The experience caused him to assess his own outlook on the world:

> This variety of company confirmed me in the resolution I had before taken of examining all things with the utmost impartiality and following it which upon the best judgement I could make appear to me to be right. It used me to bear contradiction easily; not to be conceited of my own opinions, nor overvalue my own parts and abilities. In a word, it taught me to converse with the world, and much enlarged my mind in the studies I pursued.[11]

Now with a wider perspective, William set himself the task of learning Hebrew, which he quickly mastered. He was also able to observe the Catholic Church and its practices at first hand. Whilst admitting to himself that the religion suited his temperament in many respects, particularly the monastic way of living, the beauty and solemnity of their services, and the zeal of priests, there were other aspects which were totally unacceptable, particularly the idolatry, the total submission required and the confining of salvation only to members of that religion. William's duties included the care of the sick and preaching. Such was his power of oratory that he was persuaded to publish, in English, some of his sermons; this was the first of many ventures into print.

On his return to England in September 1685, the young priest found that changes were taking place in the constitutional and religious climate. Charles II had died in February and was succeeded by his brother James II, an avowed Roman Catholic. James appointed an ecclesiastical commission to prevent Church of England clergy from attacking the Catholic faith in their pulpits, which led to the suspension of the Bishop of London. Further, the King in due course proceeded to allow Catholics into the Privy Council, fill posts at Oxford colleges and act as military and naval officers. Wake, who had become acquainted with Thomas Tenison, later Archbishop of Canterbury, now wrote *An Exposition of the Doctrine of the Church of England*. Tenison encouraged him to publish it in 1686. As a result, he fell into disfavour with the King.

In the winter of that year, Wake had a lucky escape from death. Returning on a dark night from the City, he was crossing a narrow street in the Strand by Somerset House when two hackney coaches drove violently out of the Strand at the same time up the street. 'I could not see them, and I much question whether they saw me. I stood still in the middle of the street: the danger was over in a moment. Both passed by me, however. I bless God, neither touched me'.[12]

Wake's reputation continued to grow and he was, amongst other things, asked to preach before Princess Anne. Busy with his writings and tiring of London, he went to live with Dr William Clagett, a preacher at Gray's Inn, at Highgate in late 1687, where the two men collaborated on theological works. This happy state of affairs was soon to end with Clagett's death from smallpox in March 1688. In a second version of his autobiography, Wake wrote, 'This accident quite unhinged me'.[13] The immediate question, however, was where to live. 'To remove again myself and books, but whither I could not tell. And this uncertainty of my way of living (for I had moved my lodgings and books four times within the compass of three years, to my great charge and trouble) was one of the first things that put me upon the serious thoughts of marrying'.[14]

Such a plan was facilitated within a matter of weeks by his appointment as a preacher at Gray's Inn on 7 May 1688, for he now had an income and was given chambers there. The story of his courtship is a fresh and very human one. Through Clagett, Wake had formed a friendship with Dr John Sharp, who became Archbishop of York in 1690. In the words of William Wake himself:

> Mrs Sharp, the then Dean of Norwich's wife,[15] being with us at Highgate the Christmas last, had often been speaking of a person whom both she and Mrs Clagett thought would make me a very good wife, and wished they could get her for me. But they feared Mr Folkes, who had married her sister, would oppose it, and here the matter still ended as often as they spoke about it.
>
> After Dr Clagett's death, Mrs Sharp frequently fell upon the subject of my marrying, and seriously persuaded me to it. She was an excellent and prudent woman, and everything she said had a very great weight with me. Making a visit one day at Mrs Folkes, her sister, she was willing to try what she would think of a match between us, and was so far encouraged in the discourse that she resolved

plainly to propose it to the young lady, Miss Hovell; and by consent it was agreed that Dr Sharp should propose it to her brother-in-law, Mr Folkes. He did so, and though many difficulties were raised as on such occasions there generally are, yet it ended at last in marriage between us, the 1st of October 1688, when we were happily married by Dr Sharp in his church of St. Giles in the Fields.[16]

His bride was Ethelreda, daughter of Sir William and Ethelreda Hovell of Hillington, Norfolk.[17] The day after their wedding, the couple left the capital and spent the following month at Shapwick. Whilst there, there was constant speculation about the imminent landing of William of Orange; but when this took place on 5 November at Torbay, William and Ethelreda were back in London. Like many other clergymen, he was wary of the arrival of the Prince. James was still King and the principle of Divine Right could not easily be brushed aside. If James' Catholicism caused offence to the Church of England, then it was also a fact that Prince William was a Dutch Calvinist. So uncertain was Wake at first that he advised a Guards officer to join King James' army which had gathered at Salisbury to counter the invasion. Later, after preaching before the Prince at St. James' Chapel, Wake 'had the honour to kiss his hand' and after being assured by his superiors that it was in order to take the oath of allegiance, he did so. On 4 May 1689, he was appointed canon of Christ Church Cathedral and one of the King's chaplains.

*   *   *   *   *

The following years were to set the pattern for the rest of his career, with his time occupied in preaching, writing and attending conferences. In 1689, he was granted permission to accumulate together the degrees of Bachelor and Doctor of Divinity, taking only two terms to accomplish them. Wake usually preached twice a week to various audiences; one such occasion was on 4 May 1690 at Whitehall, before the King and Queen, William and Mary, who ordered the sermon to be published 'to encourage others to do their duty'. Whilst in France, Wake had been able to preach without notes, but was now aware that increasing pressure of work made this procedure a risky one. 'I was afraid what this in time would bring me to; and especially if I should live so long that my invention would grow dry and I should have no stock of sermons made while I was younger, to relieve me in old age'.[18]

Wake was offered various bishoprics, but with true reticence refused to contemplate them. He was aggrieved however when, after such refusals, he was not considered when the deaneries of St. Paul's and Canterbury fell vacant. In 1691 the King nominated him for the rectorship of the recently-built Wren church of St. James', Piccadilly, but a bout of fever proved to be serious and he was unable to take part in any Church matters, apart from writing, for the next two and a half years. However, at the Queen's insistence, he took up the post at St. James' on 24 January 1694; he was saddened by her death at the age of thirty three in December of that same year. After seven agreeable years at Gray's Inn, Wake took leave, preaching 'a plain sermon, suitable to the melancholy occurrence', leaving his chambers and moving into the parsonage, on which he spent £100 in fitting up.[19] One of Wake's most important publications, which appeared in 1703, was *The Authority of Christian Princes over their Ecclesiastical Synods Asserted, with particular respect to the Convocations of the Clergy of the Realm of England.* The Convocations of York and Canterbury had not met since shortly after the Restoration and as a result there was no forum where Church affairs could be discussed. Wake had opposed Convocation's revival, though unsuccessfully, and it had assembled in 1700.[20] In this year, Archbishop Tenison put great pressure on his old friend to take the vacant see of Oxford, as St. James' was now earmarked for another clergyman. In an angry interview with the Archbishop, Wake refused this promotion; he was so weak with 'the cholic' at the time that afterwards he had to be carried home by chair. Despite this outburst, Wake was appointed to the deanery of Exeter in February 1702, at the same time holding St. James'. He had to relinquish the canonry of Christ Church, a post which he wished to retain, and his appeal to the Queen against this decision was to no avail.[21]

At Exeter, he found an almost bankrupt church and, as in so many other instances, he undertook the repair of the fabric at his own expense. Each summer, Wake travelled down to Exeter, where he took the opportunity of visiting his father. On 16 May 1705, Wake was summoned to Shapwick, having heard that his father's health was failing. As he later recalled:

> The month of May had been observed by him to be 'very fatal' to the family. My Mother died the 16th of the month 1671, my Grandmother the 25th of the same month 1693, my eldest sister the 2nd of the month 1656, and now it pleased God to take my Father to himself the 29th of the same month, A.D. 1705 in the 75th. of his age. I was with him about ten days before he died. He sank gradually, and seemed as well on the morning he died as he had been for some years before. He had his senses intire to the last, ordered all matters relating to his own burial as well as his other concerns, invited the minister of the parish, who had been attending him, to dine that day with us. As we were at dinner, he seemed to fall asleep, and so without ever awaking, afterwards went insensibly off and departed this life about six o'clock in the evening.[22]

William made the necessary arrangements for the burial and settlement of the will. All his father's lands and leases had been left to him, and he was now a comparatively wealthy man. Two months earlier on 14 March, he had to his surprise, received a letter from the Archbishop offering him the bishopric of Lincoln with a further year of the living of St. James'.[23] When he had visited his father, William had told him of the offer; whereas in the case of previous offers the former had advised his son against accepting them, he now encouraged him. Even so, William, in his interview with the Archbishop later in March, felt compelled to state his reasons for contemplating acceptance:

> Should I now decline what was proposed to me, I could not tell whether some very unacceptable, if not unfit person, might not be put upon him. Besides, I know not whether it would otherwise be excusable in me to resist so many calls to this office.[24]

Believing that there was 'a particular call of the divine providence about it', William agreed to accept the post. At Kensington Palace on 17 August 1705, he kissed the hand of Queen Anne for the bishopric. He suffered an attack of jaundice in September and on his recovery, he was consecrated on 21 October at Lambeth Palace by Archbishop Tenison, assisted by the Bishops of Chichester, London, Norwich and Sarum. One of Wake's reasons for hesitation had been the delicate state of politics at this time. Whilst a canon at Christ Church, he was the only member of the chapter not to be in favour of Anglican conservatism. The connection between the High Church party and the Tories was a very strong one, but the defeat of the Tories in the Commons in November 1704 had opened the way for the Lincoln appointment. Wake was a Church Whig and later voted with the Whigs in the House of Lords on 5 April 1714 when the Protestant succession was in danger.[25]

The diocese of Lincoln was the largest in England, with six archdeaconries – Lincoln, Stow, Huntingdon, Bedford, Buckingham and Leicester – and more than 1,300 benefices. Administration of the diocese was not helped by the comparative inaccessibility of the episcopal palace at Buckden, near Huntingdon. In order to establish personal contacts with his clergy, the bishop made visitations every three years with which he combined confirmations. The strain of travel and long days of work must have had a severe effect on an already frail constitution. During his three visitations of 1706, 1709 and 1712, Wake carried out in all 18,330 confirmations. To take one example, on 4 September 1709, he laid hands on some 800 candidates.[26] Besides returning to Buckden for ordinations during the visitations, there were many other duties to be undertaken whilst on tour. On 20 May 1706, he visited the Archdeaconry of Stow and on the 22nd entertained the Corporation of Lincoln to dinner. On 31 May, Wake, as Visitor, heard a dispute at Louth between the Warden, assistants and the Usher of the school, noting that 'the spire of the church is very fine'. Five days later, he gave 'a good sermon' at Stamford, only for the occasion to be spoilt afterwards: 'Our entertainment was very bad and the clergy offended at it. To shew my dislike I went away the same evening to Grantham'. On 9 June, Wake was invited by the Duke of Rutland to Belvoir Castle 'where I was received with a very peculiar respect'. The night before, Ethelreda Wake had had a miscarriage and was extremely ill. As a result, 'being very uneasy upon Mrs. Wake's account I got away as soon as I could after evening prayer, and found her by God's blessing, not worse'.[27]

We know very little of William Wake's wife or his children, as they are rarely mentioned in the voluminous corespondence which the Archbishop conducted throughout his life. There were thirteen children altogether. The first three, Etheldred, William I and Edward, did not survive infancy; Amie and Etheldred II, Hester, Dorothy and Magdalene all grew up and married. The ninth child, Anne, died an infant and Elizabeth lived only till she was fifteen. Mary later married the Reverend John Lynch of Groves in Kent, who became Dean of Canterbury Cathedral. The twelfth was William II, and finally there was Catherine, both of whom died in infancy.[28] All the six surviving children were daughters.

It was for his youngest son, William II, that he wrote *A Brief Enquiry into the Antiquity, Honour and Estate of the Name and Family of Wake*, probably in 1694 when Rector of St.

37. St. Andrew's Church, Winterborne Tomson, Dorset. The Norman Church was restored by Archbishop Wake

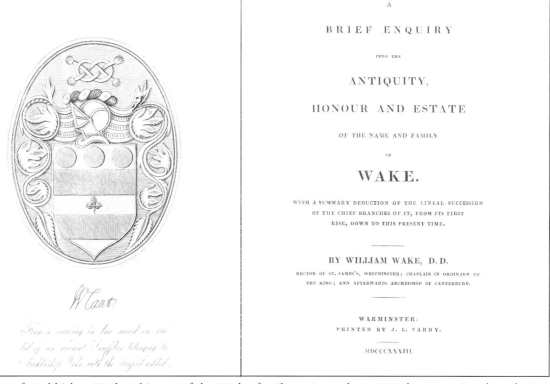

A

BRIEF ENQUIRY

INTO THE

ANTIQUITY,

HONOUR AND ESTATE

OF THE NAME AND FAMILY

OF

WAKE.

WITH A SUMMARY DEDUCTION OF THE LINEAL SUCCESSION
OF THE CHIEF BRANCHES OF IT, FROM ITS FIRST
RISE, DOWN TO THIS PRESENT TIME.

BY WILLIAM WAKE, D.D.

RECTOR OF ST. JAMES'S, WESTMINSTER; CHAPLAIN IN ORDINARY TO
THE KING; AND AFTERWARDS ARCHBISHOP OF CANTERBURY.

WARMINSTER:
PRINTED BY J. L. VARDY.

MDCCCXXXIII.

38. Title page of Archbishop Wake's history of the Wake family, written about 1694 but not printed until 1833

James'. Addressed to 'My Son', Wake abandoned the project when William died at about four years old. The manuscript was found amongst the Archbishop's papers after his death. A limited edition was privately printed by his great-great granddaughter Etheldred Benett in 1833.[29] In the opening paragraphs, Wake wrote:

> I cannot but think it a pardonable curiosity for anyone to desire to know from whom he is descended, and what figure his ancestors, in their several ages, are reported to have made in the world . . . Examples are not only very instructive, but operative and encouraging. They excite a man to do what is generous and worthy, as well as shew him what he ought to account so. They raise a secret emulation in his breast, and prick him on to a desire of rivalling those whose actions he reads of, and whose virtues he admires.
>
> It will be your part to endeavour still to increase the honour and estate of our family . . . let me therefore raise this ambition betimes in you, and let me desire you diligently to read and carefully to consider what you will here (i.e. in this book) meet with, concerning your family, from which you are descended.[30]

The book was carefully researched, with many documents and authorities quoted in footnotes. Not surprisingly, there are some inaccuracies – for instance, an extra Baldwin Wake is inserted between 1172 and 1213 – but as the first attempt to set out the Wake descent, it is an impressive account.

In the final chapter, the Archbishop carries the story to his own day. Noting that this Dorset branch of the family had not been entered on the Herald's books, he had in 1691 gathered up the records assembled by his uncle Edward and took them to Sir Henry St. George, Clarenceux Herald. After the documents had had been scrutinized, the Duke of Norfolk, Earl Marshal of England, granted him the Wake coat of arms but with the distinguishing mark of a trefoil vert on the shield.[31]

*   *   *   *   *

With the Whigs now in the ascendant from 1714, there were fewer political battles for the Bishop to fight. On the death of Archbishop Tenison on 14 December 1715, Wake was appointed to Canterbury two days later. He was now able to devote much of his attention to a project which he greatly wished to bring to fruition. In his preachings, Wake had stated a conviction that the fundamentals upon which all Christians were agreed ought to overrule all lesser differences. He therefore sought to bring together men of varying opinions and kept up a constant correspondence with Protestant churches on the Continent, including the leading Lutheran, Reformed and Moravian pastors.

A dispute between Louis XIV of France and the Vatican on the question of the right to exercise authority over the French clergy was uneasily patched up in 1693. The bishops and Gallican theologians of the Sorbonne resented Louis's apparent timidity when confronted by the Pope. Starting in 1716, Wake communicated with leading members of the Gallican Church and members of the Sorbonne, particularly Dr Ellies

Du Pin, who was a great authority on ecclesiastical matters. Wake realised that the union of the Anglican and Gallican churches was never likely to occur, but he aimed at a working relationship which could make progress towards ecumenism.[32] His scheme, as communicated on 18 November 1718 to William Beauvoir, chaplain to the English ambassador in Paris and Wake's intermediary, included agreement on the independence of every national church; the right to determine all matters internally; and on points of doctrine, to agree as far as possible on all articles of importance whilst allowing differences on lesser ones. 'Such a scheme as this I take to be a more proper ground of peace at the beginning, than to go into particulars. If such a foundation we could once agree, the rest would more easily be built upon it'.[33]

These negotiations, conducted in private, by some means became more widely known and rumours began to spread in Paris of the imminent reunification between the two churches. Action followed. Du Pin was interrogated early in 1719 and his papers confiscated. In June that year, Du Pin died and with his death, the main chance of a *rapprochement* between the two churches disappeared. The Archbishop carried on the dialogue with one of Du Pin's colleagues, Giradin, until as late as 1731. Though deeply disappointed, Wake did not give up hope that reconciliation would eventually be achieved.[34]

On domestic matters, meanwhile, there was a wide range of activities to be undertaken. As Visitor to All Souls College, Oxford, he was approached in November 1717 by the Warden, Bernard Gardner, to state his views on the legislation being proposed by the Government to alter college statutes. 'You may be assured,' Wake replied, 'that I shall esteem it my duty and happiness to support the constitution, privileges and immunities of the Universities which I shall greatly rejoice to see, whatever may be found amiss, yet I desire may continue and flourish in all virtue and learning, so long as the Nation itself remains'.[35]

With a keen interest in the aesthetic aspects of church architecture and design, he was the recipient of comment and appeals from notable architects. In October 1717 Sir Christopher Wren, then eighty five, and no longer involved in the building of St. Paul's Cathedral, had been informed by the Commissioners responsible for embellishing the building that 'a balustrade of stone was to be set up on top of the church'. Wren's own comments were elicited. Dismissing such a design as in 'vulgar taste', he hotly declared to the Archbishop, 'I never designed a balustrade. Persons of little skill in architecture did expect, I believe, to see something they had been used to in Gothic structures, and Ladies like nothing well without an edging'.[36] Nicholas Hawksmoor, appointed one of the two surveyors to the Fifty New Churches scheme of 1711, appealed to Wake for protection of his office in January 1720. English Baroque, of which Hawksmoor was an enthusiastic practitioner, was being replaced by the more fashionable neo-classical style and his forty years' service in designing public buildings was about to be set aside. 'I shall leave some Monuments of Beauty behind me', he wrote, 'so that I hope I may deserve some Encouragement from the Publick'.[37] Shortly before this, the Archbishop was the dedicatee of a work on the history of abbeys. In thanking the author, he stated, 'I am so great a lover of Antiquities that I am scarce judge of what is done in this kind. All attempts please me, and I scarce know how to find fault even where I think these want exactness'.[38]

Wake was a leading figure in fostering the work of the Society for Promoting Christian Knowledge (the SPCK) which was founded in 1698. The Society's aims, to remedy evils 'which cry aloud from Heaven', were to create charity schools for poor children where instruction in reading the Bible and the catechism could be given. Funds for the schools were provided by the gentry, business and the Church. As Bishop of Lincoln, Wake prepared a letter for his clergy on his visitations, requesting information on the progress being made in providing schools in their localities. By 1714, over 200 charity schools had been established in his diocese.[39] Problems were caused by the fact that many of the trustees and teachers of the schools were Jacobites, who supported the Old Pretender. As Archbishop, Wake was now much concerned in taking measures to counter this subversion; in 1718, he recommended that every master and mistress should take an oath of loyalty to the Government 'and heartily acknowledge King George as the only rightful King'.[40] An offshoot of the SPCK was the Society for Propagating the Gospel in Foreign Parts formed in 1701, which confined its activities to missionary work in the English plantations in America. Wake, as president of the Society, was involved for many years in a scheme in providing bishops for these plantations. By 1712, the Society had approved a project for establishing two bishops on the mainland – at Burlington, New Jersey, and Williamsburg, Virginia – and two on the islands of Barbados and Jamaica. Queen Anne supported the plan in the final year of her life in 1714, but after her death no further action was taken.[41]

These many calls on his time and energy occupied most of his waking hours. Reflecting on this situation to a correspondent shortly after becoming Archbishop, Wake wrote, 'The vii Days of the Week hardly afford me so many Hours out of my Bed, either for Rest or Reading. Many days I cannot be allowed to write a Post Letter (which was my Case last Thursday) and now I am forced to shut up myselfe to get my Debts of this kind a little under. I can therefore, at present, only heartily wish well to you who are so happy as to be Master of your own Time'.[42] On Lady Day, 1709, Wake entered in his Diary the note, 'A day of persecution'.[43] Frequently laid up with illness, Wake was by 1721 suffering from kidney stones, visiting Bath on several occasions to take the waters.[44]

Nevertheless, he was able to write several influential pamphlets and books, though this activity virtually ceased after he became Bishop of Lincoln. Wake was an avid book collector, mainly on religious and legal matters.[45] He gathered material for an ambitious project to publish all the Councils and synodical decrees, starting from the earliest times, but was unable to realise this plan. Another of the Archbishop's interests was coin collecting. Starting with Greek and Roman examples, he acquired an enthusiasm for English coins towards the end of his life. Wake wrote to the antiquarian, William Stukeley, in 1727, requesting the latter to pass on information which might lead to possible purchases, 'You will have the goodness to excuse this liberty, and impute it to the desire I have to finish a collection intended for the use of the public when I myself must have done with it'. This fine collection, together with his library, was left to his old college, Christ Church after his death.[46]

Wake did not face the prospect of old age with great enthusiasm. 'I have seen too

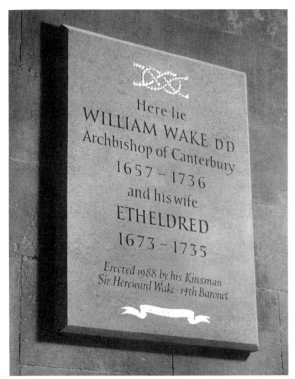

39. Memorial to Archbishop William Wake and his wife, Croydon Church, 1989

40. Archbishop William Wake by Vanderbank, early eighteenth century

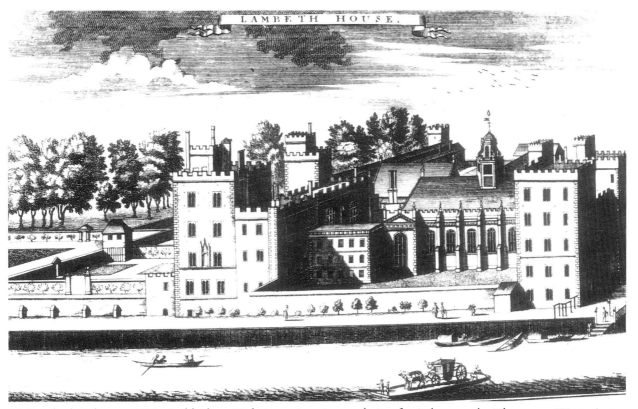

41. Lambeth Palace, c.1715. Archbishop Wake's carriage is seen being ferried across the Thames to Westminster

much of this world to be very fond of it,' he told an Oxford friend in 1719. 'I think 'tis enough for a wise and good man if he be content, while God pleases, to endure it'.[47] By slow degrees, the Archbishop withdrew from many commitments as his constitution weakened. On 7 December 1726, Wake gave a poignant description of his situation:

> For myself, I live almost a monastic life. I have a numerous family, and I keep it under the best regulation I can. We have the service of God within ourselves, and that in public in my chapel and house, four times a day. We live orderly and peaceably together; and though the necessity of business draws a great number of persons to me, yet I reduce even that as much as possible to certain times, and then eat openly with my friends two days in the week. To the Court I seldom go, save when obliged to attend my duty, either in the public or Cabinet councils; and when in Parliament time, I am rather faulty in not going so often as I should to it than in attending constantly upon it; so that I use my best endeavours to live clear of the world, and die by degrees to it. My age and infirmities (being now ready to enter on my seventieth year) admonish me to look upon myself as a citizen of another and better country, and ready to go from hence to it.[48]

He officiated at the Coronation of George II at Westminster Abbey on 12 October 1727 when the King presented him with a gold snuff box but because of his infirmity he was excused by the King from walking in procession from Westminster Hall to the church. In 1730 Wake suffered his most serious illness and his sight had begun to fail. His last public appearance was in January 1732 when he officiated at the consecration of two of his friends, Thomas Tanner and Nicholas Clagett, as bishops of St. Asaph and St. David's respectively. The death of his wife, Ethelreda, a year earlier, on 15 April 1731, left him a broken man.[49] Thereafter, his affairs were looked after by his son-in-law, Dr John Lynch, Dean of Canterbury, though Wake continued to hold the post of Archbishop.[50] On Monday afternoon, 24 January 1737, William Wake died at Lambeth Palace, two days before his eightieth birthday. The funeral cortège crossed the River Thames by boat, the last occasion when an Archbishop of Canterbury was so conveyed. He was buried on 9 February in Croydon parish church alongside his wife in the south chancel, called the Bishops' chancel, where his illustrious predecessors John Whitgift and Gilbert Sheldon were also buried. The memorial bearing a simple inscription to William and Ethelreda was destroyed in 1867 when the Church suffered a serious fire. A new memorial was dedicated in the church on 20 July 1989 by the Archbishop of Canterbury, Dr Robert Runcie, in the presence of William Wake's kinsman, Sir Hereward Wake, fourteenth baronet, and other members of the family.

*　　　*　　　*　　　*　　　*

Archbishop Wake is represented in histories of the Church of England as one of its most celebrated figures and rightly so. As a scholar first and foremost he disliked the melée of political controversy which characterized his age. Sometimes, his aversion to intrigue made him appear to his contemporaries too timid in his approach. But he was not afraid to court unpopularity, as in 1721, when he opposed a Government bill for granting relief to Quakers, in the belief that it might undermine the unity of the Church. He was most considerate towards the clergy for whom he was responsible. As one of them acknowledged in describing Wake's letters written to his colleagues, 'there is an appearance of great good nature, humanity and condescension, virtues more becoming the high station he was advanced to, than stigmatizing his brethren'.[51] He was noted for his hospitality and generosity and spent large sums of money on archiepiscopal and other residences. The Archbishop gave £11,000 for repairs to Lambeth Palace and Croydon Church.

A moderate High Churchman, he was convinced that all Christians could agree on fundamentals and overlook smaller differences in order to achieve unity. His attempts to bring about a closer union with the Gallican church and the Protestant churches of Europe clearly demonstrates his philosophy. His conscientiousness in carrying out his ecclesiastical duties cost him dearly in health. He kept up a copious correspondence with many of the leading figures of his day on a wide range of subjects. From those letters which have survived,[52] we can see at work a lively and sympathetic mind, full of curiosity.

Wake's great interest in education sprang from his own experiences. Brought up in rural surroundings, he had relished his own schooldays. One of his motives for promoting charity schools was to extend such an opportunity for learning to a wider spectrum of the population. He also never forgot his own roots in Dorset, returning to Shapwick whenever the opportunity arose. The nearby small Norman church of Winterborne Tomson, adjacent to the farmhouse owned by his father, was restored and fitted out with seats by the Archbishop and he enjoyed preaching sermons there.[53]

William Wake was liberal in bestowing patronage on several of his kinsmen. Robert Wake, son of Sir William, the third baronet, became Dean of Bocking (see Chapter 5); his cousin Edward was made Rector of Stoke Hammond, Buckinghamshire and his nephew, also Edward, was Rector at Monks Risborough in the same county. His son-in-law, John Lynch, was the recipient of many church posts. Such preferment of relatives was not uncommon at the time. One disappointed candidate for promotion wrote to Wake, 'I don't presume to find fault with the Bishop of Worcester for preferring his nephew. I only wish it were my good fortune to be a bishop's nephew too'.[54]

William Wake's achievements are now part of the history of the Church of England. Few writers have drawn sufficient attention to his human qualities and the background from which he came. He was always proud of his forebears and the family name; and in his book for his son, written at a time when the Wake fortunes were at a low ebb, he remarked:

> tho' it be long since it has pleased God to reduce us to a very moderate Fortune yet somewhat there will occur, even in what is come down to us, that may serve to set us some domestic examples of valour and piety, and to inspire us with a desire of reviving again the honour of a name, that was once so great in the annals of our country.[55]

He would have been pleased to have seen such a revival of the family fortunes which occurred a few decades later in the century.

9

Politics and Parliament:
Sir William Wake, The Eighth Baronet

ON THE DEATH WITHOUT ISSUE OF THE SIXTH BARONET
Sir Charles Wake Jones on 27 January 1755, the question of succession became a
complicated one. Neither Sir John, the fourth baronet, nor Sir Baldwin, the fifth
baronet, had surviving male heirs. Their younger brother, Robert, Dean of Bocking
(d.1725), had one surviving son, William, who now succeeded his cousin to the title.

Little is known about Sir William as few of his papers have survived. He was an
attorney at law at Southampton Buildings in Holborn and was appointed as one of the
executors of the will of Sir Charles Wake Jones in 1754, only a few months before the
latter's death.[1] The seventh baronet dropped the name Jones from the title, a precedent
followed by all subsequent holders. Since his time, the Wake family have held
Courteenhall in direct descent. Unlike his cousin, William spent a large part of his time
at Riddlesworth and at Waltham, though he died at Courteenhall at the age of fifty on
26 September 1765.

In April 1738, William had married Sarah Walker of Weston, North Yorkshire, at
St. Giles in the Fields, London. After her death at Riddlesworth on Christmas Day 1793
aged eighty five, she was buried with her husband in Courteenhall Church. They had
five sons and one daughter. The eldest, William, who became the eighth baronet, will
be described fully later in this chapter. Charles Wake, the second son, was born in 1743;
William and he were the first members of the family to go to Eton (June 1755).[2]
Charles matriculated at St. John's College, Oxford, the year after leaving Eton and
became Rector of Riddlesworth, remaining there until his death on 30 August 1781.
The third son, Arden, died an infant. Drury Wake, the fourth son, entered the 17th
Light Dragoons as a cornet in 1763. He rose to the rank of Major and fought in the
American War of Independence.[3] Later he settled at St. Bees, Cumberland, where he
died and was buried in July 1787. His daughter, Frances, was mother of Admiral Sir
Baldwin Wake Walker, the first baronet of that family. Baldwin Wake, the fifth and
youngest son, followed his brother Charles as Rector of Riddlesworth, and is supposed
to have married three times. His first wife, Elizabeth, was the daughter of General Philip
Schuyler (1733–1804) a member of one of the wealthiest New York families. In the
War of Independence, during the Saratoga campaign of 1777, Schuyler was accused of

See Appendix A – Family Trees VII and X. Notes and References pages 404–406 negligence when Ticonderoga was surrendered to the British without a shot being fired. He was subsequently cleared at a court martial and though resigning from active service in 1779, continued to advise George Washington.[4] Baldwin Wake's mother bequeathed to him the Drury family portraits from Riddlesworth in her will of July 1793. He died at Bath in 1815 without issue; it was probably then that these pictures came to Courteenhall, in the time of the ninth baronet. The one daughter of Sir William and Lady Wake was Mary, who married a Suffolk gentleman in April 1796.

After the death of Sir William in 1765, he was succeeded by his son, also called William. He was born in 1742 and quickly showed evidence of intellectual promise. Following five years at Eton 1755–9, he was admitted as a fellow commoner at Trinity College, Cambridge in 1760, then as a student at Lincoln's Inn four years later. William married, on 6 June 1765, Mary Fenton, daughter and heiress of Richard Fenton of Bank Top, Yorkshire. Within three months, he became the eighth baronet and from this time led the life of a country gentleman.

That this was possible was due largely to a fortunate marriage. The Fenton family was of very ancient descent. In the early eighteenth century, William Fenton had acquired Underbank Hall, near Penistone, in West Yorkshire, through marriage to Frances, only daughter and heiress of Captain Richard West.[5] Richard Fenton, born in 1708, was William and Frances' fifth son. A man of great drive and ability, he was Clerk of the Peace for the West Riding, where his involvement in county business won him much praise.[6] Richard lived at Bank Top in the parish of Worsborough, near Barnsley, the whole of which he owned.[7] The old turnpike road between Wakefield and Sheffield passed through the village, which was a popular resting place for travellers. Richard had married Anne, daughter of the Reverend Thomas Brooke, Rector of Richmond, and their only child Mary was born in 1745. In the will of her unmarried Aunt Frances, in January 1779, she was left £100, a diamond hooped ring and Frances' 'worked bed'.[8] Mary Fenton was a considerable heiress and the fortune which she brought with her on marriage to William Wake may help to account for the programme of building which was now undertaken at Courteenhall.

*   *   *   *   *

The fine Stables, which still stand on a ridge to the south of the House, were very probably built during the occupancy of Courteenhall by the eighth baronet. The Elizabethan building where the Wakes then lived was dwarfed by the new block and caused problems later in the century when Humphry Repton came to advise on the site of the new House. As he wrote in the Red Book of Courteenhall, 'To make it (as a stable doubtless ought to be) subordinate to the mansion would have required a palace too large for any situation that accords with the true character of the place'.[9] His solution is described in detail in Chapter 11. Various dates have been suggested for the new stable block and J.A. Gotch believed that its plainness, except for the principal doorways, pointed to the first half of the eighteenth century.[10] However, a plan of the estate of 1766 at Courteenhall does not depict such a building. For a number of reasons, it is fairly certain that a later date is more likely.

In 1753 Hugo Meynell, an eighteen year old gentleman, rented Quorn or Quorndon Hall in North Leicestershire. Meynell, who was keen on hunting, set about breeding hounds which were fast enough to keep up with foxes. This revolutionary change quickly made fox-hunting a popular sport, especially in 'the shires', (the great grasslands of the Midland counties of Leicestershire, Northamptonshire and Rutland), and particularly with the fashionable packs which hunted there.[11] The great growth of interest in the sport was from about 1780. William Wake, who lived mainly at Waltham, probably saw the possibilities of using Courteenhall as a hunting box. To house the horses, a stable block could be erected which would signify at the same time the owner's status. Perhaps, too, Sir William wished to rival the magnificent neo-Palladian stables at nearby Althorp, built by Roger Morris in 1732–3.[12] There would probably have already been a more modest stable block which was demolished at the time of the new building. In the dining room at Courteenhall, there is a painting of six black horses being made ready for a drive. In the background is a building which was probably the old Stables.[13]

One interesting piece of evidence which has recently come to light is a note of a conversation in August 1904 between Sir Herewald Wake, twelfth baronet, and his aunt, Matilda Charlotte Wake. Matilda, the younger daughter of the tenth baronet, was christened on 19 August 1832 and was fourteen at the time of the ninth baronet's death. Reminiscing on the past, she stated without qualification that the Courteenhall Stables were built in 1784, a year before her great-grandfather died.[14]

Identifying the architect of the Stables presents problems, but the most likely candidate is John Carr of York (1723–1807). The Palladian style had become popular with the gentry through such works as Isaac Ware's translation of Palladio's *Four Books of Architecture* published in 1738. After the 1740s, Georgian Palladianism spread to the provinces.[15] Carr built more than twenty stables throughout England during his long career. There are stylistic similarities between Courteenhall and some of his other stables, particularly the bold geometry and architectural motifs, such as the round arched windows linked by a bold string course. Courteenhall has the typical quadrangle arrangement with, on the facade, a central arch and over it, a window flanked by projecting pavilions, each with oval shaped windows. Inside, the mangers have niches above hay-rack level as at Wentworth Woodhouse, Yorkshire, built by Carr between 1766 and 1789, though the latter is on a much larger scale.[16]

Carr, who completed his first stable at Harewood House in 1755, was from the 1760s commissioned by many newly-prosperous Yorkshire gentry to design country houses and other buildings. Unlike his predecessors, Carr did not attempt to group the Stables with the House. A writer on Carr has observed, 'The stables of an eighteenth century Yorkshire establishment almost rivalled the house itself in importance'.[17] At Denton Park, West Riding of Yorkshire, the house and stables were started in 1770. The stables though of one storey only, have a very strong visual link with Courteenhall. Denton is some four miles from Weston, where the eighth baronet's mother's family resided. Sir William's wife, too, would have been well aware of Carr's reputation as a fashionable architect. A further Northamptonshire link was with the Fitzwilliams, who employed Carr at Wentworth Woodhouse and later at Milton House, near

42. Bedford c.1765, showing the *Swan Inn* from across Bedford High Street with St. Mary's Church in the distance

43. The Library, St. John's College, Cambridge, by Ackermann, at the time when the 9th baronet was an undergraduate at the College c.1787

44. Courteenhall Manor House, drawn before 1791. The home of the Ouseley family and then Sir Samuel Jones. Inherited by the Wake family, 1672

45. John Carr of York, architect (1723–1807), who probably built the Stables at Courteenhall

46. Courteenhall Stables in 1986. The east block as seen from the north east. In 1980, the archway was partially filled in when the Stables were converted to provide new living accommodation

Peterborough.[18] Lacking firm evidence, it is impossible to do more than speculate on the architect. If the designer were not Carr,[19] then it was probably by someone who closely copied his style.

Other candidates who have recently emerged are the brothers William (1712–76) and David Hiorn (?-1758), who were leading masons and architects in Warwick at about the middle of the eighteenth century. Besides rebuilding the parish church of Holy Cross, Daventry, between 1752 and 1758 and Great Houghton Church in 1754, the Hiorns have been credited with other Northamptonshire commissions, particularly the stables at Harlestone House and also with those at Courteenhall.[20] However, the claim of Carr or one of his followers still seems the stronger one. The Stables were sensitively converted into a house by the fourteenth baronet in recent times and is now a family home.

From the surviving list of all men between eighteen and forty five years of age living in the parish of Courteenhall in 1771, it is clear that the overwhelming majority were employed in one capacity or other by Sir William. Of the nineteen, six worked as servants at the House. There were two other servants, who may have been in the service of either Sir William or the two 'gentlemen' in the parish, the Reverend John Vaux, Rector of Courteenhall, and John Hipwell. The remainder consisted of five labourers, three farmers and a shoemaker, William Surridge.[21] No doubt several women and girls of the village also found employment at the House.

The eighth baronet and his wife led a full life, travelling between their estates at Courteenhall, Riddlesworth and Waltham and raising a family. This consisted of two sons and two daughters. The elder son, William, later the ninth baronet, forms the subject of the next two chapters. Richard William, his younger brother, born in July 1775, studied at St. John's, Cambridge and was a Rural Dean and Rector of Courteenhall for thirty seven years, 1813–50. In 1798 he married Jane, daughter of Sir William Dunkin, a Judge of the Supreme Court of Calcutta. She died in 1823. At the age of fifty one, Richard married again, to Harriet, daughter of Henry Grattan, the notable Irish orator and statesman (1746–1820), and an MP in both the English and Irish Parliaments, who opposed Union with England. Richard died in Ireland in November 1850. Maryanne, the elder daughter, born April 1773, married an Army officer and her sister, Charlotte born six years later, probably remained a spinster.

*   *   *   *   *

Sir William was not content to devote his time only to his estates. He also had political ambitions and decided to stand as Member of Parliament for the town of Bedford in the 1774 elections. The Wake family had some connections with the county, possessing property in the parishes of Bromham, Cardington and Stevington, derived from the marriage of Baldwin Wake to Ela de Beauchamp, daughter of the baron of Bedford, in the second half of the thirteenth century.

The election of a comparative outsider at Bedford presented difficulties. For many years, John, fourth Duke of Bedford (1710–71), had been a dominating influence in the town. An able and determined man, he was a prominent politician at national level. In 1742, already a leading Whig, he helped to bring about the downfall of the Walpole ministry. He became First Lord of the Admiralty, 1745–8, then Secretary of State, 1748–51, and was Lord-Lieutenant of Ireland, 1757–61. In 1763 the new government, a coalition between Bedford and Granville, known as the Bedford Ministry, was formed in which he served as Lord President of the Council.[22] Within the county he was Lord-Lieutenant and a substantial landowner. He was also one of the the largest property holders in Bedford and 'treated' the town's burgesses when they visited his Bloomsbury estate in London.[23] When the Recordership of Bedford became vacant in 1767, Bedford succeeded to the post.

There was friction between the Duke and the Corporation on a number of matters.[24] In 1767 the former demanded that a number of his friends should be created freemen to ensure the success of his two candidates as the town's MPs, Richard Vernon, the Duke's brother-in-law, and Samuel Whitbread. The Corporation refused, but despite this, both Vernon and Whitbread were elected. Two years later, the Corporation had its revenge. In September 1769 it voted to create a substantial number of freemen, gaining the support of another powerful Whig, Sir Robert Bernard, a member of an old Huntingdonshire family. A radical in politics, he was supported by John Wilkes at the 1770 election when he was returned for the City of Westminster. Freemen were created by birth, apprenticeship, purchase or gift; honorary freemen, who also had the right to vote, could be created by the Corporation without any restriction as to residence, service, number or property. No fewer than 500 freemen were now created from inhabitants of Bedford and tenants and neighbours of Bernard, who were called at the time 'guinea-pigs' because of the payment they received.[25] This intervention was decisive. At the election on 18 October 1774, Sir William Wake was top of the poll with 527 votes; also elected was Robert Sparrow, Bernard's brother-in-law.[26] The two unsuccessful candidates were both Bedfordshire men, Samuel Whitbread and John Howard, the prison reformer.[27] Whitbread had amassed a fortune with his London brewery and had expected to be elected. As he told his son a few years later, 'the way to come into Parliament respectably was by invitation, not by contention'.[28] From the beginning of the election campaign, Whitbread was aware of the danger brought about by the Corporation's action. 'I began to canvass the Town yesterday,' he told the Duke's agent on 2 October, 'and found very great encouragement ... But I am sensible the Voters of the Town cannot stand in competition with the new made ones'.[29]

After the election, both Whitbread and Howard petitioned the House of Commons, accusing Wake and Sparrow of bribery. They also challenged the right of non-resident and honorary freemen to vote as well as those in receipt of the town's charities. On 23 March 1775, a Committee of the House determined that some recipients of alms were disqualified from voting.[30] This ruling was sufficient to wipe out Sparrow's narrow majority over Whitbread – Sparrow had received 417 votes, Whitbread 409 – and Whitbread was elected in his place, along with Wake.

There were fewer problems for Sir William within his constituency after his election. The fourth Duke had died in 1771, leaving his five year old grandson as his successor to the title. However, at the next election in September 1780, Whitbread was more confident that his rival would be defeated. Only three candidates were standing for the two seats, Whitbread and his colleague, John Kenrick, with Wake as the only Independent Tory. Writing to his brother-in-law William Haytor the week before the election, Whitbread mentioned that 'Sir W. Wake has neither taken trouble nor been at any expense and Mr. Kenrick has, and I think will beat him easy'.[31] Whitbread's forecast was wrong, but Sir William's share of the vote dropped. Whitbread headed the poll with 673 votes and Sir William gained 421, 77 ahead of Kenrick. The eighth baronet had entered Parliament at the age of thirty two and was to be a Member for the next ten years.[32] Sir William's first recorded speech was on the subject of the Bedford election itself. During a debate initiated by Whitbread on 1 May 1775 calling for a Committee of the House to investigate the facts, Wake had opposed this move. He claimed that the motives of the Corporation for making honorary freemen on this occasion were laudable 'as they arose from an intention to rescue it out of the hands of a certain noble Duke, who had obtained an undue influence over the elections for members to represent the said borough in Parliament'.[33]

Nine months before Sir William was first elected, news of the Boston Tea Party reached England and in the spring of 1774 Lord North, the Prime Minister, introduced measures in the Commons to restore order in the American colonies. In 1775, the War of Independence began. To finance the war, North moved that the land tax for the following year should be raised from three shillings to four shillings in the pound. Wake opposed this new burden on the landed gentry.[34] He also supported a bill to exclude Government contractors from sitting in the House, stating that 'he could not help being of the opinion that the temptation of a profitable contract of £20,000 to £30,000 was too much, and might influence men to vote contrary to their real sentiments and to the interest of their country'.[35]

Wake's contemporaries remarked on his strong character. A writer in the *Public Ledger* in 1779 noted, 'He … piques himself on his independence'; and two years later the *English Chronicle* described him as 'a very independent Member with a small mixture of tenaciousness, or perhaps obstinacy, in his disposition'.[36] He could also be generous in his assessment of people. On the death of the Marquess of Rockingham in July 1782, his place as Prime Minister was taken by the Earl of Shelburne, one of the most unpopular politicians of his time. Much of this was due to Shelburne's outspokenness and open contempt for political parties.[37] In a debate in the House on 9 July 1782 in Shelburne's absence one MP, John Lee, declared that 'he had not heard one person step forward to say that the Earl of Shelburne was a fit and proper person for the high office he held'. Sir William immediately followed this challenge 'which truth and justice compelled him to take up'. He declared his great friendship with Shelburne over the years and asserted that 'he never met with a man more open and sincere, more uniform and steady or more honest and upright in all his transactions, and throughout the whole of his conduct, than the present first Lord of the Treasury'.[38] The motion of censure was subsequently withdrawn.

From the start of the American War of Independence, Wake had been one of its most persistent critics. After seven years of fighting, success still eluded the British. On 19 October 1781, the siege of Yorktown ended with the surrender of General Cornwallis and 7,000 men. A debate on the Address in the Commons on 28 November gave Wake the opportunity to express his sentiments:

> The minister has informed the House that there would still be resources in the nation sufficient to support the war ... If the noble lord would go down to his estate in the country and ask his tenants if there were resources, he was confident they would answer him in the negative ... He therefore advised the noble Lord not to suffer himself to be deluded by the vain hopes of finding supplies for feeding a war which had swallowed up almost all the resources of the country.[39]

In his final speech in the House on 20 February 1784, Wake drew protests from some Members. The American War had ended in the previous year; in reflecting on it, he declared that 'A mistaken sense of dignity in the American War had really ruined this country',[40] a statement which he refused to withdraw.

A month later, on 25 March, Parliament was dissolved and a general election was immediately called. Sir William did not stand again, though he took an active interest in the electioneering at Bedford. At the 1784 elections in Northamptonshire Sir James Langham of Cottesbrooke and a new candidate, Thomas Powys, later first Baron Lilford, were nominated. Powys was accused of having a 'crossbench' mentality and some Tory squires were reluctant to associate with him. Sir William, however, spoke in his favour, and whilst admitting defects in Powys's public character, stated 'take him for all in all, we shall not meet with his Equal'.[41] Both Langham and Powys were elected.

During his decade in Parliament he had witnessed many dramatic scenes and played a modest part in its proceedings, the only Wake baronet to sit in the Commons. Sir William had also seen no fewer than five Prime Ministers take office during this period.[42] Apart from his parliamentary duties, we know only a few details of his other activities. He was Sheriff for Northamptonshire, 1771–2. As Lord of the Manor at Waltham Holy Cross, in 1772, he appealed at Chelmsford Quarter Sessions against the poor rate of the parish. A local newspaper reported that 'notwithstanding the influence exerted in support of the appeal, the Court, after a hearing of four hours, unanimously confirmed the rate, to the great satisfaction of the parishioners, which was testified by the ringing of bells, and every demonstration of joy'.[43]

Sir William took a close interest in his estates. He was active in keeping the farm buildings at Courteenhall and Riddlesworth in good order. At the latter, in 1777, he undertook the widening and deepening of the nearby Little Ouse River.[44] The family link with Oxfordshire was severed with the sale of Fritwell to John Freke Willes of Astrop, Northamptonshire, in 1770. He generously helped pay off the debts of his imprudent brother, Drury, and granted him a yearly allowance for the rest of his life.[45]

On a lighter note, there was an occasion not long before his death when he had a wager with his son William's tutor respecting the prizes gained in the previous twenty years by his own Cambridge College, Trinity, and that of the tutor's, St. John's. Enquiries were made at Cambridge and it was found that Sir William had lost. It had been agreed that a silver cup, costing twenty guineas, suitably inscribed, should be presented to the winner. In the event, it was Sir William's widow who had the cup made.[46]

1785   The Executors of the Late Sir Wm Wake —— Dr

to Jno Heaven & Son—for

the following part of the funeral of the said Sr Willm

To d Hearse & 6 horses & one coach & 6 out 6 days from London to waltham Abby & down to Courteen Hall with Corps & Company — duty included	39=12=0
To one coach & 6 out 7 days to Courteen Hall & Returned to waltham	23=9=0
To d Set of Best Black ostrich feathers for hearse & horses through	2=12=6
To d Set of the Best velvets for ditto — through	2=2=0
To d Lid of Best feathers carried before the Corps through	1=16=0
To 2 Horse-porters with Gowns staffs & Covers through	8=0=0
To 6 horsemen and attender through, and men to bear the Lid	27=0=0
To 17 Silk hatbands for self, assistans porters horsemen featherman Coach men and postillions — 37/	6=7=6
To hanging the Room at Dunstable in deep mourning to deposit the Corps for the night and hanging the Great parlour at Courteen Hall in deep mourning compleat till the interment of Corps	8=8=0
To 18 Silvered d ble Scroll Scones with wax lights in ditto	4=10=0
To 2 men sitting up with the Corps at Dunstable & Courteen Hall	0=10=0
To 16 Crape hatbands for men to save their Silk ones on the Road	2=8=0
To 16 pr of Gloves for ditto men duty included	1=8=0
To allowance for all the mens liquor & Beer the journey 42/6	7=7=0
To Expence of Dinners for self assistans & 13 men at Barnett on our Return home from the funeral	1=4=10
To Expence of toll gates for Carriages & all the horsemen through the whole Journey	3=8=11
To the use of 12 Cloaks for horsemen Coachmen & postillions thro	2=2=0
To pd Carriage of hangings by Return post chaise from St Albans to Dunstable to prepair the Room for reception of the Corps	0=1=6
To post-chaise for the day to wait upon Lady wake at waltham Abby to Recieve instructions about the funeral	0=18=6
To the driver toll gates & Road Expences	0=10=6
To the Expence of my passage by the Leeds Coach to Dunstable to meet the Corps in order to see it Conducted with due Respect through to interment in family vault	0=15=0
To my attendance to the Completion of the funeral	2=2=0
To two yard & half atchievements frames & boords covered with cloth the mouldings gilt with pure gold, the arms in 4 quarterings with Lady wakes arms in an excecution of pretence	10=10=0
To d packing mat cord porterage & booking with the pen for the Atchievement sent down to Courteen Hall	0=2=6
To self & man going down to waltham Abby to put the other hatchments together & to fix it up in the church including chaise hire dinner for self & assistant & beer given to Carpenters who helped to fix it up in church	1=10=6
	£ 158=16=5

LD7. List of the funeral expenses of Sir William Wake, 8th baronet, 1785

121

The reason for Sir William's refusal to stand again as Member for Bedford is obscure. Perhaps it was the ill-health to which he was subject throughout his life,[47] or a wish to spend more time on his other interests. Only a year later, after an illness lasting seven days, Sir William died at Waltham Abbey on 29 October 1785. He was forty three years of age. Two days later, a coach bearing the body and pulled by six horses left Waltham. The procession rested for the night at Dunstable and reached Courteenhall the following day. On 6 November he was buried in the family vault in Courteenhall Church. As the *Gentleman's Magazine* wrote of him:

> In public life, his name stands high in the list of those very few, who unbiassed by party prejudice or private interest, made the good of their country the sole aim of all their actions. The uniform tenor of his political conduct justly entitles him to the noblest praise, that of an independent and honest man.[48]

10

'Old Sir William', The Ninth Baronet:
I. The Formative Years

'I WAS MUCH MORE SHOCKED THAN SURPRISED AT THE melancholy contents of your favour', wrote Jacob Preston of Beeston, Norfolk,[1] to his friend and fellow lawyer, Samuel Phipps, on 6 November 1785, 'having some time feared a sudden crisis would eer long deprive us of a most valuable friend, the World of a worthy character, and his family of a most affectionate Father, Husband and Relation. I feel exceedingly for poor Lady Wake's irreparable loss who cannot yet be presumed capable of recollecting with full force the value of what remains in so hopeful a young family'.[2]

The death of the eighth baronet a week previously had left his wife Mary with four children, ranging in age from Charlotte who was six, to the eldest, William, aged seventeen who now inherited the title as the ninth baronet. Sir William, the third Wake in succession to bear this Christian name, was born on 5 April 1768. He was still a minor but surviving letters from this time suggest that he was mature for his years and aware of the negotiations involved in administering his father's estate.

Lady Wake, who was unwell, stayed with her friends, Lord and Lady Cremorne[3] at Chelsea after the funeral. She then returned to Waltham Abbey, where, with assistance, her husband's papers relating to the Essex estates were sorted out, put in a large trunk and taken by wagon to Courteenhall. Reporting this, a solicitor informed Phipps, who together with Preston had been appointed a trustee, 'the Demands come in pretty fast upon us . . . they already amount, exclusive of Mortgage, to about £5,600'.[4] After returning to Northamptonshire on 18 November, Lady Wake applied herself to the new task of supervising the day-to-day running of Courteenhall. In early December, she told Phipps, 'Several of the Tenants have paid the Remainder of their Rents amounting to £206 11s. 0d; another Tenant whose rent is £126 per annum pays at St. Thomas. I am not easy at having so much Money in the House and shall be glad to know where I may place it'. By the end of 1785, the Waltham house was being viewed by a prospective buyer; but it was in a bad state of repair and would require considerable expenditure before it could be sold or let.[5]

For the next few years, Lady Wake relied heavily upon Phipps's advice and judgement on many matters. When a new coachman or servant was required she

See Appendix A — Family Tree X. Notes and References pages 406, 407 frequently sought his help. She took a London house at 2 Hanover Street in February 1787 'to avoid isolation' and decided that instead of hiring a coach to transport her at the cost of £33 a year, she would have one built. In sending Phipps an estimate she had received, Lady Wake added, 'I must beg a further favour of you which is to chuse the colour etc. for me. I believe I could have a chariot made at Northampton for much less money, but the workmanship certainly is there very inferior to Town work'.[6] In Norfolk the Riddlesworth tenants presented difficulties from time to time. Phipps was urged to deal with one who had not paid his rent, Lady Wake declaring, 'I have seen some years ago a great deal of the difficulty attending with Norfolk Farmers'.[7]

Besides the worries of estate matters, Mary was faced with the problem of dealing with the future education of her son. 'It is of the greatest importance', she wrote to Preston in February 1786, 'that my son should be placed under the Tuition of some proper Person as soon as possible, a Home Life being under his present situation attended with inconveniences that will readily occur to you'.[8] For the previous four years, William had been fortunate enough to have as his private tutor at Courteenhall an outstanding young scholar, Thomas Catton. Born in Norfolk in 1760, Catton had attended school at Burnham Thorpe, where one of his schoolfellows was Horatio Nelson.[9] He was elected as a Fellow and tutor at St. John's College, Cambridge, during his time at Courteenhall and was a friend of the Wakes for the rest of his life. In later years, he entered the Church, devoting himself to the study of astronomy, and was elected a Fellow of the Royal Society in 1821. Catton had charge of the College observatory, the only one in the University at the time, and collected much data on eclipses and other astronomical phenomena which was later published by the Royal Astronomical Society.[10] A benevolent and somewhat timid man, he was probably not sufficiently firm to handle his obstinate and self-willed charge.

As Catton was shortly due to return to his duties at Cambridge, it was becoming urgent to settle the question of Sir William's education. He was now almost nineteen and therefore eligible to go to university, but Lady Wake was reluctant to take this step. 'At present', she informed Phipps, 'I own it appears to me most prudent to postpone making him so entirely his own Master till another year. Besides, as I find he need not, as a Fellow commoner, reside more than half the year in College, and Mr. Catton could not be with him at Home, I should be greatly at a loss what to do with him in the vacation'.[11] One solution suggested by a neighbour of Lady Wake's parents, Edward Lascelles of Harewood House, was for William to join his son at a small school at Arnhem in Holland. This step was strongly urged by the Fentons, who told their daughter that 'the scheme of your Son's going abroad to a Protestant Seminary [is] the most likely to succeed'.[12] It was Phipps, however, who objected to Sir William being so far away from family restraint.

Lady Wake herself, after making a number of enquiries, eventually discovered a more suitable establishment. The school, at Hitcham House, near Maidenhead, was under the supervision of a cleric named Gretton who took a small number of gentlemen preparatory to their going to college. 'He is,' she stated, 'a man who has distinguished himself in Literary Merit, and of whom I heard an excellent character; his terms are £100 per annum'.[13] The small village of Hitcham, situated on the southern border of

CP17. The Library at Christ Church, Oxford to which Archbishop William Wake bequeathed his library and coin collection on his death in 1737

CP18. A medallion engraved in 1725 in honour of Archbishop William Wake. The inscription reads in translation:
'The enlightened men who have laboured to rebuild and restore learning and the true religion of Christ in Europe make this dedication to the most true servant and reverend father in Christ William Wake, Archbishop of Canterbury and Primate of All England and Metropolitan.'
John D'Assier, Geneva, 1725

CP19. The walnut cabinet, now at Courteenhall, which housed the Archbishop's collection of coins and medals

CP20. A miniature of Sir William Wake, 8th baronet (1742–1785), MP for Bedford, who built the Stables at Courteenhall

CP21. A miniature of Mary Fenton, who married the 8th baronet in 1765, by John Smart; she died in 1823, a widow for 38 years

CP22. Carriage horses and the Old Stables at Courteenhall, c.1760

CP23. William Wake, later 9th baronet, aged 16, 1784. He succeeded his father, the 8th baronet, who died the following year

CP24. Trout fishing in the River Lea at Waltham by James Pollard, 1841

CP25. Two fox hounds by J. N. Sartorius, c.1792. The 9th baronet kept his own hounds at Courteenhall

CP26. Prospect of Northampton by G. Arnald (1763–1841), showing cattle grazing on Hunsbury Hill. The four Northampton churches are seen towering over the old town

CP27. The Sitwell children at Renishaw, Derbyshire, by John Singleton Copley, 1787. The portrait shows Sitwell, Francis and Hurt, and Mary who married the 9th baronet in 1790

Buckinghamshire, perches on a hilltop overlooking the Thames. At this time it comprised a few scattered houses, a church and to the north-east, a manor house.[14] On the death of the lord of the manor, Robert Friend, in June 1780, the estate had been purchased by Lord Grenville, who was later in 1806 to become Prime Minister. Grenville subsequently built for himself a large country house, leaving Hitcham House empty.[15] When the house was advertised in the *London Gazette and New Daily Advertiser* on 3 August 1780, it was described as 'dry and in good repair, set in sixty acres of meadow with a well stocked orchard and pond, a dovecot and stables for fourteen horses and standing for four carriages'. It was now let to Gretton as a school.

*   *   *   *   *

The Reverend George Gretton who had been ordained deacon at Peterborough in 1776 was a larger than life character. He had graduated from Trinity College, Cambridge earlier that year and was eleventh wrangler. Besides running the school, he was vicar of a church in South Devon, Townstal with St. Saviour, Dartmouth, for twenty five years, and was also briefly Rector of nearby Hedsor, Buckinghamshire. He became Doctor of Divinity in 1791, chaplain to George III, and was advanced in 1809 by the Earl of Lonsdale to the Deanery of Hereford, a post which he filled until his death in 1820.[16] Gretton's forthright and somewhat eccentric views were fortunately recorded by Joseph Farington, RA, the topographical artist, who on 26 September 1806 was a fellow guest of Gretton at a country house in the neighbourhood of Hitcham. Afterwards Farington wrote in his Diary:

> Publick Schools were spoken of. He said the bane of the Publick Schools is that the parents of many of the boys fill their pockets with bank notes, & opportunity is allowed for the expenditure of it viciously. He described the characters of three great schools by saying that the youth at Eaton 'are dissipated Gentlemen'; – those at Westminster 'dissipated with *a little of the blackguard*'; and those at St. Pauls School 'the most depraved of all' . . . He said that, in His School, No Boy, though some are 18 years of age, expends more while at School, than two guineas a year. He desires the parents not to give them more than one guinea & if they require more He gives them a shilling at a time.[17]

On the following day at Gretton's invitation, Farington rode over to Hitcham House:

> There I walked about the grounds with Mrs. Gretton who shewed me several of Her Children. Her eldest son, a Clergymen, aged 25, & Her youngest Child, a Boy, 3 years old. She said she had had 15 Children. I then rode with Dr. Gretton through Burnham Wood, & by Dropmore till 2 o'clock. – He spoke of His general good fortune in life, & told me that He was very happily circumstanced in respect of property. He set out in life without having anything & now could retire to a House at [   ] in Nottinghamshire, near which He has a small estate, & could sit down possessed of £700 a year. He said He has now 26 Boys under His Tuition. The vacations are 6 weeks dated from the 20th. of July, and a month from the 20th. of December.[18]

It was unlikely that William would readily accept the regime advocated by Gretton. After discussing the matter with her son on 25 March, 1786, Lady Wake wrote anxiously to Phipps:

> I have slightly opened our Plan to William, leaving the full explanation of it to you and Mr. Preston. He talks <u>big</u>, that he shall not submit to <u>School Master</u> but shall expect his horse, to make what use of it <u>he</u> chooses: <u>to all which</u> I make no other answer than that his Guardians would, I am certain, require his conformity to nothing but which is highly proper and reasonable to be comply'd with; and I have desired him to make all <u>his objections</u> to you beforehand, as after he is once fixed, they will not be attended to. If there are young people nearby of his own age at Mr Gretton's, I think he will acquiesce.[19]

Just four days before his eighteenth birthday, on 5 April 1786, William travelled with his tutor Catton to Hitcham. The house was largely Elizabethan, but had been subsequently modernized. In the hall hung a number of good paintings, including a large picture of Charles I on horseback, a full length portrait of Henrietta Maria in the character of St. Catherine, two life size ones of Lord and Lady Sunderland and another, supposed to be an original of Oliver Cromwell.[20] William found the other six boarders to be good company. By the following month he was engaged in preparing an exhibition for visitors to the school: as part of it, William was to give a lecture on the orrery (clockwork model of the planetary system), make a speech in Greek and produce an epitome of the history of England. During the summer vacation, he toured the Midlands on horseback with one of his school friends, visiting Kedleston and some silk mills, later meeting up with Gretton at Buxton. They went on to visit his grandparents at Bank Top and then to Southwell, Nottinghamshire, ending up at Courteenhall, where they stayed for a week before returning to Hitcham.

A few weeks later, William remarked to Phipps, 'The prevailing sameness, where one day rolls over the Head of another without anything to mark it, renders it impossible for me ever to make my Letters anything but horribly stupid; for in this Bottom we are out of the way of all news, or what is transacting in the Busy World'. Nevertheless, he was ambitious to do well. 'I intend to apply very closely to my studies during the remainder of my time here, in order if possible to qualify myself to gain some little reputation at Cambridge. I begin now to look forward to the period of my going there with some impatience, as it will not be many months now before I enter my 20th. year'.[21]

During the Christmas vacation, William and a fellow student from Hitcham stayed at Courteenhall, where he was pleased with the affectionate welcome he received from his mother. The weather had been good which allowed the young men to participate in William's favourite sports, shooting and hunting. They also paid visits to a number of his friends. William did not relish the prospect of returning to Hitcham as the new term approached. There were good reasons for this. On the afternoon of 14 January 1787, William 'with much agitation of spirits', broke the news to his mother that he was now engaged to be married. The lady in question was Charlotte Raynsford, daughter of Justinian and Elizabeth Raynsford of Brixworth, who were old family friends.[22]

The news was received with dismay, particularly when it was revealed that the courtship had its beginnings as recently as 4 January, when the Northampton Assembly had been held. In the days following it, William had contrived to meet Charlotte under the pretence of hunting. Lady Wake immediately wrote to Phipps:

> I never should have suspected him of this, nor did I entertain the smallest suspicion of his having any liking to this woman, in whom there are certainly very few attractions . . . For God's sake, my dear Sir, consider with Mrs. Willes [Charlotte's sister] what is to be done to save him from this fatal step. I am in great distress indeed.[23]

Unable to contain her impatience, Lady Wake wrote at the same time to Jane Willes, who lived with her husband at Astrop Park, King's Sutton, pointing out that William was still a minor and that 'from the knowledge I have of his hasty likings and fickle turn of mind . . . I will venture to pronounce she will speedily and bitterly repent her choice'.[24] The Willeses protested that they had not in any way been party to the happenings and informed Lady Wake that Charlotte Raynsford had told William that the matter could not be considered until he was of age. Nevertheless William's mother was not pacified. She wrote to Phipps, 'Miss Raynsford is two years older than himself [i.e. William], not handsome and in size almost a Patagonian, and it is only a fortnight since we heard him speak of her merely as a pleasant partner for an Assembly; and he has often since he came Home expressed a dislike for matrimony, and I am confident he never thought of Miss R. tho' he has known her a little for years'.[25]

Within a week, news of the engagement was generally known. 'I have already received one letter from a family in the neighbourhood upon the subject', Lady Wake wrote to Phipps. 'This being the case, I trouble you now to know whether you do not think it most advisable that this disagreeable intelligence (which will inevitably travel to Bank Top, possibly with exaggerated circumstances) should be communicated to them either by you or me in as gentle a manner as we can, and as little calculated to alarm my Father'.[26] Meanwhile William had informed his guardian that 'nothing but Death the greatest of all human misfortunes, or a change in the sentiments of the dearest object of my vows, can ever prevent my being the happiest of men'. Nevertheless, he promised to postpone taking any further step 'till fully authorized both by Law and Reason to act and judge for myself'. He would endeavour, for the next two years, to apply himself to his studies when he went to College.[27]

The immediate question to be settled in the light of developments was whether to allow William to enter Cambridge, where the new term started shortly, or to despatch him back to Hitcham. 'I hope,' wrote Lady Wake to Phipps, 'a change of scene will soon erase this hasty gust of Passion'. Catton's advice was sought and he weighed up the alternatives:

> Now on the one hand a removal to College would have a tendency . . . to wean him from his present pursuit by introducing him into a new scene of things and a new Society that would dissipate those impressions which he has full leisure to cherish in the solitude and sameness of Hitcham. On the other hand, there seems

reason to apprehend that when he finds himself so near Northampton, he will not be sufficiently master of himself to forebear making excursions thither, which he might do, and return before he was missed.

Catton, who knew William well, came to no decision on the merits of either alternative but added, 'I am persuaded that unless he marries her in a little time, he never will. As far as I have been able to see into his disposition, his passions are strong and his temper fickle. He takes violent likings but they soon cool. This is not, I believe, the first instance of an <u>eternal</u> attachment to a Lady for whom all regard has now ceased'.[28]

Events now moved quickly. William returned to Hitcham, but by early February he was urging Phipps to grant him permission to go immediately to Cambridge. 'There are', he wrote, 'such an inundation of new comers, that I must own that my stay is extremely irksome to me'.[29] The headmaster, Gretton, lent unexpected but independent support for William's request. On 13 February, he told Phipps, 'I am convinced the sooner he is removed from this place the better – this opinion will not perhaps appear improbable when you consider on his part the state of his mind which naturally will represent him to himself as advanced beyond the state of a schoolboy'.[30] Much to the relief of Gretton and the satisfaction of William, this strong hint was acted upon. On 10 March 1787, William, accompanied by Catton, travelled to Cambridge, where he was admitted as a fellow commoner at St. John's College.

*　　　*　　　*　　　*　　　*

Under the mastership of William Powell (1765–75), the College had become one of the most popular in the University. During his decade in office, Powell introduced many reforms aimed at promoting systematic study and genuine research. Shortly after being installed, he ordered twice-yearly college examinations for all undergraduates, which included texts from Greek and Roman authors, algebra, Euclid, mathematics and logic.[31] Dr John Jebb, a former Fellow of Peterhouse, could write of St. John's in 1775, 'he [the observer] will behold a numerous set of learned persons improving youth of the most respectable families and fortunes in every branch of useful literature, themselves hourly improved by their assiduity in their important trust'.[32] Powell's successor, John Chevallier (1775–89), though lacking the drive of the former, helped to maintain the high reputation of the College; by 1782, St. John's produced no fewer than seven out of the eighteen wranglers.

In practice, however, there were great differences among the students in their attitude to study. Colleges admitted undergraduates under four different categories, each roughly corresponding to their social status; noblemen, fellows commoners, pensioners and sizars. The majority of students were from the latter two categories, often the sons of poor clergymen and professional men. Noblemen, normally aristrocrats or related to the Sovereign, were exempt from the usual entry qualifications or residency regulations, and frequently left without taking a degree. Fellow commoners, from wealthy county families, enjoyed many privileges denied to others. It was quite common, as in the instance of William, for the student to arrive at College with his private tutor, who might be a fellow of that College, and who maintained close contact with his charge thereafter. Fellow commoners ate with the Fellows at their table and were often loath to attend lectures. They were also allowed to 'huddle' their examinations, that is, on the day that they were to sit their degree, they were given mock exercises from which the answers were learnt in parrot-like fashion.[33] They frequented the many coffee houses which sprang up in Cambridge and, with more time on their hands, the fellow commoners sometimes were accused of riotous behaviour in the town. An almost exact contemporary of William at St. John's was Wordsworth. Admitted as a sizar in July 1787 and soon busy pursuing his own interests in literature, he later dismissed fellow commoners in his poem the *Prelude* as 'chattering popinjays'.[34]

However, Catton, writing from Cambridge, was able to assure his guardian that William was in good hands. At St. John's, he declared, 'there are motives held out to excite emulation and stimulate industry, and not without success ... our present set of Fellow-Commoners are in general very respectable, manly, regular and diligent. This is as favourable a circumstance as could attend Sir William at his first entrance on a College life'. At the same time he confessed, 'We cannot indeed boast of a very strict discipline, as you well know. Young men are perfectly their own masters here'.[35] However, the removal from Hitcham and entry into the adult society of Cambridge brought about a change in William's outlook, as Catton had forecast. Within six weeks William informed Phipps:

> I have received a very proper and satisfactory letter from Miss Raynsford in answer to mine, fitted with protestations of friendship and a total release from everything that has passed. She has desired an exchange of letters, which I shall certainly comply with. So now, thank God, this foolish affair is closed forever'.[36]

As the summer vacation approached, Lady Wake was anxious for her son to spend his time profitably. Catton, who under normal circumstances would have supervised his charge, was required at College in the holidays to prepare a new course of lectures for the following year. Catton wrote to Phipps:

> You know, Sir, that our Summer Vacation starts from the beginning of June to the 10th. of October, our Christmas Vacation a month, Easter, three weeks; and all these <u>may be</u> and <u>are</u> considerably lengthened by the students, so that there are nearly 8 months in the year in which he may be absent from College. What is he to do in all this time and where is he to be disposed of?[37]

His own suggestion was that William should be sent on a tour with a companion either abroad or into Scotland and Wales. Eventually, a fellow student at St. John's, Lord Leslie, later the 13th Earl of Rothes, was selected for this purpose. On 27 June 1787, Catton wrote, 'Lord Leslie is going by himself into Wales, and I believe will be glad of Sir William's company. For my part I can see no objections. He is a very respectable Gentlemanlike man, steady, lively and good-natured. Indeed I do not think anything better could be thought up for Sir W. than to accompany him'.[38]

Before this, however, there was more serious business at hand. William told Phipps on 20 May, 'I am very much engaged at present as our public examinations are the 10th. of next month, which is a time much to be dreaded as we are all then examined in our Hall before the whole College, classed according to our deserts and written Lists publicly stuck up for general inspection. I should be very glad was it over'. This prospect did not curtail his other interests. He had recently sold his two mares, making a profit of sixty guineas; in their place he bought 'two of the most thoroughbred horses five years old each that I ever saw ... I think I have changed my horses to great advantage and only five pounds out of pocket'.[39]

Now that the tour with Leslie had been confirmed, the two men began the planning of an ambitious itinerary. On the morning of 15 July, they set off from London after first calling on Phipps. William sent a detailed account of each stage of the journey to him 'to serve as a Hand Book should you have the curiosity to trace us on a map'; taken together, they provide a graphic picture of places and personalities in Britain towards the end of the eighteenth century.

The first stopping place was Windsor, where they saw Eton College, and at which Leslie had been a pupil. On Sunday, the following morning, they attended service at the Chapel Royal; Leslie then went to dine with Lord Walsingham, a Groom of the Bedchamber, and William rode to Hitcham House, where he was well received by his former friends. Returning to Windsor, they spent the evening with Leslie's mother, the Countess of Rothes and her second husband, Sir Lucas Pepys, physician to George III. The King had virtually retired to Windsor at this time and on the Monday morning, Leslie had a long conversation with the monarch at the Chapel on the subject of their tour. Between Maidenhead and Henley, the two men encountered the King and all the royal family who were taking an airing.[40] William reported, 'The King being on horseback stopped and talked to us, examined my Gig, and asked a great many questions'. The monarch, who was a knowledgeable horseman, provided encouragement to them. 'I can assure you', wrote William, 'His Majesty approved much of our mode of travelling'.[41] After seeing Oxford and Blenheim and visiting Shakespeare's tomb at Stratford they stayed at Warwick, where they had a conducted tour of the Castle.

A journey of seventeen miles took them to Birmingham, 'the extent and appearance of which we were much astonished, as the largeness of it, the number of busy fares and stands of Hackney coaches made it resemble London in miniature'. From 1770, Birmingham, as with many of the new centres of industry, had experienced a period of very rapid growth, due largely to the building of the canals which provided cheap and ready transport.[42] William noted:

> Leslie went tired to bed and I adonized myself and went to the Play where I was much entertained by seeing all the Coppersmiths and their wives and daughters. For singular as it may appear, tho' Birmingham is of so large extent, there actually does not have a single person in it who is not in trade; indeed it is in fact only a country village, as there is no Town Hall or Magistrates. The next morning we spent most delightfully in seeing the different Manufactures; all that I can now

say of them is that I believe there is not a single process in any of the Manufactures that we have not endeavoured to make ourselves masters of, and with which we were not highly entertained.[43]

In contrast, they were struck by 'the romantick beauty' of The Leasowes at Halesowen, Worcestershire, the landscaped garden of the poet, William Shenstone. Hagley Hall, the recently built home of the Lytteltons, was a disappointment to William, who had been eager to see it. After a day's fishing near Bridgnorth, they travelled to Coalbrookdale to see one of the great curiosities of the time, the world's first iron bridge, built by Abraham Darby in 1778. They then inspected the immense forges for casting iron at Lord Dundonald's British Tar Company factory, which greatly impressed them.[44] Scenically too, it was splendid. 'The Dale itself is a most sweet place: immense high rock and covered with hanging wood, at the bottom of which the noble River Severn runs'. Passing through Chester, they reached Wales and saw Chirk Castle 'a noble ancient place, the seat of Mr. Middleton', the first building visited on the tour with Wake family connections. Both Manchester and Liverpool with their network of docks proved interesting, but on their returning to Chester, Phipps was contacted so that urgent funds could be sent. Despite economies, they were spending more than a guinea each daily, for as William stated, 'Our greatest expense we find is the money we give to housekeepers, gardeners, etc. for seeing places'.[45]

The early part of August was spent in Wales with Leslie and another College friend, Whitmore. Confining their journey to the northern half of the country, they visited Holywell, St. Asaph, Denbigh, Llangollen ('the finest thing we have seen in Wales') and Bangor, then toured Anglesey calling at Caernarvon on their return to the mainland. 'Wherever we have been', wrote William, 'we have derived the highest entertainment and (I trust), improvement, and I can assure you I never spent any time more pleasant or more to my satisfaction'. One drawback was Leslie's state of ill-health, which, William believed, was aggravated by his doctoring himself so continually. William's own superabundant energy made him impatient with the stamina of lesser mortals. 'The only complaint that I have to find with my companions is their being so intolerably slow in their motions, which does not agree with my volatile spirits. With all the spurring I can give them, I cannot make them travel above 12 or so miles a day on an average, as <u>Leslie</u> is afraid of his <u>horses</u> going further, and <u>Whitmore</u> does not like to travel before breakfast or after dinner'.[46]

An extension of the journey to the south-west of England, proposed for late August, was given up as William's thoughts now turned to home. He told Phipps:

> Though Courteenhall does not produce so great a change of scene as Wales, I shall spend my time very pleasantly in the society of my Mother and Sisters and shall find my time agreeable occupied with my Dogs and my Gun, as shooting, of which I am passionately fond, then begins.[47]

William arrived back at Courteenhall on 27 August where he was greeted by his family and Catton. The journey, William calculated, had taken them across more than a thousand miles of Britain.

Towards the end of the vacation, William travelled to Norfolk to visit his grandmother Lady Sarah Wake, who was very ill at the time at Riddlesworth[48] and also to have some shooting. From there, he rode to Yorkshire, where he stayed with Phipps and also saw his Fenton grandparents. In late October, he left for Cambridge; few people had returned and lectures had not yet begun. Soon after this, William became ill, and his studies suffered. 'I am glad he is not wholly idle', wrote Lady Wake to Phipps in February 1788, 'but I much regret his non-attendance at the last examination, it being the only subject, I fear, that he was likely to have gained credit'.[49] William was unable to sit the final examination, but fortunately for him in May 1786, the heads of Colleges had taken action in deciding on those who would qualify for honorary degrees. They declared that persons related to the Sovereign by consanguinity or affinity and the sons of noblemen, baronets and knights were entitled to such a degree.[50] Because of this ruling, William was awarded an honorary Master of Arts. This news had to be conveyed to his guardian. Before leaving Cambridge for the last time in June 1788, he wrote to Phipps, 'I send this line in case you should have any thoughts of putting your kind intention of visiting me at Cambridge on Tuesday, as I fear it would not answer your expectation as I was in hopes it would have done; as no one takes an <u>Honorary</u> degree, consequently the sight will be but trivial'.[51]

William's college days were over, and he was free once more to pursue his sporting activities. He paid several visits to friends and in December stayed at his lodgings in Lincoln's Inn under the close supervision of Phipps. Now almost twenty one years of age, William was preparing to take on new responsibilities which would have wide-ranging consequences, not least for Courteenhall itself.

11
'Old Sir William', The Ninth Baronet:
II. The Rebuilding of Courteenhall

ON 5 APRIL 1789, ONLY THREE MONTHS BEFORE THE beginning of the French Revolution, Sir William came of age. He was now to put his considerable energies to practical purposes. In the previous June, an estimate of the value of Riddlesworth, Norfolk, and the adjoining Knettishall estates in Suffolk had been drawn up. The mansion at Riddlesworth was described as 'a large Ancient Bricked House, but by no means Modern; and the situation ... is well calculated for a Gentleman who wishes to have much Game and is fond of Sporting'. The value of the land, apart from the timber, was calculated at £18,018.[1] Just before William was twenty one, his trustees were approached to consult with him as to 'what Plann he would best approve off'.[2] A sale was effected fairly rapidly thereafter, for by May 1791, the properties had been purchased by a new owner, Sylvanus Bevan,[3] who proceeded to demolish the old house at Riddlesworth, replacing it with one of white brick with stone dressings to the design of Thomas Leverton.[4] Thus after 130 years, starting with the marriage of the third baronet to a Drury, the Wake connection with Riddlesworth came to an end.[5]

Sir William, as we have seen, had a wide circle of friends. One in particular was to lead to the establishment of close links between the Wake and Sitwell families. In 1786, William had been introduced by Samuel Phipps, his principal guardian, to a young man, Sitwell Sitwell, of Renishaw, Derbyshire. William and Sitwell, who were similar in temperament, outlook, and age, were happy to seek new adventures and outlets for their abundant energy. Following a visit to Courteenhall by Sitwell in September 1786, Wake told Phipps:

> I fear Sitwell was heartily tired of Northamptonshire, and was very sorry that I [sic] could not stay, as I wish to embrace every opportunity of improving my acquaintance and Friendship with him, not only from my own knowledge of his worth, but from the high opinion I entertain of him, and from your deserved partiality for him.[6]

Whilst Sir William was at Cambridge he bought Sitwell a greyhound and had it conveyed to Renishaw.[7]

See Appendix A — Family Trees X, XI and XII. Notes and References pages 407–411

Phipps had close links with both the Wakes and Sitwells and was instrumental in bringing the two families together. It has already been shown in the previous chapter that Phipps had his main residence at Ravenfield, West Yorkshire, near to the home of Sir William's mother. On his visits to Yorkshire, the ninth baronet was as likely to stay at Ravenfield as at Bank Top. Phipps was also a cousin of Sitwell's father, Francis Hurt, who on succeeding to his uncle William's fortunes and estates in 1777 adopted the Sitwell surname. Phipps died in March 1791 without children or immediate heirs, and bequeathed his considerable fortune to Francis: this consisted of a large property in Northumberland, smaller estates in Shropshire, his Yorkshire property and land near Renishaw inherited from his Reresby ancestors.[8]

Sitwell and William were to rival each other in the 1790s in their ambitious plans to remodel their respective family homes. William admired Sitwell for his hunting and racing abilities and his courage; when a 'royal Bengal tiger' escaped from a menagerie at Sheffield in 1798, it was Sitwell who killed it. Earlier, Sitwell had been sent on a Grand Tour by his father because of an attachment to Alice Parke, who was some four years older than him and a daughter of a Liverpool merchant of yeoman stock. When at Constantinople Sitwell was informed by his aunt that Alice had died. He hurried home to find her alive and thereupon married her in August 1791.[9] Two years later, he succeeded to the family fortune on his father's death, became MP for West Looe, Cornwall, 1796–1802, and was created first baronet in 1808; only three years later, he died at the age of forty two.[10]

Sitwell was the eldest of three brothers, the other two being Francis and Hurt and there was one sister, Mary. The delightful portrait of the Sitwell children, painted by the American J.S. Copley in 1787, depicts Mary at the age of fifteen. She has fine features with long curly hair and is elegantly dressed.[11] Mary was unusually well educated for a girl of her time and was adored by her parents. Not long after the painting was completed she became engaged to William and on 1 July 1790 they were married at St. George's, Hanover Square. Mary's niece, Georgiana Caroline Sitwell, later recorded that a few days before the marriage, when the marriage portion had been paid by her parents, Mary accidentally saw William in his cabriolet in London, driving a woman 'with whom he ought not to have been acquainted'. Mary was urged by her father to break off the match, and was offered a second portion of £25,000 if she would consent. However she refused to change her plans, though she was heard to say on her way to church that she wished she was going to her grave.[12] In the following year, on 22 November 1791, Mary died in London on the day after the birth of her son, Charles. She was nineteen years of age. Her wish was to be buried at the family's church at Eckington, which lies just below Renishaw.[13]

*   *   *   *   *

Sir William's marriage to Mary had brought with it a settlement from Francis Hurt Sitwell of £25,000. Of this sum, £7,000 was invested in long-term annuities and a further £8,110 on a purchase of the moiety of tithes at Waltham Abbey.[14] The settlement, dated 26 June 1790, also declared that if William should at any time have occasion for a sum of money for 'repairing or altering his family seat or for building a new one', it would be lawful 'to raise by sale of part or parts of the estate a sum not exceeding £10,000 for this purpose'.[15]

There were a number of reasons why it was desirable to undertake rebuilding at this time. The old manor house, which had been added to by the seventh baronet and in Repton's drawing of 1791–3 was now L-shaped, was becoming uncomfortable. Lady Mary Wake, the eighth baronet's widow, informed Phipps on 4 January 1787, 'You will be sorry to hear the last dreadful high wind shook the lower part of our miserable old Mansion so much, that a sensible Mason I have had to examine it sayes it must be taken down and new roofed, so that at present it is unsafe for anybody to lodge in the two Bedchambers over the Laundry etc., which puts us to some inconvenience'.[16] The sale of Riddlesworth would have provided a ready source to pay for the ambitious scheme which William was proposing. With the blossoming of scholarship and the arts in the last quarter of the eighteenth century in England, a new generation of artists, architects and craftsmen came into prominence. The landed gentry were able to act as patrons. As Sir Albert Richardson wrote in his *Introduction to Georgian Architecture*, 'Not only was there a residue of wealth in the form of property but there was a general realization of the cumulative value of beauty'.[17] William's marriage to Mary was also an appropriate occasion for building a new family house set in a splendid remodelled Park[18] which would also be of great benefit to future generations of Wakes.

The two men chosen to carry out these tasks were at the early stages of their respective careers, Samuel Saxon as architect and Humphry Repton as landscape gardener. Repton served as private secretary to William Windham, Chief Secretary to the Lord-Lieutenant of Ireland, before starting his new career in August 1788. The death of Lancelot 'Capability' Brown five years earlier provided an opportunity for such employment. By 1790, Repton, at the age of thirty eight, was carrying out an important commission for Lord Fitzwilliam at Wentworth Woodhouse, Yorkshire, and at Milton, Northamptonshire; in the following year, he was also employed at Courteenhall.[19] There is little doubt that it was on Samuel Phipps' recommendation that Repton was chosen. In 1789, not long before he died, Phipps had engaged Repton for his property at Ferney Hall near Ludlow, Shropshire,[20] and had expressed great satisfaction with the result. Phipps then told Repton, 'Let me earnestly beg you always to consider well the powers and abilities of your Clients, and do not on your death bed have to reproach yourself for having been accessory to the embarrassment of those who may often apply to you to gratify their vanity, rather than their actual comfort. I have myself too often witnessed such instances among the miserable Victims of folly and extravagance'. Repton commented in his Memoirs, 'These words made a very deep impression on my mind...and have so far operated on all my schemes of improvement, that I do not know a single instance in which I have ever forgotten it'.[21]

Repton disagreed with Brown's insistence on following Nature, preferring a more picturesque approach. In his view, no set formula could be prescribed for gardens. 'Variety' and 'cheerfulness' were important: above all was the comfort of his client, and suggestions were made for the siting of the house and even its appropriate shape.[22] Repton's 'Red Books', so called for the red morocco with which they were bound, were beautifully illustrated reports of his important commissions which were presented to his

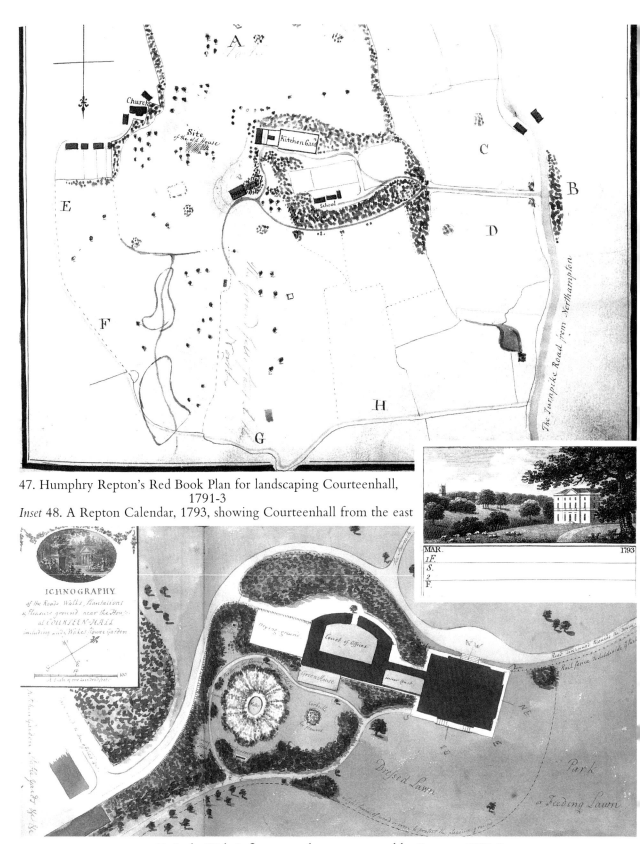

47. Humphry Repton's Red Book Plan for landscaping Courteenhall, 1791-3

Inset 48. A Repton Calendar, 1793, showing Courteenhall from the east

49. Lady Wake's flower garden, as proposed by Repton, 1791-3

136

clients. A novel feature was that his proposed improvements could be seen by the inclusion of flaps which allowed the client to compare his existing Park with the 'improved' version. The 'Red Book' for Courteenhall, lavishly decorated with Repton's watercolours, is dated 'At Courteenhall 23 March 1791' and 'At Harestreet by Romford [Repton's home] March 1793'. In his Introduction, Repton states that he paid a number of visits to Courteenhall between these dates.*[23]

Starting with an overall consideration of the House in relation to the Park, Repton raises the question of the large scale of the Stables to that of the House, a matter discussed in Chapter 9. The Stables were to be partly obscured by a plantation. He sums up the character of the new House at Courteenhall as 'that of an elegant, convenient, and very respectable Family seat; possessing a degree of magnificence compatible with comfort, but not aiming at that which belongs rather to useless Ostentation'.[24] As to its situation, Repton bluntly remarked, 'the County of Northampton is certainly not picturesque for few hunting counties indeed are so'. He condemns the unsightly custom of ridging the grassland in Northamptonshire 'which however excusable on a dead flat to drain the surface, can never be necessary in that beautiful Shaped ground, which I must call the park at Courteenhall'.[25]

On the House itself, Repton approved of 'that which has been so elegantly designed and executed by my ingenious friend Mr Saxon', particularly the convenience of placing the offices leading from the House.[26] It was recommended to rebuild on lower ground, away from the Stables, with the principal view to the south-east over the Park to the church tower, which itself was to be improved by the addition of four pinnacles. The entrance to the Park would be made more conspicuous by building lodges on the higher point halfway along the existing drive to the House. The effect of surprise was to be gained by making the approach skirt along the plantation which would screen the School House, following a natural terrace 'till it bursts suddenly on the house'.[27] By judicious replanting and the addition of simple buildings, the general appearance of the Park would be transformed and the farm hidden from view. An unusual feature of the Red Book was the inclusion of a description and plan of a flower garden for Lady Wake, consisting of beds and parterres to the south and south-east of the House.[28]

Either through indifference to or disagreement with some of Repton's suggestions, Sir William did not carry out all the improvements. The impressive lodge gates were never built; it was not until the time of the twelfth baronet, Sir Herewald Wake, in 1878,[29] that the drive was rebuilt with a new lodge and high wooden gates and the lime avenue was planted. About 1930, the thirteenth baronet replaced the wooden gates with fine iron gates and stone pillars. In 1975 the fourteenth baronet removed and widened his father's gate to give access to the modern day much wider vehicles. Another entrance gate on the north-east side and a suggested folly at the top of the Park, looking south from the House, were never executed. Repton also recommended that two ponds of different levels be made in the Great Meadow downhill on the north-east side of the House which could be blended by plantation to appear as one lake or pool. In fact, in dry summers the stream which fed it would have run dry so the idea was impracticable. One

*See Appendix C for the full transcript of the 'Red Book'.

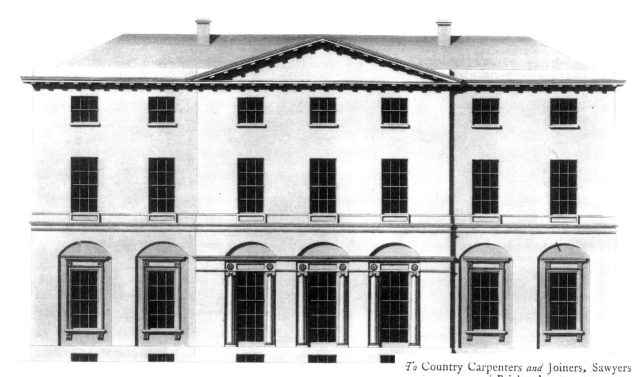

50. Courteenhall House, south elevation, from George Richardson's
New Vitruvius Britannicus, 26 December 1801
Inset 51. Advertisement from the *Northampton Mercury* 20 July 1793
for labour in connection with the completion of the House

52. The same view by George Clark(e) of Scaldwell, 1831

138

Repton feature which has disappeared since the last war is the ha-ha, on the north-west side of the House, which separated the sheep and cattle from the House and garden.

Repton's imaginative scheme for Courteenhall, though not fully adopted, was largely successful and helped to transform the Park. It was appropriate that when Jane Austen wrote *Mansfield Park*, published in 1814, she should site it four miles from Northampton.[30] By this time, Repton was a celebrated figure and one of the characters in the book, Miss Bertram, recommends his services to a friend, stating that Repton's terms were five guineas a day.[31]

The precise date when the emparking took place is not clear. The Royal Commission on Historic Monuments claims that shortly after 1766, the whole village except for the manor house, the church and the houses east of the church was removed by the eighth baronet and the area emparked.[32] Bridges, writing about 1720, stated that 'the Church . . . is now seated at the upper end of the town, but within the memory of man had several houses standing beyond and about it, which since the inclosure of the parish have been destroyed'.[33] Joan Wake, on the other hand, has written that the 'ninth baronet proceeded to pull down a number of houses to lay out the Park and grounds. He did away with the road up the old avenue, grubbed up hedges to make the Park out of the surrounding fields, altered other roads and footpaths, laid out the flower and kitchen-gardens and planted the beech plantation round the Park . . . I believe he built the row of six cottages at the bottom of the village as you go down the hill, perhaps for some of the displaced families across the Park'.[34] It is possible that the eighth baronet started the process of emparking but that the large-scale operations were carried out by 'Old' Sir William. Some notion of the scale of replanting which took place can be gathered from an entry for the Courteenhall Farm Account for February 1792:

Paid for 300 Young Oak Trees at 1/– per Hundred	3s. 0d.
Paid for 300 Young Quick-Sets at 1s. 2d. per Hundred	3s. 6d.[35]

* * * * *

Repton's partner in the enterprise, the architect, Samuel Saxon, was born on 30 June 1757 and entered the Royal Academy of Arts as an architectural student in November 1776.[36] Between 1778 and 1782 Saxon exhibited several designs whilst at the Academy, including those for a hunting seat, a mausoleum and a nobleman's villa. His first design for a villa was executed jointly with his teacher, Sir William Chambers, who had played a leading part in founding the Royal Academy in 1768.[37] Chambers, as a successful architect, was employed by many country house owners. He was also Comptroller of the Office of Works from 1769, responsible for the maintenance and construction of all Royal buildings. It was due to Chambers' patronage that Saxon, whilst still an Academy student, gained employment on the rebuilding of Somerset House in the Strand in 1776.[38] His post as Labourer in Trust (December 1777 to June 1781) was rewarded with the modest sum of 2s. 2d. per day.[39] Promotion would normally have followed but the reform of the Office of Works involved the abolition of many posts. Saxon practised as an architect from Berkeley Square, though his commissions during the 1780s are not now known.

In April 1790, the governors of the Northampton General Infirmary invited plans from architects and surveyors for a new hospital to house a hundred patients. On 15 May, Saxon was chosen to carry out the work which occupied him between 1791 and 1793,[40] the period during which he was to be employed in a similar capacity at Courteenhall. Apart from the Northampton Infirmary and the Courteenhall commissions, Saxon's only other known building was at Buckminster Hall, Leicestershire, where he again worked with Repton between 1793 and 1798. His date of death is unknown but it was some time after 1804.[41]

Repton had recommended that the House at Courteenhall should be one 'with three fronts', that is, a rectangular block, the fourth side of which would be the domestic quarters and not visible. Saxon followed this pattern in his design. As for the siting of the House, Repton favoured a prominent position, 'the crown of a knowl' [i.e. hill]. In this way, the House would no longer be dominated by the Stables. Such a positioning would also rule out the feasibility of wings which Repton had earlier favoured.

In his plans for the House, Saxon followed the spirit of his former master, Chambers. The latter in his treatise *The Decorative Part of Civil Architecture* (1759), had advocated purity of style and masculine qualities of design, combining French neo-classicism and English Palladianism. The exterior of the House is sober, a three-storey building with flattened pediments on the two main fronts, built in local golden limestone with greyer Weldon stone in the base, around the horizontal band above the ground storey, and on the cornice. The entrance side is of five bays and three storeys high, with a basement. The ground floor windows have pleasant recessed blank segment-headed panels as has the doorway, with in addition Tuscan columns. The garden side has a three-bay pediment; the principal windows are similar in treatment to those at the entrance side except that the centre bay windows have Ionic columns.

The inside of the House displays the elegance commended by Repton, but demonstrates a more Adamesque influence. The large T-shaped entrance hall, containing a number of family portraits, is divided by a screen of Doric columns. All the principal rooms on the ground floor – the Dining Room, Drawing Room and the Library – face south-east, affording a fine view of the Park and the Church. These rooms are entered from the extensions to the right and left at the end of the hall, where there are three doorways recessed beneath semicircular arches. On the far right is the Dining Room with a screen of Corinthian columns. Next to it is the Drawing Room with its splendid fireplace; on its left, striking in its originality, is the Library, which has an apsidal end instead of a screen of columns. Both the Library and the Dining Room are decorated with charming friezes and panels by an unknown hand. The Drawing Room was not completed, but the thirteenth and fourteenth baronets carried out schemes which blended well with the other rooms. On the left of the entrance hall is the main staircase with an iron balustrade and walls of marbled pink. At the top of the stairs, a passage runs the whole length of the House with bedrooms on either side. Saxon's motif of arches over the doorways is recognizable and there is a fine oval skylight.[42]

It is very probable that the building of the mansion began soon after Repton's original survey had taken place. A detailed account of the progress in its construction can be found in a 'Special agreement respecting the Building of a New Family Seat at

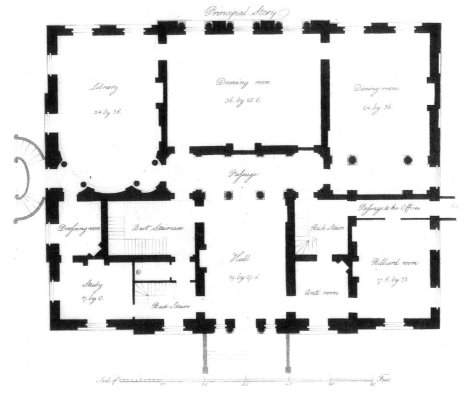

53. Courteenhall House, ground floor plan by Richardson

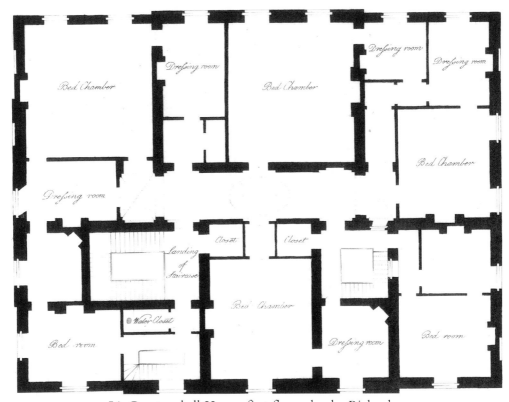

54. Courteenhall House, first floor plan by Richardson

Courteen Hall in Northamptonshire', dated 17 March 1792.[43] It refers to the 1790 marriage settlement between Sir William and Mary Sitwell mentioned earlier, and reiterates the section which stated that a sum of £10,000 could be raised for altering the existing house or building a new one.

A description and estimate, drawn up by Saxon, amounted to £10,117 10s. 0d. The sum of £9,007 2s. 0d. had been obtained from the settlement and the building was to be completed on or before Christmas Day, 1793. Some of the money was to be used for 'the purpose of paying the Expenses of pulling down the old Family Seat'. Mention is made of 'the old Materials of the said old Family Seat of the said Sir William Wake at Courteen Hall aforesaid part of which have been applied towards Building and compleating the said new Mansion House'. It also states that 'the two first Stories of the said Building having been already erected and a great part of the Materials having been prepared towards finishing the Remainder of the said House', the first instalment of £3,500 had been released to Sir William.

The schedule to this agreement contains a detailed description 'of a House now erecting at Courteen Hall', and is given below in full:

> **The Schedule** to which the above written Indenture refers.
>
> **Description** of a House now erecting at Courteen Hall in Northamptonshire for William Wake Baronet.
>
> **The Ground Plot** of the House extents Ninety two feet five Inches in Length and sixty eight feet eight Inches in depth containing Sixty three Squares forty five feet of Building – The external Walls of the Building which is four Stories high making together fifty one feet or therabouts and is built with hewn Stone and the Windows and Doors of the Ground Floor are finished with proper Dressings the whole terminating with a Stone Cornice and Blocking Course – The roof to be slated and the Gutters and Flats to be laid with either lead or Copper – Attic North West side are to be attached the Kitchen, Laundry and their Offices – The Basement Floor which is sunk and is Eight feet high contains a Servants Hall twenty two feet by eighteen Inches Stewards Room twenty five feet by twenty four feet Housekeepers sitting Room twenty five by twenty two feet and Bed Room twenty five by fourteen feet Butlers Pantry ten by eight feet and Sleeping Room twenty four by fifteen feet Six Inches Stone Closet Seven Feet six Inches Square Two Stair Cases with a general Passage and Cellars in all occupying One thousand and Nine Hundred and Sixty two feet superficial or thereabouts –
>
> **The Ground Floor** which is seventeen feet High has a Hall thirty seven by Nineteen feet Library thirty five by twenty four feet with drawing Room thirty six by twenty four feet. Eating Room thirty five feet by twenty four feet Study seventeen by thirteen feet – Dressing Room thirteen by ten feet Billiard Room twenty three by Eighteen feet Water Closet and three Stair Cases to the Chamber Story –

The Chamber Story which is Eleven feet six Inches high has seven Bed Rooms and Six dressing Rooms a Water Closet and two Stair Cases to the Atticks –

The Attick Story which is Eight feet six Inches High contains Thirteen Bed Rooms – The principal Appartments on the Ground Floor are to be finished suitable to the general appearance and the whole will be compleated in a Neat and substantial Manner – The Building as above described the Materials of which being all to be purchased would on very moderate Estimate cost One hundred and Fifty Pounds per Square –

Sixty three Squares forty five feet superficial of Building at per Square One hundred and fifty Pounds	9517. 10. 0
The offices Yards etc will Cost about	600. 0. 0
	£10,117. 10. 0

In the above Estimate is not considered the necessary pay to a Clerk of the Works nor the Architects charge for Journeys Commissions etc This amount whereof will greatly exceed the value of the Old Materials.

Whether or not all the stone came from Northamptonshire quarries has not so far been established.[44] On 19 September 1792 a bill was paid for 'the Insurance upon the Dwelling House now Building, the above Insured for Five Thousand Pounds' at a cost of £12 7s. 10d.[45] The timetable for completing the house must have been adhered to, for by July 1793, the *Northampton Mercury* was advertising for carpenters, sawyers and joiners 'mainly for inside work'. Brickmakers were also required and it mentions that the brickworks were at Blakesley, near Towcester.[46]

In the absence of documentary evidence, it is not known where Sir William would have lived during the building of the new house. The Royal Commission on Historic Monuments states that the old manor house was completely removed in 1791.[47] In addition the special agreement quoted earlier mentions the re-use of some material from the old house. On the other hand, *The Gentleman's Magazine* for January 1799 published an article on the Ouseleys, and remarked in passing that 'the antient mansion has, within five or six years, been taken down',[48] i.e. 1793 or 1794. There is therefore a range of possibilities. Sir William may have stayed in the old mansion until the new one was ready (the Butler's Room in the basement of the present Hall still contains a mantelpiece, wainscotting and a door from it).[49] The Account Books for Courteenhall during the years of rebuilding do not indicate any diminution of expenditure on household, hounds, servants and other such items. Another possibility is that Sir William spent some time at or near Renishaw, as did subsequent Wakes, or resided at Waltham. A further suggestion is that he lived in temporary accommodation on the Courteenhall estate or hired a nearby dwelling.[50]

*   *   *   *   *

Only a few months before the new mansion was completed Sir William remarried on 23 April 1793. His wife was Jenny Gambier, who was some three years younger than himself. She was stepmother to the young Charles, and they had ten children, three boys and seven girls. All three boys died in her lifetime. William, the eldest, born 5 August 1796, was eighteen;[51] Drury, born 7 December 1797, died at the age of twenty; John William, born 19 April 1801, became a clerk in holy orders, a curate in Northampton, but died at the age of twenty seven. Three of the daughters also died in their youth. Louisa, the eldest, born 4 March 1794, was sixteen, Mary, born 12 August 1799, was aged twenty six and Emma, born 22 July 1805, died at the age of seven. In contrast, both Jane Sophia, born 26 August 1802 and Emily Georgiana, born 24 February 1806, reached their ninetieth year, Cecilia was eighty eight, whilst Charlotte Joan, the youngest child, born 14 March 1815, lived to the age of sixty eight. A memorial stone to Sir William's children was placed in Courteenhall Church in 1991.

Shortly before their first child, William, was born, Jenny's brother, James Gambier, who was Admiral of the Red Squadron, suggested that his sister might be taken to London for her confinement. Sir William was furious with him, for he wanted the child to be born at Courteenhall, and this led to a duel being fought between the two men in the garden below the Library steps on the north-east side of the House. Fortunately, neither was hurt. The silver-mounted pistols are still at Courteenhall.[52] Jenny herself is supposed to have been jealous of her stepson and when Charles visited Courteenhall in later years he was given a room over the Stables. There is also a family story that on one occasion she tried to push Charles' wife, Charlotte, who was pregnant, down the front stairs.

The fear of subversion and social disorder which swept the country in December 1792 aroused by events taking place in revolutionary France resulted in a display of public loyalty to the English Constitution at Northampton. A meeting summoned by the Mayor held in the Town Hall on 7 December, pledged its firm attachment 'to the King and Parliament', adding, 'we will resist at the Hazard of our Lives and Fortunes, every Attempt that may be made, at Home or Abroad, to Disturb the Peace and good Order of Society'. A total of 1,176 adult male inhabitants signed this declaration; among them was Sir William and his servant J. Staples.[53]

The outbreak of war with France in 1793 seemed to have had little immediate impact upon Courteenhall. However, a few years later, when Napoleon was preparing at Boulogne for an invasion of England, Sir William wrote spiritedly to a friend:

> I want to know what you are about, whether you have been out much with the Beagles, or have been constantly wheeling, marching and countermarching. This I think (strange to tell) has been my occupation these last three months. I have been indefatigable in my military exertions and have now a very good troop of Cavalry. The Country in general seems now in such a state, that I have no doubt that the thing most to be wished is, that this Corsican Rascal should come and that in sufficient force to make a <u>fair trial</u> – till that is done, we can never be at rest. Of the <u>event</u> I have no fear. If we are not to have a campaign on the Sea coast, I am prepared to take the Field against more harmless Foes.[54]

The Northamptonshire Yeomanry had been formed in April 1794 to combat any invasion threat.[55] The second Earl Spencer was appointed its Commanding Officer.

55. Sir William Wake, 9th baronet (1768–1846), by Richard Deighton, c.1830

56. Reverend Richard Wake (1775–1850), younger brother of the 9th baronet and Rector of Courteenhall for thirty seven years

57. Pistols used in the duel between Sir William Wake, 9th baronet and his brother-in-law, James Gambier, Admiral of the Red Squadron, at Courteenhall in 1796

Old Sir William served as a Captain of the Wymersley Troop until his resignation through ill-health in September 1827.[56]

Sir William devoted his considerable energies to improving the efficiency of farming on the estate and in doing so transformed its appearance. There were several small farms in the parish of Courteenhall at the time: these were reduced to five, namely, the Grange, East Lodge, West Lodge, the Dairy Farm and Home Farm. The *New Inn*, beyond the Lodge, was a popular resting-place for road travellers. Sir William took away the Inn's licence, fenced in the green in front of it and changed its name to Woodleys, after that of the field behind it. When the village in the Park was removed[57] many of the inhabitants settled at Roade. As well as building additional cottages in the village for some of the displaced families, Sir William also erected an Infant School, a small thatched building in the centre of the village.

By 1804 the Rector of Courteenhall, the Reverend Edward Bayley, stated that 'Sir William Wake is enclos'd in his Pleasure Ground and planted with thriving Timber Trees: in exchange for which the Rector has from ye said Sir Wm. Wake several small but convenient Parcels of Ground'. In the following year Bayley, who was probably envious of the splendid new House, vacated his Rectory in the village 'the former wretched cottage having been in a ruinous and dilapidated state for many years', and built himself a larger and more commanding house to the south of the Church.[58]

The several volumes of annual accounts which were meticulously kept by Sir William's steward, Christopher Smyth, provide a full picture of life on the estate and at the Hall . In the fields were oxen, cows, horses, sheep, pigs and boars, many of which were sent all the way to Smithfield Market in London to be sold. Cattle were frequently purchased; in 1817, twenty four Highland Scots were bought at Leicester. Cow Doctors were called in to administer 'drinks' in 1792. Joseph West was paid ten shillings for 'taking care of the cows and sleeping in the house 4 weekends.' At the end of 1801, the hiring of a ram cost £31 10s. There were $19\frac{1}{2}$ score of sheep sheared in June 1822 at a cost of 3d. per score. The care and maintenance of the estate involved considerable outgoings. Besides planting, mowing, hedging and many other allied activities, there were wages to be paid for the gamekeeper, the ratcatcher and for the catching of moles. In July 1817, T. Drayton received £4 10s. 0d. for the use of a 'thrashing masheen' for six days. On the other hand, there was income from the sale of crops, wool, timber (including faggots), malt, kitchen fat or tallow and hides.

Household expenses were even more varied. A painter was brought from Stony Stratford for two days in 1792 (2s. 6d.) and sweeping the chimneys cost 8s. 6d. A silver soup ladle was purchased (£2 4s. 0d.) and Mr Douglas, described as 'Cabinet Maker', was paid 17s. 0d. for making a small mahogany table for Lady Wake in 1794 and a further £22 3s. 0d. for other work soon after. In April 1791, the newsman received 3s. $9\frac{1}{2}$d. for supplying copies of the *Northampton Mercury*, and Sir William paid six guineas subscription to Baker's *The History and Antiquities of the County of Northamptonshire* in 1822. Twelve 'pleasure horses', for use with the work or riding and hunting, were purchased at £10 each in 1820. Musicians were hired for a ball held in January 1800 and again in the following year. Food was bought in large quantities from Northampton Fair. In 1794, a 210 pound cheese costing £4 7s. 6d. was purchased in this way. Meat figured largely in expenses, though quantities of fish were also bought. Mr Smith of Whittlebury Forest provided venison at 10s. 6d. and London porter was a popular drink. In 1820, Mr P. Phipps was paid £45 18s. 0d. for malt. Candles and soap were large items, one consignment in October 1793 amounting to £20 3s. 0d. Coal, often in two-ton loads, arrived by canal at either Northampton or Blisworth Wharf. A pipe of wine was bought at Northampton in May 1802 and Lady Wake purchased a supply of bees in the previous year. Flower seeds and bird seed purchases are also recorded. The original seed cabinet still stands in the potting shed in the Kitchen Garden. Expenses connected with hunting were high. Calves and sheep were bought for feeding the hounds, and the wages as well as boarding for huntsmen had to be found. Tom Taylor, Sir William's huntsman, received forty guineas a year and ten guineas extra as gamekeeper. Boys were paid 2s. 6d. per week for working in the kennels. Subscriptions to the Pytchley Hunt are first mentioned in 1803; Sir William forfeited £3 3s. 0d. for failing to attend the Pytchley Spring Meeting in 1807.

Household staff included the footman, housemaid, cook (who received thirty guineas in wages for 1817), housekeeper, butler, nurse, postilion, kitchen maid, laundry maid, dairy maid, nurse maid and stillroom maid, (a bill for servants' bonnets amounted to £1 2s. 4d. in 1824), and these were supplemented in the maintenance of the household by, for example, the blacksmith, carpenter, wheelwright, glazier, mason and thatcher. Outside the immediate establishment, there were other obligations. The Usher of the Free Grammar School was paid £5 quarterly and the Rector of Courteenhall a modus in lieu of tithes, amounting to £13 13s. 0d. in 1794. The Keeper of Salcey Forest received a stipend and the Master of St. John's Hospital, Northampton, a quit rent. Monies were donated to apprenticing poor boys and helping, in one instance, a poor man in the parish of Hanslope (10s. 6d.). In 1792, Mr Evans, baker, provided 120 loaves at 6d. each for the poor of Courteenhall. A rather different subscription was that for the Harleston Association for the Prosecuting of Felons in April 1820, a sum of 11s. 6d.

The upkeep of roads was paid for by the turnpike system. A toll gate, where the fees were collected, stood across the high road by the lodge on the Northampton side of the junction with the Blisworth road and there was another between the river bridge and the present level crossing at the entrance to Northampton. Block payments for tolls were made by Sir William covering a period of two years; in May 1817, £3 3s. 3d. was paid to the Wootton toll gate. On the other hand, the ninth baronet had invested some £3,000 with the trustees of the Stony Stratford turnpike road in 1791. At the beginning of the Napoleonic Wars Sir William subscribed to a fund for the relief of soldiers' and sailors' wives. Teams of horses were hired for transporting soldiers' baggage to Newport Pagnell in 1804 and 1806.

Various rates and taxes were regularly paid. For example in February 1793, the poor rate in Courteenhall was 6d. in the pound, resulting in a demand for £3 2s. 0d. In April a church rate of £1 was paid and in May, the half year's land tax amounted to 19s. 2d. and the parish rate, at 1s. 8d. in the pound, totalled £7 5s. 0d. In July, the tax on servants, horses and carriages was £15 5s. 3d. In 1790 a Game Certificate for Sir William was £2 3s. 0d. and for his gamekeeper another 11s. 6d. On 9 November 1794, £4 8s. 2d. was paid for the excise on bricks. The half year's window and other assessed taxes due on Lady Day 1807 was £85 19s. 3d. A payment for income tax appears for the first time in 1800.[59]

Those who worked on the estate were recipients of traditional hospitality. Beer was provided for stone diggers, labourers filling the ice house and those gathering hay. In the 1790s, Mrs Paggett, the blacksmith's wife, provided 'dinners and liquors' for Sir William's tenants in April and December. There was also the village feast each year in July when the cottagers put their tables outside in the street and eating, singing and dancing would go on into the night. Rather different in character was the annual statute fair held at the New Inn. Here, the labourers would stand about, each wearing a distinguishing mark to show his branch of work (for example, horsekeepers would wear a piece of whipcord in their hats), waiting to be hired by the farmers. Maidservants were also engaged at these fairs in this way. It was at one of these fairs that the Courteenhall postmaster, William Surridge (1830–1915), as a small boy saw his first Punch and Judy show.

The religious welfare of the parish was provided by Sir William. A Sunday School was held in Shadrack Dunkley's house, for which £2 2s. 0d. was paid as well as 6s. 0d. rent to Shadrack. There were two Rectors of Courteenhall of note during the ninth baronet's lifetime, Edward Bayley[60] and Richard William Wake, Sir William's brother. Between them they spanned the years 1793 to 1850. It was Richard who, finding the Rectory too small for his family of six children and his mother-in-law, added on the north side a new staircase and drawing room and the room over it. Sir William paid a carpenter £42 6s. 6d. and a plasterer £41, both in 1821, perhaps when the church roof received its ceiling. There is now in the Church a copy of a watercolour of about the early 1840s, showing the high pews, the three-decker pulpit with a large red cushion for the bible and the sounding-board above it and the recently-installed Gothic altarpiece. The family pew contained a fireplace, and Sir William would poke the fire to stop the sermon.[61]

From early in his life, as has been shown, he was a keen horseman. Sir William kept an excellent pack of harriers for more than forty years, though at times there were difficulties. To his friend, John Dickenson, he wrote in December 1802:

On the tenth of January we are to have a famous Ball at Northampton in our new assembly rooms.[62] Lady Wake hopes you will be with us at that time. You will be sorry to hear that the Coursers, Shooters and Poachers have at last I believe annihilated the Animal Hare and fairly beat me out. Excepting a few near my House and by the side of the Road there is hardly an Hare to be found and these Home Hares are you know of no use for Sport. I have therefore at last come to a resolution to part with the Hounds and you will speedily see them advertised. Should you know any one that will come down with the *Stumpy* think of me, 100 guineas, for next to Annesleys I believe the cleverest pack of Dwarf Fox Hounds in England. You may conceive how vexed I am to be drove to this, but must console myself by hunting the Fox with Lord Southampton in the morning.[63]

58. The Duke of Grafton's Hounds at Shenley, January 1840

59. The Railway Cutting at Roade, with Dirty Lane Bridge, by Bourne, 1839

This last reference to Lord Southampton, a cousin of the Duke of Grafton who lived at Whittlebury and was Master of the Grafton until his death in 1810, indicates Sir William's keen interest in fox-hunting, and he was an active member of both the Grafton and Pytchley Hunts.[64] (The boundary between the two is at Wootton Brook).

Despite Sir William's resolution to give up his hounds, he did not do so. In 1817, Sir George Sitwell, the second baronet and Sir William's nephew, wrote to his future wife, Susan Tait:

> I have had another letter from Wake, who still writes in very bad spirits. I am sorry to add Sir W. is so unwell as to be obliged to try the water at Bath, and he is so despairing as to send me the refusal of his hounds next September. I am sorry for the cause, but the offer has delighted me as they are reckoned the best in England. I don't know what poor Sir William will do without them, as he will have no excuse to go out of the house; this is a secret, so don't tell anybody.[65]

In spite of this pessimistic forecast Sir William recovered and continued to enjoy his favourite sport. The two brick kennels were built and still stand against the kitchen garden wall; they are commemorated by a track alongside the three-acre field, Icewell, which is still known as Dog Kennel Lane.

The final blow was the building of the London to Birmingham Railway between 1833 and 1838. Some 20,000 'navigators', better known as 'navvies', were imported to make the cuttings and tunnels and to construct the line. Wildlife on the estate would have been an easy target. Giving evidence before a Select Committee on Railway Labourers in 1846, Robert Rawlinson, for four years responsible for the Blisworth contract, was asked if complaints had been received from those living in the locality. He replied:

> I think the farmers and landed gentry and inhabitants about, gave themselves quietly up to it; I know Sir William Wake, who lived within a mile of the district did; when I first went, I remember walking across his park and seeing fifty hares out in the afternoon, and I know somewhere about the time that the railway was opened, there were very few. He came down with his daughters to see the first train go down; I secured him convenient accommodation; Sir William brought two partridges in his pocket, and he said, 'I would have brought you a hare, but I do not believe I have one on my estate; I have not had one in my house for the last two years'. I mentioned it to one of these men, and he said, 'There is not above one, and we will have that this week'.[66]

*   *   *   *   *

The coming of the railways made a great impact on the face of Britain, not least in the countryside. By 1830, the Liverpool to Manchester line had been opened to traffic; and in the same year, a London to Birmingham route, some $112\frac{1}{2}$ miles in length, was proposed. In the summer of 1830, Francis Giles was commissioned by the newly-formed London Coventry and Birmingham Railway Company to survey a possible route. On 11 October that year, George Stephenson and his son Robert were appointed as engineers to the Company. Their own survey agreed with that of Giles, who concluded that the main line should be through Rugby and thus avoid the descent into the valley of the Nene, and the line to Northampton should be a branch from Blisworth, some four miles distant. The town, which was expanding, wanted the railway and went to some lengths in an attempt to divert the route from the Stephenson plan.[67]

Not surprisingly, the fiercest opponents to the proposal were the country landowners, as the line would run straight through the estates of Sir Charles Knightley of Fawsley, the Duke of Grafton of Wakefield, Thomas Thornton of Brockhall and Sir William's at Courteenhall. The resistance to the railways was summed up by one landowner, Sir Astley Cooper, at Berkhamsted, Hertfordshire, whose country house was near the intended line. Robert Stephenson recalled attending a conference at which Cooper asked, 'Do you think for one moment of the destruction of property involved in it? Why, gentlemen, if this sort of thing is permitted to go on, you will in a very few years destroy the noblesse!'.[68]

To counter the impending threat, a meeting of some thirty Northamptonshire proprietors and occupiers of lands through which the projected railway was likely to pass was held at the *White Horse Inn*, Towcester, on 30 December, 1830, with Sir William in the chair. Many reasons were advanced for the damage to property which was likely to occur. Fields would be cut in half and hunting grounds ruined. Much acreage of good land would inevitably be obliterated by the immense railway cuttings and embankments, and the water supply endangered. The noise and smells were undesirable, cattle and horses would be frightened, and hayricks might be set alight. It was agreed that there was already in existence an integrated transport system of canals and turnpikes; numerous coaches plied daily between Birmingham and London at the rate of ten miles per hour and water carriage for goods was in plentiful supply. A Committee, consisting of Sir William, Knightley, Thornton, Edward Bouverie of Delapre and three others was set up to contact landowners similarly affected in other counties and to petition the House of Commons against the forthcoming bill.[69]

Stephenson's original survey bypassed Northampton; it was merely being linked with a branch line from Blisworth. Another survey, carried out in 1831, took into account the town's wish to be as near to the railway as possible, with a line passing through Bugbrooke; at the same time Brockhall was avoided at the insistence of Thornton. A bill was introduced in the Commons on 20 February 1832, and received its third reading on 19 June. It then passed to the Lords, where opposition was much stronger. The lobbying of Sir William and the Duke of Grafton led to the defeat of the bill in Committee by nineteen votes to eleven. A different tactic was now employed by the Company. Compensation of an undisclosed amount was offered to the affected landowners. At a Company meeting on 14 January 1833, it was reported that 'the Duke of Grafton and Sir William Wake now assented'.[70] The new bill received the Royal Assent on 6 May that year.

Between 1833 and 1838, when the line was being built, Courteenhall would have experienced at first-hand the upheaval which such a project entailed. One of the most formidable excavations was the Blisworth Cutting. Some $1^1/_2$ miles in length and in places 65 feet deep, the cutting involved the removal of more than a million cubic yards of earth, clay and limestone. Beneath the clay was water, which required steam engines to pump it out. One hundred thousand pounds of explosive was used in blasting, and there was heavy loss of life among the navvies working on the cutting. The presence of hundreds of navvies, mostly Irish, in the neighbourhood was bitterly resented by the local inhabitants. Where the Company built good-sized huts for the men, the buildings were soon filthy and abounded with vermin because of overcrowding. Most of them slept in fields under the hedges, got drunk and committed criminal offences in the neighbourhood, and many of these went undetected. A Select Committee in 1839 also noted that very few of the navvies attended places of worship. One witness, when asked if 'the decent and well-disposed labourers of the village would have taken employment in building the railway,' replied that they preferred to work for farmers for ten to twelve shillings per week and 'they never would join in the work: nothing would induce them to submit to what they conceived a degradation of working upon the works'.[71]

As was mentioned earlier, when the line was opened in 1838 Sir William and his daughters witnessed the passing of the first train, probably from Courteenhall Bridge which carries the road to Blisworth. A speaker at the Towcester meeting in 1831 had claimed that the railways would 'ruin the squires and spoil the shires'; whilst this did not happen, nevertheless Sir William was not able to adjust easily to the new circumstances. The merits or otherwise of siting a railway station at either Roade or Blisworth was resolved by building one at each place. The first class fare to London was sixteen shillings, twice that of the coach, and the earliest train from Roade was 9.55 a.m. Another disadvantage voiced by a Northampton paper was that the railways deposited passengers 'at Euston Square, a place very far from the points in London which nine travellers out of ten are desirous of reaching'. Nevertheless the *Northampton Mercury* admitted that 'the people seem railroad mad'.[72]

*   *   *   *   *

In politics, Sir William supported the Whig cause though, unlike his father, he had no parliamentary ambitions. He had struck up a friendship with a near neighbour, John Charles Spencer, styled Viscount Althorp (later third Earl Spencer). Althorp, some fourteen years younger, was of a similar disposition to Sir William; they shared a passion for hunting and rowing and were keen supporters of the Pytchley.[73] When Althorp was one of the parliamentary candidates for Northamptonshire in 1806, it was Sir William who proposed his adoption, in his own words, 'activated partly by private friendship, but more because he believed him to be guided by the genuine principles of our happy Constitution'.[74] Althorp was nominated by Sir William on eight successive occasions; each time, Althorp was returned as MP.

From being a young sporting country gentleman, Althorp became deeply immersed in politics and emerged as a leading figure in the nation's affairs. After the ending of the Napoleonic Wars, he became more radical, taking up the causes of criminal law reform, the amendment of the Corn Laws and that of Catholic emancipation. Althorp was appointed Chancellor of the Exchequer and Leader of the House of Commons in

November 1830 by Earl Grey after refusing the prime ministership. With Grey in the House of Lords, Althorp committed himself in the Commons to carrying through legislation for parliamentary reform. The government was defeated on this issue in the Commons in April 1831; Parliament was dissolved and a general election followed. Althorp was returned at the head of the poll for Northamptonshire. Congratulating him on the result, Sir William wrote, 'It gives me infinite satisfaction to hope I may have been of some service to my kind friend Althorp during the late very severe contest. I confess my whole heart has been in it, not only from private friendship but from all our anxiety for the great cause of reform'.[75] In the face of stiff resistance, a Reform Bill passed through the Commons in March 1832. Much of the credit was due to Althorp who had steered it through committee after many sittings. By 4 June, the bill had been agreed to in the Lords and it received the Royal Assent three days later.[76] The Reform Act swept away the rotten boroughs and redistributed the seats to the many growing towns which had little or no representation. Voting qualifications were standardized and new classes of electors introduced into county constituencies. In all, more than 200,000 people received the vote for the first time.[77]

Celebrations were held throughout the country to mark this step towards democratic government. Nowhere was the enthusiasm greater than in the Southern Division of Northamptonshire, Althorp's own constituency. On 28 June 1832, a dinner was given to Althorp and his fellow County MP, Lord Milton, at the *George Hotel*, Northampton. A large crowd of people had gathered outside to greet the distinguished guests; the balcony was draped with flags proclaiming 'Althorp, Milton and Reform' and the church bells added to the clamour. More than 500 gentlemen sat down to dinner, after which speeches followed. In view of his long friendship with Althorp, it was appropriate that Sir William should take the chair. In his opening remarks he stated that:

> When he viewed the Meeting around him, he was apprehensive that it was presumptuous in him to have undertaken the duties of Chairman [cheers] as he was conscious that they could be much more efficiently performed by many other Gentlemen present. Yet he would yield to no man in his attachment to the great cause of Reform [cheers] He had strenuously supported that measure through his long life, and he could not then resist the honour of presiding upon the occasion of its completion [cheers]. He begged to assure them that he felt the highest possible gratification at presiding at a festival which celebrated such an event [cheers]. It was a measure the importance and value of which would be felt by the country at large. It would be only a waste of time for him to dwell upon the advantages certain to be obtained by such a measure. It was a great blessing conferred on the nation, and would descend to future generations. For the achievement of that measure to no person was the country more indebted than to his Noble Friend Lord Althorp [great cheering]; and also to the honest and intelligent Ministry of which he was a member, who possessed the confidence of the country, and who not only so ably projected the measure, but brought it to a happy issue [cheers].[78]

*   *   *   *   *

60. St. Andrew's Hospital, Northampton, by George Clark(e) of Scaldwell, 1838

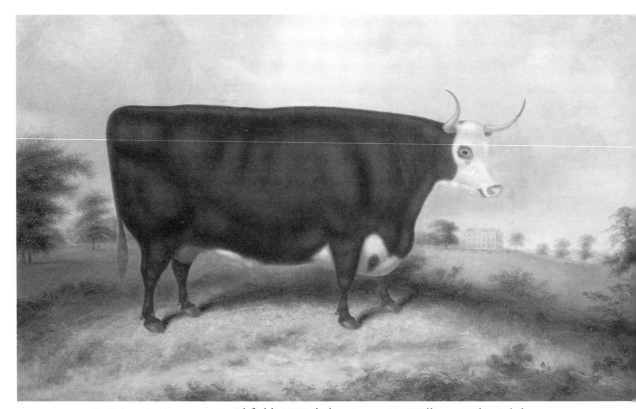

61. Prizewinning steer, Smithfield, 1832, belonging to Sir William Wake, 9th baronet

154

The 1830s witnessed many changes in Sir William's fortunes. In the year of Queen Victoria's accession to the throne, 1837, Jenny, Lady Wake, died. She was buried on 13 May in the vault in Courteenhall Church near Sir Samuel Jones' tomb, alongside her own children. Her room at the east corner of the House on the first floor was kept locked and its contents untouched until after Sir William's own death nine years later. For the rest of his life he was looked after by his three unmarried daughters, Sophia, Emily and Charlotte.

With the intrusion of the railway line through part of the Courteenhall estate, Sir William finally disposed of his harriers. Instead, he turned his attention to the improvement of his lands, introducing a better system of farming and grazing. On more than one occasion Sir William gained first prize for each class of fat oxen annually exhibited at the Agricultural Cattle Show.[79] He took a keen interest in county matters, acting as a county magistrate in dispensing justice[80] and had conscientiously carried out his duties as Sheriff during his term of office, 1791–2.[81] By the beginning of the nineteenth century the need for a mental hospital, as well as a General Infirmary, in Northampton had long been recognized. On 3 May 1828, Sir William, who was a governor of the Infirmary, announced that the Northamptonshire Yeomanry which had been disbanded, had a surplus fund of £6,000 which would be used for 'erecting a lunatic Asylum'. Six years later, in 1834, Sir William was appointed to the Asylum Committee when land was purchased in Northampton for this purpose. Sir William was present on 26 May 1836 when the foundation stone of the Asylum (later renamed St Andrew's Hospital) was laid.[82]

It was believed that Sir William was offered a peerage by one of the Whig Governments in the 1830s, but refused it on two grounds: first, that he did not possess a sufficient fortune to support the title, and second, that he valued the name of Wake too much to be willing to change it. Sir William dressed in an old-fashioned manner, with a long square-tailed coat, low hat and gaiters. Sir George Sitwell's daughter wrote of him, 'He was a charming old man, and it was a delight to see him, with his white hair and fine Saxon features, reading prayers from the large family Bible in the Courteenhall dining room with his swarm of grandchildren around him'.[83] His mother, Lady Mary Wake, was also a frequent visitor, surviving until December 1823, aged seventy eight. She was buried at Courteenhall.[84]

Sir William was a good host but kept regular hours, retiring to bed at ten o'clock promptly each night.[85] He had a good sense of humour which he frequently displayed. One anecdote which he told about himself was of the occasion when he was taken ill at Bath in his youth. He recovered, but the doctor insisted on continuing his visits. Tired of the sight of him and of paying the guinea fee, Sir William ordered the servant to tell the doctor on his next appearance that the patient had died. The report soon circulated round the town that Sir William had expired that morning.[86]

In a long life, the ninth baronet had achieved much. Undoubtedly the rebuilding of the House and the laying out of the Park was his greatest legacy. His participation in many good causes within the county was made possible by the boundless energy which he possessed.

The coming of the railways had changed the face of the countryside around

Courteenhall and Sir William never became fully reconciled to the new conditions. Loyalty to friends was one of his outstanding characteristics and he was a popular figure in society. An observer wrote, 'In dress he was somewhat singular, but it was the singularity of a gentleman, and of one that, as in his politics, declined changing his coat with the mere fashion of the day'.[87] Having inherited the baronetcy at the age of seventeen, he had been able to superintend the estates for the next sixty years.

Sir William died on 27 January 1846, in his seventy eighth year. In life, he had always shunned all forms of ostentation or extravagance. He stipulated in his will that the funeral should be in private 'with as little expense as may be' and that it should, if it were at Courteenhall, be 'a walking funeral and attended only by such of my children or near relations as shall wish to attend'.[88] The funeral took place at Courteenhall Church on 2 February. His happiest memories were associated with his home. It is recorded that when Sir William was dying, his brother, the Reverend Richard Wake, hurried across the Park to bring him the consolations of religion. 'It's all right, Willie,' he said, 'You are going to Heaven'. 'I don't want to go to Heaven,' replied Sir William, 'Courteenhall's good enough for me'.[89]

12

Chattie and The Tenth Baronet

THE LIFE OF OLD SIR WILLIAM PRESENTS A PICTURE OF A successful man of action, whose wide interests, combined with a restless energy, left their stamp on his generation. There could be no greater contrast in every respect than with that of his eldest son, Charles, who succeeded him as the tenth baronet in 1846.

As already noted, Charles's mother Lady Mary Wake died a few days after he was born, in November 1791. In childhood, he received little affection from his stepmother, the former Jenny Gambier. At the age of twelve he entered Harrow, the only Wake baronet to have attended this school.[1] In that year, 1803, Harrow for the first time equalled Eton in numbers, reaching a total of 350. Thanks to the humane regime of the headmaster, Dr Joseph Drury (1785–1805), the school had attracted an exceptional proportion of the upper classes, including at the time of Charles' entry one reigning and three prospective dukes, a marquess, two earls and five future earls and viscounts; Peel, Palmerston and Aberdeen had been among his pupils as well as Byron, who later in life expressed his admiration for Drury.[2] On his retirement in 1805, Drury was succeeded by Dr George Butler. This appointment was very unpopular with the senior boys, some of whom went so far as to lay a trail of gunpowder under a passage with the intention of blowing up the new headmaster. In 1808, shortly before Charles left Harrow, Butler proceeded to curtail some of the monitors' privileges; this led to a serious rebellion and subsequent damage to the school. Unperturbed, Butler expelled the ringleaders and quelled the mutiny.[3] Unfortunately we do not know if Charles, who must have witnessed the events, played any part in them.

Like his father, Charles was admitted as a fellow commoner to St. John's College, Cambridge, matriculating in 1810. He did not take a degree,[4] but returned to Courteenhall. The war with Napoleon was entering its decisive phase with the French invasion of Russia in 1812, and Charles joined the Northamptonshire Militia with the rank of Captain. In many ways, Renishaw continued to hold attractions for the young Charles. Sir Sitwell Sitwell, his uncle, was a welcoming host and the long-standing friendship between his father, Old Sir William, and Sitwell was a close one. It was not too surprising, therefore, that at Eckington Church, Renishaw, on 23 August 1815 Charles married his cousin, Mary Alice, Sir Sitwell's elder daughter. Thus both his

See Appendix A – Family Tree XIII. Notes and References pages 411–414 father, Sir William, and Charles, had married successive generations of Sitwells. But the parallel continued, with the tragically early death of his bride after little more than a year. As a friend wrote at the time, September 1816, 'Poor Wake is as well as he can be expected to be after such a dreadful misfortune. They were a very happy couple, and only twenty four years of age, both of them'.[5]

*   *   *   *   *

It was not until six years later, that Charles remarried. The bride was Charlotte Murdoch Tait, second daughter of Craufurd Tait of Harvieston, who lived in a remote spot by Loch Fyne in West Scotland. As an old Highland family, the Taits strongly supported the Jacobite cause; Charlotte's grandmother, for instance, had been given the unlikely Christian name of Charles, after that of the Young Pretender. It was by a series of chances that Charlotte and Charles first met. In January 1814, Charlotte's mother had died, leaving her husband to tend nine young children. Two years later Sir George Sitwell, then an undergraduate, who had inherited the baronetcy on his father's death in 1811, visited Edinburgh. There he called on his brother Frank's father-in-law, Sir Ilay Campbell, the Lord President of the Court of Session. Campbell, later Lord Succoth, was an extremely wealthy man and a noted jurist;[6] it was his daughter, Susan, who was Charlotte's mother. Sir George fell in love with Charlotte's eldest sister, also called Susan, and in June 1818, married her.[7] A year later they moved back to Renishaw, taking Charlotte with them. It was on their way down to Derbyshire, travelling by a somewhat circuitous route, that Charlotte encountered Charles in Cheltenham.

This was not the first occasion. In 1813, when Charlotte herself was only thirteen, he had arrived at Edinburgh Castle with the militia in charge of French prisoners; in the extensive journals which she kept, Charlotte describes him then as 'just of age, very good looking and as full of fun as his Father could desire. [He] at once took his place in our family as prime favourite with old and young'.[8]

At Cheltenham, Charles in a single day showed Charlotte as many of the sights as possible. In the spring of 1819, Sir George and Lady Sitwell came to London for the season, bringing Charlotte with them, though she chafed at the restrictions placed on young unmarried women. 'I cannot say I liked it, nor I think did they very much. The amusements did not seem half as real as those we had been used to. It was a great consolation to me that Charles Wake was there, bringing with him part of our early life'.[9]

Life at Renishaw was full of excitement. It was from there in 1821 that Charlotte received an invitation to attend the coronation of George IV, and she vividly describes in her Journal the scene at Westminster Abbey when Queen Caroline attempted to gain admittance to the ceremony but was excluded by her husband. Sir George Sitwell, a weak but kindly disposed man, was easily persuaded by Susan to go to Scotland for shooting, becoming one of the first Englishmen to do so. They leased Balmoral, long before Queen Victoria fell in love with the Highlands,[10] and Charlotte accompanied them and their growing family. At Renishaw, Charlotte enjoyed the brilliant balls which were held there, carefully listing in her Journal her more notable partners.[11] She was a gifted mimic and her high spirits added to her attractiveness. An incident in her youth demonstrated that she was not lacking in physical courage. One winter, when Charlotte was with a skating party, the thin ice on the lake gave way beneath a young man. Whilst the other guests looked on in horror, she instantly dived into the water and rescued him. Taking this act as a sign of affection, he promptly proposed to her. In refusing, Charlotte stated that she would have done the same for any other gentleman in peril. From that time onwards, she was known as 'the diving belle'.[12]

Charlotte's Journals are silent on the details of her courtship with Charles, simply recording that early in April 1822 she paid a farewell visit to Scotland before her marriage on 1 June that year at St. George's, Hanover Square, London. In the unpublished version, however, she noted, 'Circumstances had so blended my Husband's life with mine even during my years of childhood that affection for him was a part of myself and I felt as though I had been born married'.[13] An insight into her character is provided by her description of Charles:

> [He was] no longer full of fun and frolic, but softened and saddened by the sorrow that had fallen upon him. The early death of his young wife seemed to have added a shade of romance to every thought connected with him, and though at the time of her marriage I had looked upon her, without ever having seen her, as an interloper, for the very good reason that he had been used to call me his little wife, yet, as she was dead, I heartily forgave her, and felt a tenderness for her memory.[14]

*   *   *   *   *

Charlotte and Charles settled at Tapton Grove, seven miles from Renishaw. Their first child William was born there in 1823. Charles, remembering the death of his first wife, was very nervous whilst awaiting the birth and, retiring to his room to take some cordial, swallowed by mistake a large quantity of laudanum. Almost unconscious, he was made to walk up and down the corridors whilst a servant was dispatched for a doctor. Charles never fully recovered from this incident and his health thereafter was indifferent.[15]

By the time their second child, Charles, was born on 23 October 1824, Charlotte's younger sister, Marianne had recently arrived at Renishaw. She was a frequent visitor to Tapton, and her Diary affords interesting glimpses of life there at the time. In May 1825, Marianne recorded, 'Chattie [Charlotte's family nickname], Charles and their boys came from Courteenhall on the 31st, all looking well this time'. On 24 September, she had taken them to the Chesterfield Races and later to the Doncaster Races. Early in the following year, their first daughter, Susan Emily, was born. A strange entry for 9 July 1827 states that Susan Sitwell and her husband 'arrived in safety at the Grove, where Chattie was ready to receive us, dined early and had a long walk and howled at the moon'. In September their fourth child, Drury, was born. Six days before the event Charles wrote to his London solicitor requesting 'two pounds of Arrowroot from Apothecaries Hall, preparatory to Mrs. Wake's confinement,' adding, 'I think we shall soon want a larger house at this rate.'[16] On 20 March, Chattie and Charles joined the family at Renishaw at 6.00 a.m. 'to see Sir George Sitwell set off in state as High Sheriff with a flourish of trumpets and his Javelin men.' Marianne remarked shortly before the

159

birth on 23 March 1828 of the Wake's fifth child, Herwald Craufurd, 'My poor little Chattie looking enormous. I trust she may have a safe and easy time and that this may be her last brat.' This wish was in vain for in fact there were seven more children to follow. Charlotte and Marianne's father, Craufurd Tait, arrived at Renishaw on 31 March 'looking much older than we last saw him. Chattie, Charles and children here, Papa quite a Patriarch among us all, children and grandchildren'. Marianne visited the Grove in March 1829 where Charles had read out to them Robert Peel's speech on the Catholic emancipation question. Her comment was, 'The bill will be carried as sure as fate so the people need not put themselves in such a state about it!'[17]

Charlotte and Charles were of very different temperaments, as she herself acknowledged. When annoyed or excited, he would speak quickly and loudly, startling his audience. Charles' uneven temperament could also lead to trouble, as in the instance when he opposed the marriage of his first wife's younger sister Anne Sitwell to Colonel Frederick Stovin, which almost resulted in a duel. Of a withdrawn disposition he was much less socially inclined than Charlotte, disdaining the frequent parties at Renishaw and neighbouring country houses, such as Chatsworth, the private theatricals and visits to the Races. Politically, too, they supported different parties; Charles, like his father, Old Sir William, was a staunch Whig whilst Charlotte's family were determined Tories. On the matter of religion, Charlotte had been brought up a Presbyterian. Charles was a devout member of the Church of England.[18] His knowledge in religious matters was described by Charlotte as 'far ahead of ours' and her mother was impressed by receiving from him the four volumes of Cooper's Sermons, the contents of which he knew well.

Life at Tapton Grove was greatly enjoyed by Charlotte. The house, which was large enough for her growing family, was sited on very high ground overlooking the Derbyshire dales. A beautiful flower garden with a mulberry tree surrounded the house and there were wooded walks and a common which were the delight of the children. With a farm producing sufficient food for the household and Renishaw so close by, living was inexpensive. The marriage of Susan to George Sitwell had been followed two years later in 1824 by that of her eldest brother, John to Mary Sitwell, George's cousin. Renishaw became a second home for Charlotte's orphaned brothers and sisters, much to her satisfaction, though this put a great strain on Sir George's purse.

Amidst all this activity, Charlotte managed to find time to become a writer. In 1829 appeared her book *The Beavers and the Elephant. Stories in Natural History for Children*, published by William Blackwood of Edinburgh. Her name does not appear on the title page, and it simply states 'By a Mother'. In an Introduction, Charlotte notes that though there were many books written for children, few dealt with natural history, those that do 'contenting themselves with describing the length, height, and colour of the animal and ... do not seize on the advantages the subject presents'.[19] Individual stories rather than general descriptions were needed if the child's interest was to be held. Charlotte shrewdly observed two common characteristics in children, 'a strong love of the marvellous, and the other, a no less strong desire for the truth'. Drawing on the work of naturalists – 'my plan is not to compose but to compile'[20] – Charlotte wrote two stories, each with a number of chapters, one concerning a settlement of beavers which was hunted by Red Indians, and another about the adventures of a female elephant,

Soubahdir, and her calf. Both stories, which Charlotte herself skilfully illustrated, end with a moral as well as an uplifting religious message.

* * * * *

Shortly after the book's publication, the long-established routine at Tapton came to an end. Charlotte had observed that with every year that had passed, Charles became more averse to mixing with society and even his close friends, and his health suffered from 'suppressed gout'. The remedy and the cause, as described by Charlotte, were puzzling: 'it was decided that we must leave the Grove in which the air was too exciting and the life too quiet to be good for him'[21] In May 1830, they crossed over to Dieppe, where they found the whole court of Charles X. France was at that time in turmoil. The unpopular monarch had dissolved the Chamber of Deputies in March and new elections in May had returned a majority unfavourable to the king. Given the uneasy political situation, it is surprising that the Wakes continued their leisurely way towards Paris, which was a stopping place on the way to their intended destination, Switzerland.

They arrived at St. Germain-en-Laye, on the outskirts of Paris, in mid-July, where at their hotel they received the news that Charles X had issued the Five Ordinances, which virtually banished the basic freedoms in the country. A revolution broke out, centred in Paris, which led to the abdication of the monarch. Hordes of refugees from Paris filled the hotel and the Wakes listened to the terrifying stories of the fighting in the city. When the Red Flag was hoisted over the Chateau in St. Germain-en-Laye, the Wakes were the only English family left in the town. One of the chief reasons for not joining the refugees who were speeding towards the coast was that Charlotte was ill and expecting her sixth child. They were pleased when a large carriage drove into their hotel yard from which three girls, a young boy and an old gentleman, alighted. He was General William Knollys, who had just left Paris. The two families quickly struck up a friendship which was later cemented by several marriages between their respective grandchildren.

Early in August, the Wakes proceeded to Paris, where they were able to witness the celebrations, following the successful ending of the uprising. As Charlotte noted, 'Every street rang with the Marseillaise . . .There was universal joy, and a sense of safety changed the expression of countenance of every man and woman in the crowds still collected everywhere'.[22] Both Charles and Charlotte deeply shared the feelings of those around them; when their fifth son was born on 20 August 1830, he was named Philip Augustus after the new King, Louis Philippe. They stayed for the winter in a pleasant apartment on the Champs Elysées; after a very adventurous year the family came back to England. If life at Renishaw had been too quiet for Charles's disposition, then the French expedition had provided a stark contrast.

For a time after their return they settled at Atholl Crescent, in the newly-built quarter of Edinburgh, Western New Town. But a more permanent residence was required and it was whilst staying at Malvern that Charlotte and Charles viewed Powick Court, near Worcester, and immediately decided to take it.[23] The owner of the property was John Pakington, a young lawyer who had assumed that surname in 1830

161

on becoming heir to his maternal uncle, Sir John Pakington, the eighth and last baronet of Westwood Park, near Droitwich.

In early 1835, when the Wakes leased Powick Court at £200 per annum,[24] Pakington had already unsuccessfully fought three elections as a Conservative for Worcestershire county seats.[25] After becoming MP for Droitwich in 1837, he represented the borough for thirty seven years. Subsequently, he was a member of three Cabinets, and was elevated to a peerage in 1874, taking the title of Lord Hampton.[26] Pakington's amiability, quick intellect and sociability led to a friendship which made their stay at Powick enjoyable. They were frequently invited to Westwood Park, a fine Elizabethan house remodelled in the style of a seventeenth century French chateau, and situated some twelve miles from Powick. Pakington, like Charlotte, enjoyed singing. In old age, she reflected on her last visit to Westwood where, grouped round the piano, was Pakington, with three women: his wife, Mary, who was accompanying him in a duet, Augusta Murray, later to become his second wife, and, turning over the pages of the music, Augusta Davies, who became his third.[27]

As with Tapton Grove, Charlotte and the family were happy to explore the neighbourhood, particularly enjoying the expeditions down the Wye Valley. There had been further additions to the family with the birth of a second daughter, Matilda, born 28 March 1832, and a sixth son, Edward Baldwin, on 14 December 1833, shortly before moving to Powick. Tragically, two more children died in infancy, Isla Campbell, aged eight weeks, on 24 October 1837 and Frederick William George, aged fourteen months, on 29 December 1839; they were buried in Powick churchyard.[28] Charles' health once more was causing concern and it was considered advisable to seek the sun abroad. After five happy years at Powick, the Wakes left there in March 1840. Charles wrote in his farewell letter to Pakington, 'Tho' our connection as Landlord and tenant must be dissolved (and your kindness and liberality in the former capacity I shall not readily forget) yet I trust our occasional intercourse may not be interrupted, and that I may consider I have at least made one friend in Worcestershire'.[29]

Switzerland seemed a suitable country for Charles' recuperation and the family settled at Geneva, by the lake, where another son, Montague, was born in July 1841. However, the cold did not agree with the invalid and a doctor advised that the following winter should be spent in the warmer climate of Nice. They set off to cross the Alps, with Charlotte and Charles occupying the seat at the rear of the carriage: also outside were two boys and a servant, and 'precious Emily' their elder daughter, with a nurse, whilst a Swiss maid and three more children travelled inside. After an adventurous journey, they arrived in Nice, where they were greeted by their old friends and neighbours, Captain (later the fourth Earl) Spencer and his wife. Charles' health rapidly recovered, though as spring came, the biting winds once again made a further move essential. Shortly before they left, their seven month old son, Montague, died in January 1842. The Wakes settled in Pisa in February and March – 'a duller abode cannot be imagined' – noted Charlotte.[30] Tragically and unexpectedly on 1 April, Emily died in Florence at the age of sixteen. She had been her parents' favourite child. Charlotte put up a memorial tablet in Courteenhall Church inscribed 'She leaned upon the cross and died'. Charles' health deteriorated once more and the sad party arrived back in England

62. Bust of Archbishop
Archibald Tait (1811-82),
by Morton Edwards, 1867

63. Archbishop Tait with family, convalescing at Cannes, c.1870

at the end of May. In October, Pitsford House became the family home for the next three and a half years. Their twelfth child and last son, Archibald Emilius, was born there in 1843.

*　　　*　　　*　　　*　　　*

With the death of Old Sir William in January 1846, Charles succeeded to the title as the tenth baronet. They now had few financial difficulties, as the ninth baronet had left personalty (i.e. property not including land) after deductions, in the sum of £42,492 6s.11d.[31] From the time he moved to Courteenhall, Charles led the life of a semi-invalid and, unlike his father, did little to make improvements either to the Estate or to the House.[32] Charlotte, in contrast, found difficulty in accommodating her many interests. A second venture into authorship led to the publication of *A Simple Commentary on the New Testament* in 1849. She also composed the words of a song, based on a traditional Scottish air, called 'Grizell Cochrane, or the Daughter Dear'; the subject of the piece had saved the life of her Jacobite father, who had been found guilty of treason, by intercepting his death warrant on its way from London to Edinburgh.[33] Although both Charles and Charlotte held strong religious convictions, they were by no means hidebound. In February 1856, they supported a petition for the Sunday opening of galleries and museums to the public. This drew a strong protest from the Rector of Courteenhall, the Reverend George Robbins, in the form of a sixteen-page letter. Dismissing Charlotte's quotation, 'The Sabbath was made for man and not man for the Sabbath,' Robbins stated, 'My opinion is that the opening of the British Museum and the establishment of lectures in it such as you describe would be calculated to draw off the minds of men from that quiet experimental communion and meditation which seem to me so peculiarly characteristic of the privileges and duties of the day'.[34]

Both Charles and Charlotte showed a keen interest in the past and it is to their credit that they were the first Northamptonshire Wakes to undertake systematic research into their family's history. As was mentioned in Chapter 1, Sir Charles commissioned a genealogist to compile the Wake pedigree well before Kingsley's novel was published. Charlotte also sought out information on 'the warrior of the Fens, Hereward de Wake' and gathered evidence from parish registers of the Wakes who were buried at Clevedon.[35]

Daily life in the household followed a strict routine. The family rose at 7.30 a.m and prayers followed at exactly 9.00 a.m. Breakfast was taken at 9.30 a.m and various businesses transacted until dinner at 2.00 p.m. From 3.00 p.m until 6.30 p.m or 7.00 p.m, there were visits to the poor of the village or to neighbours, or drives. At 8.00 p.m, a 'powerful tea' was provided, then reading, and bed at 11.00 p.m.[36]

At times of illness of a member of the Tait family, Charlotte would quickly leave Courteenhall to assist. On such occasions Charles' letters to her giving the news provide interesting and often amusing insights into happenings. In May 1856 he wrote, 'I send you one line to say that Mr. Archibald Wake [aged twelve] suffered much from Toothache yesterday, and was in bed all day, tho' I made him better with a glass of Port Wine'. He was not always as successful with his offspring. Later, Charles complains that 'The Boys are really ill-behaved Idiots'. In June 1860, he was faced with a revolt from the

CP28-29. Humphry Repton's Red Book, 1791-3. Prospects showing the existing house (above) and landscaping (below) of the proposed new building as planned by Samuel Saxon, pupil of Sir William Chambers

CP30. Charles Wake, later 10th baronet, at the age of 7 by J. Clarke, 1798

CP31. Sir Ilay Campbell of Garscube, Lord President of the Court of Session, Edinburgh; the grandfather of Charlotte, Lady Wake. He died in 1823 at the age of 89

CP32. Philip Augustus Wake aged 17, by W. Drummond, 1850

entire household staff, being told by one that servants 'were not to be had, as they now never professed to stay in a place more than two or three months, and all tried to get on the Railroad.' Charles concludes his letter, 'I think an example <u>must</u> be made, for all authority seems at an end. In short it seems we get on badly without you. "Not be trifled with" ought to be stuck up downstairs.' And on another occasion, 'Matilda will write to you on domestic matters for I do not feel competent to accede to or dissent from the proposition as to Scullery or Laundry'. Once when Charlotte was away, there were no fewer than thirty two guests staying in the House.

Inevitably, the state of his own health was a frequent topic. 'I am unwell today,' Charles wrote in May 1856. 'Yesterday we called at Delapre but I was half dead the whole time and I am fast coming to a stand still'. Nevertheless, he held firm views on medicine. 'You are so completely independent of me that it appears absurd my making reply respecting your go ahead proceeding in regard to sending for a Homeopathic Dr . . . I have so often expressed in your hearing my opinion of Homeopathy, that I say nothing on the present occasion.' Charlotte's lack of attention to detail – her letters rarely bore the date and invariably lacked the full address – led to misdelivery of mail, points which were frequently remarked upon. It was also difficult to predict her movements, as Charlotte was liable to change her mind at the last moment and appear unexpectedly. Charles once remarked, 'I hardly know if you will get this. Your arrival in a <u>Balloon</u> would not surprise me'. Despite the apparent surface irritability, Charles' fondness for Charlotte clearly emerges in his correspondence. '<u>Pray, pray</u> take all the care you can of yourself,' he ended one letter, 'God bless and keep you, Dearest'. Invariably, Charles signed himself 'Ever your affectionate Hub'.[37]

*   *   *   *   *

One outstanding member of the Tait family was to play an important part in the couple's lives. Archibald Campbell Tait, Charlotte's youngest brother, was born in December 1811 when she was twelve. Much to her mother's grief, Archie was born with club feet, though this disability was cured in childhood by a farrier in Lancashire. Charlotte adopted a protective role, which was reinforced by the death of their mother when Archie was only three years old. In childhood, he was often at Renishaw and after his sister's marriage to Charles, became almost part of the Wake household. Charles spent much time with the very intelligent and happy boy and watched his progress with a paternal interest. Predictably his career rapidly advanced. Tait became a Fellow of Balliol College, Oxford, in 1834, and was ordained two years later. This was at a time when the Oxford Movement was causing much concern within the Church of England. When John Henry Newman's *Tract XC*, opposing religious liberalism, was published in March 1841, Tait was one of the signatories to the famous 'Protest of the Four Tutors', which declared opposition to Newman's tract; it was a turning point in the Move-ment,[38] and confirmed Tait's growing authority. As his proud sister had earlier written to him, 'I trust that I may live to see my Archie not only an ornament to the sacred profession for which he is destined, but one of those <u>true Shepherds</u> who follow the steps of their Lord in sustaining the needy, leading back the wandering, and bringing many to the fold'.[39] In June 1842, Charlotte was with Archie, who was returning to

Oxford, on Blisworth Station, when their attention was attracted by a number of Rugby school boys filling up carriages of the train, all silent and sad. Dr Thomas Arnold, their headmaster, had died suddenly. Archie had known him well and he was encouraged by his sister to apply for the now vacant post. Much to Charlotte's delight, he was appointed; he was only thirty years old. Following a man of Arnold's stature was not easy, especially as at first Archie seemed rather remote and had not the ease of manner to get on well with boys. Despite these handicaps, Tait's achievements at Rugby were many. Numbers rose from 362 to 500, and a programme of school building was undertaken, including a library and a museum.[40] He reduced the power of the Sixth Form and abolished a number of out-of-date customs.[41] Tait was greatly assisted in his work by his wife, Catharine, whom he had married in 1843.

Seven years later, Tait accepted the Deanery of Carlisle. Tragedy struck in 1856. Within the space of one month, March to April, five of their seven daughters died from scarlet fever. Charlotte journeyed to Penrith to comfort the bereaved couple.[42] Charles, whose own children had suffered from the same fever when at Tapton, wrote to Charlotte, 'My heart bleeds for the dear Dean and his wife, for tho' reason and religion will successfully enforce resignation to the Divine Will, they cannot efface the past from the Memory, nor blunt the feelings implanted by Nature – neither were they meant to do so'.[43]

One thought filled Charlotte's mind; how to prevent the return of Archie and Catharine to the Deanery. Only the year before, she had said to her brother, 'What a first rate Bishop you would make. Can no steps be taken?' A plan now formed in her mind. Lord Palmerston, the Prime Minster, had as his chief ecclesiastical counsellor the seventh Earl of Shaftesbury, the philanthropist and reformer. As the young Lord Ashley,[44] Shaftesbury had spent two years in Derbyshire with his cousin and her husband, then Rector of Eckington, and he became great friends with Sir George Sitwell.[45] Charlotte had met him at Renishaw in 1819 and thought him 'the handsomest young man I had ever seen: he was very tall, and his countenance radiant with youthful brightness'. Now, some thirty seven years later, when she and Charles were in London, Charlotte was determined to arrange a meeting with Shaftesbury. As she wrote in her Journal:

> Without saying a word to my Husband who I feared may possibly object I drove to Lord S's house at a time in which he would most probably be at home, sent in my card, upon which I had written a request to return at any time that might be most convenient to him; a servant brought a message that in a quarter of an hour he would be glad to see me. Well I remember the intervening time, and the feelings with which I entered his Library. We had not met since I was eighteen and he was twenty. He had of course risen to receive me, and there we stood for half a minute face to face each holding the other's hand, he I suppose like myself endeavouring to trace the original countenance in the present. It was difficult to recognize the face of the handsome sparkling Boy I remembered so well, in the grave care worn countenance before me, but there was encouragement in its kind thoughtful expression. I told him at once that I had come to speak to him of

my youngest brother known to him by reputation and of whose family bereavement he had heard and that knowing his influence I trusted that he would use it to prevent his return to his desolated home. 'Everyone tells me that Lord Palmerston is chiefly guided by your counsels in selecting who he ought to recommend to the Queen when there is a vacant Bishoprick and I want to tell you what I myself personally know of my Brother'.

He listened attentively but rather coldly to my representation of his management of the working man &c, disclaiming the power attributed to him, but he became interested as I passed on to his family circle telling him how even the children had been associated in his work among the poor, how fever had fallen upon them one by one, and how each child old enough to know the name of God had glorified God in the suffering illness, by which they had literally passed from death into Life, describing as well as I could the loving submission of all, as child after child had been given up into the Saviour's hands 'and now the nursery is empty, the house is utterly desolate. How can the Father & Mother return there, Oh Lord Shaftesbury I am sure you will go to Lord Palmerston, and ask him to do that great kindness, which will give to the Church and the Country, the very best and most efficient of Bishops when ever he may have power to do so'. The tears had fallen from the kind eyes that had been fixed in earnest attention, he had himself lately lost a son. No man on earth possessed a heart more full of feeling and he said, 'I will indeed do what I can. I cannot promise to succeed, but I will try, I entirely believe all you say of your Brother'.

Thankful and comforted I left him, I knew that he would keep his promise, and wrote to my Brother that I was sure he might turn his thoughts to a coming change relating all that had passed.[46]

Charlotte, in recalling the long interview, told Archie, 'I remember that he gave particular heed to all I said on the subject of your powers of arranging, and classifying and getting through work, and influencing men's minds'.[47] A few days after the interview, Shaftesbury, bearing in mind that Tait was a Broad Churchman, wrote to her, 'I stated your brother's qualifications in the strongest manner to Lord Palmerston, adding that as he desired all sections of the Church of England to be represented, he could not do better than take one who, being neither Puseyite, High Church, nor Evangelist, was an admirable man and full of zeal for the advancement of religion'.[48] Shortly afterwards, in September 1856, Palmerston offered him the post of Bishop of London.

Although, with only one exception, Tait was the first man for nearly two hundred years to be made Bishop of London without having previously held another See, he successfully dealt with many difficult ecclesiastical issues during his decade in that office. But the pressure of work put a strain on his less than robust constitution. Towards the end of Tait's headmastership of Rugby, in February 1848, he had contracted rheumatic fever. On Ash Wednesday, it was believed that he might die at any moment and he dictated a letter of farewell to the Sixth Form and sent messages to many friends.[49]

Although Tait recovered, his health was now undermined. Thus, when Palmerston offered him the Archbishopric of York in 1862, Charlotte, anxious for her brother, saw the post as an escape from the hectic life of the metropolis. 'If the consciousness of failing strength inclines you towards this new path', she wrote, 'remember that it will not lack deep interests, and they will bring hard and anxious work, for there are hordes of half savages to be reclaimed in those Yorkshire wilds described by Charlotte Brontë'.[50] Charles strongly advocated York on health grounds though when Tait decided to remain in London, Charlotte agreed with her brother. As she quaintly put it to Catharine, 'It seemed to me very like a man making a second marriage while the first wife and family were not only yet living, but possessed of all the husband's thoughts and affections'.[51]

*   *   *   *   *

Shortly after Charles and Chattie had moved into Courteenhall in early 1846, Sir George Sitwell's financial situation became desperate. He had lived extravagantly and incurred much debt, mainly through keeping his own foxhounds, fighting and losing an expensive contested election in 1832 against the Devonshires, and providing lavish hospitality. Sitwell was obliged to live on £700 a year instead of his accustomed £12,000. In the autumn of 1846, he went abroad, sold many of the contents of Renishaw and never returned to the house. Courteenhall now became the meeting place for the Taits, especially when Archie was at Rugby. Inviting Susan Sitwell to stay at Rugby, Archie wrote, 'We are so near Courteenhall that we should be almost one party'.[52] He convalesced there after his illness with his brother-in-law and sister.

Much of Charles' time was occupied in supervising the day-to-day running of the Courteenhall and Essex estates, as the impressive bulk of his correspondence testifies. Difficulties could arise from living some distance away from Waltham. Evidence was given to the Select Committee on Royal Forests in April 1863 that Charles' agent, without permission, had tried to compel visitors to High Beach in Epping Forest to go to the public house, *The Wake Arms*, for refreshment. This had been accomplished by destroying the springs from which water was obtained to make tea. By doing this, the agent was hoping to promote the interests of the licensee, who was a tenant. Charles, on being informed, deprecated the act of his agent and ordered the springs to be restored to the public.[53] Shortly after they were married, Charles and Charlotte had stayed from time to time at Waltham Abbey. Amongst their friends there was the Reverend Joseph Arkwright of Mark Hall, Harlow, son of the inventor of the spinning frame, with whom Charles rode.[54]

Like his father, the tenth baronet remained closely interested in politics. 'You name the Northamptonshire election,' wrote a friend whilst the Wakes were abroad in August 1847. 'Too bad in any case to have Vyse [Colonel Richard Vyse, Conservative MP, South Northamptonshire, 1846–57] as your County Member and as you say, you can't go home to take part'.[55] Charlotte, meanwhile, was occupied with the fortunes of her large family, whose exploits will be the subject of the next chapter. She never lost her Scottish ways; one Courteenhall villager in 1926 remembered Lady Wake celebrating New Year's Day every year by giving all the old people a dinner. She would

64. Pitsford House, c.1890 home of Charlotte, Dowager Lady Wake and subsequently her son Drury Wake

65. Drury Wake with his mother, at Pitsford, c.1875

also send her housekeeper round the village to ask each woman what she wanted; later they would all go to the House to collect their presents.[56]

During the last twenty years of his life, Charles' search for good health was a constant quest. Long parts of the year were spent on the Continent, where they might be joined by members of their family, especially Archie and his wife. In the autumn of 1863, Charles was told by his doctor that the Northamptonshire dampness necessitated a change of venue for them. They removed to Dover and then on to Brighton. There, Sir Charles died on 23 February 1864, aged seventy two; he was buried at Courteenhall on 1 March.

A little over a year later, Charlotte's eldest son, William, the eleventh baronet, died; he was followed within twenty months by his wife, Margaret. In 1864, Charlotte had taken up residence at Pitsford, occupying the old house where she and Charles had lived before going to Courteenhall. The house was enlarged and rebuilt and Charlotte had for her companions her only surviving daughter, Matilda, and son, Drury, both of whom were then unmarried. Drury, together with his brother, Charles, and Charlotte, were guardians of Sir William's seven children, who ranged in age from twenty three to nine. They all now moved into Pitsford House, where Charlotte presided over the household.[57] She was to remain there for the next twenty four years.

Charlotte, who had always disliked the Northamptonshire winters, left Pitsford each autumn with Matilda, in search of a better climate. Between 1864 and 1876, they stayed at Malvern, Weston-super-Mare, Brighton, St. Leonards-on-Sea and Bournemouth, venturing abroad only once, to Cannes in 1870.[58] The occasion of this last visit was after the illness of her brother, Archie, when Charlotte accompanied him and his wife.

Two years earlier, in October 1868, following the death of the Archbishop of Canterbury, Charles Longley, Disraeli offered the vacant post to Tait. He accepted it. Charlotte's long-held faith in her brother's outstanding abilities had been justified. In turn, the new Archbishop continued to look to her for support in his work. At the 1878 Lambeth Conference, she was summoned to the Palace to help Catharine with the arduous duty of receiving the assembled bishops from many parts of the world.[59] On one memorable occasion, the Archbishop came to Pitsford to visit Charlotte. The word quickly spread that he was to preach on the Sunday evening at the parish church. People from many parts of Northamptonshire descended on the village; those who were unable to obtain a place within the church listened from outside.[60]

After Catharine's death towards the end of 1878, Archie depended on Charlotte still more heavily. On 23 July 1882, he wrote in his Journal, 'Sleeplessness at night, sickness, nervous affection, but mercifully the clearness of my head and power of speech are not affected ... Dear Chattie is still with us here – thirteen years older than me, and as fresh as a lark, but I doubt if she could make as good speeches'.[61] Early in September, alarming accounts from Addington Place, Surrey, of her brother's health reached her and she immediately went there. Sir William Jenner, the physician, gave little hope for Archie's recovery. Archie greeted her when she entered the room, 'I am glad you are come back, you are a sort of Mother in the House'.[62] During the next few weeks, Charlotte tended him with the same loving care as in his childhood, seventy years before. She was with him when he died peacefully on Advent Sunday, 1 December 1882.

Queen Victoria expressed a wish to see her late Archbishop's only surviving sister, and Charlotte was summoned to Windsor. At the audience, the Queen was accompanied by Princess Beatrice. Charlotte afterwards wrote to her grandson's wife, Lady Catherine Wake, 'It was very kind and very pleasant, nevertheless it was rather alarming being shut up with those two. She gave me an affectionate kiss at parting and I was much drawn to her'.[63] At the interview, the Queen was interested to hear from Charlotte about Balmoral as it was in Sir George Sitwell's time, before she and the Prince Consort had bought it.

Even in old age, Charlotte was as vigorous in her views as ever, though she was becoming physically frail. Admitting in 1884 that she had not read Octavia Hill's book on promoting improvements for the poor in London, she declared, 'What I read becomes, when I know it is true, such a part of myself that it makes one wretched unless I can help it'.[64] Politically she remained staunchly Conservative. She attended a wedding fête at Pitsford in July 1885, when the whole village prayed and feasted together. 'I cannot tell how this pleases me in our radical village and convinces me more than ever that the correct way to keep radicalism from conquering liberalism, is the kindly natural bond that ought to unite the Classes'.[65] Not surprisingly, she deplored the return of Bradlaugh and Labouchere as MPs for Northampton, but her *bête noire* was Gladstone. At the time when the Prime Minister had declared himself in favour of Irish Home Rule, she described the 'evil [which] has been done to the public conscience by Gladstone's shilly shally shifting, self deceived and most deceiving policy'.[66] In May 1886, when the crisis was at its height, Charlotte expressed her views even more strongly. She wrote to her niece, 'What do you think of Gladstone now? I know what I think – that he should either be sent to the Tower or to Bedlam, as the case may be!'[67] However, she was pleased at the election to Parliament of Sir George Reresby Sitwell, the third baronet, in December 1885, adding, 'I trust that it will not cause him to forget Renishaw – very few MPs reside among their constituencies'.[68]

By this time, Charlotte was confined to her bed, though she would write later, 'I do trust soon to get out or I shall have to give in altogether. At eighty seven, what else is to be expected? God is very good to me in every way'.[69] She continued in good spirits until Easter Sunday, 31 March 1888, when she passed away peacefully, aged eighty eight; Charlotte was buried at Courteenhall on 6 April, in the new family vault on the north side of the churchyard, next to her husband.

*   *   *   *   *

Sir Charles, the tenth baronet, had inherited in middle age and when his health had become delicate. A charming and affable person, he took as his second wife a remarkable woman of strong character, who provided a steady basis for their marriage. It was due to her initiative that members of the Tait and Wake families received due and deserved recognition in their respective professions. She was a generous person by nature and was motivated by a deep religious conviction; her work amongst the poor at Pitsford was but one example.[70] It was through the intermarriages between the Sitwells, Taits and

66. Sir Charles Wake 10th baronet (1791–1864), aged about 65

67. Charlotte, Dowager Lady Wake in old age, c.1885

Wakes that Courteenhall became a gathering place for the families during the tenth baronet's time. There was also much sadness during Charlotte's lifetime. She outlived her husband by twenty four years and witnessed the death of no fewer than nine of her children, including William, the eleventh baronet. In 1938, Charles St. Aubyn Wake, 'Bulldog' Wake's eldest son,[71] recalled driving over to Courteenhall from Pitsford some time after Sir Charles's death:

> My great-grandmother, Charlotte, Lady Wake, and a lot of them went. The house was empty, and when Gran-gran went into the house she went what the Scotch called 'Fay' and said, 'Oh my children, oh my children, I can feel them all round me', meaning the dead ones, and it was all very dreadful and depressing and they went off to Pitsford as soon as they could.[72]

There is little doubt that several of them had inherited Charlotte's unusual personality; this is reflected in the varied and colourful careers which many of the children pursued and which will now be described.

13
Defenders of the Empire

IN ALL, EIGHT OF CHARLOTTE AND CHARLES WAKE'S children, seven boys and one girl survived until adulthood. Matilda, the only daughter, devoted her life in later years to looking after her mother and died unmarried at Courteenhall on 6 March 1924. An interesting feature of this generation of Wakes is that no fewer than four sons chose to serve in the Forces, for longer or shorter periods, and with varying degrees of success. Of these, perhaps the most notable was the tenth baronet's second son, Charles.

He joined the Navy at the age of thirteen in 1837, when the family were living at Powick. Charles was described by one of his daughters as 'the most unworldly person she had ever known, very simple, very religious and loved by everybody. He was small and fair, with regular features and strikingly blue eyes; brave as a lion, and with great moral courage'.[1] On many occasions whilst still a cadet, Charles was the subject of complaint by his officers. In July 1842, the captain of his ship remarked on his neglect of duty, 'appearing on the Quarter deck in a filthy dirty state, out at the Elbows, and without a button on his Jacket: I have repeatedly spoken to him on the subject'.[2] Explaining the situation to his father, Charles later wrote, 'True, I have perhaps been rather insubordinate to my superiors, mutinous perhaps; and that I have been badly dressed . . . You say that you dare say a collier's boy is cleaner on any week day than I am on Sunday . . . But take a more lenient view of the case, and be not so severe, I entreat of you'.[3] Two years later, Charles was once more in trouble because of 'excesses in Wine' whilst at HMS *Excellent*, the school for naval gunnery at Portsmouth, and getting into debt 'brought on by intemperate living'; fortunately, his father's friend, Captain Frederick Spencer, was able to intervene on his behalf and thus saved him from disgrace.[4] Charles, who throughout his life was on very affectionate terms with his mother, ended a letter at this time, 'I have little more to say, my dearest Mother, except that I feel uncertain that no reproaches, however well merited, can make me feel more deeply my errors than I do at present'.[5]

Charles' character was very accurately described to his father by Sir Thomas Hastings, his Captain, and superintendent at the Royal Naval College, Portsmouth: 'I regret to say he has no fixed principles as to discipline and he is naturally of an impatient

See Appendix A – Family Trees XIII and XIV. Notes and References pages 414–417 and insubordinate temper. Unless he endeavours to guard against these evils, he will make shipwreck of himself, more especially as he is equally lax in reference to higher and more careful considerations'.[6] After briefly serving on the Home Station, Charles spent many years in the Mediterranean. Promotion soon followed.[7] In August 1846, he was appointed Lieutenant at the age of twenty one, and posted to the *Hibernia*, the flagship of Admiral Sir William Parker.[8] He became a Commander in 1855, sailing with the sloop *Devastation*, and four years later, on 23 June 1859, he was gazetted Captain. Charles was now put in charge of the *Bulldog*,[9] a small six-gun paddlewheel steam sloop of 1,124 tons, of the North America and West Indies Squadron.

Amongst the other qualities which he brought with him to the *Bulldog* was an enthusiasm for promoting religious feeling among the crew. In 1860, a Royal Navy Scripture Readers' Society was established to provide sailors with suitable literature. Charles told his uncle, Archie, the Bishop of London, 'I have been a subscriber since it first began, and from my own knowledge can speak of its usefulness. Already good has been done on board the *Bulldog*'.[10] Charles was conscious of his lack of formal education, but did not consider it a handicap. From the *Bulldog* in July 1865 he wrote to his mother:

> What are the particular duties of a country gentleman that are to be learned at Eton and Oxford and can't be learned at sea? I think without vanity that if ever I had succeeded to the estate ... I should have made a fair country gentleman, and done the duties of the position tolerably, tho' I have been all my life at sea.[11]

By September, the *Bulldog* was based at Vera Cruz, in the Gulf of Mexico, and Charles expected to be there for a further three months.[12] The course of events decreed otherwise and would thrust Charles unexpectedly on to the international stage.

An uprising had taken place in October 1865 in Haiti, an island which forms part of the West Indies. Native rebels, commanded by a black chief, Salnave, had stormed the house of the British Consul at Cape Haitien, on the north side of the island; they had taken out and shot some Haitian refugees who had been given protection there. The Consul's house was then wrecked and the English flag pulled down. The *Bulldog* was lying off the Cape at the time and the Consul explained what had occurred to Charles Wake. Charles immediately demanded an explanation from Salnave and received for reply 'a mere burst of vulgar insolence'. In Charles' private report to the Commander-in-Chief, he wrote, 'It was clearly my duty to demand redress for such gross outrage and defiant hostility of demeanour, and it seemed to me that when my temperate demands were met with contempt, it was equally my duty to inflict a punishment that would teach respect to the English Flag and home'.[13]

Accordingly, at 8.45 a.m on 23 October, the *Bulldog* sailed into the harbour. It was fired upon when passing Fort Picolet; returning fire, the *Bulldog's* gunner put the main fort out of action as well as a smaller one. Charles then steamed full ahead towards the *Voldrome*, a vessel captured by the rebels, and sank it. A schooner, armed by Salnave, met with the same fate. However, in the excitement of the action, Charles had misjudged the distance from the shore and the *Bulldog* ran on to the shoals. The shore batteries were

68. Margaret, Lady Wake (1825-66), wife of
Sir William Wake, 11th baronet, c.1835

69. Sir William Wake, 11th baronet (1823-65),
aged about 35

70. Drury Wake at Pitsford, 23 July 1890, a year before his death

71. HMS *Bulldog*, commanded by Captain Charles Wake, engaging the rebels at Cape Haitien, Haiti, October 1865

72. *Punch* cartoon, 27 January 1866, supporting Captain Charles Wake's action against the rebels

now trained on the helpless ship and some members of the crew were killed and injured. As evening came, the firing ceased. Charles pondered his hopeless situation: three of the lifeboats had been rendered useless, the men were exhausted, almost all the ammunition had been expended and the ship was hopelessly aground. Charles therefore ordered the men into the remaining boats and with the assistance of a gunner set fire to and blew up the *Bulldog*. The officers and crew landed on friendly territory and were then taken by steamer to Jamaica. The *New York Herald* on 17 November, reporting their arrival, stated, 'All the English are in high glee at the gallant conduct of the *Bulldog*'.

This view was not shared by the naval authorities and a court martial was held in Jamaica. There, Charles accepted full responsibility for the loss of the ship and his master was acquitted of blame.[14] The Board of Admiralty determined to hold a further court martial at Devonport, with the Commander-in-Chief, Admiral Sir Charles Fremantle, as president. This took place on 15 and 16 January 1866. After long deliberation, the Court decided that both Charles Wake and the master were negligent in allowing the ship to go aground and in prematurely destroying it. Charles was therefore dismissed the ship and severely reprimanded.[15]

Typically, Charles refused to accept the verdict. 'I cannot believe that the case has been put fairly to them [the Law Officers]', he told his Uncle Archie, ' . . .All I should like, in the matter of the affair being spoken of in the House of Commons, is that in case Mr. Bright [John Bright, Liberal MP] or any of his Crew should put questions and ask for papers on the subject, someone should be able to put my case forward clearly, strongly, but <u>temperately</u>, in the event of the Government offering me up as a victim and throwing me overboard altogether as a Jonah to appease the Peacemongers'.[16]

Such fears were in fact groundless. A well-placed friend informed Bishop Tait:

> From all I could make out at the Admiralty I do not think that the result of the Court Martial will do him much harm, but of course it will require time before he can hope to get another ship unless we have a war. In that case he would, I doubt not, soon get a command for his courage cannot be doubted. Unfortunately there is an order on the Station that no Captain is to fire a shot without first consulting his Admiral, but I am glad to say the Admiralty do not intend to try him for having disobeyed that order, so I think they are anxious not to do more than they are obliged.[17]

The Admiralty's decision was certainly not endorsed by public opinion, which saw Charles Wake as a modest hero, falling foul of officialdom in the course of defending the British flag. This view was well expressed by *Punch* at the time, which printed a lengthy ballad called the 'Pounding of Port Haytien' accompanied by a cartoon headed 'Admiral Punch Does Justice to Captain Wake.' Beneath a drawing of Mr Punch handing a sword to Charles Wake are the following verses:

> And here's three cheers for Captain Wake, and while we sail the sea,
> May British Bull-Dogs always find Captains as stout as he,
> That's all for biting when they bite, and none for bark and brag,
> And thinks less about Court-Martials than the honour of the Flag![18]

DEFENDERS OF THE EMPIRE

It was not in Charlotte's nature to wait upon events, especially where her own family was concerned. Shortly after the court martial, a Conservative government was once more in office. In July 1866, Charlotte and Charles attended a large dinner party at Fulham Palace, given by her brother. She recorded in her Journal:

> To my great pleasure I found myself before dinner in earnest conversation with Sir John Pakington, and sat next him at dinner. He is one of those old friends who I value most, and who in the thirty years we have known him has always been the same, clever, true hearted, agreeable, and friendly. I am glad that he is the new First Lord of the Admiralty, for he is very fond of Charlie, and was so indignant at the verdict of the Court Martial, on the blowing up of the *Bull Dog*, that he will be sure to give him a ship. Indeed he told me he would – and moreover that the Duke of Somerset [Liberal First Lord, 1859–66] had left a recommendation of him for employment to his successors in Office.[19]

Sure enough, within a few months, Charles was given command of another ship, the frigate *Endymion*. But the traumatic experience at Haiti had left its mark. As he wrote to Drury, his brother, in November, 'The fact is, and I cannot conceal it from myself, that my ill-success in the *Bulldog* has taken all my kick out of me. I suppose the wound to my *amour propre* (as the French say) was too deep, and nothing can reconcile me to the jog trot of the Service in Peace time'.[20] Nevertheless, he enjoyed the opportunity of visiting several countries in the Middle East. He admired the intelligence and looks of the Syrians, though he was sad that the country, with so many Christians, was under Turkish rule. 'Beyrout ought to be the most thriving city in the East and a great commercial emporium but there is hardly any trade here'.[21]

Charles was much happier in his domestic life. In February 1860, he had married Emma St. Aubyn, eldest daughter of Sir Edward St. Aubyn, the first baronet, of St. Michael's Mount, Cornwall. Her uncle was the General William Knollys, whom Charles had met when a boy near Paris during the 1832 uprising (see Chapter 12). Emma was a delightful person, taking a great interest in people, but as unbusinesslike in worldly affairs as her husband. They settled at Devonport and raised a family, consisting of six sons and four daughters. Emma's relatives were close by and there were frequent social gatherings. Charles informed his sister on one occasion, 'Devonport is full of St. Aubyns now, the Mount party, including two sons, having come here and taken up their quarters for a month at "Pounds", a nice country house belonging to Hodge the Banker! A good name for a Banker's house, is it not?'[22] For his part, Charles made visits to Pitsford, where he particuarly welcomed the opportunity of seeing his only sister, Matilda.[23] After one such visit, he walked along the line from Pitsford to Northampton Station, a distance of some five miles, and casually commented, 'If there were many trains running it would be a dangerous line to walk on'.[24]

Like his father, Charles suffered frequently from bouts of ill health and depression. After commanding the *Endymion* in the Mediterranean from 1866 to 1869, he became Captain of the corvette *Penelope* until 1875, and was stationed at Harwich. On 21 September 1876, Charles was promoted to Rear-Admiral with a posting at Devonport. In order to economize, the family moved for a time to Honfleur, near Le Havre, in the late 1870s. Money was a chronic problem; thanking his mother for an unexpected New Year's gift for the family, he wrote, 'Emma and I are as grateful as any of the recipients, for it was a grief to us to think that the children had no Xmas presents, and that we could not afford even to send the younger ones to the pantomime'.[25]

Charles was advanced to the rank of Vice-Admiral on 3 January 1881 and placed on the retired list. Five years later, in April 1886, he was appointed an Admiral. Like their father, all six of Charles' sons became members of the Forces: five were Army officers and one followed Charles' footsteps in the Navy. Unlike his father, though, Drury St. Aubyn Wake made an auspicuous start to his career. Charles had the satisfaction of witnessing the beginnings of his spectacular progress.[26] Drury, appointed an Admiral in April 1917, gained many honours and decorations as well as a knighthood.

Charles had become desperately ill in 1884 and only partially recovered. He died, aged sixty five, on 26 March 1890 and was buried at Pennycross, near Devonport. Emma survived him for another thirty years until 15 March 1920.

*   *   *   *   *

The third son of the tenth baronet, Drury Wake, born in 1827, was some three years younger than his brother, Charles. They differed considerably in temperament; Drury was a more solid, reflective person who enjoyed company and was always popular. A friend recalled him in his youth as one 'so full of life and spirits [and] the best hand at chaff I ever knew'.[27] After attending a private school in Bath, Drury was exactly fifteen years of age when he entered Rugby, on 7 September 1842. The ninth baronet had been the first Wake to send a son, John William, to the school in 1814,[28] and Sir Charles was happy to follow this precedent. Drury arrived at Rugby at the same time that his uncle, Archie Tait, became its headmaster. He was fortunate to have as one of his teachers the most famous son of the previous head. 'I like Mat Arnold very much indeed,' Drury wrote to his Aunt Matilda in 1845, 'I hope he will stay here till I get out'.[29]

In the following year he entered Christ Church, Oxford, where, as in the case of his grandfather, Old Sir William, he devoted much of his time to horses. Drury became a figure of great admiration throughout the university for an impressive equestrian feat which he achieved during his second year at Oxford. One evening at a party, the students were discussing the adventures of one member of Exeter College who had recently ridden to London and back in eight hours. On learning of this, Drury immediately wagered £250 to £50 that he would ride the same distance in two hours less. The bet was instantly accepted and Drury soon set out for Marble Arch. Eleven horses were made ready at intervals along the route, and showing great skill and determination, he completed the course in only five hours.[30] However, the College authorities were far from pleased with this achievement and suspended Drury from Oxford for a year;[31] he returned and gained his BA degree in 1851.

Within three years, his prowess as a horseman was employed on a much more serious and important task. Drury was in Constantinople in March 1854 when Britain and France declared war on Russia. Sir Hugh Rose, a soldier and diplomat, then secretary to the British embassy in Constantinople, asked Drury to deliver a dispatch of

CP33. The Defence of Arrah, 1857, during the Indian Mutiny. Herwald Craufurd Wake and his colleagues were besieged in the house for 7 days

CP34. The Summerhouse in the garden at Courteenhall, painted in 1880 by Sir Herewald Wake, 12th baronet

CP35. Sir Herewald Wake (1852–1916) 12th baronet
by G. W. Miller, c.1883

CP36. Catherine (Kitty) Lady Wake, wife of 12th
baronet by G. W. Miller, c.1883; she died in 1944,
aged 92

great importance to the Foreign Secretary, Lord Clarendon, in London. The gravity of the international situation made it imperative for Drury to undertake this duty. Accompanied by a guide and a horse carrying provisions, Drury rode across the Balkans for six days and seven nights, before they arrived at Belgrade. From there, he proceeded by train, arriving in London eleven days after setting off from Constantinople.

Calling on Lord Clarendon, Drury found him smoking a cigar before going to bed. The Minister read the dispatch thoughtfully, then turning to Drury asked, 'And what is your opinion? You are come straight from Constantinople: is peace or war intended?' 'War, without doubt', replied Drury. Clarendon rejected this view, pointing out that Sir Stratford Canning, the ambassador at Constantinople, who was then in London, had told Clarendon that war was very unlikely.[32] In the event, Drury was proved right; in September that year, the allied troops landed in the Crimea, where a long and bloody war ensued.

He now entered the County Militia as a Captain, serving with his regiment first at Gibraltar in 1855 and then in Ireland. Later, he studied for the Bar at the Inner Temple and became a barrister on the Midland Circuit in 1859. Before his law career could be established, the effects of the long ride across the Balkans took its toll; Drury's spinal cord had been seriously weakened. His mother, Charlotte, graphically recorded the event in her Journal:

> Drury was gone down to hunt in Northamptonshire. Suddenly we heard that he was prostrated by sudden illness. I went to him at once, and found him paralysed from head to foot. So suddenly had this come upon him that in the house of a Friend (the Reverend Maze Gregory, Roade Rectory) with whom he had intended to remain two nights he lay helpless for six weeks before he was able to be carried across his Father's Park to Courteen Hall where Sir Charles with Philip and Matilda joined us. Will I ever forget the procession when as tho' upon his Bier my bright, active Drue was carried by six men with the kind ministering friend Gregory following down the hill across the Park, into the House, through the windows of the Saloon, and there laid down motionless![33]

Charlotte tended him with great care during the five years he was crippled. She paints a vivid picture of Drury sitting in the garden at Courteenhall in summer, wrapped in coloured shawls, Sir Charles, with his long white beard, near him, leaning on his staff, surrounded by the young men, women and children who frequently visited Drury to keep up his spirits. During these years, he never lost his enthusiasm for horses and was determined to hunt once more with the Pytchley at the earliest moment. By the end of the fifth year of his illness, Drury was able to join the meets in a carriage especially constructed for the purpose.[34]

After his recovery, he was not able to resume his law career and Drury settled into the life of being a country gentleman. During the late 1860s, he supervised the refurbishment and reconstruction of Pitsford House, or 'The Pit' as he called it. In December 1867, the building was finished. The fir poles in the garden were sold off and Drury discussed plans to provide an arbour on top of a hill for Charlotte.[35] The interior of the house too was now 'very comfortable' after its additions.[36] Drury also played an active part, as joint guardian with his mother, in the upbringing of the six young children of his late eldest brother, William, the eleventh baronet, who had died in 1865. Still a bachelor, he was able to devote himself to their welfare. He called in Dr William Barr, in January 1866, the skilful Northampton physician who had treated him during his illness, when two of the children had chicken pox. He frequently took the children in a wagonette to Brampton to see the Pytchley, describing it as 'a capital day for us all.' In February 1868, Drury arranged for the girls to be taken into Northampton to buy Valentines.[37] In the previous December, he wrote to Charlotte, who was abroad, describing how the children were being kept busy. 'The girls are in the village schoolroom making decorations for the Church and the boys are playing in the barn as it rains fast'.[38]

Drury married, at the age of forty seven, Louisa Nethercote, the second daughter of H.O. Nethercote of Moulton Grange. The Nethercotes were near neighbours and Louisa's father was a distinguished fellow member and historian of the Pytchley. Drury was some twenty three years older than Louisa and they had four children, a boy, Drury, and three daughters, Emily, Susan and Mary. His legal qualifications were usefully employed in the county, first as a Justice of the Peace from 1871 and then, in 1888, as Chairman of the Northamptonshire Divisional Bench.[39] Between 1875 and 1880, Drury was Honorary Secretary of the Pytchley[40] and he continued to hunt, though a fall almost resulted in another serious injury. His last public honour, and an acknowledgement of his services to the county, followed the setting up of the Northamptonshire County Council in January 1889, when he and the Duke of Grafton were unanimously elected as the first aldermen of the Council.[41] Drury died on 22 April 1891 at the age of sixty three and was buried at Courteenhall three days later.

*　　　*　　　*　　　*　　　*

Few Wakes have chosen the Civil Service as a career. One who did was Herwald Craufurd, the fourth son of Sir Charles, who entered Government service and was to achieve nationwide fame. Born in 1828, Herwald, the first member of the family to bear this name, did not make a promising start. He followed his brothers to Rugby in March 1842. From the beginning there were complaints of his behaviour and attitude. His tutor, C.T. Arnold, wrote despairingly to Charles in March 1844, 'Hopelessly, I cannot help thinking that you would be acting for his Interest as well as of those with whom he lives, to move him . . . I have given up all Hope of his Improvement here'.[42] Tait, both Herwald's headmaster and his uncle, was equally worried. He endorsed Arnold's concerns, stating that Herwald suffered from 'unconquerable idleness' and 'an insane love of talking which causes him to make no distinction between Chapel, School or any other place'.[43] In a letter to the boy's father, Tait suggested that a more rigorous regime at another institution might be beneficial 'both for his own sake, that he may have a fresh start, and for the sake of his brothers'.[44]

Entry to university was out of the question, but another rather unusual institution was chosen which helped in the formation of a maturer character. The East India College, commonly known as Haileybury, had been established in Hertfordshire in

1802 by the East India Company for the purpose of improving the quality of Civil Servants sent out to India.[45] As an institution of higher education, candidates were normally at least twenty one years of age and with a public school background. The College placed great importance on the need to produce an *esprit de corps* amongst its students. Teaching was of a high standard – its staff included T.R. Malthus and Sir James Mackintosh – and the course itself offered training in Oriental subjects, such as the languages and laws of India, as well as the 'history, customs and manners of the different Nations of the East'. During the College's 50 years' existence, almost 2,000 students graduated, of whom approximately 90 per cent went to India.[46]

Herwald was at Haileybury from 1849 to 1850 and in the following year joined the Bengal Civil Service. During the next seventeen years in India, he served first as an assistant magistrate, then as a magistrate and collector, in various places in Bengal. Herwald had now found his true niche. Writing from Chuprah in June 1855, he informed his father, 'You will be happy to hear that I have not only passed the examination but that out of nine who went up in Bengal, I was second and ran the first man close'.[47] He would in future be given more powers, which consisted of imposing fines of up to 200 rupees and imprisonment of up to a year. The drawbacks of the work were acknowledged but were not too serious. 'When the climate and the life we lead is taken into consideration,' he wrote, 'the bargain is certainly not on our side. However I am getting accustomed to it and I dare say some day shall be as prosy and as fond of talking shop as most of our men'.[48]

At the outbreak of the Indian Mutiny in May 1857, Wake was at Arrah, a small town in Bengal in the north-east of the country, where he was in charge of the district of Shahabad. The rising had been started by sepoy troops, and when the three native regiments stationed nearby at Dinapore mutinied, Koer Singh, a seventy five year old landed proprietor, much liked by the Europeans, persuaded them to join with others in attacking the small body of English people in Arrah. It was decided that, rather than abandon the city, a stand would be made in a previously fortified bungalow belonging to Mr Boyle, the district engineer of the railway company. Accordingly, on Sunday 26 July, the party moved in. It consisted of fifty members of the Sikh Police, with a water-carrier and a cook: the remaining fifteen were officials, amongst whom were a judge, surgeon, opium agents, collectors, and Herwald Wake. Quantities of grain and water had been laid in for the officials but, owing to shortage of time, there were only a few days' supply for the police, who made up the majority of the defenders.

The beleaguered party did not have long to wait. On Monday 27 July at 8.00 a.m the insurgents entered the town and attacked the bungalow from every side, keeping up a stream of fire during the whole day. Several assaults were made on the party with a range of weapons. As Herwald described it afterwards, 'They tried to starve us out, burn us out, smoke us out and blow us up, but the only thing they carried out continually was the firing, night and day'.[49] The rebels were now joined by the Station Guard of 150 men and thousands of Koer Singh's own men. The doors and windows of the bungalow were riddled with bullets, though only one man was wounded. Herwald afterwards recalled, 'I had made up my mind not to be taken alive, and after a long conversation as to its justifiability, had agreed with another man, that if possible, when we were overpowered, we should shoot each other at the same moment'.[50]

Two cannons throwing four pound shot were hauled by the enemy into position, and one was even placed on the roof completely commanding the inside of the bungalow. In Herwald's official report, he stated, 'Nothing but cowardice, want of unanimity, and only the ignorance of our enemies prevented our fortifications being brought down about our ears'. The defending group gradually became bolder as the siege advanced. As the grain ration was becoming monotonous, a sally was made at night by the Sikhs and four sheep were brought in for the hungry men. The water supply, which was in a precarious state, began to run out so a well, eighteen feet by four, was dug by the defenders in less than twelve hours.

The first British relief force sent out from Dinapore to Arrah in late July fell into an ambush and retreated with severe losses. It was agreed by the authorities that the besieged party at Arrah would have to be abandoned and left to its fate. Fortunately for them, Brevet-Major Vincent Eyre, Bengal Artillery, the hero of Kabul, at that moment arrived by steamer at Buxar, on the other side of the district, with forty European gunners and guns. Taking command of 150 soldiers of the 5th Fusiliers, Eyre and some other volunteers started for Arrah. On 13 August, they heavily defeated a much larger rebel force. The way to Arrah was now open. Herwald's reactions were typical:

> Some of the volunteers then rode to us with the news, and I jumped on one of their horses, and I had the jolliest ride I ever had in my life, to join the force and come in with them. I got a jolly cheer on my appearance, and a basin of men's soup and a bottle of beer (not before it was wanted) . . . then we marched in, and the 'detainees' came out rejoicing.[51]

The siege, which had lasted seven days against a force of several thousands, was over, and with hardly a casualty. As Herwald remarked, 'The whole thing was a miracle'.

Although Koer Singh's forces had been beaten, they had retreated to his stronghold at Jagdispur, in the jungle, and still presented a threat. Herwald admitted later that it was a 'foolhardy expedition', consisting of a force of 500 men, which set out to pursue Koer Singh's army.[52] Major Eyre put Herwald in command of his gallant Sikhs. Reaching the jungle on 12 August, the force engaged the enemy in a two hour hand-to-hand battle, during which many of the defenders were killed and wounded and the fort at Jagdispar was finally captured. Herwald conducted his part in the battle on a small mare, which he had bought on the spot, and was pleased that the animal remained calm though often out of its depth in the river and with bullets flying all around it. Herwald reflected later on his own temperament:

> I have been in situations of danger often but I was curious to know how I should feel in a situation where it was in my power to court, or to keep out of it, as I chose, and I was glad to find, that when heading one part of a force under a perfect shower of bullets, my only feeling was one of boisterous happiness. Verily, man is a destroying animal.[53]

A further example of his coolness under fire was the daily diary which he kept during the siege, written with a pencil on the wall of the bungalow.[54]

LD8
DIARY
KEPT ON THE WALLS OF THE BUNGALOW, AT ARRAH
BY H.C. WAKE, MAGISTRATE

We went into our fortified bungalow on the night of Sunday, the 26th of JULY, one jemadar, two havildars, two naiks and 45 privates, and Bhistie,* and cook, of Captain Rattray's Sikh Police Battalion; Mr. Littledale, judge; Mr. Coombe, officiating collector; Mr. Wake, officiating magistrate; Mr. Colvin, assistant; Dr. Hall, civil assistant surgeon; Mr. Field, sub-deputy opium agent; Mr. Anderson, his assistant; Mr. Boyle, district engineer to the railway company; Synd Azeem Oodein Hosein, deputy-collector; Mr. Dacosta, moonsiff; Mr. Godfrey, schoolmaster; Mr. Cook, officiating head clerk of the collectorate; Mr. Tait, secretary to Mr. Boyle; Messrs. Delpeiron & Hoyle, railway inspectors; and Mr. David Souza.

The police abandoned the town on the Sunday, and as we were wholly unable to estimate the force coming against us, we thought it right to remain in the station, trusting to Dinapore for relief.

JULY 27th

The insurgent Sepoys arrived in the morning, and all attacked us in force. They were joined by the Najebs† or some of them, and numbers of Koour Sing's men. The Sepoys have repeatedly declared that they were acting under Koour Sing's orders, and endeavoured to seduce to their side the Seikhs‡ who have hitherto behaved nobly, refusing to have anything to do with them, and shewing perfect obedience and discipline.

9 a.m. same day — The Najebs are firing on us with the rest.

JULY 28th

Two small cannons are brought to play upon the bungalow; they load them with hammered iron balls and brass door handles and such like: fired at us all day from behind their barricades, but could not get the range with the biggest, which seems to carry heavyish metal. The *little one* has done us no serious damage, hitherto only one man (a Seikh) wounded, but seriously, a ball in the head. The scoundrels skulked behind trees and walls, and Boyle's house, which, unfortunately, is within eighty yards (afterwards measured fifty,) so we cannot tell how many are hit.

JULY 29th, 7 a.m.

This morning they were up to something new; thousands are collected, probably the greater part villagers and disbanded Sepoys, collected by Koour Sing.

5 p.m. — No harm done; they can't touch the bungalow with the big gun; the skulls won't come within shot, though now and then one is knocked over by rifle shots.

11½ p.m. — Heard commencement of engagement between troops sent to our relief and the rebels.

DEFENDERS OF THE EMPIRE

JULY 30th.

About 5 a.m. one of the Seikhs sent to our relief came in and told us that only 300 Europeans and 90 Seikhs had been sent to our relief – God aid them! Our well under the lower story is nearly finished. The relief has evidently had to retire, but we hear, (from the Seikhs,) that artillery is coming. There are four feet of water in the well! N.B. – The well is about eighteen feet deep, and was dug within twelve hours. In the afternoon made a sally into the compound, and brought in some sheep, and two birds in cages, that had had neither food nor water for five days.

JULY 31st

The rebels have got the largest of the guns close up to the house, and fire on us, protected by the garden wall, (N.B. – Through a hole.) Several of the balls, round and cast iron, have struck the lower story, but, hitherto, have done no serious damage. The balls are about four pounds; how they do so little damage we cannot imagine. We have reason to apprehend that the Sepoys are mining us from the outhouses to the south. We have commenced a counter mine. The Seikhs are offered their lives and liberty if they hand over the judge, magistrate, and collectors – the ladies and children too!!! are not to be injured!!!!

SATURDAY, AUGUST 1st

No cannonade till 5½ p.m. Occasional small arms firing all day. No one injured, except one Seikh had the wind knocked out of him by the bricks displaced by a cannon shot. Several rebels supposed to have been killed by long shots. They are raising strong barricades on the roof of the opposite house, from which they are likely to give us serious annoyance, as they can see right into the upper verandah. The shaft of the counter mine has been sunk to the depth of about seven feet, and the gallery carried off towards the south, and there stopped, under the outer face of the wall. In the evening we were informed that it was the Soubadar's wookum!!! that all our lives were to be spared if we would give up our arms, and we should be sent to Calcutta! Firing from the big gun, (which they had placed on the roof of the big house,) kept up all night. Two alarms during the night, but finding us prepared on both occasions, no attack was made, except with musketry.

SUNDAY, AUGUST 2nd.

Guns fired three times between daybreak and 11 a.m. Little musketry; few rebels to be seen. Gallery progressing.

SUNDAY, AUGUST 2nd.

Major Eyre defeated the rebels; and on the 3rd we came out.

"Written with the stump of a pencil, on the wall, at any moment that could be snatched, in case we should be scragged."

HERWALD WAKE.

---

*Water carrier.   ‡Of Captain Rattray's Bengal police Battalion.
†An armed police corps, furnishing jail and the army guards to the civil station.

73. Herwald Craufurd Wake, CB (1828–1907), hero of Arrah, fourth son of Sir Charles Wake, 10th baronet

74. Freedom of the Borough of Northampton presented to Herwald Craufurd Wake, 2 August 1858

75. Arrival of 10th Sudanese Battalion and Egyptian Mounted Infantry, Suakin, Sudan, sketched by Richard Wake, 1888   *Inset* 76. Richard Wake (1865-88), artist, second son of Herwald Craufurd Wake, who died of wounds and was buried at Suakin, 7 December, 1888

187

Major Eyre highly praised Herwald in his dispatches for his part in the expedition.[55] After his efforts, Herwald recuperated at Buxar before returning to duty. He was given the freedom of the Borough of Northampton in 1858 in recognition of his gallantry and he was made a Commander of the Bath in 1860.[56] His exploits provided the basis for a three-part novel, *The Dilemma*, written by Sir George Chesney in 1876[57] and as late as 1901, a book entitled *Our Public Schools: Their Influence on English History*, recalls Herwald's prominent part in the siege of Arrah and its sequel.[58]

The links between the Sitwells and the Wakes were once more reinforced with the marriage in August 1860 of Herwald to his cousin, Lucy Charlotte Hurt Sitwell, the youngest daughter of the second baronet, Sir George Sitwell and his wife Susan. There were two sons of the marriage, Herwald, born 1862, and Richard Frederick, born in 1865. Richard, a gifted artist, and war correspondent for the *Graphic*, died on 7 December 1888 of a bullet wound received from enemy trenches whilst riding out to sketch the Gemaizeh Fort in the Sudan, and was buried at Suakin on the Red Sea.

Not surprisingly, the exertions of the Arrah affair had permanently weakened Herwald's constitution and he prematurely retired from the Indian Civil Service in 1868 at the age of thirty nine. Like his father, Herwald was a Liberal in politics. 'Stay a Whig by all means', wrote his sister Matilda in 1880, 'but you will be an extinct bird like the Dodo: there are nothing but Tories and Rads now'.[59] He had contemplated standing for Parliament in the 1868 election but decided that the costs involved would be far beyond his means. Nevertheless, as he wrote to his mother, Lady Charlotte, 'I am <u>most</u> anxious to commence a new career and will leave no stone unturned to do so'.[60] But by now something of a *malade imaginaire*, Herwald obtained no further employment. He lived on, uneventfully, for another thirty three years, and died at Freiberg, Germany, on 9 December 1901.

*   *   *   *   *

Herwald was not the only member of the family to serve in India. His younger brother, Edward Baldwin, known as Baldwin, the sixth son of Sir Charles, born in December 1833, had joined the Army at the age of eighteen. Like Herwald, he had chosen to serve in the East and was a Cornet in the 3rd European Light Cavalry in Bengal from 1853 and became a Lieutenant three years later. As he was stationed near Herwald, they met on more than one occasion in Calcutta. From his correspondence with his mother, Lady Charlotte, Baldwin emerges as a much more sentimental and sensitive person than his brother. In one letter, in which he asks for a copy of a recent painting of Lady Charlotte, he continues, 'The pillow you sent me I often look at and sometimes sleep upon it and everybody who sees it admires it very much'.[61]

His constitution was not strong and in 1857, he was temporarily invalided home from India.[62] Shortly after Baldwin's return, Sir Charles and Charlotte were holding a dinner party in London when the door burst open and Baldwin, flushed and excited, gave the first news of the outbreak of the Indian Mutiny. Baldwin considered it his duty to return there at once, but the doctor refused to allow him to do so.[63]

Baldwin's connections with India continued through his marriage on 26 January 1861 to Mary, second daughter of Ross Donnelly Mangles of Woodbridge, Suffolk, a member of the Council in India. She had been born in India in 1831. Baldwin was posted back to India after their marriage. Two sons, Gerald and Philip, and two daughters, Mildred and Ethel, were born there, but shortly after the birth of Ethel, in September 1868, they left for England. Mary died on board ship in the Red Sea on 8 December and was buried at sea. Two years later at Moulton, Baldwin married Ellen Mary Nethercote, eldest daughter of H.O. Nethercote. It will be recalled that Drury had married Ellen's younger sister in 1874; thus two brothers married two sisters. On their returning to India, a daughter, Mary Charlotte, was born at Lucknow in May 1872. Baldwin and Ellen left India for the last time shortly afterwards: three more daughters, Henrietta, Dorothy and Chattie, the latter named after her grandmother, were born in England.

Baldwin was promoted to the rank of Captain on his appointment to the 21st Hussars in July 1862. By 1875, he had been in the Army for twenty three years and was now the senior Captain of his regiment. He was aggrieved that the Government had broken faith with officers, late of the Indian Army, who had volunteered for the British Army on the matter of promotion. He urged his Uncle Archie, now Archbishop of Canterbury, to use his influence with Gathorne-Hardy, Secretary of State for War, and the Duke of Cumberland, Commander-in-Chief of the Army.[64] Matters moved quickly. Two months later, in July 1876, Baldwin was gazetted as Brevet-Major, and in the following year, December 1877, as a full Major. Six months later he was promoted to Lieutenant-Colonel, 21st Hussars.[65] But Baldwin was not to enjoy his new status for long. Never a good sleeper, he was in the habit of drinking from a bottle of hairwash, containing chloroform, before retiring to bed. Whilst staying at his father-in-law's on 6 August 1883, Baldwin misjudged the amount of the liquid and died that evening. He was forty nine.[66]

*   *   *   *   *

Two of Sir Charles and Charlotte's sons, Philip Augustus and Archibald Emilius, sought adventure in Australia. Archibald, the tenth child and youngest boy, became a sheep farmer in Queensland; he died, unmarried, aged twenty eight on 18 June 1871.[67] Philip Augustus, the fifth son, born in France in August 1830, led a full and more adventurous life. There is a delightful watercolour drawing of him at Courteenhall when he was about seventeen, in which he is shown standing beside a post and rail fence with a gun under his arm. Philip had fair hair and blue eyes and a frank and open expression.

He attended a school at Chenies, Buckinghamshire.[68] and sailed for Australia on 1 August 1848 after dining on board ship with his brother, Drury, at Portsmouth. On his nineteenth birthday, 20 August, he wrote in his Diary, 'I pray Almighty God I may meet all my Dear Family one happy day and to part no more'.[69] At the end of the month whilst on the forecastle, a fellow passenger next to Philip stepped backwards, caught his foot on a rope and was drowned. Philip noted, 'Nothing but the rail saved me from going

189

over too. How wonderful are the ways of God'.[70] Arriving in Australia, he spent several months in Melbourne, where he was very happy with his new life and his surroundings.

For the whole of 1850, Philip helped a friend on a cattle station, though he found time to go turkey shooting, possuming and participating in kangaroo hunts. On his twentieth birthday, Philip received a long letter from his father 'proposing a partner for me who I am afraid will not answer. I am very sorry as his heart seemed set on it'.[71] The work was very arduous: it consisted of rounding up, cutting, branding and spaying cattle, some of which were very wild. On one very hot day, 27 October 1850, no fewer than 1,100 sheep were dipped. Examining his future prospects earlier in the year, Philip admitted that they were not bright. 'I wish', he wrote, 'some kind person would leave me a couple of thousand pounds. How I would bless their memory'.[72] Matters, however, did temporarily improve. By the following year, he had entered into partnership with two friends, renting a station at Janevale, by the River Loddon, between Ballarat and Bendigo, capable of containing upwards of 30,000 sheep. But this venture proved to be a financial worry. In November 1851, he recorded, 'I got my allowance from home a few days ago and am very much obliged to my Father for being so punctual as it has set me well on my legs again, as we shall get nothing from this station this year at all'.[73]

By chance, Philip now found himself in the centre of a momentous event in Australian history – the discovery of gold. In February 1851, it had first been found near Bathurst in New South Wales, but the fields had proved to be disappointing to prospectors. However on 9 August the same year some gold in huge quantities was found at Ballarat, some sixty miles from the then small town of Melbourne. In many cases it lay on the surface in nuggets, varying in size from a few ounces to a solid block of over 184 pounds in weight.[74] Towns such as Melbourne and Geelong were soon deserted as the gold rush got underway. One lady who visited the diggings at Bendigo observed:

> Many – perhaps nine-tenths – of the diggers are honest industrious men, desirous of getting a little there as a stepping-stone to independence elsewhere; but the other tenth is composed of outcasts and transports – the refuse of Van Diemen's Land – men of the most depraved and abandoned characters, who have sought and gained the lowest abyss of crime, and who would a short time ago have expiated their crimes on a scaffold. They generally work or rob for a space, and when well stocked with gold, retire to Melbourne for a month or so, living in drunkenness and debauchery.[75]

An official report on the social conditions prevailing in the Victorian gold fields drew attention to the influx of people from many countries 'met together in a wild tract of broken forested country . . . under such strong inducements to cupidity, disorder and crime, the imagination is free and unrestrained to picture the extent to which crime may, however improbable, prevail in secret without the possibility of discovery or chance of detection'.[76]

Philip records in his Diary on 26 September 1851 that the landlord of his local inn showed him 'a beautiful sample' of gold. Despite this he was never tempted to join the prospectors, being content to occupy himself with the farm. The last entry in his Diary in 1852 reads, 'The diggings flourish. Cay [his partner] has gone there to try and sell some of the sheep. Very hot all day'.

As the diggings advanced nearer to the farm, the latter became almost untenable. Philip abandoned his work and joined the Gold Mounted Police with the rank of Lieutenant. The force's main task at first was to deliver consignments of gold from the sites to the strong rooms of local banks, where it was then collected by the owners. It was dangerous work as robberies and ambushes of gold convoys were a frequent occurrence. One particular instance was the robbery of an escort from the M'Ivor diggings in July 1853, when eleven armed bushrangers shot the police escort and escaped with the gold; the robbers were subsequently captured and the gold was recovered. Philip may have been on duty in the district, for he subsequently wrote to *The Times* on the affair.[77] Shortly after this, he was obliged to return to England having contracted ophthalmia which endangered his health. He made a good recovery and, determined to enter public life in Australia, set himself a course of reading books and official publications which would stand him in good stead: these included Blue Books on Australian Colonies, de Tocqueville's *La Démocratie en Amerique*, Lewis's works on the Colonies ('dull but useful') and J.S. Mill's *Principles of Political Economy*, 'most of these to be thoroughly mastered'.[78]

The journey back to Australia in November 1854 was a very uncomfortable one. After seven weeks out of Plymouth the ship had only reached Cape Horn. A sail was almost lost and though the ship was well armed against privateers – it carried besides two cannons, many muskets, pikes and cutlasses – all the armaments were in a rusty condition. Philip's attitude towards sea voyages was very different from that of his elder brother, Charles, then a Commander in the Navy. In a letter to his parents in November Philip wrote, 'This is the most miserable way of passing one's existence I ever came across. I can't settle to anything now; how on earth people ever come to be sailors I can't say'.[79]

Philip soon discovered that Melbourne was a greatly changed place from that of a year before. The European invasion had gathered impetus and the town's population had trebled in three years.[80] Moreover, the Gold Mounted Police Service had been reduced in numbers and with totally different grades; as he expressed it, the ranks of the Mounted Police were crowded with gentlemen who had 'gone to the wall' in the vain hope of making their fortunes at the diggings. Philip now searched for other suitable work. Sir Charles, who considered that his son had qualities to offer the public service, was able to arrange for Philip to meet the Lieutenant-Governor of New South Wales, Sir William Denison.[81] The interview took place in Sydney in May 1856. Although Denison was sympathetic he immediately dashed any hopes of government employment. In desperation, Philip asked his father, 'What am I to do? Can you think it right for a man with £400 in his pocket to settle afresh in a country where as many thousands would hardly suffice if he had them? I feel so loth to risk the small remnant of my money in a place where every speculation has turned out ill'.[82] He made one more attempt at renting a cattle station, but without success. He wrote home, 'The heat is fearful here and being very fat it tells on me'.[83]

191

Philip left Australia and in April 1859 was appointed as assistant superintendent of police in Mauritius in the Indian Ocean. Over sixty years later the Inspector-General under whom Philip served recalled an incident of the time:

> His name was Philip A. Wake. He knocked up the Detective Inspector at 3 o'clock one morning, just as the man had gone to sleep, to see if he ever went to bed. He got the name, in consequence, of Philip awake.[84]

His health had greatly deteriorated and by the following year he was back in England, dangerously ill, and he came to Courteenhall. Sir Charles arranged for Philip to be in the care of Dr Barr, who was also attending Drury there.[85] Convalescence was slow and Philip was now a permanent invalid. To pass away the time, he wrote a very lengthy and badly-written novel[86] entitled *Was She Right?*, based on his Australian experiences in the Gold Mounted Police. Attempts to have it published were unsuccessful.[87] In his Diary, he complained often of 'the blue devils' which were around him; further suffering had resulted from a blow received whilst commanding a troop of the Mounted Police. Now in constant pain, Philip went to Nice, where he died on 5 December 1863 at the age of thirty three. A memorial tablet, with a touching inscription, was placed by his mother on the south aisle wall of Courteenhall Church.

*   *   *   *   *

Of all the sons of Sir Charles and Charlotte, without doubt the one that caused the most concern was their eldest, William. He was born at Tapton, Derbyshire, on 20 May 1823 and christened in the parish church at Eckington. According to a family anecdote, William started his existence by kicking a Bible off his mother's lap before he was born.[88] He was sent to a small boarding school at Bath at the age of fourteen, when the family were at Powick. His 'little negligences and irregularities and want of discipline' were commented upon by the proprietor in the following year.[89] In June 1838 he entered Rugby when Dr Thomas Arnold was headmaster,[90] but, as with his younger brother Drury, his stay was not a happy one.

Shortly before he was eighteen years old, William joined the Army as Second Lieutenant in the 1st Battalion of the Rifle Brigade. His career started inauspiciously. Quickly falling into debt when he was in Ireland and at one stage arrested on account of it,[91] William sent a Dublin tailor's bill for £211, and two others of £100 and £65 to his grandfather, Old Sir William, for payment. Charles told his son that Sir William 'feels so indignant at your reckless extravagance that he declines to have anything to do with you or your concerns'. Charles urged him, 'Give up your boy's habits; try to live like a man if you can instead of the wild boys of your Regiment. Give up your foolish practice of asking to eat dinner and drink champagne that <u>you</u> do not pay for but which I <u>now do</u>!'.[92] These promptings were in vain; after William was posted to Malta, a family friend there reported that William had admitted to him that he was 'very anxious to leave the army, as he found himself unable to resist the temptations in it'. He had been in trouble several times and was discovered in a state of drunkenness in the streets on more than one occasion.[93]

William, for his part, admitted the 'enormity of my folly', promising to mend his ways, especially to avoid getting into debt.[94] A few days later, he left Malta for Corfu with his regiment and it was there on 11 April that his Commanding Officer informed Charles of the necessity of removing his son from the Army because of his behaviour; he was also once more in debt.[95] He left Corfu on 6 May via Malta and Gibraltar for England. Ten days later Charles heard from a friend that William had become engaged to a girl whilst in Malta, Rose Low, whose stepfather was a naval surgeon with the Mediterranean Fleet. William, he told Charles, was considered one of the family and added whimsically, 'I presume you do not wish to be a Grandfather yet'.[96] Charles acted quickly. Rose's mother was informed that the match was impossible, as William's future prospects were so uncertain that he was not likely to be in a position for many years to marry.[97] On 21 July, William, writing from Pitsford, returned the photograph of his former fiancée to her and the matter was closed.

William was now twenty and showed little sign of settling into a career. His behaviour, present and past, also caused his father to despair. Charles penned a lengthy letter at this time to his son, who was about to leave the family home, recalling William's history. He pointed out that complaints had constantly been made by those who had had authority over him, ranging from his preparatory school head and Dr Arnold to Colonel Buller, his commanding officer. His faults were listed: thoughtlessness, carelessness, self-conceit, disrespect and an abominable temper. Charles had previously discussed matters with William after his return from Malta; William had resisted all criticism and, in his father's words 'proclaimed every body a fool but yourself, set public opinion at defiance and now send every body to the Devil (to use your own expression)'. Religion too had long been abandoned. Though William's finances were in better shape, Charles stated, 'I have noticed the habit of buying things unnecessarily in Northampton'. Charles, from observation, had also been distressed to find that 'more than two glasses of Wine have the same effect on your constitution as a bottle on most others. The same applies to Tobacco . . . On your head now be the consequences, if you exceed in either the above articles'.[98]

It would be reasonable to conclude that these rebukes, coupled with a promise by Charles never to repay any more of his son's debts, the family home forbidden at Christmas and stays of only up to ten days at other times allowed, would have ended in the parting of ways. Instead, and somewhat surprisingly, Charles agreed to William's request to be sent to London to study law, with financial assistance provided by Old Sir William. Accordingly, payment of rent for William's chambers, at 53 Lincoln's Inn Fields, was made for a year to 25 June 1844, when William came of age and would be in possession of his own income.[99] The venture into law was a failure and by July, William wrote to his brother, 'Bulldog' Charles, 'The truth is I am desperately in want of money at present as I started in debt and to retrieve that have got into trouble and shall always be in difficulties till I can raise a sum to clear off everything'.[100] William, like his brother, was very fond of the sea, especially yachting. It was for this reason that he had recently bought a house at 24 Bugle Street in Southampton which provided a base for the sport. In early August, William again wrote to his brother, hinting at more serious matters: 'I now need a friend's advice most and I have a deal to say to you and more than you think'.[101] Charles, on receipt of this letter, told his mother who went to see William in Southampton. There, William informed her that he was to be married in the following month.

His intended bride was Margaret Ann Fricker, daughter of Henry Fricker, a purser in the service of the P. & O. Shipping Company. Henry Fricker had married Margaret Nouchette at All Saints Church, Southampton, on 23 December 1824. She was the daughter of a French planter living in Haiti, in the West Indies. During an insurrection of slaves in 1800, both her parents were killed, but Margaret herself, then aged two, was saved by her nurse taking her to the harbour where the infant found safety in an English ship. A young man on board named Henry Robinson took her back to England, where she was raised by his parents in a comfortable house in London.

Henry Fricker was a man of many parts. Born to the son of a furrier in the parish of St. George's, Hanover Square, London, in March 1804, he went into business as a silk mercer and furrier in Southampton, later becoming a draper. He was a member of the town council from 1843 to 1846 and then went to sea.[102] Before this, Fricker had become proprietor of the Star Hotel[103] in Southampton which his wife Margaret managed whilst he was away. It was probably here that William met the young Margaret Fricker. Margaret was described by one of William's friends as 'an amiable young woman, very right minded, sensible, and perfectly free from affectation'. and 'one that I think will guide him discreetly if he is to be governed, and he seems most affectionately fond of her'.[104] The eldest of five children, she had received a good education and was an accomplished musician, having qualified as a teacher. Further, her demeanour was 'far above what might have been expected in the station of life in which she had moved'. As a future mother, Margaret was, in his friend's opinion, 'not unsuitable to the office of training up of children'.[105]

On receiving news of his son's impending marriage, Charles Wake took immediate steps to stop it. A doctor provided a medical certificate on 12 September 1844 which stated:

> Mr William Wake is now labouring under a state of mind bordering on Delirum Tremens combined also with an imbecility and incertitude of act and purpose which renders him at this moment wholly incapable to judge for himself on so important a subject as his marriage but which imbecility will, in my opinion, justify his friends in the adoption of all such measures as prudence and justice would suggest.[106]

Charles followed this with a letter to his son justifying his conduct, adding, 'I trust the day will come when you will be able to see how truly I have acted for your interests'.[107] In reply, William emphasized 'the very great and terrible pain . . . your late measure has caused'.[108] Six days later, on 21 September 1844, in spite of the obstacles placed in their path, William and Margaret were married at Southampton.

Even before the marriage, the relations between William and his father had further deteriorated on the question of family finance. William had reached his majority in June 1844. As the Wake estates were entailed upon him, it was thought desirable to put out of his power the opportunity of squandering them. A deed of settlement was drawn up guaranteeing William an annuity of £300, to be doubled on the death of his grandfather, Old Sir William, in return for consenting to divest himself of his powers under the entail. William readily agreed to this arrangement.[109] On 13 June, all the parties involved signed the deed of settlement at Courteenhall; but six days later, Charles received a letter from William's solicitor requesting a copy of both the deed of settlement and of the title deeds of the estates. This was refused on the grounds that such a move was 'for the sole purpose of raising by extravagant means Money on his reversionary Interest'.

It was clear that Charles' assessment of the situation was correct. He soon learnt that William was intending to raise money in order to buy a yacht jointly with his solicitor.[110] Charles' action in attempting to stop William's marriage had exacerbated the situation. William now instructed his father to communicate with him only through his solicitors and threatened to bring a lawsuit over the deed of settlement. By January 1845, he was again in debt having borrowed £1,000, for which he was to repay the colossal sum of £6,000 when he came into possession of the property.[111]

Probably through Margaret's good influence, however, William was soon making the first tentative moves towards reconciliation with his father. An intermediary suggested that if William could be forgiven, he would drop the lawsuit, provided a financial settlement could be made for his wife in the event of his death. In return, William and Margaret would have no further dealings with the Frickers and would move into Northamptonshire. As Charles' friend put it, 'I feel no hesitation in stating my belief that your son, William who to you and his family was "lost", will, like the prodigal son in the scripture, be "found".'[112]

Old Sir William, now nearing the end of his life, wrote to the family solicitor that though William might obtain the money to fight a High Court case 'neither myself nor my son have any. A very expensive Chancery suit in the present state of my heart and nerves would, I am convinced, shortly kill me'.[113] On 23 August 1845, writing from Boulogne to his father, the young William mentioned that he too would find it impossible to pay the costs of a law suit. William proferred an olive branch: 'I trust that you will not be offended at my taking what appears to be the most straightforward way of avoiding future misunderstanding by writing direct to you, and I sincerely hope by so doing that all will be satisfactorily settled to both parties, and that this is the last communication I shall have to make with you on law matters'.[114] The reason given by William for the prolonging of the business was that his 'being once in the power of the lawyers, I had no opportunity to get free'.[115] By November, William had accepted the new settlement, which included an annuity for Margaret of £800 on his death.

That same month, their first child, Hereward William, was born; he lived for only eight months. Shortly afterwards, William expressed his anxiety about Margaret's state of health. He wrote to his father, 'I may rely on your kind sympathy as a one time friend and though estranged, but still my father and also father of my dear brothers and sisters for your kind and good wishes for myself and my innocent, as far as regards herself, harmless wife'.[116] William was still in debt. He had invested heavily in mining shares and in February 1846 learnt that he had been cheated out of the sum of £1,100.

However, some good had come out of it. As a friend wrote, 'He is now becoming economical. I have succeeded in breaking him of taking spirits in any shape . . . I really think in about six months he will be quite another man'.[117]

Old Sir William had died a few weeks before and Charles succeeded as the tenth baronet. William and Margaret went to Jersey where, in June 1847, he was arrested and imprisoned for debt. For some unknown reason, he had wanted a human skeleton and bought one from a doctor but failed to pay for it.[118] A regular visitor to William in prison, a medical man, informed his mother, 'The dreadful state of things into which he is plunged will soon completely fit him for an Asylum. He is not even allowed a cell to himself and the set and class on whom he has been thrust are truly revolting'.[119] Thanks to the kind act of a total stranger, who stood security for him, William was released on bail at the end of June.[120] He was later returned to the gaol, but Margaret plotted an escape. William asked for a piano to be brought into the prison but, being dissatisfied with it, declared that it must be sent back. William was hidden in the piano case when it was taken out of the prison. Margaret had meanwhile prepared detailed plans. A sailing ship was waiting off a lonely part of the coast and he arrived safely back in England.[121] Astonishingly, William wrote an account of his adventures, entitled 'My Escape and Imprisonment', which was published in a contemporary periodical.

Settling in France, William and Margaret returned to Southampton for the birth of their second son and the future twelfth baronet, Herewald Craufurd Wake, on 19 July 1852, so that he might have British citizenship.[122] Previously they had had two daughters, Amy Margaret, born 1847, and Frances Josephine, born 1849, both born and privately christened at Vimoutiers, near Argentan, Normandy.[123] In 1855, the family was living at Rue Madame, Paris, where their third daughter, Lucy Helena, was born. Between 1855 and 1860, they resided at Maison des Portes, about two miles outside Honfleur. Archibald James was born there in 1856, as was their fourth son, Charles Baldwin, two years later. William and Margaret were now reconciled with his father and mother. The question of William being divested of his powers under the entail was not pursued. On the death of Sir Charles, William would come into possession of the family estates.

The marriage had proved a happy one and William was reluctant to be away from Margaret. In 1856, when his mother was staying with Catharine and Archie Tait after the death of five of their children, William was a companion at Courteenhall for Charles. From there, he wrote:

> I will look after my father, and do all I can to make him feel your absence less, but I must beg of you to not to delay your absence longer than a week. It is now about two months since I have seen my dear wife, and I intended going to see her the beginning of next week. I cannot of course leave my father alone, so have pity upon me and do not keep me away from my wife longer than necessary.[124]

As a family man, William enjoyed playing games with his children. Some years after William's death, his brother Charles recalled the former's skill in charades, particularly in acting the character of Pecksniff.[125]

After over a decade abroad, William and Margaret settled in 1860 at 8 Carlton Hill East, St. John's Wood, London, residing there for the remainder of his life. Their fifth son, Thomas Herbert Drury was born in 1862. Sir Charles, his father, had died on 23 February 1864 and William now became the eleventh Wake baronet. That summer, Sir William came with his family to Courteenhall. It was not a happy time as he was bored with the country. Margaret, who loved the house and the estate, considered it to be very beautiful. 'Twould be all right if you were a bullock', Sir William is purported to have replied.[126] Sir Charles had anticipated that his son would not wish to reside at Courteenhall. In his will, made shortly before his death, he offered the furniture to William at the modest sum of £1,500 'with a view to facilitate my said son William letting the Mansion house at Courteen Hall'.[127]

Had Sir William long survived, the fate of Courteenhall would have been uncertain. Soon after becoming the eleventh baronet, he had marked every tree to be felled on the estate in order to pay money lenders. However before this action could be carried out, Sir William died on his yacht at Southampton on 13 April 1865 at the age of forty two and was buried at Courteenhall. He had been baronet for thirteen months. Margaret, his widow, remained in London, surviving only until the following year, 12 December 1866, when she was buried alongside her husband at Courteenhall.

* * * * *

The colourful lives led by the sons of Sir Charles and Charlotte Wake were typical of many other early Victorian families. Two of them, Charles 'Bulldog' Wake and Herwald Crauford Wake, in different parts of the world, played prominent parts in the defence of the Empire whilst a third, Drury, made his contribution by his famous ride from Constantinople to Belgrade shortly before the outbreak of the Crimean War. A fourth, Edward, also served his country in the Indian Army. It was ironic that the eldest son, William, the eleventh baronet, was the least notable of them all, leaving on his death an uncertain future for Courteenhall.

14
High Victorian Courteenhall:
The Twelfth Baronet

THE DEATH OF SIR CHARLES, THE TENTH BARONET, AND
Sir William, the eleventh baronet, within the space of just over a year caused a number
of problems. Courteenhall had not been occupied by Sir William so in April 1865 the
house stood empty. Herewald Craufurd, Sir William's eldest surviving son, became the
twelfth baronet when he was still only twelve years old and it was necessary to let the
House until he came of age.

All the furniture at Courteenhall had been sold after Sir William's death, and the
tenants were expected to provide their own.[1] A family called Willis rented Courteenhall
for two years[2] and in 1868 it was let to Clement and Florence Cottrell-Dormer of
Rousham, Oxfordshire. During the hot summer, a baby girl, Dorothy Mary, was born in
June but died in August; she is buried in the churchyard at Courteenhall. Two more
children, a boy and girl, were also born during the family's tenancy.[3] Clement became a
Justice of the Peace and Deputy-Lieutenant of the County and hunted with the Grafton
and the Pytchley. He also first began there his herd of beef Shorthorns, bought from the
Howards of Clapham Park, Bedfordshire.

In her *Reminiscences*, Florence noted, 'The Wakes came over from Pitsford
occasionally, and we always got on comfortably with them'.[4] The Cottrell-Dormers
were friendly too with the Wentworths at nearby Stoke Bruerne Park, which, related
Florence, was said to be haunted by a white rabbit, 'a very harmless ghost', and they also
stayed with the Graftons at Wakefield Lodge. Courteenhall became the social centre for
the duration of the Northampton Races. In December 1874, Clement inherited
Rousham from his father and it was decided to give up Courteenhall in the following
autumn after a stay of eight years. Florence recorded the occasion:

> We left dear old Courteenhall on a hot September day. We had been very happy
> there, for a rented house has its charms; you only have to keep in order what you
> rent, not all the gates you go through on the estate, or the hedges you see that
> want repairing, or the cottages – all that is nothing to you when you are only a
> tenant. We sold all the furniture we didn't want, and took away all we were
> attached to. Two of the Wakes came over to our last scanty luncheon before
> leaving for the train.[5]

See Appendix A – Family Tree XV. Notes and References pages 418–422

During this time, the new Wake baronet, who was still a minor, completed his formal education. Herewald soon showed signs of his unusual character: he could be unpredictable, often amusing and independent-minded. From an early age, he was keen on hunting. When he was eleven, he wrote to his grandmother, Lady Charlotte Wake, after the purchase of a new pony, 'We went out foxhunting with the hounds and grounded the fox in front of Salcey Forest . . . My new pony is a spinner; he did everthing to get me off and even buck-jumped, but he never made me lose a stirrup'.[6]

Shortly afterwards, he was sent to a preparatory school, Wellesley House, at Twickenham. The headmaster considered that it was essential for Herewald to be thoroughly grounded in Latin and Greek, and the following course was set for him: Henry 1st Latin Book, Bradley Exercises, Greek Delectus, Greek Grammar (verbs), Latin Grammar (syntax) and Evans 1st verse book. Herewald, who admired his Uncle 'Bulldog' Charles, wanted to join the Navy. With that objective in mind and disliking the school routine, he and another boy ran away. They spent the night at Banbury but the manager of the hotel, who was suspicious, locked them in their room. They managed to escape but soon after they were caught, and returned to Twickenham.[7]

Herewald settled back into school routine. He told Grandmother Wake, 'I am getting on pretty nicely in Classics. I don't do much else except in Arithmetic and algebra. Of the latter I don't see the use except that in a higgledy piggledy sort of a maze of brackets, plusses and minuses, you can prove that everything is equal to everything and that black is white – at least that is all I can make out of it at present'.[8] For a brief period Herewald attended a crammer at Turvey, Bedfordshire, which prepared boys for the Navy. During the summer vacation, he spent part of the time with his guardian, the Reverend Frederick Thursby, Rector of Abington, Northampton,[9] from where he informed his mother, 'I have now decided to give up the Navy altogether and go to Eton to learn that which is necessary for me'.[10] Herewald's sensitive nature was combined with a maturity beyond his years. A month after his father's death, he was aware that Charlotte Wake had never come to terms with her son's marriage to Margaret Fricker. 'I am going to tell you something which is strictly private', he wrote to his grandmother, 'so do not tell anyone – this is it':

> When I was with Mama she would always be ill and very unhappy after any of the letters you sent her, for she seems to read them on the wrong side. So I am sure it would make her much happier if you wrote and said somebody told me you did not like the tone of my letters and say you will not talk about any more painful subjects to her . . . Please do not take offence at this letter.[11]

Herewald's touching words made an impression on Charlotte, for a few weeks after, Margaret wrote to her mother-in-law, 'Thank you for your letter received this morning. I do very much like you to write to me as you used to do'.[12]

By the following year, 1866, Herewald had made sufficient progress to be accepted for Eton. But his restless spirit led him to run away once more, only a month after starting at the school. Craufurd Tait, Charlotte's nephew, gave her the news that Herewald had been found at Fulham Palace, Bishop Tait's residence, and had been

77. Eton College by W. E. Harris, 1874

78. Eton Badge, given by Sir Herewald Wake, 12th baronet, aged 17, to Catherine St. Aubyn, 1869

79. St. Michael's Mount, Cornwall, c.1880, the home of the St. Aubyns

returned to Eton, 'though he will, I am afraid, have to be whipped as that is the punishment always given for running away', adding, 'but it will not hurt him much'.[13]

His mother, Lady Margaret, died in December 1866 and Charlotte and his Uncle Drury at Pitsford looked after Herewald's welfare. In the following May, Drury reported after one of Herewald's vacations that 'Amy [Herewald's youngest sister] had a most happy letter from Harry. Eton is certainly answering most thoroughly to him. Short holidays, however, I think are better than long ones ... I was sorry for the boy as he had so very little hunting, but it was a very good thing in every other respect'.[14] It was during this time at Eton that Herewald began to develop a special talent which was a source of great pleasure to him in later years. His tutor, Edward 'Badger' Hale, wrote to Charlotte:

> He is certainly a clever boy and has a talent for literature, at present of a light kind, I fear, but as it shows itself chiefly in original composition, I encourage it as much as possible. To write even burlesques or parodies requires some thought. What I think he most requires to be cautioned against is acquiring a reputation for being singular.[15]

Herewald was long remembered by other Etonians for his famous fight with a tall, strong boy called Ridley. Typically, Herewald's sense of justice was outraged when he found Ridley, nicknamed 'the World', bullying a small boy; he stopped it and challenged his opponent to a fight. Herewald, who at the time was described as 'shortish, thickset and clumsy' was nevertheless a good boxer. The school did not allow bare fist fighting, but after more than one attempt, a contest took place behind the old Fives courts on the Dorney Road. A contemporary later wrote, 'I am thankful to say that I did not attend the show. But I happened to see the World conducted back to his Dames' house and the spectacle was gruesome. The punishment inflicted had been very considerable, and I do not think the World appeared in public for a fortnight. The bruising baronet was almost untouched'.[16]

*   *   *   *   *

Whilst Herewald was still at school, his Uncle Charles and Aunt Emma St. Aubyn had invited him to stay with them at Devonport. There he met Catherine, Emma's younger sister by sixteen years. Catherine, or Kitty as she was called, had stayed at Courteenhall as a young girl.[17] Herewald instantly fell in love with this pretty, petite and intelligent girl and kept in touch with her. Herewald, also known as Hal or Harry in the family, invited Kitty, aged seventeen, to the Eton v. Harrow cricket match at Lord's. There he gave her a silver badge with the Eton coat of arms and a pale blue ribbon which is still preserved at Courteenhall.

Kitty's family, the St. Aubyns, had been connected with the ancient monastery, later castle, of St. Michael's Mount, Cornwall, since the sixteenth century.[18] The baronetcy of the first creation became extinct on the death of Sir John St. Aubyn, the fifth baronet, in 1839. He was a man of wide interests; as a Whig politician, he represented three Cornish boroughs as a Member of Parliament between 1784 and

1812. Sir John was also an early collector of fossils and minerals and was elected Fellow of the Society of Antiquaries in 1783 and Fellow of the Royal Society in 1797.[19] The Cornish painter, John Opie, was one of his friends. Sir John married Juliana Vinnicombe, by family tradition the daughter of a blacksmith of Marazion, near St. Michael's Mount, but not until after all their fifteen children were born.[20] Kitty's father, Edward, the fourth son of Sir John, was a barrister, and succeeded to his father's estates; for political services he was created a baronet in July 1866. Sir Edward St. Aubyn's wife was Emma, daughter of General William Knollys, and they had five sons and three daughters, Emma who married Charles 'Bulldog' Wake, Juliana, who died a spinster, and Kitty.

In 1870, at the age of eighteen, Herewald left Eton. He made a tour of the world in 1872–3, accompanied by a young doctor and lifelong friend, Francis (later Sir Francis) Lovell, who became an eminent specialist in tropical diseases.

It was on his way home from the world tour that stopping in Italy Harry and his friend Lovell met up with Lady St. Aubyn, recently widowed, who was accompanied much to Harry's delight, by two of her daughters, Juliana and Kitty. Harry proposed to Kitty on Isola Bella, Lake Maggiore, and was accepted. On his return to England, Harry sent her Northamptonshire news in his frequent letters. One splendid occasion was the double celebration of his own twenty first birthday and the announcement of his engagement to Kitty on 19 July 1873 when the Cottrell-Dormers generously placed Courteenhall at the Wake family's disposal in order to give a party for the cottagers and tenants. Harry wrote an account of the day's events in typically whimsical style:

> At half past twelve I marched up the steps into the Hall door, which was prettily decorated with the following:
>
> **Long live Sir Herewald Wake**
>
> My Grandmother and Aunt Tilly burst into tears and the band struck up discordant noises ... I made a neat and touching speech, in turn reflecting on the good feeling which has always existed between my family and the people of Courteenhall and how I should endeavour to give equal cause with my forebears for its lasting continuance. This, my maiden speech, was made on a very empty stomach, so directly we repaired to the house and had a splendid feed. There we observed the butler to be very drunk and he dextrously poured a gallon of claret cup all over me ... After tea I repaired to the Housekeeper's room and delivered another neat speech to the tenants, telling them in a few well chosen words that they were all angels in plain clothes and it was the sole object and ambition of my life to imitate the stirling excellence which they possessed. This went down well and old John Robinson, the oldest farm tenant on the estate said, 'Dang it. I loave him' ... At 10.30 p.m. we started for home [Pitsford] I driving back in a dog cart.[21]

Harry's aunt, Josephine, also wrote to Kitty after the party, though in a more serious vein:

80. Sir Herewald Wake and Catherine St. Aubyn, photographed on their engagement, 19 July 1873

I wish you could have seen Harry, for it must have increased your love for him. He was such a dear boy, and I think he realized the responsibility which had come upon him. Grandmama proposed your health as a very pretty and a very charming young lady, who would come to be another Lady Wake, and when there had been a hearty cheer, an emphatic voice was heard, 'I hope she'll come soon', and we hope it too, heartily.[22]

Kitty and Harry were married in the following year on 14 April 1874 at St. George's, Hanover Square, with his great uncle Archbishop Tait officiating; he was twenty one and she twenty two years of age.[23] The couple left on the first stage of their honeymoon in a carriage pulled by four horses, with two postilions. Unfortunately, the driver was involved in an accident as they were leaving London and they were thrown out of the carriage. Muddy and dishevelled, they finished the journey in a cart drawn by one horse. After spending the first night at a hotel in Weybridge, Surrey (lamb cutlets and rhubarb tart for supper, Kitty recalled sixty six years later),[24] they stayed with friends near Ascot, then drove down to Cornwall, where they visited the St. Aubyns. Guilsborough Grange, north of Northampton, was taken for six months, their neighbours at the Hall being the Dowager Lady Spencer and her stepdaughter, Lady Sarah Spencer. The next three months were spent in London at Chatham Place, where their first child, Thurfrida (Ida), was born on 28 March 1875. As Honfleur in Normandy was then the family base, Kitty and Harry moved into Courteenhall Rectory.

By this time, the Cottrell-Dormers were preparing to move out of Courteenhall, and plans were made by Harry for taking repossession. It had been eleven years since his grandfather, Sir Charles had resided there and much restoration work was necessary.[25] The House had to be reroofed and rooms refurnished in a contemporary style. The majority of the furniture and furnishings were bought at a sale of the contents of Courteenhall commencing there on 21 September 1875. In addition, there were purchases from stores in London and Northampton.[26] A new heating and hot water system was installed. The cost of the restoration of Courteenhall was about £8,000. Later, the water supply was causing problems as the London and North-Western Railway Company had dried the wells and springs by deepening the Blisworth (Roade) cutting. The Company agreed to pay about £2,000 towards putting the matter right.[27]

A main reservoir was built by the Railway Company at the top of the Park with a daily supply of 1,920 gallons from the springs in the railway cutting. The Company installed a ram which pumped the water up into the reservoir over a distance of over $1^3/_4$ miles, and from which the house received its supply by gravity. Two other reservoirs were constructed at Woodleys and at West Lodge Farms.[28]

A matter of lesser concern but one which raised some difficulties within the family was the complication caused by the marriage of two sisters to two generations of Wakes. Uncle Charles was Herewald's uncle and brother-in-law, and Emma was Kitty's aunt and sister-in-law. As Emma wrote to Herewald, 'I think that as you have put us all into this quandary about relationship between uncle, aunt, sister in law, and upsetting all the nephews, nieces and cousins, turning one into the other, it is your bounden duty to

81. Building of underground reservoir near Sharman's Barn, Courteenhall, 1890. Fifty men were employed for this purpose by the London and North-Western Railway Company

82. Courteenhall Village Feast, 1883, at The Pightle near Crippletoe Lane, leading to the Church beyond

make the chaos clear – it is far beyond me'.[29]

Whenever a new baby was expected, Harry always took a house in London for the occasion. After the birth of their eldest boy, Hereward, on 11 February 1876, at Cadogan Place, London, Kitty became desperately ill with typhoid fever. Whilst recuperating at St. Leonards-on-Sea, Harry was also struck down with the same illness which permanently weakened his constitution.[30] It was not until July that the family were sufficiently recovered to return to Courteenhall.[31]

*   *   *   *   *

One of Herewald's great interests was the Northamptonshire Militia, which he joined as a Sub-Lieutenant in 1874. He rose to the rank of Captain, 4th Battalion, Northamptonshire Regiment and continued to serve with enthusiasm until 1888.[32] He also held the distinction, probably unique, of simultaneously holding a commission as Captain in the 1st Northamptonshire Volunteers, Towcester, and Captain with the Northamptonshire Regiment. As a first-class marksman, he took particular pride in supervising rifle practice. His Diary for 18 May 1880 records, 'This morning my Company went to the Butts at Horton . . . remained all day shooting the Course over twice, making fifty three and fifty six'.[33] In the previous two years, he had won the Company Challenge Cup of the Towcester Rifle Corps at their annual match. The social aspect of soldiering also had its appeal. Herewald noted on one occasion, 'Dined at Mess, band and Cock fighting, then to bed at the Angel 11.30'.[34] After the annual training exercises had been held, there was a Militia ball for the participants. One of them was given by Herewald and Kitty at Courteenhall in 1884.[35]

The Colonel of the 1st Northamptonshire Volunteers was Henry Fitzroy, Lord Euston, nephew to the Duke of Grafton. On the back of a large photograph of Fitzroy at Courteenhall, Herewald recorded his growing disenchantment with the movement:

> I had no luck, as England was not once invaded during the time I had a leg to stand on . . . I sham fought under the Duke of Grafton at Windsor, acting as Major, Queen Victoria's Jubilee, and camped out with Euston at Althorp several times. When half the Towcester Corps, Wolverton men, deserted to the Bucks Volunteers, that Corps demised, so I took command of one of the Northampton Companies. Then I was declared medically unfit by the War Office to retain my Militia commission, although the Army Doctors who examined me told me that they passed me. I think I must have owed this action of the War Office to personal malice on the part of [   ].[36] So in disgust I chucked my Volunteer Commission as well.
>
> <u>Now</u> 1908. The Radical Cads in power have done away with both Militia and Volunteers from the same motives. They think ½ an army and an armed mob will serve old England better. So Euston has lost his command as well. If ever England is invaded, I will join the enemy and tell them who to <u>go for</u>.[37]

For their first years at Courteenhall, Kitty and Herewald had few worries. With about £5,000 a year to spend, Herewald indulged in various sports. In 1882, for instance, besides taking part in military exercises, he went on a five day canoeing trip with his brother Archie, salmon fishing on numerous occasions and, in September and October, killed nearly 500 head more game than he had ever done before.[38] Herewald also began to fish and hunt for quite lengthy periods in Ireland. As he confided on one occasion in his Diary, 'What a blessing I have a sensible little wifie who sees the advantage of change occasionally'.[39] In addition, there were trips to London, where he met friends at his clubs, Arthur's and Brooks's, playing billiards and black pool. On 7 June 1879, a second son, Godwin Rupert, was born at Eccleston Square, followed three years later by St. Aubyn Baldwin on 1 November 1882 at 65 Eaton Place.

Another of his great interests was cricket. A notable 'stonewall' batsman, he played as often as time allowed. His Diary for 1883 records that in one match he made seventy four runs for the Militia versus a team of Regulars, and at Althorp there was a match against 'celebrated Ladies' – 'Juliana [St. Aubyn] 16 runs, Kit 0. Great victory for our side'.[40] He was a member of the MCC from 1874 and his endeavours for Northamptonshire County Cricket Club were later acknowledged in *Wisden*.[41] After the club had been formed on 31 July 1878, matches were at first played in gentlemen's parks. Sir Herewald contemplated establishing a County ground in the Park at Courteenhall but the soil was found to be too stony.[42] When the opportunity arose in 1885 for the purchase of ten acres of land at Abington for a County Cricket ground, Herewald was one of its keenest advocates. A Northamptonshire County Cricket and Recreation Grounds Co. Ltd. was formed, and in its prospectus stated that 'As a proof of the confidence felt in the undertaking it may be mentioned that Sir Herewald Wake, Bart and Joseph Hill Esq of Wollaston Hall have already advanced the amounts necessary for purchase of the Ground, and have entered into agreement for the necessary works to be done in making the Ground and Fences etc'.[43] Herewald lent the sum of £1,000 on a loan secured by a debenture. Elected as one of the directors, he chaired the first meeting of the Company on 30 April 1885, when the six present considered where the pavilion should be placed. 'The Directors also requested Lord Burghersh [of Apethorpe Hall, Northamptonshire] to be good enough to make enquiries as to a second-hand Roller which his Lordship stated he believed to be for sale'.[44] In 1887 when the club was in debt, owing £311 5s. 0d, Herewald called an extraordinary general meeting of shareholders to discuss ways of raising the money.[45] He also helped to find new players when they were most needed.[46]

As a young man in his early twenties, Sir Herewald began to develop phlebitis in his legs and was often a semi-invalid for weeks at a time. He sought advice from a number of medical men. On 13 April 1881, he noted, 'Spurgeon came over in the morning to see Tom [his brother] and my legs. Says he is going to put 'em all right in no time, Bass, Burton, Venning and others having failed. Hope he will'. Unfortunately, no cure was found, but it was during those frequent periods when he was obliged to rest up that he wrote and illustrated a series of books for his children which still give pleasure to his descendants. Herewald was a skilful draughtsman and he could capture a likeness in a moment. As he grew older, writing began to take the place of drawing and in his study at Courteenhall he committed to paper his philosophy as well as his views on current happenings, both locally and nationally.[47]

83. Family group at celebration of 21st birthday of Hereward Wake, eldest son of the 12th baronet, August 1897. It includes: *Back row:* third from left Lucy Wake, fourth from left Juliana St. Aubyn and second from right Madame Amy Ball. *Second row:* from the left Mrs Emma Wake, Phyllis Wake, Sir Herewald and Lady Wake, Hereward Wake and Mrs Louisa Wake, wife of Drury Wake. *Third row:* from the left Josephine Wake, Godwin Wake, Thurfrida Wake and Drury Wake. *Seated:* Reverend Archibald Wake and Joan Wake with Tilly the kitten

84. Sir Herewald Wake (1852–1916) in the Library, Courteenhall, c.1900

A sport which both he and Kitty shared was hunting, which he described as 'a foretaste of Heaven'. Herewald was a fearless rider – his motto was 'When you're going to take a fence, throw your heart over and jump after it' – and in the field his energy was boundless.[48] He was a member of both the Grafton and the Pytchley Hunts. Kitty hunted for a number of seasons with the Grafton and was reported to have been a good rider.[49] The sport provided Herewald with suitable inspiration for poetry; a forty five-verse poem entitled 'A Run From Halse Copse' begins:

> No worthier theme than hunting can a poet's soul inspire,
> The stirring music of the chase shall tune my Muse's lyre;
> Men, hounds, and horses I will sing, and ever as you listen,
> Your pulses shall beat faster yet, your eyes with fire shall glisten.
>
> For you shall hear the story told how Reynard fate defied,
> And ran a gallant race for life, how gamely Reynard died;
> For with that day's achievements all the country side resounds,
> And I will sing the praises of the Duke of Grafton's hounds.[50]

From his youth, Herewald was a close observer of the countryside[51] as the detailed listing of plants, birds and insects in his Diary testifies. A friend, Dudley Elwes, Rector of Billing and later Roman Catholic Bishop of Northampton, described Herewald's great knowledge of his surroundings:

> The land held far more for him than the mere business labour that it entailed. For him it enshrouded all the mysteries of nature, or rather, it gave up to his patient and devoted study of natural history a vast number of those secrets hidden to so many who live daily among them unconscious of their existence. This was more particularly the case during his early manhood, when the careful study of the life habits of birds and beasts was less practised among country folk than it is at present. His walks abroad were a communing with Nature in all her moods and tenses. To accompany him on one of them was to have the veil lifted upon almost every form of life swarming unnoticed around. Not a bird or insect or animal big or small but he could tell you its mode of life, its loves and fears, its enemies and friends, told, not in the dry-as-dust manner of the text book, but with a fund of interesting detail and anecdote brimming over always with that wonderful kindly humour which was so much in evidence when he spoke of these things.[52]

Herewald's philosophy was cheerfully summed up in a poem he wrote at the turn of the present century:

GREEN

As I hop from clod to clod with hayseeds in my hair,
I thank Almighty God I'm in the open air.
I pity all the City folk who often pity me,
For being as I wish to be as green as green could be.

The preservation of the countryside and its wildlife was of great concern to him and he was an early believer in the importance of making young people aware of their responsibilities through education. A leaflet which he wrote in 1905 entitled *Fiat Justitia!*, written in his inimitable style, is a good example. It begins:

> I have been asked by the Royal Society for the Protection of Birds to write something which will enlist the sympathy and be likely to obtain the co-operation of public schoolboys in giving our birds fair play. I am an old Eton fellow myself, and though from one cause or another I have had to stand aside while many of my contemporaries have distinguished themselves in public life, I do not regret the years I have spent in the country and in the study of Natural History, and shall certainly not think they were wasted if anything I can say on the subject of justice to the birds should win your attention.[53]

Nearer home, a more direct message was necessary. A handwritten notice, signed by Sir Herewald and no doubt once displayed in a prominent position near the boundary of the estate for the benefit of Courteenhall children, has survived. It reads:

> NOTICE
> If there is any more picking of wild flowers in the plantations or orchards without special leave, or if there is any birdnesting this season at all: the little boys or girls who do these things will not be my friends any longer. I shall be very sorry, because my Christmas or other parties will have so few young people to come to them, as I only ask my friends.[54]

When the Northamptonshire Natural History Society was formed in 1876, Sir Herewald became a founder member and was active in furthering its aims, namely, to conduct research into all aspects of natural phenomena and to publish the results. From the beginning, he was a Vice-President of the Society and President of its Entomological Section, the latter a position he filled for the rest of his life. An outstanding event in the history of the Society was the meeting of the twenty four Midland Societies at Northampton in 1880. The two-day meeting was widely reported in the press and was chaired by the twenty seven year old Sir Herewald.[55] On the death of Lord Lilford in 1896, he became the Society's President.

The range of topics which he chose for lectures was wide, and many of them were reprinted in the Society's *Journal*. In his earliest article, 'The Entomology of Northamptonshire with list of Northamptonshire Butterflies', Sir Herewald expressed the hope that members would each investigate one or more genus. 'I am sure,' he wrote, 'that Entomology is a science that is very far from being worked out, and every tyro that takes it up is as likely to make some startling discovery as the oldest professor'.[56] A more philosophical paper was 'Instinct and Reason Considered in Connection with the theory of the Evolution of Man', written in 1886: here, he attacked Darwinism, as leading inevitably to materialism and he explored the differences between man and lower animals.[57] Other articles included 'Flowers', 'The Spider and the Fly', 'Foxes'

85. Empire Day at Roade, 1909, with the 12th baronet addressing the local children

86. Sir Herewald Wake at harvest-time, c.1910

and 'On the Wing'. The latter was presented as a paper to the Society's annual general meeting on 3 March 1898. In it, Sir Herewald remarked that the builders of flying machines had so far been unsuccessful, as they had not sufficiently made a study of Nature. Although he favoured such attempts, he was not hopeful that there would be immediate results. He told the audience, 'I do not myself think that any of us now alive will ever be able to take return tickets to, let us say, Timbuctoo, by an aerial liner'.[58]

Sir Herewald regarded the coming of the motor car as an unmitigated disaster for the countryside. He refused to own one himself and when an MP, J.W. Scott-Montagu, who was also editor of *The Car*, suggested that there should be no specific speed limit fixed for cars on 'the open deserted roads of rural areas', he wrote to the press:

> I should be in favour of some such measure. But at present, when one ventures out in a vehicle drawn by horses, or on horseback or on foot, there is only an intolerable uncertainty as to whether one will reach one's destination alive. Let us, therefore, have no half measures, and to ensure that the roads in rural areas shall be really deserted and no animated hindrances to the most rapid progress of the motor car shall exist, may I suggest that the good old British custom of attaching scythe blades to the axles of the modern mechanical Chariot be re-introduced and legalised.[59]

*   *   *   *   *

He was never long away from Courteenhall, which he dearly loved, calling it the 'Hub of the Universe'. A close interest was taken in the farming of the land, as will be seen later. There were three outlying farms, each with two or three cottages, East Lodge, West Lodge and, some one and a half miles from the Hall, the Grange. Beyond the Grange were two more cottages and some farm buildings, not far from the Wootton Brook, which was the parish boundary on the north. The Estate was 1,629 acres in extent, with mixed farming land, much of it under grass with plantation and hedgerow. In addition, the Essex estate was 1,512 acres.[60]

On 27 May 1880, a Hare and Rabbits Bill was introduced into the House of Commons which was to give the occupier of land, concurrently with the landlord, the right to kill ground game. At a well-attended meeting of the Chamber of Agriculture held on 7 August at Northampton to discuss the issue, Herewald expressed his belief that trapping would interfere with fox-hunting. Afterwards, he noted: 'Poopoohed. We shall see. Majority petitioned in favour of bill, which by the way was what the meeting was called for, Lord Spencer having been taunted by Lord Elcho with having no petitions from the agricultural interest'.[61]

The great agricultural depression, caused by a combination of cold, wet seasons between 1875 and 1880, foreign competition and low prices, had serious consequences for landowners and farmers in Northamptonshire. At a meeting of the Chamber of Agriculture on 2 April 1881, Sir Herewald made a speech on distress for rents and in the following January took part in a deputation of Agricultural Chambers which met the Prime Minister, Mr Gladstone, and Sir William Harcourt.[62] Between 1884 and 1896, with a much reduced income, Sir Herewald was obliged to let Courteenhall whenever

From Dec 13th — 18th 75

The Dukes.	Sytably.	Oakley.
Monday: Austin Copse..	Syrell Wood	Crawfield
Tuesday:		
Wednesday: Castletherpe	Yelvertoft.	Ravensden..
Thursday:		Snelson
Friday: Blakesley	Weedon	
Saturday:	Harrington	Simmesmead.

CP37. The Duke of Grafton's Hounds, by the 12th baronet. Each week he inserted details of where the hounds were to meet

CP38-39. 'Greedy Tom', from a book of poems written and illustrated by the 12th baronet, 1879-92, for his children and called *Papa's Picture Book*

GREEDY TOM

Of all the greedy boys I know Tom is the greediest boy I know,

He never cares for games of play, but goes on eating fruit all day.

He's longing, too there's no denying, for on his side you see him lying,

At full length in a strawberry bed where to replenish he has fed.

The berries he's too tired to pick them so is contented now to lick them.

A fairy chanced to pass that way while Tommy on his stomach lay,

And asked him, "Why so like a beast he was contented thus to feast?"

Tom got upon his hands and knees and boldly answered, "Cos I please?"

"Perhaps you please the fairy said to be a pig? And Tom replied

"Yes." She cried "It shall be so and vanished from the scene.

When it!

His nose and ears are seen unfurling, a tail to from his back is curling;

Tom thinks his nose is rather strange but is unconscious of a change.

His fingers now have turned to toes and this more like a pig he grows;

The spell poor Tom can not resist his tail has got another twist.

Tom wonders what it's all about until he finds his nose a snout

His grunts the lonely echoes waken and now his only fit for bacon.

possible, taking Kitty and the family to smaller rented houses. The first to occupy Courteenhall was an American, Mr John Caper, who was followed by a rich shoe manufacturer from Northampton.[63] It was during this period that the last two of their six children were born, Joan, on 29 February 1884 at 65 Eaton Place and Phyllis Katheren, on 20 February 1887 at 5 Lowndes Street, the house of Kitty's mother, Lady St. Aubyn. Writing to his brother Tom from Courteenhall in January 1888, Herewald stated, 'In a short time I expect to have to leave this place to go to ruin as I cannot let it, and my income has gone down with a run of late to many degrees below zero and expenses increasing all the time'.[64] Matters had not improved three years later, though some of the earlier pessimism about the future of the house had been modified:

> Courteenhall is in a bad way. Like the wonderful one hoss shay, it has served its purpose for just 100 years and now requires almost rebuilding from foundations to chimney pots. Rents have fallen so low, that I doubt our ever being able to make our permanent home there again especially as I shall have to spend all the little capital I can scrape together on the restoration of the place.[65]

A lady whose mother had known Herewald since childhood recalled in 1969, 'I think it must have been my Mother who told me about Uncle Harry resigning his Clubs, and all I remember is that a tenant was asking to have his roof repaired and your Father said he couldn't afford it. "Well, Sir Herewald," said the man, "you belong to two London clubs and say you can't afford to mend my roof". Uncle Harry said nothing but resigned from his Clubs and repaired the roof'.[66]

Even before the agricultural depression, Herewald was faced with problems on the estate. Joseph Arch (1826–1919), the son of a farm worker of Barford, Warwickshire, was the prime mover in organizing agricultural labourers into a Union in the southern part of the county in 1872. In March of that year, a strike was called for better wages and a fighting fund was started. So successful was Arch in his efforts that a National Union of Agricultural Labourers was formed at the end of May. The movement quickly spread, especially in the Midlands, causing much consternation amongst the landlords and discontent amongst the villagers. Herewald was echoing the sentiments of many squires when he wrote, 'Mr Joseph Arch and gentlemen "of his kidney" disturbed once and for all the life-long and friendly relations that had often existed between the farmer and his servants'.[67]

Courteenhall was one of the places which was caught up in this movement. In 1877, Arch visited Roade, and many workers went from the estate to hear him. John Whiting, who for many years was the twelfth baronet's gamekeeper, later recalled that occasion and subsequent events to Joan Wake:

> Well, Miss Joan, it was this way. Joseph Arch came round and held meetings in the villages, he and his speakers, and told the men if they would join his club or union as he called it, they would all get £1 a week, and they would all have three acres and a cow. They were then getting 15/– a week, and all the estate men, them as worked for Sir Herewald, they all joined. And when they went to get their money on a Friday – Friday was payday – from old Mr. Gardiner [William

Gardiner, agent] they said they must have more money. He said he couldn't give 'em it without asking Sir Herewald. Next payday they went and there was no more money, so then they said if there was no more by next payday, they would leave. The next payday there was no more, so they all left except one, and that was Henry Tite – all of 'em, gardeners, and milkers, and carters, and all. Payday being Friday, the next day was Saturday, and Mr Gardiner he managed to do the milking himself, and he went down to Roade and found where John Kightley was in Wales, wrote to him, and became as gardener in place of old Tom Clarke, and he got one of the Dentons in place of old George Spencer, who had worked in the garden for 40 years, and Joe Howes. Howes' father came as milkman, and Howes as shepherd, and by the same evening, every place was filled, and none of the others came back – not one of 'em.[68]

*   *   *   *   *

Sir Herewald also took a close interest in Northamptonshire public affairs. He was a magistrate from 1876 and for many years a member of the Bench at Northampton every Saturday, lunching later at the Club and having a game of billiards before he came home. He had very clear ideas on the most suitable background for Justices of the Peace. When the fifth Earl Spencer as Lord-Lieutenant was supporting the nomination of two Nonconformist manufacturers and a corn factor to the County Bench in 1882, Sir Herewald was opposed to the action. 'There is no doubt', he told Lord Spencer, 'that at present the bourgeois class in England are excessively vulgar in their notions, that is to say, they are respecters of persons and therefore hardly qualified as a rule to administer justice impartially'.[69] He was Sheriff of the County in 1879 and from August 1914, a Deputy-Lieutenant.

On the death in September 1890 of Pickering Phipps, the former Conservative MP for Northampton and managing director of a brewery, there was a vacancy on the County Council for a councillor for Wootton. Sir Herewald agreed to stand as a non-political candidate, a move supported by the Liberals on the Council. He hoped that, as in Phipps's case, he would be returned unopposed. However, a lawyer, G. J. Phillips, came forward as a candidate. The election campaign, which lasted a week, was, in the words of a newspaper 'characterised by an exchange of red hot shot'.[70] Both candidates held meetings every night, both ending their campaign with speeches at Piddington. There, Sir Herewald 'spoke of his desire, as exemplified by his action at Roade, that agricultural labourers should have allotments'.[71] Voting, which took place on 17 and 18 October 1890, was at four polling stations. The result was:

Sir Herewald Wake	351
George Jason Phillips	295
Majority	56

Sir Herewald, the ninth titled member of the County Council,[72] intimated in January 1892 that he had no intention of standing for re-election.[73]

Like many Wakes before him, he was a Liberal in politics, especially in his youth. In March 1880, when a general election was announced, he convened a meeting at Northampton with a view to standing against the two Conservative MPs for South Northamptonshire, Sir Rainald Knightley and Major F.W. Cartwright, but could not find sufficient support.[74] Sir Herewald was equally opposed to the radicals, Charles Bradlaugh and Henry Labouchere, who were Liberal nominees at the general election that year. Sir Herewald led those members of the party who refused to accept Bradlaugh. He threatened to use violence at Courteenhall against those Bradlaugh supporters who distributed their 'blasphemous and obscene literature' on the estate.[75]

Shortly after Gladstone had been returned to office in April 1880 Herewald attended a 'grand and enthusiastic Liberal meeting' in Northampton where he was voted into the chair. It was resolved that a Liberal Association be set on foot, and the motion was carried without dissent. 'The ball is set rolling,' remarked Sir Herewald, 'but it is a precious little one'.[76] After the fall of Gladstone's government in June 1885, he wrote a letter to *The Times* stating that he intended to contest the Northampton election against Bradlaugh and Labouchere,[77] but later withdrew his candidature. With the adoption of Home Rule by the Gladstonian Liberals from 1886, Sir Herewald ceased to play an active part in Liberal politics, describing himself henceforth as a Liberal Unionist. One of Gladstone's last pieces of legislation, the Local Government Act of 1894, established parish councils. In a pamphlet *The Parting of the Ways*, addressed to 'Friends and fellow Labourers', Sir Herewald warned that 'the labouring classes, if they continue to do it, have the power some people think to be unjust and extravagant with other people's money.' The democratic principle, he argued, reduced the benevolent influence of the country squire:

> An open village I know of, say of six hundred inhabitants or so, will have about 150 parish electors, men and women. Out of these about twenty five are owners or tradesmen, and twenty five are women. That will give a majority of votes to working men of about 50, so the Parish Council Act may well be called the rural charter, but it certainly annuls the hitherto existing charter of all those who are really interested in the permanent welfare of a country village.[78]

Sir Herewald took the opportunity to attack City gentry, armchair officials and secretaries in Government departments 'with their souls hidebound by bricks and mortar, their brains befogged with smoke, and their blood running with printers' ink [who] know little or nothing about the country or village life'. The introduction of death duties by the Liberals was given as one example of this attitude:

> I am an Agricultural Landowner. The Budget Bill '94 will cost my son one of his best farms if anybody will buy it, at one-half what it has cost his dead father, and that money is to be spent in protecting foreign competition which is bankrupting the farmers and driving the land, his only means of livelihood, clean out of cultivation.[79]

Sir Herewald's personal circumstances were probably at their lowest point at the opening of the last decade of the century. After a gap of some nine years in his Diary he recorded at the end of it:

> *August 1891.*
> How many sad events have occurred since I last wrote in this book. In '82 I was quite a junior member of the family, and now only one of what my sister Amy called the 'dear chaplet of Uncles' remains, and he lives by himself abroad in ill health.[80] My brother Charlie, my uncles Charlie and Drury, my grandmother, the Archbishop, my guides and counsellors and my dearest friends, all passed away and many other gaps besides have been made in the family circle … Serious illness has again played havoc with the health and strength of my dear wife and myself, but thanks be to God, our six dear children are with us strong and well.[81]

In January 1891, Catherine had become desperately ill at Courteenhall with typhoid fever caused by bad drains. Near neighbours and friends, Roger and Mary Eykyn of Gayton House, Blisworth, temporarily looked after three of the children, Baldwin, Phyllis and Joan, as well as providing accommodation for Kate Groves, their nurse and Dora the pug. Mary Eykyn told Herewald, 'You will like a line to know how happily we all get on. They are such good obedient chicks, no trouble to any one'.[82] Later, Herewald took a villa, Fernwood at Dallington, where he stayed with the children whilst Catherine was recovering, first at Little Houghton House and then at Medina House, Brighton. During this time Herewald was himself unwell with a recurrence of phlebitis which severely restricted his activities.[83]

There were several moves for the family during the next few years. In the summer of 1892, Sir Herewald occupied a small house for six months at Ravenstone, near Keswick, on the slopes of Skiddaw, overlooking Lake Bassenthwaite. Whilst Courteenhall was let to the Whitehouses in 1892–3, they resided at 133 Queen's Gate, London,[84] and in the winter of 1893–4, they rented Cotterstock Hall, near Oundle, Northamptonshire for the same reason. Whilst at Cotterstock, Herewald took Phyllis and Joan to nearby Lilford Hall, home of the distinguished ornithologist and field naturalist, Lord Lilford,[85] where they were shown the *vivaria* (areas artificially prepared for keeping animals in their near natural states). To Herewald's delight, on the same visit, he saw a Lammergeier Eagle or Bearded Vulture from one of Lilford's aviaries fly on to the roof of the Hall and spread out its wings. Sharing similar interests, Lilford and Herewald frequently exchanged papers on the research which each had undertaken.[86] During 1894 and 1895, the Wakes' home was Courteenhall Rectory, whilst the Coopers rented the Hall. In 1896, the family at last settled at Courteenhall where they remained until Sir Herewald's death twenty years later.

*　　　*　　　*　　　*　　　*

Although he never talked about the subject, Herewald was a devoutly religious man. Extensive restoration work was carried out on Courteenhall Church during his lifetime

87. Interior of Courteenhall Church, c.1875. Note box pews, high pulpit and credo behind the altar. The walls and ceiling were plastered

88. Courteenhall Church with chairs, altar table, tiled floor with steps and oil lamps, c.1890. The box pews, pulpit and lectern were removed by the Rector, the Reverend George Hooper during the family's absence in Cornwall in 1887

89. Courteenhall Church, 1912. Repairs to the interior included the removal of plaster from walls and ceiling. The Norman font is on the right of the picture

at a considerable cost. Before 1883, the south side of the chancel was the only place in the church where any architectural features could be seen, for the whole church had a low ceiling and the walls were covered in plaster of various hues. Even the pillars and the font appeared as rectangular pieces of plaster. The south-west bay in the nave was blocked up and the tower arch at the west end, being higher than the ceiling, had a false plaster arch, and the opening was concealed with lath and plaster. The top half of the east window was also blocked up, but with rubble. Between 1883 and 1885, at a cost of £335 9s. 4d, the south-west bay was opened out, some work was done on the tower and the bells and new heating apparatus installed. The old flooring, which was rotten, was replaced by a tiled floor, with steps up to the east end. The architect responsible for these alterations was Piers St. Aubyn. Sir Herewald was very angry when during the family's absence in Cornwall in 1887, the Reverend George Hooper removed the old square box pews (which were replaced with chairs) and in addition disposed of the family pew and pulpit.[87]

A more urgent set of repairs was undertaken in 1896–7. The tower was in a poor state, so six iron tie rods were inserted and secured to plates on the outside; it was repointed in cement and a new vane-post was erected. The walls of the nave and of the north aisle were leaning considerably, so the north-west angle of the aisle was underpinned and two buttresses built. The walls of the north porch were also under-pinned. All the plaster in the interior was removed and was then pointed with cement. Some new tracery and glass was placed in the east window. A new lectern and choir stalls were put in the chancel and a new pulpit added to the church. The work, costing £452 17s. 0d. was carried out under the direction of William Hull of St. Giles' Street, Northampton.[88]

It was hoped that this now completed the task of restoration. However, in 1911, a further settling of the nave and north aisle was observed and immediate action was necessary. The two north piers were underpinned and the walls made good. The thirteenth century roof needed to be repaired and the leadwork on the roof was found to be perished and was replaced. At the same time, the false arch and the partition across the tower opening were removed. Finally, the windows throughout were releaded and glazed where necessary. The restoration of the building, carried out by W.R and E.E. Bowden of London, had cost £700; the Church was rededicated on 14 December 1912.[89]

Sir Herewald was responsible as patron of the living for the installation of his younger brother, the Reverend Archibald Wake, as Rector of Courteenhall after Hooper's resignation in August 1887. Archibald, known to the family as Archie, had previously been a curate at Eardisley, Herefordshire, since 1884. He moved into the Rectory on 26 November 1887 with his sister Lucy and their three servants. Neither Archie nor Lucy ever married.[90] As a youth, he had been presented with a Gownboy Foundation Scholarship at Charterhouse by his uncle, the Archbishop.[91] His cheerful disposition made him popular with his fellow pupils. Another Gownboy and exact contemporary was Robert Baden-Powell. Both were good sportsmen and played together in the School's Football XI in 1875.[92]

Archie was responsible for keeping the Courteenhall Parish Book,[93] and he embellished it with jottings about his own activities and adventures. There are many references to his ill-health, such as: 'Sunday 1st January 1888. We inhabited the Library for the first time, wherefore I caught a bad cold'. On the 30th of that month, he was confined to bed with a chill. 'I do not know whether it was caught from eating an ice in London, or travelling, or from running in and out to view the total eclipse of the Moon on Saturday night'. He was pleased to call on the Rector-designate of St. Mary's, Far Cotton End, Northampton, the Reverend William Deane, who had been with him at Oxford. Furnishing the Rectory with Lucy's help occupied quite a lot of his time. After one such visit to the salesroom, 'I got Lucy to drop me at Wootton Hall Lodge gates and called on McCallum [James D. McCallum], the Chief Constable, who warned me to keep the Church plate and Cash box safe, upstairs for choice; because Parsons, being so careless, the burglars lately seem to have made a dead-set at Rectory houses. I followed his advice'.

Archie tended to be accident prone. He attended Deane's installation at Far Cotton on 3 February 1888. 'I walked back thence with Miller [Reverend Augustus Miller of Wootton] (who pushed me into the ditch in the dark, and who nearly had a fit because he thought I had one, because I didn't holloa). Nevertheless I had a pleasant supper with him of eggs and bacon, and (luckily) borrowed his lantern to walk home across the fields'. He led a full social life, playing golf, cricket and tennis, and enjoyed hunting and shooting. Archie was a frequent caller at the Hall, where he was pleased to see his nephews and nieces. On 29 February 1888, which was a Leap Year, he noted in the Diary, 'We took our presents down to that sensible, bewitching child Joan, in commemoration of her first birthday in four years'. Archie was on very good terms with his sister, Lucy, though there were occasional grumbles: 'Lucy badgered me to put that remaining stair carpet down, and other work about the house, against Mr. Palmer's arrival, so I had to do it'.

There were frequent entertainments at the Rectory for the villagers. On 7 December 1888, fifty people were present, many of whom volunteered to read or sing (without a piano). Magic lantern shows were popular, though Archie accidentally caused the programme to be abandoned on 9 February 1889 by damaging the machine. Instead, he read an essay 'How to cure a cold'. On each New Year's Eve, the choir and bell ringers would have supper at the Rectory, finishing with Midnight Mass.[94]

The Parish Book contains vignettes of village life which are reminiscent of those of the Reverend Francis Kilvert, who had also been a curate in Archie's former county, Herefordshire. In February 1888, a girl, Edith Newcombe, had died in Courteenhall of diphtheria and on the following day Archie visited her bereaved parents:

> I used one of Harmer's Norwich coats, which I had got for distribution, as a disinfected coat: it will do in like cases again. I have also apportioned off one Bible for use in contagious and other catching diseases, but pray God we shall be spared from such. Meantime we must examine the Sanitation. The odd thing is there are no drains.

Three days later, 'Walked to Campion's Farm, [John Campion, farmer] distributing Parish Magazines, and called on Williams, the poor woman's face much aged in death'.

On St. Andrew's Day in November that year, the Rectory drains and well were found to be very unsatisfactory and he reported, 'I have had them put right on a better system and drawn plans.' However, in the following June 1890, Archie was struck down with an astonishing list of illnesses. According to him, he was ill in bed for five months with 'pleurisy, congestion, inflammation of the right and then of the left lung, nerve pain, thrombosis, phlebitis of left and then right leg, heart affection, dropsy, eczema, etc. etc'. Leaving Courteenhall in November to recuperate, he and Lucy arrived on the last day of the year at Bordighera, Italy, where he had to be carried upstairs to his room. It was not until July 1891 that he was once more able to walk, though only shakily. Catherine Wake, it will be recalled, had been taken ill with typhoid fever that same January. Archie remarked that 'the Hall hopelessly to pieces, with drain inspecting'.

There was a happy ending to Archie's bout of illness. Some two years previously, on 20 June 1888, there had been a Bishop's visitation to Courteenhall. In Archie's own words, 'I was "visited" about having no pulpit in the Church'. However, on his return to Courteenhall from Bordighera on 4 June 1891, he was 'Greeted with Bells ringing, inhabitants out in street, children at the gate, flowers, flags flying, and a subscription of £27 17s. 0d. towards Pulpit, as Thankoffering for return and recovery'. On 19 November a new pulpit was dedicated in Courteenhall Church by Dr Mandell Creighton, Lord Bishop of Peterborough, who preached the sermon: the clergy of all the parishes adjoining Courteenhall were also present and there were about 280 in the congregation.

Unfortunately, Archie's further exploits and adventures are not described in any detail after this date, for as he wrote, 'I think that a Diary is out of place in this book, so I intend to make it a Parish Book'.

Archie remained at Courteenhall until his death in 1925, a period of thirty eight years in all, one of the longest serving parsons at Courteenhall since the first rector, John de Biscebrok, took office in 1269. A good description of the Sunday church routine and the congregation in the 1890s has been left by his niece, Joan Wake:

> Every Sunday the whole households of Hall and Rectory and a fair proportion of villagers attended at least one service, as a matter of course, we in our best clothes, Papa and the boys dressed as when they went to London in dark trousers, black frock coats, and how well I remember the row of top hats on the hall table near the front door put ready for them. Mama was also in a Sunday dress and so were we, but two of us, Ida and me or Phyllis and me, had already gone across the park to Sunday School in the infant school in the village at 10.15. Either Ida or Phyllis would then collect the five or six dogs we always kept in the house and take them up to the stables to be shut up during church, and then we would all collect in the church, including the servants, the housemaids and kitchen and scullery-maid in their regulation Sunday morning costume, black coats and skirts and black straw bonnets, tied with long strings under their chins.
>
> At a few minutes to 11, the Sunday school children came pouring up Cripple-Toe Lane from the village, and would sit in the two or three rows in the front of the south aisle, Aunt Lucy sitting behind them. There were three or four

90. Courteenhall Rectory on the south side of the Church, built largely in 1805 with Regency windows

91. Drawing by Sir Herewald Wake, 12th baronet, of a tennis match at Stoke Bruerne Park, August 1877. On the right is Catherine, Lady Wake and the 12th baronet. On the left are Squire Vernon and the Reverend Augustus Dampier, Rector of Courteenhall

bell-ringers in those days, and they rang steadily for half an hour before Morning and Evening Prayers. Papa and Mama and the boys would take their seats in the family pew, and Ida and Phyllis and I in the choir, where there were never less than a dozen men, and women, boys and girls, who seldom missed a service. At two minutes to eleven in through the south door came the Rector with his mortar-board and cassock green with age, a portly dark-bearded man of about 5 feet 10 inches in height.[95]

In an essay entitled 'Irreverence' written by Sir Herewald on 15 October 1905, he recounts a recent Sunday lunch with his three daughters following a Church service, when he asked them about Uncle Archie's sermon and concluded:

> They are apt to adopt too critical a standpoint as regards the conduct of the services. Their keen sense of humour is also apt to lead them astray somewhat, as possibly my own has ... Yet they are good girls enough in their way. They take Sunday school, are in the choir, one plays the organ and they are the personal friends of every man, woman and child in the parish. What they lack is the reverential spirit. Perhaps it is because with a good-natured Uncle for their priest, they are too much behind the scenes.[96]

Archie was also popular with the children at Courteenhall School, (see Chapter 16) of which he was the Correspondent. In July 1925, only twelve days before he died and when he was very ill, he made a request to the headmistress to see the dances which the children performed at their Entertainment. The School Log book records that the children left for the Rectory in the afternoon for this purpose.[97]

*   *   *   *   *

Sir Herewald believed in the value of education and was a staunch supporter of the Courteenhall Grammar School, endowed by Samuel Jones in 1672 and situated within the grounds of the estate. Boys,[98] educated without charge, were drawn from the neighbouring twelve parishes which lay within four miles of Courteenhall but excluded Northampton. The smaller boys boarded in the large attic above the schoolroom and the older boys made their way on ponies or walked. The schoolmaster and the usher were chosen by the Mayor and Aldermen of Northampton with the consent of the Lord of the Manor of Courteenhall.

When the Schools Inquiry Commission on the state of the endowed schools (1864–8) sent an Assistant Commissioner, T.H.Green, to Courteenhall, he reported that the standard of education at the school was higher than that of an ordinary elementary school.[99] Much of the credit was due to the schoolmaster, William Haskins, who had been appointed in 1856. Haskins as a young man had wanted to be a teacher, but his parents sent him to work as a tailor at Wootton. One day when he was frightening off birds, his gun exploded and blew off his left hand. He walked the two miles to Northampton Infirmary, where he watched the doctor amputate the hand without anaesthetic. The accident pleased Haskins, as he was now able to follow his preferred occupation. He trained as a pupil teacher, and taught at St. Sepulchre's, Northampton, where Sir Charles offered him the post of master at Courteenhall.[100] He was a good schoolmaster with a wide range of interests and abilities. As the school could not afford an usher, Haskins, a self-educated man, taught during his career, Greek, Latin, French, pure and applied mathematics, drawing and design, book-keeping, land surveying and science. Haskins carried out land surveys for the parish and took some of the boys with him in order to give them practical experience. A man of many parts, he was also an architect and was known to help the villagers to draw up their wills.[101]

The pupils, mainly sons of labourers, attended full-time up to the age of nine; and for about six to nine months per year up to the age of twelve. As Haskins told a Royal Commission on the Employment of Children, Young Persons and Women in Agriculture, 'The boys are attracted away from school to go to work ... it is a wonder we get them to school at all, they are never so happy as when they are in the fields'.[102]

Haskins had a red face and long beard and his wooden arm terminated in an iron hook. When he heard the Grafton Hounds during school hours, he would immediately stop the lesson and shout, 'Boys! the Hounds! Out you go!' On the first occasion Sir Herewald met him, he enquired who he was. 'Askins', he replied. 'How do you spell it?' asked Sir Herewald. 'Haitch, Hay, Hess, Kay, Hi, Hen, Hess', said Mr. Haskins.[103]

There is evidence that Haskins' predecessor, the Reverend Miles Walker, had neglected the repair of the school, with dilapidations estimated at his death at £307 10s. 0d.[104] With the passing of the Elementary Education Act in 1870, which established a system of elementary education in England, Board Schools were provided in neighbouring villages and the numbers in the Grammar School dwindled to four or five by the 1890s.[105] On 25 October 1898, Haskins died after forty two years' service at the school. The building was in a derelict state. As one of Her Majesty's Inspectors, Mr. A. Cartwright, reported, 'It might have been the original of Dotheboys Hall!'[106] The Mayor and Aldermen of Northampton refused to appoint another master and the school was closed down.

As was noted in Chapter 11, the ninth baronet had established a school room in the village for infants and girls. The boys eventually entered the Grammar School and the girls were sent to a private school in Roade, the fees being paid by the Lady Wake of the day.[107] With the retirement of the Infant schoolmistress, this school too was closed down. In 1899, there were forty seven children of school age. 'Poor Courteenhall!', wrote Sir Herewald to the Board of Education, 'for 200 years in advance of the rest, is now the only parish in the County unprovided with education of any sort!'[108]

However, neither Sir Herewald nor his brother Archie gave up the struggle. As the former pointed out towards the end of his life, 'A school, situated as it is right in the grounds of this private house, is of no advantage to myself or my heirs – rather the contrary, for obvious reasons. The matter is merely a question of duty on my part'.[109] The 1902 Education Act revived hopes of a reassessment of the situation, but it was not until May 1907 that the Board of Education agreed to hold a public inquiry on the issue. In anticipation of this, Sir Herewald had raised a petition from all the parishes affected and had personally interviewed every member of the parish councils within four miles of Courteenhall.[110] The inquiry took place in the Free Grammar School on 10 May where Sir Herewald, Archie and Lucy all gave evidence. Sir Herewald vigorously attacked the Board, drawing applause from the audience. He wished that the £100 per annum which the Wakes had given to the Grammar School should now be applied to establishing a good elementary school in Courteenhall, maintaining that the founder had had no class distinctions in mind. The Board of Education and the Borough of Northampton, on the other hand, preferred the monies to be applied to scholarships for boys attending existing grammar schools, on the grounds that Courteenhall was a grammar school under the 1840 Grammar Schools Act. Sir Herewald demonstrated that since the closure of the school, young children were obliged to walk up to three miles to Roade across the muddy fields in winter. The accumulation of endowment funds made the restoration of a local school a real possibility. He also challenged the officials present by stating, 'With regard to the rates, he had not yet become a passive resister, but he should not promise that he would not become one if they did not have a school'.[111]

The Board made no further moves following the inquiry, though meanwhile Sir Herewald and Archie made plans to reopen the Infant School. Archie complained to the Board in November 1908, 'We had one of your Inspectors down and he <u>in my hearing</u> said it [the room] was 2 inches too low as a minimum: when you replied to my last letter a year ago now it was stated <u>officially</u> it was 2 inches too short'.[112] At the same time, Sir Herewald succeeded in restoring the Grammar School building to a sound condition. A Board official noted in a Minute in July 1910, 'Sir Herewald proved very persistent, ultimately persuaded us into sanctioning £445 to be spent in making the premises watertight'.[113] In 1915 Archie requested a Judge of Assize to reappoint a master to Courteenhall Free School, but was not successful. By then the village population had diminished[114] and it would have been difficult to justify the School's reopening. It was left to his son, the thirteenth baronet, to take up the matter once more.

*   *   *   *   *

Politically, Sir Herewald moved further away from his Liberal origins as the present century approached. In 1892, when Gladstone was returned to office for the fourth and last time, Herewald wrote to his wife, 'These confounded elections are not going right at all. The Gladstonians gain eleven seats to the Unionists three, out of about fifty eight. At that rate the G.O.M. walks in, and then you, my dear, and everyone else will soon find out why I was excited about politics'.[115]

He congratulated the sixth Marquess of Exeter of Burghley House for a letter to the Press in 1906 on the future of country houses and their estates under the new Liberal Government. Sir Herewald remarked:

> Landowners are believed to have the purses of Fortunates by the crowds, and the Manufacturing and Trading Classes and <u>Politicians</u>, confound them all, have been exploiting that popular folly *ad nauseam*, and mean to continue doing so till the Nobility – Gentry of this country are submerged. You probably noted how the parks and pleasure grounds of country seats were excluded from the action of

the Small Holdings Act.[116] The reason is obvious. These radical leaders mean to have our houses and parks for themselves. Burghley House will be made into a lunatic asylum for the Socialistic ex M.P.s whose heads have swollen a trifle too much. Some Socialist Bounder has got his eye on this plot already as I get confidential enquiries on 'behalf of my clients' nearly every other week, as to when I will turn out, said client being evidently astonished at my having hung on for so long.[117]

Lloyd George's Budget of 1909 – known as the People's Budget – was strongly condemned by Sir Herewald. A twenty per cent tax on the unearned increment of land value, the setting up of labour exchanges and the introduction of unemployment insurance and child allowances,[118] he declared, would result in Catherine and himself having to leave Courteenhall and be thrown on the roadside.[119] Sir Herewald's opposition to the National Insurance Act of 1911 achieved prominence in the national Press; he declared that as a magistrate he would not sit on the Bench to compel people to pay their contributions.[120] In one of his later speeches, at a Conservative gathering at Stoke Bruerne Park, he stated that he had tried to keep out of politics but felt compelled to speak out at a time when the nation had to choose between good and evil. The people who were calling themselves Liberals were now joining hands with Socialism.[121]

Nevertheless, the management of the Courteenhall estate, together with that at Waltham, remained Sir Herewald's main concern. He was closely involved with day-to-day affairs[122] and took an interest in every aspect of the land and those who worked on it. A frank account of this is given in his Notes to Executors and Trustees of the Estate, written in October 1910:

Mr Drury Wake was Agent during ——'s occupation and I supposed that he was looking after my interests, in which I was mistaken, the dear old gentleman being under the impression that everybody he had to deal with was as honourable a man as he was himself. Consequently all manner of thieves swarmed on my Estate, like flies attracted to a piece of meat.

It was only that I saw what was going on with my own eyes, that prevented the whole Estate being equally spoilt, but after Mr Wake's death and Mr Tunnard [Ambrose Tunnard, agent] left me, I managed for myself. With this result, I got rid of the bad tenants, one after another, taking the land into my own hands as they left and letting again, but with my eyes open.. As a consequence, the said tenants had to quit, not that I ever turned anyone out, but I soon let them see I intended them to farm fairly, or not at all on my land, so they left. For some years my returns were very small but all the time I was restoring the land, and getting it clean and looking after the buildings, fences, ditches and watercourses. There are 72 miles of fencing on the 1,700 acres concerned and 12 miles of roads and cart roads, so to this day there still remains a lot of work to be done.

Anyhow, at last on the 1,130 acres of land now actually in hand, with my present Farm Steward's able assistance, I have made the full rent as assessed during the last five years on the average. This, after paying full salary to Steward, good wages to the men, and giving them all a share in nominal profits. I should strongly advise my successor to continue my system.[123]

This experiment in co-operative farming, based on profit-sharing, had begun in 1901 and attracted widespread interest. In a newspaper interview ten years later, Sir Herewald expressed the hope that the scheme would be adopted by many more landlords.[124]

Much of Sir Herewald's success was due to his lifelong study of the science of agriculture and of cattle breeding. About a third of the Courteenhall estate was arable, the rest pasture. He grew high quality seed corn and bred Shire horses and pedigree Shorthorns, and kept pedigree Hampshire sheep and Berkshire pigs. Not surprisingly, many prizes were gained at Shows, particularly for the wool and fatstock.

One of the major worries was that of taxation. In December 1903, he informed his eldest son, Hereward:

> I have been working hard on my accounts for the last five years in order, in case of my going off the books before I have pulled this property round, to prevent you being mulched by the Government of a large sum of money, succession duty, not really due from your Estate.
>
> I wanted the Government to proceed against me, years ago, but they declined the combat and have let me pay my taxes in my own way, I should imagine, for the simple reason that every land owner and farmer in the country would have adopted my plan if published and refused to pay a cent more than was actually due.[125]

Sir Herewald's objective was to work up the income of the Courteenhall and Waltham estates to £5,000 a year gross, it being then £4,200. Annual expenditure consisted of housekeeping £1,300, garden £250, stables £300 and £600 for his children. He was also writing a history of the two estates for the guidance of his successors which contained useful hints.[126] As he wrote exuberantly later:

> Nothing succeeds like success, and my crop of hopes not having been blighted in 1906, I am sowing more for 1907, 8–9 and 10 very freely. My sheep, 680 head, Thorpe [C.E. Thorpe, valuer] writes, is the best and soundest flock he has ever seen! Not a sick or sorry one among them and I always get top prices for everything now – and have beaten the record for ten years past several times of late. Cock a doodle do![127]

Sir Herewald was 5 feet 10 inches in height, broad-shouldered and had strikingly grey eyes. To the end of his life, he had thick brown hair with a slight curl in front and hardly a grey hair. A relative, then a child, describes him at this time as 'pallid, full face, a chestnut moustache and "Imperial", and a very lively, quizzical expression. He smoked rather a lot, and had a very distinctive voice. He treated us delightfully, and we always looked forward to his visits and his amusing sayings and stories. I dare say he could have been alarming to older people if you got on the wrong side of him, and he had very decided opinions and prejudices; but he was most generous and kindhearted, and always ready to help people he was fond of'.[128]

Meal times, when the whole family would assemble, were an elaborate affair:

Prayers were supposed to be at 9 o'clock but Sir Herewald was so frequently late, sometimes as much as 25 minutes, that Lady Wake finally said she was going to have breakfast at 9 and the family would come away from breakfast to prayers whenever Sir H. came down. Prayers were in the hall and on the tinkling of a bell the servants filed in, cook, ladies' maids, housemaids, kitchen and scullery maids, footmen and finally the butler. They knelt at a long bench facing the wall down one side of the room. On one occasion a cat came in with them and jumped from kneeling back to kneeling back along the whole length of the row. The family faced the opposite wall. Prayers began with the General Confession, followed by a prayer from an MS family collection, the Lord's Prayer and the Grace. They took about five minutes. The family then returned to the breakfast table.

Breakfast consisted of porridge with cream and salt (when small the children had sugar), fried eggs with bacon or eggs boiled at the table, fish (kippers, bloaters &c, kept hot on a tray over spirit lamps), ham, tongue and cold beef. Toast and marmalade followed and the meal ended with fruit. Both tea and coffee were available. On one occasion Lady Wake asked a new guest whether he would take tea or <u>corfee</u>. The guest replied that he would take tea, but his wife, a cousin, afterwards revealed that he always had coffee, but he couldn't bring himself to say <u>corfee</u> and didn't dare say <u>coffee</u>. Lunch consisted of a joint, saddle of lamb being particularly good, or sometimes Shepherd's Pie or hashed mutton with potatoes and greens. On Sundays there was always a boiled pudding, 'grey Christmas pudding', that is a less rich pudding with less fruit and spice. On other days there was invariably rice pudding with stewed fruit (most often apple). Lunch ended with a slice of Luncheon cake, a cake made with yeast, with sultanas in it and yellow in colour. There was claret to drink.

Tea was also a large meal with hot scones, thin bread and butter and jam, fruit or seed cake. Cream not milk was put into the tea.

Dinner was the most elaborate meal of the day: soup, fish, an entrée if there were visitors, roast meat or game, pudding such as Creme Caramel, savoury and dessert (at which Grace was said). There was claret to drink and port with dessert, but when there were visitors other wines were provided with the different courses. Sherry went with the soup and was not served before meals until after the First World War.

The gardener was particularly good at providing fruit early and there was plenty of it. Sometimes in the season they had strawberries four times a day, at three meals, plus a subsidiary outing to the locked kitchen garden in the afternoon.

At lunch there were two large crocks in the dining room into which were put what was left of the meat and vegetables. These were taken down to the village for the old people. In cold weather sheeps heads &c were bought and soup made for a special list of people in the village.[129]

As the first generation of Wakes to have been wholly brought up in the happy atmosphere of Courteenhall, Sir Herewald's children were able to develop their talents and share their achievements. Although not outwardly displaying much emotion, Sir Herewald was proud of his offspring[130] and was closely involved in providing support when necessary. In congratulating his eldest son Hereward on his advancement in the Army, he added:

> I think your mother or Joan said something about you having said or written that if you did not get the nomination (you have got), you would not be able to afford to go in for the next one, as it was so expensive paying tutors, etc. I mention this, my dear boy, because I wish you to understand that you and I can easily arrange for the provision of any reasonable amount of funds which may be required by you to help you on in your profession. That would not be forestalling the fortune, or any part of it, that you will inherit on my decease, for the simple reason that any money so laid out would be the finest investment you could make, if such outlay was found to be necessary to give you a chance of becoming Commander-in-Chief some day when the daisies are blooming on my grave oh.[131]

The outbreak of the First World War in 1914 was a great blow to him. Walking through Courteenhall village one Sunday afternoon, Sir Herewald passed a group of young men. He looked at them and, out of hearing, muttered 'Cannon fodder'.[132] However, he was very proud of his three sons who were on active service with the Army and the Navy. Speaking at a citizen corps meeting at Roade in December 1914, he said that if the Germans landed in England 'he would come out in a bath chair with a rook rifle, and if a shell did not finish him off, he would kill one or two Germans. His only regret was that he was unable to fight for his country'.[133]

Sir Herewald suffered a serious illness in the spring of 1915, when he had completed his fiftieth year as baronet. On 16 December, he dined with his Waltham Abbey and Nazeing tenants on the occasion of the rent audit. Exactly a fortnight later, after a day's shooting in Northamptonshire, Sir Herewald caught a chill, contracted pneumonia and died at Courteenhall at 11.05 a.m on 5 January 1916. All his family except Baldwin, who was at sea, were by his bedside. Hereward, the new baronet, afterwards told his wife, Daisy, 'Almost the last thing he said that we could understand was "Give Daisy my love"'.[134] He was sixty three years of age.

At the funeral on 10 January, his coffin was carried to the churchyard along the path from the House in his own splendid farm wagon, drawn by two Shire cart horses. He was buried in the graveyard opposite the west door of Courteenhall Church. As his daughter Joan wrote of him:

CP40. Hereward Wake, later 13th baronet, as a boy by G. W. Miller, c.1883

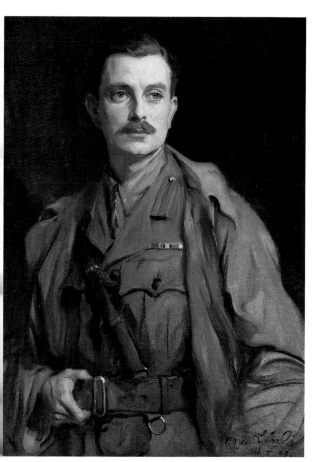

CP41. Lieutenant-Colonel Sir Hereward Wake,
13th baronet by P. A. de Lazlo, 1916

CP42. Lady Margaret, wife of Hereward Wake by
P. A. de Lazlo, 1914, a wedding present from her
parents, Robert and Evelyn Benson

CP43. Medals of Vice-Admiral Sir Baldwin Wake (1882–1951), including Knight Commander of the British Empire and Companion of the Bath

CP44. Major-General Sir Hereward Wake, 13th baronet aged 81 by Simon Elwes, 1957

CP45. Medals of Major-General Sir Hereward Wake, 13th baronet (1876–1963), including the Companion of St. Michael and St. George, the Distinguished Service Order and the Companion of the Bath

Thus lived and died a good man who loved and understood the land, adored his wife, family and home, worked hard, faced and coped with his difficulties, enlivened the world with his wit, and made Courteenhall for many years a tribal centre for countless relations and friends.[135]

15

Major-General Sir Hereward Wake, The Thirteenth Baronet: I. Youth to end of World War I

FROM THE EARLIEST TIMES, THE WAKES HAVE PRODUCED from generation to generation many distinguished members of the Army and the Navy. Few, however, can match the military career in length of service, variety of experience and personal bravery of Sir Hereward Wake, the thirteenth baronet.

In 1884, at the age of eight, he was sent to a preparatory school at Brighton. He missed the family life at Courteenhall especially when Phyllis was born in February 1887. 'I never was so surprised in my life when I heard I had a new sister. What is she like? I wish I could be at her christening but I suppose I cannot ... Our family increases slowly. We have six already'.[1] However, with the birth of Phyllis, the family was complete.

Hereward went to Eton in September 1889, which he found 'awfully jolly', though disappointed that in his first three weeks no one had asked him if he could fight. Many years later, Hereward recorded an interesting conversation he had had at the Deanery in October with the Dean of Windsor, Randall Davidson, (Davidson's wife was a daughter of Archbishop Tait):[2]

> During breakfast Dean Randall Davidson told a story of how he had lately been present when the tomb containing Charles I, Henry VIII and Lady Jane Seymour in St. George's Chapel was opened and the Prince of Wales (Edward VII) replaced on Charles I's coffin a bit of his neck which had been chopped off at his execution, kept by somebody, and sent to Queen Victoria, who had ordered it to be put back in the tomb.[3]

Hereward liked the life at Eton and this was reflected in his teachers' reports to his father. Writing privately to Sir Herewald, his housemaster F.W. Cornish, stated, 'He is a capital boy, always full of energy and good spirits and does sensible work far above the average'.[4] Even more enthusiastic was the young A.C. Benson, then an inspiring classics master, later Master of Magdalene College, Cambridge.[5] Hereward had come top in a particularly industrious and intelligent division. Benson observed:

See Appendix A – Family Trees XV and XVI. Notes and References pages 422–427

He has not only showed interest and intelligence in his work, but he has made teaching a pleasure by his quick perception and great friendliness, and I have not often had a boy up to me who interested me more; as he has none of the mildness which is apt to accompany industry, but is all alert in every way and has as much liveliness as any boy in the Division; I am thoroughly sorry to see the last of him, and wish him well most sincerely in every respect.[6]

Hereward also enjoyed physical recreation though he was no athlete. On St. Andrew's Day 1890, he helped Cornish's (his house) to win the Lower Boy Football Cup, beating Hale's by two goals and a rouge to a goal and two rouges.[7] In March 1891, Queen Victoria and the Empress Frederick of Germany unveiled the statue of the monarch in the Queen's Schools. Hereward, who was at the ceremony, noted that 'there were Eton boys as a guard of honour, 300 strong, and the band playing God Save the Queen, and the Duchess of Teck too fat to get into the chapel'.[8] On another occasion, he wrote to his father 'Uncle Archie, [Reverend A. Wake] whom I asked about Sunday Closing of Publics, differs from you in his opinion. I am sending you his somewhat lengthy arguments, and I have sent him yours. The debate on Saturday was a particularly rotten one'.[9]

When Cornish retired in July 1893, J.H.M. Hare took over the house and Hereward became captain of the house.[10] For a brief period he was now with his younger brother, Godwin, who had entered the school in April. During his last two years at Eton, when he won many prizes, Hereward was with the talented and redoubtable H.E. Luxmoore as tutor, an arrangement which Hereward greatly appreciated.[11] By now his future career had been settled by his decision to enter the Army, and in preparation for this he had joined the Army class in 1893. On 12 July 1894, Corporal Wake was one of the eight boys from the school shooting for the Ashburton Shield at Bisley.[12] He left Eton a few days later; throughout the whole of his life, he continued to take a keen interest in the school and its affairs.

The autumn was spent at a crammer at Great Malvern, Worcestershire, preparing for the Sandhurst examinations. He took the task seriously, working eleven hours a day, leaving one hour free, in which time he would run for five miles.[13] It was not surprising therefore that he was successful and he began his course as a Gentleman Cadet at the Royal Military College in January 1895. It is significant for his later career that in the second half-yearly examinations two of his best subjects were Tactics and Military Topography.[14] On 17 March 1897, Hereward was gazetted as Second Lieutenant, 60th Rifles, The King's Royal Rifle Corps. He was an excellent rifle shot and won the Officers' Cup for the whole Army three months later, making eight bulls eyes running.[15]

It was because of his military commitments that he was not able to celebrate his coming of age until 30 July, some five months late. The occasion at Courteenhall was a splendid one, shared with relatives, friends, parishioners and tenants of Waltham, Nazeing and Courteenhall. His father, Sir Herewald, made a speech recalling the occasion of his own twenty-first birthday party some twenty four years previously. Tea was provided for between 500 and 600 people, followed by a variety of sporting

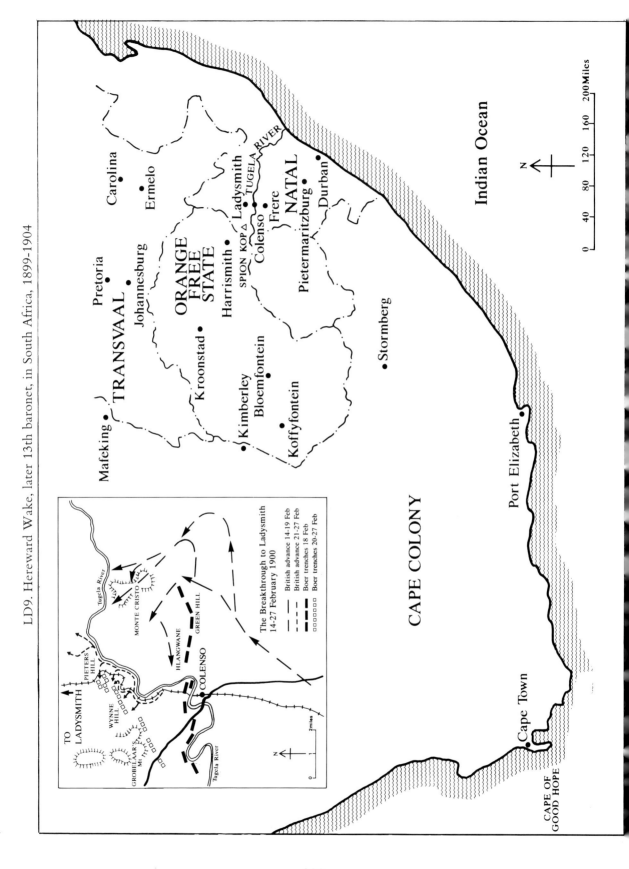

LD9. Hereward Wake, later 13th baronet, in South Africa, 1899-1904

**The Breakthrough to Ladysmith
14-27 February 1900**

————— British advance 14-19 Feb
- - - - - British advance 21-27 Feb
▭▭▭▭▭ Boer trenches 18 Feb
▰▰▰▰▰ Boer trenches 20-27 Feb

activities. The evening ended with dancing on the lawn.[16] By way of celebration, Hereward spent a holiday in Paris and was particularly taken with the theatre: *Le Misanthrope* and *La Malade Imaginaire* were 'just ripping and I understood it all'.[17]

But events overseas were taking place which would profoundly affect Hereward's life. Attempts by Britain to negotiate for the maintenance of peace in South Africa during 1899 came to an end with the ultimatum issued by the Boers on 9 October for the withdrawal of British troops. The prospect of active service was an attractive one for Hereward. He was stationed in Ireland at the outbreak of hostilities; now a Lieutenant he wrote to his brother:

> I'm sick of this waiting. They say we shan't march up till January. Meanwhile, the Boers will have chucked it, having been repulsed by General White [Lieutenant-General Sir George White, VC, Commander-in-Chief of Forces] and sick of making fools of themselves. We shall get a medal in commemoration without seeing a shot fired, and march with glory (?) through a crowded and enthusiastic metropolis. Ehem! and damn.[18]

Such optimism proved to be illusory. The Orange Free State and Transvaal joined forces and the South African (Boer) War broke out on 12 October. At this stage, the Boers had a two-to-one superiority in fighting men with greater mobility and artillery power. It was not until 29 September that the British Cabinet had authorized a force of some 47,000 men to be sent from England.[19] The Boer invasion led to a series of setbacks for the unprepared and poorly organized British Army. Mafeking, defended by Baden-Powell, was besieged on 13 October, as was Kimberley two days later and Ladysmith on 2 November.

*   *   *   *   *

Hereward left England with the 3rd Battalion of The King's Royal Rifles on 4 November 1899 in the Royal Mail Steamship *Servia*. Stopping briefly at St. Vincent, where he bought 200 enormous bananas for his company at a cost of three shillings, the ship sailed into Cape Town on 23 November. There he narrowly missed seeing his brother Godwin, who was serving in the 2nd Battalion, 5th Northumberland Fusiliers, and later he landed at Durban. The plan was for Hereward's battalion, which formed part of the 6th Brigade under Major-General N.G. Lyttelton, to join the field force in northern Natal with a view to relieving Ladysmith. He wrote to his youngest brother, Baldwin, an officer in the Royal Navy:

> The 60th. have lost half their officers in the 1st. and 2nd. Battalions already, including some of my best pals. In fact the Boers fight uncommonly well, if they <u>are</u> obliged to run every time, so if Godwin and I get knocked on the head mind you carry on as the future head of the family should do, and as I know you will. Don't sell Courteenhall, don't marry for money only, and stick to your profession; for that is what I mean to do myself.[20]

The Boers made good use of their knowledge of the terrain and of the War Office's lack of detailed intelligence to exploit the situation. Casualties mounted and the 'Black

Week', 10 to 15 December, was the lowest point of British fortunes. On 10 December, they were defeated at Stormberg, Piet Cronje was successful at Magersfontein on the 11th and there was disaster at Colenso, in which Hereward was a participant, on the 15th.[21]

General Sir Redvers Buller, the new Commander-in-Chief, a brave but reluctant leader,[22] had taken personal command in Natal. The plan was to cross the Tugela River, defeat Louis Botha's forces on the north bank and then relieve Ladysmith. Buller's muddled orders, the lack of detailed maps of the area and above all the Commander-in-Chief's loss of nerve during the battle were responsible for the subsequent defeat. Hereward's account of the battle, written on the following day, gives an objective assessment of events:

> Hildyard's Brigade advanced in lines of skirmishes at right angles to railway. Two Batteries trotted up to Railway without any precautions (Col. Long.) when suddenly a terrific fire burst out from Boers in wood and trenches at 500 yards. This was about 7a.m. Two guns out of twelve escaped, remainder lost all horses and men at once. The rest of the attack at this point was an attempt to recover the guns. Colenso was attacked and found full of Boers. But the Devons, West Yorks and Queens established themselves close to the river and along the railway in front of the guns. Two attempts were then made to take off the guns, the last by Freddy Roberts and some of Thorneycroft's mounted Infantry. He was wounded in three places, lost ten men out of twelve, most of his horses shot. It was this attempt of which I saw the end. A more gallant affair it is hard to imagine. The 60th. and Scots Rifles then moved up to cover retirement. Orders were then given to retire and the Brigade had finally done so by 2p.m. except two companies of Devons. An ambulance went down to the guns, which were covered by a battery on the hill. A party of Boers thereupon dashed out with a cheer and took away all the guns – ten. We could not fire owing to the ambulance. The Devons were captured with their colonel. This happened just before the 60th. were ordered to retire. At 2.30 firing had practically ceased, although we were followed by a few shells.
>
> It is is said that had the infantry held on till dark without retiring the guns could have been saved, that the retirement, although carried out splendidly and with the utmost coolness, cost many more lives than would have been the case had they stayed where they were. The Brigade lost 3 to 400 (?) and the whole affair was caused by the two batteries advancing so close to a practically impregnable position under the belief that it was unheld. It is understood that no such attack would have been made had there been no guns to save. Hart's (Irish) Brigade on the left moved up in quarter column! to the river, hitting off the wrong drift. When they had almost reached it, up jumped the Boers and let drive with everything they could lay hands on. The Connaught Rangers were slaughtered, their colonel, major and adjutant killed and most of their officers. Other regiments in rear lost heavily and all retired at once – but in good order. They fell into the ambush about 7 and all retired by about 11, I believe. Barton's

Brigade on the right did the same thing, and lost very heavily. They retired on our right. Lyttelton covered the retirement, 20,000 men, British! under the best of England's generals, repulsed with the loss of 1,500 men and 10 guns. Incredible as it appears each Brigade fell into ambush. On the 13th. and 14th. our heavy naval guns bombarded the intrenchments. The Boers, although possessing heavy guns, made no reply. Hardly one man could be seen. It is probable Buller himself thought they had all gone. The generals must have. We march gaily up unsuspecting. Suddenly every trench is manned, guns appear, large and small, there are thousands of the enemy ready hiding, and not one fires till we get into the trap. Then all is up. The position can never have been reconnoitred sufficiently. We have been repulsed with loss – not defeated – but 24 hours ago not a man could have imagined it possible.[23]

Whilst the Battalion was resting after the battle at Frere, Hereward, who had heard that Godwin had been taken prisoner at Stormberg and was at Pretoria, met and talked to Winston Churchill, then a young newspaper correspondent, who had just escaped from there.[24] Within a month they were to meet again at Spion Kop, a conical-shaped mountain 1,470 feet above the Tugela, to the west of Colenso. Here, Buller hoped to seize the mountain and open the road to Ladysmith, but once more, because of weak generalship, a bloody battle ended in defeat. Churchill, writing from Durban on 28 January 1900, stated, 'The scenes on Spion Kop were among the strangest and most terrible I have ever witnessed'.[25] Hereward's usual optimistic and cheery tone in his letters home was muted. In a letter to his sister Ida he gave this account of the battle:

We all feel rather low. My best friend Robin [Grant] is dead and buried fifty yards from where I write, near the Colonel and French Brewster. What they will put in the papers I don't know. Anyhow on the 25th Warren fought a great battle. His left was ten miles away; his right on a hill about one mile long close here called Spion Kop over the river. Guy's men seized the top of the left of the hill with the bayonet on night of 23rd. The Scottish Rifles went up to help them. All the 24th and 25th they were attacked by thousands of Boers with guns, and half of them killed. On the 25th General Lyttelton was asked for help and as he ordered my battalion to take the rest of the hill we did so. The hill is very high indeed and so steep that it is mostly climbing up precipices. The left half battalion attacked A, the right B, F Coy. was in front with Briscoe's. We started up about 2p.m. and I got to the top with nine men, first, at 6.30. We were under a cross fire all the way. Why the deuce we are alive I don't know. Anyhow the Boers ran from the trenches before we got there, but up at the top we weren't much better off, and the nine men speedily came down to five. However Cathcart and Warre soon came up with more, and finally we had nearly 100 on the top. Anyone who looked over was shot at once. I tried jumping up to fire and down again but could only see a lot of big rocks and trees 150 yards below which contained the enemy. My half battalion lost two officers killed and two wounded and about fifty men. The right half were just the same on the other hill – the

92. 'My brave Irish', Royal Dublin Fusiliers, Battle of Pieter's Hill, 27 February 1900, printed by Caton Woodville

93. Bivouac of 3rd Battalion, The King's Royal Rifle Corps, after the Battle of Spion Kop, 25 January 1900. Photographed by Lieutenant Hereward Wake

Colonel was killed and two officers wounded and about forty men killed and wounded. I can't describe it much. I didn't feel nervous at all – one doesn't – the difficulty was to get enough men on, some are keen enough. It was horrible seeing men rolling down like rabbits. At dark we were ordered to retire, (we had just planned a bayonet charge) much to our amazement and rage, but now I see it's as well we did. Anyhow we saved the lives of all those on the left of the hill who could not otherwise have held on till dark, when they retired also. I hope I shot a Boer or two but very much doubt it. I could easily have killed a horse but hadn't heart to, so I put a bullet under him and he trotted away. I believe his owner shot Brewster and several men – he was a crack shot anyhow and very nearly had me several times. I had about twenty shots in his direction but he was lodged between two stones, I expect, and I couldn't spot him. The General had us up today and said he was proud of us and that it was the finest bit of skirmishing and fighting he had ever seen. Poor Robin Grant was hit twice. Thistlewayte and Beaumont are badly wounded, and Briscoe and Kay, slightly. The poor old Colonel looked over the edge and got a bullet through his head. I was talking to Brewster when he was killed. I had an awful job getting two wounded men in and didn't arrive at the drift till 2.30a.m. The funny thing was that I felt very ill all day till the attack, and was sick going up the hill, but a mighty strength came over me and I have been well ever since. So I should recommend fighting for a liver upset by tinned beef.[26]

Writing to his mother a few days later, Hereward reflected, 'We walked or rather climbed up Spion Kop and came down again feeling, I suppose, as miserable as it is possible to feel during one's life'. He also mentioned that another great battle was to take place shortly: 'Buller declares he has the key of the way to Ladysmith'.[27] This third attempt to relieve Sir George White and his forces proved to be a costly failure. The place selected by Buller was Vaal Krantz, a ridge five miles east of Spion Kop. Once more, the operation required a crossing of the Tugela River. By the end of the first day of the battle, 5 February, a pontoon bridge had been thrown across it, the Boers having been taken by surprise. Hereward was among those who reached the hill by late evening. All the following day, the troops lay on the hill in the burning sun, unable to obtain any water or food. At 5.00 a.m, the Boers had started a bombardment which continued until the British withdrawal from the hill at 9 o'clock that evening. Hereward was bandaging a soldier who had both feet badly torn by a shell when a rush of Durham soldiers in retreat from the Boers swept past him. Hastily finishing the bandages, Hereward took a rifle and with the help of a sergeant managed to get a few men back into the firing line, with the Boers only some forty yards away. By this time, more of the soldiers had rejoined the small group of defenders. In Hereward's own words, 'When we fixed swords [bayonets] and cheered they all came back'. The bayonet charge was successful. Hereward's prompt action had temporarily saved the situation. Binding up one man with a bullet through his head, Hereward and his companions now retired. Typically, Hereward called the incident 'The worst 5 minutes I ever spent in my life and yet the best'.[28] The battle, ending in humiliation, had cost 333 British dead.[29]

The final breakthrough to Ladysmith occurred after a period of continuous fighting from 14 to 27 February. It was during this campaign, at Wynne's Hill, a mountain of some 4,400 feet, 3 miles north of Colenso, that Hereward encountered the greatest personal danger. As he wrote at the time:

> The facts are these – 4 of our companies, mine included were sent out late in the evening 3 days ago [22 February] to take up a line of outposts on a hill captured during the day. As we approached, the Boers were attacking the hill and its gallant defenders fled, the Lancashire Brigade. So we just charged up (it was almost dark) and retook it with the bayonet. But unfortunately the Boers were in large numbers, and fired at us from all sides in the darkness at ranges from 50 to 100 yards. We charged again and killed many and took some prisoners. It was a most exciting time; I think the Boers must have shot many of themselves. I fired my revolver at flashes close to me. Unfortunately about 100 men with Cathcart, Blundell, Alec and two others got too far and were quite surrounded. Cathcart was killed. When things got quieter, and only an occasional shot was fired, I was able to crawl through the Boers where they had left a space, and visit the beleaguered party. I found them in a round stone sangar, the Boers fifty yards away all round. I think they must have been in just as big a funk as we were. They were whistling and making signals. Our cartridges were nearly expended. Can you imagine a more awful state of affairs? Alec was as cool as possible and only seemed rather bored. Well, we finally agreed in a whispered council of war that I should crawl back and bring assistance at daybreak. This I was able to do. (Doesn't it sound like a novel?); whenever I trod on a stone crack! crack! pat! and you may believe I lay pretty close. Well, after wandering about till 1a.m., I found the Col. commanding the 11th. Brigade, and he gave me two companies of the East Surreys and three of the Devons, and I guided them to position; we were to do a bayonet charge at dawn on each side of the hill up to the sangar and bring back our men. At 4.30 we advanced and all was quiet. We walked up to within 150 yards and not a sound. I feared some trap and asked the E. Surreys to halt, while I went on and the whole lot retired through. I got inside the sangar – all was still! Whispered retire.
>
> Hardly had one man crept out before a most awful fire burst out all round us. A dozen of us fired from the wall while the others ran back, and when all had started Blundell and I ran with the rest, and I'm sure I never went so fast. The hail of bullets was awful. Luckily it was dusk and only about half were shot down. Alec was hit in the arm. How anyone escaped I don't know. We passed the E. Surreys, who poured in volley after volley, and then ran back in their turn through a second line we had made behind. They lost an awful lot of men in saving us. This second line we held on to, but it proved most unfortunately situated later. Only Curling, Alec and I remained here, and we got together. When fully daylight, a bad fire began all round and of the 50 men who lay across that hill with us (only six were Riflemen) there were only about 20 unhit, as we were not permitted to retire for three hours. Our wounded we had to leave and

few survived. One of my men was captured by the Boers and escaped, and he tells me they shot the wounded if they moved an inch, and it was only on the third day that we had an armistice to collect them. I lost my best sergeant. I now command F. Coy. as poor Cathcart was our skipper. When we did retire many were killed, and Alec shot again in the leg, but not badly. He is one of the bravest men I know. You must under stand we didn't abandon the hill, but just left an uncomfortable part of it where we had arrived by a fatal mistake. We hold it still. Yesterday was the armistice, worse than fighting in my opinion. I shall not forget it.

> When I got down with Alec and Curling safe I was covered with blood and dirt, and utterly tired out.[30]

By this time, the tide of war had turned in favour of the British. On the same day that General Cronje was defeated at Paardeberg on 18 February 1900 the Tugela was finally crossed. Two days after Hereward had sent his vivid account of Wynne's Hill, he was part of the force which entered Ladysmith, with the Boers in full retreat. The first phase of the Boer invasion was now over.

* * * * *

On 10 March, Hereward's mother received a letter from Edwina Roberts, daughter of Field Marshal Lord Roberts, who had succeeded Buller as Commander-in-Chief, South Africa, at the end of December. Roberts, nicknamed 'Bobs' by the soldiers, was an Indian Army man. He had won the Victoria Cross during the Indian Mutiny in 1857–8 and had served as Commander-in-Chief of India, 1885–93. From 1895 until his appointment to South Africa, Roberts was Commander-in-Chief in Ireland. It was whilst he was stationed there that Hereward was invited to stay with the Roberts'. As he told his mother at the time, 'Lord Roberts asked very nicely after Uncle Harry [Herwald Wake], and said he would never forget the Arrah episode'. Hereward was also chosen to act as aide-de-camp to the Field Marshal at a big field day.[31]

In her letter Edwina Roberts informed Lady Wake, 'I thought you might like to hear your son is going to be on Father's Staff. Father was very anxious to get a 60th. man and knew your son when he stayed with us at The Curragh last year'.[32] Hereward received the news of his appointment at Pietermaritzburg. He quickly caught a train to Kimberley and then rode 100 miles on horseback to Bloemfontein, which Roberts had recaptured on 13 March. Joyously, he told Ida, 'Here I am, ADC to the most famous and popular man in the whole world, Commander-in-Chief of the largest army England has ever put in the field. My extraordinary luck makes me think I am dreaming'.[33]

Hereward soon settled into the work, much of which was concerned with deciphering telegrams from field commanders and from the Cabinet. He was the object of much interest at headquarters as the first man in that area who had been in Ladysmith. He chafed at the lack of exercise and was pleased at the opportunity of travelling to Cape Town, a journey of almost 1,000 miles, with Roberts' mail and to escort an important Boer prisoner-of-war. The Field Marshal discussed with Hereward the battles of the

60th Rifles; it was obvious that the death at Colenso of his son, Freddy, a brother officer and a close friend of Hereward, had deeply affected the old soldier.

Roberts' campaign to march north-east to take Pretoria began in early April. Hereward, on horseback, witnessed several of the battles, with Lord Roberts at the head of his staff, Kitchener on his left and behind, several generals, colonels and ADCs. 'It is a new sensation,' he wrote to his mother, 'to view a fight from a position of inglorious security, and not exactly a pleasing one; but you know what's going on which you don't with your own regiment, a fact which my limited view of the Natal battles as expressed in my letters reveals'.[34] He also noted the advanced guard, 'crawling up kopjes, hunting through scrub and looking into holes and scouring about for all the world like Snap and Glynn [Hereward's two favourite dogs, a fox-terrier and spaniel respectively] drawing the Bath Spinney'.[35]

By 12 May, Kroonstad had been captured. A procession was formed and Roberts entered the town in triumph. 'Of course,' wrote Hereward, 'a cinematograph was rigged up, so you had better go round the Music Halls and look for me on a white horse, between Westminster [Duke of] and Settrington'.[36] When Roberts took Pretoria on 31 May, his 'Grand Army' had covered 260 miles in 26 days. Much to Hereward's chagrin, he was taken ill at Kroonstad and was unable to accompany his hero into Pretoria. Following on a few days later on 17 July there was an emotional reunion with his brother, Godwin, who had been released as a prisoner of war at Pretoria. Even then, Hereward's sense of humour was irrepressible. 'We went to see his prison', he told Ida, 'and I photoed him scrabbling at the bars of his cage from the outside'.[37]

There was some consternation on 6 August when De Wet managed to evade the British forces and escape across the Vaal. As Hereward noted, 'It's not a very edifying picture, 50,000 men and a dozen of our best generals after one farmer and 2,000 uneducated Boers'.[38] 'He [De Wet] is a true soldier in every way', he had written earlier, 'and no coward nor treacherous. When we catch that man he ought to have command of our Mounted Infantry'.[39] A souvenir which he had collected was a Boer Long Tom shell (unfired) from one of their new Creusot 155mm guns, 'but as it takes two men to lift it, I don't know how I shall get it home'.[40] The final phase of the Natal war began in early August. On the 25th, Roberts arrived to take charge of his own forces combined with Buller's. Hereward was present at the last great set battle of the campaign, at Belfast, east of Pretoria on 27 August.[41]

With the overrunning of Transvaal and the flight of the Boer leader, Kruger, to Europe, Roberts considered that the war was as good as over and he prepared to leave South Africa. He particularly requested to see the 1st Battalion of The King's Royal Rifles as it left Pretoria at the end of October. It was a sad occasion, as Hereward recounted:

> The Chief was out to see them pass his house at 6.30. The regiment halted and he shook hands with all the officers but he was unable to say a word, although he had intended to make a speech. The memory of Freddy seems to be brought back to him every time he sees the regiment, and when the 1st. Battalion afterwards marched past, he broke down altogether.[42]

Hereward was greatly looking forward to returning to England with his chief, but was delayed by two events. Prince Christian Victor, Queen Victoria's favourite grandson, who had been an extra ADC to Roberts since August, died of typhoid in Pretoria on 28 October. Both Roberts and Hereward attended the funeral. At the same time, Roberts' daughter Aileen, who was also very ill with typhoid, had to recover at Johannesburg before the journey could be made. Hereward arrived in England in early January 1901. On 3 January he drove with Roberts in procession in State carriages through cheering crowds from Waterloo to Buckingham Palace, where a banquet was given.[43] At the time Queen Victoria was seriously ill at Osborne and she died on 22 January. A week after the banquet, Hereward rode once more through the streets of London, this time on horseback, in the Queen's funeral procession from Westminster Abbey to Paddington, where the cortège was taken to Windsor.

On Hereward's return to South Africa in May, the situation had changed. With the Boers now resorting to guerrilla tactics, Kitchener, the new Commander-in-Chief, attempted to contain the enemy by erecting a line of blockhouses, with barbed wire between them, across the country. In addition, 'concentration camps' were set up, housing 120,000 Boer women and children, of whom some 20,000 died of starvation or disease. Hereward did not favour either unnecessarily stern measures or cruelty. Replying to a letter from his father, Hereward commented, 'There are a certain number of the enemy who will not submit to be conquered by their despised foes, and who never will, any more than you would accept the rule of a French governor at Northampton'.[44] After witnessing the plight of the Dutch refugees, he remarked, 'It is a sight for anyone who wants to moralize on the horrors of war'.[45]

The Boer guerrillas, known as Commandos, were inflicting heavy casualties on the British. Hereward's own regiment had lost nearly all their Mounted Infantry officers by October 1901, with seventy wounded or killed. It was now that Hereward's courage was put to its greatest test.

On 26 October, Hereward was with a force of 200 men near Koffyfontein, Orange Free State, in search of Commandos who had been worrying the garrison:

> After a long two days march we spotted several of the enemy about 9 a.m. and Col. Henry at once ordered an attack. Ronaldson with self and thirty five men and officers were to seize a ridge and work down to the right, Henry with remainder (bar 50 left behind) and the pom-pom on our right. The river was behind the Boers. We advanced on the ridge and when my four Scouts reached the crest, there were the Boers coming up hand over fist the other side. One scout was killed and all four horses immediately. On the first shot we galloped, dismounted under the hill and advanced. The delay was fatal, and luck against us. As we came into view a hot fire broke out at 200 yards and we lay down and blazed back. Then we essayed to advance. The men hung back of course a little. I hadn't gone five yards before I saw a bearded scoundrel with his eye cocked along the barrel. I suppose I moved pretty quick but he just got me.[46] Creighton was down on my left and two of my men dropped out of three near me, so I found it wasn't good enough and took cover. After that it was a duel at

150 yards for an hour. To my grief I found I had a rifle with a damaged foresight, and I <u>couldn't</u> hit a Boer. There they were, close to, on the sky-line coming up to fire and down again time after time, but where my bullets went to I'm hanged if I know. I'd have given a year's pay for my rook-rifle. I could have wept. I did swear. I swear now … This went on for an hour, while Henry worked over on our right. The welcome baying and crackle of musket and the pompom getting nearer and nearer cheered our aching frames and particularly my neck. Our men shoot so atrociously and I fancy few took aim, that at length they got the better of us and the smallest movement brought a crack, followed by the intolerable smell of a bullet hitting a rock close to, a smell that brings hateful memories. Then they fired a loose volley and fled. I knew it. I felt sure. I put up my hat six inches. Nothing happened. Cautiously, cautiously we looked up. All was still! Crawled on with rifle ready – you never know what they'll do, and we are all damn funks – stood up, advanced, ran a bit, ran more. Got on the crest. There they go! On their horses and off! Pom pom pom pom pom – pom pom pom – (repeat this several times). A final rattle of musketry. The retreat was well-timed and they all got over the river, bar one. I found a field-dressing on a rock near the man who shot me – nothing more. We got their dinners at a farm below. Another force was to have been across the river but turned up too late. We had four officers wounded and two men, one man killed, all the men of my company. Nine horses killed.

This is a long description of an interesting little skirmish. You will observe that the Boers had the best of us <u>by two minutes</u>. Had we been on that crest just before them instead of vice versa we should have bagged the lot, as the hill was very steep their side, and their horses were at our mercy. Oh what infernal luck![47]

This cheery account hid the fact that Hereward had received a bullet wound in his neck, very near to the spinal column. A trophy which he sent home to his mother was the handkerchief which he was wearing around his neck with no fewer than twenty four holes in it.[48] As a result of his encounter he was kept in hospital for some weeks until the wounds had healed. In December, he had lunch in Pretoria with Lord Kitchener who was very sanguine about the end of the war, possibly in six months' time, which in the event was an accurate estimate.

The Boer Commandos were proving to be very troublesome in the Transvaal. Hereward was to spend the last six months of the war in this territory. Conditions were very difficult, given the new tactics, particularly ambushes, which had to be employed against an invisible enemy. He told his mother, 'We move at night so often that I have acquired the habit of sleeping peacefully in the saddle, and wake up fresh for the rush at dawn, which is exciting to a degree and somewhat dangerous'.[49] It was exhausting work too. The heavy rains, mountainous terrain, the long distances covered by horseback and the close-range fighting took its toll. Hereward was upset at the casualties amongst the horses. In one week in January 1902, he calculated that his Company of Mounted Infantry had lost twenty five horses out of seventy.[50]

94. Boer Commandos at Newcastle, Natal, October 1901

95. Badge of the Northamptonshire Rifle Volunteer Corps, worn by Sir Herewald Wake, 12th baronet

96. Badge of The King's Royal Rifle Corps, worn by the 13th baronet and later by his sons Hereward and Peter

243

The final stages of routing out the remaining Boers, involving the burning of farmhouses, searching mountain caves and intercepting wagons, and the increasing use of Zulu impi by the Army, was not to Hereward's taste. Towards the end of March he wrote exasperatedly, 'O Lord! Send 100,000 more men please and let's get it over at once'.[51]

Hereward's personal courage received public recognition at this time when he was awarded the bronze medal of the Royal Humane Society. On Christmas Eve 1901, he had plunged into the swollen river at Bosman's Spruit in the Transvaal and succeeded in saving the life of one of his men who had been swept away crossing the bridge, which was already two feet under water. Learning of the award he could scarcely believe it. 'It was a natural and easy thing to one who could swim to pull a poor devil out of the water what couldn't, and on seeing him sink I naturally hauled him out. It never struck me as dangerous, and my only wonder was that everyone else on the bank hadn't done the same'.[52] There was no let-up in the fighting, even when the Boer generals were holding meetings to discuss possible peace terms. Attacks on the Boers, resulting in heavier casualties for the British, often involved raids of up to forty miles in a day in cold weather; at one place, Val, when an encounter necessitated lying down in the dark for several hours, water was selling at half a crown a liqueur glass.

A fitting end to Hereward's nineteen months' campaigning in South Africa was the award of the Distinguished Service Order for outstanding bravery. Even this was briefly dismissed in a letter to his father. 'Colonel Mackenzie presented me with my D.S.O. on parade the other day – what the devil am I to do with it on the bleak veldt?'[53] By the end of the campaign, he had been promoted to Captain (January 1902), mentioned in dispatches three times and had gained two medals with seven clasps.

A month later, on 31 May 1902, the Treaty of Vereeniging brought hostilities to a close. The day before, Hereward told Ida, 'There is one reason why I long for peace, namely that the sickening sufferings of the wretched horses will cease'.[54] During the campaign, Hereward had several horses, with such names as Little Piggy, The Bouncer and his favourite charger, Marcus.[55] With more leisure available, Hereward passed the time playing football and polo. Shortly before returning to England on leave, Hereward revisited Spion Kop, now with over 300 crosses and stones marking the burial places, and then on to Vaal Krantz. Buller's poor generalship had left bitter memories. 'I never realized this before', he wrote to Ida, 'but the monuments of Spion Kop are records of a great British victory and nothing less, wantonly turned into a miserable defeat. I doubt if any other Army would have gone up Pieters Hill after such shows as we had'.[56]

After a brief spell in England, Hereward reluctantly returned to South Africa in January 1903. Anxious to settle once more in England, he asked General Lyttelton in April for news of postings, to be told that no more infantry battalions would be leaving South Africa for another year – 'so I think you had better sell my horses in August or September, unless you hear further'.[57] Courteenhall was never far from his thoughts. On 1 October, he wrote, 'Today, my dear Ida, being the feast of St. Pheasant, I wish you luck in the Three Cornered Plantation'.[58] At last, in January, 1904, Hereward left South Africa for the last time. Jokingly Hereward surmised, 'I don't know how I shall do at home with my extravagant habits, as the pay is good out here. Hunt I will, at any cost'.[59]

*   *   *   *   *

Hereward's arrival back home coincided with the reorganization at the War Office and the formation of a new general staff. He was now appointed to the Office in order to enlarge his experience. A friend who had fought alongside him at Colenso and Spion Kop before becoming Lyttelton's Brigade Major was Henry Wilson, later Field Marshal Sir Henry Wilson. He wrote to Hereward:

> I am so glad to hear you are going to the War Office and that you like the prospect. There is more to be learnt there than anywhere and I think possibly more chances of helping and doing good. It always delights me to see men like yourself (I write in no flattering sense) going up to the War Office. When you, and your like, gain experience and keep your ideals, then we shall be in a fair way to make this old country safe. You must come and pay us some Saturday to Monday visits. You are always welcome.[60]

Wilson was appointed as Commandant of the Staff College, Camberley, in January 1907. A year later Hereward was selected to attend the College as a student. Wilson's breadth of vision and outstanding grasp of military tactics, combined with a remarkable personality inspired awe and admiration in his students,[61] including Hereward. Wilson was convinced that there would be war with Germany and the potential enemy was carefully studied by the students. A tour of the 1870 Franco-Prussian War battlefields stimulated Hereward's interest in tactics. Whilst in Alsace, he saw a Prussian regiment on manoeuvres and was impressed with their bearing and efficiency.[62] After spending 1909 at the Royal Naval War College, he returned as GSO3 at the War Office until 1911,[63] when he became Brigade Major, 2nd Infantry Brigade at Aldershot. He was gazetted as Brevet-Major in May 1913 and joined his 1st Battalion in January 1914. Hereward's love of horses found many outlets and he was Master of the Staff College Drag Hounds. He was also unlucky, breaking his pelvis while riding at Olympia in 1909 and injuring his back in a regimental point-to-point race in 1913.

So far, Hereward's military career had occupied most of his waking hours. In January 1911 now aged thirty five, he had published an article in the *Cavalry Journal* on the need for horses in the event of mobilization. With the ever increasing threat of war from Germany, he was conscious like his hero, Lord Roberts, of the need for an Army prepared to meet any military aggression. It was probably about this time that he first met the nineteen year old Margaret Winifred Benson, known as Daisy, at Cortachy Castle, Angus, the home of the Earl of Airlie. Hereward described her as 'small and fair with brown hair and eyes that are often blue. She is good at tennis, having athletic brothers, and I'm hanged if I know if she rides or not'.[64] She was the eldest daughter of Robert and Evelyn Benson of Buckhurst, Withyham, Sussex, and South Street, Park Lane. Benson, sole partner of Robert Benson & Co., merchant bankers,[65] (later Kleinwort Benson) had at Oxford won both the University Mile and Three Mile races and played in the first Association football match against Cambridge in 1874.[66] An art connoisseur, he had acquired many Early Italian paintings,[67] as well as Chinese porcelain and antique furniture and was a Trustee of the National Gallery and a Council member of the Victoria and Albert Museum. His wife, Evelyn, was the sister of Major Sir George Holford, Equerry to King George V, owner of Dorchester House, London, and Westonbirt, Gloucestershire. Their father, Robert Stayner Holford, had been Conservative MP for East Gloucestershire, 1855–72.[68]

Daisy's background contrasted sharply with Hereward's. Her father had rented Buckhurst, a large house built by George Stanley Repton in the 1830s,[69] from Lord De La Warr at the beginning of the century. Robert had spent lavishly in restoring the house, commissioning Lutyens in 1903–4 to undertake the work, and create a series of superb gardens.[70] Buckhurst during the next two decades remained their main family home. Daisy's childhood in the company of her brothers, Guy, Rex and Con and her sister Rosalind was a happy one and she had a wide circle of friends. Her letters to her parents, written at the age of sixteen, indicate that she led a hectic social life: dances at Hatfield ('the house is heavenly') until the early morning and at Lady Desborough's Taplow Court, deer-stalking with her father in Scotland, and visits to Paris to improve her French, see the art galleries and attend yet more dances. Daisy took piano lessons and though not a skilful player, loved music and frequently went to concerts. She was responsible for calling a meeting at Stafford House in order to begin a journal, called the *Parachute Magazine*, devoted to current issues and the arts. 'We have not yet had the time to take the question of the Suffragettes seriously in *The Parachute*', she wrote to her father in 1907, 'but when you get here, you must help me to put in something about them'.[71] Whilst still in her teens, she was briefly and unofficially engaged to Bobby White, a younger brother of the third Lord Annaly, Master of the Pytchley, who lived at Holdenby; Bobby subsequently became a family friend.[72]

One of the earliest surviving letters from Hereward to Daisy, dated 22 June 1912, enclosed £2, 'which is what you won on the last race before you went away . . . I hope you liked Ascot. I liked it better than any I've been to yet'.[73] The salutation is 'Dear Miss Benson'. Exactly a week later, Hereward wrote excitedly to his mother from camp:

My dearest Mama,

Daisy Benson of Buckhurst has promised to marry me.

She is an angel and much too nice for me, but oddly enough she is very fond of me, and almost as much so, I do believe, as I am of her. She is only 20.

I am now tackling her father and mother, and I don't know what's going to happen, so please don't breathe a word except to Sir H. and the girls.

You must help me though, and impress on Sir H. that it will not be necessary to give a gloomy account of the financial state of affairs on that dim and distant date when I succeed to the family estate.

It is much more to the point to consider my professional prospects as a soldier.

97. Field Marshal Earl Roberts, VC (front row, second from the right) with Sir Alfred Milner (front row, second from the left) and some staff officers, Cape Town, December 1900. Lieutenant Hereward Wake, then one of Roberts ADCs, is on the extreme left, back row

98. Sir Hereward Wake, 13th baronet (1876–1963) on horseback at Courteenhall. In the background is Godwin's Oak

Congratulate me, as I am a very fortunate and happy man.
Love.

Yours

Hereward[74]

He had proposed at a dance given by Lady Leicester on 27 June. To celebrate, Hereward purchased a hunter, which he asked Daisy to name, though adding, 'I think "Leicester" would do, to commemorate the ball of the season'.[75] In August, Hereward was invited to Ardgowan, near Glasgow, where Daisy's friend Una Shaw-Stewart lived. Hereward's memories of the occasion three years later were chiefly concerned with the fact that they shot 203 brace of grouse and caught a trout each, Daisy's weighing ½lb. and his 1¼ lbs.[76]

With plans for the marriage settled Hereward's time was fully occupied as Brigade Major to Brigadier T.L. Morland, Commander of the 2nd Brigade, at Aldershot, taking part in night manoeuvres and mock battles. Shortly before the wedding, when Daisy's personal possessions were being moved into their house at Blackdown, Hampshire, Hereward reported, 'Lord, what a lot, but they melted away indoors. Nothing broke except a tiny chip off your writing table, and of course three or four dozen Ming jars which I sent to the kitchen, mistaking them for utensils, and they got smashed to atoms, dear, atoms'.[77]

The wedding, which took place at St. Margaret's, Westminster, on 30 October 1912,[78] was attended by many distinguished guests, including the Prime Minister, Asquith, and his wife Margot. Hereward was delighted that Lord Roberts, now eighty, and his two daughters were able to be present. The marriage ceremony was conducted by clergy from both sides of the family; Randall Davidson, now Archbishop of Canterbury, assisted by Daisy's uncle, Edwyn Hoskyns, Bishop of Southwell. The *Northampton Herald* stated, 'The popularity of the bride may be estimated from the fact that she received something like 600 wedding presents, and South Street, Park Lane, her parents' town house, though a spacious structure of the Queen Anne period, could not accommodate them'.[79] The presents were displayed at Dorchester House, which Sir George Holford had let to the American ambassador, who placed the house at the couple's disposal for the reception.

Following his father's example, Hereward had determined that he would not be the first member of the Wake family to drive away from his wedding in a motor car. Accordingly, he hired two horses to take Daisy and himself to Paddington. Sir George Holford had lent them Westonbirt for their honeymoon and unfortunately for Hereward, he had overlooked the fact that a motor car would be sent to convey them from Tetbury Station to Westonbirt. During the journey, the chauffeur lost control because of the wet road and the car ran into a ditch. Hereward was thrown through the window but escaped serious injury. Daisy was also thankfully unhurt. Two horses were required to pull the car out of the ditch and the couple finished their journey in a farmer's cart. Sir Herewald Wake told a reporter afterwards that it seemed to be the hereditary experience of the Wake family to have a mishap on their honeymoon; the same had happened after his own wedding thirty-eight years previously.[80] Daisy and

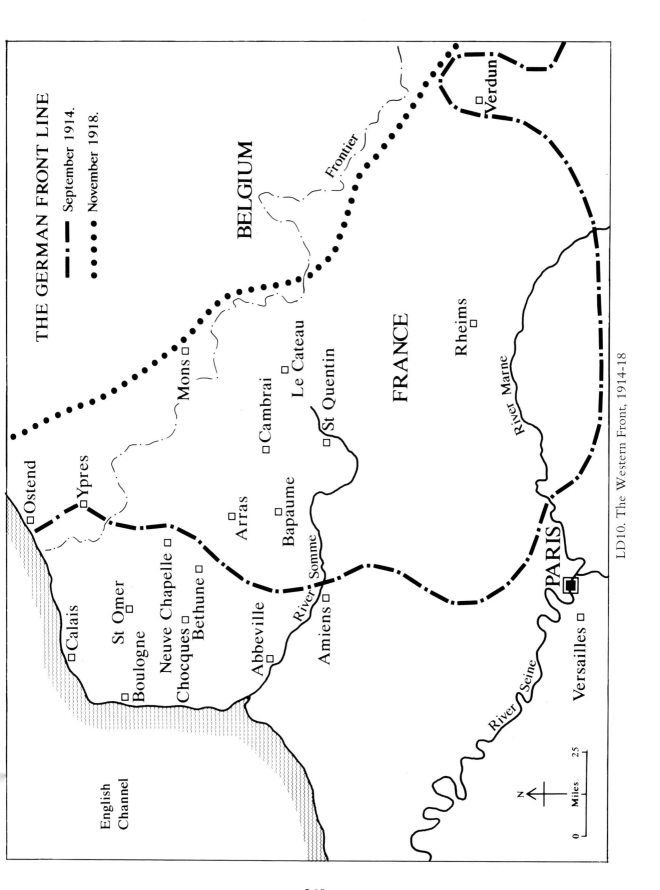

THE GERMAN FRONT LINE

- – · – September 1914.
- • • • • November 1918.

English
Channel

BELGIUM

Frontier

Ostend

Ypres

Mons

Calais

St Omer

Boulogne

Neuve Chapelle

Chocques

Bethune

Arras

Bapaume

Cambrai

Le Cateau

St Quentin

Abbeville

Amiens

River Somme

FRANCE

Rheims

Verdun

River Marne

PARIS

Versailles

River Seine

N

Miles

0   25

LD10. The Western Front, 1914-18

Hereward later returned to Courteenhall on 21 November where there were celebrations, including a supper in the Old Grammar School for all the tenants and those who worked on the estate.[81]

*　　　*　　　*　　　*　　　*

Events in Europe were soon to cast a shadow over their lives. In the summer of 1914, Germany had positioned 1½ million soldiers on the Belgian border. On 1 August, Germany declared war on Russia and requested that her army should be granted passage through Belgian territory. This was refused and Germany declared war on both Belgium and France. Troops crossed the Belgian border on 4 August. Britain as a guarantor of Belgian neutrality declared war later that same day. Kitchener assumed charge at the War Office and appointed Field Marshal Sir John French to command the British Expeditionary Force, which he had devoted several years to organizing and training.[82] Hereward, who was now Brevet-Major, was contacted soon afterwards. On 14 August, French crossed the Channel by the cruiser *Sentinel* from Dover to Boulogne with part of his General Headquarters. It consisted of Lieutenant-General Sir Archibald Murray, Major-General Sir William Robertson, Brigadier-General Henry Wilson and Major Hereward Wake.[83]

Staying the night at Amiens, they arrived next day in Paris to be greeted by vast crowds shouting *'Vive l'Angleterre'*.[84] As Hereward wrote to Daisy that day:

> The main purpose of our journey here is to fix up a plan with General Joffre, the French Commander-in-Chief, and he happens to be somewhere else, so I expect Henry [Wilson] will go off to see him. As he cannot speak English and French cannot speak French (one is apt to get confused here) it would be worse than useless for the two commanders to try and settle anything of great importance over the telephone. One French General said he only knew three English sentences, but they were quite enough to get on with anywhere. They were 'Rost bif and potitoes', 'Beauteefool women' and 'Kees me queek'. Beside this sort of thing, my dear, I am an accomplished linguist. As a matter of fact I am speaking French better every time I try.[85]

The following day, Hereward was present at the historic conference between French and Joffre and the two staffs at Vitry-le-Francois, Joffre's GHQ near Rheims. 'The plan of campaign was unfolded and you can imagine the scene – in a small classroom of a school with childish pictures on the wall. Some day I will write an account of what took place'.[86] That night at dinner, Hereward sat next to French and had a long talk with him and admired the Field Marshal's grasp of the situation.

Soon afterwards, however, the situation became desperate. A French offensive was unsuccessful and in the first battle between British and German armies at Mons on 23 August, the former were obliged to retreat: British and French forces fell back to the Marne. As the Germans advanced towards Paris, the French Government left for Bordeaux. During this traumatic period, Hereward was sent out to act as a traffic manager at places such as St. Quentin, where guns and men converged and which took a

250

night and a day to unravel. It was there that he was shocked by the sight of hundreds of British soldiers, exhausted and demoralized, lying on the pavements fast asleep, having thrown away their packs, rifles and equipment. He resented the intervention of the Army Censor in restricting his letters to Daisy and found a way round it by posting them privately by the King's Messenger. Daisy was the envy of her friends thereafter in often receiving Hereward's letters on the same day that they were written.

On 9 September he confided to Daisy, 'To tell the truth I have never lived through such a bad time as the fortnight of our retreat from Mons . . . We were very near a big disaster, and are lucky to have got off with a loss of about 16,000 men. The Germans moved five Army Corps of about 290,000 men against our five divisions, two of which were only just out of the train and minus some of their artillery'.[87] Hereward privately blamed Kitchener for the débâcle, especially the initial delay of a week in sending out the Expeditionary Force: because of this, soldiers were rushed into battle. Hereward's dislike of the Germans was based on such incidents such as that which occurred at Rheims on 19 September:

> Today saw the last of the Cathedral and the story comes from one of our officers who saw what happened. There has been fighting round Rheims for some days. The French drove the Germans out of it a few days ago and the latter have since been holding a strong positon round the N.E. side which prevented the French coming out. They have amused themselves by shelling the town and killing inhabitants, but not very much. There were no soldiers inside. Today the Germans deliberately turned their heavy artillery on the Cathedral till it caught fire, the roof fell in and the destruction was complete.
>
> There was no military object in this proceeding, and I suppose it was done out of rage and spite. One hardly need comment upon it, for I expect the newspapers of the world in general will do the needful in this respect. They are a curious people, these Germans, with their cursed 'culture', and I cannot think that any race can become great which shows itself to be so small in big matters.
>
> The French had put 800 wounded Germans in the Cathedral to save it from destruction, and it is said that they locked them in and shot any that tried to crawl out. But it is more likely they carried the wounded to a place of safety though they are getting so angry that I would not be surprised at anything. When our troops catch prisoners the latter beseech them not to hand them over to the French.[88]

With worries of possible invasion if the Germans should reach the Channel ports, the Cabinet in London ordered British troops to northern Belgium in an attempt to relieve Antwerp; Major-General Sir Henry Rawlinson was in charge of the field force. Hereward was sent by Sir John French to Ostend with further instructions on 11 October shortly after Antwerp had been evacuated;[89] he admired the way in which the Belgians continued to defend their country.

Amidst all the chaos and discomfort, Hereward found time to write to Daisy on 29 October, their second wedding anniversary. He recalled:

It was a happy day, dear, wasn't it? I felt absurdly happy and confident – absolutely confident. There was a kind of feeling one has if one attained a great object after years of concentrated effort. I can imagine a snail feeling intense satisfaction all over on getting to the top of a wall after climbing for three weeks. I feel also very sorry for the other snails who would never get to such a good place as mine. Luckily for them they don't realize it.[90]

From 13 October 1914, the British GHQ, after many peregrinations, settled at St. Omer, some 25 miles from Calais. This was of particular interest to Hereward as the town was the birthplace of Torfrida or Thurfrida, who had there met and married Hereward the Wake nearly nine centuries previously. The war was going badly, with the enemy pushing troops into Flanders. By the 19th the Germans had reached Ypres, where Rawlinson was approaching from Bruges. The first Battle of Ypres, lasting from 30 October to 24 November, was a bloody one, as Hereward observed at close quarters:

The battle yesterday was terrible. The Germans sent their Guard Corps round to hammer us. They got through in one place and over 700 of their corpses were counted behind our line this morning. Ten times that number lie in front, I suppose. In some places, the trenches are only 10 yards apart.[91]

A few days before, Daisy had travelled down for the weekend to Englemere, near Ascot, the home of Hereward's old chief, Lord Roberts. Although now over eighty, he wished to play an active part in the war. Kitchener appointed him as Colonel-in-Chief of the Overseas Forces and Roberts, excited at the opportunity, spent much time welcoming men from different parts of the Empire. On hearing that an Indian Division had landed in France, he made plans to visit them at the Front. Rawlinson, on leave for a few days, was also at Englefield. Daisy, visiting the Roberts' at the beginning of November, reported to Hereward:

I have never seen anyone in better spirits than Rawly and he looks *so* well. He wants to take the little man over to you on Friday, to see the Indian troops. He is *wonderful*, Lord Roberts, and goes about the house singing to himself like a boy of sixteen.[92]

The critical military situation made it necessary to delay Roberts' departure until 11 November, when he crossed to Boulogne with his elder daughter, Aileen. There he spent the afternoon visiting hospitals and Hereward had the pleasure of taking tea with him and informing him at first hand of the battle then raging nearby. After an early breakfast, Roberts toured his beloved Indian Divisions and later watched the shelling at Ypres, some six miles distant.[93] His daughter noticed that he was not well on their way back to St. Omer. He had caught a chill, and as he displayed a high temperature was put to bed. 'We are rather alarmed', wrote Hereward on 13 November, 'as after all he is 84'.[94] Pneumonia set in. Sir Henry Wilson, who had escorted the Field Marshal on his visit, wrote in his diary the following day:

The little Chief got steadily worse. I was in and out all day with Aileen, and took her for a walk at 4 o'clock. At 7.45p.m. Hereward sent for me. When I got there the Chief was dying. Aileen, Hereward, and I, with 3 doctors and 3 nurses were with him to the end. He died at 8p.m. in absolute peace and quiet. The story of his life is thus completed as he would have wished himself, dying in the middle of the soldiers he loved so well and within the sound of guns.[95]

Hereward was given the responsibility of escorting Aileen back to England. They left for Calais the following day. On the 19th, Hereward attended the state funeral at St. Paul's Cathedral, where the pallbearers were five Field Marshals, an Admiral of the Fleet, an Admiral and five Generals.

*   *   *   *   *

Following the first Battle of Ypres, the Western Front was static as the opposing armies became deadlocked. A series of complex trench systems was constructed, combining the functions of defence and communications, and were separated by No Man's Land; stretching from the English Channel to Switzerland, the lines of the Allied armies varied but little between November 1914 and September 1918.[96] Hereward noted that the German parapets and trenches were distinguishable from the Allies because they were made of white linen and coloured cloth of every sort, including old petticoats. With the opposing trenches only a matter of yards apart, verbal exchanges were often made. On one occasion, Hereward heard the men in a German trench shout across in English, sing the Austrian national anthem and then roar with laughter.[97] The discomfort experienced by the occupants is easily imagined. As Hereward told Daisy:

> Charlie's dug-out holds about 250 men. It is 30 steps down in the blue clay, which drips and stinks and there is a continual blue river along the passage and down the stairs of the various entrances, which runs to an electric pump which pumps up the water and also supplies the electric light. Being made by us and not the Boche, the dug-out is only 4'6" high and one is constantly stooping in it. The air is pretty thick too.[98]

Summing up the situation at the end of the year, Hereward believed that but for a fluke, Paris would have fallen to the Germans in September and that they were within inches of capturing Calais, with a possible invasion of England to follow. Much of the blame could be attributed, in his opinion, to Kitchener, who was caught unprepared when war broke out, having refused to listen to Lord Roberts' warnings. On learning of Kitchener's death on his way to Russia, drowned in the *Hampshire* which was sunk on 5 June 1916, Hereward wrote, 'His loss to the country is nothing ... History will some day size him up and wonder why his country thought so much of him'.[99] Politicians, too, had been too complacent: 'The wonder is', he noted, 'that Haldane and Grey and Co. have not been hung on lamp-posts in Trafalgar Square for deceiving the people, as well as for interfering with the Army matters'. On 20 February 1915, Hereward rode with Henry Wilson, who unburdened himself on his own position. 'Asquith has never forgiven him for his share in the Ulster business [in 1913],[100] and prevented him being made C.G.S. here and getting a K.C.B. the other day. Imagine his dirty revenge coming now'.[101]

Some good news for Hereward was his promotion to General Staff Officer 2nd Grade, a full Major, attached to 1st Corps HQ commanded by Lieutenant-General Sir Charles Monro. After 6½ months at GHQ a change was welcome. He arrived at his new posting on 23 February at Chocques to join the 1st Corps, a part of the First Army, which had been formed at the end of 1914. Its commander was General Sir Douglas Haig. No British offensive had been mounted since December, and it was probably in order to impress the French that an operation was begun at Neuve Chapelle on 10 March 1915. An intense bombardment on a narrow front caught the enemy by surprise and some ground was gained. Hesitation on the part of the two Corps Commanders, bad communications and, more importantly, the shortage of munitions, led to the territory being retaken by the enemy after three days of fighting. Haig had ordered the attack to be pressed 'regardless of loss' and the casualties were heavy,[102] with some 13,000 British killed. In the ferocity of the battle, the Germans slaughtered many wounded; 'the first Battalion got very angry and the Leicesters did not bring in a single prisoner', Hereward reported.[103] A week after the battle, Hereward toured Neuve Chapelle, which was 'an indescribable place of ruins without a single house or tree left standing.' By 27 March 1915, the village had already changed hands six times with the German trenches even then only 250 yards away. Amidst all the wreckage, he observed that 'there had been a nice old church, something like Courteenhall, I think, judging by part of a window which somehow got itself sticking up in the air'.[104] Hereward's lecture entitled 'The Battalion in Battle' was printed at this time; it was used as primer for Army training and was on sale to the public at 6d.

*   *   *   *   *

Without any apparent warning, there was a dramatic turn of events in his fortunes. On 12 April 1915 whilst he was in conversation with Lieutenant-General Monro, Hereward found himself unable to answer a few questions which were put to him. Monro immediately ordered Hereward to return to England for medical care and rest. In common with many other soldiers, Hereward was diagnosed as having neurasthenia, or nervous exhaustion. After a short stay at Buckhurst, he went on to a hospital at Ascot for a consultation, from where he wrote to Daisy, 'Dr. Crouch asked me if you were of a sedative nature or very talkative, and I said I never get a word in sideways, so he orders you to come as part of the treatment'.[105] Later, one of Hereward's vertebrae was found to be slightly displaced and there was also a displacement close to his skull. Seven months later he was informed by a specialist that he had never had any of the symptoms of neurasthenia, but that his injuries, probably caused by the fall from his horse at Olympia in 1909, had debilitated him.[106] Returning to his old room at the War Office in December, he learnt that Haig had succeeded Sir John French as Commander-in-Chief of the BEF and that Wilson was to command the 4th Army Corps.

*   *   *   *   *

It was suddenly necessary to become involved in domestic matters. On New Year's Day, 1916 Hereward received a message in London from his sister Ida that their father was very ill with pneumonia and he immediately returned to Courteenhall. He was at Sir Herewald's bedside when he died on 5 January. Hereward was now the thirteenth Wake baronet and father of two young children, Margaret and Diana. A house, 10 Westbourne Street, Hyde Park had been given to them by Robert Benson in 1913. In early 1916, Daisy and the family settled there.[107] Hereward was concerned about the future of Courteenhall. His mother, together with her daughters, had temporarily left there in August for Scotland. Hereward's first thoughts were to shut the house for the winter and later to let it, much to Ida's dismay, as a hospital.[108] 'I have not much time to think about family affairs', he wrote to Daisy in August 1916, 'and I only tried to make clear what ought to be done in the event of the estate outgoings exceeding the incomings, which is what is going to happen'.[109] Earlier he had informed Daisy, 'I want to have a son, and call him Hereward, and for him to grow up kinder and nicer and braver and bigger (I don't mean in body because he must <u>not</u> weigh more than 10 stone) than his father, and have all the adorable qualities of his mother as far as a man should have them'.[110] Whilst on leave in London, to his great delight their first son was born on 7 October and was named Hereward. Sir Henry Wilson consented to act as one of his godparents and Aileen, Lady Roberts another. When the Dowager Lady Wake finally left Courteenhall in the following month, Hereward wrote, 'She says all the poor people of Courteenhall wept when she said Goodbye to them. I wonder if she will ever go back, or any of us? I should like to think young Hereward will live there some day'.[111]

On 22 May 1916, now a Lieutenant-Colonel, Hereward had once more returned to France, landing at Le Havre. There, he took the opportunity of calling on his eighty year old Aunt Amy Ball, who lived nearby, for lunch. 'Imagine my surprise,' he told Daisy, 'when the maid told me that Aunt Fif (Josephine) died on Sunday and that Aunt Lucy was on the point of arriving … After the tearful embraces and the story over (I gather she would not have died if she had had ordinary medical treatment) we became a very cheerful party'.[112] Aunt Fif's body was taken over to England on the following day for burial at Courteenhall.

Back at 1st Corps Headquarters in early June, Hereward was able to attend an Old Etonian dinner at which fifty two were present. A note on the back of the menu was sent to Mr. Luxmoore and a telegram in Latin to the headmaster.

Later that month, the deadliest battle of the war, the Somme, was begun with a seven day bombardment of the German lines. Haig had been given a free hand by the Cabinet and had decided to attack on a fifteen mile front towards Bapaume. Rawlinson was ordered to carry out the operation. The Battle of the Somme, lasting from 1 July to 18 November, claimed over a million soldiers, approximately equally divided between the two sides. Hereward was in the front line when the battle began. In the chaos of the fighting, he was within about twenty yards of the Germans, remarking, 'It was very exciting and not very dangerous as no-one could see what they were shooting at'. He was proud of the fact that, though wet and covered in mud, he had been able to remain active throughout the first twenty four hours of the battle.[113] Even though the British outnumbered the Germans six to one, the attack was a failure. The bombardment had not caused the enemy to withdraw, the soldiers were overburdened with equipment and, at the insistence of Marshal Foch the assault took place at 7.30 a.m. in broad daylight, when the advancing troops could easily be seen by the Germans.[114] By the end of the campaign, only a few miles of territory had been gained.

At the height of the battle, the Prime Minister, Asquith, and his wife Margot went to Buckhurst for the weekend of 23 July.[115] Daisy noted with indignation that the visit had developed into an enormous weekend party of pre-war days' magnitude, numbering nineteen people. 'I see no reason', she wrote to Hereward, 'to order expensive fruit from London and revert to dinners of eight courses and buy expensive new evening clothes because one of your (so called) friends is to spend the weekend with you'.[116]

The use of aircraft, blowing their Klaxon horns as they flew low, introduced a novel element. As Hereward observed, 'My chief impressions of the Somme were an arid desert covered with shell-holes, a most infernal din, and the air full of great sausage balloons almost bumping one another and aeroplanes flying backwards and forwards, hooting like lost souls'.[117] In spite of these conditions, wildlife still flourished. Hereward spotted a grey-backed shrike and a hen harrier near the front line, though he was unable to share his love of natural history with his colleagues, none of whom, he claimed, 'could tell the difference between a hippoboscus and a kipper'.

Even during the most trying times, Hereward's sense of humour rarely deserted him. On 30 August, he reported the following incident:

> I was up early trying fireworks and it was quite amusing. The first one was labelled 'Hold in left hand and light with match – smoke-candle'. A loud explosion ensued, several people were knocked down, and the missile finally burst in the air 300 feet above us giving out a shower of red and green lights.
>
> Warned by this unexpected occurrence we carefully read the instructions on the next, which ran 'Caution! This bomb will be ignited with a long fuse, and good cover should be provided for troops within 200 yards of it. Beware of falling fragments'. Placing it in a gravel pit and ordering a man who was 23rd in the last marathon race to light it and seek shelter, we retired a ¼ mile behind a house and awaited events. Judge of our astonishment when the only result was a gentle smoke.[118]

Hereward's liaison duties required great stamina. During the Battle of the Somme, he would rise at 7.00 a.m. or, on occasions, 4.30 a.m., walk some part of the trenches, breakfast at 8.00 am. and then carry out any urgent written work. After lunch, there were further visits to the trenches or to see another Division or Corps headquarters. Dinner, – 'the food is a disgrace' – served at 7.45 p.m., was followed by more office work or to a Brigade headquarters or further visits to the trenches. The day ended at 11.30 p.m. or 12.30 a.m., at which time he would write to Daisy. One occasion which particularly appealed to his sense of adventure was an expedition down a 'mine'. Both sides developed the practice of burrowing under their opponent's lines, placing explosives and blowing up the trenches. This operation involved climbing down a slippery ladder, then crawling along a long low gallery:

The man digging at the end by the light of a solitary candle sends out the clay in sandbags which are gently removed by his companion. He digs noiselessly as far as possible and we talk in whispers. For the Boche might be quite close, and if he hears us coming before we hear him, he puts in a charge of 2,000 to 6,000 lbs. of ammonal and lets if off when our men are close to and blows in the whole thing. I may say that during the last three months we have several times caught the Boche that way but he has not caught us once in this part, in that way. The listener at the end of a gallery sits and listens and it is nervous work till they get used to it, as the number of noises one hears is extraordinary. Pumping out water and in air has to go on unceasingly or there is soon too much of the one and too little of the other, and altogether it's a poor life, but not as bad as it sounds.[119]

By the time the Somme offensive ground to a halt in November, British casualties alone amounted to 420,000 men. On 19 September, Rawlinson had reported Haig's Chief of Staff as saying that the C-in-C 'means to go on until we cannot possibly continue further either from the weather or want of troops'.[120] It was no wonder that the soldiers faced the future with little optimism. Writing shortly after the Somme campaign was over, Hereward described the devastation which he witnessed:

The mud here gets deeper and deeper and it's pretty hard to know how to cope with it.

The battlefield presents the most extraordinary appearance. I walked right through a large village without discovering that I was not still in the open country. On looking back I perceived one or two stumps of trees sticking out between shell craters, and one mound of a slightly more brick-colour than the others and concluded this might have been the church or the chateau. It is not only the villages that are like this. The whole ground on an area seven miles by nine is the same – shell holes and mounds of earth, touching each other, not a blade of grass, not a tree, even the roads so completely obliterated that they are invisible and one can't find them. It is very difficult to walk across all this, in fact only possible on the paths that have been made since, and they are deep in mud. Over everything there is scattered a collection of broken rifles, shells, clothing, accoutrements, helmets, bits of guns and wagons, and still in many places dead soldiers and Boches, and horses.

This country can never be tilled again and I suppose the villages will never be rebuilt. I should think they will plant it with trees (the holes are ready!) when they have finished showing American tourists round the battlefield. For my part I never want to be reminded of this business again, and the people who write histories of this cursed war may write them for future generations, not for us.[121]

However, there were some brighter interludes. A makeshift fox-hunt was organized by a local farmer in which Hereward and some of his colleagues participated. As it was near the front line, it was forbidden to blow a horn, but the chase was an enjoyable

99-102 Christmas cards drawn by the 13th baronet

outing, resulting in a bag of two rabbits, a stoat and finally a fox. Many of his letters home contain references to the wildlife and fauna of the countryside. A month after his son was born, he wrote to Daisy, 'I hope little Hereward will know every rabbit hole and birds' nest for two miles round [Courteenhall] as I did, and in fact as I do now'.[122]

Hereward was to become well-known amongst the soldiers for other than his fighting qualities. Like his father, he was a talented artist and he now put this gift to good use. He greatly disliked the conventional Christmas cards and never sent them. To Hereward, a more personal card, drawn by the sender, had much more merit and saved the writing of many letters. He had first drawn a Christmas card some five years previously at the Staff College. For Christmas 1916, he produced one for the 61st Division. Twenty thousand were initially printed and were to be sold at 1d. each, the profits to be used for a soldiers' charity. They were an enormous success and a reprint was soon necessary. On 23 December he wrote, '40,000 of my Xmas cards have been sold – think of that. They will be all over the world'.[123] Many letters of appreciation were received, several from complete strangers. Hereward continued this custom of designing a topical card every Christmas up to 1962.

Hereward also now found time to do some reading. H.G. Well's *Mr. Britling Sees It Through* had recently appeared and he found it instructive. 'It brings out the agony of this cursed war, and it explains the curious attitude of those people who never would believe a war was possible – Mr. Britling himself was one'.[124] When Ida informed him that his cousins, Edith and Osbert Sitwell, had produced a book of poetry which was 'neurotic, erotic, idiotic and extremely nasty stuff', he told Daisy, 'Do send it to me; it will cheer us all up here'.[125]

As a man of action, time-wasting was anathema to him. Hereward found the French habit of sitting for hours over meals intolerable as he preferred to bolt his food in order to carry on with the task in hand. He also had decided ideas on the sort of religious education he wanted for his children, especially when contemplating Daisy 'whose religious education was almost entirely neglected, but who displayed in every bit of her mind and character all the essentials of true Christianity, or what I think are the essentials'. His list of principles included: speak the truth always, be kind to others, be brave, be cheerful and happy and make others so, be energetic and do the best that one is able and finally not be a snob. The more formal aspects of Christian teaching, he believed, were less instructive:

> I spent years trying to learn the Ten Commandments by heart without having the least idea what they meant, and consider it did me no good at all. It was frightfully wicked to do anything amusing on a Sunday – I must not covet my neighbour's ox or his wife, nor bow down to a graven image, nor do a quantity of things I had not the least inclination or opportunity to do. Honestly, I think the Ten Commandments need not be read to Peggy till she is 21. The Lord's Prayer wants explaining too. For years I thought 'Hallowed be thy name' was a mistake for Herewald.[126]

* * * * *

103. Headquarters of 21st Infantry Brigade, 7th Division, during the Battle of Neuve Chapelle, 10-14 March 1915

104. Battle of Albert, Somme. Explosion of a mine ten minutes before the assault on Beaumont Hamel, 1 July 1916

105. Signallers of the Royal Garrison Artillery wearing gas masks in a shell hole in a forward signal post, early 1917

106. Well-concealed and revetted captured German trench at Gommecourt, March 1917

At the end of 1916, there were important political and military changes. Asquith was replaced as Prime Minister by Lloyd George, whom Hereward 'would not trust with a piece of cheese to bait my mousetrap, but he appears to want to win the war'. A War Cabinet of five was substituted for the existing War Committee. Joffre was superseded by Nivelle, as Commander-in-Chief, French Forces, and Haig was promoted to Field Marshal. On 1 January 1917, Hereward's own promotion to Brevet-Colonel was announced in the press. Ida told him that if he had not been ill for nine months earlier in the year, he might have been a General by this time.

Hereward was a participant in what was perhaps the most horrific campaign of the war, the third Battle of Ypres, which lasted from 31 July to 10 November 1917. Lloyd George in his *Memoirs* reflected, 'No soldier of any intelligence now defends this senseless campaign . . . Passchendaele was indeed one of the greatest disasters of the War'. The bitter demoralization of the French in April after Nivelle's abortive offensive in Champagne was only saved by Pétain's stout defence at Verdun. Haig had two motives for staging the battle in Flanders. The first was to capture the German submarine bases on the Belgian coast and the second was to prevent the enemy launching a further attack on the French.

The opening bombardment from 2,174 Allied guns and howitzers was accompanied by four days of ceaseless heavy rain. For the infantry the consequences were disastrous. As Haig wrote in his dispatch at the time:

> The low-lying clayey soil, torn by shells and sodden by rain, turned to a succession of vast muddy pools. The valleys of the choked and overflowing streams were speedily transformed into long stretches of bog, impassable except for a few well-defined tracks, which became marks for the enemy's artillery. To leave these tracks was to risk death by drowning.[127]

The Germans, who had been aware for the previous two months that a large-scale attack would be mounted, erected a system of concrete pillboxes in depth instead of trenches. This proved to be a further obstacle to British troops hoping to make advances. Hereward, with the 61st Division in the front line, remarked, 'It beats me how any human being can stand it'. The Headquarters, cramped and insanitary, were on the banks of what was once a canal.

Apart from German bombing raids, there was an additional hazard, the use of mustard gas, which caused large blisters and burns. 'The first night', he wrote, 'we had gas shells from midnight till 3.30 a.m. and had our masks on all the time. My nose was very sore from the clip that had to pinch it inside . . . and my eyes were sore. Otherwise it did me no harm'. He was fortunate that a mustard gas shell, which burst on his shelter when he was sleeping, did not penetrate the roof.[128] The static war increased in ferocity: by October, Hereward reported the slaughter of German soldiers, seeing 'heaps of 20 and 30 of them, all bayonetted, who could hardly have resisted, all over the place'.[129] By the time the campaign came to a close in early November, only 5 miles of ground had been captured at a cost of 300,000 men.

Within a matter of a few days, the final battle of 1917 took place, one which was to transform the military strategy employed in future wars. Haig had been planning an

107. Tank F4 climbing a slope at Wailly on 21 October 1917. In November, tanks were deployed on a large scale by the Allies at the Battle of Cambrai

108. Field Marshal Sir Henry Wilson inspecting a French Guard of Honour at Versailles, 2 June 1918

attack further south at Cambrai. A new secret weapon had been developed with trained troops which was ready for use – the tank. Accordingly, at 6.20 a.m. on 20 November, 381 tanks, supported by infantry, moved forward towards the enemy line. The element of surprise was complete and the enemy retreated. Haig's failure to exploit the initial success led to a strong German counter attack; little had been achieved by the British at the end of over a fortnight's fighting.[130] Hereward viewed the Battle of Cambrai on its last day in his usual cheerful spirit. He confessed:

> It is beastly beyond words but the thrill and go of the whole thing is to me (and I can't help it) jolly good sport, and the splendid feeling I have now of confidence, and the folliness of being able to really laugh when people are looking haggard and anxious.[131]

*   *   *   *   *

Three days after the battle, Hereward received the exciting news that he had been appointed to the staff of Sir Henry Wilson, the chief British military representative on the Supreme War Council at Versailles. He was also promoted to temporary Brigadier-General. In the previous month, November 1917, Lloyd George had helped to establish the Council, thereby lessening the authority of Haig and his supporter, Robertson, Chief of the Imperial General Staff.[132] The Council consisted of political and military representatives from Britain, France, Italy and the United States, the latter having entered the war in April. One of the Council's major tasks was to examine and recommend Allied military and naval strategies on a co-ordinated basis. Not surprisingly, the Council was regarded with great suspicion and rivalry by the War Office and military men. Hereward gave an example after a visit by King George V to France in March 1918 when Hereward was temporarily attached to the 3rd Army Headquarters: 'The King asked me where I had been and when I said Versailles, that finished the conversation'.[133]

The first meeting of the Supreme War Council was held on 1 December with Clemenceau in the chair and Lloyd George, Milner and Wilson as the British representatives. Their support staff were divided into three sections, A (Allies), headed by Colonel H.W. Studd, M (Materials), led by Brigadier F. Sykes and E (Enemy) under Hereward. The latter's task was to gather as much information about the enemy's military disposition in all theatres of war, and attempt to view the strategic situation as seen through German eyes. Wilson requested that all those in Section E when at work should wear their caps with their peaks at the rear, so that when they looked up in the large mirror that was in the room they imagined themselves as Germans.[134] Foreign generals were often surprised to be introduced to Hereward by Wilson as 'That Boche'.

The transition for Hereward from a life of survival on the Western Front to preparing plans for the whole of the war zones was a difficult one, especially as he was conscious of the jealousies generated by the War Office and GHQ which hampered his work.[135] His ability to grasp strategic possibilities was soon apparent. On 20 January he told Daisy that his paper on the situation in Turkey was being sent all over Europe. He had also received a visit from General Jan Smuts, whom he considered very intelligent and charming. Harking back to the Boer War, Hereward added, 'I had never met him before, though I have fought against him many times'.[136]

Wilson had capitalized on Hereward's strategic skills by encouraging him to play war-games, with Studd representing the Allies, and Hereward as the German Commander-in-Chief. This was soon turned to good use. In January 1918, the American military representative, General Tasker Bliss, had returned to Versailles and pronounced himself in favour of the United States of America sending 150 battalions, to be incorporated into the BEF. He was ready to recommend this course if Wilson considered it desirable. Wilson promised Bliss that he would be able to convince his American colleague on the following day. Afterwards, Wilson wrote in his Diary:

> Bliss and four of his officers came this morning, and I gave them a lecture, with maps, on our war game. Then Bertie Studd and Hereward played the game for them, and they were immensely struck by the whole thing, and Bliss told me that he had never dreamt of such a thing and that it was intensely interesting, and that we had made out an overwhelming case for America helping us with every single man possible in every possible shape. So we did a real good morning's work.[137]

There was an even more impressive display of Hereward's and Studd's skills to follow. On 28 January, Lloyd George, accompanied by amongst others Lord Milner, arrived at Versailles. One of the main agenda items for the Supreme War Council which was to meet on the 31st was the Western Front campaign for 1918.[138] As a prelude to it, the war game was once more re-enacted for the Prime Minister and his party on the following day. 'You would have been alarmed to see me delivering a lecture to the P.M. this morning', Hereward told Daisy. 'He sat in an armchair with a pipe in his mouth, leaning back and now and then asking a question, or making a little joke'.[139] Hereward heard afterwards that Lloyd George was much impressed with the prognostications suggested by the war-game. On 30 January, Haig was invited to a similar session. Leo Amery, then on the staff of the Council, was angry at the Field Marshal's reactions:

> D. Haig and Staff came in to hear a new edition of the Wake and Studd lecture. D.H. showed little interest, twiddled his moustache and read a paper which he had prepared for the afternoon . . . I grew hot several times as Studd pointedly explained the precautions which he would take, but Haig never even realised that he was being taught his business as C-in-C.[140]

Hereward wrote later of Haig, 'I am afraid he thought more of downing Versailles than of beating the Boche'.[141] In Hereward's reading of the enemy's mind, he had forecast to Lloyd George, Milner and Haig that the Germans would mount a massed attack using up to 100 divisions by 1 April. These would be employed against the British right flank north of its junction with the French, and would then drive a wedge between the two armies, forcing the French back on Paris and the British to the Channel ports.

265

This would then end the war. Hereward's assessment proved to be remarkably accurate: when the enemy offensive began on 21 March, he was correct to within two German divisions and to within two or three miles as to the centre of the front attacked.[142] Unfortunately, Haig was caught unprepared and the Germans made great advances. Lloyd George later paid public tribute to Hereward, though without actually naming him. In a Commons speech on 9 April, the Prime Minister called Hereward's January report 'the most remarkable forecast of enemy intentions that has ever been made'.[143]

Hereward was sorry to lose Wilson in February when the latter was appointed CIGS, being replaced by Rawlinson. There were other changes. In March, because of the military disasters suffered, Foch was empowered to co-ordinate Allied strategy, and on 14 April he became Commander-in-Chief of the Allied Forces. Hereward visited Foch's HQ that day where he saw both Pétain and Foch. The latter was, in Hereward's estimation, 'a most extraordinary man who doesn't listen to anybody but himself much, I think'.[144] Lloyd George, on the other hand, had risen greatly in Hereward's esteem. After dining with Wilson and Lloyd George in February, Hereward wrote of the latter, 'Really, I like him better than any of those highly-placed soldiers (bar H.W.[ilson] of course) and he seems quite simple and direct and full of commonsense, without any of that common kind of indirect politeness which prevents a man giving a jolly good smack-in-the-eye retort to anyone who makes a statement which he knows is foolish or incorrect'.[145] Hereward was also impressed with a fellow officer and secretary to the British delegation, George Lloyd, (later Lord Lloyd) who gave a thrilling description of his adventures in Palestine. 'He and a man called Lawrence (who got three firsts at Oxford and is an expert in medieval pottery) lived for months with the Bedouins in the desert spending their time wrecking trains of Turks'.[146]

Although Hereward's forecast of the German offensive had been ignored, he continued to be confident of his powers of prophecy. 'I would not tell anyone but you,' he confessed to Daisy, 'but up to the present I have succeeded in fortelling the events of the battle with an accuracy that rather startles me though it is painfully easy if you follow the Boche who never breaks a rule. My last effort I concocted last night … I find it totally opposed to what Foch thinks is going to happen, totally. I pray God I am wrong. It would be awful to defeat a military genius. But my success as a prophet has shaken my nerve. I feel I can't go wrong!'[147]

When the German March offensive petered out in early April, a second great attack was mounted on the 9th by Ludendorff on a front of only 7,500 yards south of Ypres. During the ensuing fighting the Germans took the Messines Ridge and Armentières, and opened up a breach in the British front. On 17 April, Hereward recorded:

> I have been keeping up my reputation as a prophet, I can tell you. On 4th April I announced that the attack in the south was over and a biggish show would presumably come off north of Arras. On 9th. the Boche attacked at Béthune. On 13th I said they would renew the attack in the same place between 15th and 17th. On 15th and 16th the Boche made two big attacks there.

Yesterday I gave them another forecast and I'll tell you later if it comes true.[148]

*　　　*　　　*　　　*　　　*

On 29 May, Hereward was ordered to proceed to Salonika in Greece, and prepare a report on the situation. British troops had been sent there in October 1915 at the invitation of the Greek government. During the following year, when King Constantine and his ministers determined to remain neutral, the French commander, General Sarrail, put pressure on the monarch to join the Allies. Sarrail's political interference and plans for a Salonika offensive against the Bulgars caused uneasiness in London. With 90,000 British troops under Sarrail's command, Lloyd George was reluctant to allow these troops to play more than a limited role in the fighting, especially as the plan to divert Austro-German attention from the Western Front had had only limited success.[149] A large-scale attack by Sarrail at Dorian in April 1917 resulted in 5,000 British casualties. The French were much more enthusiastic to continue the campaign. In June, a French commissioner arrived at Athens with many troops and forced Constantine to abdicate in favour of his son; the Greeks abandoned their neutrality and joined the Allies. However, Sarrail's policy was disliked by Clemenceau, the French Prime Minister; shortly after the latter took office in November 1917, Sarrail was dismissed.

Hereward's expedition, which occupied some three weeks, was an exciting one. Landing by destroyer on the Greek coast, he had a two day journey to Florina for a conference with the French commanders there. In contrast to the war in the West, Hereward observed that the peasants were able to go on working in the fields close to the front line without apparent disturbance. On 9 June, he visited Monastir, the capital of Macedonia, which the Allies had captured in the previous year and was just behind the French front line. 'This is Serbia,' Hereward told Daisy, 'and the people all wear white clothes embroidered in red and black – very picturesque and becoming, but very hot in summer'.[150] Two days were spent at the Headquarters of General George Cory, the British commander, where he interviewed many people. Much diplomacy was called for, as besides the French, there were Italian, Greek and Serb officers who made up the force. The final day was spent in a tour of the Vardar front, where a heavy attack by the Bulgars on the Greeks was witnessed. He arrived at Florina on 22 June and then had a nervous ride over the mountains: 'At one time at the Pasa di Lagania we were over 3,000 feet up ... if we met anything we were done, and I am not fond of having 2 inches between the wheel of the car and a drop of 1,000 feet'. During the journey, which lasted from 6.00a.m. to 9.30p.m., six tyres were cut to pieces. Although the tour had been an exhausting one, Hereward left the Balkans with much regret, having to leave a host of friends of different nationalities behind him.[151] Two further days were spent at GHQ, Italy, where he saw the Italian attack on Col Rosso. Hereward arrived back at Versailles on 2 July.

The major activity in progress there was the gathering of the Prime Ministers for a meeting of the Supreme War Council which ended on 4 July. The situation in the Balkans formed part of the agenda, and Hereward was able to speak to the CIGS, General Sir Henry Wilson, on his firsthand impressions as well as to deliver a secret document entrusted to him by Cory.[152] Hereward's visit to the Balkans had reinforced his conviction that the winning of the war depended on political as well as military considerations. He drafted a paper entitled *Strategy Without Policy*. In it, he pointed out that it was only after three years of misfortunes and errors that the Allies had established unity of command on the various fronts, while unity of strategical direction, in principle at least, was effected by the decisions of the Supreme War Council. In his opinion, inconvenient political questions could not be shelved until after a military victory had been gained. The solution was simple:

> It is time that the Allied nations have agreed to accept the decisions of the Supreme War Council as binding upon all of them in the political no less than in the military sphere. But in the political sphere they are not advised, as in the military sphere they now are, by a single conjoint staff. The result is that strategy has often to be decided without the political side of the question, on which strategy should be based, having been properly considered. No common policy in fact, agreed in advance by the Council's advisers, is laid before the Council for consideration. At once national divergencies of view tend to arise, and the conduct of the war is hampered because the Council is unable to lay down a clear and agreed statement of what it wants, for the achievement of which its military advisers are to be called upon to work . . . It seems vital that in addition to the Military Staffs at Versailles who are engaged in working out in co-operation with one another the details of military schemes, there should be diplomatic staffs engaged in working out in co-operation with one another and with the Military Representatives, conjoint schemes of political objects to be attained, so that if and when these schemes are approved by the Council, the military plans may be shaped accordingly.

These diplomatic representatives would sit permanently together to work out schemes of Allied policy. The War Council would be able to accept, reject or modify as it pleased any schemes put forward by this body.[153]

Balfour, then Foreign Secretary, read another of Hereward's papers, *Allied Policy in the Balkans*, with much interest.[154] However, when a further meeting of the War Council was held on 11 July, thanks to Hereward's initiative,[155] he confessed, 'I am feeling slightly depressed at the discovery that Lord Robert Cecil (Balfour's Assistant Secretary of State) and his confrères have no instructions such as I hoped but are merely attempting to report on the political aspect of a general offensive in Macedonia'.[156] A well-placed sympathiser was Leo Amery, who served on the staff of the War Council at Versailles and was also Assistant Secretary to the War Cabinet. He agreed with Hereward that there was a need for a permanent political as well as a military staff at Versailles, but saw difficulties. When the war was over 'each Power is bound to think of its own interests. Naturally, for the sake of harmony among the allies, it does not lay stress at present on those of its interests which conflict with those of other allies'. He therefore suggested that it might be useful to arrive at a common policy in the first instance in those regions of the world such as Russia and the Balkans, where the Allies had no direct territorial ambitions, and where military and political issues were most closely entangled.[157]

Hereward accepted Amery's argument, but pointed to the urgent need for action, especially with the possibility of Germany offering tempting peace proposals aimed at

109. After the Battle of St. Quentin Canal, 2 October 1918, Brigadier-General J. V. Campbell, VC, on the Riquerval Bridge addressing his troops

separating the Allies. He laid the blame for the lukewarm attitude displayed by the British towards his proposals on the Foreign Office:

> By avoiding difficult and inconvenient issues, we are laying up trouble and delaying victory, for they cannot be avoided, they can only be postponed – sooner or later they have got to be faced. I see nothing but danger in avoiding them as we do. It is the old Foreign Office way, substituting politeness and secret double-dealing for honesty of purpose and frank statement of facts, that brought about this war, and is now preventing us ending it.[158]

Hereward's pessimism at the lack of vision shown by Allied governments for the future of Europe was not assuaged by moves made by Sir Edward Grey, the former Foreign Secretary, to produce a forum for such discussions. 'I see the damn fellow is still writing articles about Leagues of Nations in intervals of trout-fishing', Hereward wrote in August. 'The only league we shall ever see is an alliance against a common enemy, and the result of this war will be the world once again divided into two camps, the balance of power, another war ever on the horizon, and all the old story over again'.[159] As a last contribution to the deliberations at Versailles, he wrote an interesting document *British Interests at the Peace Conference* a fortnight before the Armistice. In it, he stated that the way to secure the future peace of the world was 'to effect a just teritorial settlement which will leave as little resentment as possible',[160] a principle which the politicians unfortunately ignored.

*   *   *   *   *

The war was now entering its final phase, following the last German offensive on the Western Front begun at Rheims on 15 July 1918. 'We heard the thunder of the guns in Champagne last night,' Hereward told Daisy that day, 'The thought of 2,000 million bottles of champagne in Rheims fills me with anxiety'.[161] The second Battle of the Marne led to a strong Allied counter-offensive, long prepared by Foch. Hereward correctly forecast that within two months, the Germans would be putting forward requests for an armistice. By the end of August, he was impatient with the Allied progress. 'I want to get on with the war and go to Courteenhall and grow turnips', he informed Daisy.[162] For this reason he was pleased to be sent on a mission to the 4th Army, commanded by Rawlinson. He arrived at Headquarters on 6 September, to find that the Allies had advanced eight miles the previous day, with the Germans in full flight.[163] Two days later, Hereward made a tour of the front line with the Divisional Commander. 'It was our old ground near St. Quentin', he wrote cheerfully, 'and I know every inch of it. I had not seen a shell or seen a dead Boche for ages, and feel very bucked up by my visit already'. On 9 September, Rawlinson invited Hereward to give an impromptu talk to a conference of Corps Commanders on his impressions gained during the visit.[164]

The capture of the Hindenburg Line on 29 September and the surrender of Bulgaria led to Ludendorff demanding the initiation of peace negotiations. British, French and

American troops pressed forward and on the German acceptance of President Wilson's Fourteen Points, the war ended on 11 November. The Peace Conference, in which the Supreme War Council played a part, kept Hereward busy until the Treaty of Versailles was signed on 28 June 1919. After almost five years in France, Hereward returned home. Amongst the honours he had received were the Companion of the Order of St. Michael and St. George, Commander Légion d'honneur and the Order of the Crown of Italy, and he had been mentioned four times in dispatches.

16

Major-General Sir Hereward Wake,
The Thirteenth Baronet:
II. Courteenhall and the Second World War

THE ENDING OF HOSTILITIES DID NOT MEAN THAT Hereward would immediately be able to deal with the many pressing problems which had accumulated at Courteenhall since the twelfth baronet's death. At the end of 1920, as Lieutenant-Colonel, he was given command of the 4th Battalion of The King's Royal Rifle Corps in India. Hereward and Daisy's third son, Peter, was christened on 8 September 1921; four days later, Daisy left for India. The Battalion was stationed at Quetta, the capital of Baluchistan, in the north-west of the country, 'the most Godforsaken spot on earth', he told his mother. Daisy landed at Bombay on 21 October, and with Hereward visited many of the sights of the country. A fortnight later, they arrived in Delhi, where they stayed with the Commander-in-Chief, India, Hereward's former Army commander in France, Lord Rawlinson. Daisy's visit coincided with that of the Prince of Wales. Both she and Hereward were invited as guests on the occasion of the Prince's stay with the Maharaja of Bharatpur from 5 to 9 December 1921. The two day journey from Quetta was followed by much lavish entertainment. On 8 December, in a single day's shooting some 2,500 wild fowl were claimed. After the Prince had left, the party went into the jungle for nine days where both Daisy and Hereward joined in the sport. Daisy proved to be a good shot, killing at least one hyena and a chinkara (Indian antelope).[1] After touring the sights of Northern India, Daisy and Hereward left India for England on 9 January 1922.

On their return, Hereward devoted much of his spare time to setting Courteenhall in order. With a family of six children, – Roger, the second son, having been born in 1918 and Patricia, the third daughter, born in 1919 – and heavily dependent on his Army pay for income,[2] the family finances were stretched. Towards the end of the Great War, he had contemplated selling or letting Courteenhall to ease the burden. Hereward had found on inheriting that his father and grandfather had burdened the Estates by decreeing in their wills that their younger children should each receive an annuity. As early as 1912, his solicitor warned him, 'On the death of your Father, your Mother takes a jointure of £1,000 and your brothers and sisters the interest on £10,000 which will have to be raised for them ... Personally, I should be inclined if a favourable

See Appendix A – Family Tree XVI. Notes and References pages 427–430 opportunity occurred to dispose of the Essex Estates'.[3] Now head of the family, Hereward sold the whole of the Nazeing Estate and was able to pay his two brothers and three sisters capital sums in full settlement, thereby freeing the income from Courteenhall and Waltham.[4] The income from the land was small and death duties added to the difficulties. Some of the account books belonging to Hereward's father could not be found: as a result he was obliged to pay death duties on property which he never owned and also lost some fishing rights and other dues.[5]

'We must have a home somewhere with nothing but happiness in it and no regrets ever mentioned', Hereward wrote to Daisy in May 1917.[6] Courteenhall was the obvious place, if it could be afforded. He contemplated closing up the top floor and living mainly on the first floor with a dining room on the ground floor, converted from the billiard room, and a small kitchen beneath it.[7] There was encouragement, too, from Godwin, who generously offered to place the whole of his resources at the disposal of the Estate to prevent the sale of Courteenhall and to provide £500 a year for eight years to help pay the death duties. As a temporary expediency, the Hall was let from 1 April 1918 to Alleyn Court Preparatory School from Westcliff-on-Sea, Essex, for the duration of the war. The school left Courteenhall at the end of the year.[8] It was an enormous relief for Hereward to know that during the war, Ida had taken charge of both the Courteenhall and Essex estates and was running them efficiently.[9]

From India, looking ahead, Hereward had told Ida, 'Soldiering is a job I know from A to Z and at farming I don't know where to begin'.[10] On his return, he set about learning the subject with great thoroughness. By May, 1922, he remarked to Daisy, 'I am just beginning to grasp things'.[11] Prices for animals remained high, and the good weather meant that by the beginning of September forty acres of wheat had been harvested.[12] However, the fluctuating state of agriculture proved to be a constant worry. Nearly six years later, Hereward was disturbed to find that he had amassed an overdraft of £5,767.[13]

In 1922, the Law of Property Act had abolished copyhold tenure. Since 1672, the family, as Lords of the Manors of Waltham and Nazeing had held Manorial Courts regularly and administered the complicated and extensive common lands along the Lea River Valley and the rights of commoners, for example, to take firewood and graze cattle. After 1922, Hereward ceased to administer the common lands which became derelict.

Farming was not Hereward's only preoccupation. In April 1921, whilst he was in India, Daisy and their young family had moved into Courteenhall. Hereward was determined to make to make the Hall into a comfortable home. He called in Edward Ranyell, a London firm specializing in high quality decoration and design. On 16 February 1922 he informed Daisy:

> Ranyell and his foreman have been here. He went into raptures over the library and dining room and hall and gallery. But wept over the door-handles and plates which he swears must have been substituted for the originals – very likely by the Dowager. He says the marble work on the stairs is very good and dates from 1791 and must not be touched. But the pink doors are awful. He says they should

be dark and he'll think it out. He thinks the hall, library and dining room very fine examples and in perfect proportion. I have asked him to estimate for the hall as well, but God knows if he can do all this or if we ought to. I don't![14]

The work proceeded slowly. Radiators in the hall proved difficult to move and in the gallery, a fresh-looking coat of pale green paint was found under the distemper. One night in April, Hereward worked until 2.00a.m. in the basement where he found many of the windows unlatched or open and the silver scattered in various cupboards.[15] By the middle of May, Daisy's bathroom had been finished as had the study stairs, and a staff of servants was scrubbing the paint in the dining room, which had not been attended to for many years. The cost of decoration was £713.[16] Later, when the new boilers had been installed, there was a delivery of eleven tons of anthracite. A letter from Hereward to Daisy indicates that work on the newly restored Hall would be completed by October 1922.[17]

Whilst Hereward was occupied with Courteenhall affairs, his Battalion arrived back in England from India, prior to being disbanded. He returned to the Regimental Headquarters at Winchester where, on 9 December, he took part in the Battalion's last parade. His close bond with the soldiers is clearly seen in a letter he wrote the next day to Daisy:

> The men kept up their expectation to the end, turned out as smart as if they were still at Quetta and their marching and drill, absolute steadiness and discipline, a wonder to behold, considering they have been three weeks on a ship and are just going off. For a few minutes I had that wonderful feeling of command again which can't be described. It's a sort of personal sympathy between me and every man on parade which I feel so intensely. I know they will do anything I want and they know I will never ask them to do anything that isn't right.
>
> And so they marched past in fours, the remnant of my splendid fighting machine, and were gone.[18]

In July 1924, he was appointed General Staff Officer (Lieutenant-Colonel) at Western Command Headquarters, Chester. This posting enabled him at the same time to supervise the Courteenhall Estate.[19]

One cause which Hereward immediately took up was the long running battle with the Board of Education over the question of a school at Courteenhall. Although the twelfth baronet had been unsuccessful in persuading the officials to reopen the old Grammar School building as an elementary school, Hereward and his sister Joan were determined to remedy the matter. On 27 January 1923, they attended the Board's offices in Whitehall where they were received by two officials, W.G.B. Ritchie and W.R. Barker, both from the Legal Department. Joan Wake made a note of the interview:

> Barker was rather offensive, and he lost his temper and Hereward very nearly lost his, and I had to mediate and restore peace. Barker said, 'Really, Sir

Hereward, the suspicion and distrust with which you continue to regard the Board is beyond anything', or words to that effect, to which H. and I both replied we had had twenty five years' experience of the Board. It was really only by attacking the Board and putting them on the defensive, using tactful persuasion with the County Council and utterly ignoring the Corporation of Northampton, that Hereward got the business through.[20]

The new Courteenhall Elementary School, adjoining the old Grammar School, was opened later that year, on 11 September 1923. Six pupils were admitted on the first morning when the Rector, Archie Wake, showed the children the old registers kept by the former Grammar School masters, and he gave each child a packet of sweets to take home. This was followed a few days later by a visit from Hereward, as chairman of managers, and Daisy, when the registers were checked.[21] Throughout the school's existence, Hereward took a keen interest in it and its pupils. By 1947, only eleven children were on the roll and were taught by the headmistress, Mrs Irene Salter, the sole member of staff. On family occasions, such as the marriage of Mary Wake at St. Margaret's, Westminster, on 18 Feburary 1947, the headmistress was invited to it, so the pupils were given the day off. By 1950, there were but four pupils in the school, and much to Hereward's regret, it was finally closed that summer.

Hunting was resumed with great enthusiasm, the Grafton Hounds often meeting at Courteenhall. In the autumn of 1927, Hereward was asked to take on the Mastership, but considered that his bank manager might not totally approve of this step.[22] He was also approached shortly after this to stand for Parliament as Conservative candidate for the Kettering Division, but declined the offer.[23] A few months earlier, Daisy's father had sold his entire collection of celebrated Italian paintings to Sir Joseph Duveen for a reported sum of £500,000.[24] Looking ahead, Hereward wrote to Daisy, 'I suppose we needn't really worry about having two eggs for breakfast instead of one'.[25]

Military duties were occupying more of his time as tours were undertaken with his GOC, General Sir Richard Butler, throughout the Western Command and in Northern Ireland. In February 1928, he attended Lord Haig's funeral. Later that month, on being appointed to command the 12th Infantry Brigade at Dover and becoming Deputy-Constable of Dover Castle, Hereward left Chester. The five years at Dover, 1928 to 1932, were busy ones. Although he was now over fifty, he took a very active part in the manoeuvres involving his Brigade, some days starting at 7.30a.m. and finishing at 5.00p.m.[26] He also rode in the Brigade's Point-to-Point. In 1930, he was appointed ADC to the King. Hereward played a leading part in restoring the Constable's Tower, Dover Castle, where he lived.[27] He encouraged the Office of Works to reinstate the castellations and to floodlight the Castle. By removing the rifle store and making other alterations Hereward was instrumental in allowing the keep to be opened to the public. His endeavours were recognized when he was made an Honorary Freeman of the town in July 1932 at the end of his tenure of the office.[28] In that same year, he was promoted to Major-General.

In June 1933, he was appointed a Commander of the Bath (Military Division). From 1934 to 1937, Hereward was General Officer Commanding the 46th (North Midland)

110. The 4th Battalion, Northamptonshire Regiment in camp at Arundel, 1929. The 13th baronet is seated fourth from the left

111. Sir Hereward Wake, 13th baronet, when ADC to King George V and Margaret, Lady Wake at a Levée, Buckingham Palace, c.1933

112. Catherine, Dowager Lady Wake's 87th birthday, with her 6 children at Weston Turville Manor House, near Aylesbury, 22 August 1939 *Back row:* Godwin, Joan, Baldwin, Phyllis. *Centre:* Catherine Lady Wake. *Seated:* Hereward and Thurfrida

276

Territorial Division, which allowed him to be based once more at Courteenhall. Daisy's first six children had been born within nine years of their marriage: a seventh, Mary, followed in 1927. Hereward was keen to make the Estate a paying proposition. He now put more capital into it, established a dairy herd and built a silage-tower at the Home Farm. A Ford tractor with solid iron wheels was popular with the Wake children: where the land was heavy, two steam-engines were employed at each end of the field which pulled a plough attached to a steel cable backwards and forwards from one end of the field to the other. To ease the burden of work, Hereward had immediately after the War let Woodleys Farm to Mr. Percy Clark, West Lodge Farm to Mr. Herbert Penn and the Grange Farm to Mr. William Dainty, keeping in hand only two or three hundred acres of park land around the house down to the Washbrook Lane and the Village Road.[29]

At more than one stage, it seemed possible that Hereward's role as a country squire could be ended. On 31 October 1933, he informed his mother:

> I saw the Secretary of State today and he asked me to undertake Lieutenant-Governor of Victoria.[30] I have been spending the rest of the day finding out all I can about it, and Daisy and I will have a week or so in which to decide Yes or No. It would mean five years away with six months home in the middle ... Write and say what you think about it.[31]

After much consideration, Daisy and Hereward did not accept the Australian post, though considerable official pressure was brought to bear. Hereward admitted that 'I would like to do a job like that, but there are other people to consider, not forgetting the children and yourself ... It has been a great relief to me once the decision was made'.[32] Two years later he was again approached, this time to become Lieutenant-Governor of New South Wales, an offer which was also declined. Finally, the post of Governor-General of New Zealand was refused on similar grounds. Hereward's Army connections were not severed when he retired in February 1937. He was pleased to be appointed Colonel Commandant of the 1st Battalion of The King's Royal Rifle Corps, a post which took him abroad. By this time, war in Europe was once more a real possibility, though at sixty three, Hereward could hardly have surmised that his military skill and knowledge would once more be fully employed.

*   *   *   *   *

On 3 October 1939, exactly a month after England had declared war on Germany, Hereward put on his uniform again upon being summoned to the War Office in London. There, much to his surprise, he was asked to be one of the four King's Messengers whose job it was to convey highly confidential material to commanders in the field. He accepted without hesitation.

The following day, almost exactly twenty five years since his previous crossing with the advance party of the British Expeditionary Force, Hereward took the boat from Folkestone to Boulogne. He arrived at British GHQ at Arras where he delivered his six bags of documents and was invited to dinner by Lord Gort, Commander-in-Chief of the

BEF.[33] Gort, who was in fine spirits, believed that the Germans would push the French back to the Maginot Line but would not attempt a big offensive before the winter. Hereward enjoyed the company which included Gort's Chief of Staff, Lieutenant-General Sir Henry Pownall, and the Duke of Gloucester, who was Chief Liaison Officer; he drew comparisons with the position in 1914 and reminisced about Henry Wilson, John French and the retreat from Mons. Hereward also recorded talk of possible changes in senior posts: 'Gort thinks some of the old politicans ought to be out of the Government and their places taken by men of iron and go, including Winston. I suggested George Lloyd and Trenchard'.[34] On the return journey to Folkestone, some floating mines which had come within twenty feet of the ship on its outward journey were once more sighted. The Captain told Hereward that the Admiralty had refused him a rifle to blow them up, on the grounds that it would make the ship an armed merchantman.

Apart from the strain brought about by travelling under war conditions, the life of a King's Messenger was a hectic one. Journeys across the Channel in both directions were almost continuous with little chance for Hereward to return to Courteenhall.[35] However, the opportunity to be involved in discussing military affairs with the leading figures was irresistible. For instance, from General Ironside, CIGS, on a visit to France he heard at first hand of the General's difficulties with the War Minister, Hore-Belisha. He was also able to revisit the sites of the First World War battles around Arras and the beautifully-kept British cemeteries. He was worried at the build-up of German forces on the Western Front and believed that half a million Allied troops should be massed on the Franco-Belgian border. Gort in a conversation was very doubtful if the Germans would now embark on a big offensive.[36] On a lighter note, Hereward heard that Eton had discarded top hats 'because they did not go with gas masks. The Empire is shaken'. On 25 October, he dined with the writer, André Maurois, who told him that the character of Major Parker in his first novel, *Les Silences du Colonel Bramble* (1918) was partly based on his brother Godwin.[37] Ida had subsequently translated the book into English.[38]

Hereward did not take easily to the large-scale employment of women in the armed forces. On 21 December 1939 he noted:

> It was a shock to see Dame Helen Vaughan stride into the dining room of the Hotel at Arras dressed as a Lieutenant-General complete, red gorgets, medal-ribbons, hat and everything! She is head of A.T.S. [Auxiliary Teritorial Service] With her an attractive young A.D.C. with armlet of the Army Staff. Don't quite know why I object to this so much. Well, I suppose we shall win the war somehow – by getting a laugh out of everything, I expect. Why did I feel inclined to tear off my General's badges, put them in my soup and send them by waiter to Mrs. Vaughan?[39]

The first Christmas of the war was spent at Courteenhall with all seven of the family; the hounds ran on Boxing Day from Astcote Thorns, with the children taking part on their ponies. On 3 January 1940, Hereward took his three sons to Castle Ashby for pigeon-shooting. He was not pleased to hear that Hore-Belisha had been sacked by Chamberlain. 'C.I.G.S, [Ironside] the least discreet man I ever knew, and Gort too, have been openly critical of him for a long time and C.I.G.S said they had told the Prime Minister he must go'.[40]

Travelling was made very difficult by the harsh weather experienced at the beginning of the year. The journeys across the Channel were undertaken in driving rain, fog and snow. On 29 January, back in England, Hereward recorded:

> The country is covered with snow and freezing hard. Here at Courteenhall a foot deep with drifts to four feet. Last night the temperature touched zero. Main roads passable where snow is beaten down, Blisworth road blocked. Birds are dying.[41]

Not surprisingly, given the nature of the work and the effects of the weather, Hereward's health was weakened. He caught influenza in February which necessitated a twelve day stay in bed, followed by a few days in Brighton to recuperate. Returning to work, he discovered that Anthony Eden, then Secretary for Dominions, had put his name down for a Governorship of a Dominion, probably in eighteen months' time.[42]

Within a week or two, the war situation had changed dramatically. On 9 April 1940, German forces invaded Denmark and Norway, and Italy began to show signs of joining in on Germany's side. Hereward's reaction was typical: 'Let 'em all come'.[43] A month later, Belgium, the Netherlands and Luxemburg were attacked and German forces soon entered Northern France. On 15 May, shortly before Abbeville was taken and Calais and Boulogne had already been bombed, Hereward made his last journey across the Channel. The sea was calm and there was a bright sun. His ship, called *Queen of the Channel*, although only small, was heavily guarded: six trawlers acted as minesweepers, and these were escorted by two destroyers, whilst three planes flew around the small fleet at between two hundred and six hundred feet. Now there were new challenges to be faced.

*   *   *   *   *

With the outbreak of war a number of changes had taken place at Courteenhall. The parish became crowded with schoolchildren evacuated from London and Hereward and Daisy moved from the Hall into the two flats above the Stables. Hereward remarked at the time, 'Our move has astounded the village, etc. and created a great moral effect'.[44] The Hall was offered as a hospital but it was occupied by a boys' public school, St. Lawrence College, Ramsgate, Kent from September 1940. Altogether there were seventy two boys and a small staff under the headmaster, the Reverend Ronald Perfect.[45] The happy relations which had been established between Hereward and Daisy and the school continued well after the War ended; as late as 1957, they were guests at the College's Old Boys' Annual Dinner.[46]

Hereward's mother, Catherine, had from 1919 settled at Weston Turville, near Aylesbury, where she was looked after by Ida. She had celebrated her eighty-seventh

279

birthday there in August, 1939 when her children and grandchildren joined her to celebrate the occasion. On the outbreak of war, Hereward offered her a cottage at Courteenhall: 'How nice it would be to have you back here', he wrote.[47] In May 1940, Weston Turville had to be evacuated because of the proximity of an aerodrome, and Catherine, accompanied by Ida, two servants and two dogs, arrived at Courteenhall Rectory on 6 June.[48] The house, which she shared with fifteen boys from the school, proved to be very comfortable and she enjoyed sitting in the garden during the hot summer of 1940. Ever practical, she recorded in her Diary, 'I shall probably spend my last days here. Will save a lot of trouble being so near the churchyard'.[49] Having her family round her was a source of great pleasure. However, she was worried about the safety of Hereward's three sons, Roger in the Navy, and Hereward and Peter, both in their father's Regiment. She recalled her own anxiety some forty years previously when her own sons Godwin and Hereward were in South Africa and Baldwin took part in the China War. One of her last engagements was in August 1943 at the Army Cadet Camp at Overstone, near Northampton, when Hereward led the march past of over 960 boys. 'I felt very proud of him', she wrote, 'I see in the *Northampton Herald* that "a spectator of 92 took a great interest in it, Catherine Lady Wake, Sir Hereward's mother"'.[50] Four months later, on 18 January 1944, she died and was buried at Courteenhall.

During the Battle of Britain, there was great excitement at Courteenhall on 23 August 1940 when there was an air raid. Edwards, the groom, was by the Hall when he saw a large German aircraft, clearly displaying two black crosses on its wings about 300 feet up, coming very slowly towards him. He threw himself against a wall, hoping that the plane had no rear-gunner. There followed a burst of machine gun fire. As the aircraft came over the corner of the Stables, there was more firing through the trees, followed by a shot at the grazing sheep; it then passed over to the left of the Church and disappeared. No damage was done on the estate. Ida, who was feeding her chickens at the Rectory, heard the firing and darted into the chicken house. Catherine Wake was still in bed and when Ida went in to her later, the former casually asked, 'Was that a bomb?' Mary, Hereward's twelve year old daughter, in describing the raid, summed it up thus, 'It was all over in a few seconds but Courteenhall feels much more important at having been a German target'.[51]

Since Hereward's return to England on 15 May, the war had gone badly for the country. The French and British Armies had retreated and were finally trapped around the Channel ports. A week later, in order to delay the German forces, Churchill, now Prime Minister, dispatched forces to Calais. Frequent commands were given from London for the troops not to contemplate surrender. The gallant defence of Calais was subsequently praised by the Prime Minister in a speech to the Commons on 4 June 1940:

> I have said this [German] armoured scythe stroke almost reached Dunkirk – almost but not quite. Boulogne and Calais were the scenes of desperate fighting. The Guards defended Boulogne for a while and were then withdrawn by orders from this country. The Rifle Brigade, the 60th Rifles, and the Queen Victoria's Rifles, with a battalion of British tanks and 1,000 Frenchmen, in all about 4,000

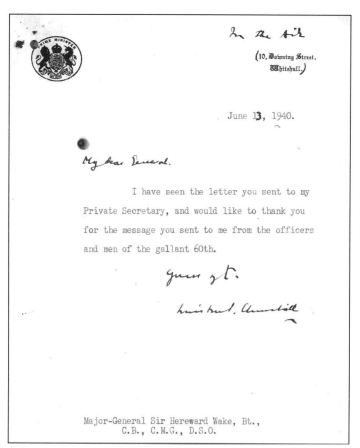

In the Air
(10, Downing Street,
Whitehall.)

June 13, 1940.

My dear General,

I have seen the letter you sent to my
Private Secretary, and would like to thank you
for the message you sent to me from the officers
and men of the gallant 60th.

Yours ,t.

Winston S. Churchill

Major-General Sir Hereward Wake, Bt.,
C.B., C.M.G., D.S.O.

13. Churchill's reply to the 13th baronet when Colonel Commandant, 60th The King's Royal Rifle Corps written 'In the Air', 13 June 1940. The Prime Minister was returning from France after attempting to persuade the French Government to continue the war

115. Badge of
HMS *Hereward*

114. The destroyer HMS *Hereward*, sunk off Crete by German aircraft, 29 May 1941

strong, defended Calais to the last. (Cheers.) The British Brigadier was given an hour to surrender. He spurned the offer – (cheers) – and four days of intense street fighting passed before the silence reigned over Calais, which marked the end of a memorable resistance.

Only thirty unwounded survivors were brought off by the Navy, and we do not know the fate of their comrades. Their sacrifice was not, however, in vain. At least two armoured divisions, which otherwise would have been turned against the British Expeditionary Force, had to be sent for to overcome them. They have added another page to the glories of the Light Division, and the time gained enabled the Gravelines waterlines to be flooded and to be held by the French troops. Thus it was that the port of Dunkirk was kept open.[52]

On hearing Churchill's words, Hereward, as a Colonel Commandant of the 60th Rifles, wrote to the Prime Minister's secretary:

> Will you, if a convenient moment occurs, tell the Prime Minister that the Officers of the 60th. – and the men too – are proud of his reference in the House to the defence of Calais, and very grateful to him for it.
> This requires no answer. I just want him to know.

Churchill, who was on his way to Tours to make a final effort to persuade the French Government not to surrender,[53] replied as follows:

> In the Air
> June 13 1940
>
> My dear General
> I have seen the letter you sent to my Private Secretary, and would like to thank you for the message you sent to me from the Officers and men of the gallant 60th.
> Yours very truly
> Winston S. Churchill[54]

Hereward's second son, Roger, then a Sub-Lieutenant in the Royal Navy, played a leading part in bringing back many British and French troops from Dunkirk. In order to rally the exhausted men on the jetty awaiting the boats, Roger used his hunting horn 'which', in his own words, 'incidentally a damn Frenchman trod on while I was securing a ship'.[55]

*　　　*　　　*　　　*　　　*

One of the most startling aspects of the German invasion of Western Europe was the employment of so-called 'blitzkrieg' tactics, which involved a highly mobile ground force, intensive air bombardment, the wide use of parachutists and the establishment of a 'Fifth Column' which undermined the morale of the defending country. To prepare

116. 5th Marquess of Exeter, Lord-Lieutenant for Northamptonshire and Sir Hereward Wake, 13th baronet, Deputy Lieutenant taking the Home Guard salute at Peterborough, 1940

117. Visit of H.M. King George VI, Colonel-in-Chief, The King's Royal Rifle Corps, to the newly formed 2nd Battalion on 16th August 1940 at Tidworth, accompanied by Major-General Sir Hereward Wake, Colonel Commandant. The old 2nd Battalion was lost at Calais in June 1940

for the seemingly inevitable invasion of Britain, Anthony Eden announced the formation of Local Defence Volunteers (LDV) on 14 May 1940, consisting of men between seventeen and sixty five, whose tasks would include the following: engage and report enemy parachutists, carry out counter espionage, provide the military with local knowledge of the area, organize road blocks and protect factories and other important posts. Immediately afterwards, on 16 May, a small meeting was convened at Northampton consisting of the Lord-Lieutenant of the County, the Marquess of Exeter, Mr A.A. Ferguson the Chief Constable, two military men and Hereward. The latter, as Chairman of the Northamptonshire Territorial Army Association, agreed to serve as Zone Commander for the County.

The County was divided into six (later reduced to five) divisions, corresponding roughly with the Police divisions, each with a Group Commander responsible to Hereward. Recruitment, which was drawn entirely from the civilian population was a great success: within a month, there were well over 15,000 LDVs within the county. But there were many aspects of the organization which concerned Hereward. No uniforms, only armbands, were available for the men and the military authorities insisted on calling the officers 'Organizers' instead of Commanders to emphasize the difference between the two forces. (Hereward ignored this ruling, calling his own post County Commandant). Total armaments consisted of 990 rifles, fewer than 1 to 15 men, and only about 20 rounds per rifle. Shotguns would be of only limited use, and he was not impressed by a neighbouring county, where the LDV had been ordered to use knives, axes and bludgeons.[56] This situation was quickly improved and operations were put on a more professional footing. On 23 July 1940, the name of the force was changed from Local Defence Volunteers to that of Home Guard.[57]

Ironside, now Commander-in-Chief, Home Forces and responsible for this organization, heard of the system of warnings of a possible enemy attack by the ringing of church bells, which Hereward had evolved, and wished to know more about the system. In reply, Hereward pointed out that in the nine counties bordering Northamptonshire, each had different signals, and that a single method of ringing should be laid down for the whole country.[58]

If our present perceptions of the Home Guard are perhaps coloured by *Dad's Army*, the reality of the situation at the time was much more fraught. An article in the *Preston Deanery Parish Magazine* for July 1940, written by the Reverend James Berry of Roade, stated, 'With the threat of invasion hanging over us, I meet people really afraid of being bayoneted on their doorsteps . . . but the Germans are highly disciplined and we should not fear it'. To avoid civilian panic, Hereward wrote a letter[59] which appeared in the centre pages of the *Chronicle and Echo* confirming Berry's remarks and urging people to stay put.[60] However some evidence of the danger of the situation was the secretly-circulated Intelligence Report to Northamptonshire Home Guard that an enemy agent, dressed as a civilian armed with an automatic pistol and equipped with parachute and harness, had been arrested near Northampton on 6 September at 5.30p.m.[61] Hereward wrote in a private memorandum that the only hope of success was for Home Guards to take the offensive against any invaders. 'Every experienced soldier must realise that if they hold defensive positions against well armed German troops,

Home Guards, armed as they are, are certain to meet with swift disaster'.[62]

The distrust and rivalry between the Army authorities and the Home Guard may seem astonishing in the light of the perilous situation at this juncture of the war. Early in November 1940, East Midland HQ instituted a system of dealing direct with the fourteen Battalion Commanders of the Home Guard, against which Hereward protested in vain. At Christmas, it was proposed that the five Group Commanders should be abolished; Hereward once more protested pointing out that this was contrary to War Office instructions. The final blow came on 23 January 1941, when he was informed by General R.F. Adam, GOC Northern Command, that the War Office had ruled that the 'Chairman of a Territorial Army Association could not also be a Zone Commander, Home Guard, and that therefore Hereward must resign the latter post. He then sent his letter of resignation to Lord Exeter, who begged Hereward not to take this step.[63] Hereward, disgusted with 'the maze of intrigue and double dealing', would not change his mind. He was amazed to hear subsequently from General Adam 'that his real reason for asking me to resign was that I was too senior for the East Midland Area to deal with'.[64] Hereward received many letters of appreciation from section and platoon commanders, though he never publicly disclosed the reasons for his resignation.

*   *   *   *   *

As the war progressed, the prospect of victory continued to look bleak. The year 1942 was a low point for the Allies. Japan had entered the war in December 1941 and Singapore and many other Far Eastern countries had fallen. In North Africa, Field Marshal Rommel's brilliant tactics in Libya resulted in the retreat of Imperial forces to Egypt. In July 1942, the Germans resumed their drive into Russia and later swung towards the Caucasus and Stalingrad. As in 1940, an invasion of mainland Britain was once more a real possibility.

No one was keener to make preparations to meet this threat than Hereward. The Government issued a confidential Green Book in July 1942, *Consolidated Instructions to Invasion Committees in England and Wales*, setting out the steps which should be taken by localities to defend themselves. Although there was a Northamptonshire County Invasion Officer, Brigadier-General M.F. Gage, DSO, in post, the County Council decided not to take any action as a body. Hereward, who had been an Alderman since 1937, was concerned at this attitude as by August only 240 out of the 700 parishes in the county had set up Invasion Committees. In July Hereward had spoken at a County Council meeting deploring the apparent prevailing apathy on the matter. Lord Arthur Brooke of Great Oakley Hall, near Kettering, Chairman of the Council's Emergency Committee, responded by pointing out to Hereward that 'invasion is not the business of the County Council'. In reply, Hereward stated that as the Council had elected a County Emergency Committee, the members of which were automatically members of the Invasion Committee, the Council had a responsibility to the people. 'As a private member of the County Council,' wrote Hereward, 'and having military experience, I cannot hold my peace and say nothing when I believe, as I do, that the situation is serious and that our preparations are inadequate'.[65]

285

INVASION!

A PUBLIC MEETING

WILL BE HELD ON

SUNDAY EVENING, JULY 19th,

1942, at 8 o'clock prompt,

In the Council Schools, Roade, when the Village Invasion Committee will report on the steps taken, or to be taken, for your protection in the event of Blitz or Invasion.

Sir Hereward Wake, Bart.

has kindly consented to attend and speak.

Every Adult Parishioner is invited and urged to be present.

 SUNDAY, JULY 19th, in the Council School at 8 p.m.

PILLINGHAM & SON, PRINTERS, BRIDGE ST, NORTHAMPTON

LD11. Poster advertising the setting up of a Village Invasion Committee at Roade, July 1942

By this time, he had already visited some of the neighbouring villages, urging them at meetings to take steps to prepare for the grave situation. As Chairman of Courteenhall Parish Council, Hereward called a meeting of parishioners ('Persons under 20 years of age not admitted') on Sunday 16 August at the Courteenhall Old School, where he outlined the measures which an Invasion Committee could undertake. It would make a register of motor vehicles, deal with food supplies in an emergency, arrange for water supplies if reservoirs were out of action, deal with supplies of fuel and light if electricity were to be cut off, arrange for cooking food if added population occurred, provide money where necessary, disseminate information and allay panic. Telephones and public transport would be forbidden, and so a messenger service was essential. Troops, British and foreign, might have to be billetted in every house, barn and shed, and Hereward advised householders to lay in two or three weeks' supply of food. Milk and vegetables would be readily available, so this would alleviate the problem. A quantity of sawn wood for emergency cooking would be provided by the Courteenhall Estate. A Committee was quickly formed. It consisted of Hereward (Chairman), Mr Isaac Dodson (Home Guard Commander), Mr T. Tasker (Special Constable), Mr William Merryman (Air Raid Warden), Lady Wake (WVS), Miss Thurfrida Wake (Food Organizer) and Major L.T. Hamblen (Bursar, St. Lawrence College). Eight sub-committees were also set up:

a) <u>Food and Cooking</u> Miss T. Wake
b) <u>Fuel</u> Sir Hereward Wake
c) <u>Housing and Population</u> Lady Wake
d) <u>Water Supply</u> Mr Jack Ashton
e) <u>Motor Vehicle Register</u> Mr W. Merryman
f) <u>Tools Location List</u> Mr Walter Clements
g) <u>First Aid and Medical</u> Mr Edwards
h) <u>Fire Service</u> Mr Frank Lane
i) <u>Messenger Service</u> Mr Pat Merryman

Two more Sub-Committees, for Air Raid Precautions and Home Guard, were soon added, and fortnightly meetings of the main Committee were to be held.[66]

Hereward organized the Hall and the village for this new task with great enthusiasm. By the time of the second Committee meeting on 30 August much had been achieved. Liaison had been established with the Blisworth and Wootton Committees and notice-boards had been erected at the Post Office and the Lodge Gate. Ida had issued advice to all Courteenhall householders on what food to keep in reserve, and was arranging for outdoor cooking stoves to be built in the village and at the Old School. Daisy had undertaken a detailed survey of the houses, rooms and inhabitants of Courteenhall. Pat Merryman had recruited three messengers, and during term time, boys from St. Lawrence College would be available for this work. Every house had a supply of dry sand and buckets for fighting incendiary bombs and the location of water supplies was listed. Anti-gas ointment was issued later. The Home Guard were that

118. Winston Churchill in the Western Desert, 5 August 1942. From left to right General Sir Claude Auchinleck, Commander-in-Chief Middle East; Lieutenant-General W. H. E. Gott, Commander 8th Army; Major-General Miles Dempsey and Churchill

EIGHTH ARMY

PERSONAL MESSAGE
from the
ARMY COMMANDER

TO BE READ OUT TO ALL TROOPS.

1. When I assumed command of the Eighth Army I said that the mandate was to destroy ROMMEL and his Army, and that it would be done as soon as we were ready.

2. We are ready NOW.

The battle which is now about to begin will be one of the decisive battles of history. It will be the turning point of the war. The eyes ot the whole world will be on us, watching anxiously which way the battle will swing.

We can give them their answer at once, «It will swing our way».

3. We have first-class equipment; good tanks; good anti-tank guns; plenty of artillery and plenty of ammunition; and we are backed up by the finest air striking force in the world.

All that is necessary is that each one of us, every officer and man, should enter this battle with the determination to see it through — to fight and to kill — and finally, to win.

If we all do this there can be only one result — together we will hit the enemy for «six», right out of North Africa.

4. The sooner we win this battle, which will be the turning point of the war, the sooner we shall all get back home to our families.

5. Therefore, let every officer and man enter the battle with a stout heart, and the determination to do his duty so long as he has breath in his body.

AND LET NO MAN SURRENDER SO LONG AS HE IS UNWOUNDED AND CAN FIGHT.

Let us all pray that «the Lord mighty in battle» will give us the victory.

B. L. Montgomery.

23-10-42.
Middle East Forces.   Lieutenant-General, G.O.C.-in-C., Eighth Army.

119. Lieutenant-General Bernard Montgomery's message to the 8th Army on the eve of the Battle of El Alamein, 23 October 1942

120. British Infantry advancing in open formation towards enemy positions during the first day of fighting, Battle of El Alamein, 24 October 1942

week moving three boxes of ammunition including Molotov Cocktails, to the Stables, which acted as GHQ for the Committee.[67]

Fortunately, the tide of war changed in the Allies' favour, particularly with General Montgomery's successful North Africa offensive at El Alamein in October 1942 and the Russian counter-attacks at Stalingrad in the same month. As a result the Courteenhall Invasion Committee was never put to the test.

One casualty of the war was the destroyer HMS *Hereward* of the Hero class, with a displacement of 1,340 tons. Daisy had launched the ship at Newcastle upon Tyne on 9 December 1936 and Hereward had presented its captain with a silver salver on which was engraved the Wake Knot. During the first two years of the war, *Hereward* took part in many different operations. When the decision to evacuate Greece was made on 24 April 1941, *Hereward* helped with the embarkation of the troops.[68] With the invasion of Crete by the enemy on 20 May, naval forces were subjected to heavy enemy air attack. Seven days later, the cruisers *Orion*, *Ajax*, and *Dido* with six destroyers, including the *Hereward*, sailed for Heraklion to evacuate the garrison. Under incredibly dangerous conditions, the entire Heraklion complement of some 4,000 men were brought on board the ships. Difficulties now began to mount. At 03.45 a.m. on 29 May, the rudder of the destroyer *Imperial* jammed and another destroyer, the *Hotspur*, was sent back to sink her. As daylight dawned, the force was dive-bombed by a wave of Junkers 87s, known as Stukas. At 06.50 a.m., *Hereward*, which had picked up 450 troops, was hit by low flying Stukas near the foremast funnel. Rear-Admiral H.R. Rawlins, who was in command of the operation, was now faced with the choice of salvaging the crippled *Hereward*, thus endangering the rest of the force, or abandoning her five miles off the Crete coast. The decision was made to leave the *Hereward* to her fate. She was last seen heading towards the coast, its guns still firing at the aircraft. Later, as Italian torpedo boats approached the destroyer, *Hereward* blew up.[69] Its captain, Lieutenant-Commander W.J. Munn, and a large number of those on board were saved, but four officers and seventy two ratings were lost.[70]

*   *   *   *   *

Even during the blackest moments of the war, Hereward was able to find consolation in the countryside and its wildlife. In April 1943, he wrote an article for a Northamptonshire journal on rooks, debating whether they were a curse or a blessing. Hereward had no doubt of their value. He wrote 'Personally, I never allow rooks to be disturbed from young corn, and I have never known a bad crop to follow'. This was because they ate the wireworms. Similarly, he calculated that one pair of rooks killed 60,000 leatherjackets, another crop pest. He concluded, 'If what I have written as a result of my own observations over many years is mainly correct, how can there be too many of them? Surely they ought to be protected'.[71] The demands of the Armed Forces left the Estate with few young men to carry out the agricultural work. There were ways, however, of overcoming this difficulty, although officially they were not to be encouraged. Joan Wake reported:

One of the Courteenhall farmers' wives told me her little girl aged 9½ had been doing a man's work driving the tractor in the harvest field. Her legs are too short to reach the gears, of course, but they put it in gear for her, and off she goes.[72]

Hereward took much interest in the welfare, well-being and education of youths. He was an eloquent advocate of the Cadet Force and devoted much time to the Northamptonshire force. Joan Wake visited her brother in the Stables for supper in October 1944 where there was Hereward, Daisy, their son Roger and new daughter-in-law, Olwyn. She recorded, 'A pleasant evening except that H. would talk about his blooming cadets all the time, which I am sure didn't interest Olwyn in the least'.[73] In a speech at a ruridecanal conference at Preston Deanery in 1943, he stated his belief, echoing the views of his own father, that children brought up in the country benefited both physically and morally. He called for compulsory education up to sixteen (it was then fourteen) and for free continuation schools thereafter.

On other aspects of rural life, he was both enlightened and perhaps in some respects, ahead of his time. He campaigned for better cottages with electric light, gas, water and improved sanitation, taking the lead himself at Courteenhall village. A good and regular bus service to villages was essential. Playgrounds and organized games also needed to be provided. Churchgoing had fallen away; many people were bored by the services though they did not voice this. Shorter services, he believed, would be a useful start. Further, he postulated that:

> If ever the countryside in England is reduced to one parson for each group of villages, it may be that his occasional services in the village church may come to mean more to the people than the regular services they now fail to attend, and that the parson may be more really in touch with his flock than some are now.[74]

After serving as a Justice of the Peace from September 1924, and Deputy Lieutenant, Hereward was appointed High Sheriff of Northamptonshire in 1944. He attended the Assizes held at the beautiful seventeenth century Court House at Northampton, where he sat next to the judge, with his chaplain, the vicar of All Saints, Northampton, on his other side. Joan Wake was present at a Sheriff's luncheon in October 1944 in the Council Chamber at County Hall for the Clerk of Assize, Mr Bancroft, the Deputy Sheriff, JPs and Mayor, the Clerk of the Peace for the Borough and Clerk of the Peace of the County, as well as officials of the County Council. At the end of the meal:

> Hereward proposed the King. Murmurs of 'The King, God bless him.' Then Mr Bancroft in a delightful speech, saying he had been thirty years on our circuit and how much kindness he had received 'in your great county', and mentioning that Hereward was the 11th of his line to be sheriff thereof, (murmur from the audience), the first Wake sheriff having been in the 12th century, (collapse of assembled company) and here the old boy slipped up a couple of centuries, for

the first wasn't till 1329, proposed H's health. Then Hereward, standing there with Daisy next him, made quite a long and very charming speech, saying he hoped when all these days of grief and anxiety were over, Mr. Bancroft would still be clerk of assize. Then he said the sheriff's duties were more onerous in the old days when he used to meet the judge on horseback at the borders of the County. Ah, he added, that was in the days before the railways had come to spoil the fox-hunting. (Shades of old Sir William!)[75]

At the age of seventy in 1946, Hereward decided, after nineteen years as an Alderman, to resign the appointment. Lord Henley, Chairman of the Council, in a letter to Hereward of refreshing candour, expressed his regret 'because you are one of the few members who have had the vitality and imagination to think for himself'.[76] In the following year, after residing at Courteenhall for a quarter of a century, Hereward and Daisy handed it over, together with Waltham, to his eldest son, Hereward, and moved to Axford Lodge, Preston Candover, near Winchester.

Sir Hereward's interest in Northamptonshire affairs remained as strong as ever, and there was at least one piece of incomplete business which required his attention. In January 1938, the Ministry of Health had appointed a committee, known as the Kennet Committee, to inquire into the future of iron-ore workings in the County. It found that the area of ore-bearing land amounted to about one-sixth of the total. Reporting in March 1939, it noted that some 2,250 acres had been devastated and not restored; legislation was needed to remedy the situation.[77] Two and a half years later, the matter was referred to Lord Justice Scott's Committee on Land Utilization in Rural Areas: it reported in August 1942. It reiterated the findings of the Kennet Committee and then made more positive recommendations: 'In principle, it is wrong that any body or person should be allowed to work land for the extraction of minerals and leave it in a derelict condition. Legislation should be passed imposing an obligation on all those who derive benefit from the working of land for minerals to restore that land for agriculture or afforestation or other purposes within a short period of time after the land has been worked out'. It called for a technical investigation of the industry in order to ascertain the extent to which it was mechanically and financially practicable to effect restoration.[78] Again, no immediate action was taken but in June 1944, the Minister of Town and Country Planning appointed a Committee on the Restoration Problem in the Ironstone Fields, chaired by A.H.S. Waters, VC, to carry out 'a technical investigation of the ironstone industry in Northamptonshire and adjoining Counties with a view to reporting on the measures employed by the industry for the restoration of land damaged by quarrying operations and ascertaining to what extent these measures could be extended or improved under present conditions and in the future'.[79]

Hereward took an early interest in the subject. He was appalled at the devastation and dereliction left by iron-ore workings and the ruin of agricultural land in the County. In October 1941, as Chairman of the Northamptonshire Branch of the Central (later Country) Landowners' Association (CLA), he headed a sub-committee on the issue. It consisted of seven of the largest landowners in the County; of these, he was the only one who had no personal interest in the matter, the other six having iron-ore deposits on their properties. This was to be a source of friction in the coming discussions. After the Scott Committee had reported, Hereward successfully proposed an amendment during a discussion of the County Council Planning Committee that all land excavated in future should, within a reasonable time after the war, be levelled sufficiently for agricultural use.[80] No fewer than forty Northamptonshire villages were under threat.

The main point of contention between Hereward and his colleagues on the Northamptonshire CLA was his insistence that restoration should be compulsory; some other members believed that this might unduly restrict landowners' rights. In February 1943 these differences came to a head with the resignation of the President, Lord Spencer, and two members, Lord Brooke and Lord Brassey. Hereward also offered to resign as Chairman, but was reappointed to the post which he had held for many years.[81] Hereward remained firm in his views. He wrote in the following year:

> The opposition of interested landowners to legislation is minded to all of us. The abolition of private ownership of land would be disastrous but if that is to include the right to leave land devastated, it is difficult to defend it: or indeed to support any organisation or party which claims such rights for it.[82]

Hereward's activities in the matter were not confined to his work on the CLA and the County Council. He visited a number of quarries on the Duke of Buccleuch's estate operated by Stewarts and Lloyds of Corby and saw the work of extraction and levelling; this was followed up with a technical report for the information of CLA members.[83] His efforts drew grudging admiration from fellow landowners. The Duke of Buccleuch wrote to Hereward in February 1944, 'I am afraid your views and mine differ at present in regard to your tactics, but if our ultimate aim is similar, I hope they and we will be reconciled before long'.[84] Referring to the attitude of the CLA, another member told Hereward:

> Having come to the meeting, their [the members] main object is to get away quickly and they are too frightened to ask questions. 'What was Hereward driving at: what is all the fuss about?' The answer is of course that there is no disagreement and Hereward is only doing what 'you' have approved . . . I want to see you get some of the thanks for having set this ball rolling instead of, as appears at present, most of the kicks.[85]

More positive gains were now being made. In 1944, the extensive workings in South Northamptonshire were abandoned, and levelling began. When the Waters Committee began taking evidence in June 1944, the Chairman expressed a desire to hear the views of the Northamptonshire Branch of the CLA. A deputation was appointed and evidence, in the form of a printed pamphlet *Iron-Ore Workings in Northamptonshire,* was published in September. The evidence contained in the pamphlet frankly set out the divisions within the County branch of the CLA, but put forward positive proposals: that the question of 'to restore or not to restore' could not be left to royalty owners and mining companies to decide between themselves: that obligatory restoration would have no appreciable effect on the supply or price of the ore: and that

CP47. Diana Wake on Nimrod at The Grafton Hunt Hunter trials,
11 April 1938 by Arthur Haigh from a photograph. Diana was killed
when riding in a race in 1950

CP46. Joan Wake by Mrs Arthur Harris, to mark Joan Wake's
resignation after 43 years as Founder and Honorary Secretary of the
Northamptonshire Record Society, 1963

CP48. The Church Tower of St. Peter and St. Paul, Courteenhall, from the Park, painted by Peter Newcombe, November 1982

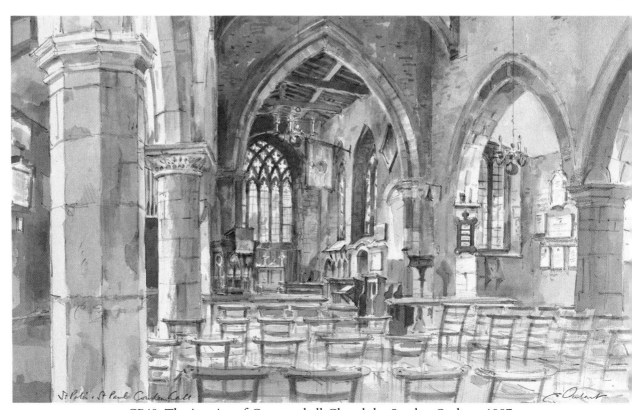

CP49. The interior of Courteenhall Church by Stanley Orchart, 1987

legislation fair to all parties could be achieved to enforce restoration.[86] The CLA leaflet, which had been drafted by Hereward, became the bible of advocates of restoration and the Waters Report's recommendations published in May 1945 were largely based on it.[87]

To keep up the momentum, Hereward conducted an intensive letter-writing campaign to the national and local press. In February 1949, he pointed out under a newspaper heading 'Hereward Wake calls for County Action Group', that as the Planning Committee of the County Council had 'achieved nothing', a special high-level County Committee should be set up.[88] He also bombarded with correspondence two Northamptonshire MPs, Reginald Manningham-Buller, QC (later Lord Dilhorne), Conservative Member for Daventry, 1943-50, and South Northamptonshire, 1950–62 and Gilbert Mitchison, QC, (later Baron Mitchison) Labour Member for Kettering, 1945–64. Both subsequently expressed their concern during debates in the Commons. A prominently placed article in one local paper in July 1946 was headed 'Two Northamptonshire MPs Press for Land Restoration'.[89]

The campaign was a long drawn-out one. As late as 1949, Kettering Rural District Council were faced with a large-scale mining application affecting 37,000 acres.[90] Finally the need for effective legislation in the matter was acknowledged in 1951 when the Minerals Workings Act reached the Statute Book. It gave power to County Councils to ensure that, before new workings were started, full levelling with restoration to agriculture was to be carried out. Northamptonshire County Council took effective advantage of this power. Levelling of workings soon began at a cost of £140 an acre: opponents to the scheme had claimed that it would amount to £1,000 an acre. The cost of the work was defrayed from the Ironstone Restoration Fund, established under the 1951 Act, and was assisted by government grants. Hereward's long campaign had been successful in saving much of the Northamptonshire countryside. He continued to take an interest in the work of restoration long after he had moved to Hampshire. In 1960 he accompanied members of the County's Minerals Sub-Committee in their annual tour of restored ironstone areas. He was both astonished and delighted at the results.[91]

*   *   *   *   *

Now with more time available, Hereward turned his attention to writing. He rejected an offer of a publisher to write an autobiography but produced two books of poems with drawings, *Laugh with Me* (1946) and *Laugh again with Me* (1947). More substantially, he embarked on research into the history of the Wakes which he intended as a book about Joan, the Fair Maid of Kent, her relations, forebears and descendants. His sister, Joan, was enthusiastic about the project and she wrote to him in September 1961, 'We would very much like to have the family history . . . for you to give to your children and grandchildren, with a few over to be kept at Courteenhall for future generations'.[92] Although Hereward consulted many sources and made contact with historians, the book was never written. Hereward also developed an interest in the history of the Green Man as depicted on inn signs, especially in Northamptonshire, and published an article on the subject.[93]

One major project which did come to a successful conclusion was a history of The King's Royal Rifle Corps in the Second World War. He told a newspaper reporter in 1947 about the book a year after he had started:

> It is too early, Sir Hereward thinks, to produce a final history. For this volume he is primarily indebted to his own energies throughout the war.
>
> Every war year, against mounting difficulties, Sir Hereward produced a Regimental Chronicle. It contained first-hand accounts from all theatres of war in which the Battalions were fighting. When the war ended he had amassed in the Chronicles the story of every campaign – all written by eyewitnesses from generals to riflemen. These he has edited.[94]

To assist him with selecting material and editing the book, Hereward enlisted Major W.F. Deedes, MC (who later became Lord Deedes), who had fought with the Regiment in Normandy and Germany, 1944–5. Deedes, an experienced journalist, at the time was waiting for an opportunity to stand as an MP. He met Hereward on a number of occasions in London, starting in 1946. Hereward, who had obtained much information from the Regimental records at Winchester, left the greater part of the selection of material to Deedes.[95] The first-hand accounts of the participants in different theatres of war make fascinating reading. Two of Hereward's own sons, Major Hereward Wake and Lieutenant Peter Wake, appear in the accounts. The book is divided into six theatres of war – Calais 1940, the Desert War 1939–43, Greece and Crete 1941, Italy 1943–5, North-West Europe 1944–5 and the liberation of Greece 1944–5. Altogether, it consisted of 180,000 words and was published in 1949, using as its title a translation of the Regimental motto *Celer et Audax – Swift and Bold.*

*　　*　　*　　*　　*

A fitting climax to a life already full of achievement was Hereward's visit to the United States of America in June 1960. A British Exhibition was to be held in New York at this time, and it was therefore an opportune occasion to celebrate Anglo-American links. The King's Royal Rifle Corps was originally raised from American colonists in Pennsylvania, Virginia and Maryland by John Campbell, Earl of Loudoun in December 1755 in order to fight the French and Red Indians. It consisted of four battalions of 1,000 men each and was styled the 62nd or The Royal American Regiment of Foot. In 1756 it was re-ranked the 60th.[96] Before the outbreak of the American War of Independence in 1783, it had helped Wolfe to capture Quebec and seen service in the West Indies, after which it returned to England.

The links were re-established when America entered the war with the Allies in 1941 after the Japanese attack on Pearl Harbor. But even before this, in the spring of that year, special arrangements had been made between the War Office and the United States government for a small number of American citizens to be given temporary British nationality in order to enlist in The King's Royal Rifle Corps. After undergoing a course of training in England, they were granted officers' commissions. Of the seventeen recruited, six served at El Alamein and were all wounded; later, two of these were killed in Tunisia, a further one at Anzio, Italy and another died fighting for the

121. The 13th baronet speaking at a dinner in New York, 14 June 1960, for American officers who served in The King's Royal Rifle Corps before the United States entered the war

122. Badge of the 60th Royal American Regiment of Foot, raised in America in 1755. After the American War of Independence the Regiment changed its title to The King's Royal Rifle Corps

123. Dinner at Courteenhall on 9 November 1962 to celebrate the Golden Wedding of the 13th baronet and Margaret, Lady Wake

French *Maquis*.[97] As Colonel Commandant, Hereward knew well many of these officers, entertaining them at Courteenhall,[98] and he kept in touch with them or their relatives after the war had ended.

Sir Anthony Eden, himself a member of the 60th in the First World War[99] and who had met the American recruits before they left for the North African campaign, wrote in June 1960 to Charles G. Bolté, one of the survivors, 'It is wonderful news that the 60th Rifles is having its first American reunion since before the Revolution. Please give my best wishes to all present for a memorable evening. I am sure that it will be'.[100] Hereward and Daisy were the guests of honour at a splendid Regimental dinner held at the Knickerbocker Club, New York, on 14 June, which forty six American, Canadian and British attended.[101] According to one ex-60th officer who was present, 'The dinner, which was one of the greatest occasions we have all experienced in our lives, or will ever, went off perfectly. We all rose to your father who made the speech of his life'.[102] Hereward proposed a toast to 'The Regiment', and, after thanking all those who had worked so hard to make the dinner a success, went back into the past and gave some amusing reminiscences of his early Army service. In one of his stories, Hereward told how, as a young officer, he was introduced to the very elderly Duke of Cambridge, then Commander-in-Chief of the Army, who said to him. 'They tell me you need brains now in the Army. I never had any. Do you?'

To which Hereward dutifully, replied, 'No, Sir'.

'I thought not', said the Duke, approvingly.[103]

The visit, which lasted three weeks, was a packed one. He was unwell on his arrival in America but soon recovered. There were endless reunions to attend and ceremonies to perform. One which gave him much satisfaction took place on Governor's Island, New York, where the original Regiment was stationed from 1756 to 1783. Here he laid a poppy wreath with the regimental badge and ribbon.[104] Hereward and Daisy charmed everyone; as one observer remarked, 'He twinkles and enjoys himself'. A member of the British Consulate-General staff and a former member of the 60th wrote to one of Hereward's sons:

> I do want to tell you one final thing. I walked with your father back to the Carlton House after the Dinner. He said to me, 'You know, this is different to what I expected. I am learning a bit more all the time'. I only hope that we will all, at the age of 84, have the warmth and humility and imagination to say something half as wise.[105]

Two years later, Hereward and Daisy celebrated their Golden Wedding at Courteenhall with thirty two members of their family. On 4 August 1963 he died peacefully in his sleep at the age of eighty seven. It was on his last birthday that he told a reporter that his chief recreation was 'seeing friends'.[106] His highly-developed sense of humour made him good company, but in matters of importance and principle he was willing to court unpopularity. He was not sentimental and never emotional, and had little time for anniversaries. 'After all,' he once told Daisy, 'our counting of days and years is based on things which might be quite accidental – I mean our distance from the sun, the rate the earth travels and rotates, and so on'.[107] Hereward had six great passions in life: his family, his Regiment, hunting, horses, dogs (not cats), and Courteenhall. He was also concerned in the affairs of the County, holding many different offices. His achievements in the service of his country during three major wars were outstanding and were publicly recognized. As a person, he inspired others by his example. Colonel Victor Cazalet, MC[108] whom Hereward had brought on to the staff at Versailles in 1918, afterwards wrote:

> You are one of the few people in this world whom it is a privilege to know, and you, although you don't agree with me in many beliefs, always helped me to live up to my principles, and were always an example of so many things I wanted and want to be. This I say, unblushingly, as I mean it.[109]

Hereward's ashes were buried at Courteenhall Church on 10 August 1963. It was his wish that the mourners did not dress in black. The Church bells, of which he was very fond, rang out and the flag on the Church tower flew at full mast and at the close of the service, as a final seal on Hereward's life and career, the bugles of his Regiment were sounded. Daisy lived on for another thirteen years until the age of eighty four; her ashes lie buried beside his in Courteenhall churchyard.

17

Joan Wake, Historian

THE THREE SONS OF SIR HEREWALD, THE TWELFTH baronet, Hereward, Godwin and Baldwin, achieved distinction in their military and naval careers. There was much less scope for the three daughters, Ida, Joan and Phyllis, brought up in a Victorian country household. It was considered inappropriate in all but a few cases for young ladies to proceed to university or to follow a profession. It was in spite of these handicaps that Joan, the fifth child and second daughter, became a national figure in the field of local records and a historian in her own right.

Joan was born at Courteenhall on 29 February 1884, a leap year. She was therefore able to label the messages of congratulations which she subsequently received on reaching her eightieth birthday, 'Letters, telegrams and cards on my 20th birthday, February 29th 1968'.[1] Joan was immensely proud of the fact that she was the first bearer of that name in the family since her illustrious forebear some 550 years before, Joan of Kent. Whilst two of her brothers, Hereward and Godwin were sent to Eton, Joan and her sisters were educated by governesses and tutors at Courteenhall – 'and a remarkably good education it was', she once said. One of her earliest memories was an overnight visit to Devonport at the age of five with Baldwin, Phyllis and their nurse, Kate Grey, to stay with Uncle Charlie 'Bulldog' Wake and Aunt Emma. Some seventy seven years later she recalled:

> Uncle Charlie took us to the station next morning, and I remember him very well, talking and laughing through the carriage window while we were waiting for the train to start – short, square-shouldered, fair complexion, and blue eyes – the instantly recognisable sailor's face.[2]

Whilst the house was let, the family occupied the Rectory, and on one occasion her great aunt Matilda Wake told her the story of how the day nursery had once been used for an unusual wedding. In the 1820s, Charles Dunkin Wake, of the Rectory, fell in love with his cousin, Jane Sophia, of the Hall, the third daughter of 'Old Sir William'. Marriages between first cousins were frowned upon and they had to wait many years before the wedding took place at Courteenhall in 1845, he being thirty eight and his

See Appendix A – Family Tree XV. Notes and References pages 430–437 bride forty three years of age. Later, Charles' elder brother, Richard William, also fell in love with one of Old Sir William's daughters, Charlotte Joan, and, as they were unable to meet, the lovers used to post each other letters in the trees in the Park. Aunt Matilda recounted that they were not allowed to marry but that in their old age, they defied convention and went to the Continent where they passed as brother and sister.[3]

It was a happy childhood for Joan and her brothers and sisters with Courteenhall as the social centre for many relatives and friends. Their father introduced them to the different aspects of the countryside, including hunting and shooting.[4] Joan as a young girl was included in one party which shot sixteen rabbits. Visits to the villagers were frequently made. Joan particularly enjoyed these visits with her mother, Phyllis and their governess to old Betsy Dunkley on her birthdays. Other guests included Mrs William Dunkley, Palmer, an old villager, and Miss Haskins the schoolmaster's daughter, and the small room was full to overflowing. Joan noted:

> After tea we used to ask riddles (the same every year) and Palmer used to sing the alphabet to a funny old tune and he always ended by saying, 'I were a great singer in my day, but when tunes came in I were done'. I have often thought since that he must have known a lot of old English folksongs and when he said tunes he meant music printed on paper.[5]

Queen Victoria's Diamond Jubilee celebrations in 1897 were also a memorable experience. A huge bonfire was lit in the village and Uncle Archie reported that he had counted thirty one others from Courteenhall Railway Bridge. The fireworks in the distance at Northampton were spectacular; Baldwin, Phyllis and Joan, armed with pillows, watched the display from the window, climbing back into bed when it was all over. The thirteen year old Joan had earlier reported:

> The *Poultry Journal* came today. It is very nice. The Diamond Jubilee has affected most things but I never thought it would affect poultry. But it appears from this paper that a new hen! has been invented to commemorate the Diamond Jubilee, which is to be called 'The Diamond Jubilee Orpington Hen'. It is a mixture of black, buff and rose-combed Orpingtons.[6]

A more dramatic occasion was the receipt of the news that her brother Godwin had been taken prisoner by the Boers in South Africa in December 1899. Then, in the following July, Joan watched from the schoolroom window as her father and Ida started off in the dog-cart for a day after snipe along the Tove, to take their minds off the situation. That same day, a telegram arrived announcing that Godwin was safe and Joan recalled her Papa reading it on his return and 'dancing for joy in front of the house'.[7]

One of Joan's great interests was music. In 1898, she joined the recently-formed Northampton School of Music, where she studied the piano. Standards were high and many famous musicians, including Gervase Elwes, Harry Plunket Greene and Donald Tovey, often visited the School.[8] It was here too, that Joan struck up a friendship with a fellow student, Delia, the eldest daughter of the sixth Earl Spencer. At the age of sixteen, Joan succeeded Mr B. Foddy when he left the parish as organist at Courteenhall

124. Page from a family scrap book of 1898, when Joan Wake was fourteen years old

125. Page from a later family scrap book, c.1905, depicting the 5th Earl Spencer on the right

300

126. Vice-Admiral Baldwin Wake (1882–1951),
fishing at Bjora reservoir, Norway, June 1937

127. Vice-Admiral Baldwin Wake, 1939

128. Major Godwin Wake (1879–1949), painted
by A. Hankey, France, February 1915

129. Godwin Wake's house 'Vigila', Southern Rhodesia,
which he designed and built

Church, and she held the post for the next twelve years until 1912. She also trained the choir. Sundays were particularly hectic. Early service began at 8.30 a.m, followed by a dash back to the house for breakfast. Sunday School started at 10.15 a.m (in the Sunday School Room in the village) and then back to the Church to play for the 11 o'clock service. After lunch, there was Sunday School once more at 2.15 p.m, then a call at the Church to prepare for the evening service at 6.00 p.m and a final rush back to the Hall to get dressed in time for dinner at 8.00 p.m.[9]

When Joan became 'organist', there was only a harmonium in the church, the Reverend George Hooper having done away with the organ in his 1887 restoration. She was determined to raise money for an organ and, as in almost all her other fund-raising ventures during her life, she was successful. Her stipend of ten pounds a year was put into an organ fund and other money was collected by means of subscriptions and concerts which she arranged. In 1909, Joan bought an organ from a church in Harringay, North London. On 12 July 1909, an inaugural service and recital to celebrate the installation of the new organ was held in the Church, attended by many local celebrities.[10]

She was fond of her Uncle Archie, Rector of Courteenhall Church, especially for his broadmindedness on religious matters.[11] Joan recalled that Uncle Archie was a very careless driver and was on occasions flung from his dog-cart on to the roadside. After one such accident, he hobbled into Church on Sunday, done up in blue bandages, with a patch on his nose and his arm in a sling. Archie had a life-long grievance against his brother, the twelfth baronet, who refused to let him drive across the Park, thus necessitating an extra two miles travel if he wanted to go to Blisworth or Roade. Joan was told that after dark, Archie would venture on the forbidden route. One Irish clergyman friend recollected the most exciting drive of his life, galloping across the Park in pitch dark, among the rabbit holes with the Rector's groom hanging on behind for dear life, crying out, 'Stop, sir, stop, for God's sake stop!'[12]

An incident which she remembered with great vividness all her life was a visit about this time to the Reverend Horace Wilkinson, the Rector of Stoke-by-Nayland, Suffolk. In his study he pulled out a box from the kneehole of his writing desk. Wilkinson took out an object covered with cloth, unwrapped it and handed to Joan the mummified head of Oliver Cromwell. It had probably been saved by one of his supporters after his body had been disinterred by Royalists after the Restoration in 1660.[13]

There were opportunities for travel to the Continent. Aunt Amy Ball, who lived in France, took Joan to that country for a month in September 1902. Joan's visit to Paris resulted in a carefully kept journal entitled 'The Adventures of A Parisite'. A much more extended tour of the Continent was made shortly before the outbreak of the First World War in the company of her mother and Aunt Josephine St. Aubyn. Leaving London on 8 May 1914 'at sparrow chirp', they visited Bruges, Budapest, Prague and Vienna and arrived back in England on 29 June. In her journal, Joan made detailed notes of the architecture of the many famous buildings which they saw and of the museums visited.

She was acutely aware of the deficiences in her formal education, and began to read widely, mainly in the fields of literature and art. Amongst her early papers are essays written for and marked by Professor John Churton Collins, Professor of English Literature, University of Birmingham.[14] They include such titles as On the Nature of Art, The Teaching of Tennyson's *The Princess* and *In Memoriam*, and The Plot and Scheme of Browning's poem *La Saisaz*, all of which were awarded A grades. Her cousin, Edith Sitwell, whose first small volume of poems appeared in 1915, sent many of her early verses to Joan for criticism. 'I hope,' Edith wrote, 'you will always say *just* what you think; I should hate it if you didn't.'[15] As a mark of her gratitude, Edith dedicated a number of poems to Joan.[16]

It was not until she was almost thirty that she began to find her proper niche. Living in an isolated part of Northamptonshire some years later, Joan informed a friend:

> It is strange how I am experiencing here the feelings which drove me from home in 1913. The pettiness, prejudice, maliciousness almost, and stupidity of country society (not the village people). Thank goodness Courteenhall is free from this. I miss my high-brows![17]

Joan's interests were almost entirely academic and she decided to devote herself to the pursuit of knowledge. In 1913, at the age of twenty nine, she settled in London, initially at 42 Emperor's Gate, South Kensington, and enrolled at the London School of Economics and Political Science for a two year part-time course in palaeography and diplomatic and medieval economic history.[18] Her tutor, Hubert Hall, inspired her by his seminars on the parish and parish documents, and she made extensive notes of the works of Pollock and Maitland on land tenure, Vinagradoff on the growth of the manor and Seebohm on the English village community. Her medieval economic history tutor was the young Eileen Power, who was then studying the economic position of women in the Middle Ages. At the sessional examination in July 1915, Joan gained first place out of the five candidates.

With the course now completed, she hoped to use her newly-gained knowledge to some purpose. 'I don't believe it is impossible to get research work', a fellow student told Joan, 'I have heard of some going since the War [began]. And you can always fall back on the local archaeological society or even the parish magazine'.[19] She had already made a start in December 1914 by copying out charters and writs relating to Blisworth and other Northamptonshire places and enquiring into place names in the county. By a stroke of good luck, she found an opening for her talents almost on her own doorstep. Many years later she recalled:

> My first exploration of a private collection had taken place as early as in 1915, when a neighbour, Sir Thomas Fermor-Hesketh, asked me over to Easton Neston to look at some boxes of old deeds in his possession. Here I very soon came across a twelfth-century charter – a confirmation by Walchelin Maminot, a magnate of King Stephen's reign, of a grant to the neighbouring Abbey of St James, Northampton, by a local peasant, Geoffrey of Hartwell, and his sons William and Simon. The names of other peasants occur in the deed, and those of three priests among the witnesses; a church, a chapel, a mill, and two crofts are

303

130. Joan Wake examining a document, c.1925

131. Confirmation by Walchelin Maminot, a twelfth century magnate, of a grant to the Abbey of St. James, Northampton, by Geoffrey Hartwell and his sons. One of the first manuscripts translated by Joan Wake, amongst the papers of Sir Thomas Hesketh at Easton Neston.

132. Joan Wake with Sir Maurice Bowra, Vice-Chancellor, Oxford University, on the award of honorary Master of Arts degree, Oxford, 23 January 1953

mentioned – all in this little scrap of parchment under nine inches by four in measurement. As I had lived within five miles of all these places for the whole of my life, my interest may be well imagined. I had obviously hit upon an important collection at the very start.[20]

As a late beginner at Latin, she found difficulty at first in reading manuscripts. Joan was much encouraged by the Northampton ecclesiastical historian, the Reverend R.M. Serjeantson, who had urged her to examine the Fermor-Hesketh collection in the first instance. He wrote to her in September 1915:

> Don't be disheartened about the Latin. These contractions and terminations bother us all. You are doing excellent work. If I can help you at any time don't be afraid to ask. There is a kindly feeling among Record searchers and it is quite understood that we should all help one another.[21]

That same year, Joan had visited her friends, Mr and Mrs Stephen Ward at Reading, where he was a member of the Philosophy faculty at the University College. The Wards had also invited their distinguished Professor of Modern History, Frank Stenton. 'F.M.S.', as Joan came to call him. He became very interested in her work at Easton Neston and invited her, unofficially, every Tuesday to his lectures at Reading. The afternoons were spent in his room with one or two other students, including Doris Parsons (who was to become his wife), copying and discussing charters. 'One Tuesday the word "history" was mentioned – it gave me quite a shock. Could this wonderful and exciting business we were up to, this intimate contact with real people in the remote past which I was experiencing, have anything to do with the dull and prosy stuff called history which I used to learn out of books in the schoolroom? Yet so it was'.[22]

Because of the outbreak of war, her researches took a secondary place to assisting the war effort. After serving as a clerk in a Cambridge hospital, she became honorary secretary of the Northamptonshire District Nursing Association from 1916 to 1919. The principal object of the Association was to reduce the very high rate of infant mortality. Whilst travelling throughout the county from village to village, she became aware of the vast amount of valuable historical material which was being lost to the salvage campaigns.[23] For a short period after the war, Joan worked as a research assistant for Sir Francis Piggott's series of books on maritime law,[24] but she had in mind a far more spectacular project which would satisfy her as yet unformulated ambition.[25]

*   *   *   *   *

It was whilst Joan was working on the Fermor-Hesketh papers that Frank Stenton, wrote to her:

> I do not know any work at the present time more valuable than the copying of records in private custody. It is no good writing any more about the manor in general as if the manor meant the same thing in Lincolnshire or in Hertfordshire.

What we want is a supply of local monographs – plenty of them, and well distributed. I do not know what plans you have formed for your own work.[26]

For Joan, Stenton's great message to the historical world was simple; that there was no real distinction between local and national history. She was encouraged by him to go further. On one of her visits to Reading, 'F.M.S., who had told me about the Lincoln Record Society founded [in 1910] by Canon C.W. Foster, with whom he was closely associated, turned to me and said: "You must start a Record Society in Northampton" '[27]

The notion of a Northamptonshire Record Society had first been mooted many years previously. Edwin Holthouse, a surgeon and antiquarian, whose family had been vicars at Hellidon for two generations, suggested in *Northamptonshire Notes and Queries* of 1886 that there was ample material in the County for the publication of historical papers.[28] Because of the War, it was not until October 1920 that a number of influential town and County people held meetings at Northampton and Peterborough to explain their aims; the Stentons and Canon Foster supported Joan in both towns. The Northampton meeting was held in the Council Chamber of the Guildhall on Tuesday afternoon, 19 October. The Mayor, Councillor F. Kelly, who took the chair, acknowledged that 'it was owing to the energy and perseverance of Miss Joan Wake that they had gathered together'. In her speech, Joan mentioned that it was whilst working in London on a volume of reference, having been given the Northamptonshire part to do, that she had first realized the extraordinary richness of manuscripts which were scattered about the County. Characteristically, she drew the attention of the audience to the need to save records before it was too late:

> There were great opportunities for Northamptonshire to go one better than other counties, and they might lay the foundation for future social historians to build upon, but it was no good their having their heads buried in parish registers while the dust-cart rumbled by, laden with valuable family manuscripts, and people lighted their pipes with some 12th. century charters. (Laughter and applause)[29]

On 10 December 1920, the Society was established at a Council meeting, held at the Public Library. Two committees were appointed to organize the work of the Society, in Northampton and Peterborough respectively. The aims of the Society were to accumulate manuscripts, as well as copies and photographs of them; to arrange lectures; to train students; to make lists of local records; and to recommend the publication of manuscripts to the Council.[30] It differed from the Lincoln Record Society in that one of its prime aims was to accumulate in a strong room a collection of documents relating to the County.

The early Annual Reports of the Society indicate the range of Joan's activities. In the first year she gave five lectures for the Northamptonshire Education Committee on the development of rural society. This was followed by a visit to the Bibliothèque Nationale in Paris to secure a photograph of Henry I's confirmation of William Peverel's grant of the manor of Courteenhall to the Cluniac priory of Lenton; she also copied extracts from a twelfth century cartulary relating to English manors of that house. In April 1925, Joan visited Holland, to see the national archives at The Hague and municipal archives elsewhere in the country and in September, she went to Sweden for a tour of record repositories, two of which were housed in sixteenth century castles. The trip was rounded off with a call at Copenhagen where she saw the national archives and in addition one of the principal local record repositories. Joan was impressed with the custody and arrangement of local archives and the training of local archivists. She reported, 'In spite of far greater riches, both in archives and money, England is in these respects a long way behind France, Holland, Sweden, Denmark and other European countries'.[31]

The work of collecting documents in England was becoming more urgent with the break-up of many of the larger estates and especially after the passing of the Law of Property Act 1922 which abolished copyhold tenure and so made the keeping of manorial records legally unneccessary. As a result, many existing manorial and other records were in danger of destruction. The Master of the Rolls was empowered to make provision for the proper custody of these records. The Society was selected to act for Northamptonshire and the Soke of Peterborough, a move which provided Joan with a great stimulus to increase the Society's collections.

One advantage which Joan used to good effect was that, as a member of one of the oldest families in the County, she had entrée to many country houses where there were accumulations of estate and family records. A typical example is contained in her Diary for October 1932:

> I have just returned from Burghley. I had not been there for three years, and was longing to go again. I went on my motor bike. Met by the butler who took me to my room, the same one I have always had . . .
>
> Dinner at eight in a small dining room. We ate off silver plates – four courses and a dessert. I had some claret and was the only wine bibber, the others roughing it on water. I also the only one to smoke. Next day, Lord Exeter [President of the Record Society] discussed Record Society finance. He said to me, 'I have complete confidence in you'. I bowed low, and was very pleased as this is not the first unsolicited testimonial I have had.
>
> The Duke of Buccleuch has said the same thing once or twice in other words. Result, I can now borrow what I want from these places . . .
>
> [Next day] So I made a list, stuffed an armful (of documents) into my suitcase, said goodbye, and left at three o'clock on my motor bike with the precious burden which I got safely to the Record Rooms later this afternoon.[32]

Another rich source for documents was the solicitors' offices in the County. In 1933, she noted:

> I have just got back from Norton from a visit to Beatrice Thynne, during which I started clearing out my solicitor's lumber room at Daventry. 3½ days and then I

chucked it, as it was most tiring and the dust and filth gave me a sore throat, and made arrangements for the job to be finished by a furniture remover. But it is well I did a good part of it myself, because the solicitor and his head clerk kept on producing wonderful things from odd corners. A Daventry town apprentices' and craft guild book of Elizabeth's reign for instance. I have found parish records, charity records, highway books, militia, volunteer, early railway and election papers, deeds back to Edward II, inclosure papers, awards, and maps, private and tradesmen's (and one doctor's) account books, (all from 100 to 150 years old), and buried in piles of rubbish and filth and documents on the floor, nearly up to my knee, and court rolls of seven manors going back to the first years of 18th century, including those of Fawsley hundred court. I took the precaution of putting all the best into a sack and bringing it away today. The rest will follow in twenty or thirty sacks to be sorted at leisure with the help of volunteers. The lawyer is pleased because I have found some old black penny stamps worth several pounds apiece; in fact I'm not sure I have not enriched him to the tune of something like £100 in this way, in addition to getting his rooms cleared for nothing. I wonder how many more such rooms there are in the county?[33]

She was also assiduous in tracking down collections which were no longer in the County and inveighing their owners to deposit them with the Record Society. One such case was a visit to Lord Winchilsea at Buckfield, Basingstoke, on 1 August 1930. After tea:

Almost immediately Lord W. took me down to the basement, where in a kind of cellar with a wooden door, which he unlocked, were piles of packing cases, more than half of which contained the collection of manuscripts which he had said he would deposit with the Northants. Record Society. Mrs. Carvell, the clerk who had helped me at Haverholme [Lord Winchilsea's former residence] came and pointed out the different lots:

1. Those catalogued by Canon Foster (shortly before 1925), including originals and extracts from the public records.
2. Uncatalogued mss. from the loft at Haverholme, including large quantities of court rolls.

Lord W. said, 'Now you only want the Northamptonshire documents?' I gave him a short homily on the iniquity of breaking up collections. He then inquired as to conditions of custody – who would use them etc. etc. I said they would be kept in a fire-proof strongroom, produced two or three at a time, and used in the presence of me or my assistant, by properly accredited students. He said, 'Oh, that sounds as if they would be safer with you than they are here'.

We discussed stamps, and he said he would have one made 'Finch-Hatton Collection' at the Army and Navy Stores, to be used for his mss. He said he would send the boxes direct by road with Mr.Carvell, and would find out if there was a reliable man to move them. If not, I was to send someone from Northampton with a fair-sized furniture van.[34]

CP50. Major Hereward Wake, MC
(later 14th baronet) aged 27,
on his return from the
North African Campaign
by Oswald Birley, 1943

CP51 (below). The children of Sir Hereward and
Margaret, Lady Wake by Simon Elwes. Presented to
Sir Hereward by his children on his 80th birthday in
1956. From left to right: Peter Wake, Sir Mark
Turner (in whose house the picture was painted),
Lady Margaret Turner, Mary Weatherby, Patricia
Dawnay, Roger Wake and Hereward Wake

CP52. The Garden, Courteenhall. The 13th baronet and his wife redesigned the Garden in the 1930s

CP53. The Arboretum, below the House, planned and planted at Courteenhall since 1965 by the 14th baronet

Apart from fruitful visits to such places as Althorp, Rockingham Castle, Drayton[35] and Canons Ashby, Joan's boundless curiosity took her to many parts of the county to inspect, amongst other things, dovecotes and the sites of meeting places of the hundreds courts. In 1925, she witnessed the last manor court to be held in Northamptonshire. This was at Gretton in the Hatton Arms, where a widow in deep mourning either surrendered or was admitted to a tenement by the rod held by the lord of the manor.[36] In the early 1930s the village of Corby was also investigated and recorded in anticipation of the new steel works being built there, and old inhabitants of villages were sought out for their reminiscences of working conditions, names of roads and lanes and family history.

In old age, Joan corresponded regularly with Emily Surridge, a former resident of Courteenhall village, then approaching one hundred. Emily set out in great detail her memoirs, which included an account of the eleventh baronet's widow, Margaret, driving down the village with Aunt Matilda in her pony carriage.[37] Earlier, in 1947, Joan had visited Miss Rice, then a nonagenarian, who was born at East Lodge, Courteenhall. Joan recorded, 'She can remember Sir Charles [tenth baronet] distinctly, coming to inquire after her brother William when he was dying, and how he insisted on going round to the back door so as not to disturb him by going in at the front. She must be the last person alive who can remember Sir Charles, who died in 1864'.[38]

In response to a circular from the Record Society asking for new members, Joan in April 1933 called at Oundle on a Mrs Smith, a brewer's widow, who had become a brewer herself. Mrs Smith remembered the Wake family when they were at Cotterstock Hall in 1893 and Joan's father in his militia days. After partaking of lunch, consisting of beefsteak pie and mince pies, washed down with Guinness stout, Joan noted, 'She said she was afraid the house smelt of smoke. "You will think me a horrid old woman – I smoke a pipe". "So do I", said I, and we made friends at once.' The house itself, Cobthorne in West Street, had once belonged to William Butler, Commander of the Parliamentary forces, and the staircase had come from Sir Thomas Tresham's unfinished Lyveden New Bield. Mrs Smith produced a handful of late seventeenth and eighteenth century leases which Joan thought were wonderful. Just as the two were shaking hands, Mrs Smith said, ' "Oh I've got some more documents you had better see. I had forgotten about them". So back we went to the dining room, and she opened a large iron chest which had come from the Brewery, full of deeds and documents, relating to Norfolk, Devon, Middlesex and Northants, including a Court Roll of King John and an Account Roll temp. Hen.VIII of a royal bailiff. This was my general impression in a quarter of an hour's examination. Result: she is bringing the lot to the Record Rooms [at Northampton] tomorrow where she will leave them to have a list made, and then Northants, to keep what they want, the rest to be distributed to the Counties through the British Records Association . . . A good afternoon's work.'[39]

Joan's appearance changed little over the years. She was stocky and heavily built. She had straight hair and a rather sallow complexion; but it was an interesting face with a determined jaw which displayed a great strength of character. Clothes were of little interest to her. She usually wore her old wartime District Nursing Association coat and a battered hat, though she always carried her best hat in a box on her motor bike for when she visited the grander houses. Joan was an untidy worker; her rooms were filled with piles of papers and books both on the desk and the floor. She was a great but impatient user of the telephone. Many a missive was delivered to some errant individual on one of her famous postcards.[40] Exasperating to work for – she was a perfectionist who demanded total commitment to the task in hand from those around her – she was nevertheless generous and kind towards many people. Joan was also broadminded and not at all unworldly in everyday matters. Like her father, she rarely discussed religion though she was very knowledgeable and had her own deep convictions. Universally, Joan was known as 'Miss Wake' and did not brook undue familiarity.[41]

In those early days of the Society her energy was boundless. In February 1933, she made the three hour journey from Northampton to Milton, the home of the Fitzwilliams, via Peterborough:

> Took off coat, and into the room where Toby Fitzwilliam is arranging the later papers and correspondence. We seized seven boxes of letters from 1550 to end of Jac.I and took them to the Library, where I set to work at a large writing table, Mr. Fitzwilliam writing letters opposite me, to examine contents of boxes. Several original letters of Henry VIII and Elizabeth, lots of correspondence about Ireland, and a certain amount about local affairs, but not much. A letter from a Wake and another from Thos. Brudenell, both of which I copied. Took notes of several more, also of a book of dealings with Council, letters etc. to Protector Somerset, 1548–9, which may be very important. Lunch at one, Lady Fitzwilliam and her son there, (wife of Sir – F., equerry to King,) and a young George Curzon, an actor. Cup of coffee and back to the letters. Then to the muniment room proper over the stables, where I was left alone. Took lots of notes from catalogue, and noted contents of a Peterborough Abbey account roll 1308 of thirty three long membranes. Worked quickly and Mr. Mellows [W.T. Mellows, Honarary Assistant Secretary of the Record Society for the Soke of Peterborough] was astonished at the amount I had got down in the time. At three Mr Fitzwilliam took me back to Peterborough.
>
> He dropped me at the Bishop's registry, where I found Mr. Savory, who took me into the Knights' Chamber, which has been restored and fitted with steel cupboards for the muniments which were formerly kept over the archway into the precincts. They are neatly stowed away in cupboards, with air holes, but the windows were shut, and there was a mildewy smell and I suggested ventilators in the windows at each end. There is only a rough list of the documents and I suggested a proper catalogue. He said no, he did not want anyone but him to be able to find the things. (This is rot of course, and I must ask the bishop about it.) I said he might be run over by a motor bus.
>
> From there to the Probate Registry where I found Rev. H.I. Longden, [Henry Isham Longden, Deputy Custodian of the Record Society] hard at work at the wills. He shewed me a book of wills, recently found in a solicitor's office and given back to the Registry beginning about 1470. He motored me to the station and I returned to Northampton by the 6.5 getting back to Collingwood

Road at 8.15p.m. after a strenuous but most interesting day.[42]

Such a hectic routine left little time for a settled existence. Joan stayed with many friends both before and after she rented The Green Farm, at Cosgrove, an old stone house on the Buckinghamshire border, from Captain Philip Atkinson in 1937. One of her favourite residences was at 39 Collingwood Road, Northampton, where her old friend Miss Mary Hern provided accommodation as well as help with Record Society business. Joan additionally used the Judge's Lodgings in Northampton, the Ladies' Club at Hazelrigg House, Marefair, and enjoyed the hospitality of Mr and Mrs W.T. Pearse in their house at 502 Wellingborough Road and later at Adstone, Towcester.[43] In London she often stayed at Crosby Hall, Chelsea, The International hostel of the British Federation of University Women, where she met many overseas scholars.

Joan also advanced the work of the Society in two other ways. As the first Honorary Secretary, she was involved in its day-to-day running and largely dictated the Council's policy. She was, too, the Honorary General Editor of the Record Society's publications. Five volumes were issued in the first decade of the Society, two of which – *Quarter Sessions Records of the County of Northampton 1630, 1657–8* (1924) and *Musters, Barons, Subsidies etc. in the County of Northampton 1586–1623* (1926) – she herself edited. She was not the easiest of editors to please though, and often changed her mind, sometimes when the text was ready for final printing.[44] Joan was also active in drumming up support for the Society by persuading people in the County and overseas to become subscribers; by 1930, there were 233 members.

Recording the county's history was one of her pre-eminent aims. As early as 1922, she read a paper at a meeting of the Library Assocation on 'Collaboration in Historical Research', outlining the need for local records to be listed and deposited in local offices, with archivists trained in archaeology.[45] One journal commented on 'this pioneering endeavour': 'A large number of women who, having no need to earn, are missing the interest of regular war activities, may possess the student nature and find in this Record work a life interest'.[46] A more ambitious extension of this scheme was a shilling booklet written by Joan entitled *How to Compile a History and Present-Day Record of Village Life* with the object of encouraging the Women's Institutes of Northamptonshire 'to rescue from oblivion traditions, legends, stories of present-day life and other records of historical interest.' The booklet attracted a long editorial in *The Times*. It began, 'Northamptonshire, as a county, has always had a sense of its own history. If a scheme which has been drawn up for the use of its Women's Institutes for the compilation of the histories of its villages proves successful, it may perhaps lead the way towards a similar movement in other counties'.[47] The booklet, which appeared in June 1925, met with a more enthusiastic reception than the author had expected.[48] A second edition appeared in October and was followed by a reprint in November. A third edition followed in 1935.

When the editor of the *Northampton Independent* reviewed the work, he ventured to ask if Joan Wake 'could advise historians how to make their publications pay'. In reply, she quoted an article from her friend Sidney Peyton, Librarian at Reading University College:[49]

311

The only reward this man can have will be ... the recognition by those who are most entitled to appraise the worth of such work. This surely is the only reward worth having.[50]

Some of her publications were not considered commercially viable ventures. Joan informed Peyton in June 1934, 'I am going to take the risk of printing the Railway article [*Northampton Vindicated, or Why the Main Line Missed the Town*] privately in the autumn in the hope that I shall get my money back'.[51] A successful work was her *Guide to St. Michael's Mount*, the home of her mother's family, the St. Aubyns, which went into six editions between 1934 and 1939.[52] In 1935 she told a friend, 'By the end of May I shall have paid for my new edition of 2,000 Guide Books and still have about 100 in hand or 200. So if I can sell the 2,000 this year I shall clear £66, but shall be more than content with £50. I might even buy a car next year if I do well over this.'.[53]

Joan's standing as a scholar had by this time been widely recognized. She had lectured in 1926 to the Anglo-American Conference of Historians in London, was a member of the Local History Committee of the Historical Association and in 1929 gave evidence to the Committee on House of Commons Records with reference to manuscript material in Northamptonshire collections for the history of early Members of Parliament.[54] The time was now ripe for the realization of Joan's plans for an archive service in the County.

* * * * *

In August 1929, a letter had appeared in the main London daily newspapers from three members of the Society's Council, the Marquess of Exeter, J.A. Gotch (Chairman of Council) and Joan, describing the work of the Society, and appealing to owners of Northamptonshire collections, particularly those who had left the County, to deposit their manuscripts in the custody of the Society for the use of history students. Shortly afterwards, on 29 March 1930, the Record Rooms of the Society at County Hall, Northampton, were officially opened by the Master of the Rolls, Lord Hanworth. The collections of the Society, which so far had been housed in the Public Library and the chamber under the Borough Museum, were now moved to the County Council buildings. The accommodation consisted of a fireproof strong room, a students' room and a general store room. As the entire staff consisted only of Joan Wake as Honorary Custodian, Miss Mary Grace as Assistant Secretary and a cataloguer, it is surprising that the rooms were able to be open to students for six days a week.[55] But the finances were shaky. Joan hoped to produce one Record Society volume a year, though the total income in 1932 was only £230. 'Our clerk costs us £100 a year or just over', she wrote, 'The Reading Rooms and other expenses another £70 <u>at least</u>, which does not leave much for publishing.'[56] Nevertheless by the outbreak of the Second World War, ten volumes had been published including *The Montagu Musters Book, 1602–1623* (1935) which Joan had edited.

The archives were widely used by many scholars and local historians. One visitor in the early 1930s, Professor R.H. Tawney, the economic historian, became a member of the Council from 1943 until his death in 1961. The Place-Name Survey of

Northamptonshire, which occupied much of Joan's time, brought its own reward. When *The Place-Names of Northamptonshire* edited by J.E.B. Gover, A. Mawer and F.M. Stenton appeared in 1933, it was stated in the Preface, 'The choice of Northamptonshire as the county for treatment in the year 1932–3 was largely determined by the possibilities of local help which offered themselves through the inauguration of the Record Rooms of the Northamptonshire Record Society'.[57]

Publicity through novel means was exploited. Joan gave a broadcast talk from Birmingham (Midland Region) on 28 March 1934 on 'The Romance of Local Records' which was followed up with an appeal for new members.[58] She also organized ambitious displays of historical material in the form of annual exhibitions for a wider audience. The official Diary of the Society records on 28 March 1936:

> The Elizabethan Exhibition, lasting for a week, 28 March – 4 April, opened with a private view for members, followed by a lecture on 'Queen Elizabeth' given by Professor J.E. Neale of London University, in the Town Hall, Northampton. Between 400 and 500 people were present and afterwards the exhibition of portraits and mss. was open till 6pm. Portraits had been lent from many Northants country houses, Althorp, Drayton, Courteenhall, Boughton House, Milton, Rockingham Castle etc. These showed the important men in Elizabeth's reign who either lived in Northamptonshire or had Northants connections. Lord Spencer superintended the hanging of these in the Record Rooms and Miss Scroggs came down from London for two days to help with the documents that were exhibited.

By the following year, the Annual Report stated, 'The Record Rooms are now full to overflowing'.[59] Storage alone had become a problem: among the archives, more recent acquisitions were the Fitzwilliam of Milton estate records (thirteen sackfuls) and the Willoughby (Daventry) collection (seventy five sackfuls).[60] The County Council now agreed to provide accommodation for students and the manuscript collections in their new premises which, it was hoped, would be ready by 1940. In anticipation of more space being available, a photographic survey of fast-disappearing Northamptonshire landmarks was initiated by Joan. Dated houses and cottages formerly used as village workhouses were to be particularly noted.[61]

Before these developments could be put into operation, the Second World War began. During the 1914–18 War, Northampton had been bombed, and it was therefore considered a risk to leave the Society's records on the top floor of a building in the centre of the town. Consequently, between 2 and 12 September 1939, some thirteen tons of records were removed to two separate places for safe custody under Joan Wake's supervision. She used her own home, The Green Farm at Cosgrove, as one depository.[62] The other was Brixworth Hall north of Northampton. On 23 November, Joan was notified that soldiers were to be billeted at the Hall and she was concerned for the safety of the documents there. In December, she received a message that workmen installing the water supply at the Hall had heard water dripping in one of the rooms. 'I went over by bus immediately, unsealed the Butler's Pantry where the dripping water had been heard and found it was a tap dripping over the sink: found everything was quite all right, sealed it up again and examined the seals on the other doors'.[63] As the deposits of archives continued to accumulate, it was found necessary to have two more depositories: these were located at Brixworth Rectory and at nearby Overstone Park. All four depositories were regularly inspected by her.[64]

*　　　*　　　*　　　*　　　*

One of Joan's great anxieties over the years was the destruction of records by default or by ignorance.[65] Now, in wartime, this problem was compounded by the exhortations of both government and the local authorities for firms and individuals to help the salvage drive. The Master of the Rolls made an appeal to lawyers not to destroy documents without first seeking the expert advice of the British Records Association, of which Joan had been a Council member since its formation in 1932.

Joan decided to take immediate action by herself. By the end of 1940, she had visited numerous firms of solicitors in eighteen Northamptonshire towns as well as in eight adjoining counties.[66] Although she met with many disappointments and difficulties, not least the rationing of petrol, these failed to dampen her ardour for the work. At Thrapston on 9 July 1940 she met the partner of one firm 'a conceited young know-all, who told me with pride and satisfaction that he had had a clear out a year ago, and had destroyed two lorry-loads, but "nothing of the slightest historical interest" '. Motoring on to Oundle, she met Mr Coombs, 'very civil and sympathetic. He had nothing to show me, and said the only hope was a cupboard under the stairs which was full of stuff, but he had lost the key. Wild hunt in his drawer on the spot. Asked his clerk. No result. We gazed at the door of the said cupboard . . . Mr. Coombs promised me faithfully he would let me come when he had found the key'.[67]

A German invasion was considered imminent at this time, as was made clear when Joan called in at Cotterstock Hall to visit Lady Etheldreda Wickham, then in her late seventies. Lady Etheldreda had been chairman when Joan was honorary secretary of the Northamptonshire District Nursing Association during the First World War.[68] In Joan's words:

> She gave me a delightful welcome. She said she had got out her rifles, cleaned them, and had been having a little practice and found her eye was as good as ever. 'Going to give them to the military?' I asked. 'Not I', said she, 'I'm going to have a pot at them myself!'[69]

The most profitable call of the day was on Mr Loveday of Loveday and Son, Islip, who proudly told Joan that his family had been making horse-collars in the village for 300 years:

> 'Got any records?' said I. 'Yes', said he, 'but the waste-paper merchant is fetching them next week for the government.' 'Let me see them first', said I, and after a fierce argument face very close to face for ten minutes, he led the way up one pair of stairs, up another steeper pair of stairs then up an impossible

perpendicular ladder through a trap-door in the ceiling, to an attic, where lay about half a ton of records in chaotic disorder. We shifted the lot in a very short time.[70]

On at least one other occasion, Joan was able to turn the salvage drive to the advantage of the Record Society. The *Northampton Independent* reported in June 1941:

Miss Wake 'Passes The Hat'

The irrepressible resourcefulness of Miss Wake in overcoming any obstacles to her devoted work in salving ancient documents from destruction was again illustrated at the annual meeting of the Northamptonshire Record Society.

A Northampton solicitor had sent her a deed of the reign of Henry VIII concerning the transfer of some property at Rushden to the Abbess of Delapre.

Holding up the ancient parchment to the meeting she apologetically explained that the lawyer's client wanted 15s. for it, and as the Society did not make a practice of buying such things, lest they should be inundated with them, she was in some difficulty, for although she would like to have the document for the Society, there were no specific funds for its purchase.

Then in an appealing tone she added that it seemed a shame to get people to an indoors meeting on such a fine afternoon and then to suggest a silver collection, but she wondered if they would be so very kind as to give, say, a shilling or so in a hat at the door.

The appeal of Miss Wake was not made in vain. Had she asked for more it would have been forthcoming from appreciation of the fine example she sets as a saviour of historical treasures.[71]

A pleasant interlude from the punishing routine she set herself was to assist the Duchess of Gloucester, who had joined the Record Society in 1940, in sorting out some of the records at her home, Barnwell Castle. One collection of particular interest to Joan was that belonging to Thomas Bell, (?1783–1862) a minor poet, village historian and schoolmaster who lived there. She had written about Bell some years previously[72] and in December 1942, went to Barnwell to discuss with the Duchess where best to place the documents. Joan suggested that those items which had come from Boughton, the Duchess's former home, should be returned there.[73]

Only three months before Joan died, she wrote to the Duchess:

I live much on happy memories of old days. And now I must tell you of one of the most wonderful sights of my life. It was in the last war and for some years I had not been to the other end of Northamptonshire. I was passing by Boughton in my little car, and thought I would go down to the House to see how things were getting on . . . The housekeeper, whom of course I knew, let me in, and there lying in the sunshine on the floor were the sculptures of all the Kings and Queens from the tombs at Westminster Abbey! It was marvellous because of course in the Abbey they are so high up, and in my day the light not very good, so

315

that one could never really see them properly. They were moved soon after because Grafton [Underwood] air field was so close.[74]

On 20 May 1944, Joan had a narrow escape in this area. She had received special permission to cross the Grafton Underwood airfield runway in order to reach Boughton, but on this occasion 'I was never so frightened in my life as a huge, immense great aeroplane came taxi-ing towards me, and was so high the driver could not possibly have seen the tiny little Allegro and me! I fled towards a jeep and stuck close to that, and then the plane went off down the runway and soared into the air, – a beautiful sight'.[75]

Despite the severe difficulties connected with publishing during the war as well as the considerable calls on her time, Joan continued to ensure that there was a steady stream of volumes for publication by the Record Society; four titles appeared between 1939 and 1945. When the Reverend Henry Longden, Sir Gyles Isham's cousin and then Vice-President of the Society, died in 1942, he had completed thirteen volumes of his scholarly work *Northamptonshire and Rutland Clergy from 1500*. Joan, as his literary executor, undertook the completion of the remaining two volumes, which appeared in 1943, the latter volume containing a full length memoir of Longden by her.[76]

The opening of 1944 was a sad one for Joan. Her mother, the Dowager Lady Catherine Wake, died at Courteenhall. However, only a few days later, her youngest brother, Baldwin, who had joined the Navy as a midshipman and had risen to be a Vice-Admiral, was appointed Knight Commander of the British Empire (KBE), 'not', as Joan told Doris Stenton, 'for standing on the poop with his back to the lee-scuppers, blazing away at the enemy's rigging (he did that at the Battle of Jutland!), but for sitting in board-rooms, getting constructors to build the right sort of ship for the Navy, a job he has had since Munich-time, [Admiral Superintendent of Contract-Built Ships, 1937–44] and more difficult and less congenial to a man like him than the former'.[77] It was a proud day for Joan as she joined Ida to witness the investiture of her brother at Buckingham Palace on 21 March.[78] An active and energetic person with a good sense of fun, Baldwin had remained a bachelor. On his mother's death, he inherited Weston Turville, where Joan often went to visit him until he died there in 1951.[79]

Joan continued her work of salvaging solicitors' records, covering many miles in her small battered convertible car, the *Allegro ma non troppo* as she called it: the car itself was crammed with cartons, attaché cases, a portable typewriter, rolls of postage stamps and her very large handbag.[80] Her driving, which could be erratic, often terrified passengers, especially when she became diverted by what she was saying. Visiting a firm in Market Harborough, she called on Mr X of the Public Record Office, which had taken part of the workhouse on the Leicester Road to store 150 tons of records. Joan observed:

> Last time I saw Mr. X he was a fine-looking, middle-aged, well set up man with dark hair. I found a rather bent, grey-haired, thin, old man with a white moustache. (He used to be clean shaven). I wondered if he had an equal shock on seeing me. No doubt this war has aged us all very much more than the five years it has so far lasted.[81]

CP54. The Entrance hall, Courteenhall by Jeremy Whitaker, 1976

CP55. The Dining room, Courteenhall by Jeremy Whitaker, 1976

CP56. The Library, Courteenhall by Jeremy Whitaker, 1976

CP57. The Drawing room, Courteenhall by Jeremy Whitaker, 1976

The intensive labour and stress did, in fact, take its toll. Uncharacteristically, Joan's diary for Friday 24 November 1944 reads: 'Very tired. Lay about all day and did O'. Consultations with various doctors were frequently made. On 15 December after checking the Society's records at Brixworth she noted, 'Back to see Dr. ??? who said I had not got cancer this time'. But none of this blunted Joan's wry sense of humour. During the German V2 raids on London in February 1945,[82] she went to London to a meeting of the Royal Historical Society for Frank Stenton's last appearance as President:

> Room crowded. New president thanked officers for gallantly carrying on during the crashing of the bombs. C-R-U-M-P. Roooaaarrr – down came one just as the last word was out of his mouth. A pause – then the whole room rocked with laughter.[83]

It was typical of her busy life that the ending of the war in Europe received but the briefest of entries in her Diary: 'May 8 and 9 till May 16th inclusive – Germans capitulated in bits. May 8. V. day. Church and bonfire'. Perhaps the exhausted state of the nation at this time is captured in the description of a visit made by Joan to Grafton Regis, south of Courteenhall, where she had lunch with Lord and Lady Hillingdon and their daughter:

> His coat (tweed) was literally in rags and tatters. He apologised for it but it is the smart thing to do now, either to be in rags or to have large leather patches of odd sizes on your coat sleeves, *vide* Mr Brudenell or Hereward.[84]

*   *   *   *   *

The most immediate and pressing problem now was the rehousing of the dispersed records of the Society. At the end of the European war, it was clear that the County Council was reluctant to make the rooms once more available. In addition, so much more material had been accumulated during the War that the old space at County Hall was insufficient. A new home had to be found. Sir Gyles Isham, formerly a Shakespearian actor, a knowledgeable historian of the County and an active member of the Society, offered accommodation at his residence, Lamport Hall, some nine miles north of Northampton. A five-year lease at a rent of £143 per annum was granted.[85] Before this could be effected Joan interviewed George Tomlinson, then Minister of Works in the Attlee government, to arrange for the prisoners of war who were at Lamport to be transferred to Brixworth Hall. She even managed to persuade Tomlinson to provide compensation for damage to Lamport and then used the money for repair and redecoration. On 3 November 1946, together with a helper, Joan labelled and listed 167 boxes and parcels of records in the servants' hall at Brixworth, finishing the job at supper time: on the following day, they were dispatched to Lamport.[86] Because of the severe weather, the move to Lamport was not fully accomplished until 28 April 1947.

The premises leased included the front hall, the seventeenth century stair hall, the eighteenth century library, the adjacent dining room and pantry, and a flat for the archivist. The Society had little furniture, four bookshelves and insufficient shelving for

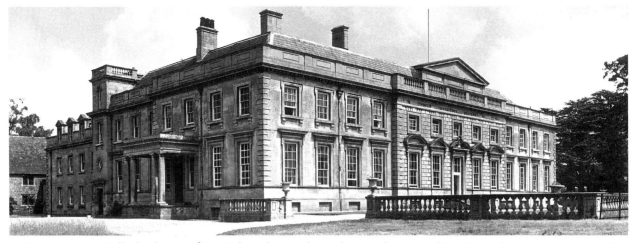

133. Lamport Hall, the home of Sir Gyles Isham, where the Northamptonshire Record Society was housed from 1947 to 1959

134. Dust jacket of *The Brudenells of Deene* by Joan Wake, published by Cassell and Co. in 1953

135. The Library, Lamport Hall, one of the rooms occupied by the Record Society

136. Joan Wake collecting 76 sacks of documents from Messrs Stops and Burton, solicitors, Daventry 1935

storing records. The latter were mainly kept in old trunks, suitcases, tin boxes of every size and shape, wooden crates, sacks, cardboard boxes, and even hatboxes; standard card-board boxes were in due course ordered from a container company.[87] Later, Joan negotiated an extension of the lease to include more ground floor rooms to the rear. By 1950, there were ten rooms full of records.[88]

There were many difficulties to overcome. Little or no heating was available and in the first months of 1947, when the weather was very severe, five ceilings in the house collapsed and water poured into the rooms. The condition of the premises after its wartime occupation left much to be done. Joan told her brother Godwin:

> I was busy last week trying to get our rooms at Lamport cleaned. No labour to be had for miles around for scrubbing, so at last I managed to get the services of a couple of German prisoners who are quartered at Boughton. They slopped the water on the filthy floors, shoved the dirt about feebly with a scrubbing brush, and left it to dry again, so down I had to go on my rheumatic knees, and shew them how to do it properly, (though in confidence I must tell you I have never scrubbed a floor in my life); however with many groans and much hard breathing I did a square yard so that at least you could see the grain of the wood, the prisoner hauling me up three times to go down again in the right place to get at the next bit. 'Schmutzig, sehr schmutzig', [Dirty, very dirty] I said, as I sent him to empty the bucket, hastily remembering the German I learnt with Fraulein in '91, adding when I had finished, 'So schones Holz und rein'. [Such pretty wood and clean][89]

Security also presented problems. The records could not be left unattended so Joan, without the owner's permission, put a bed in the former butler's bedroom.[90] Christmas 1948, was, by her own admission, the 'strangest I have ever spent', consisting of a week's residence on her own at Lamport.[91] Joan also used the room as a *pied à terre*, saving her the long journey in the evenings to Cosgrove. Meals were mainly out of tins, with lunch being taken at nearby Maidwell, where there was a roadside café.

Finance was another constant source of worry. The staff had to be paid and a number of volumes were in course of preparation. In spite of grants from local authorities, the Society had a deficiency of £200 between income and expenditure by the beginning of 1947.[92] Money-raising became a major preoccupation. A year later Joan informed her brother:

> I have been grinning like a dog and running about the County, too busy for words, having turned commercial traveller for the moment. I have visited forty one shoe and engineering firms at Northampton, Peterborough and Kettering and have sold £675's worth of advertising space in a circular the Record Society is issuing. This is the quickest, cheapest and best modern way of raising money for charities, and the trade tell me I have done very well.[93]

These advertisements were to appear in a new publication, *Northamptonshire Past and Present*, a journal of a more popular character than the Society's regular series of volumes, but nevertheless containing some valuable contributions to the history of the County. The first issue, in October 1948, was an immediate success, with 4,000 copies issued, a half of which were distributed overseas to induce subscriptions for subsequent issues.[94] Joan was editor from 1948 to 1959 and also wrote many of the articles herself.

These activities by no means exhausted her other interests, particularly in buildings and archaeological sites (she tried to get the County resurveyed by air) and, to a lesser extent, museum objects. Joan had battles with the County Surveyor over the removal of ancient milestones from road verges, and deplored the failure of the County Council to replace them after the war. She also wrote an article in the *Northamptonshire Past and Present* about threatened churches. In 1947, she was one of the founders of the Society of Archivists, becoming its Vice-Chairman. Joan enjoyed cultivating friends and acquaintances amongst academics, such as R.H. Tawney, Lewis Namier, T.F.T. Plucknett and V.H. Galbraith; these friendships were sustained by correspondence.

By 1949, it was becoming obvious that the burden of the work of the Society could no longer be the responsibility of one person. She was now sixty five and, in her own words got 'extremely tired in the head after these bouts of work at Lamport'. Joan, too, needed more time to edit the Society's volumes. Inflation was playing havoc with finances and she was conscious that the staff dealing with the records were not adequately paid. She wrote to an American friend in March, 'When you get the N.R.S. Report, look at the accounts. We have saved the situation for one year, but I can't go on for ever, and we shall have to find some means of putting the work on to a permanent basis. This is my next objective'.[95]

Joan privately sought the help of the Marquess of Exeter, President of the Society, who was Lord-Lieutenant for Northamptonshire and formerly Chairman of the Soke of Peterborough County Council.[96] She was anxious that any new arrangement with the County or Northampton would lead to the loss of her absolute control over the Society's collections and search room, as the local authorities would take over the burden of the Society's finances. A compromise was eventually arrived at. The three authorities concerned, the County Councils of Northamptonshire and the Soke of Peterborough and the County Borough of Northampton, agreed that the custody of the records and the remainder of the Society's lease of Lamport would be transferred to a new body, the Northamptonshire Archives Committee, on 1 January 1952. Northampton Borough Council was particularly suspicious of the possible expenditure which might be involved, and with some grounds: for, whilst the negotiations were in progress, Joan had appointed a second archivist in September 1950 and a further one the following year.[97] Patrick King, who had been Assistant Secretary to the Society since August 1948, now became the first Chief Archivist of Northamptonshire.

Joan was reluctant to hand over the records to the local authorities without a show of resistance. Only the day before the transfer of power to the Archives Committee, she finalized the deposit with the Society of the Earl of Westmorland's collection. There was also a great struggle over the transfer of catalogues and indexes which had been prepared during the Record Society's era of curatorship.

Lamport Hall now served both as a record office and the headquarters of the Record Society, so that in theory each had different functions. In fact, despite the changed constitution, Joan retained a large say in the policy and running of the Record Office through her presence at Lamport, and through her membership of the Technical and Advisory Committee which was set up in 1952 to advise the Chief Archivist. She continued to rule the Society through her Council and was skilful in transferring responsibility to them when more weight was needed in presenting a case. Joan dictated 'resolutions' to the Council which would therefore arrive in their name not only at local council offices but also in government ministries.

*   *   *   *   *

Sustained writing was rarely achieved because of the perambulatory nature of her life. Her one major book, a history of the Brudenells of Deene Park, Northamptonshire, had a long gestation. In 1933, the squire of Deene, George Brudenell, a colourful and outspoken person, notable for his eccentricities of dress and behaviour,[98] asked Joan to prepare a catalogue of the family papers. The latter immediately became a friend of the Brudenells[99] and frequently stayed with them. She set to work with typical enthusiasm, listing, stamping, and numbering all the documents over a period of three weeks from late October to early November. Joan wrote at the time:

> It is such fun getting near the end of the first stage of my work at Deene. It is such a beautiful collection and I am beginning to feel quite proud of my catalogue. I turned up a ms. I had quite forgotten last week. A sort of notebook with surveys etc. in it for a small village near by, with receipts for medicines for humans, horses, dogs, etc. and what is *most* interesting, copies of little contracts with shepherds, stone masons and labourers, to work for definite periods, giving the rates of wages, mostly in the reign of Henry VII, some for Richard III. Quite unusual I think and I hope some day to write an article about them. Hush!.[100]

Joan soon realized that a much larger project was possible, but progress was slow. Seven years later, on 16 June 1940, shortly after hearing on the radio of the capitulation of the French Army, she recorded, 'It is impossible for one small mind to take in the full implications and all the sorrow and horror of the situation, and we carry on with our jobs. Now that Mama is settled, I am settling down to the Brudenell book again'.[101]

Some notion of Joan's writing methods is captured in a letter:

> Am tremendously busy, having now arranged all my notes and references for the 3rd. Earl of Cardigan [George Brudenell, 1685–1732], I hope to get some written in the next three days. The writing is what I do most quickly. The preparation of the material is an immense physical job, as you know. To organise it so that I can visualise an integrated picture and then select the essentials to get the proper proportions and effects of light and shade.[102]

During the war, Joan was horrified to discover that the Deene documents were in a room which was a dangerous fire hazard, so with the help of a man and a boy, carted the whole collection away to one of the Society's four depositories. Joan's researches took her to Castle Howard, near York, between 6 and 9 June 1944. She had visualized a beautiful eighteenth century spacious library; instead she found herself in a cellar with a vaulted stone roof, dimly lit by a window at one end. The long narrow room was crammed with boxes and chests of drawers; family correspondence of the eighteenth and nineteenth centuries altogether occupied between 150 to 200 cases. 'I worked very hard', she wrote, 'and a good deal of physical labour was, as is usual, involved, lifting heavy parcels down from the high shelves and shunting the ladder about. So when I got back to my room in the evening I was too tired to do much'.[103] It was not until 30 November 1946 that she could state, 'Tis midnight and I have just buried the 7th Earl of Cardigan [of the Charge of the Light Brigade fame] with ten generations of his ancestors in the family vault at Deene'.[104]

By the end of the year, the first draft of the book was finished, the last chapter being devoted to the seventh Earl's widow, Lady Adeline, whom Joan had met at Apethorpe before the First World War[105] shortly before her death at the age of ninety one. Lady Adeline had achieved notoriety by her book of reminiscences, published in 1909. Amongst other things, she recounted with relish her unrequited courtship, when a widow, of Disraeli whilst he was Prime Minister. Her great aim in life was to look different from other people. She received guests at Deene on summer evenings in her late husband's red uniform trousers and cuirass or in full evening dress and scandalised some Northamptonshire villagers by appearing out shooting in a Highland kilt with bare knees.[106] As Joan stated in the Preface:

> The Brudenells are no doubt typical of other Midland families, with their gradual evolution from obscure beginnings to the highest social eminence, without producing any great man of overpowering stature. Thus their story will probably appeal to the student of the average and normal rather than of the phenomenal. The lover of the egregious must content himself with the last two chapters about the seventh Earl of Cardigan and his extraordinary Countess.[107]

The book, entitled *The Brudenells of Deene*, was finally published in 1953 and was well received. A typical review was that of Anthony Powell, who devoted over a page to it in *Punch* and began:

> It would be a great pity if this book were overlooked by readers who want to be entertained. The title suggests merely one of those family histories that are inclined to fall into one of two categories; the well-documented, appealing only to the genealogist: or the chatty, from which all serious historical matter has been removed. Here, however, is both historical interest and light relief. Miss Joan Wake has used her material with remarkable skill; and the Brudenells themselves, partly from their habit of preserving records, partly from the individuality – not to say eccentricity – of various members of their race, provide all the elements of an enthralling narrative.[108]

*   *   *   *   *

Although Joan had travelled a great deal, she had never been outside Europe until 1947. It was then that she decided to visit her brother Godwin, who had suffered a stroke, at his home in Southern Rhodesia. She recalled her father's address in 1898 to the Northamptonshire Natural History Society on birds, when he had discussed the possibility of human flight and stated, 'I do not myself think that any of us now alive will ever be able to take return tickets to, let us say, Timbuctoo, by an aerial liner'. Joan commented, 'Forty nine years later (and I was very much alive in 1898) I walked into a station in London and bought a return ticket to Southern Rhodesia, about 3,000 miles further away than Timbuctoo'.[109]

Apart from climbing a tree or a church tower, Joan had never had her feet off the ground, so the three day flight to Salisbury was an exciting experience. Landing on 19 May 1947, she was met by her brother in his beautiful new Chevrolet with his native driver, Marusa, who was dressed in a white duck coat with blue facings and silver buttons, each of which bore the Wake Knot. After the First World War, Godwin, a life-long bachelor with some talent as an artist, had briefly grown rubber in Malaya before emigrating to Southern Rhodesia in 1925. He settled in the hilly district dominated by the Umvukwe Mountains, some sixty five miles north of Salisbury, and bought an estate of about 3,000 acres. He named it Vigila, after the first word of the family motto, *Vigila et Ora* and developed the estate as a tobacco farm.[110] Joan was fascinated by the house Godwin had recently built under his own direction with native help; constructed in brick, it was directly inspired by the architecture of Courteenhall, (which Godwin had always loved), especially the front entrance doorway, the panelling and the library, with its Georgian-style apsidal end.[111]

Early in July, she and Godwin set off for a drive of 1,800 miles across the Transvaal, Orange Free State and Cape Colony which took ten days, with nightly stops. At Pretoria, Godwin took Joan to the fine government buildings on the site where he was in prison during the Boer War, and showed her the gap in the hills where they had watched Lord Roberts' army come to their relief. Thirty miles on was Johannesburg. Joan commented, 'We hurried through as quickly as we could, a huge modern industrial town, and I felt a lot of sympathy with Kruger [Boer President of the Transvaal 1883-1900], wanting to keep the money grubbers out of his pastoral country'.[112] During a month's stay at Sea Point, Cape Province, Joan found a journal in the Cape Provincial Archives describing the death at Cape Town of Governor William Wake of the East India Company at Bombay on 5 February 1751.[113] Subsequently Godwin discovered in the vestry of the Dutch Reformed Church at Cape Town the hatchment of this William Wake. In spite of further investigations, no firm links could be established with the Wakes of Courteenhall.[114]

After leaving Godwin, she flew to Kenya, where again she mixed pleasure with work, exploring Central African archives and enrolling new members for the Record Society.[115] On the flight back, she observed as she flew over the North African battlefields the wheelmarks of tanks still plainly visible in the sand; and crossing Spain into France at Bordeaux, she was able to pick out the route of Edward III's and the Black Prince's campaigns. Joan arrived back at Heathrow on 15 September. 'A wonderful trip', she wrote, 'and I came back feeling ten years younger'.[116] Godwin died two years later, on 8 December 1949, and was buried at Vigila. Godwin left the estate to his younger sister Phyllis, who was married to Richard Archdale. Joan paid two further visits to Vigila, in 1963 and 1967.

Another exciting venture was a two-month lecture tour of the United States in 1957. There were other incentives to undertake this tour. In Virginia, where her cousin Evelyn Sitwell lived, Joan wished to see some of the celebrations of the 350th anniversary of the colony which was founded in the reign of James I. She also wanted to visit Kenwood, Oneida, in the north of New York State where her old friend, Miss Hope Emily Allen was in very poor health. A medieval scholar with Northamptonshire ancestors, she had been a frequent visitor to England, and after their first meeting in 1920, travelled with Joan to the Continent. In 1934 Miss Allen identified the original manuscript of *The Book of Margery Kempe*, by centuries the earliest autobiography of a woman in the English tongue, and she devoted the next seventeen years of her life to a study of the mystic.[117] Joan was also very keen to visit the Henry Huntington Library in San Marino, California, in order to study documents relating to Northamptonshire.

Joan arrived in the United States on 7 April, proceeding to Kenwood, and then to Smith College, Northampton, Massachusetts, where she delivered her first lecture, on the Brudenells. The town, according to local history, was given its name by Captain John King, who was from Northampton, England, as he considered it compared favourably with his native city.[118] Joan's most important engagement was to give an address to the annual two-day meeting of the Medieval Academy of America at Harvard on 26 April 1957. The topic was 'Northamptonshire Records', and the talk was later published. The organizer wrote afterwards, 'She certainly made quite a hit with everyone . . . It was agreed that she was the most interesting speaker on our program'.[119] Joan was not impressed by the famous Plymouth Rock, calling it 'a miserable pebble held together by cement', and passing through a place called Spencer, she sent a postcard to Earl Spencer.

She flew to Los Angeles and then visited the Huntington Library, where she made a number of exciting discoveries. There was a unique copy of Shakespeare's first published work, the poem *Venus and Adonis* (1593) which was once at Lamport, as well as three paintings that came originally from Althorp. There were also many documents relating to Northamptonshire: a history of Wollaston, covering a period from 1620 to the early eighteenth century, an Elizabethan survey of Cogenhoe, lists of Papists from many parts of the county, including the name of Mary Brudenell, and bills of sale connected with Rockingham, Kelmarsh and Desborough among others. Joan commented with sadness, 'I do begrudge them the manuscripts so intimately connected with our Northamptonshire countryside'.[120] After her stay in San Marino, she flew to Washington, then to Virginia and finally back to see Hope Allen near New York.

Joan was impressed by the fact that altogether she had flown over 13,000 miles in nine weeks without travelling on a train. In an interview reported in a local American paper just before she returned to England, Joan expressed her admiration for the good architecture she had seen and had been surprised by the number of old houses and the classical influence on them. She was also delighted to find so much interest in America in local history and records. But Joan was touched most of all by the friendliness felt towards England. She told the reporter, 'I have been greeted with the greatest kindness and hospitality everywhere I have gone'.[121] On the following day, 10 June, she flew back from New York to London.

Joan reported on her American experiences at the Record Society's annual general meeting at Lamport Hall on 6 July. The chairman, Sir Gyles Isham commented 'that to have to introduce Miss Wake to the Record Society was like introducing General Booth to the Salvation Army'.[122] One interesting outcome of the visit was that microfilms of some of the documents which she had scrutinized in the Huntington, those relating to Brackley and Wollaston in the Ellesemere Collection, were in due course sent to the Record Office.[123]

*   *   *   *   *

Joan was a great campaigner for what she considered to be worthy causes, especially if they were against bureaucrats. As Chairman of Cosgrove Parish Council, she once took action when in the summer of 1947 the water supply in the village failed. No satisfaction was forthcoming from the Water Authority and as she was about to depart by air to Rhodesia to visit her brother Godwin, she sent a telegram to the Minister saying, 'Cholera imminent'. This resulted in an immediate visit by three or four anxious bowler-hatted officials, who arrived at Cosgrove just as Joan's aircraft took off from Heathrow.

When the debate over the devastation of the countryside as a consequence of ironstone workings was at its height, the second National Conference of Parish Councils took place at Central Hall, Westminster on 20 October 1949. On behalf of the Northamptonshire Association of Parish Councils, Joan proposed a resolution which deplored the destruction being caused by the workings:

> My turn came, and an attendant rushed at me with a sort of huge lampstand (A microphone), and began pushing me about, still in the back row, to get me in position. I waved my arms a bit and shook them off, and made my way to the table in front where someone made room for me, and a smaller microphone was put in front of me. I consulted the back rows of the audience as to whether they could hear me (well over 2,000 there, all the galleries as well as ground floor filled), and then fired off my speech.
>
> About ⅔ of the way through, that old devil Scott [Sir Leslie Scott, formerly Lord Justice Scott, the chairman] stood up, and told me my time was up. I looked at him. 'I will give you ten seconds more,' he said. I took two minutes, and finished my speech, but had to cut a few sentences. I got a good clap … After two or three more speeches, it was put to the meeting, and every hand seemed to go up. 'Any against?' A fool woman at the back put up her arm. But either Scott was blind or pretended to be, and declared the Resolution 'carried unanimously', and as the Reporters were sitting with their backs to the audience, it so appeared in the press.[124]

The largest and longest drawn-out battle of her life took place when Joan was over seventy. As early as April 1944, she had made up her mind that a permanent home was needed for the Record Society and its records, and she soon earmarked a likely site.[125] At a Council meeting on 26 September, she advanced the idea of establishing it at Delapre Abbey, Hardingstone, on the southern edge of Northampton.[126] The Abbey, the remains of a Cluniac nunnery dating from about 1100, had been acquired by the Tate family at the Dissolution of the Monasteries. It was sold in 1764 to Edward Bouverie and remained in the family until the death of the last member, Miss Mary Bouverie, in January 1943.[127]

To expedite her plan, Joan handpicked a sub-committee of the Society to investigate possible accommodation. On 5 October 1944, accompanied by two of the Society's Council members, she made an inspection of Delapre, which at the time was requisitioned by the Army. 'I had no idea it was so large', she wrote afterwards in her Diary, 'all except the south side, which is a straightforward series of large rooms opening one out of the other (the three of them), a veritable rabbit warren'.[128]

Kingsthorpe Hall, a mile north of Northampton, was mooted as an alternative, but this was quickly dismissed. Joan now sought an interview with W.R. Kew, the Town Clerk, at the Guildhall. She pointed out that the Society had been founded at a meeting in that very building with the Mayor in the chair; that they had been instrumental in restoring to the Borough an important set of medieval borough records; and that the Society had co-operated with the Education Department in arranging free lectures and exhibitions for schools. The obligation of the Town Council to help the Society as a matter of public duty was also emphasized. In reply, Kew stated that Delapre might be wanted as a youth club after the war for the 7,000 young people between the ages of 16 and 21 in the borough. He therefore suggested that if the Society's plans for Delapre fell through, the Midland Station or a large house in Cliftonville might be considered.[129] At the Record Society's Council meeting on 23 November 1944, Joan noted with satisfaction, 'Council decided to go for Delapre, so that is another fence safely negotiated in the long, long obstacle race ahead'.[130] Lord Exeter, armed with a detailed brief drawn up by Joan, subsequently had an interview with the Mayor and Town Clerk, and the Society's application was filed for consideration until the Abbey premises had been derequisitioned.[131]

In 1946, the Town Council purchased the Delapre estate, including the Abbey. Although the Army vacated the premises two years later, it was immediately occupied by the Ministry of Works and the County War Agricultural Committee. Frustratingly, when both these bodies no longer needed the premises, Delapre was not offered to the Society. The Society's Annual Report for 1953, written by Joan and dated 31 May 1954, stated, 'Your Council have been watching with some anxiety the negotiations for the acquisition of premises for the records of Northamptonshire at Delapre Abbey, which would form such an admirable centre for students, and as the headquarters of this Society'.[132] This anxiety arose from a meeting of the Town Council on 6 April, which voted for the complete demolition of the Abbey, after rejecting a compromise scheme put forward by Alderman Frank Lee[133] 'that the Council should consider sympathetically a scheme from a suitable body for the substantial preservation of the Abbey'.[134] Joan publicly described the Council's decision as 'deplorable and an act of sheer vandalism'.[135]

New tactics were required. A fortnight later, the Northamptonshire Rural Community Council, of which Joan was a leading figure, launched a 'Save Delapre Abbey' campaign. She also contacted many well-known County estate owners, church dignitaries, aldermen and councillors. One consequence was that the County Council entered the fray supporting the Society, sending a letter to Harold Macmillan, then Minister of Housing and Local Government, stating that demolition should not be contemplated until all possibilities had been examined. A conference at Whitehall, consisting of Macmillan, four representatives of the Borough and four of the County Council, took place on 8 July. The outcome was a suggestion from the Minister of a scheme which would involve the sale or lease for a nominal sum of the Abbey to the Council.[136]

However, there was a dramatic turn in the situation when, on 16 November 1954, the County Council unexpectedly announced that it had withdrawn its objection to the demolition of Delapre. Urgent action was now needed. Joan was able to obtain from a Ministry of Works architect an estimate for making essential repairs to the Abbey. This amounted to £15,000, but the Society's Council resolved that another £5,000 would be required for contingencies. The Ministry was prepared to grant £5,000 and the Borough Council agreed that if the Record Society were able to raise the £15,000 by 30 June 1956 and carry out repairs to the Council's satisfaction, it would make Delapre available to the Society for ninety nine years at a reasonable rent.[137]

Time was short, as this left just over six months to raise the money, or the building would be demolished. A small campaign committee, consisting of Joan, her nephew Peter Wake, Sydney Elborne, a barrister, and C.E.G. Mumby, the Honorary Society's Treasurer and a solicitor, was immediately formed, with Joan as one of the joint secretaries for the campaign. Launching what was called 'the third battle of Northampton' at a public meeting on 4 January 1956, chaired by her eldest nephew, Major Hereward Wake, then High Sheriff of Northamptonshire, Joan appealed for support adding, 'If we allow Delapre to be swept away it will be like destroying a historical document . . . tangible evidence of centuries of local history'.[138] Letters of support were read out from eminent historians, including V.H. Galbraith and Dom David Knowles, respectively Regius Professors of History at Oxford and Cambridge, and Sir Lewis Namier. A pamphlet to explain the 'Lightning Campaign' also bore messages from other distinguished persons such as John Betjeman, Sir Albert Richardson, President of the Royal Academy, R.H. Tawney and Professor Michael Postan.

By the end of February, a total of £3,346 had been received, and in May the Pilgrim Trust gave the fund a boost by donating a further £3,000 on condition that the remaining £12,000 could be found. With only forty two days to go, a sum of nearly £9,000 was still needed. A series of fund-raising events was arranged, such as a matinée of Shaw's *Pygmalion* at the Repertory Theatre, whist drives, illustrated lectures, dances and competitions ('Please no raffles', Joan stated in a pamphlet).[139]

Behind the scenes, Joan was taking unilateral action to secure County wide support. Amongst her papers is a handwritten memorandum of one such initiative:

327

27 April 1956

Delapre Abbey – Northamptonshire County Council
Interview at 11.30a.m. with Chairman and Clerk of
Northamptonshire County Council in Chairman's room.

Hostility among members of C.C. so far, Mr Marlow [Ewart Marlow, MC, Labour Chairman of County Council, 1954–65] says, is an individual affair. If he raises the question of Delapre Abbey campaign at next N.C.C. Meeting on May 10th, it might raise a storm. Mr Turner's [J. Alan Turner, OBE, Clerk to the County Council and Record Society Council member] advice – get on with campaign and come to County Council when it is a *fait accompli*, when any opposition would be howled down.

In the circumstances, without raising the matter with the County Council, Mr. Marlow cannot sign a letter to *The Times*. They both think that if Lord Exeter, Gyles Isham, Lord Brand, Sir G. Clark and myself sign it – that it will do for the County, and that no-one would then dare to write in opposition.[140]

Four weeks later, a lengthy letter on behalf of the Society and bearing many important signatures appeared in *The Times*.[141] Nevertheless by the deadline, 30 June only £7,000 had been raised but Joan persuaded the Town Council to extend the deadline until the beginning of 1957. She had been ill earlier in the year, but now devoted all her energy to reaching the target.

The headquarters of the campaign, at 44 Bridge Street, was a constant hive of activity with Joan directing the strategy. By mid September, she reported that 1,243 individual subscriptions, ranging from two shillings to £2,000, together with the proceeds of sixteen functions, had produced a total of £12,600; this left a target, after paying expenses, of £2,900.[142] One of the final events of the campaign was a treasure sale, held at the Angel Hotel on 23 November. Appropriately, the centrepiece of the sale was a solid gold snuff box, formerly belonging to King Louis Philippe, and once owned by General Everard Bouverie, squire of Delapre from 1858 to 1871.[143]

By the mid-morning of 31 December, 1956, only £317 more was needed. With a flourish of publicity, Joan announced to the newspapers that she would be waiting by the telephone at the campaign office until 6.00 p.m that night, and then at the home of a friend in Northampton until 12.30 a.m into the New Year to receive further donations.[144] The campaign had been a total success. At the beginning of February 1957, the Trustees of the Delapre Abbey Trust Fund were able to request Northampton Borough to prepare the documents for granting a ninety nine year lease of the Abbey to the Society.[145] Joan's final triumph was to negotiate the lease at a nominal rent of £100 per annum which was non-reviewable.

At a subsequent Town Council meeting, Joan's long campaign to save the Abbey was acknowledged by many members. Among the tributes was one from Alderman Walter Lewis, recently Mayor of Northampton, who commented, 'Many people have many kinds of monuments and many kinds of activities. Miss Wake's monument will be Delapre Abbey, without question'.[146] Restoration of the golden brown local ironstone façade, the clearing of buildings to open up the courtyard, the insertion of new windows in the eighteenth century brick walls of the 'cloister' passage round the ground floor courtyard and the installation of ducts to supply warm air to the store rooms was undertaken. By May 1959, the Abbey, the new home of the Society and the County Record Office, was ready for its official opening.[147]

In planning the celebrations, Joan asked her old friend Sir Frank Stenton to speak and he accepted without hesitation. Recalling their first tentative moves to set up a Record Society, he went on:

> It is really extraordinary that after thirty nine years, we should be making plans to join in the celebration of what was then a dimly realisable possibility.
>
> But of course, it has all turned on you, and I only hope that the others who are present will realise that essential fact. I think they will, for they must be conscious that it is you alone who have held up the walls of Delapre.[148]

Originally, it was planned to hold the ceremony indoors at Delapre, but so great had been the response to the 1,500 invitations which were sent out that the guests were accommodated in a giant marquee on the lawn. Representatives from more than half the counties of England were present; officials included the Master of the Rolls, the Keeper of the Records of the Public Record Office, university and civic figures, descendants of the Tates and Bouveries, local societies, schools and the many individual subscribers to the Appeal.[149] As Joan wrote of 'Delapre Day':

> Saturday, the ninth of May, 1959, is likely, one would imagine, to linger for quite a long time in the memory of people in and around Northampton. The gathering at Delapre Abbey on that beautiful spring day was a demonstration the ethos of which is not to be conveyed by words; it was of a quality to be experienced to be properly realised . . .
>
> May 9th was perhaps above all, Northampton's day. We were told that the excitement in the town that morning was great. The joy of the Borough that the old Abbey was to continue to be part of its life as it had been for so many centuries was splendidly reflected in the local Press and abundantly demonstrated in other ways. The huge Union Jack hoisted on the top of the house by Messrs. Jeffery and Sons; the exquisite floral decoration indoors by Mrs. William Hubbard and her friends; the delightful music on the lawn provided by the Town Band, – all freely given – expressed the local feeling in no uncertain terms.[150]

With the opening of the Abbey, the forty tons of archives relating to Northamptonshire which Joan had collected could now be housed, as could the Record Society itself, in the thirty-five room mansion. A leading article in *The Times* entitled, 'A Home for History', well summed up her achievement:

> When 1,300 people in a small county town, with only a sprinkling of professed students among them, choose to spend a sunny afternoon in May listening to

137. Delapre Abbey, west front. The Northamptonshire Record Society occupied this part of the building from 1959 to 1991

138. The Search Room, Northamptonshire Record Office, Delapre Abbey, 1959. Joan Wake is second from the right. On the right is Mr Patrick King, the first Chief Archivist of the Northamptonshire Record Office

139. Joan Wake at the opening of Delapre Abbey, 9 May 1959. From left to right: C. E. Vivian Rowe, Northampton Town Clerk, holding the peppercorn rent; Alderman E. Newman, Deputy Mayor of Kettering; Councillor V. J. H. Harris, Mayor of Northampton; Alderman John V. Collier; Lord Evershed, Master of the Rolls; Sir George Clark, President of Northamptonshire Record Society; Mr. Ewart Marlow, Chairman of Northamptonshire County Council; Joan Wake and Mr. Sidney Elborne, Chairman of Northamptonshire Record Society

speeches about the care of ancient documents, more explanation is required than the presence on the platform of the MASTER of the ROLLS, two eminent professors of history, and the official representatives of local authority and scholarly societies. The truth is that Northamptonshire has developed a sense of the vitality of history, a pride in its own traditions, and a determination to preserve them for posterity which no county in the land can surpass; and that, as speaker after speaker declared on Saturday, is the fruit of the life's work of the shire's most distinguished antiquary, MISS JOAN WAKE ... The peal of bells that ended the day's celebrations saluted a true victory for history over the encroaching forces of time.[151]

*   *   *   *   *

To have succeeded in such an endeavour required a strong personality and an iron will. Joan possessed both these qualities, which could make life difficult sometimes for those around her. Her Assistant Archivist at Lamport recalls, 'One looked forward to her visits with mixed feelings, apprehensive of minor peccadilloes coming to light yet always fascinated to catch a glimpse of the breadth of her interests'.[152] In 1959, another Assistant Archivist at Lamport, P.A. Kennedy, became County Archivist for Nottinghamshire. Writing from there, he reassured Joan that he had no intention of trying to acquire part of the Finch Papers (Burley-on-the-Hill), agreeing with her that collections should never be split on any grounds, territorial or other. Satisfied with this assurance she replied: 'Thank you for yours of Nov. 27 and I am so glad you have not been blown away by any wind of vain doctrine'.[153]

Notwithstanding her determination and singularity of purpose, she was sensitive and well aware of her own shortcomings. Writing to Hope Allen in July 1948, she remarked:

> I am sorry to say I have struck an *awful* bad patch – in my own character, I think. The last trouble and a serious one is with the Stentons over the publication of The Book of Seals.[154] I have upset them both badly, at a very long meeting in Oxford last week ... I have been difficult, awkward, tactless in the extreme, and begin to think I must resign from everything and give my last years to research. I have got across everyone in *every* direction, and made myself most unpopular. I pity myself, which I shouldn't do, but I do so need a *friend*; living alone is bad, bad.[155]

She made a number of enemies amongst historians and archivists, but this was due, in her view, to their lack of understanding of the problems of preserving local records. In 1947, after two false starts, she was writing an article for *The Times* on the subject, and felt too exhausted to proceed. 'But,' she told a friend, 'I MUST write it. It is a plain fact that I know more about the whole subject after thirty years concentrated study than anyone else, and it is the only way to get a better scheme across than ...'s'.[156]

On matters of principle, Joan would brook no compromise. For instance in 1938, she requested that her shares in a company allied to Stewarts and Lloyds, the steel manufacturers, should be sold: 'I really cannot draw any of my income from a firm which is directly or indirectly devastating large areas of this County [for iron ore] and for present profit, rendering it absolutely useless for agricultural purposes for ever'.[157] Ten years later, even stronger words were used against an opponent of the campaign to curb iron-ore workings: 'A teaspoonful of poison in his soup would save Northamptonshire, but I am now talking like Queen Elizabeth with regard to Mary Queen of Scots'.[158]

Dr Kathleen Major, Archivist at Lincoln from 1936 when she became acquainted with Joan, recalled saying to a mutual friend, Lewis Loyd, the medieval scholar, how fortunate Northamptonshire was to have so many people within the County interested in records and the Record Society. He replied, '"Oh, Joan bullies them: she has done so since she was in the nursery", adding, for she was standing near, "Don't you, Joan?": an accusation which she took in good part, for she recognized her own dogged determination to achieve her objects'.[159] Stories of her endeavours on behalf of the Record Society are legion. A typical one was the occasion when the Inland Revenue dared to challenge the Society's claim to some fiscal exemption; she parted from the harassed Whitehall official with the threat that 'Questions will be asked in *both* Houses of Parliament'.[160] Never in a strong personal financial position, Joan made many sacrifices in her work for the Society.

But there were often many lighter moments, such as the occasion when a new Record Society volume was delivered from the printers for dispatch to members. 'Volunteers were marshalled to parcel up the volumes, the capacity of each to make a good job of it being tested by the simple expedient of seeing their effort thrown vigorously across the room to see how the packing and knots survived. Miss Wake was not going to have the recipients or the Post Office complain of any laxity in that direction'.[161]

Joan also left an account of the Society's 1954 annual general meeting where Arthur Bryant gave an excellent talk on Pepys. The Heskeths had entertained the speaker to lunch before the lecture at Easton Neston:

> We had a fine day – <u>crowds</u> came – and we had about 30 or 40 in the next room with a re-lay machine, so they heard very well including, I was told, all Lord Exeter's and my asides to each other but I trust not Freddie Hesketh's loud reverberating snore in the middle of the lecture, which I quashed with a smart blow on his knee (luckily I was next to him), greatly to the amusement of one or two people in the front row.[162]

* * * * *

The fortieth anniversary of Joan's Secretaryship of the Record Society was celebrated at the annual general meeting in May 1960 with a number of gifts, a dictation machine for recording her reminiscences,[163] fifty books (including a complete set of the *Dictionary of National Biography*) and a gold bracelet.[164] In her speech, she announced that she was going into battle again, this time against the Local Government Commissioners

CP58. Sir Hereward Wake, 14th baronet, in the uniform of Vice Lord-Lieutenant for Northamptonshire, 1983–1991, wearing the Wake Baronet's badge

CP59. Julia, Lady Wake (b.1931) seated in the Library by Richard Foster, 1978

Courteenhall 1987 JW.

CP60. Courteenhall House, Stables and Church, by Jonathan W

987. The M1 motorway is in the background screened by trees

CP61 (above). Courteenhall House
from the Park
by Jeremy Whitaker, 1976

CP62. Three generations:
the 14th baronet, his son Hereward
Charles and eldest grandson John
Hereward on the Drawing room steps,
Courteenhall, Christmas 1989

who were proposing to alter the County's boundaries.[165] At the same time, she gave up editing *Northamptonshire Past and Present*.

Over the years Joan had become increasingly lame with rheumatism and needed to use a walking stick. On 9 May in the following year, she broke a thigh and was confined to hospital in Oxford for three months. Although this event prevented her from attending the 1961 annual general meeting in person, she nevertheless presented the Annual Report as usual, in a speech delivered from her bed and reproduced at the meeting on a tape-recorder.[166] Joan continued to carry on with her work as usual, as her bed was surrounded by pockets, into which various categories of correspondence would be placed for further action.[167]

Joan entered at this time in her Book of Aphorisms a quotation attributed to George Brudenell: 'In advancing years, refuge is taken in procrastination'. The Record Society's Council was changing with more younger members who wished to play a greater part in the policy-making decisions than was previously the case. In April 1962 at a Council meeting, Joan announced that, after forty two years as Honorary Secretary, she was anxious to resign. Within a year, she was suffering from spondylitis of the cervical spine and migraines. She was now more lame and became very tired talking to people. In her medical observations of herself, she noted, 'Three hours finishes me for two or three days and I have to stay in bed to recover'.[168] Joan resigned as Honorary Secretary in 1963 though remaining General Editor of the Society's main series of publications. Her achievements were listed at the annual meeting. In 1920, membership stood at ninety six and the income was £127: now, membership had reached 1,097 and an income of almost £3,000 was recorded. In thanking the President, Sir George Clark, Joan modestly replied that her connections with the Society had enabled her 'to indulge in a most delightful hobby'.[169] She relinquished the General Editorship two years later, but her researches still continued: an edition of the letters of Daniel Eaton, steward at Deene, to the third Earl of Cardigan, was published by the Society in 1971 when she was eighty seven.[170] Meantime, there were two personal sad losses for Joan. Her eldest brother, Hereward, the thirteenth baronet, had died in 1963 and there was a further loss within two years, of her eldest sister Ida, a handsome and intelligent person, who had devoted almost the whole of her life to looking after her mother.

*   *   *   *   *

Although Joan had been elected a Fellow of the Society of Antiquaries in 1945 and made a Commander of the British Empire in 1960, it was from the academic world that she hoped for recognition. This came in January 1953, when she was awarded an honorary Master of Arts by Oxford University. The Public Orator, drawing on pertinent quotations from Cicero and Ovid, stated, 'I can well imagine that in her dreams she acquires for herself and her shires those indestructible "records on massive bronze and steel engraven" which are kept by the goddesses of Destiny. No Record Office can be better stocked than theirs and no one can speak more true than they'.[171] Her brother, Hereward, who was unwell at the time and unable to attend the ceremony, wrote, 'You have shed lustre on the family and in a new line for us – The first Wake who has been distinguished for intelligence and literature'.[172] Joan described the ceremony and her own feelings to her friend Hope Allen:

> The reception I had from the whole University, as it were, was a most warming and wonderful thing, and whatever disagreeablenesses and difficulties I may have in front of me, I shall always have that to fall back upon and remember. Oh, my dear, having been and felt *such* an outsider all my life, to be inside the fold! – it is wonderful ... Professor Neale once or twice has said to me, 'Some day, Miss Wake, there will be a "footnote of gratitude" to you in some future work of history'. Posthumous rewards are not much use. Oxford has done better than that.

I have tried to do the work for its own sake, but felt that if there ever was to be any recognition, there was only one kind which I would appreciate as really worth having – i.e., from the academic world, and now it has come and in such a perfect way and I do feel so grateful.[173]

One final academic distinction awaited her. Six years after Oxford, the oldest university, had honoured Joan, the then newest, Leicester,[174] presented her with the degree of Doctor of Laws. The newspaper reporting the ceremony noted that 'she had to use her trusty stick rather more than she used to, but did not lack gallant assistance in the procession'. Among the other recipients was the Northampton-born musician, Edmund Rubbra. In describing her work, the Public Orator drew a picture of Joan and the dragon, the heroine rescuing Delapre from it by her own heroic qualities:

> The dragon was Confused Counsel; in its toils Delapre all but succumbed. But dragons facing Miss Wake had three choices – they could yield at once, they could yield before long, or they could yield eventually.[175]

In 1935, Joan had been left two houses in Oxford by her Aunt Lucy Wake. Exactly twenty years later, she moved from Cosgrove into one of them, 11 Charlbury Road where she enjoyed entertaining her younger relatives, great nephews and nieces. As she was now a member of the University, attached to St. Anne's College, she had, in her own words, 'achieved the dream of my life – to live in Oxford and take part in the academic life of the University'.[176] She was delighted, too, that her house was near the River Cherwell, as its source was at Charwelton in Northamptonshire. During her last years as Honorary Secretary of the Society, Joan would motor over from Oxford and use the office at Delapre as a temporary flat, sleeping at nights in the room surrounded by the Society's publications.[177]

She was well enough to attend the fiftieth birthday celebrations of the Society held in the summer of 1971. Two other survivors from the original members, Sydney Elborne and Daisy Wake, were also present. In a 'spirited speech', she deplored the proposal by the Boundary Commission to sever Brackley and other Northamptonshire villages from the County, calling the move 'outrageous and the antithesis of democracy'.[178] It was noted by the meeting that she had edited the first volume in the Society's series publications, and 1971 would see the publication of the twenty fourth volume, also edited by her, an achievement not equalled in the history of any other known learned Society.

As early as 1924, in an article on local sources of history, she had envisaged the day in the future 'when all local official archives not in current use will be transferred to County Record Offices under the care of trained archivists, and made available for historical study'.[179] By the end of her life, this had been fully realized, largely by her own efforts.

Sir Gyles Isham visited Joan in a Northampton nursing home thirty six hours before she died on 15 January 1974, five weeks before her ninetieth birthday:

> Her critical faculties were unimpaired, and she said after our discussion, 'I feel I am in the swim again'. At her death, the writer felt he could say in Shakespeare's words, 'There's a great spirit gone'.[180]

Joan had planned her departure in great detail, having chosen the prayers and the order of the service as set out in the 1662 Book of Common Prayer. It was her express wish that the occasion was not to be too solemn. The Courteenhall church bells were not muffled and after the ceremony, on a fine, crisp day, the mourners made their way to the Old Grammar School for wine and food. All those present agreed that Joan's spirit would have approved of the celebration of her memory.

18

Courteenhall Today

THE WORLD WARS OF 1914–18 AND 1939–45 HAVE BEEN
responsible for many changes at Courteenhall, involving the Hall and the Estate. An
important landmark was the occupation of Courteenhall by the thirteenth baronet, Sir
Hereward and Lady Wake with their family at Courteenhall in the early 1920s. It has
remained the family home of his eldest son, also called Hereward, who became the
fourteenth baronet in 1963, up to the present day.

The first five of the thirteenth baronet's children, Margaret, Diana, Hereward,
Roger and Patricia, were all born in London, (Peter and Mary were born later at
Courteenhall) and it came as something of a surprise for the children when the bustle
and noise of the capital was exchanged for a rural setting. Their French nanny, Marie
Leprêtre, conversed entirely in French to the two eldest girls. One of them, Margaret,
then aged seven, on arrival at Courteenhall, asked, 'Mais où sont les omnibuses? Il n'y a
pas que l'herbe ici' ('Where are the buses? There's nothing but grass here'.)

The three boys, like their father and grandfather, went to Eton and also like their
father, served with distinction in the forces. Roger joined the Royal Navy in 1934 as a
midshipman from Eton at the age of sixteen and served throughout the Second World
War, in particular with the Royal Naval Commandos for the landings in Normandy,
becoming a Lieutenant-Commander. Peter joined The King's Royal Rifle Corps at the
outbreak of War and was later wounded in Italy. Before this, he served in the same
Battalion as his brother Hereward in the Western Desert. Diana also spent five years in
the Army, ending the war as Staff Captain with the British troops in Palestine and
Transjordan.

The future fourteenth baronet, Hereward, left Eton in 1935 for the Royal Military
College, Sandhurst, obtaining a Commission as a regular officer in the following year in
his father's old Regiment, The King's Royal Rifle Corps, and on 23 January 1937 sailed
to join the 1st Battalion of the Regiment in Burma. From the middle of 1938 until
August 1939, he served with the Battalion in Egypt where at one time he acted as Air
Liaison Officer with the RAF at Heliopolis. Earlier, in February 1939, when Major-
General Sir Hereward Wake was Colonel Commandant of the 1st Battalion, he decided
to inspect it at Cairo. Sir Hereward had the pleasure of inspecting, amongst others, his

See Appendix A – Family Tree XVII. Notes and References pages 437, 438

140. Delayed 21st birthday of Second Lieutenant Hereward Wake, eldest son of 13th baronet at Courteenhall, 4 August 1938, with Courteenhall and Waltham Abbey farm tenants

son Hereward, and accompanying the now motorized Battalion on their desert manoeuvres.[1] The Commanding Officer of the 1st Battalion was Lieutenant-Colonel William 'Strafer' Gott, a brilliant tactician who prepared the soldiers for the coming war in the desert with great thoroughness.[2] On 5 August 1942, Churchill personally appointed him to take command of the Eighth Army, but two days later Gott was killed when his aircraft was shot down. His successor was the comparatively unknown Lieutenant-General Bernard Montgomery.

At the beginning of the War, Hereward was sent back to England and he was appointed Assistant to the Chief Instructor at Sandhurst, being promoted to Captain. In 1940, he volunteered to join a special ski battalion established by General Ironside, Chief of the Imperial General Staff, to form part of a British Expeditionary Force to Northern Norway. Finland was at war with Germany and Russia, and it was planned that the force would assist the Finns in their struggle. The troops trained at Chamonix with the French Chasseurs Alpins and then embarked on a Polish boat for a secret destination, probably Narvik; at this point, on 13 March, the news came through that the Finns had made peace so the force was disbanded. It was the nearest that Britain came to being involved in conflict with Russia during the Second World War.[3]

The war in Cyrenaica, North Africa, after some early Allied successes, was by mid 1942 turning very much in favour of the Axis Powers. Hereward, together with 2,000 other soldiers and airmen, sailed in the old P. & O. liner *Moultan*, via Durban escorted by the battle cruiser HMS *Repulse*, shortly to be sunk by the Japanese off Singapore. The troops disembarked at Suez and Hereward joined his Regiment in the Western Desert. Promoted to Major, he commanded a Company of the 1st Battalion, which formed part of the 7th Support Group of the 7th Armoured Division (The Desert Rats). They operated at the extreme southern end of the Desert Army's line. Following a powerful offensive by Rommel in May, the Allies had rapidly retreated to Egypt. At El Alamein, some seventy miles from Alexandria, the Allied forces dug in and checked the enemy advance.

On 31 August, Rommel launched his final attack in an attempt to break through the defences but was halted at Alam Halfa. It proved to be one of the crucial battles of the Western Desert.[4] During the fierce fighting, forty five German tanks were destroyed and this resulted in a convincing victory for the defending army. A contemporary wrote of Major Hereward Wake's part in the battle:

> When the enemy broke through the minefield, Toby Wake, collecting seven carriers from the top of a mountain, and leading them down for three-quarters of a mile in the middle of the night, at once charged the enemy, killing and driving them away. As he could get no further on account of the minefield, he did ground action for the remainder of the night. It was the speed and smoothness of their action which saved the night.[5]

For his part in the action, Major Wake was awarded the Military Cross.

Two months later, the Battle of El Alamein, described as one of the decisive battles of the world, took place. Hereward Wake commanded C Company of the 1st Battalion

141. Drawing of a Rifleman of the 1st Battalion, The King's Royal Rifle Corps, 8th Army in the North African Desert before El Alamein, by Oswald Birley. Lieutenant Peter Wake acted as a model

142. Standard of No II (AC) Squadron, the Royal Air Force, laid up in Courteenhall Church, 28 October 1984

143. Lieutenant-General W. H. E. Gott, CB, CBE, DSO, MC (1897–1942), Commander, XIII Corps. Killed on 7 August 1942 when his plane was shot down by German fighters in Egypt shortly after he was appointed GOC 8th Army

144. Memorial to 17 Wakes buried in the family vault beneath the organ and to Lieutenant-Commander Roger Wake, RN (1918-88), by his Royal Naval Commando shipmates, Courteenhall Church, 1988

during the battle and his brother Lieutenant Peter Wake was one of the officers in B Company. The German defeat at Alamein led to the pursuit of the enemy through Cyrenaica and Tripolitania, some 1,600 miles, ending in Tunisia where the 8th Army joined with the 1st Army in May 1943; the destruction of German and Italian forces in North Africa was now complete.

A few weeks before, in March 1943, both Peter and Hereward Wake were invited to lunch with the new Commander-in-Chief, Montgomery. They were impressed with the confidence which 'Monty' exuded, especially as he described, with gesticulating hands, exactly the strategy he was going to employ to win the forthcoming Battle of Mareth, which began on 21 March. Shortly before the final surrender of Tunis, Hereward Wake was wounded on 29 April in a night attack at Argoub el Megas by a bullet which grazed his chin and then entered his shoulder, breaking a collar bone.[6] He arrived back on a hospital ship in England in June. He recuperated at the Stables at Courteenhall and studied at the Senior Officers' School and the Staff College.

When the long awaited Second Front started on 6 June 1944, D-Day, with the invasion of Europe, The King's Royal Rifles were once more in action. Hereward Wake, commanding A Company of the 2nd Battalion, took part in the break-out from Normandy and the encirclement of part of the German Army at Falaise in August.[7] The liberation of France and Belgium was followed by a winter of waiting in Holland where his hearing was damaged by a shell. In the spring, the Rhine was crossed and an advance made all the way to Lübeck. Major Wake was posted to Montgomery's Tactical HQ at Luneberg Heath, where he was one of a select body of Liaison Officers taking orders from the Commander-in-Chief, and personally reporting to him in his caravan. With the ending of the war in Europe in May 1945, there was work to do in connection with the military government of Germany. This was followed by six months in Greece from May 1946, when the Communists were striving to overthrow the monarchy.

*   *   *   *   *

By this time, Sir Hereward was seventy one and, because of the burden of possible death duties and taxation, decided to hand over Courteenhall in its entirety to his eldest son. Both Sir Hereward and Daisy were exhausted at the end of the war, having endured the unheated top floor of the Stables for six years. They had bought a small house at Preston Candover in Hampshire during the war and since it was impossible for them to reoccupy the Hall, they now planned to live there. The move took place in late 1946. Soon after, at the beginning of 1947, Major Wake was invalided out of the army partly due to his deafness, a subsequent handicap, and set about taking on his new responsibilities at Courteenhall. The six years of war had left the Estate, as with so many others, in a depressed condition. There was practically no income from the little invested capital, rents were low and there was a large backlog of repairs, and modernization and improvements were long overdue.

By the end of the year, St. Lawrence College had left Courteenhall and the Hall was now empty. It was considered likely that Courteenhall itself would never again be lived in by the family, so new tenants were sought. From 1 January 1948, the Hall was let to the Presbyterian Church of England as a residential community centre, with a full repairing lease. The weekend before this arrangement came into operation, Major Wake and his sister Diana decided to hold a Grafton Hunt Ball in the empty house to celebrate the ending of the war. Some 150 people attended, including Sir Hereward and Daisy, neighbours, family and friends. Music was provided by Major Wake's Regimental band, and refreshments were served in the Hall on long trestle-tables bearing an abundance of sandwiches, sausage rolls and tea, in spite of the food shortages.[8]

In order to gain some experience of running the Estate, Major Wake had become, in January 1947, a pupil of Jackson Stops at his Cirencester office. The following year, he returned home and attended the Northamptonshire Institute of Agriculture at Moulton as a day student to learn about farming. Soon afterwards, he personally took over the running of the Estate and the Home Farm.

Alterations and improvements were made to the Stables, which were converted into a two-storey house. A boiler and some radiators were fitted and three loose horse boxes were converted into an office. Living in the Stables Major Wake was able to devote his energies to carrying out the necessary work on the Estate. In 1948, some trees were cut down in front of the Stables in order to let in the sun and a big larch in the top garden which had begun to lean rather badly was taken down. Major Wake counted between 160 and 170 rings, which dated it to about 1785, probably planted shortly after the Stables were built. Whilst the improvements in the Stables were being made, Hereward and Diana found that the space under the floor boards of the flat were packed with large quantities of husks of corn; mice had, in the course of two centuries, carried it along from the granary.[9]

During this time, Diana was very active in turning the kitchen garden into a commercial enterprise, selling the produce in London; she was of enormous help to her brother in many aspects of life at Courteenhall. She excelled at sports and games and was a fearless rider. At the age of thirty two, on 11 March 1950, she was tragically killed riding in a point-to-point at Bicester in the presence of her mother and father.

On his engagement to Julia Lees of Falcutt House, near Brackley in October 1951, Major Wake undertook further improvements to the Stables flat, which they occupied after their marriage on 6 February the following year.

* * * * *

The lease with the Presbyterian Church of England terminated on 1 January 1953. At this stage, there was no intention of reoccupying the House, which was in a dilapidated condition, without furniture or carpets and with damage caused by burst pipes and leaking roofs. No suitable new tenant could be found and it was decided that it should be demolished. However, it was Simon Elwes, the artist and an old family friend from Billing, who in September 1952 had called for tea at the Stables and suggested that Major Wake and his wife might live in the House. Later, Professor Albert Richardson, the leading expert on Georgian architecture, travelled from his home at Ampthill and was asked to give his opinion. Richardson's reaction was similar to Elwes'; that they

Courteenhall House as a Conference and Holiday Centre

ALTHOUGH the Adam Brothers designed a residence suited to the slow and spacious days of the eighteenth century, Courteenhall could scarcely have been better conceived by them had they designed it expressly for the purpose for which it has now been acquired.

The ground floor with its imposing Entrance Hall, its grandly proportioned rooms, is ideal for Conferences and Discussion Groups. There is the Wedgewood Dining Room with its lovely ceiling mouldings and exquisite fireplace; then the Drawing Room, beautifully designed, with an atmosphere of its own, looking out contemplatively over the lovely parkland of Northamptonshire. Visualize too the Library, containing a fine collection of calf bound volumes, chosen not only for their contents but also for the decorative value of their bindings. The sense of harmony in this room is complete.

The walls of all these rooms are almost hallowed by a magnificent collection of portraits by Van Dyke and other masters of the bygone centuries. Can one imagine more restful or more inspiring surroundings?

On the other hand, in the basement are large rooms ideally suited for catering for the physical well-being of the residents. While some are, of course, devoted to domestic needs they have mainly been set apart for recreational purposes such as table tennis or can be used as classrooms for the teaching of handicrafts. Here noise and mess can be indulged in without disturbing the sober atmosphere of the rooms above. The upper floors have been furnished as comfortable bedrooms. There are a limited number of single and double rooms, while larger rooms accommodate

an average of six people. The beds have interior spring mattresses, conducive to that supreme holiday essential—a good night's rest.

Under Conference conditions up to 80 people can be accommodated at one time.

Near to the house is the old family church where the Wakes and the villagers have worshipped for many generations. It is approached from the house by a footpath across the fields. In the grounds are three grass tennis courts and a four-acre playing field.

The surrounding countryside is full of beauty and historical associations ready to be explored by the walker or cyclist. Northamptonshire is ideal for both. The nearby town of Northampton, sometimes called "a cradle of dissenters," has existed as a community since a tribe of ancient Britons first pitched their camp on Hunsbury Hill some two thousand years ago. Those with a "nose" for things of the past will find an immense amount to interest them, all within short distance of the house.

But Northampton lives not only in its history. It is very much alive to-day and offers all the services and attractions expected of a modern township with over 100,000 population.

Apply The Secretary

COURTEENHALL HOUSE

at

PRESBYTERIAN CHURCH OFFICES
134 GEORGE STREET, W.1

Terms

For a period of 7 days or more £4-11-0

For a period of less than 7 days 13-6 *per day*

A reduction of 1 0 per day will be made to Presbyterian visitors

145. Brochure advertising Courteenhall House as a holiday and conference centre, 1948. The Estate let the House to the Presbyterian Church of England from 1948 to 1951

146. Seed cabinet, early nineteenth century, still in use in the potting shed in the kitchen garden, Courteenhall House

should try, in the first instance, to camp in the House. An estimate for the demolition of the House was, however, obtained from the firm of Thomas Oakley in January 1953; it amounted to £2,000. Sir Hereward, from Hampshire, sadly agreed with his son that demolition was probably the best solution and that he should concentrate on converting the Stables into a permanent home.

Such a draconian measure could be justified on financial grounds. Taxation was heavy at this time, modernisation and redecoration as well as maintenance would be expensive, and there were forty houses and cottages on the Estate which needed attention. Several other alternatives presented themselves: either to buy a house elsewhere or build a new house, possibly at the old Sand Pit, or reoccupy Courteenhall Rectory or buy Quinton Glebe. A more dramatic compromise which was mooted was to remove the top floor of the House and lower the roof. (Merryman, the family's former Irish groom, ingenuously suggested that it might be better to remove the ground floor).

Encouragement to preserve the Hall also came from a third quarter, Hugh, Earl of Euston (later 11th Duke of Grafton), a member of the Historic Buildings Council. He suggested that estimates should be obtained for minimum improvements, for which a grant might be provided to cover part of the cost. The Wakes should then move into the Hall for a trial period and, if it was found to be impracticable, then should move back into the Stables.

Shortly after the birth of Major and Mrs Wake's son, Hereward Charles, in November 1952, an estimate had been submitted by Edward Green, Northampton, the builders, for restoring the Hall on the most economical scale. After the Presbyterian Church of England tenants had vacated Courteenhall, it was found that dilapidations were more extensive than had at first been realized. The necessary alterations included the conversion of the old coke boiler to oil and the Study into a kitchen and pantry. A hand-operated service lift was to be installed on the back stairs at the rear of the House from the ground floor to the first floor only. The old Kitchen and Scullery were to be turned into garages. Finally, three bedrooms and two bathrooms only were to be painted and the plumbing modernized. The estimate was £4,000.

In due course, a grant of £2,000 was made by the Government on the recommendation of the Historic Buildings Council, and Major Wake's father-in-law, Captain Geoffrey W.M. Lees, presented them with an equal sum. The estimate was accepted and the builders moved into the House in the summer of 1953. By December it was ready for occupation. There was much restoration work to do as well as refurnishing and maintenance. Whereas Sir Hereward and Daisy had found it almost impossible to live in Courteenhall without a dozen servants, the post-war regime began with two 'daily' helpers. Over the following years, the House, the architect Samuel Saxon's finest surviving building, was gradually and lovingly brought back to its original splendour.

The Stables did not remain empty. Captain Lees paid for further improvements: the old garage was converted into a new kitchen, a new dining room was constructed and a new front entrance was made. It was occupied by Captain Lees's mother, Mrs Edith Lees from Whittlebury from 1954, and then later by Peter Wake and his wife. More recently, the Stables underwent further improvements, incorporating the Stables Cottage,

148. Thatched cottages, Courteenhall Village, c.1930. The village, situated off the main road, has no through traffic
Inset 147. Sundial, Courteenhall Village, marking the completion of the reroofing and modernization of 16 cottages
in 1961

149. Courteenhall Village, by Stanley Orchart, 1985

344

150. Cottages during reroofing, Courteenhall Village, 1957. The thatched roofs were replaced with tiles and gutters after being heightened

151. The Stable Yard at Courteenhall, 1957

152. Outbuildings, Courteenhall. The centre building, once the Bakery and Game Larder, in course of conversion into a cottage, 1957. The Laundry is on the left

153. The Laundry, Courteenhall, 1957. Built 1791 when the household numbered nearly 50

154. The Old School House, 1957 (left), now a private residence, with the Free Grammar School (right), now the Parish Hall

155. Visitors being shown in 1957 where the proposed London to Yorkshire motorway would cut the Estate in two

without damaging the character of the buildings. The central archway was not filled in, but within it was constructed a covered passage linking the north and south ends of the ground floor.[10] In 1978, it became the home of the fourteenth baronet's son, Charles Wake, and his family.

During the war the gardens were neglected; flower beds were done away with and vegetables grown to produce much-needed food. With the House once more occupied, Julia replanned and replanted the garden. The thirteenth baronet had planted a large yew hedge on the south side towards the Stables, surmounted by elaborate topiary birds. These latter were reduced in number but the remaining ones were restored to their original shapes. Daisy had made a herbaceous border along this hedge; now flowering trees and shrubs were planted. In order to give privacy to the Stable Yard and archway, a new footpath with beech hedges was devised through the gardens, separating the Stables from the House.

Dutch elm disease has destroyed all the elm trees in the Park, woodlands and in the hedgerows, including one a hundred feet high. Further damage was caused during the severe drought of 1976 when a number of adult beech trees perished, and the 1987 gales blew down many trees. The remaining hedgerow ash trees and some old oaks are dying, possibly as a result of pollution or modern arable farming. More positively, during the last twenty five years, about twenty new woodland spinneys have been planted and a six acre arboretum below the House with a collection of some two hundred and fifty varieties of trees from many parts of the world.

There have also been many changes on the Estate itself, as a comparison between the pre-war and modern maps show (see Appendix B). The seven farms required updating and much was spent on new buildings for dairy and beef cattle, modern implements, grain storage and the connecting of mains water to all fields and cottages and the House. Connection to the village was made possible by an arrangement with the District Council about 1954 when the mains and a sewage disposal plant were constructed and six Council houses were built at the east end of the village. In the late 1950s, modernization of the sixteen thatched cottages in Courteenhall village was completed when the roofing was renewed with tiles. The village pond, once used for collecting buckets of water, was filled in as it was dangerous, and unsightly with rubbish. More recently, a major undertaking has been the renewal of the roof of the House in 1987 which required new lead, slates, much new timber and the rebuilding of forty five chimneys. Courteenhall Rectory, formerly occupied by great Uncle Archie and great Aunt Lucy, was sold off by the Church Commissioners shortly after 1945. The Church remains in good repair: a gold weathercock surmounts the tower, placed there in memory of the thirteenth baronet who died in 1963. There was an interesting ceremony in 1985 when No. II Squadron of the RAF, which in 1931 had adopted the name Hereward and the Wake Knot crest because of its long history of army co-operation duties, laid up its standard in the Church.[11] The Old Grammar School continues to be used as the Parish Hall. The Schoolmaster's House and the adjoining Infant School to the east were sold to the Estate when the school was closed down in 1950 and have now been converted into one large house.

At Waltham shortly after the war the government compulsorily acquired a large

156. Aerial view of Courteenhall, 1959, showing House, Stables and in the foreground, the Old Rectory and Church. Note on the left the ancient ridge and furrow

157. The Wake Family Memorial Book placed in Courteenhall Church by the 13th baronet, in which are recorded the lives of members of the family from 1944 (see coloured illustration on title page)

158. Some of the many Wake monuments, in Courteenhall Church

acreage at 'existing use' agricultural value for an extensive new housing estate to rehouse Londoners. Later, it acquired the whole of the Abbey Farm, which now forms part of the Lee Valley Regional Park. Subsequently, Sir Hereward sold his interest in the common land to a gravel company and only very little of this Essex Estate now remains. These sales at Waltham made possible improvements at Courteenhall and the purchase of Blisworth Lodge Farm, Wards Farm at Collingtree and the Glebe Farm and Manor Farm at Quinton, bringing the acreage of the Courteenhall Estate up to about three thousand acres, of which two thousand acres are farmed in partnership by Sir Hereward and Lady Wake and their son Charles.

*   *   *   *   *

If Courteenhall itself has remained largely unchanged over the centuries, it has, like so many other rural parts of Northamptonshire, been affected by external forces. The prime cause of change was the coming of the M1 motorway.

In February 1955, the Government of the day announced that Britain's first motorway, from London to Yorkshire, was to be built. The initial stage of some seventy miles would start from a point north of London,[12] cross Bedfordshire and Buckinghamshire and terminate at Crick in Northamptonshire. By the following January it was revealed that at least a half of the one hundred objections registered with the Ministry of Transport had come from Northamptonshire. Professor Nikolaus Pevsner in his introduction to the volume on the county has written, 'It must be admitted that the soil of England is so closely and intimately worked and so subtly landscaped that the intrusion of the motorway was bound to be specially violent. It was for this reason that opposition to it remained for so long'.[13]

The proposed motorway cut diagonally across the Courteenhall Estate with an intersection where the A508 crossed the M1 at Junction 15. In 1957 the Estate was warned that a compulsory acquisition order was being prepared by the Ministry of Transport, and on 27 February 1958 the order itself was received: later that year, Major Wake was taken in the contractor's helicopter to survey the route of the motorway.

A remarkable feature of the project was the speed with which it was built. Sir Owen Williams and Partners were briefed in 1951, but work on the M1 did not go ahead until 24 March 1958. By September the following year – a period of eighteen months – the road was open from London to Crick. The scale of the operation was very impressive: it involved five thousand men, five million pounds worth of machinery and twelve thousand maps. Working day and night, the contractors, John Laing and Son Ltd., surfaced two and a half million square yards of motorway, carried one hundred and thirty two bridges over or under existing roads, railways, canals and footpaths, and built a service station every twelve miles.

The compensation which the Estate received from the Ministry of Transport in November 1963 for the conveyance of the Courteenhall land was £15,246, with an additional sum of £1,403 for interest accrued. A separate cheque for the derisory sum of £3 13s. 4d. was sent by the Ministry 'for inconvenience suffered'. Five of the seven Courteenhall farms – East Lodge Farm, Grange Farm, Home Farm, Wards Farm and

159. The M1 motorway under construction across Courteenhall parish looking south east towards London from the A508 road bridge (later Junction 15), 1958. Courteenhall House is amongst the trees on the right. On the left is Mrs Julia Wake and son, Hereward Charles

160. Margaret, Dowager Lady Wake's 80th birthday party, Courteenhall, 19 April 1972. Most of her 22 grandchildren are in the picture

161. Sir Hereward Wake, 14th baronet and Professor Peter Gordon, in the Library at Courteenhall, 18 April 1991.

162. The Old Grammar School, Courteenhall, by Stanley Orchart, 1989

163. The Library, Courteenhall, drawing by Stanley Orchart, 1989

West Lodge Farm – were affected by the motorway. Accommodation works carried out included the building of a bridge for the drive to East Lodge Farm, where two cattle grids were built. Six other bridges were erected on the Estate, all existing footpaths and bridle roads being preserved.

The building of the M1 created many problems for Courteenhall. Two streams which now took the surface water from the motorway had to be regularly cleaned. Piped water had to be connected to several fields and existing power lines had to be altered. When the cuttings were being excavated, the top soil was dumped in adjoining fields. Eighteen months later when it was cleared away, some of the original soil disappeared too. The design of the early bridges over the motorway was unpleasing as they were built at speed; subsequent motorway bridges are of better design. The road itself, altogether six lanes in width, has large embankments on each side of it. No consideration was paid by the Ministry of Transport at this time for the privacy of landowners along the motorway, and no landscaping was undertaken. At first, it was contemplated that as Courteenhall House was now completely visible from the M1, it would provide a pleasing view for the passing motorist. There was also the problem of the noise generated by the constant stream of traffic day and night. To alleviate these problems, in the last twenty five years, Sir Hereward has planted belts and spinneys, largely of evergreen trees. The appearance of the Courteenhall Estate has thus been totally changed. The names given to the spinneys, containing approximately a quarter of a million trees, have mainly Wake associations, consisting either of place names, such as Bourne, Clevedon, Waltham and Alamein, or the names of the children and grandchildren (see Estate maps 1930 and 1992, Appendix B).

At a lunch given at Newport Pagnell on 30 September 1959 to celebrate the completion of the first section of the M1, Sir Owen Williams, the consulting engineer, anticipated that 'the road would last for about a thousand years'.[14] This optimistic estimate was dampened a month later by the main contractors on the day of the official opening of the M1, 2 November, who stated, 'There is no guarantee that settlement and cracking will not occur'.[15] With between sixteen and seventeen thousand vehicles using the motorway on the first day, it was not surprising that within thirty six hours it was reported that the hard shoulder had collapsed at one point under the weight of a heavy lorry.[16]

One consequence of the motorway has been the heavy increase in traffic in the area, both on the road itself and those leading off it at Junction 15 past Courteenhall; bypasses, road widening and extra exits and entrances to and from the motorway are the only means of alleviating the problem. Recently it has been stated, 'It [the M1] was destined to give new emphasis to the "At-the-Crossroads-of-Britain" image of Northampton, highlight its role as an ideal distribution centre and compensate for its decline as a manufacturing town'.[17] The building of the motorway has indeed doubled the size of Northampton during the past thirty years, and has led to the expansion of nearly all the other towns and villages in the County, and the building of Milton Keynes to the south.[18]

*   *   *   *   *

One of the remarkable features of the Wakes is their unbroken line of descent. The present baronet, Sir Hereward Wake, is the fourteenth member to hold that title and represents the twenty-ninth generation of the Wake family to live in Northamptonshire. When he was appointed High Sheriff of the County in 1955, he was the fifteenth Wake to hold this post since his ancestor Thomas Wake in 1330. He has been a Deputy Lieutenant since 1969 and in 1984 was appointed the County's first Vice Lord-Lieutenant.

Sir Hereward also followed his father, grandfather and forebears in becoming closely involved in County affairs. For fifteen years, from 1955, he was a Councillor on the Northampton Rural District Council and has been for over forty years Chairman of Courteenhall Parish Council.[19] For forty years, he took an active part in the work of the Country Landowners Association as Chairman and President of the Northamptonshire branch. He was Chairman of the managers for ten years of St. John's Approved School, at Tiffield, which was founded by his great uncle Archie and, as with several previous generations of Wakes, was a governor of Northampton Grammar School and of St. Andrew's Hospital. He was Vice Chairman of Nene College when it was first founded and is a Patron of the Northamptonshire Grammar School. Also like his father and grandfather, Sir Hereward is Patron of the living of Courteenhall, the Church now being united with Collingtree and Milton Malsor. The widespread destruction of many historic buildings in the County, which Courteenhall so nearly suffered, has led Sir Hereward to support initiatives to save them. He was on the committee formed to conserve Canons Ashby House and Church, the former of which, with the help of the National Heritage Memorial Fund, the National Trust has taken into its custody. As Chairman of the trustees of Lamport Hall, he helped to preserve the house, its contents and estate for the benefit of the public. Similarly, Sir Hereward was a patron of the three appeals to restore the historic Ely and Peterborough Cathedrals and Waltham Abbey Church.

Another of his interests has been the provision for the youth of the County. Together with the Reverend Harry Whittaker, Sir Hereward in 1961 founded the Northamptonshire Association of Youth Clubs, of which he was Chairman for fifteen years and then President. This Association is the largest and most successful of its kind in the country. Its new buildings at King's Park, Moulton, include the Hereward Wake Centre which was completed at a cost of over three million pounds and opened on 7 June 1990 by Her Majesty Queen Elizabeth the Queen Mother.

As was shown in the last chapter, Joan Wake, Sir Hereward's aunt, was instrumental in setting up in 1920 the Northamptonshire Record Society and the saving of many thousands of documents relating to Northamptonshire history. Sir Hereward joined the Society in 1946 and was a member of the Council from 1964, earlier taking an active part in the campaign to save Delapre Abbey. In 1978 he became Chairman of the Council and is now President. For many years he served on the Executive Committee of the Standing Council of the Baronetage.

Lady Julia Wake is a Justice of the Peace, and is involved with many aspects of Northamptonshire life. She is President of the Northamptonshire Girl Guides and a Governor of Northampton High School for Girls, and is much involved with other

164. Aerial view 1986, of the east front of the Stables, Courteenhall, with Stable Yard, Home Farm buildings and Kitchen Garden, and with the Old Grammar School beyond. The greenhouses have since been pulled down and the cowshed converted into a new Estate Office

165. Aerial view of Courteenhall House, 1986, showing the south and east fronts shortly after the roof was renewed and the 44 chimneys rebuilt

organizations. Sir Hereward and Lady Wake have one son, Charles, three daughters, Diana, Caroline and Sarah and ten grandchildren at the time of writing.

*   *   *   *   *

Some years ago in an article in a local newspaper about Courteenhall it was stated, 'It is hard to believe that the tiny and remote village of Courteenhall, situated as it is at the end of one narrow lane, is only ten minutes ride away from Northampton'. The village itself, with no shops, has remained much as it was two centuries ago. The population of the parish has hardly changed either: in 1851, it was one hundred and thirty five and a century later only five fewer. Next to the village stands the Church where generations of Wakes are buried, and across the fields the Hall, which was newly built by the ninth baronet in 1792. The eight hundred years which have passed since the Wakes first settled in Northamptonshire have witnessed many fluctuations in the family's fortunes. The motorway and the subsequent increase in traffic have changed the landscape around Courteenhall and its former air of tranquility, and the ever-expanding Northampton now laps up to the Estate's boundaries. The extent to which Courteenhall can survive these and other future developments remains in the hands of the fourteenth baronet's son and grandson; it is hoped that the Wakes may continue to play an active part in Northamptonshire affairs.

APPENDIX A
Wake Family Trees

FAMILY TREE I

THE WAKE FAMIL

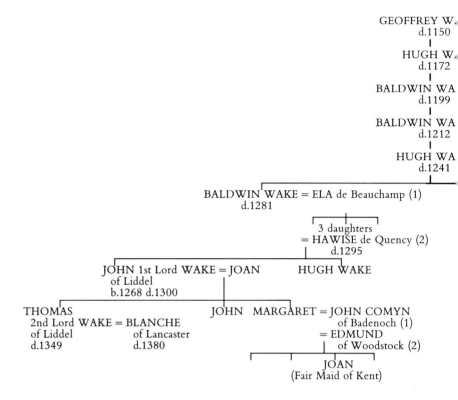

GEOFFREY W.
d.1150

HUGH W.
d.1172

BALDWIN WA
d.1199

BALDWIN WA
d.1212

HUGH WA
d.1241

BALDWIN WAKE = ELA de Beauchamp (1)
d.1281

3 daughters
= HAWISE de Quency (2)
d.1295

JOHN 1st Lord WAKE = JOAN   HUGH WAKE
of Liddel
b.1268 d.1300

THOMAS   JOHN   MARGARET = JOHN COMYN
2nd Lord WAKE = BLANCHE   of Badenoch (1)
of Liddel   of Lancaster   = EDMUND
d.1349   d.1380   of Woodstock (2)

JOAN
(Fair Maid of Kent)

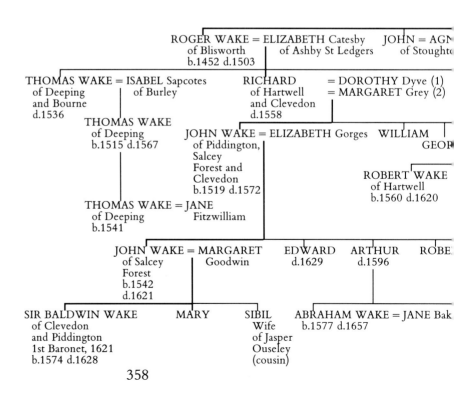

ROGER WAKE = ELIZABETH Catesby   JOHN = AGN
of Blisworth   of Ashby St Ledgers   of Stoughto
b.1452 d.1503

THOMAS WAKE = ISABEL Sapcotes   RICHARD   = DOROTHY Dyve (1)
of Deeping   of Burley   of Hartwell   = MARGARET Grey (2)
and Bourne   and Clevedon
d.1536   d.1558

THOMAS WAKE   JOHN WAKE = ELIZABETH Gorges   WILLIAM
of Deeping   of Piddington,   GEOR
b.1515 d.1567   Salcey
                              Forest and   ROBERT WAKE
                              Clevedon   of Hartwell
                              b.1519 d.1572   b.1560 d.1620

THOMAS WAKE = JANE
of Deeping   Fitzwilliam
b.1541

JOHN WAKE = MARGARET   EDWARD   ARTHUR   ROBE
of Salcey   Goodwin   d.1629   d.1596
Forest
b.1542
d.1621

SIR BALDWIN WAKE   MARY   SIBIL   ABRAHAM WAKE = JANE Bak
of Clevedon   Wife   b.1577 d.1657
and Piddington   of Jasper
1st Baronet, 1621   Ouseley
b.1574 d.1628   (cousin)

th to 17th CENTURIES

Guernsey

Bourne = EMMA fitzGilbert

Bourne & Deeping = AGNES de Hommet

Bourne = ISABEL Briwere

Bourne = JOAN de Stuteville

```
SIR HUGH WAKE = (unknown)
    of Blisworth and Deeping
    d.1315
SIR THOMAS WAKE I = ELIZABETH Cransley
    of Blisworth and Deeping
    d.1346
SIR THOMAS WAKE II = ALICE Pattishall   HUGH
    of Blisworth
    d.1379
```

SIR THOMAS III = MAUDE Pigot   MAUDE   BLANCHE   SIBIL   ANNE
WAKE
of Blisworth
d.1383

HN WAKE   THOMAS WAKE IV = MARGARET Philpot
375 d.?   of Blisworth
                          b.1378 d.1425
                      THOMAS WAKE V = AGNES Lovell
                          of Blisworth   of Clevedon
                          b.1402 d.1458
                          THOMAS WAKE VI = (unknown) (1)
                              of Blisworth   = ELIZABETH Beauchamp (2)
                              b.1435 d.1476

WILLIAM   = (unknown) (1)   ISABEL = JOHN BROKE
of Hartwell = ANNE Southwood (2)   of Great Oakley

WILLIAM   JOHN   ELIZABETH   MARGARET
of Cardington of Flore
b.1481

CHARD = ELIZABETH ROGER | ANTHONY | HUGH | ROBERT | 6 daughters
1581 | Lowe   BALDWIN LEONARD THOMAS   FRANCIS ELIZABETH
      | of Clevedon   CECILY
CHARD   CHARLES   MARY   FRANCES   MARGARET
1570   d.1627   MARY
1628   DOROTHY
                                                      ANNE

LLIAM   JANE   MAGDALEN LUCRECE   ISABEL   MARY
1645   d.1606
                Second wife of
                Richard Ouseley
                d.1598
ISAAC WAKE = ANNA Bray   SARAH
1580 d. 1632   d.1642
```
```

FAMILY TREE II

THE BLACK PRINC

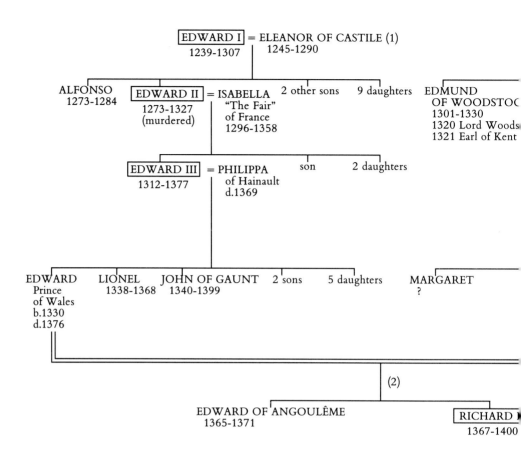

EDWARD I = ELEANOR OF CASTILE (1)
1239-1307   1245-1290

ALFONSO   EDWARD II = ISABELLA   2 other sons   9 daughters   EDMUND
1273-1284   1273-1327   "The Fair"   OF WOODSTOC
             (murdered)   of France   1301-1330
                          1296-1358   1320 Lord Woods
                                                                   1321 Earl of Kent

EDWARD III = PHILIPPA   son   2 daughters
1312-1377   of Hainault
             d.1369

EDWARD   LIONEL   JOHN OF GAUNT   2 sons   5 daughters   MARGARET
Prince   1338-1368   1340-1399   ?
of Wales
b.1330
d.1376

(2)

EDWARD OF ANGOULÊME   RICHARD
1365-1371   1367-1400

FAMILY TREE III

TH

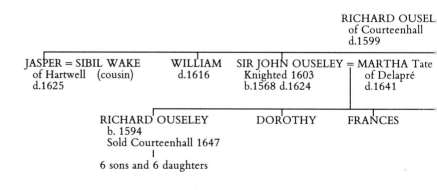

RICHARD OUSEL
of Courteenhall
d.1599

JASPER = SIBIL WAKE   WILLIAM   SIR JOHN OUSELEY = MARTHA Tate
of Hartwell (cousin)   d.1616   Knighted 1603   of Delapré
d.1625   b.1568 d.1624   d.1641

RICHARD OUSELEY   DOROTHY   FRANCES
b. 1594
Sold Courteenhall 1647

6 sons and 6 daughters

ND JOAN OF KENT

MARGARET OF FRANCE (2)
1282-1317

MARGARET WAKE   1 daughter   THOMAS
d.1349   Earl of Norfolk
(her first husband having
been John Comyn killed
at Bannockburn, 1314)
(Sister and sole heir of JOHN WAKE
and JOAN of Liddel and great great
granddaughter of LLWELYN THE GREAT,
1173-1240)

EDMUND   JOHN   JOAN   = SIR THOMAS HOLAND KG (1)
PLANTAGENET PLANTAGENET   "Fair Maid of Kent" Created Lord Wake of Liddel
Baron Woodstock Baron Woodstock 1328-1385   and Earl of Kent
2nd Earl of Kent 3rd Earl of Kent Countess of Kent b.? d.1360
1327-1331   1330-1352 d.s.p. Baroness Woodstock
               1349 Lord Wake   Baroness Wake

ANNE OF BOHEMIA (1)   THOMAS   EDMUND   JOHN HOLAND
1394   HOLAND   HOLAND   1353-1400
ISABELLE OF FRANCE (2)   1351-1397   b.1352   Earl of Huntingdon
1409   Created Earl of Kent   and Duke of Exeter 1397
               in 1385   Lord Wake
               Lord Woodstock
               Lord Wake

USELEYS

ANE Partridge (1)
MAGDALEN Wake (2)
d.1607

CHARD   MARY   ELIZABETH   BRIDGET
   ROBERT   DOROTHY   ANNE

IIGHILAE   ANN

FAMILY TREE IV

THE FIRS

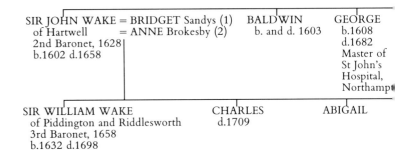

SIR BALDWIN WAKE
of Clevedon and Piddingt•
1st Baronet, 1621
b.1574 d.1628

SIR JOHN WAKE = BRIDGET Sandys (1)   BALDWIN   GEORGE
of Hartwell   = ANNE Brokesby (2)   b. and d. 1603   b.1608
2nd Baronet, 1628   d.1682
b.1602 d.1658   Master of
                               St John's
                               Hospital,
                               Northamp•

SIR WILLIAM WAKE   CHARLES   ABIGAIL
of Piddington and Riddlesworth   d.1709
3rd Baronet, 1658
b.1632 d.1698

FAMILY TREE V

THE DRURY

SIR DRU DRURY
of Riddlesworth
b.1531 d.1617

SIR DRU DRURY (II) = ANN Waldegra
of Riddlesworth
1st Baronet, 1627
b.1588 d.1632

SIR DRU DRURY (III) = SUSAN Jones (1)
of Riddlesworth   (Sister and co-heir
2nd Baronet, 1632   Samuel JONES of
b.1612 d.1651   Courteenhall)

                     = MARY (2)
                     d. 1651

SIR ROBERT DRURY = ELIZABETH Dunston •
of Riddlesworth   = ELEANOR Harsnet (2)
3rd Baronet, 1651   = DIANA Violet (3)
b.1634 d.1712   d.1744 d.s.p.

'AKE BARONETS

```
BIGAIL ——— (1)
LIZABETH Digby (2)
d.1631
```

BALDWIN WAKE	ABIGAIL	ELIZABETH
Captain Wake)	b.1609	b.1614
nighted 1646		
1611 d.1649		

| ELIZABETH | BRIDGET |

F RIDDLESWORTH

```
ELIZABETH Calthorpe (1)
CATHERINE Finch (2)
```

| ELIZABETH | ANN | FRANCES |

WILLIAM	KATHERINE
b.1615	
d.1653	

DRU	DIANA = SIR WILLIAM WAKE
d.s.p.	d.1675 3rd Baronet, 1658
	b.1632 d.1698

FAMILY TREE VI

THE WAKE – JONE

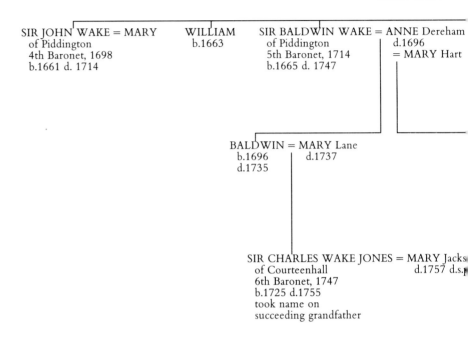

SIR WILLIAM WAI
of Piddington
3rd Baronet, 1658
b.1632 d.1698

SIR JOHN WAKE = MARY
of Piddington
4th Baronet, 1698
b.1661 d. 1714

WILLIAM
b.1663

SIR BALDWIN WAKE = ANNE Dereham
of Piddington
5th Baronet, 1714
b.1665 d. 1747

d.1696
= MARY Hart

BALDWIN = MARY Lane
b.1696   d.1737
d.1735

SIR CHARLES WAKE JONES = MARY Jacks
of Courteenhall   d.1757 d.s.p
6th Baronet, 1747
b.1725 d.1755
took name on
succeeding grandfather

FAMILY TREE VII

THE WAK

SIR JOHN WAKE
of Piddington
4th Baronet, 1698
b.1661 d.1714

WILLIAM
d.1663

SIR BALDWIN WAK
of Piddington
5th Baronet, 1714
b.1665 d.1747

BALDWIN
b.1696 d.1735

SIR CHARLES
WAKE JONES
of Courteenhall
and Waltham
6th Baronet, 1747
b.1725 d.1755

ONNECTION (1)

)IANA Drury
d.1675
(Sister of Sir Robert Drury 3rd Bt.
niece of Samuel Jones of Courteenhall)

ROBERT	SAMUEL = ELIZABETH Champion	ISAAC
Dean of Bocking	later	(left estates by great uncle,	b.1671
b.1666 d.1725	Samuel Wake Jones	Samuel Jones
see next	of Waltham Abbey	of Courteenhall)
Family Tree	b.1670 d.1713	

SUSANNA	ELIZABETH	MARY	DIANA	GEORGE	DRURY
b.1668	b.1664	b.1662	b.1660	b.d.1675	b.1673

IARLES = ELIZABETH Sambrooke	DIANA	MARY
iter d.s.p.	b.1699	b.1702

Charles Wake Jones
f Waltham Abbey
.1701 d.1739
ook name in 1718
eft estates by uncle
amuel Jones in will
f 1712 and educated
y him

JONES CONNECTION (2)

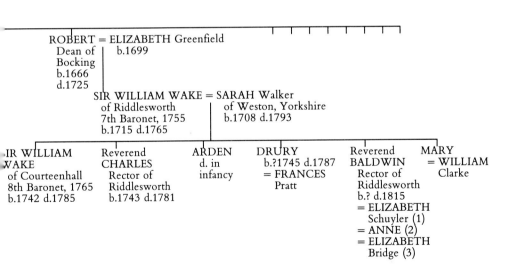

ROBERT = ELIZABETH Greenfield
Dean of | b.1699
Bocking
b.1666
d.1725

SIR WILLIAM WAKE = SARAH Walker
of Riddlesworth | of Weston, Yorkshire
7th Baronet, 1755 | b.1708 d.1793
b.1715 d.1765

IR WILLIAM WAKE	Reverend CHARLES	ARDEN	DRURY	Reverend BALDWIN	MARY = WILLIAM
of Courteenhall	Rector of	d. in	b.?1745 d.1787	Rector of	Clarke
8th Baronet, 1765	Riddlesworth	infancy	= FRANCES	Riddlesworth
b.1742 d.1785	b.1743 d.1781		Pratt	b.? d.1815

= ELIZABETH
  Schuyler (1)
= ANNE (2)
= ELIZABETH
  Bridge (3)

FAMILY TREE VIII

THE WAKES C

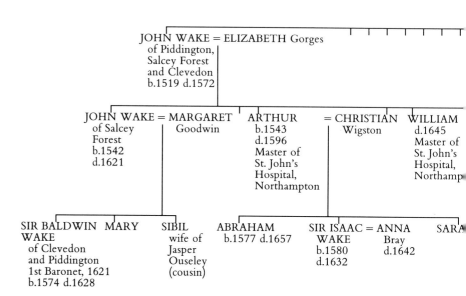

DOROTHY Dyve

JOHN WAKE = ELIZABETH Gorges
of Piddington,
Salcey Forest
and Clevedon
b.1519 d.1572

JOHN WAKE = MARGARET   ARTHUR   = CHRISTIAN   WILLIAM
of Salcey   Goodwin   b.1543   Wigston   d.1645
Forest   d.1596   Master of
b.1542   Master of   St. John's
d.1621   St. John's   Hospital,
                            Hospital,   Northamp
                            Northampton

SIR BALDWIN MARY   SIBIL   ABRAHAM   SIR ISAAC = ANNA   SARA
WAKE   wife of   b.1577 d.1657   WAKE   Bray
of Clevedon   Jasper   b.1580   d.1642
and Piddington   Ouseley   d.1632
1st Baronet, 1621   (cousin)
b.1574 d.1628

FAMILY TREE IX

THE WAK

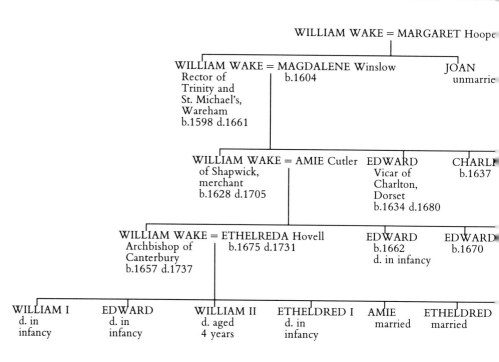

WILLIAM WAKE = MARGARET Hoope

WILLIAM WAKE = MAGDALENE Winslow   JOAN
Rector of   b.1604   unmarrie
Trinity and
St. Michael's,
Wareham
b.1598 d.1661

WILLIAM WAKE = AMIE Cutler   EDWARD   CHARL
of Shapwick,   Vicar of   b.1637
merchant   Charlton,
b.1628 d.1705   Dorset
                              b.1634 d.1680

WILLIAM WAKE = ETHELREDA Hovell   EDWARD   EDWARD
Archbishop of   b.1675 d.1731   b.1662   b.1670
Canterbury   d. in infancy
b.1657 d.1737

WILLIAM I   EDWARD   WILLIAM II   ETHELDRED I   AMIE   ETHELDRED
d. in   d. in   d. aged   d. in   married   married
infancy   infancy   4 years   infancy

ᴬRTWELL, PIDDINGTON AND ANTWERP

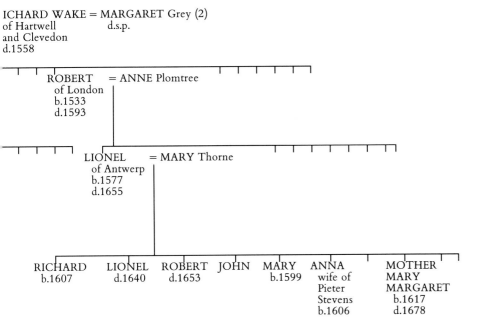

ɪCHARD WAKE = MARGARET Grey (2)
of Hartwell   d.s.p.
and Clevedon
d.1558

ROBERT   = ANNE Plomtree
of London
b.1533
d.1593

LIONEL   = MARY Thorne
   of Antwerp
b.1577
d.1655

RICHARD	LIONEL	ROBERT	JOHN	MARY	ANNA	MOTHER
b.1607	d.1640	d.1653		b.1599	wife of	MARY
					Pieter	MARGARET
					Stevens	b.1617
					b.1606	d.1678

F DORSET

EDWARD   MAGDALENE
d. in infancy   b.1629
       d.1693

MAGDALENE
b.1655

ᴇSTER	DOROTHY	MAGDALENE	ANNE	ELIZABETH	MARY	CATHERINE
ᴍarried	married	married	d. in	d. aged	married	d. in
			infancy	15 years		infancy

FAMILY TREE X

THE EIGHTH BARON

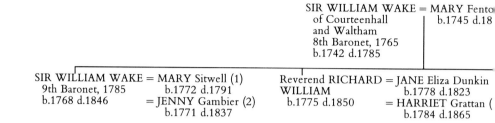

SIR WILLIAM WAKE = MARY Fento
of Courteenhall
and Waltham
8th Baronet, 1765
b.1742 d.1785
b.1745 d.18

SIR WILLIAM WAKE = MARY Sitwell (1)
9th Baronet, 1785
b.1772 d.1791
b.1768 d.1846
= JENNY Gambier (2)
b.1771 d.1837

Reverend RICHARD = JANE Eliza Dunkin
WILLIAM
b.1775 d.1850
b.1778 d.1823
= HARRIET Grattan (
b.1784 d.1865

FAMILY TREE XI

THE WAKE – SITWE

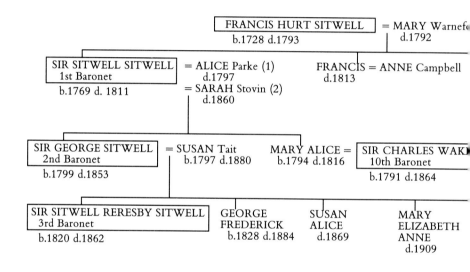

FRANCIS HURT SITWELL = MARY Warnefo
b.1728 d.1793   d.1792

SIR SITWELL SITWELL = ALICE Parke (1)
1st Baronet   d.1797
b.1769 d. 1811   = SARAH Stovin (2)
                      d.1860

FRANCIS = ANNE Campbell
d.1813

SIR GEORGE SITWELL = SUSAN Tait
2nd Baronet   b.1797 d.1880
b.1799 d.1853

MARY ALICE = SIR CHARLES WAK
b.1794 d.1816   10th Baronet
               b.1791 d.1864

SIR SITWELL RERESBY SITWELL
3rd Baronet
b.1820 d.1862

GEORGE
FREDERICK
b.1828 d.1884

SUSAN
ALICE
d.1869

MARY
ELIZABETH
ANNE
d.1909

368

SIR WILLIAM WAKE

```
                            |
MARYANNE = ROGER          CHARLOTTE
b.1773      Elliott Roberts   b.1779 d.1853
```

ONNECTION

```
        |                      |
HURT = ANNE Hardy         MARY = | SIR WILLIAM WAKE |
d.1803                    b.1772 |   9th Baronet    |
                          d.1791 |_____|
                                   b.1768 d.1846
```

```
            |                      |
GEORGIANA          LUCY CHARLOTTE = | HERWALD            |
CAROLINE           HURT            | CRAUFURD WAKE      |
d.1890             b.1827 d.1907   | 4th son of 10th Baronet |
                                   |_____|
                                     b.1828 d.1901
```

FAMILY TREE XII

THE NINTH BARONE

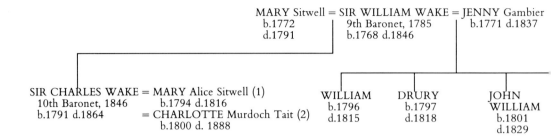

MARY Sitwell = SIR WILLIAM WAKE = JENNY Gambier
b.1772   9th Baronet, 1785   b.1771 d.1837
d.1791   b.1768 d.1846

SIR CHARLES WAKE = MARY Alice Sitwell (1)
10th Baronet, 1846   b.1794 d.1816
b.1791 d.1864   = CHARLOTTE Murdoch Tait (2)
     b.1800 d. 1888

WILLIAM
b.1796
d.1815

DRURY
b.1797
d.1818

JOHN
WILLIAM
b.1801
d.1829

FAMILY TREE XIII

THE TENTH BARONE

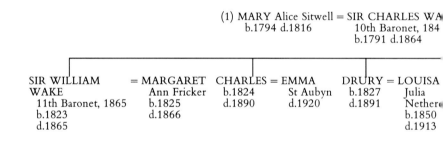

(1) MARY Alice Sitwell = SIR CHARLES WA
b.1794 d.1816   10th Baronet, 184
     b.1791 d.1864

SIR WILLIAM = MARGARET   CHARLES = EMMA   DRURY = LOUISA
WAKE   Ann Fricker   b.1824   St Aubyn   b.1827   Julia
11th Baronet, 1865   b.1825   d.1890   d.1920   d.1891   Nether
b.1823   d.1866   b.1850
d.1865   d.1913

MATILDA
CHARLOTT
b.1832
d.1924

FAMILY TREE XIV

THE ELEVENTH BARONE

SIR WILLIAM WA
11th Baronet, 186
b.1823 d.1865

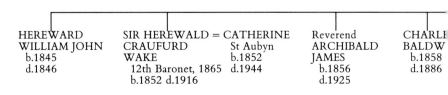

HEREWARD
WILLIAM JOHN
b.1845
d.1846

SIR HEREWALD = CATHERINE
CRAUFURD   St Aubyn
WAKE   b.1852
12th Baronet, 1865   d.1944
b.1852 d.1916

Reverend
ARCHIBALD
JAMES
b.1856
d.1925

CHARLE
BALDW
b.1858
d.1886

SIR WILLIAM WAKE

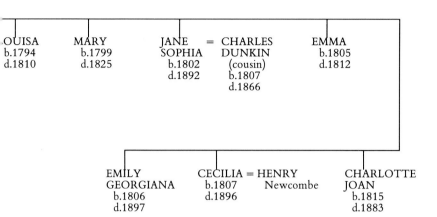

LOUISA
b.1794
d.1810

MARY
b.1799
d.1825

JANE = CHARLES
SOPHIA   DUNKIN
b.1802   (cousin)
d.1892   b.1807
         d.1866

EMMA
b.1805
d.1812

EMILY
GEORGIANA
b.1806
d.1897

CECILIA = HENRY
b.1807   Newcombe
d.1896

CHARLOTTE
JOAN
b.1815
d.1883

SIR CHARLES WAKE

CHARLOTTE Murdoch Tait (2)
b.1800 d.1888

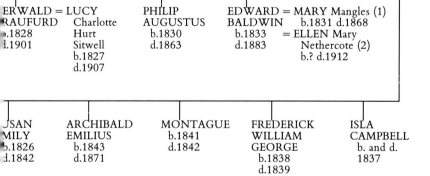

ERWALD = LUCY
RAUFURD   Charlotte
b.1828   Hurt
d.1901   Sitwell
          b.1827
          d.1907

PHILIP
AUGUSTUS
b.1830
d.1863

EDWARD = MARY Mangles (1)
BALDWIN   b.1831 d.1868
b.1833 = ELLEN Mary
d.1883   Nethercote (2)
          b.? d.1912

SUSAN
EMILY
b.1826
d.1842

ARCHIBALD
EMILIUS
b.1843
d.1871

MONTAGUE
b.1841
d.1842

FREDERICK
WILLIAM
GEORGE
b.1838
d.1839

ISLA
CAMPBELL
b. and d.
1837

SIR WILLIAM WAKE

MARGARET Ann Fricker
b.1825 d. 1866

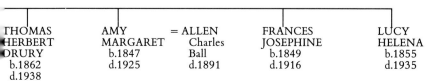

THOMAS
HERBERT
DRURY
b.1862
d.1938

AMY
MARGARET
b.1847
d.1925

= ALLEN
  Charles
  Ball
  d.1891

FRANCES
JOSEPHINE
b.1849
d.1916

LUCY
HELENA
b.1855
d.1935

FAMILY TREE XV

THE TWELFTH BARON

SIR HEREWALD CRAUFURD WA
12th Baronet, 1865
b.1852 d.1916

SIR HEREWARD WAKE = MARGARET 13th Baronet, 1916 Winifred (Daisy) b.1876 d.1963 Benson b.1892 d.1976	GODWIN RUPERT b.1879 d.1949	ST AUBYN BALDWIN b.1882 d.19	

FAMILY TREE XVI

THE THIRTEENTH BARON

SIR HEREWARD WA
13th Baronet, 1916
b.1876 m.1912 d.19(

SIR HEREWARD = JULIA
WAKE   Rosemary Lees
14th Baronet   b.1931 m.1952
b.1916

ROGER = OLWYN
b.1918   Wynne-Finch (1)
d.1988   b.1924 m. 1944
      = BELINDA
      Crossley (2)
      b.1928 m. 1985

FAMILY TREE XVII

THE FOURTEENTH BARON

SIR HEREWARD W.
14th Baronet, 1963
b.1916 m.1952

HEREWARD = Lady DOUNE
CHARLES   Mabel Ogilvy
b.1952   b.1953
m.1977

DIANA Julia = RODERIC
b.1955   John Fle
m.1979   b.1953

JOHN HEREWARD b.1978	Henry David b.1980	Thomas Mark b.1984 d.1985	Laura Katherine b.1986	Chloe Dorothy b.1989	Hermion Kirsty b.1989

SIR HEREWALD WAKE

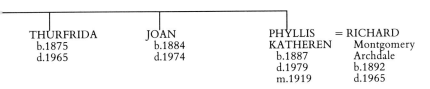

ATHERINE St Aubyn
b.1852 d.1944

THURFRIDA	JOAN	PHYLLIS	= RICHARD
b.1875	b.1884	KATHEREN	Montgomery
d.1965	d.1974	b.1887	Archdale
		d.1979	b.1892
		m.1919	d.1965

SIR HEREWARD WAKE

MARGARET Winifred (Daisy) Benson
b.1892 d.1976

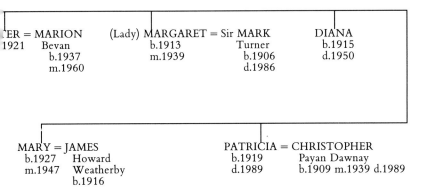

ER = MARION	(Lady) MARGARET = Sir MARK	DIANA
1921 Bevan	b.1913 Turner	b.1915
b.1937	m.1939 b.1906	d.1950
m.1960	d.1986	

MARY = JAMES	PATRICIA = CHRISTOPHER
b.1927 Howard	b.1919 Payan Dawnay
m.1947 Weatherby	d.1989 b.1909 m.1939 d.1989
b.1916	

SIR HEREWARD WAKE

JULIA Rosemary Lees
b.1931

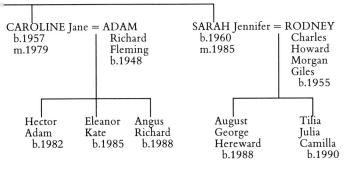

CAROLINE Jane = ADAM	SARAH Jennifer = RODNEY
b.1957 Richard	b.1960 Charles
m.1979 Fleming	m.1985 Howard
b.1948	Morgan
	Giles
	b.1955

Hector	Eleanor	Angus	August	Tilia
Adam	Kate	Richard	George	Julia
b.1982	b.1985	b.1988	Hereward	Camilla
			b.1988	b.1990

APPENDIX B
Maps of Courteenhall

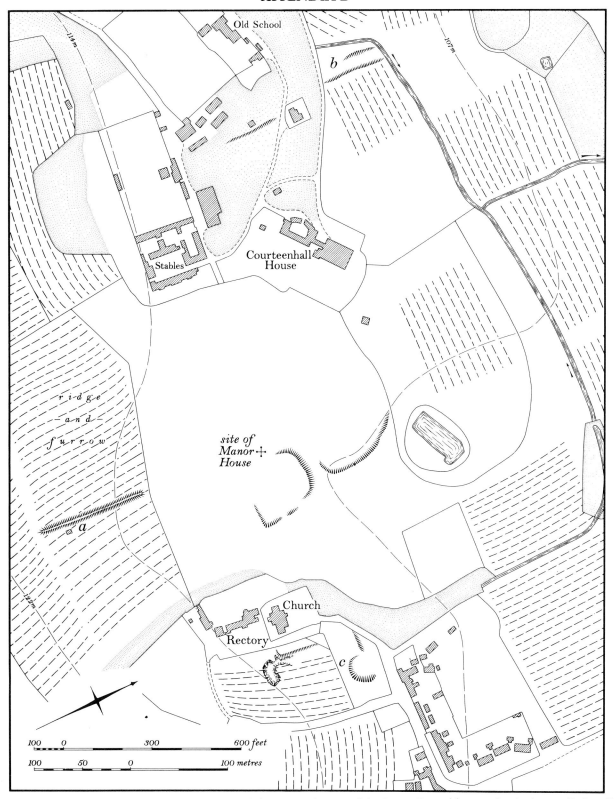

1. Map of Courteenhall, showing the ridge and furrow and parts of the lost village. (a) an embanked gravelled walk leading to the old Manor House, with a line of elm trees on either side forming an avenue; (b) represents a section of the roadway which led to Northampton; and (c) was the site of a farm and outbuildings

2. A plan of part of the Estate
of Sir William Wake,
8th baronet,
at Courteenhall,
5 December, 1766

A

PLAN of part of the Estate of Sr William Wake Bart at Courtenhall, Surveyd Decr 5th 1766 P Barker

Contents	A	R	P
House and Yards &c	1	1	30
Garden	0	3	33
Plantation	0	2	24
Orchard	2	3	08
Hungry Hill	28	1	21
Widow Churches House & Yard	0	0	27
Wm Robarts's Orchard	0	1	33
Pond Close	8	2	15
Huds Close	7	2	09
Billinghams Home Close	2	0	34
Becknights Close	1	2	06
Huds Home Close	2	0	15
Jno Evans & Willm Burmans Ho &c	0	1	21
Chas Billinghams House & Yards	0	2	03
Billinghams Home Close	1	2	00
Joseph Shaws House & Yards	0	1	30
Mr Shaws Stack Yard	1	0	05
Susan Causbys House & Yard	0	0	37
Widow Barss, Wm Churchs Fotterwell &c	0	0	20
James Tibsons House &c	0	0	08
Wm Pains House & Yards	1	1	21
Pains Home Close	2	1	38
Wm Westleys House & Do	0	0	34
Thos Hall & Jno Harris's Do	0	0	22
Jno Hancock & Wm Hilliars Do	0	0	21
Robt Robarts's Do	0	0	20
Wm Hasfords Do	0	0	30
Jno Hancocks Do	0	0	08
Chris Hilliars Do	0	0	06
Richd Burrages Do	0	0	08
Wm Cawdry Jno Clarks Do	0	0	36
Wm Rovans Do	0	2	35
Mr Nauxes Tightle	1	2	00
Brooks	11	3	37
Brooks Meadow	10	1	32
Phillips's Home Close	2	1	10
Do House & Yard	0	2	06
Robt Fotterwell's House & Do	0	1	30
Do His own Yard & Malting	0	1	25
Wm Gibbs's House & Yard	0	2	10
Jno Hylliars House	0	0	04
Will Buckers House &c	0	0	34
Mordants House & Yard	0	0	33
Little Close South of Do	1	0	00
Tenstile	11	2	29
Long piece	16	3	30
Stockings	15	3	00
Hardens Well	11	0	30
Sheep Walk	17	1	20
Little Sheep Walk	19	0	38
Roads &c	3	0	32
Total	181	3	18

	F	R	F
The Old Road from Robarts Barn at A to Mr Shaws House at B Contains in Length Width of Do about 30 Feet	1	32	0
The New intended Road begins at Mr Shaws House at B continues from thence to the Corner of Quinton Road at C and from thence to D it then turns West to Robarts Barn at A containing in Length	8	5	6
The New Road furthest by	6	13	6
The Church Path from Mr Shaws House at B to Robarts's Barn at A in Length	2	3	0

To NORTHAMPTON

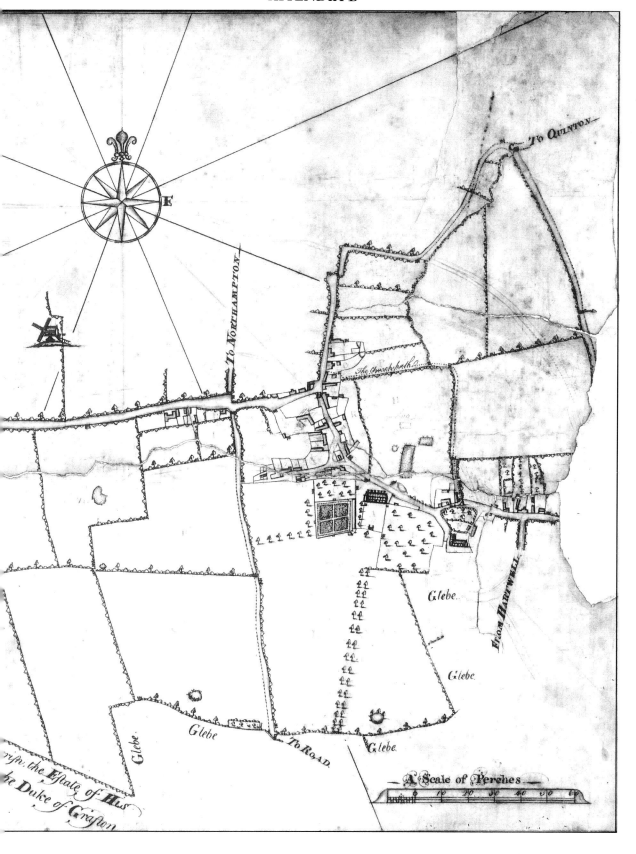

To QUINTON

To NORTHAMPTON

The church path

Glebe.

From HARTWELL

Glebe.

Glebe.

Glebe.

To ROAD.

Glebe.

Glebe.

...rso, the Estate of His
...he Duke of Grafton

A Scale of Perches

0   10   20   30   40   50   60

3. Courteenhall and neighbouring parishes as shown on a map of Northamptonshire drawn by Eyre and Jefferys 1779

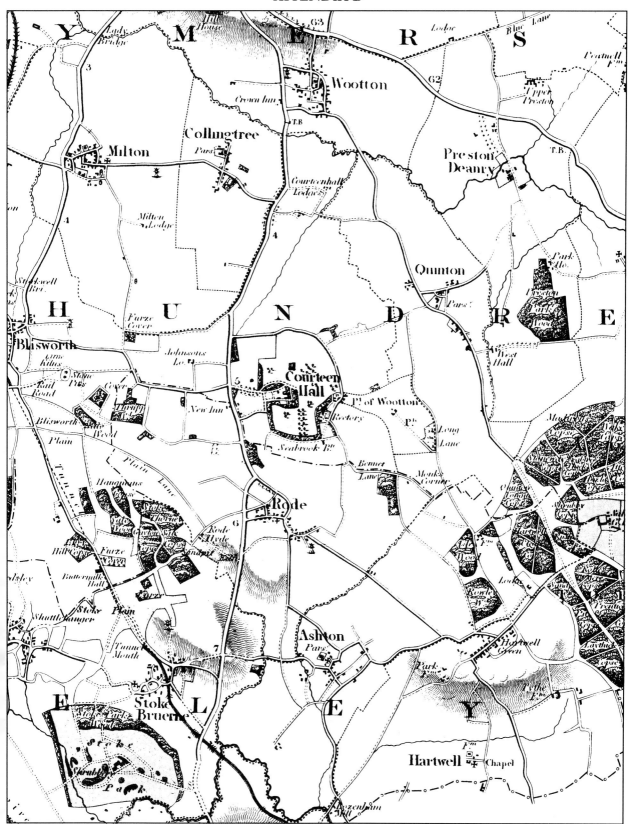

4. Courteenhall and neighbouring parishes as shown on a map of Northamptonshire drawn by A. Bryant 1827

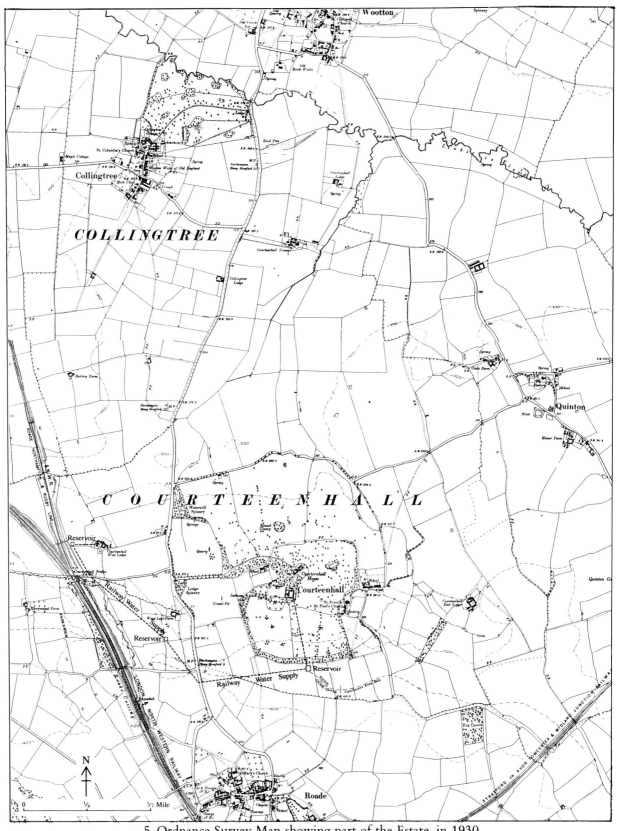

5. Ordnance Survey Map showing part of the Estate, in 1930

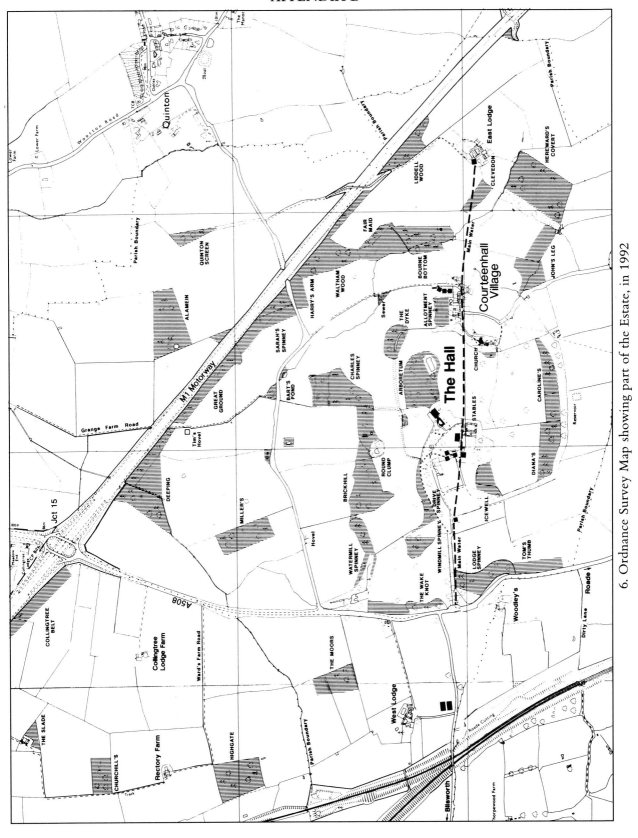

6. Ordnance Survey Map showing part of the Estate, in 1992

APPENDIX C
Repton's Red Book of Courteenhall, 1791-3

COURTEEN–HALL

in Northamptonshire

A Seat of

Sir William Wake Bart.

INTRODUCTION

Sir

In compliance with your obliging wishes, I have now the honour to deliver my opinion on the improvements at Courteen hall, together with the reasons on which that opinion is founded. It may be observed, that a considerable time has elapsed betwixt the date of my first visit at Courteen hall, and the completion of this small volume but having from time to time had opportunity of marking out much of the detail on the spot, the apparent delay has I trust been of no consequence, particularly as these kind of books serve less as a guide for the execution, than as a record of the improvements, and a justification of the principles on which they are conducted.

I have the honour to be
Sir Your most obedient
and obliged humble Servant

H. Repton

At Courteen hall March 23rd 1791

At Hare Street by Romford March 1793

APPENDIX C

CHARACTER

The agreement of parts to the whole, and a conformity of these parts to each other, is what constitutes Unity of Character, which is one of the first objects of good taste in every branch of the polite arts. It becomes therefore highly requisite to take such a comprehensive view of every design before the separate parts are carried into execution, that no incongruity may arise in adapting them to each other; I am led to this observation by an error in the stile, and perhaps the situation of the stables at Courteen-hall. It could never have been the intention to place so large and so magnificent a pile of building on this conspicuous and elevated spot, at the same time meaning, that it should be concealed by plantation; yet to display this whole edifice, and make it (as a stable doubtless ought to be) subordinate to the mansion, would have required a palace too large for any situation that accords with the true character of the place, which is that of an elegant, convenient, and very respectable family seat; possessing a degree of magnificence compatible with comfort, but not aiming at that which belongs rather to useless Ostentation.

SITUATION

The general face of the County of Northampton is certainly not picturesque, few hunting countries indeed are so, but I am convinced that this County owes its want of beauty to the bad habit of lopping trees, and ridging up the ground, more than to the shallow soil or natural shapes of the surface: whether the defect be natural or artificial, it is certain that in proportion as the unimproved parts of a County are less beautiful, there will be more pleasure to the proprietor and more credit to the Artist, if the environs of the house be judiciously improved. It is not only the duty of Landscape gardening to heighten and display those features of a place which are naturally beautiful, or to hide and soften those which are naturally otherwise, but he must also endeavour to counteract those deformities, which injudicious artificial management has in a manner naturalized to the spot; of this kind is that unsightly custom of ridging all the grass land in Northamptonshire, a custom which however excusable on a dead flat to drain the surface, can never be necessary in that beautiful shaped ground which I must call the park at Courteen-hall.

THE HOUSE

Having had the honour to be consulted with regard to the stile of house proper for Courteen hall, as well as the situation and aspect; it may not perhaps be inapplicable to this volume, to retrace those considerations which induced us to prefer that, which has been so elegantly designed and executed by my ingenious friend Mr. Saxon. Some palaces of very large dimensions have been built with corresponding wings, producing a magnificent effect of Symmetry; but unless the building be of such dimensions as to allow apartments in one of the wings, and a compleat set of offices in the other, it has ever been found by experience that no plan can be so inconvenient to a family as that which places the offices in two distinct buildings, separated by the body of the house.

APPENDIX C

There is always some danger of destroying the unity of design, by making a house with wings appear to be <u>three distinct</u> buildings, joined by a meagre line of connection; but even if the design be perfect, it requires a proper situation, such would have been the amphitheatre of plantation on the summit of the hill at A, on the map, [see illustration 47] if the aspect had been south, and if there had been a sufficient depth of wood to rise above the building, and form an ample background.

The mansion at Courteen hall being intended as a Family residence, and not built merely to please the eye, it was necessary to let the proper aspect take the lead of every other consideration: and south inclining to the east, is from experience found to be the most desirable of all aspects in England. This position of the house gives the greatest extent of Park-lawn in front of the principal apartments, and in proportion as the south front turns towards the east, that to the north will incline towards the west, which will shew that side of the house occasionally illuminated by the setting sun, and thus render it conspicuous from the turnpike road; which would seldom be the case while the house is in shadow. The crown of that knowl on which the house is situated, would not admit the addition of two wings, and absolutely required the kind of house with three fronts which has been adopted.

APPROACH

From the situation of Courteen hall, and the general state of the cross roads, it happens that only one approach can be made for coaches from the turnpike, yet there is a nearer line across the fields which may be used in summer, and as the place where this road would quit the turnpike is a spot from whence there is the best distant view of the whole park, it should be marked by some striking object to call the attention of travellers.

In the following sketch, I have merely hinted the kind of rude portico which might be added to a thatched cottage of any form that Mr. Saxon may suggest, but the design for such a cottage must be simple, lest it should assume too much the character of a

385

lodge, for this reason I conceived that the gate ought rather to be <u>dark green</u>, than <u>white</u>, especially as the intention is rather to direct the eye to distant objects, than to fix its attention on this as an entrance. The person who resides at this cottage would of course keep the gate locked, and give necessary information when the green road might be practicable.

The map will sufficiently explain the form of the plantation, and the course of the two roads, diverging immediately after passing the lodges.

These are represented in the preceding sketch from the design of Mr. Saxon. On so small a scale it is impossible to do justice to the architecture, but it serves to shew the effect which will be immediately produced by the additional plantation, in excluding the light from beneath the trees already growing near the spot, and this will make a sufficient background to the lodges.

The approach skirts along the plantation which serves to skreen the school house etc., and proceeds along a natural terrace with a fine view of lawn and distant country, till it bursts suddenly on the house, and tho' it is impossible to shew the house at a greater distance, yet as the road will pass along this interesting line of terrace with prospects to the north, it may perhaps be desirable to reserve the new and more appropriated scenery to the east and south to be seen from the apartments.

ENTRANCE LODGES

I have elsewhere* observed that "There are two reasons for marking the principal entrance to a park with some importance; the first, has a reference to those who visit the place, and may be considered with respect to the grounds, in the same light as a handsome vestibule or hall is to the other rooms in a house, they both have a preparitory effect. The second reason relates to the public, and where the mansion itself is not visible from the high road, I think a lodge of some kind should mark the distinction betwixt the approach to a Gentleman's place, and the residence of a farmer, in this case the necessity for making it ornamental, is the same with that for decorating the outside of the house itself."

As there would be no real advantage gained by extending the park to the hedge near the turnpike, so I am convinced that an entrance will be far more conspicuous, and produce a more striking effect, placed on the brow of the hill and backed by plantation, than it could have if placed near the two little clumps by the side of the turnpike, but to extend the idea of continued property, I must recommend a plantation at B. on the opposite side of the road, and if the fields C. and D. were grass, instead of arable, and planted in a better stile, it would do away with the present appearance that the road has of being made thro' the land of another person.

*The Hassells Bedfordshire I.Pym Esq.

VIEWS from the HOUSE

In looking towards the south, the Church is so near and so conspicuous an object, that its improvement ought not to be neglected, and as the present outline is blunt and unpleasing, I should advise that it be corrected by the aid of four well proportioned pinnacles, and which would give it a lightness not easily to be imagined.

The plantation A. which crowns the hill, is in its present form defective; it is one of those belts which give an air of confinement by the want of variety and intricacy in its outline, the eye darts along its whole extent without any object to arrest its attention, and a walk in such a plantation is apt to satiate by the first impression, that the whole of its course is pre-conceived; this may without difficulty be improved by bringing forward some additional depth of plantation, and perhaps by breaking thro' some part of the skreen to give variety to its outline, or even a pavilion in the bosom of its concave form; would tend to vary the present sameness which is certainly objectionable.

APPENDIX C

VIEW to the EAST

The ground falls so rapidly from the house towards the north and east, that very little of the lawn in this direction can be seen, and indeed it is one of those subjects which painting does not well represent, altho' I have attempted it in the following sketch: but the ground beyond the road and the hedge E.F. rises very boldly, and I think ought to be considered as part of the park in appearance, altho' it is not necessary that it should be so in reality; but the hedges should be removed, and the land converted into pasture, leaving the handsomest trees and thorns to stand single on the lawn. The brow of the hill which is now ragged and unsightly by some starved or lopped pollards, ought to be clothed by a plantation, and a simple building should be erected on this spot, to mark the continuance of ornamented ground, tho' in fact it might only be a shed for horses, or a hovel for granary, or perhaps a keepers house: but its outward form should be ornamental, and not bear the character of an appendage to a farm.

OF FARM BUILDINGS

I have already frequently* expressed my opinion on the incongruity of blending the farm with the park, as being two objects incompatible with each other: the one leads to beauty, the other to profit, and it is as absurd to expect dignity or importance from a corn field, a barn, or a farm house, as to look for elegance of furniture in the timber yard of a cabinet-maker: the materials of beauty indeed are there, but they are collected for the purposes of trade and profit, and till the fields become park, or till the timber becomes furniture, neither can be displayed as objects of taste: the same holds good with respect to the buildings belonging to each. If a farm house or even a barn be at such a distance, as not to be seen distinctly, or to be evidently <u>beyond</u> the ample range of the park, it may perhaps be a pleasing object, but if it be a building apparently standing <u>in the park</u>, it ought to be visibly appropriated to its situation; especially if it is a leading feature from the principal apartments of the Mansion, for this reason I propose by planting to hide more of the farm house on the hill, and to introduce in its stead a building of the kind I have mentioned. When an ornamental building can at the same time be made useful, it is certainly advisable, but I wish always to keep in view, that elegance, simplicity, congruity, and beauty are the immediate objects of my profession, and tho' they must occasionally be adapted to convenience and utility, yet they shrink from the sordid idea of yielding profit.

* Antony house, Cornwall, R.P. Carew Esqr., Shavington, Shropshire, Lord Visct. Killmorey, Widdiall hall, Herts., J.S. Ellis Esqr. etc. etc.

OF THE WATER etc.

I must reserve my decided opinion on the possibility of converting the small brook into an object of beauty, till I am more perfectly acquainted with the actual fall and levels of the ground, and I have been less attentive to this subject, first from the apparent difficulty of making one large piece of water without great expence, and secondly from the consideration that a sheet of water to the north or east of the house, is seldom cheerful or pleasing; because when the grass and trees are rendered most lively by the suns rays, the water takes a darker hue, and never glitters but with the sun beyond it.* I have however slightly marked on the map the shape of two ponds of different levels, which might be so blended by plantation as to appear one lake or large pool, but as the arrangement of plantations in this part of the ground must depend on the determination respecting the water, I have not marked any on the map, tho' I think a skreen to divide the park from the arable ground at G. or H. will certainly be advisable.

* This subject is more fully treated in Brocklesby, Lincolnshire, J. Anderson Pelham Esq.

THE FLOWER GARDEN

The following map [see illustration 49] will appear so whimsical at the first glance, that it may be necessary to support my opinion by an explanation, first observing, that the ichnographic representation of a garden furnishes no more idea of its effect, than a ground plan of a house does of its several fronts. The degree of symmetry and formality which pervaded the geometric stile of gardening seems to have left a total aversion to every thing that is formal or regular in gardens, but there are certain situations in which regularity is still necessary. A flower garden consisting of beds and parterres is too formal an object to occupy the principal view from the windows, yet in a pleasure ground it is always a desirable circumstance if properly secluded from the general scenery, and being so small that the eye surveys all its parts at once, symmetry becomes necessary, because a great degree of irregularity would have more the air of confusion and disorder than natural ease and elegance. This is nicely distinguished by Montesquieu on Taste. "Wherever Symmetry is useful to the soul and may assist her functions, it is agreeable to her; but wherever it is useless, it becomes distasteful, because it takes away variety. Therefore things that we see in succession ought to have variety, for our soul has no difficulty in seeing them; those on the contrary that we see at one glance ought to have symmetry. Thus at one glance we see the front of a building, a parterre, a temple, in such things there is always a symmetry, which pleases the soul by the facility it gives her of taking the whole object at once." Lord Kaimes in the Elements of Criticism also explains this subject "Nature indeed, in organized bodies comprehended under one view studies regularity; which for the same reason ought to be studied in <u>Architecture</u>: but in large objects, which cannot be surveyed but in parts and by succession, regularity and uniformity would be useless properties, because they cannot be discovered by the eye. Nature therefore in her large works, neglects these properties; and in copying Nature, the Artist ought to neglect them."

APPENDIX C

THE OFFICES

Unless a house be of that ancient collegiate form which allowed space for the offices in one or more sides of the quadrangle, I am of the opinion, that there is no necessity for the total concealment of the offices, which are an appendage not only of convenience but of magnificence, provided they are neither too mean for the Character of the mansion, nor too mighty to hold a subordinate place in the composition: on this principle the offices at Courteen hall are placed in a line from the house, to unite every object of convenience, forming a way under cover almost to the stables and kitchen garden, yet they may to a certain degree be concealed by a plantation, over which they will appear as an inferior part of the design, not unworthy the mansion to which they belong. The following sketch No. III will give some idea of the combined effect of the House and offices as seen on the north side. The drawing No. II was finished before the foundations of the new house were laid, and while the old house was yet standing; it serves to shew the effect the house will have, when seen together with the stables in keeping them subordinate, but this effect will be yet more powerful, if some part of the offices or perhaps a greenhouse be added to the Mansion, to make it appear less detached.

Notes and References

INTRODUCTION

1. Sir Hereward Wake to Joan Wake, 12 January 1959, Joan Wake Papers, Northamptonshire Record Office.

2. Joan Wake to Sir Hereward Wake, 16 January 1959, Northamptonshire Record Office, V219.

3. See Chapter 8, pp. 104ff.

4. Monson Papers, Mon 7/43/601, Lincolnshire Archives Office. Sanderson was Bishop of Lincoln, 1660–3.

5. J. C. Brooke, Somerset Herald, to Sir William Wake, eighth baronet, 1782, Northamptonshire Record Office, V219: and Sir William Wake to J.C. Brooke, September 1782, Brooke Papers, c.455, f.104, Bodleian Library, Oxford.

6. PINE, L.G. *They Came With The Conqueror* (1954), p.18.

7. MS Notes, 10 December 1883, Courteenhall Papers.

8. VAUGHAN, R. *Matthew Paris* (1958), pp.1–13.

9. STONE, L. and STONE, J.C.F. *An Open Elite? England, 1540–1880* (1984), p.237.

Chapter 1
BEGINNINGS: HEREWARD THE WAKE

1. TOUT, T.F. 'Hereward', in *Dictionary of National Biography* (1891), vol.26, p.692. Domesday Survey states that in Kesteven 'Hereward had not Asford's land in Barholm hundred on the day on which he fled'. FOSTER, C.W. and LONGLEY, T (eds.) *The Lincolnshire Domesday and the Lindsey Survey* (1924), Lincoln Record Society, vol.19, p.225.

2. There are many versions of the Hereward stories contained in various documents. Besides the *Anglo-Saxon Chronicle*, they include the Anglo-Norman verse chronicler, Geoffrey Gaimar's, *L'Estoire des Engleis; De Gestis Herewardi Saxonis* (modern version in English, BEVIS, T.A., 1981), with a Preface by Sir Hereward Wake; Ingulf's *Historia Croylandensis*, supposedly twelfth century but a later medieval forgery; and the fourteenth century *Chronicon Petroburgense*.

3. WHITELOCK, D. (ed.) *The Anglo-Saxon Chronicle. A Revised Translation* (1961), entry for 1070, p.151.

4. KINGSLEY, C. *Hereward the Wake* (1866), vol.ii, pp.148, 152.

5. KEEN, M. *The Outlaws of Medieval Legend* (1961), pp.24–5.

6. PLATTS, G. *Land and People in Medieval Lincolnshire* (1985), p.261.

7. Essay XIV, pp.91–120.

8. For more details, see FERRAND, M. *Charles Kingsley* (1937), p.173.

9. KINGSLEY, op.cit., vol.i, p.iv.

10. For descriptions of Barnack at this time, see CHITTY, S. *The Beast and the Monk. A Life of Charles Kingsley* (1974), pp.26–33, and COLLOMS, B. *Charles Kingsley: the lion of Eversley* (1975), pp.22–5.

11. KINGSLEY, op.cit., vol.i, pp.16–17.

12. KINGSLEY, F.E. (ed.) *Charles Kingsley, His Letters and Memoirs of his Life* (1877), vol.i, p.182.

13. Sir Herewald Wake to editor of *The World*, 5 January 1895 (draft), Courteenhall Papers.

14. See NORMAN, E. *The Victorian Christian Socialists* (1987), pp.35–57.

15. Cameo VIII, 'The Camp of Refuge'. vol.i, pp.50–7.

16. Sir Herewald Wake to editor of *The World*, 5 January 1895 (draft), Courteenhall Papers.

17. W.W. Skeat to Sir Herewald Wake, 26 November 1907, ibid.

18. See FREEMAN, E.A. *The History of the Norman Conquest in England* (1875), vol.iv, Appendix. 'The legend of Hereward', pp.826–33. In 1867 Freeman had attacked Kingsley's lectures publicly, stating that if 'Mr. Kingsley has any regard for his own reputation, he will leave history and philology to some of the historical and philological scholars of which Cambridge certainly has no lack'. Quoted in KADISH, A. 'Scholarly Exclusiveness and the Foundation of the *English Historical Review*', *Historical Research*, vol.61, no.145, 1988, p.181. The two men later became friends.

19. Sir Herewald Wake, 'Hereward the Wake and his descendants', n.d., Courteenhall Papers.

20. Chapter 10, 'Genealogical Outline', pp.80–98.

21. Sir Herewald Wake to W.W. Skeat, 6 December 1907, Courteenhall Papers.

22. See, for example, SIR IAIN MONCREIFFE OF THAT ILK, 'Hereward the Wake', *The Genealogists' Magazine*, vol.15, no.10, 1967, pp.1–10.

Chapter 2

THE EARLY WAKES:
FROM NORMANDY TO NORTHAMPTONSHIRE

1. The charter of Baldwin fitzGilbert is reproduced in STENTON, F.M. (ed.) *Facsimiles of Early Charters from Northamptonshire Collections*, Northamptonshire Record Society (1930), vol.4, p.3.

2. Ranulf's charters are printed in BARRACLOUGH, G. (ed.) *The Charters of the Anglo-Norman Earls of Chester, c.1071–1237*, Record Society of Lancashire and Cheshire, 1988.

3. KING, E. 'The Origins of the Wake Family: The Early History of the Barony of Bourne in Lincolnshire', *Northamptonshire Past and Present*, vol.5, no.3, 1975, p.173.

4. See KENNEDY, P.A. 'A Gentleman's Home in the Reign of Henry VII', *Northamptonshire Past and Present*, vol.2, no.1, 1954, p.17.

5. For an account of this Crusade, see RUNCIMAN, S. *A History of the Crusades* (1954), vol.3, pp.217–19.

6. PARIS, M. *Historia Anglorum* (ed. MADDEN, SIR F. 1866) vol.2, 1189–1245, p.459, lists Hugh Wake amongst the English nobles who had died.

7. The Wakes remained Lords of the Manor of Chesterfield until the fifteenth century. Hugh's son, Baldwin, granted an important charter to the borough, guaranteeing the burgesses freedoms and privileges. RIDEN, P. and BLAIR, J. (eds.) *History of Chesterfield* (1980). vol.5, p.19.

8. See VICTORIA COUNTY HISTORY *Buckinghamshire* (1927), vol.4, p.319. The Wakes held the manor until 1355, when it was given to Robert Mordaunt of Turvey and his wife. ANON. *Some Account of Clifton Reynes in the County of Buckinghamshire* (1821,

reprinted 1883), pp.14–16. There is a fragment of a table tomb in St. Mary the Virgin, Clifton Reynes, which bears the Wake arms.

9. For fuller details, see HUDLESTON, C.R. and BOUMPHREY, R.S. *Cumberland Families and their Heraldry* (1978), pp.353–4.

10. COLLINGWOOD, R.G. 'Liddel Strength', *Transactions of the Cumberland and Westmorland Antiquarian Society,* vol.26, 1926, p.390.

11. CURWEN, J.F. 'Liddel Mote', *Transactions of the Cumberland and Westmorland Antiquarian Society*. vol.10, 1910, p.93. Alexander II received £200 of land in Cumberland in exchange.

12. Cal. Doc. Scot., vol.2, p.63.

13. TREHARNE, R.F. 'The Battle of Northampton, 5th April 1264', *Northamptonshire Past and Present*, vol.2, no.2, 1955, pp.26–7.

14. VICTORIA COUNTY HISTORY *Northamptonshire* (1937), vol.4, p.224.

15. A Wake link with this area continued as may be gathered from a surviving petition from the inhabitants of Thaxted dated 2 February 1598 against John Wake, one of the high constables of the hundred of Dunmow. Apparently, he was a very contentious man, refusing to pay his proportion of the assessment relating to his high constableship, favouring his friends by letting them go free and oppressing those neighbours with whom he was displeased. The petition was allowed. MS of George Lowndes, formerly at Barrington Hall, Essex.

16. Between the third and fourth piers of the south nave. See plan in WEIR, Y.E. *A Guide to the Heraldry in York Minster* (1986), pp.23 and 28.

17. FRYDE, N. *The Tyranny and Fall of Edward II, 1321–1326* (1979), pp.198–200.

18. Even in the days of his greatest prosperity, Thomas had to borrow money, particularly from his Hull neighbours, the mercantile house of Pole. TOUT, T.F. 'Thomas Wake', in *Dictionary of National Biography* (1899), vol.58, p.443.

19. WHITEHOUSE, J. *A Short History of Cottingham* (1974), p.10; PAGE, F.G. *The Church of St. Mary the Virgin, Cottingham* (1951), p.14.

20. MELLOWS, W.T. (ed.) *Henry of Pytchley's Book of Fees* (1923), Northamptonshire Record Society, vol.2, p.82.

21. KIRBY, J.L. *Henry IV of England* (1970), p.14.

22. Blanche Wake's funeral tablet was discovered during demolition work in Stamford High Street in 1968. See *Rutland and Stamford Mercury*, 28 October 1968, and an account of the discovery itself, L. Tebbutt to Joan Wake, 17 May 1968, Joan Wake Papers.

23. GOLLANCZ, M. (ed.) *Rolls of Northamptonshire Sessions of the Peace* (1940), Northamptonshire Record Society, vol.11, p.xxv. He was also Northamptonshire Keeper of the Peace in 1307.

24. See MADDICOTT, J.R. *Thomas of Lancaster, 1307–1322* (1970), pp.121–30.

25. Notes by Major-General Sir Hereward Wake, thirteenth baronet, 'Wake Coat of Arms', c.1950, Courteenhall Papers. Illustrations of heraldic knots, including the Wake Knot, are contained in BROOKE-LITTLE, J.P. (ed.) *Boutell's Heraldry* (1983 edition), pp.169–70.

26. James A. Frere, Bluemantle, to Major-General Sir Hereward Wake, thirteenth baronet, 28 February 1951, Courteenhall Papers.

27. Described in METCALFE, W.C. (ed.) *The Visitations of Northamptonshire made in 1564 and 1618–19* (1887), p.52.

28. BRIDGES, J. *The History and Antiquities of Northamptonshire* (1791), vol.1, p.334. The old Manor House stood on the north side of the High Street, not far from the church. It had a fine Tudor door and windows, mullioned and square hooded. It was demolished at the end of the nineteenth century, having fallen into disrepair. CLINCH, M.C. *The Story of Blisworth* (1939), p.21.

29. SUTHERLAND, D.W. *The Eyre of Northamptonshire, 3–4 Edward III, A.D. 1329–1330* (1983), vol.1, p.xix.

30. Ibid, p.165.

31. Ibid, p.179.

32. In August 1330, Thomas Wake also claimed the constableship of Northampton Castle on the grounds that the office had always belonged to his predecessors. The jurors found in his favour and on 17 November, William Pillaston, the then Constable, was ordered to surrender the Castle, together 'with his armour, vitals etc. found therein' to Thomas and his successors. See SERJEANTSON, REVD. R.M. 'The Castle of Northampton', *Journal of the Northamptonshire Natural History Society and Field Club,* vol.14, 1907, p.112.

33. Sir Thomas sold all his rights in the manor and advowson of Cransley to a London merchant, John Pyel, on 29 March 1350. VICTORIA COUNTY HISTORY *North-amptonshire* (1937), vol.4, p.164.

34. WAKE, JOAN 'The Justices of the Peace, 1361–1961', *Northamptonshire Past and Present*, vol.3, no.2, 1961, p.71.

35. See the account in SCOFIELD, C.L. *The Life and Reign of Edward the Fourth* (1923), vol.1, pp.87–9.

36. The available evidence is set out in ROSS, C. *Richard III* (1981), Chapter 5, 'The Fate of Edward IV's Sons', pp.96–104.

37. GAIRDNER, J. 'William Catesby', in *Dictionary of National Biography* (1887), vol.9, pp.1193–4. His final wish, to be buried in his

own village, was granted. The very fine double canopied brass of William and his wife Margaret is within the altar rails of the church. See DAVIES, L. and GRAY, J.B. *Ashby St. Ledgers, Northamptonshire. A Visitors Guide*, n.d.

38. OWEN EVANS, H.F. 'Blisworth, Northamptonshire', *Transactions of the Monumental Brass Society*, vol.9, no.9, 1961, pp.489–92.

39. BARRON, O. (ed.) VICTORIA COUNTY HISTORY *Northamptonshire Families*, 'The Wakes of Blisworth and Deeping' (1906), p.324.

40. For the list of Wake office-holders see PETTIT, P.A.J. *The Royal Forests of Northamptonshire* (1968) Northamptonshire Record Society, vol.23, p.21n.

41. MS Top. Northants c.36. A survey of royal Forests in Nottinghamshire and Rutland, 1564. pp.357ff, Bodleian Library, Oxford.

42. BL Add. MS.32091.

43. Major-General Sir Hereward Wake researched this point and believed that 'the present house on Salcey Lawn, Hartwell, occupies the site of the old Wake mansion of the fifteenth century', MS Notes, Courteenhall Papers.

44. PRO L.R. 9/15/565.

45. WAKE, JOAN. 'Two Justices Fall Out', *Northamptonshire Past and Present*, vol.1, no.5, 1952, pp.1–9.

Chapter 3

JOAN, THE FAIR MAID OF KENT

1. Joan is supposed to have acted as his godmother, although she was only two years of age. *Notes and Queries*, 7th series, vol.v, Jan-June 1888, pp.149, 238.

2. LONGMAN, W., *The History of the Life and Times of Edward the Third* (1869), vol.i, p.33.

3. An informal exchange of marriage vows before witnesses was considered by the Church to be legally binding.

4. According to Holand's petition to Pope Clement VI in May 1347, he maintained that

he had married Joan 'more than eight years ago', i.e. when she was about twelve. GIBBS, V., DOUBLEDAY, H.A. and LORD HOWARD DE WALDEN, *The Complete Peerage* (1929), vol.7, p.151.

5. GALWAY, M. 'Joan of Kent and the Order of the Garter', *University of Birmingham Historical Journal*, vol.1, 1947, pp.34–5.

6. CORYN, M. *The Black Prince*, (1934), p.185.

7. For fuller details, see DUNN-

PATTISON, R.P. *The Black Prince* (1910), pp.188–9.

8. His earlier life is described in EMERSON, B. *The Black Prince* (1976), p.154.

9. PACKE, M. *King Edward III*, (ed. SEAMAN, L.C.B., 1983), p.114.

10. HARVEY, J. *The Black Prince and his Age* (1976), p.103.

11. BARBER, R. *Edward Prince of Wales and Aquitaine* (1978), p.174.

12. Joan is reputed to have been responsible for the introduction into this country of the Gascoigne or Gaskin cherry, which is still grown in the Kent orchards. WEBBER, R. *The Peasants Revolt* (1980), p.34.

13. Froissart's *Chronicles*, although a very useful secondary source for this period, are often historically inaccurate and must be treated with caution. See BARBER, R. 'Jean Froissart and Edward the Black Prince', in PALMER, J.J.N. (ed.), *Froissart: Historian* (1981), p.35.

14. POPE, M.K. and LODGE, E.C.(eds.), *Life of the Black Prince by the Herald of Sir John Chandos* (1910), pp.152–3. The name of the chronicler is unknown, but it is likely that the work was commissioned by Richard II. TYSON, D.B. *La Vie du Prince Noir by Chandos Herald* (1975), p.33.

15. Such letters from commanders in the field were circulated quite widely and provide evidence of a simple propaganda organization at Edward III's court. See PRINCE, A.E. 'A Letter of Edward the Black Prince describing the Battle of Nájera in 1367', *English Historical Review*, vol.41, 1926, pp.415–17.

16. RUSSELL, P.E. *The English Intervention in Spain and Portugal in the Time of Edward III and Richard II* (1955), pp.84–107.

17. See SHERBORNE, J.W. 'The Battle of La Rochelle and the War at Sea, 1372–5', *Bulletin of the Institute of Historical Research*, vol.42, 1969, p.26.

18. BARBER, op.cit, p.228.

19. HOLMES, H. *The Good Parliament* (1975), p.106.

20. A full version of the will is given in HARVEY, op.cit, pp.160–5.

21. *Life of the Black Prince by the Herald of Sir Chandos*, op.cit, p.170.

22. ARMITAGE-SMITH, S. *John of Gaunt* (1904), p.291.

23. EVANS, J. 'The Wilton Diptych Reconsidered', *Archaeological Journal*, vol.105, 1950, pp.3–4.

24. See SENIOR, M. *The Life and Times of Richard II* (1981), pp.62–85, for a brief account of the uprising.

25. It has been suggested that Joan was the strategist behind this move. KRIEHN, G. 'Studies in the Social Revolt in 1381', *American Historical Review*, vol.7, 1901–2, p.275.

26. Nothing now remains of her tomb, but as recently as 1890, the mummified remains of a woman were discovered in a garden at Stamford, on the site of the Black Friars monastery adjoining the Grey Friars buildings. A piece of parchment was found in cerecloth wrappings (waxed cloth used as waterproof covering), bearing a black letter inscription 'Johan'. The body may very likely have been moved at some time to prevent desecration and may well have been Joan's. Unfortunately, the local authority would not permit the burial of the remains in a local cemetery, and they were re-buried in a field outside the town without marking the spot.

27. A later fifteenth century chronicler attributes to Joan a prophecy of Richard's downfall: 'At thy coronation, my son, I rejoiced that it had fallen to my lot to be the mother of an anointed King; but now I grieve, for I forsee the fall which threatens thee, the work of accursed flatterers'. ADAM OF USK. *Chronicon, A.D.1377–1421* (ed. THOMPSON, E.M., 1904), p.143. Richard was deposed on 30 September 1399 and murdered at Pontefract Castle on 14 February 1400.

28. WORKMAN, H.B. *John Wyclif, A Study of the English Medieval Church* (1926), vol.1, p.290.

29. When Wyclif was brought before an ecclesiastic court at Lambeth in spring 1378, it was Joan's intervention which enabled him to escape with only a reprimand. McKISACK, M. *The Fourteenth Century* (1959), p.512.

Chapter 4

MIXED FORTUNES

1. VICTORIA COUNTY HISTORY *Northamptonshire* (1902), vol.1, pp.288–9.

2. Ibid.

3. GOVER, J.E.B., MAWER, E. and STENTON, F.M. *The Place-Names of Northamptonshire*, English Place-Name Society (1933), vol.10, p.146.

4. Ibid; though the Northamptonshire pollbook of 1748 records the name as 'Courtenhall'.

5. ROYAL COMMISSION ON HISTORIC MONUMENTS (ENGLAND). *An Inventory of Archaeological Sites in South-West Northamptonshire* (1982), p.38.

6. PEVSNER, N. *Northamptonshire* (1973, second edition), p.165.

7. E. Clive Rouse to Sir Hereward Wake, 3 September 1969. Courteenhall Papers.

8. CALENDAR OF INQUISTIONS POST MORTEM (Cal. Inq. P.M.) No.69 2 Edw. I.

9. Cal. Inq. P.M. No.602 9 Edw. II.

10. Cal. Inq. P.M. No.573 19 Edw. III and No.173 23 Edw. III.

11. Cal. Inq. P.M. No.752 19 Hen. VII.

12. PLAYFAIR, W. *British Family Antiquity*, (1809), vol.3 p.873.

13. WAKE, J. 'Courteenhall A Hundred Years Ago'. Lecture, 25 January 1940, p.4, Northamptonshire Record Office, Joan Wake Papers.

14. Quoted in BARRON, O. *Northamptonshire Families* (1906), p.327.

15. Bridges noted that the brasses were missing when he visited the church early in the eighteenth century and that they were probably destroyed during the Reformation.

16. See *The Pedigree Register*, June 1908, p.137, and Sir Hereward's MS note, Courteenhall Papers.

17. A deed of assignment dated 20 March 1627 relating to lands at Hartwell names 'Sibill Owseley of Hartwell, widow'. She continued to live there after her husband's death. Dayrell Papers, Buckinghamshire Record Office, D22/4/1.

18. Castell was Rector at Courteenhall from 1627 until his death in 1645. He presented a petition to Parliament in 1641 for the propagating of the Gospel in America and the West Indies and for the settlement of plantations there.

19. Pedigree of Ouseley family, Kyre Park MSS, Shropshire Record Office, 1878/8.

20. Much of the above information on the Ouseley family is based on the researches of P.I. King.

21. KENYON, R.L.L. 'Manor of Sandford and Woolston'. *Transactions of the Shropshire Archaeological and Natural History Society* 1904, vol.4, 3rd series, p.309.

22. COBBETT'S PARLIAMENTARY HISTORY OF ENGLAND (1808), vol.3, 1642–1660, p.1487.

23. VICTORIA COUNTY HISTORY *Shropshire* (1979), vol.3, p.264.

24. HENNING, B.D. (ed.) *The House of Commons, 1660–1690* (1983), vol.2, p.664.

25. TUCKER, N.R.F. *Denbighshire Officers in the Civil War*, (1964), p.76.

26. MYDDELTON, W.M. (ed.) *Chirk Castle Accounts, AD 1605–1666* (1908), p.150. Reprinted as 'A Visit to Courteenhall', *Northamptonshire Past and Present*, vol.4, no.4, 1969, p.245.

27. JAMES, R.R. 'Berwick Almshouses: Will of Sir Samuel Jones, Knight, Founder 1673', *Transactions of the Shropshire Archaeological and Natural History Society*, vol. 8, 4th series, 1921, pp.117–19.

28. TATE, W.E. 'Inclosure Movements in Northamptonshire', *Northamptonshire Past and Present*, vol.1, no.2, 1949, p.27.

29. LEONARD, E.M. 'The Inclosure of Common Fields in the Seventeenth Century', *Transactions of Royal Historical Society*, 1905, vol. 19, pp.118–20.

30. Agreement reached between Reverend William Ponder and Sir Samuel Jones for an exchange of land subsequent to an

Inclosure at Courteenhall, 10 January 1650. Discovered by Joan Wake in Courteenhall Church chest c.1970, Joan Wake Papers, and Northamptonshire Record Office, 86P/32.

31. C.8 Chancery Proc. Mitf. 148/49, 29 January 1661.

32. Ibid., 15 May 1662.

33. PEVSNER, N. *Shropshire* (1958), pp. 73–4.

34. Stanton, who had an extensive practice, was apparently prepared to adjust his designs to the taste of his patrons. WHINNEY, M.D. *Sculpture in Britain, 1530–1830* (1964, revised edition, ed. PHYSIC, J., 1988), pp.135–6.

35. VICTORIA COUNTY HISTORY *Somerset* (1978), vol.4, p.154.

36. HARBIN, S.W.B. 'Members of Parliament for the County of Somerset', *Proceedings of the Somersetshire Archaeological and Natural History Society*, (1939), p.7.

37. COLLINSON, J. *History of Antiquities of the County of Somerset* (1791), vol.3, p.119.

38. GREEN, E. 'The Descent of the Manor of Clevedon', *Proceedings of the Somersetshire Archaeological and Natural History Society*, vol.27, 1881, Part 1, p.4.

39. OSWALD, A. 'Clevedon Court, Somerset – I', *Country Life*, 30 June 1955, p.1672.

40. COOKE, R. 'Clevedon Court', in *West Country Houses* (1957), p.23.

41. ELTON, SIR A. and M.A.E. *Clevedon Court* (1990, tenth edition), p.10.

42. I am grateful to Lady Elton, FSA, for this information, which is based on an examination of the gableheads during the course of recent renovation and restoration.

43. For a photograph of a small chimney of the Great Hall which was formerly visible, see Plate XLC in WOOD, M. *The English Medieval House*, (1965), p.257.

44. ELTON, SIR A.H. 'Clevedon Court', *Proceedings of the Somersetshire Archaeological and Natural History Society*, vol.27, 1881, Part II, p.8.

45. GREEN, E. *Portbury Priory* (1905), p.7.

46. Sir J. Digby to Sir T. Edmonds, 11 May 1611, Madrid. 'The bearer of this, Mr. Wake, is my brother-in-law, married my sister.' Sherborne Castle Papers, Dorset.

47. PETERSSON, R.T. *Sir Kenelm Digby* (1956), p.31.

48. CALENDAR OF STATE PAPERS. Domestic, 1625–1649, Addenda, pp.395–6.

49. PRO C99/82/5; C99/82/10–11, and C99/82/15 no.174.

50. THE COMPLETE PEERAGE ed. GIBBS, V.C. (1912), vol.2, p.320.

51. Clevedon Court, Private and Estate MSS, Deeds 1501–1666, Somerset Record Office, DD/EN/102 S/1598.

52. GREEN, E. 'The Descent of the Manor of Clevedon', *Proceedings of the Somersetshire Archaeological and Natural History Society*, vol.27, 1881, Part I, p.26.

53. BARRON, op.cit., p.327.

54. SERJEANTSON, REVD. R.M. *A History of the Hospital of St. John in Northampton* (1913), p.58.

55. For full details of the Grand Remonstrance and subsequent events, see DAVIES, G. *The Early Stuarts, 1603–1660* (1959). pp.118–23

56. CALENDAR OF STATE PAPERS. Domestic, Charles I, 1641–3, 1 December 1641, p.186.

57. CLARENDON, EARL OF, *The History of the Rebellion*, (1702–4, ed. MACKAY, W.D., 1888), vol.2, p.223.

58. HOUSE OF LORDS, Calendar, 1642, 34 and 35, Journal, vol.5, p.179ff.

59. Ibid., p.209.

60. Document in the possession of the Duke of Somerset, Maiden Bradley, Wiltshire.

61. MORRAH, P. *Prince Rupert of the Rhine* (1976), pp.165–6.

62. GARDINER, S.R. *History of the Great Civil War 1642–49* (1889), vol.2, p.439.

63. The names of only five children are known.

64. CALENDAR OF STATE PAPERS. Domestic, Charles II, 1660–1, August 1660, p.240.

Chapter 5

HOW THE WAKES CAME TO COURTEENHALL

1. RIGG, J.M. 'Sir Robert Drury', in *Dictionary of National Biography* (1888), vol.16, pp.57–8. Sir Robert, elected Speaker on 17 October 1495, held the office for one year only. W.S. Morrison, Speaker of the House of Commons, to Sir Hereward Wake, 28 June 1954, Northamptonshire Record Office, V219.

2. BALD, R.C. *Donne and the Drurys* (1959), p.104.

3. WILLIAMS, N. 'The Risings in Norfolk 1569 and 1570', *Norfolk Archaeology*, vol.32, 1961, pp.77–8.

4. Lord Burghley's full account of the execution of Mary Queen of Scots, mentioning Sir Dru's presence, is reproduced in CAMPLING, A. *The History of the family of Drury* (1937), pp.82–4.

5. PALMER, C.J. 'Remarks on the Monastery of the Dominican Friars at Great Yarmouth', *Norfolk Archaeology*, vol.3, 1852, p.386.

6. BARRETT-LENNARD, T. 'Some Account of the Manor or Castle of Horsford', *Norfolk Archaeology*, vol.15, 1904, p.282.

7. See deed between Dru Drury and Roger Drury of Rollesby, Norfolk, being a special livery granted to Sir Dru Drury, Knight. Lands, tenements etc. in Rollesby, dated 1608. Drurys of Riddlesworth Papers, Suffolk Record Office, E2/3.

8. BLOMFIELD, F. *An Essay Towards the Topographical History of the County of Norfolk* (1805), vol.1, p.278.

9. KETTON-CREMER, R.W. *Norfolk in the Civil War* (1969), p.302.

10. CAMPLING, A. op.cit., p.86.

11. Will of Charles Wake, 30 December 1708, Northamptonshire Wills, 5th series, Northamptonshire Record Office, f.232.

12. BARRON, O. *Northamptonshire Families* (1906), p.330.

13. CHAPMAN, H.F. *St. Mary's Deanery Church, Bocking, Essex* (1954), p.4; and HOFFMAN, A. *Bocking Deanery. The Story* (1976), p.78.

14. Courteenhall Papers.

15. The back of the manor house bears the date 1683. PEVSNER, N. *Oxfordshire* (1974), p.609.

16. VICTORIA COUNTY HISTORY *Oxfordshire* (1959), vol.7, p.139.

17. Revd. B. McClellan to Sir Hereward Wake, 24 May 1985, Courteenhall Papers.

18. STONE, L. and STONE, J.C.F. *An Open Elite? England, 1540–1880* (1984), p.133.

19. JAMES, R.R. 'Berwick Almshouses: Will of Sir Samuel Jones, Knight, Founder 1673', *Transactions of the Shropshire Archaeological and Natural History Society*, vol. 8, 4th series, 1921, pp.110–11.

20. DEAN, D. *Waltham Abbey Church, Essex* (1984), p.1.

21. See illustrations in HIGGS, E. *Waltham Abbey* (1979), pp.3 and 5.

22. 'Extracts of severall Patents in King Henry the Eighth and Edward the Sixth Reigns to Sir Anthony Denny and after to Jan Joane Denny of the Monastery of Waltham at Waltham Holy Cross, 1652', Essex Record Office, D/D Jg. B41.

23. BASCOMBE, K.N. 'Sir Anthony Denny' and 'Sir Edward Denny, Earl of Norwich', in DEAN, D. (ed.) *The Worthies of Waltham* (1978), vol.2, pp.1–2 and 17–20.

24. Illustrated in 'Tudor Panels from Waltham', *Country Life*, 17 July 1909, pp.97–8. See also CLIFFORD-SMITH, H. *The Waltham Abbey Room*. Victoria and Albert Department of Woodwork (1924), pp.9–13.

25. HUGGINS, P.J. 'Waltham Abbey Monastic site and prehistoric evidence, 1953–1967', with documentary survey by K.N. Bascombe. *Transactions of the Essex Archaeological Society*, vol.2, 1970, p.217.

26. MUSTY, A.E.S. 'Exploratory Excavations within Monastic Precinct, Waltham Abbey, 1972', with documentary survey, by K.N. Bascombe. *Essex Archaeology and History*, vol.10, 1978, p.131.

27. VICTORIA COUNTY HISTORY *Essex* (1966), vol.5, pp.142 and 158.

28. By an agreement of 24 February 1876 the Corporation had purchased from Sir Herewald 768 acres of waste within the manor of Waltham Holy Cross. Final Report of the Epping Forest Commissioners, 1 March 1877. P.P.1877, xxvi, p.14.

29. LYSONS, D. *The Environs of London* (1795), vol.2, p.285.

30. According to the *Dictionary of National Biography*, Uvedale's opponents also made the further curious charge against him of having obtained an appointment as an actor and comedian at the Theatre Royal Drury Lane to protect himself from the execution of a writ. BOULGER, G.S. 'Robert Uvedale', in *Dictionary of National Biography* (1899), vol.58, pp.76–7.

31. FORD, E. and HODSON, G.H. *A History of Enfield* (1873), p.201.

32. FARMER, J. *The History of the ancient town, and once famous abbey, of Waltham* (1735), pp.159–60.

33. The House was described in 1718 as being built on the site of the Abbot's and Convent's Lodgings, 'tho' the buildings are so altered, that there is little appearance of that Antiquity'. WILLIS, B. *A History of the mitred parliamentary Abbies, and Conventual Cathedral Churches* (1718), vol.1, p.192.

34. These measurements were confirmed by crop-marks seen and plotted during the dry summer of 1984. Dr K.N. Bascombe to the author, 21 November 1988.

35. A more realistic though flattering illustration of the House is to be found in ANON. *A New and Complete History of Essex by A Gentleman* (1771), vol.4.

36. FARMER, op.cit., pp.160–1.

37. Quoted in HUGGINS, op.cit., p.219.

38. FARMER, op.cit., p.27. See also photograph in CLEALL, A. *Waltham Abbey Church Guide* (1948, second edition), p.19.

39. MS. Top. gen. e.18 f., 113, Bodleian Library, Oxford.

40. 'W.W.' *Middlesex and Hertfordshire Notes and Queries*, vol.4, 1898, p.43.

41. See, for example WRIGHT, T. *The History and Topography of the County of Essex*, (1835), vol.2, p.452.

42. D/P 75/11/4, Essex Record Office. As late as April 1788, the rating book describes the house as Abbey House. Subsequent entries mention rating only for the 'Abbey Land'. Dr K. Bascombe to author, 19 February and 12 May 1990.

43. A part of the Abbey Gardens was transferred to the parish church for use as a burial ground on 21 Jan 1814 by Sir William Wake, ninth baronet, and his son, Charles. They each received a sum of ten shillings for the transaction. WINTERS, W. *The History of the Ancient Parish of Waltham Abbey or Holy Cross* (1888), pp.164–7.

44. See BAILEY, B. *English Manor Houses* (1983), pp.172–3.

45. VICTORIA COUNTY HISTORY *Buckinghamshire* (1927), vol.4, p.353.

46. PEVSNER, N. *Northamptonshire* (1961), p.166. The architectural tablet is of an extremely high standard both in design and execution. It is the work of William Cox I (1717–93) of Northampton. See LEWIS, S.M. ' A Family of Stone-Carvers: the Coxes of Northamptonshire'. *Northamptonshire Past and Present*, vol.1, no.6, 1953, p.36.

Chapter 6
SIR ISAAC WAKE, DIPLOMAT

1. SHEILS, W.J. *The Puritans in the Diocese of Peterborough, 1558–1610*, Northamptonshire Record Society (1979), vol.30, p.29.

2. For Isaac's own religious views, see his *Divine Meditations by an Honourable Person. Whereto is adjoyned a Determination of the Question, Whether Men ought to Kneele at the Receipt of the Holy Communion* (1641). There is a copy of the pamphlet in the British Library.

3. FOSTER, J. *Alumni Oxonienses: the members of the University of Oxford, 1500–1714*, (1891), p.1553.

4. WOOD, A. *Fasti Oxonienses* (1691), vol.2, p.539.

5. Quoted in NICHOLS, J. *The Progresses, Processions, and Magnificent Festivities of James the First* (1828), vol.2, p.545.

6. WOOD, A. *Athenae Oxonienses* (1691), vol.1, p.812.

7. MALONE, E. (ed.) *The Plays and Poems of William Shakespeare* (1790), vol.4, p.436.

8. A contemporary account does not list Isaac Wake as being present at the funeral ceremony itself. ANON, *Trecentale Bodleianum* (1913), pp. vii-viii.

9. NOTESTEIN, W. 'John Chamberlain', in *Four Worthies* (1956), pp.30–1.

10. McCLURE, N.E. (ed.) *The Letters of John Chamberlain* (1939), vol.1, pp.398–9.

11. Isaac Wake to Sir Dudley Carleton, 2 December 1612, State Papers (Venice), 11/153.

12. McCLURE, op.cit., p.544.

13. ANON. *Letters From and to Sir Dudley Carleton, Knt., during his Embassy in Holland from January 1616 to December 1620* (1757), pp. v-vi.

14. Papers of Sir Thomas Edmondes, vol.11. Isaac Wake to Sir T. Edmondes, 9 September 1617, BL, Stowe, MS. 176. f.163.

15. STOYE, J.W. *English Travellers Abroad, 1604–1667* (1952), p.166.

16. McCLURE, op.cit., vol.2, p.195.

17. Ibid, pp.198–9.

18. Papers of James Hay, Earl of Carlisle, vol.1. Isaac Wake to Earl of Carlisle, 12 May 1619, BL, Egerton MS. 2592, f.59.

19. GARDINER, S.R. *History of England from the Accession of James I to the Outbreak of the Civil War* (1895), vol.3, pp.292–3.

20. GARDINER, S.R. *Letters and Other Documents Illustrating the Relations between England and Germany at the Commencement of the Thirty Years War* (1865), p.111.

21. BL Stowe MS. 176, 26 February 1621, f.221.

22. McCLURE, op.cit., vol.2, pp.425–6.

23. Ibid., p.552.

24. CALENDAR OF STATE PAPERS. Domestic. Charles I, 1627–8, 11 November 1627, vol.84, p.429.

25. THOMPSON, F.M.L. *Hampstead, Building of a Borough, 1650–1964* (1974), p.18.

26. AUBREY, J. *Brief Lives* (ed. CLARK, A.) (1898), vol.2, p.272.

27. VICTORIA COUNTY HISTORY *Middlesex. Hampstead and Paddington* (1989), vol.9, p.51.

28. 'W.R.W.' 'John Wilde', in *Dictionary of National Biography* (1900), vol.61, p.228.

29. RUIGH, R.E. *The Parliament of 1624: Politics and Foreign Policy* (1974), p.85.

30. HENDERSON, B.W. *Merton College* (1899), p.135. The first Oxford University MP, elected in 1604, had been a Mertonian, Sir Thomas Crompton.

31. REX, M.B. *University Representation in England, 1604–1690* (1954), p.69–74.

32. SHARPE, K. *Sir Robert Cotton, 1586–1631: history and politics in early modern England* (1979), p.172.

33. McCLURE, op.cit., p.547.

34. Ibid., p.540.

35. SMITH, L.P. *The Life and Letters of Sir Henry Wotton* (1907), vol.2, p.284.

36. See AKRIGG, G.P.V. *Jacobean Pageant or, The Court of King James I* (1962), pp.65–7.

37. CALENDAR OF STATE PAPERS. Domestic, Charles I, 1628–9, 7 December 1628, p.405.

38. Quoted in NICHOLS, op.cit., vol.2, p.454.

39. Wotton had complained to the Venetian ambassador at Turin that he had not received on his departure honours and gifts equal to those given to the French ambassador when he left Venice in 1607. SMITH, L.P., op.cit., vol.1, p.500.

40. WOOD, op.cit., vol.2, p.39.

41. MATHEW, D. *James I* (1967), p.315.

42. McCLURE, op.cit., vol.2, p 616.

43. LOCKYER, R. *Buckingham: the life and political career of George Villiers, 1st. Duke of Buckingham, 1592–1628* (1981), p.335.

44. WAKE, SIR ISAAC. *A Threefold Help to Political Observations contained in three Discourses* (1655), p.85.

45. Ibid., p.82.

46. Ibid., pp.89–90.

47. Sir Isaac Wake to the Duke of Savoy, 1627, BL Harley MS.1583, f.165.

48. PRESTWICH, M. *Cranfield. Politics Under the Early Stuarts. The Career of Lionel Cranfield, Earl of Middlesex* (1966), pp.364–5.

49. SMITH, L.P., op.cit., vol.2, p.95. Between June 1617 and May 1620, Sir Isaac Wake received £1,281 'for diet' and £1,150 for transportation and secret service, a total of £2,431. SCHREIBER, R.E. *The political career of Sir Robert Naunton, 1589–1635* (1981), pp.141–2.

50. Sir Isaac Wake to Sir Lionel Cranfield, Sackville Papers. 10 December 1621, and McCLURE, op.cit., vol.2, p.478.

51. CALENDAR OF STATE PAPERS. Domestic, Charles I, 1629–31, 28 September 1621, p.349.

52. SMITH, L.P., op.cit., vol.2, p.475.

53. Quoted in NOTESTEIN, op.cit., p.48.

54. Sir Isaac helped Arundel in acquiring one of Holbein's most celebrated portraits. He wrote to Sir William Boswell, secretary to Carleton, on 6 December 1628, 'The picture after which you do seem to enquire was made by Hans Holben in ye time of Henry 8 and is of a Count of Moretta. My Lord of Arundel doth desire it, and if I can get it at any reasonable rate he must and shall have it'. HERVEY, M.F.S.,

The Life, Correspondence and Collections of Thomas Howard, Earl of Arundel (1921), p.258.

55. MILLAR, O. *The Age of Charles I* (1972), p.11.

56. HERVEY, op.cit., p.201.

57. CHARLTON, J. *The Banqueting House, Whitehall* (1964), pp.48–9.

58. Rubens to Sir Dudley Carleton, 19 May 1618, in SAINSBURY, W.N. *Papers of Peter Paul Rubens* (1859), p.35.

59. For a detailed history and description of the two portraits, see BROOS, B. *Meesterwerken in het Mauritshuis* (1987), pp.119–25.

60. CUST, L. *Anthony Van Dyck* (1911), pp.44–5.

61. Sir Isaac Wake to Sir Lionel Cranfield, Sackville Papers, 21 March 1622.

62. HUXLEY, G. *Endymion Porter, the life of a courtier, 1587–1649* (1959), pp.149–50.

63. HOWARTH, D. 'Charles I and the Gonzaga Collections', in CHAMBERS, D. and MARTINEAU, J. (eds.) *Splendours of the Gonzaga* (1981), p.97.

64. Sir Isaac Wake to Lord Conway 28 April, 1628, in SAINSBURY, op.cit., pp.326–7.

65. MARTINEAU, J. and HOPE, C. (eds.) *The Genius of Venice, 1500–1600*, (1983), p.48.

66. CALENDAR OF STATE PAPERS. Domestic. Charles I, 1635–6, Daniel Nys to the King, 1635?, p.76.

67. The exhibition *Splendours of the Gonzaga* was on display from November 1981 to January 1982. For catalogue details, see n.63 above.

68. For example, Anna wrote to her father in July 1630, recommending Sir James Scott to be made an officer in his regiment which was leaving for Venice. CALENDAR OF STATE PAPERS. Domestic, Charles I, 1629–31, Anna Wake to Lord Conway, 27 July 1630, p.313.

69. Lord Conway to Sir Isaac Wake, Coke Papers, 7 December 1629.

70. Between October 1628 and March 1631, though still formally ambassador at Venice, Sir Isaac appears to have assumed permanent representational responsibilities at Turin. He travelled directly from Savoy to his

appointment in France. BELL, G.M. *A Handlist of British Diplomatic Representatives 1509–1688* (1990), p.231.

71. BIRCH, T. *The Court and Times of Charles the First*, (ed. WILLIAMS, R.F. 1848), vol.2, p.93.

72. CALENDAR OF STATE PAPERS. Domestic, Charles I, 1629–31, Rowland Woodward to Francis Windebank, 22 December 1630, p.416.

73. GARDINER, S.R. *History of England from the accession of James I to the Outbreak of the Civil War, 1603–42*, (1895), vol.7, p.197.

74. Papers of James Hay, Earl of Carlisle, Sir Isaac Wake to the Earl of Carlisle, 9 April 1632, BL Egerton MS. 2597 f.64.

75. DUKE OF MANCHESTER, *Court and Society from Elizabeth to Anne* (1864), vol.2, p.23.

76. FULLER, T. *The History of the Worthies of England* (ed. NUTTALL, P.A., 1890), vol.2, p.509.

77. Papers of James Hay, Earl of Carlisle, Anna Wake to King Charles, n.d., BL Egerton MS. 2597, f.112.

78. BARRON, O. *Northamptonshire Families* (1906), p.326.

79. Isaac Wake to Sir Dudley Carleton, 26 September 1616, quoted in SMITH, L.P. op.cit., vol.2, p.103.

80. LLOYD, D. *State Worthies, or the Statesmen and Favourites of England from the Reformation to the Revolution* (1665, ed. WHITWORTH, C. 1776), vol.2, p.220.

81. WAKE, SIR ISAAC *An Essay on Friendship. Written by a Noble Gentleman, Deceased. And now, Revised and Illustrated* (1640), pp.152–4.

Chapter 7

MOTHER MARY MARGARET WAKE, AN ENGLISH CARMELITE

1. HARDMAN, A. *Two English Carmelites: Mother Mary Xaveria Burton and Mother Mary Margaret Wake* (1939), p.131.

2. CROSS, F.L. and LIVINGSTONE, E.A. (eds.) *The Oxford Dictionary of the Christian Church* (second edition, 1974), p.240.

3. BUTLER, L. and GIVEN-WILSON, C. *Medieval Monasteries of Great Britain* (1979), p.51.

4. HUNTER, T. *An English Carmelite. The Life of Catharine Burton* (1876), pp.6–7.

5. HARDMAN, A. *Mother Margaret Mostyn, Discalced Carmelite, 1625–1679* (1937),

p.14.

6. I am grateful to the Mother Superior, Lanherne Carmelite Convent, Mawgan-in-Pyder, Cornwall for this information.

7. HARDMAN, A. *Two English Carmelites*, op.cit., p.134.

8. ANON. *A Complete Parochial History of the County of Cornwall* (1870), vol.3, p.294.

9. PEVSNER, N. *Cornwall* (1951), p.100.

10. DOUBLE, G.H. 'Saint Mawgan', in *The Saints of Cornwall* (1962), Part 2, p.44.

11. HARDMAN, A. *Two English Carmelites,*, op.cit., p.131.

Chapter 8

WILLIAM WAKE, ARCHBISHOP OF CANTERBURY

1. SYKES, N. *William Wake, Archbishop of Canterbury, 1657–1737* (1957), vol.1, p.6

2. MAYO, C.H. (ed.) *The Minute Books of the Dorset Standing Committee 23rd. Sept. 1646 to*

8th. May 1650 (1902), p.370.

3. HUTCHINS, REVD. J. *The History and Antiquities of the County of Dorset* (1774, third edition, 1874), vol.1, p.120.

4. *A Relation of a Survey of the Western Counties in which is briefly described the Cities, Corporations, Towns, Castles. By a Lieutenant and Captain of the Military Company in Norwich, begun 4 August 1634*, BL Lansdowne MS 213, ff.373–4.

5. BAYLEY, A.R. *The Great Civil War in Dorset, 1642–1660* (1910), p.45.

6. SARGEAUNT, J. *Annals of Westminster School* (1898), pp.98–9.

7. ROYAL COMMISSION ON HISTORICAL MONUMENTS (ENGLAND) *East Dorset* (1975), vol.5, p.59. Shapwick Manor was sold in 1762 by Wake's descendants to John Spencer, later first Earl Spencer.

8. William Wake to Charles Stuart, Duke of Richmond, 2 December 1671, BL Add. MS.21948, f.20. (Wrongly attributed to Archbishop Wake in the British Library Catalogue).

9. WAKE, L. *Lord Archbishop William Wake. Archbishop of Canterbury and Family* (1982), p.45.

10. Eighteenth-century copy of Autobiography, hereinafter referred to as *Autobiography*, Lambeth Palace Library, MS.2392 f.10v.

11. Ibid., ff.11v and 12.

12. Ibid., f.22.

13. Ibid., f.59.

14. Ibid., f.27v.

15. She was Mrs. Elizabeth Palmer, of a wealthy Lincolnshire family. The circumstances surrounding her marriage to Dr Sharp bear a remarkable similarity to those of William Wake's. See NEWCOME, T.(ed.) *The Life of John Sharp, D.D., Lord Archbishop of York* (1825), pp.27–8.

16. *Autobiography*, ibid., ff.29 and 29v.

17. For Ethelreda's ancestry, see LE NEVE, P. *Le Neve's Pedigrees of Knights* (1873), vol.8, p.62.

18. *Autobiography*, f.70.

19. Ibid., f.79v.

20. MOORMAN, J.R.H. *A History of the Church in England* (1953, third edition, 1973), p.271. For full details, see BENNETT, G.V. *The Tory crisis in Church and State, 1688–1730: the career of Francis Atterbury, Bishop of Dorchester* (1975), p.51ff.

21. Dering Correspondence, vol.5, 1691–1762, BL Stowe MS 747, f.155.

22. *Autobiography*, ff.90v and 91.

23. Journal of Archbishop William Wake, 1 March 1705, Lambeth Palace Library, MS.1770, f.1.

24. Ibid., 14 March 1705, f.1

25. SYKES, N. 'Archbishop Wake and the Whig Party 1716–23', *The Cambridge Historical Journal*, vol.8, no.2, 1945, p.103.

26. SYKES, N. *William Wake, Archbishop of Canterbury, 1657–1737* (1957), vol.1, pp.172 and 249.

27. Journal of Archbishop William Wake, 31 May, 6 and 9 June 1706, Lambeth Palace Library, MS. 1770, ff.17–18.

28. See BL Add.MS.16569 f.235, written by one of the Archbishop's daughters.

29. Only one hundred copies of the book were printed.

30. *A Brief Enquiry into the Antiquity, Honour and Estate of the Name and Family of Wake*, pp.1–2, 5–6.

31. Ibid., pp.67–8.

32. ADAMS, L. (ed.) *William Wake's Gallican Correspondence and Related Documents, 1716–1719*, (1988), vol.1, p.8.

33. Revd. W. Beauvoir's Correspondence, 1716–20, BL Add. MS 22880, f.14.

34. LUPTON, J.H. *Archbishop Wake and the Project of Union between the Gallican and Anglican Churches* (1896), p.117.

35. Wake to Bernard Gardner, 21 March 1716, Archbishop Wake MSS, Christ Church, Oxford, Arch. W. Epist.15, f.23.

36. Arch. W. Epist. 19, f.67.

37. 12 January 1720, Arch. W. Epist. 21. f.202.

38. Revd. W. Cole, Misc. Collections, BL Add. MS. 5829, vol.28, f.67v.

39. JONES, M.G. *The Charity School Movement. A Study of Eighteenth Century*

Puritanism (1938), p.65.

40. Wake to Henry Newman, 2 June 1718, Arch. W. Epist. 15.

41. SYKES, N. *William Wake*, op.cit., vol.2, p.209.

42. 10 March 1716, BL Add. MS. 5481 f.18.

43. Journal of Archbishop William Wake, 21 August 1706, Lambeth Palace Library, MS.1770, f.22v.

44. ADAMS, L. (ed.) *William Wake's Gallican Correspondence and Related Documents, 5 Feb 1721–12 Dec 1721* (1989), p.182.

45. For instance, Wake listed, in four closely written pages, 'My Law Books', Arch. W. Epist. 18, ff.499–500.

46. SUTHERLAND, C.H.V. 'The Coin Collection of Christ Church, Oxford. A Chapter in the History of Numismatics', *Oxoniensia*, vol.5, 1940, pp.141–2. The Archbishop's portrait hangs in the college's dining hall.

47. Wake to Dr A. Charlett, 9 October 1719, Arch. W. Epist. 16.

48. *Biographica Britannica*, vol.5, part 2, 4095b.

49. Wake to Browne Willis, Willis Papers, Bodleian Library, Oxford, MS.16328 vol.36, f.247.

50. For fuller details, see BL Add. MS.5841, f.21.

51. Ibid.

52. Surveying his correspondence in old age, Wake commented at the beginning of one volume, 'I have not had time to look these over, nor do I know how they came to escape the fire; many thousands of equal moment were burnt.' Arch. W. Epist. 17, f.1v.

53. HUTCHINS, op.cit., vol.1, p.196.

54. Quoted in SYKES, N. *William Wake*, op.cit., vol.1, p.242.

55. *A Brief Enquiry into the Antiquity, Honour and Estate of the Name and Family of Wake*, p.4.

Chapter 9

POLITICS AND PARLIAMENT:
SIR WILLIAM WAKE, EIGHTH BARONET

1. BARRON, O. *Northamptonshire Families* (1906), p.331.

2. AUSTEN-LEIGH, R. A. *The Eton College Register, 1753–90* (1921), pp.538–9.

3. Letter from Miss A. Walker, Ravenshill, Kielder, Northumberland to Sir Herewald Wake, n.d., Courteenhall Papers.

4. JOHNSON, T.H. *The Oxford Companion to American History* (1966), p.708.

5. BURKE, J.B. *Burke's Dictionary of Landed Gentry of Great Britain and Ireland* (1850), vol.1, p.405.

6. WILKINSON, J. *Worsborough: its Historical Associations and Rural Attractions* (1879), pp.158–9.

7. 'A Survey of Land called Banktop in Wosbrough Dale in the Possession of Richard Fenton Esq, c.1770', Sheffield City Archives, MD 2837.

8. Copy of Will of Frances Fenton, 1 January 1779, Sheffield City Archives, LD 735.

9. REPTON, H. *Courteenhall Red Book* (1791), p.7.

10. GOTCH, J.A. *The Old Halls and Manor Houses of Northamptonshire* (1936), p.83.

11. ITZKOWITZ, D. *Peculiar privilege. A social history of English foxhunting, 1753–1885* (1977), p.200.

12. WORSLEY, G. 'Carr at Courteenhall', *Country Life*, 30 October 1986, p.1390.

13. OSWALD, R. 'Courteenhall', *Country Life*, 19 August 1939, p.172.

14. Joan Wake Papers.

15. See HARRIS, J. *The Palladians* (1981), p.23, and SUMMERSON, J. *Architecture in Britain, 1530–1830* (1970, fifth edition.), p.371.

16. Letter, Ivan and Elizabeth Hall to Sir Hereward Wake, 4 July 1985. Courteenhall Papers.

17. KITSON, S.D. 'Carr of York', *Journal of the Royal Institute of British Architecture*, vol.17, 3rd. series, 29 January 1910, p.254.

18. COLVIN, H.M. *A Biographical Dictionary of British Architects, 1600–1840* (1978), p.196.

19. The Courteenhall Stables do not appear in the Georgian Society's handlist, *The Works in Architecture of John Carr* (1973).

20. GOMME, A. 'William and David Hiorn', in BROWN, R. (ed.) *The Architectural Outsiders* (1985), p.58.

21. 'A list of all men in the Parish of Courteenhall between the age of eighteen and forty five years with their several ranks and occupations, 1771'. Northamptonshire Record Office, X2386.

22. TRENT, C. *The Russells* (1966), pp.192–201.

23. GODBER, J. *The Story of Bedford. An Outline History* (1978), p.89.

24. GODBER, J. *History of Bedfordshire, 1066–1888* (1969), pp.326–7.

25. O'BYRNE, R.H. *Biographical and genealogical notices of the Members of Parliament, Part 1. Bedfordshire* (1848), p.8. In 1767, Bernard was prepared to spend £45,000 during the election campaign in his county to prevent the election of Hinchingbrook and Carysfort. VICTORIA COUNTY HISTORY *Bedfordshire* (1908), vol.2, p.64.

26. In the 1774 and 1780 general election Bedford was one of the few constituencies where there were Wilkite candidates. See O'GORMAN, F. *Voters, Patrons and Parties. The Unreformed Electoral System of Hanoverian England, 1734–1832* (1989), pp.293 and 304.

27. Howard, who had been appointed Sheriff of Bedford in the previous year, shortly before his second marriage made an agreement with the lady 'that to prevent altercations about those little matters which he had observed to be the chief grounds of uneasiness in families, he should always decide'. BARKER, G.F.R. 'John Howard' in *Dictionary of National Biography* (1891), vol. 28, p.44.

28. FULFORD, R. *Samuel Whitbread, 1764–1815. A study in opposition* (1967), p.45.

29. Whitbread to R.Palmer, 2 October 1774. Bedford Papers, FAL 47/4, Bedfordshire Record Office.

30. OLDFIELD, T.H.B. *An Entire and Complete History, Political and Personal, of the Boroughs of Great Britain* (1792), vol.1, pp.9–10.

31. Whitbread to W. Haytor, 8 September 1780, Whitbread Papers, W1/6398, Bedfordshire Record Office.

32. It has been calculated that of the 5,034 MPs between 1734 and 1832, 25 per cent entered the Commons between the ages of twenty six and thirty three. Sir William was thirty two. A half of the total number served for less than eleven years. Baronets made up 11.1 per cent of Members and those having attended Eton 15.6 per cent. From Cambridge, Trinity College sent the most MPs (299). JUDD, G.P.IV *Members of Parliament, 1734–1832* (1955), passim.

33. ALMON, J. *The Parliamentary Register* (1775), vol.1, 1 May 1775, p.445.

34. Ibid. (1776), vol.3, 13 November 1775, p.157.

35. Ibid. (1779), vol.12, 11 March 1779, p.129.

36. NAMIER, SIR L. and BROOKE, J. *The House of Commons, 1754–1790* (1964), vol.3, p.590.

37. See FITZMAURICE, LORD. *Life of William, Earl of Shelburne* (1912), vol. 2, pp.283–4.

38. HANSARD, T.C. *The Parliamentary History* (1783), vol.23, 9 July 1782, p.187.

39. Ibid., (1782), vol.22, 27 November 1781, p.730.

40. DEBRETT, J. *The Parliamentary Register* (1784), vol.13, p.170.

41. FORRESTER, E.G. *Northamptonshire County Elections and Electioneering, 1695–1832* (1941), pp.86–7.

42. Lord North (1770–82), Marquess of Rockingham (1782), Earl of Shelburne (1782–3), Duke of Portland (1783), and William Pitt (1783–1806).

43. Cutting from unidentified Essex newspaper, 1772.

44. For this work and for widening ditches, the bill was £25 17s. 6d. Sir William Wake to Simon Randall, 11 June 1777, Wake (Courteenhall) Papers Northamptonshire

Record Office, X9013.

45. The debts amounted to more than £1,000 with another £600 in interest outstanding. Lady Mary Wake to Samuel Phipps, 15 June 1788, Wake (Courteenhall) Papers, Northamptonshire Record Office, X9014.

46. Lady Mary Wake to Samuel Phipps, 30 March 1786, ibid.

47. Mrs. Delany, who recorded London society at this time, noted on 9 January 1784, 'went to Sr Wm Wakes, where I din'd. He din'd at table, though he was *carried* into ye room by ye servts'. LLANOVER, LADY (ed.) *The Autobiography and Correspondence of Mary Granville, Mrs Delany* (1862), vol.3, p.201.

48. *The Gentleman's Magazine*, July 1785, vol.60, p.919.

Chapter 10
'OLD SIR WILLIAM', NINTH BARONET:
I. THE FORMATIVE YEARS

1. Preston lived at Beeston St. Lawrence Hall, Norfolk, near Riddlesworth, and practised as a barrister at Lincoln's Inn. He dropped dead, aged forty five, from his horse as he was speaking to a carpenter on the return from a ride. *The Gentleman's Magazine*, November 1787, vol.2, p.1024.

2. J. Preston to S. Phipps, 6 November 1785, Lane Papers, Staffordshire Record Office (hereinafter, LP, SRO), D 357/L/1/42.

3. Philadelphia Hannah, wife of the Irish peer, Thomas, Baron Dartrey (Viscount Cremone from 1785), and a frequent visitor to the Wake household. Mrs. Delany records in her diary that on 3 Jan 1784 Lady Wake and Lady Dartrey 'took me in ye coach; they were going to see Mrs. Wright's wax-work to amuse ye children'. Two days later, 'Lady Wake came for me . . . went to Lord Dartrey's to dinner; I staid till past 11; Lady Dartrey's birthday, she is, I believe, 43. After dinner Lady Wake's children came; we had a fiddle and danced (I with Mr. W.) when ye children went to supper'. LLANOVER, LADY (ed.) *The Autobiography and Correspondence of Mary Granville, Mrs Delany* (1862) vol.3, pp.194 and 196.

4. W. Bullock to S. Phipps, 14 November 1785, LP, SRO, D 357/L/1/63.

5. Ibid, D 357/L/1/59. Lady Wake had earlier stated, 'I am anxious to have the House in Essex Lett or rather the Lease disposed of'. Lady Wake to S. Phipps, 5 December, 1785, Wake (Courteenhall) Papers, Northamptonshire Record Office, X9013.

6. Lady Wake to S. Phipps, 2 April 1788, ibid. In his will dated 19 December 1782, Sir William had left to his wife amongst other bequests 'a coach and one pair of horses as she should choose, with harness'.

7. Lady Wake to S. Phipps, 18 April 1788, ibid.

8. Ibid., 7 February 1786.

9. Of Nelson, Catton's obituary states, 'The only impression which remained in Mr. Catton's memory respecting him was that he was somewhat backward in learning.' *The Gentleman's Magazine*, April 1838, vol.9, p.433.

10. CLERKE, A.M. 'Thomas Catton', in *Dictionary of National Biography* (1887), vol.9, p.1234.

11. Lady Wake to S. Phipps, 19 February 1786, Northamptonshire Record Office, X9013.

12. Ibid., 14 March 1786.

13. Ibid., 19 February 1786.

14. SHEAHAN, J.J. *History and Topography of Buckinghamshire* (1882), pp.849–50.

15. GRIMES, C.H.D. *A History of Hitcham* (1926), p.19.

16. VENN, J.A. *Alumni Cantabrigienses* (1940), Part 2. 1752–1900, vol.1, part 2, p.145.

17. CAVE, K.(ed.) *The Diary of Joseph Farington* (1982), vol.8, p.2859.

18. Ibid., p.2860.

19. Lady Wake to S. Phipps, 25 March 1786, Northamptonshire Record Office, X 9013.

20. LIPSCOMB, G. *The history and antiquities of the County of Buckinghamshire* (1847), vol.3, p.282.

21. Sir W. Wake to S. Phipps, 26 September 1786, LP, SRO, D 357/L/2/6.

22. Charlotte, born 18 November 1766, was the youngest of seven children, of whom the eldest two were boys and the other five girls. HOWARD, J.J.(ed.), *Miscellanea Genealogica et Heraldica* (1898), vol.2, 3rd series, p.162. For her background, see BUCKLAND, A. *The Rainsford Family* (1932), passim.

23. Lady Wake to S. Phipps, 14 January 1787, Northamptonshire Record Office, X 9013.

24. Lady Wake to Mrs J. Willes, 14 January 1787 (copy), ibid.

25. Lady Wake to S. Phipps, 16 January 1787, ibid.

26. Ibid., 22 January 1787.

27. Sir W. Wake to S. Phipps, 20 January 1787, LP, SRO, D 357/L/2/10.

28. T. Catton to S. Phipps, 19 February 1787, LP, SRO, D 357/L/1/30.

29. Sir W. Wake to S. Phipps, 6 February 1787, LP, SRO, D 357/L/2/11.

30. G. Gretton to S. Phipps, 13 February 1787, LP, SRO, D 357/L/1/21.

31. MILLER, E. *Portrait of a College. A History of the College of St. John the Evangelist, Cambridge* (1961), p.66.

32. DISNEY, J. (ed.) *The Works of John Jebb* (1787), p.121.

33. WINSTANLEY, D.A. *Unreformed Cambridge. A Study of Certain Aspects of the University in the Eighteenth Century* (1935), pp.52–3.

34. MULLINGER, J.B. *St. John's College* (1901), p.273.

35. T. Catton to S. Phipps, 19 February 1787, LP, SRO, D 357/L/1/30.

36. Sir W. Wake to S. Phipps, 1 May 1787, LP, SRO, D 357/L/2/15.

37. T. Catton to S. Phipps, 19 February 1787, LP, SRO, D 357/L/1/30.

38. Ibid., 27 June 1787, D 357/L/1/24.

39. Sir W. Wake to S. Phipps, 20 May 1787, LP, SRO, D 357/L/2/16.

40. From 1784 George III gained much pleasure in his rides and encounters with the ordinary people around Windsor. VULLIAMY, C.E. *Royal George* (1937), p.192.

41. Sir W. Wake to S. Phipps, 19 July 1787, LP, SRO, D 357/L/2/18.

42. GILL, C. *History of Birmingham* (1952), vol.1, especially chapter 6, p.88 ff.

43. Sir W. Wake to S. Phipps, 29 July 1787, LP, SRO, D 357/L/2/19A.

44. See COSSONS, N. and TRINDER, B. *The Iron Bridge. Symbol of the Industrial Revolution* (1979), p.48.

45. Sir W. Wake to S. Phipps, 29 July 1787, LP, SRO, D 357/L/2/19A.

46. Ibid., 16 August 1787, LP, SRO, D 357/L/2/21.

47. Ibid.

48. She wrote of her health a little later, 'Although denied the gratification of walking I am thankful to receive the blessing of living tolerably free of excruciating pain'. Dowager Lady Sarah Wake to S. Phipps, 6 February 1789, Northamptonshire Record Office, YZ 6115.

49. Lady Wake to S. Phipps, 10 February 1788, Northamptonshire Record Office, X 9013.

50. WINSTANLEY, op.cit., p.81.

51. Sir W. Wake to S. Phipps, 29 June 1788, LP, SRO, D 357/L/2/37.

Chapter 11
'OLD SIR WILLIAM', THE NINTH BARONET:
II. THE REBUILDING OF COURTEENHALL

1. Estimate of an Estate at Riddlesworth Norfolk and Knettishall Suffolk belonging to Sir William Wake Bart., June 1788, Northamptonshire Record Office, Courteenhall (Wake) Papers, X9013.

2. John Josselyn to William Bullock, 4 March 1789, ibid.

3. Riddlesworth Glebe Terrier, 25 May 1791, Norfolk Record Office, PD 528/8. It is interesting to note that the parishioners, besides paying the normal tithes, were required to give '2 Eggs for every Hen and one Egg for every Cock at Easter'.

4. KENWORTHY-BROWNE, J., REID, P., SAYER, M. and WATKIN, D. (eds.) *Burke's and Savill's Guide to Country Houses: East Anglia* (1981) vol.3, p.175.

5. Bevan's house was destroyed by fire in 1899. It was replaced by the present building in the following year. Used as a school since 1946, it numbers amongst its former pupils HRH the Princess of Wales.

6. Sir W. Wake to S. Phipps, 26 September 1786, Lane Papers, Staffordshire Record Office, D357/L/2/6.

7. Ibid, 23 October 1787, Lane Papers, Staffordshire Record Office, D357/L/2/25.

8. Information kindly supplied by Sir Reresby Sitwell, Bart., of Renishaw Hall, Derbyshire.

9. SITWELL, O. *Left Hand, Right Hand!* The Cruel Month (1945), vol.1, p.14.

10. As the official history of Members of Parliament remarked, 'He was seen twice after his death, at Sheffield and Renishaw, but not in the House of Commons'. THORNE, R.G. *The House of Commons, 1790–1820* (1986), vol.5, p.187.

11. See SITWELL, S. 'English Pictures at Renishaw', *Country Life*, 29 October 1938, p.419.

12. 'The Dew, It Lyes on the Wood', in SITWELL, O. *Two Generations* (1940), p.33.

13. In the Courteenhall Estate Account Book for 1791, an entry for 3 December states, 'Paid the Clergyman that buried Lady Wake, £5 5s. 0d.', Northamptonshire Record Office, ML1403.

14. Account, Samuel Phipps, 13 July 1790, Northamptonshire Record Ofice, X9014.

15. Release and conveyance to uses of settlement made upon the marriage of Sir William Wake with Miss Sitwell, Wake (Courteenhall) Papers, Northamptonshire Record Office, X2774.

16. Lady Wake to S. Phipps, 4 January 1787, Northamptonshire Record Office, X9013. Further repairs were carried out by John Middleton in June 1788 at a cost of £83 18s. 0d. Courteenhall Estate Account Book for 1788, Northamptonshire Record Office, ML1230.

17. RICHARDSON, A.E. *An introduction to Georgian Architecture* (1949), p. 98.

18. Parks were originally mainly woodland enclosed to protect beasts for hunting purposes. The landscape aspect of parks became increasingly important for country house owners in the eighteenth century. Courteenhall House and Park are illustrated in HOSKINS, W.G. *The Making of the English Landscape* (1955), p.130. For the history of emparking in Northamptonshire, see STEANE, J. *The Northamptonshire Landscape* (1974), pp. 208–13.

19. STROUD, D. *Humphry Repton* (1962), p.64.

20. Repton was making maps and drawings there in October 1789, but a year later, from 21 October 1790, he spent three days with Phipps at Ferney Hall, carrying out further improvements. Humphry Repton, 'Landskape Gardening and Accounts of my Time employ'd, 1788–90'. Norfolk Record Office, MS.10.

21. Humphry Repton, Memoirs, BL Add. MS.62112, ff.7–8.

22. CARTER, G., GOODE, P. and

LAURIE, K. *Humphry Repton, landscape gardener, 1752–1818* (1982), p.42.

23. Humphry Repton, Courteenhall Red Book, 1791–3, p.5. The original Red Book is at Courteenhall.

24. Ibid., p.7.

25. Ibid., p.8.

26. Ibid., p.9.

27. Ibid., p.15.

28. Ibid., p.21. The idea for this may have come from Sir William, as he would have worked closely with Repton. As the latter wrote indignantly to another Northamptonshire client, 'I have always been in the habit of treating with Principals and not with agents. I must beg you will not again refer me to anyone but yourself'. Repton to George Freke Evans, Laxton Hall, Wansford, 9 January 1806, Freke Evans (Laxton) Papers (copy), Northamptonshire Record Office, Bundle 1.

29. For a drawing and plans of the new entrance lodge, see *The Architect*, 23 February 1878.

30. Jane Austen's biographers almost unanimously suggest that Mansfield Park was based on Harlestone House where she had stayed. It is now very probable that she had in mind Stoneleigh Abbey. MALINS, E. 'Humphry Repton at Stoneleigh Abbey, Warwickshire', *Garden History*, vol.5, No.1, 1977, pp.21–9.

31. AUSTEN, J. *Mansfield Park* (1814, reprinted 1972), p.51.

32. ROYAL COMMISSION ON HISTORIC MONUMENTS (ENGLAND) *An Inventory of Archaeological Sites in South-West Northamptonshire* (1982), p.35.

33. BRIDGES, J. *The History and Anitquities of Northamptonshire* (1791), vol.1, p.353.

34. WAKE, JOAN, 'Courteenhall A Hundred Years Ago'. Notes for talk 1940, pp.3 and 6, Joan Wake Papers.

35. Courteenhall Estate, Husbandry Accounts 1792, Northamptonshire Record Office, ML1403.

36. GRAVES, A. *The Royal Academy of Arts. A complete Dictionary of Contributors, 1769 to 1904* (1906), vol.7, p.37; and HUTCHISON, S.C. 'The Royal Academy Schools, 1768–1830', *Walpole Society* (1962), vol.38, p.142.

37. COLVIN, H.M. *A Biographical Dictionary of British Architects 1600–1840* (1978), p.205.

38. HARRIS, J. *Sir William Chambers, Knight of the Polar Star* (1970), p.100.

39. CROOK, J.M. and PORT, M.H. *The History of the King's Works* (1973), vol.6, p.20.

40. WADDY, F.F. *A History of the Northampton General Hospital* (1974), p.28.

41. CROOK, and PORT, op. cit., p.24.

42. For illustrations and fuller architectural descriptions, see EDWARDS, R. and RAMSAY, L.G.C. *The Late Georgian Period, 1760–1810* (1957), p.22; GOTCH, J.A. *The Old Halls and Manor Houses of Northamptonshire* (1936), pp.82–3; OSWALD, A. 'Courteenhall', *Country Life*, 12 August 1939, pp.144–8, and 19 August 1939, pp.172–6; PEVSNER, N. *Northamptonshire* (1973 edition), p.166; and STILLMAN, D. *English Neo-Classical Architecture* (1988), vol.1, pp.144, 170, 176, 298, 303; vol.2, p.517.

43. Wake (Courteenhall) Papers, Northamptonshire Record Office, X2775.

44. The twelfth baronet was confident that much of it had been brought from Bath. WAKE, JOAN 'Courteenhall a Hundred Years Ago', op.cit., p.3.

45. Courteenhall Estate, Husbandry Accounts 1792, Northamptonshire Record Office, ML 1403. After its completion the house was insured for a sum of £8,000. Husbandry Accounts, 4 August 1794, Northamptonshire Record Office, ML 1404.

46. *Northampton Mercury*, 20 July 1793.

47. ROYAL COMMISSION ON HISTORIC MONUMENTS (ENGLAND) *An Inventory of Archaeological Sites*, op.cit., p.35.

48. *The Gentleman's Magazine*, January 1799, vol.69, pp.18–19. The article also mentions that the arms of Queen Elizabeth, which were displayed in the hall of the old house, were taken to Blisworth Church.

49. Repton's Red Book, p.3, shows a detailed drawing of the old house, but it is not clear if it was executed in 1791 or 1793.

50. It may be surmised that the 1782 'Special agreement' respecting the building of the new house could have used a standard precedent which mentioned the pulling down of the hall, and was not suitably amended. This wording still appears in modern precedents. See *The Encyclopaedia of Forms and Precedents* (1971, fourth edition), vol.20, 'Destruction and re-erection of mansion house', pp.703–4.

51. On 29 July 1811, Sir William wrote to the Lieutenant-Governor of the Royal Naval College, Portsmouth, where his son had been a scholar for a year. Enclosing a medical note, Sir William added, 'His illness having already detained him from the College so many months, I can hardly expect that the Lords Commissioners of the Admiralty will consent to keep ye vacancy open for him any longer, especially as the Physicians are decidedly of the opinion that even should his life be spared (which is alas most doubtful) he will never be able to engage in any active profession'. Royal Naval College, Portsmouth, Public Record Office, Adm. 1/3508.

52. The event was verified at the time by a near neighbour and friend, George Isted of Ecton Hall, in a letter to the second Earl Spencer. Isted claimed that most people believed that Sir William was in the right. Seventh Earl Spencer to Joan Wake, 29 September 1954, Joan Wake Papers.

53. *Northampton Mercury*, 27 November 1792. See also HATLEY, V.A. 'The Headless Trunk: A Study in Northamptonshire Politics, 1795–6'. *Northamptonshire Past and Present*, vol. 8, No.2 1990–1, p.105.

54. Sir William Wake to J. Dickenson, 28 October 1798, Joan Wake Papers.

55. CAZENOVE, H. de L. *Northamptonshire Yeomanry, 1794–1964* (1964), p.5.

56. Sir William Wake to second Earl Spencer, 10 May 1826, Spencer Papers, British Library, G.146. Sir William was one of the leading subscribers to the Yeomanry funds in 1803, contributing the sum of £100. *Northampton Mercury*, 22 October 1803.

57. Twenty-one cottagers are listed in a rental return of 1792. Northamptonshire Record Office, ML1403.

58. Courteenhall Glebe Terrier, 19 June 1804, Northamptonshire Record Office, X580. The old Rectory had a thatched roof which was so low that cattle could reach the eaves. William Surridge to Joan Wake, 1913, Joan Wake Papers.

59. Items collated from the Courteenhall Estate Account Books, 1790–1822, Northamptonshire Record Office, ML79–84, 1230–1 and 1403–4; and Annual Accounts of Christopher Smyth, steward, 1796–1805, and Thomas Lister, bailiff, 1799–1806, Courteenhall Papers.

60. Bayley was the defendant in an action at Northampton Assizes in August 1810 when a villager, Ward, claimed that the Rector had injured his wife in an affray between the parties concerning the right of access to a pool of water at Courteenhall. The jury awarded the plaintiff £250 damages. *Northampton Mercury*, 4 August 1810.

61. Information from Lady Wake, wife of thirteenth baronet, February 1940, Joan Wake Papers.

62. This was held at the George Hotel, which had been rebuilt and was reopened on 27 September 1802, the first day of the Northampton Races. ADCOCK, A. 'Notes on the George Hotel, Northampton', *Journal of the Northamptonshire Natural History Society*, vol.20, no.159, 1919, p.98.

63. Sir William Wake to J. Dickenson, 30 December 1802, Joan Wake Papers.

64. GREAVES, R. *The Grafton Hunt* (1949), p.7.

65. Sir George Sitwell to Susan Tait, 17 April 1817, Blanche Sitwell Papers, Northamptonshire Record Office, Box 4.

66. Select Committee on Railway Labourers, P.P. 1846 xiii, Evidence, 22 May 1846, Q.903.

67. See WAKE, JOAN, *Northampton Vindicated, or Why the Main Line Missed the Town* (1935), p.21; and HATLEY, V.A. 'Northampton Revindicated. More Light on Why the Main Line Missed the Town,' *Northamptonshire Past and Present*, vol.2, no.6,

1959, p.305.

68. SMILES, S. *The Story of the Life of George Stephenson* (1873), p.239.

69. *Northampton Mercury*, 15 January 1831.

70. The Company's warrant was increased by about £500,000 to conciliate opponents.

71. Select Committee on Railway Labourers, op.cit., Q.895. For further details, see COLEMAN, T. *The Railway Navvies. A History of the men who made the Railways* (1965), pp.28, 31 and 37.

72. MARLOW, N. 'The Coming of the Railways to Northamptonshire', *Northamptonshire Past and Present*, vol. 3, no.5, 1964, p.208.

73 LE MARCHANT, SIR D. *Memoir of John Charles, Viscount Althorp, third Earl Spencer* (1876), pp.83–4.

74. FORRESTER, G.F. *Northamptonshire County Elections and Electioneering, 1695–1832* (1941), p.110.

75. Sir William Wake to Viscount Althorp 24 May 1831, Spencer Papers, British Library, G.16.

76. MYERS, E. *Lord Althorp* (1890), chapters 5 and 6, pp.72–115.

77. BROCK, M. *The Great Reform Act* (1973), pp.310–11.

78. *Morning Chronicle*, 30 June 1832, p.4.

79. *The Gentleman's Magazine*, March 1846, vol.25, p.315.

80. SHORTHOUSE, R.W. 'Justices of the Peace in Northamptonshire, 1830–1845', Part 1, *Northamptonshire Past and Present*, vol.5, no.2,

1974, p.139.

81. Deed between Sir William Wake and Samuel Rudge concerning the County Gaol, Northampton, 13 February 1792, Northamptonshire Record Office, D 3789.

82. WAKE, SIR HEREWARD 'A Short Account of the Founding of St. Andrew's Hospital, Northampton,' *Northamptonshire Past and Present*, vol.7, no.2, 1984–5, pp.95–7.

83. SITWELL, O. *Two Generations*, op.cit., p.35.

84. Lady Mary Wake's hatchment survives in Courteenhall Church. The remaining three are those of the ninth, tenth and thirteenth baronets. SUMMERS, P. (ed). *Hatchments in Britain: Northamptonshire, Warwickshire and Worcestershire.* (1974), pp. 14–15.

85. GODDARD, H. *Memoirs of a Bow Street Runner* (1956), p.197.

86. SITWELL, O. *Two Generations*, op.cit., p.34.

87. *The Gentleman's Magazine*, March 1846, vol.25, p.315.

88. Will of Sir William Wake, Ninth Baronet, dated 1 September 1845, Principal Probate Registry. William Gray, a Huntingdon gentleman who settled in Courteenhall in 1836, recorded in his diary that on 5 July that year he had witnessed Sir William's signature to his will. *Diary of the late William Gray Esq. of Courteenhall, Northamptonshire* (1875), p.36.

89. WAKE, JOAN, 'Courteenhall a Hundred Years Ago', op.cit., pp.25–6.

Chapter 12

CHATTIE AND THE TENTH BARONET

1. DAUGLISH, M.G. and STEPHENSON, P.K. (eds.) *The Harrow School Register, 1800–1911* (third edition, 1911), p.30.

2. THORNTON, P.M. *Harrow School and Its Surroundings* (1885), p.197.

3. LABORDE, E.D. *Harrow School, Yesterday and Today* (1948), p.46.

4. VENN, J.A. *Alumni Cantabrigienses* (1954), part 2, vol.6, p.308.

5. Marianne Tait to James Campbell Tait,

September 1816, quoted in WAKE, L. (ed.) *The Reminiscences of Charlotte, Lady Wake* (1909), p.61 (hereinafter referred to as *Reminiscences*).

6. LORD COCKBURN. *Memorials of His Time* (1856), pp.115–19.

7. As Charlotte noted in her Journal, 'My Aunts were by far too good diplomatists to allow a young Baronet, entirely his own master, with a splendid Place and 10,000 a year, to slip through their fingers'. Charlotte, Lady

Wake, Manuscript Journals, Northampton-shire Record Office, vol.8, f.14 (hereinafter referred to as *Journals*). *The Reminiscences of Charlotte, Lady Wake* (note 5, supra.) is based on her much fuller manuscript Journals. The published version omits many of the more interesting personal and family details. The editor of the book, Lucy Wake, was Charlotte's grand-daughter.

8. *Journals*, vol.4, f.14.

9. *Reminiscences*, pp.84–5.

10. SITWELL, SIR R. *Renishaw Hall and the Sitwells* (1985), p.5.

11. For example, recollecting a ball held at Renishaw in 1820 Charlotte wrote, 'My first partner I felt quite proud of, he being a double first-class man, young Charles Wood (now Lord Halifax)'. *Reminiscences*, p.90.

12. *Journals*, vol.8, f.36.

13. *Journals*, vol.10, f.47.

14. *Reminiscences*, p.58.

15. SITWELL, O. *Two Generations* (1940), p.73.

16. Charles Wake to Richard Andrews, 1 September 1827, Northamptonshire Record Office, X9024.

17. Diary of Marianne Tait, 1825–31, Blanche Sitwell Papers, Northamptonshire Record Office.

18. However, he was by no means an uncritical one. Asked by Bishop Tait to comment on the character of a local clergy-man, he replied, 'A greater <u>scamp</u> I do not know and even heard of, and the only excuse that can be made for him is (the very doubtful and Charlotte one) that he is out of his mind'. Charles Wake to Bishop Tait, 1 February 1861, Tait Papers, Lambeth Palace Library, vol.121, ff.226–7.

19. *The Beaver and the Elephant* (1829), p.3.

20. Ibid., p.6.

21. *Journals*, vol.8, f.71.

22. *Reminiscences*, pp.153–4.

23. A model lease for Powick Court stated that the tenant should not 'shoot, course or sport on the farm and lands, but to have liberty to take and destroy the Rabbits by means of Ferrets and purse nets, but not otherwise'.

Pakington Papers, Hereford and Worcester Record Office, BA 3835/15 (ii) 5.

24. Charles Wake to John Pakington, March 1835, Northamptonshire Record Office, X9023 Bundle 23.

25. Pakington's agent wrote to Charles Wake in May 1835, accepting the latter's conditions for leasing Powick Court: 'As soon as the Election (for Worcestershire East) is over, Mr. Pakington will have the Rooms furnished agreeably to your suggestion'. J.B. Hyde to Charles Wake, 3 May 1835, Northamptonshire Record Offiice, X9023 Bundle 23.

26. Disraeli commented to his sister, Sarah, on Pakington's debut in the House of Commons on 15 November 1837, thus: 'He was confident, fluent, and commonplace, and made a good chairman of quarter sessions speech. "It was the best speech he ever will make", said Sugden [MP for Ripon], "and he was practising it before the grand jury for the last twenty years". However, I supported him very zealously, and he went to bed thinking he was an orator, and wrote to Mrs. Pakington, I've no doubt, to that effect'. MONEYPENNY, W.F. *The Life of Benjamin Disraeli, Earl of Beaconsfield* (1912), vol.2, p.19.

27. *Reminiscences*, p.185.

28. Powick Baptism and Burial Registers, Hereford and Worcester Record Office, (copies). In October 1894, Hereward Wake, later the thirteenth baronet, sought out their burial places. He found 'a large flat tomb under a yew tree in the Churchyard, with the inscription enclosed. It is one huge stone, about 7 feet by 4 . . . and shaded by a small yew tree'. Hereward Wake to Lady Catherine Wake, 1 October 1894, Joan Wake Papers, Northamptonshire Record Office.

29. Charles Wake to John Pakington, 26 August 1839 (draft), Northamptonshire Record Office, X9023 Bundle 23.

30. *Journals*, vol. unnumbered, f.4.

31. H.P. Markham to Sir Charles Wake, 18 May 1846, Northamptonshire Record Office, X9018 Bundle 9.

32. Some redecorating was undertaken. In

September 1848, Sir Charles informed his Essex solicitor, 'We shall leave home on Monday for a time to get out of the way of painters, and we shall have some difficulty to bear the smell till then'. Sir Charles Wake to R. Andrews, 21 September 1848, Northamptonshire Record Office, X9018 Bundle 11.

33. It seems probable that other members of the family were also musical. In his will, Sir Charles bequeathed to his daughter, Matilda, 'my last grand square pianoforte manufactured by Collard and Collard'. Will of Sir Charles Wake, tenth baronet, dated 25 October 1862, Principal Probate Registry.

34. Reverend G. Robbins to Lady Charlotte Wake, 13 February 1856, Joan Wake Papers.

35. R. Lee to Lady Charlotte Wake, 12 April 1858; and T. Close to Lady Charlotte Wake, 5 September 1865, Joan Wake Papers.

36. Unknown correspondent to Matilda Wake, c.1860, Joan Wake Papers.

37. Sir Charles Wake to Lady Charlotte Wake, 18 May 1856; and 5, 17, 20 and 22 June 1860, Joan Wake Papers.

38. FOISTER, S. *Cardinal Newman, 1801–90* (1990), p.41.

39. Lady Charlotte Wake to A.C. Tait, 27 May 1832, Tait Papers, vol.76, ff.58–9.

40. HOPE SIMPSON, J.B. *Rugby Since Arnold. A History of Rugby School from 1842* (1967), p.14.

41. One particularly absurd one went by the name of 'shirking', a poor compromise between allowing and not allowing the younger boys to go for a walk in the country. 'They might go, but if they were seen by a master or a prepostor they had to run away from him as fast as they could until they heard the magic word "on", when they could proceed peacefully with their walk'. EVERS, C.R. *Rugby* (1939), p.60.

42. For Charlotte's own description of events there, see BENHAM, W. (ed.) *Catharine and Craufurd Tait. A Memoir* (1879), p.254.

43. Sir Charles Wake to Lady Charlotte Wake, 16 May 1856, Joan Wake Papers.

44. FINLAYSON, G.B.A.M. *The Seventh Earl of Shaftesbury, 1801–1885* (1981), pp.384–5.

45. POLLOCK, J. *Shaftesbury. The Poor Man's Earl* (1985), pp.24–5.

46. *Journals*, vol.10, ff.5–7.

47. Lady Charlotte Wake to A.C. Tait, 18 September 1856, Tait Papers, vol.79, f.11.

48. Lord Shaftesbury to Lady Charlotte Wake, 22 September 1856, Tait Papers, vol.79, ff.48–9.

49. DAVIDSON, R. T. *Life of Archibald Campbell Tait, Archbishop of Canterbury* (1891), vol.1, p.134.

50. Lady Charlotte Wake to Bishop Tait, 3 October 1862, Tait Papers, vol.80, ff.136–7.

51. Lady Charlotte Wake to Catharine Tait, 3 October 1862, Tait Papers, vol.103, f.246.

52. Archbishop Tait to Lady Susan Sitwell, 20 October 1848, Blanche Sitwell Papers, Northamptonshire Record Office, X272, Box 4.

53. ADDISON, SIR W. *Portrait of Epping Forest* (1977), p.105. See Minutes of Evidence taken before the Select Committee on Royal Forests (Essex). Lieutenant-Colonel G. Power, P.P. 1866, vi, Q. 769.

54. Charles Wake to Reverend Joseph Arkwright, c.1825, Arkwright Papers, Essex Record Office, D/D, Ar.C3.

55. H. Newcome to Sir Charles Wake, 10 August 1847, Northamptonshire Record Office, X9018 Bundle 9.

56. Mrs Tite, 'Reminiscences, Sunday 4 July, 1926', Northamptonshire Record Office, X2386.

57. Matilda Wake to unknown correspondent, undated letter, but 1870, Joan Wake Papers.

58. 'Itinerary of Lady Charlotte Wake and her daughter Matilda Wake for each winter after Sir Charles's death, 1864–1876', Joan Wake Papers.

59. *Reminiscences*, p.309.

60. TUCKER, T.G. 'Memories of Pitsford A Hundred Years Ago', *Northamptonshire Past and Present*, vol.6, no.1, 1978, p.52.

61. DAVIDSON, R.T. *Life of Archibald*

Campbell Tait, Archbishop of Canterbury (1891), vol.2, p.549.

62. *Journals*, vol.14, f.6.

63. Lady Charlotte Wake to Lady Catherine Wake, 18 July 1883, Joan Wake Papers.

64. Lady Charlotte Wake to Blanche Sitwell, 14 February 1884, Blanche Sitwell Papers, Northamptonshire Record Office, X272, Box 3.

65. Ibid., 24 July 1885.

66. Ibid., 22 January 1886.

67. Ibid., 7 May 1886.

68. Ibid., 22 December 1885.

69. Ibid., 25 February 1887.

70. Obituary, *Northampton Herald*, 7 April 1888.

71. Major Charles St. Aubyn Wake, CMG (1861–1938), was a very colourful character. His Army career included service in the local forces of Zanzibar, a spell in the Turkish Army and in the Royal Irish Rifles. Documents relating to Major Charles St. Aubyn Wake, National Army Museum, Chelsea, 6309/165.

72. Interview, Joan Wake, 26 August 1938, Joan Wake Papers.

Chapter 13
DEFENDERS OF THE EMPIRE

1. AYLING, K. *My Mother's Family* (1974), p.17.

2. R. Maunsell to Charles Wake, 9 July 1842, Northamptonshire Record Office, hereinafter NRO, X 9018 Bundle 5.

3. Charles Wake junior to his father, 5 November 1842, NRO, X 9023 Bundle 8.

4. Captain Frederick Spencer to Charles Wake, 5 January 1844, NRO, X 9018 Bundle 6.

5. Charles Wake junior to his mother, 10 January 1844, NRO, X 9018 Bundle 6.

6. Sir Thomas Hastings to Charles Wake, 6 May 1844, NRO, X 9018 Bundle 5.

7. Writing to his mother shortly before being promoted to Commander, Charles declared, 'Your letter goes on to talk about promotion . . . I should like to leave it in better hands, so please refrain from mentioning it in your letters, even if I should be tempted to speak of it in mine'. Charles Wake junior to Charlotte Wake, 14 May 1853, NRO, Joan Wake Papers.

8. O'BYRNE, W.R. *A Naval Biographical Dictionary* (1849), p.1233.

9. The last letter written by his father, the tenth baronet, shortly before he died in 1864, was to the Admiralty, requesting a ship for his son. Shortly after, Charles junior was given command of the *Bulldog*. Charlotte, Lady Wake, Manuscript Journals, NRO, vol.10, f.47.

10. Charles Wake junior to Bishop Tait, 21 July 1865, Tait Papers, Lambeth Palace Library, vol.138, f.379.

11. Charles Wake junior to his mother, 23 July 1865, Joan Wake Papers.

12. Ibid., 24 September 1865.

13. Report of the Engagement with the Batteries at Cape Haitien and the blowing up of H M Ship *Bulldog* by Captain Charles Wake to prevent her falling into the hands of the Enemy, 29 October 1865, Joan Wake Papers (copy), p.8.

14. *The Times*, 4 December 1865, p.2.

15. *The Times*, 17 January 1866, p.12.

16. Charles Wake junior to Bishop Tait, 24 January 1866, Tait Papers, vol.83, f.338.

17. J. M. Walker to Bishop Tait, 22 January 1866, Tait Papers, vol.82, f.186.

18. *Punch*, 27 January 1866, p.37.

19. Charlotte, Lady Wake, Manuscript Journals, NRO, vol.11, f.5.

20. Charles Wake junior to Drury Wake, 21 November 1866, Joan Wake Papers.

21. Charles Wake junior to his mother, 9 May 1867, Joan Wake Papers.

22. Ibid., c.1870.

23. He once wrote to her, 'Rest assured

that I miss you as much as you can miss me. Indeed I should have liked very much to have enjoyed more of your society. I think you and I agreed so well in all our ideas on all subjects!' Charles Wake junior to Matilda Wake, 31 December 1853, Joan Wake Papers.

24. Charles Wake junior to Matilda Wake, 14 May 1871, Joan Wake Papers.

25. Charles Wake junior to his mother, 2 January 1884, Joan Wake Papers.

26. In 1882, Charles wrote to his mother about Drury, 'Did I tell you that he came out of the last half yearly exams 1st. in his ship again, and only 2nd. in the Fleet and that Captain Tryon [Secretary of the Admiralty] had presented him with a handsome set of gold shirt studs as a mark of his approval and that the Admiral Beauchamp Seymour [Commander-in-Chief, Mediterranean] had also asked him to breakfast for the same reason?,' Charles Wake junior to Charlotte Wake, 13 December 1882, Joan Wake Papers.

27. E.H. Campbell to Matilda Wake, c.1869, Joan Wake Papers.

28. SOLLY, G.A. *Rugby School Register, 1675–1857* (1933), vol.1, p.217.

29. Drury Wake to Matilda Wake, March 1845, Joan Wake Papers. Matthew Arnold temporarily took a post at Rugby in 1845 after leaving Oxford. Two years later, he became secretary to Lord Lansdowne, Lord President of the Council.

30. NETHERCOTE, H.O., *The Pytchley Hunt, past and present* (second edition., 1888), p.297.

31. The College was concerned over the steady decline in the academic achievements of their students, particularly marked in the period 1841 to 1850. BILL, E.G.W. and MASON, J.F.A. *Christ Church and Reform 1850–1867* (1970), p.24.

32. WAKE, L. (ed.) *The Reminiscences of Charlotte, Lady Wake* (1909), p.227.

33. Charlotte, Lady Wake, Manuscript Journals, NRO, vol.10, f.45.

34. NETHERCOTE, op.cit., p.303.

35. Drury Wake to his mother, 16 December 1867, Joan Wake Papers.

36. Ibid., 21 December 1867.

37. Ibid., 11 February 1868.

38. Ibid., 21 December 1867.

39. *Northampton Herald*, 25 April 1891.

40. PAGET, T.G.F. *The History of the Althorp and Pytchley Hunt, 1634–1920* (1937), p.134.

41. GORDON, P. '"A County Parliament": the First Northamptonshire County Council', *Northamptonshire Past and Present*, vol.7, no.3, 1985–86, p.191. His politics were described as being 'Liberal with supposed Unionist proclivities'. *Northampton Mercury*, 2 February 1889.

42. C.T. Arnold to Charles Wake, 14 March 1844, NRO, X 9018 Bundle 6.

43. A.C. Tait to Charles Wake, 14 March 1844, ibid.

44. Ibid., 16 March 1844.

45. Built by William Wilkins, designer of the National Gallery, to which Haileybury bears a strong resemblance. WEBSTER, F.A.M. *Our Great Public Schools* (1937), p.129.

46. LOWELL, A.L. *Colonial Civil Service. The selection and training of colonial officials in England, Holland and France* (1900), p.304.

47. Herwald Wake to Sir Charles Wake, 3 June 1855, Joan Wake Papers.

48. Ibid.

49. Defence of Arrah House, 1857, by eight European local officials and fifty officers and men of 'Rattray's Sikhs'. Report from H.C. Wake to T. Tayler, Commissioner of the Patna Division (copy), Joan Wake Papers.

50. Herwald Wake to his mother, 27 August 1857, Joan Wake Papers.

51. Ibid.

52. For this battle, see KAYE, SIR J.W. *A History of the Sepoy War in India, 1857–1858* (1876), vol.3, pp.141–7.

53. Herwald Wake to his mother, 27 August 1857, Joan Wake Papers.

54. The full text, which was headed 'Written with the stump of a Pencil on the Wall at any Moment that Could be Spared in Case we should Be Scragged', is reproduced in DANVERS, F.C. et al, *Memorials of Old Haileybury College* (1894), pp.635–7. See also

pp.185-6 of this volume.

55. Dispatch dated 13 August 1857. Eyre himself was awarded the Victoria Cross for his action.

56. The *Northampton Mercury* on 7 August 1858 reported that 'Courteenhall, the seat of Sir Charles Wake, near this town, has been the scene of festivities during the week, to welcome the return home of Herwald C. Wake Esq., the hero of Arrah. The aristocracy of the neighbourhood assembled in great numbers on the joyful occassion, besides numerous distinguished visitors from a distance.'

57. Chesney was also the author of the sensational *Battle of Dorking* published in 1871.

58. MINCHIN, J.G.C. *Our Public Schools. Their influence on English history* (1901), pp.217-18.

59. Matilda Wake to Herwald Wake, c.1880, Joan Wake Papers.

60. Herwald Wake to his mother, 28 March 1868, ibid.

61. Baldwin Wake to his mother, 4 October 1854, ibid.

62. Herwald, after leaving his brother, wrote to their mother, 'Baldwin has, I am happy to say, given up his projected trip to Simla. I told him he had much better hold that card till he was really ill'. Herwald Wake to Lady Wake, 9 June 1855, ibid.

63. WAKE, L. (ed.) *The Reminiscences of Charlotte, Lady Wake* (1909), p.248.

64. Baldwin Wake to Archbishop Tait, 13 May 1876, Tait Papers, vol.224, ff.135-6.

65. The Duke of Cumberland wrote to the Archbishop about Baldwin, 'I was truly delighted to be able to persuade [sic] him in his Regiment in which I have no doubt he is doing a great deal of good', 15 January 1879, Tait Papers, vol.99, ff.16-17.

66. *Northampton Herald*, 11 August 1883.

67. In one of the few surviving letters from him, Archibald told his sister, 'You will be pleased to hear that I now never touch spirits .. . and what is more, I feel the benefit of it to my health'. Archibald Wake to Matilda Wake, 13 April 1869, Joan Wake Papers.

68. W. Osborn to Sir Charles Wake, 3 July 1847, NRO, X 9023 Bundle 12.

69. Philip Wake, Australian Diary, 1848-52, 20 August 1848, NRO, X 3834.

70. Ibid., 30 August 1848.

71. Ibid., 26 August 1850.

72. Ibid., 2 March 1850.

73. Ibid., 24 September 1851.

74. TILBY, A. W., *The English People Overseas: Australasia, 1688–1911* (1912), vol.5, p.135.

75. CLACY, E. (ed. THOMPSON, P.) *A Lady's Visit to the Gold Diggings of Australia in 1852–53* (1853), p.162. Hugh Proby, son of the future 3rd Earl Carysfort, Elton Hall, Northamptonshire (now Cambridgeshire), was also in Australia at this time. He wrote to his father, 'The accounts during the last week from Sydney and Melbourne have been quite wonderful – £47,000's worth of gold is reported to have been brought into Melbourne in one week. Everyone here is going mad about it'. Proby to Admiral Granville Proby, 12 December 1851, Elton Hall Papers, vol.9.

76. Latrobe to Earl Grey 2 March 1852. Further Papers relative to the Recent Discovery of Gold in Australia, P.P.1852–3, lxiv, p.170. Quoted in CLARK, C.M.H. (ed.) *Select Documents in Australian History, 1851–1900* (1955) pp.31–2.

77. For an account of the robbery, see *The Times*, 25 October 1853, p.4 and Philip's letter, *The Times*, 2 November 1853, p.7.

78. List of Books to be read between November 1st 1853 and November 1st 1854, Joan Wake Papers.

79. Philip Wake to Sir Charles and Lady Wake, 22 November 1854, Joan Wake Papers.

80. GRANT, J. and SERLE, G. *The Melbourne Scene, 1803–1956* (1957), p.74.

81. Sir Charles Wake to unknown correspondent, n.d., but April 1856 (copy), Joan Wake Papers. According to one historian, Denison 'feared gold might speed up what convictism had begun, spread equality over the whole of society, and place a low estimate on everything that distinguished one man from his fellows'. CLARK, C.M.H. *A History of*

Australia, 1851–1888 (1978), p.11.

82. Philip Wake to his father, 5 May 1856, Joan Wake Papers.

83. September (?) 1856, ibid.

84. R.E.H. Anson to Joan Wake, 2 May 1921, ibid.

85. Sir Charles to Lady Wake, 5 June 1860, ibid.

86. The novel, filling eight notebooks, is about 70,000 words in length. NRO, X 3834.

87. Undated letter to unnamed publisher, in second notebook, ibid.

88. Joan Wake. Notes on Great Uncles and Aunts, Oxford, 7 January 1965, Joan Wake Papers.

89. SOLLY, op. cit., p.355.

90. J.W. Fraser to Charles Wake, 4 May 1838, NRO, X 9023 Bundle 23.

91. William Wake to his father, 13 April 1844, NRO, X 9018 Bundle 6.

92. Charles Wake to William Wake (draft), n.d. but 1842, NRO, X 9023 Bundle 2.

93. Unnamed correspondent, probably to Charles Wake, 13 February 1843, NRO, X 9023, Bundle 8.

94. William Wake to his father, 18 March 1843, NRO, X 9023 Bundle 10.

95. Col. G. Buller to Charles Wake, 11 April 1843, NRO, X9023 Bundle 8.

96. J. Campbell to Charles Wake, 16 May 1843, ibid.

97. Charles Wake to Mrs Low (draft), [19] May 1843, ibid.

98. Charles Wake to William Wake, (draft), late 1843, NRO, X 9023 Bundle 2.

99. Charles Wake to Mr Smith, Furnival's Inn, 3 June 1844, NRO, X 9018 Bundle 7.

100. William Wake to Charles Wake junior, 9 July 1844, NRO, X 9023 Bundle 10.

101. Ibid., 9 August 1844.

102. Miss S.D. Thomson, Southampton City Archivist, to Joan Wake, 25 January 1967, Joan Wake Papers.

103. The hotel, which still stands in the High Street, was visited in 1831 by the Duchess of Kent and the 12-year-old Princess Victoria, who stayed there for three days.

104. G.A. Wake to Charles Wake, 26 February 1845, X 9023 Bundle 2.

105. Ibid., 6 September 1845.

106. Dr D. R. McNab, signed 12 September 1844, NRO, X 9023 Bundle 10.

107. Charles Wake to William Wake, 17 September 1844 (copy), ibid.

108. Ibid., 15 September 1844.

109. Charles Wake, Memorandum, n.d., but 1844, NRO, X9023 Bundle 10.

110. Charles Wake, Account of events, n.d., but after June 1844, NRO, X 9023 Bundle 2.

111. Case In re Sir William Wake, Bart., 19 January 1845, ibid.

112. G.A. Wake to Charles Wake, 8 March 1845, ibid.

113. Sir William Wake to R.B. Andrews, 6 April 1845, NRO, X 9024.

114. William Wake to his father, 23 August 1845, NRO, X 9023 Bundle 10.

115. Ibid., 8 September 1845.

116. Ibid., 27 November 1845.

117. J. Wiblin to R.B. Andrews, 26 February 1846, NRO, X 9024.

118. Charles St. Aubyn Wake. Interviewed by Joan Wake, 26 August 1938, Joan Wake Papers.

119. Dr J.J. Hallett to Charlotte Lady Wake, 20 June 1847, NRO, X 9023 Bundle 1.

120. Ibid., 30 June 1847.

121. Wake Notes. Information given me by Aunt Lucy (eleventh baronet's youngest daughter) at St. Fillans, N.B., while on a visit to her in August 1931, Joan Wake, Joan Wake Papers.

122. Ibid.

123. BARRON, O. *Northamptonshire Families* (1906), p.335.

124. William Wake to his mother, 3 April 1856, Joan Wake Papers.

125. Charles Wake junior to Matilda Wake, 1 January 1879, ibid.

126. Joan Wake. Notes on Great Uncles and Aunts, Oxford, 7 January 1965, ibid.

127. Will of Sir Charles Wake, tenth baronet, dated 25 October 1862, Principal Probate Registry.

Chapter 14
HIGH VICTORIAN COURTEENHALL: THE TWELFTH BARONET

1. The furniture from the Hall had also been sold after the deaths of the ninth and tenth baronets. Sir Herewald Wake, Memorandum, August 1904, Joan Wake Papers (unless otherwise stated, the following references are from this collection).

2. Information, Dowager Lady Catherine Wake to Joan Wake, February 1940. In Joan Wake's Papers, there is an extract from a letter without signature (? Drury Wake), to unknown correspondent from the 1860s which reads: 'As Courten Hall <u>must</u> be let, I am glad the business is done, but I wish we knew what sort of a man M. Willis is, and whether he will take an interest in the parish and people'.

3. Dorothy North, Clement Cottrell-Dormer's granddaughter, to Joan Wake, 10 September 1964.

4. COTTRELL-DORMER, F. *Reminiscences and Wanderings at Home and Abroad, 1837–1900. Provided for her dear children* (1906), vol.1, p.118.

5. Ibid., p.119.

6. H. Wake to Lady Charlotte Wake, 14 January 1864.

7. AYLING, K. *My Mother's Family*, (1974), p.5.

8. H. Wake to Lady Charlotte Wake, 20 September 1864.

9. Rector of Abington, 1847–69. A graduate of Lincoln College, Oxford, Thursby died on 17 October 1869 at the age of forty eight. LONGDEN, H.I. REVD, *Northamptonshire and Rutland Clergy from 1500* (1942), vol.13, p.225.

10. Sir H. Wake to Lady Margaret Wake, 5 July 1865.

11. Sir H. Wake to Lady Charlotte Wake, May 1865.

12. Lady Margaret Wake to Lady Charlotte Wake, 17 July 1865.

13. Craufurd Tait to Lady Charlotte Wake, 16 October 1866.

14. Drury Wake to Lady Charlotte Wake, 26 January 1867.

15. E. Hale to Lady Charlotte Wake, 30 May 1867.

16. MACNAUGHTEN, SIR M. *Sketchy Memories of Eton* (1904), p.29.

17. Sir Herewald's aunt, Josephine, wrote to Kitty at the time of her engagement, 'The old shepherd (Papworth) remembered you and was quite delighted when Grandma told him you were the lady who was coming. He said "You was a little fierce 'un" '. Josephine Wake to Catherine St. Aubyn, July 1873.

18. WAKE, J. *Guide to St. Michael's Mount* (1934, 1945 edition), pp.15–17.

19. COURTNEY, W.P. 'Sir John St. Aubyn', in *Dictionary of National Biography* (1897). vol.50, pp.121–2.

20. Joan Wake to J.B. Whitmore, FSA, 4 October 1955 (copy).

21. Sir H. Wake to Lady Charlotte Wake, 24 July 1873.

22. Josephine Wake to Catherine St. Aubyn, July 1873.

23. As her sister Emma commented to Catherine, 'I cannot delay in writing to tell you how very glad I am at the prospect of having Harry Wake some day for my brother-in-law ... Although I can't help saying I wish he was a little older, please give him my love'. Emma Wake to Catherine St. Aubyn, 22 June 1873.

24. Joan Wake, Mama's reminiscences, told me in 1939 or early 1940.

25. Towards the cost of repairing the interior of the House and decorating the ceilings and walls Clement Cottrell-Dormer paid £688 6s. 6d. out of a total of £764 5s. 11d.. Ledger, Cost of household furniture, repairs and improvements at Courteenhall, 1875, Courteenhall Papers.

26. Ibid.

27. Sir H. Wake, Memorandum, 1904.

28. Sir H. Wake, Courteenhall Estate. Estate Management Notes 1873 to 1911, Courteenhall Papers.

29. Emma Wake to Sir H. Wake, 14 July 1873.

30. In 1935, Catherine Wake believed that 'the doctors might have done more for him in those early years after typhoid'. Diary, Lady Catherine Wake, 21 December 1935.

31. Joan Wake, Reminiscences, n.d., p.4.

32. ANON. *Records of the Services of the Northamptonshire and Rutland Militia from 1756 to 1889* (1890), Appendix. In his Diary for 4 May 1881, Sir Herewald remarked, 'Today Ida wanted to know if I should go on soldiering when I went up to God.' Diary, 1880–3, Courteenhall Papers.

33. Ibid.

34. Ibid., 15 May 1880.

35. MARKHAM, MAJOR C.A. *The History of the Northampton and Rutland Militia, 1756 to 1919* (1924), p.117.

36. Left blank in the text.

37. 'Found by Joan Wake on back of large photograph of Henry, Lord Euston, at Courteenhall in 1964'.

38. Sir H. Wake, Diary, 21 October 1882.

39. Ibid., 30 April 1880.

40. Ibid., 1883. That same year, there was a Ladies' cricket match between Miss Fuller's Eleven and Miss Peel's Eleven at Courteenhall. Kitty, who played for Miss Fuller's team, was on the winning side. Sir Herewald acted as umpire. For an illustration of the match, see WAKE, JOAN 'Ladies' Cricket Match at Courteenhall, 23 July 1883', *Northamptonshire Past and Present*, vol.4, no.4, 1969–70, p.214.

41. *Wisden* (1917), p.266.

42. *Northampton Herald*, 5 February 1909.

43. Northamptonshire County Cricket and Recreation Grounds Co. Ltd. Account Book, 1885–1923, Markham, Solicitors, Papers, Northamptonshire Record Office, Box 2. Sir Herewald also advanced £560 in a secured loan towards fencing the ground.

44. Directors' Minute Book, 1885–1923, 30 April 1885, p.30, Markham, Solicitors, Papers, Northamptonshire Record Office, Box 2.

45. Sir H. Wake to fifth Earl Spencer, 14 December 1887, Spencer Papers, British Library, K 314.

46. *Northampton Independent*, 13 March 1909. Sir Herewald's enthusiasm for the club was tempered by his dislike of the increasing professional element in the team. COLDHAM, J.D. 'Early Northamptonshire Cricket', *Northamptonshire Past and Present*, vol.2, no.3, 1950, p.136.

47. Joan Wake, Note, 30 March 1965.

48. When he was in his mid-fifties, Sir Herewald hunted between 5 November 1905 and 7 March 1906 on thirty seven occasions, twenty two with the Grafton, eleven with the Pytchley, two with the Quorn and two with the Warwickshire. Sir H. Wake, My Hunting Days this Season, 1905–6.

49. See ELLIOTT, J.M.K.(ed. ELLIOTT, E.K.) *Fifty Years' Fox Hunting with the Grafton and other packs of hounds* (1900), p.282.

50. Ibid., p.96.

51. Whilst still at school, he was asked by his Aunty Tilly to suggest a book for his birthday. He replied, 'I should like one of the late Richard Jefferies. I like them all, but *have* only one called *Field and Hedgerow*'. H. Wake to Matilda Wake, n.d.

52. ELWES, D. REVD., 'Sir Herewald Wake, Bart', *Journal of the Northamptonshire Natural History Society and Field Club*, vol.18, 1916, pp.140–1.

53. WAKE, SIR H. '*Fiat Justitia!*' Royal Society for the Protection of Birds. Leaflet No.53 (1905), p.1.

54. Northamptonshire Record Office, X2387.

55. WAKE, J., 'The Early Days of the Northamptonshire Natural History Society', *Northamptonshire Past and Present*, vol.1, no.5, 1952, p.41.

56. WAKE, SIR H. *Journal of the Northamptonshire Natural History Society and Field Club*, vol.1, 1880–1, p.56.

57. Ibid., vol.4, 1886–7, pp.153–62.

58. Ibid., vol.10, 1898–1900, p.2.

59. WAKE, SIR H. ' "The Deserted Roads" and the Motor Car'. Scrapbook, n.d.

60. In 1882 the gross value of the Essex and Northamptonshire estates was £5,810.

BATEMAN, J. *The Great Landowners of Great Britain and Ireland* (1883), p.45.

61. Diary, 7 August 1880. The Bill reached the Lords on 30 August and received the Royal Assent on 7 September. See GORDON, P. *The Red Earl. The Papers of the fifth Earl Spencer, 1835–1910* (1981), vol.1, pp.157–8.

62. Diary, 31 January 1882. See Royal Commission on Agriculture 1895. Report of R. Hunter Pringle, Assistant Commissioner on the Counties of Bedford, Huntingdon and Northampton, 10 November 1894, P.P. 1895, xviii, pp. 13–14.

63. Joan Wake, Preface to Sir Herewald Wake's 'Verses', n.d., p.2.

64. Sir Herewald Wake to T.H.D. Wake, 17 January 1888.

65. Diary, August 1891.

66. Mrs Beatrix Konstam to Joan Wake, 4 March 1969. Mrs Konstam's mother was a Miss Smyth of Little Houghton.

67. Quoted in HORN, P. *Joseph Arch: the farm workers' leader* (1971), p.70.

68. Joan Wake, Joseph Arch at Courteenhall. Conversation with John Whiting, 13 September 1927. Northamptonshire Record Office, X2387.

69. Sir Herewald Wake to fifth Earl Spencer, 7 March 1882, Spencer Papers, British Library, K221.

70. *Northampton Mercury*, 17 October 1890.

71. Ibid.

72. Ibid., 24 October 1890. S.G. Stopford Sackville, the Conservative Vice-Chairman of the Council, in congratulating Catherine on her husband's election, stated, 'I do think it is most important that Country Gentlemen should not be superseded in the management of their own affairs by ambitious and talkative nobodies'. S.G. Stopford Sackville to Lady Wake, 21 October 1890, Courteenhall Papers.

73. *Northampton Mercury*, 29 January 1892.

74. Lady Knightley of Fawsley, Journal, 18 and 20 March, 1880, Northamptonshire Record Office, K 2898; and *Northampton Herald*, 20 March 1880, and 27 March 1880.

75. See ARNSTEIN, W.L. *The Bradlaugh Case: a study in late Victorian opinion and politics* (1965), pp.24 and 28.

76. Diary, 17 April 1880. Sir Herewald wrote to Bobbie Spencer, a Liberal, some years later on his political principles, 'I know I have not changed mine though, and by the way, it was I that started the organization which our friend Becke (C.C. Becke, Liberal election agent) has been working, well, not too ably, for you'. Sir H. Wake to C.R. Spencer, 22 July 1895, 6th Earl Spencer Papers, Northamptonshire Record Office, SOX 378/75.

77. *The Times*, 2 July 1885, p.12. Herewald had publicly stated in December 1884 that he would stand as MP. Charles B. Wake to H.P. Markham, 21 December 1884, Northamptonshire Record Office, H.P. Markham Papers, CAM. 277.

78. WAKE, SIR H. *The Parting of the Ways* (1894), p.7.

79. Ibid., p.6.

80. i.e., Herwald Wake, the hero of Arrah.

81. Diary, August 1891.

82. Mrs R. Eykyn to Sir H. Wake, January 1891.

83. Sir H. Wake to Matilda Wake, 16 May 1891.

84. There is a gap in the Courteenhall Visitors' Book from 7 November 1891 to 27 March 1893. This is followed by a note in Sir Herewald's hand, 'After two years' enforced absence, House restored'. Courteenhall Visitors' Book 1887–1917 (copy), Northamptonshire Record Office, ZA 4227.

85. Thomas Lyttelton, fourth Baron Lilford, was the first President of the Northamptonshire Natural History Society and author of *Notes on the Birds of Northamptonshire and Neighbourhood*, published in 1895 in two volumes.

86. Lord Lilford to Sir H. Wake, 23 November 1893.

87. Joan Wake called on Hooper in Cornwall in 1933 and discussed the former Rector's actions of more than four decades previously. Hooper stated that 'the wood was sold to Lord Addington, who panelled rooms

with it in his house near Reading'. Joan Wake, Notes of conversation, 22 September 1933, Northamptonshire Record Office, X2386. The Religious Census of 1851 showed that the Church had 14 enclosed pews with free open seats to hold 100 persons; the average attendance at services during the previous year was 100. Census of Religion: Census of the Population for Churches and Chapels in Northamptonshire, HO 195/167, 15 March 1852, Public Record Office.

88. Reverend A. Wake, 'Courteenhall Church'.

89. *Northampton Independent*, 21 December 1912.

90. Archie noted on one occasion, 'Lucy and I dined at the Hall to meet Miss Farquhar. She is very pretty: and nice'. Courteenhall Parish Book, 1887-1924, 20 February, 1888.

91. *Northampton Independent*, 8 August 1925.

92. ARROWSMITH, R.L. (ed.) *Charterhouse Register, 1769–1872* (1964), p.387; and HILLCOURT, L. W. with OLIVE, LADY BADEN-POWELL, *Baden-Powell. The Two Lives of a Hero* (1964), p.19.

93. Reverend A. Wake, Courteenhall Parish Book, 1887–1924.

94. Reverend A. Wake, 'Entertainment at Rectory, Courteenhall, 1888–9'.

95. Joan Wake, Reminiscences, n.d.

96. Sir H. Wake, 'Irreverence', 15 October 1905, Northamptonshire Record Office, X2387.

97. Courteenhall School Log Book, 1923–50, 20 July 1925, Northamptonshire Record Office, SLB/31.

98. 'Owing to the early prejudices of our forefathers, girls were always excluded from its benefits'. WAKE, SIR H. 'Courteenhall School', *Journal of the Northamptonshire Natural History Society and Field Club*, vol.10, 1898–1900, p.199.

99. Schools Inquiry Commission 1868, P.P.1867–8, xxviii, vol.12, p.331.

100. Report, Hon. W. Bruce, 3 July 1888, Ed 49/5645 Part I, Public Record Office (PRO).

101. Joan Wake, Courteenhall and Wakefield, 4 February 1947.

102. Royal Commission on the Employment of Children, Young Persons and Women in Agriculture, Evidence, P.P.1867–8, xviii, p.691.

103. Joan Wake, Reminiscences, n.d.

104. Minutes of Meeting of Northampton Town Council, Guildhall, 5 September 1853, Northamptonshire Record Office, 86 P/141.

105. As a school inspector reported to the Board of Education, 'The population [of Courteenhall] is not likely to increase as Sir Herewald Wake never had labourers with families in his cottages, as water is very scarce and in a dry season, he has to keep a water cart going'. HMI Mr. A. Cartwright to G.N. Richardson, 14 November 1903, Ed 2/328, PRO.

106. Ibid.

107. Reverend A. Wake to R.L. Morant, 24 September 1903, Ed 2/328, PRO.

108. Sir H. Wake to R.L. Morant, 1 July 1910, Ed 49/5646, PRO.

109. Sir H. Wake to Board of Education, 7 August 1915, Ed 49/5645 Part I, PRO.

110. Sir H. Wake, Memorandum, April 1907. Courteenhall School, 1912–15, Courteenhall Papers.

111. *Northampton Daily Chronicle*, 11 May 1907.

112. Reverend A. Wake to Board of Education, 24 November 1908, Ed 2/328, PRO.

113. 1 July 1910, Ed 49/5646, PRO. For Sir Herewald's correspondence, see File, Restoration 1909–10, Courteenhall Papers.

114. On 12 January 1914, there were thirty one children in the village between the ages of five and thirteen. Courteenhall School, 1912–15, Courteenhall Papers.

115. Sir H. Wake to Lady Catherine Wake, '5p.m.' 5 July 1892.

116. The Small Holdings Bill (No.2), to amend the Small Holdings Act 1892, had received its second reading on 29 March 1906. A few years earlier, Sir Herewald had sought an interview with W.H. Long, President of the

Board of Agriculture, who 'rather pooh poohed my suggestion of giving landowners a chance versus professional buyers (and fraud?)'. Sir Herewald Wake, Fragment of Diary, 5 January 1899.

117. Sir H. Wake to William, fifth Marquess of Exeter, 24 October 1906, Courteenhall Papers.

118. See MURRAY, B. *The People's Budget, 1909–1910* (1980), p.169–70.

119. He was actively involved in the Liberty and Property Defence League, consisting of a group of influential people who opposed these measures. See *Morning Post*, 11 June 1909, p.3.

120. *Northampton Independent*, 29 June 1912. The heading for this item was 'A Bold Baronet: Won't Lick Stamps'.

121. *Northampton Herald*, 29 January 1909.

122. As Sir Herewald wrote to Hereward, 'I have worked hard myself all the time and it is most gratifying to find that my own labours with Account books and calculations and conferences with Tickler [E.S. Tickler, agent] and others have <u>not</u> been thrown away. In fact without my help, Tickler acknowledges he should have had no time to do the outdoor work of superintendence and direction on so large a farm'. Sir H. Wake to Hereward Wake, 16 October 1906, Courteenhall Papers.

123. Sir H. Wake, Notes to Executors and Trustees of Estate, written October 1910, ibid.

124. *Daily Graphic*, 31 August 1911, p.4.

125. Sir H. Wake to Hereward Wake, 4 December 1903, Courteenhall Papers.

126. Ibid., 25 April 1904.

127. Ibid., 16 October 1906.

128. AYLING, op.cit. p.7.

129. Joan Wake, Meals at Courteenhall, n.d.

130. In later years, whenever all his children were together at Courteenhall, Sir Herewald would write against their names in the Visitors' Book, 'Wake covey again. Gratia Deo!' e.g. August 1908. Courteenhall Visitors' Book 1887–1917 (copy), Northamptonshire Record Office, ZA 4227.

131. Sir H. Wake to Captain H. Wake, 16 October 1906, Courteenhall Papers.

132. Joan Wake, Preface, p.6.

133. *Northampton Herald*, 11 December 1914.

134. Sir Hereward Wake to Lady Margaret Wake, 5 January 1916, Courteenhall Papers.

135. Joan Wake, Preface, p.4.

Chapter 15

MAJOR-GENERAL SIR HEREWARD WAKE,
THIRTEENTH BARONET
I. YOUTH TO END OF WORLD WAR I

1. Hereward Wake to Lady Catherine Wake, 2 March 1887, Joan Wake Papers.

2. Afterwards, Edith Davidson wrote to Hereward's mother, 'We enjoyed much the sight of Hereward on Sunday morning. He came to breakfast with us, and seems to look well and happy. I think he is <u>so</u> like Harry – it seemed just like his father grown young'. Edith M. Davidson to Lady Catherine Wake, 30 March 1889, Courteenhall Papers.

3. Sir Hereward Wake, Relics of Charles I, n.d. but c.1950, Northamptonshire Record Office, V221. See also BELL, G.K.A. *Randall Davidson, Archbishop of Canterbury* (1935) vol.1, pp.98–101.

4. F.W. Cornish to Sir Herewald Wake, 29 December 1890, Joan Wake Papers.

5. ASKWITH, B. *Two Victorian Families* (1971), p.165.

6. A.C. Benson, Classical Report for Michaelmas 1890, Joan Wake Papers.

7. H. Wake to Daisy Wake, 30 November 1914, Courteenhall Papers.

8. H. Wake to Lady Catherine Wake, 21 March 1891, Joan Wake Papers.

9. H. Wake to Sir Herewald Wake, 25

October 1891, ibid.

10. J.H.M. Hare to Sir Herewald Wake, 22 December 1893, Courteenhall Papers.

11. H.E. Luxmoore to Sir Herewald Wake, January 1894, ibid. Luxmoore, a man of many talents, had been amongst other things, associated with William Morris and the Arts and Crafts movement. JAMES, M.R. *Letters of H.E. Luxmoore* (1929), p.p. 22–3.

12. *Eton College Chronicle*, 21 July 1894, p.1060.

13. H. Wake to Lady Catherine Wake, 8 November 1894, Joan Wake Papers.

14. Royal Military College, Camberley. Report of Gentleman Cadet H. Wake, December 1895, Courteenhall Papers.

15. H. Wake to Sir Herewald Wake, 9 July 1897, ibid.

16. *Northampton Herald*, 7 August 1897.

17. H. Wake to Lady Catherine Wake, 4 September 1897, Joan Wake Papers.

18. H. Wake to Godwin Wake, 16 October 1899, ibid.

19. ENSOR, R.C.K. *England, 1870–1914* (1936), p.251.

20. H. Wake to Baldwin Wake, 25 November 1899, Joan Wake Papers.

21. For details of the battles, see AMERY, L.S. (ed.) *The Times History of the War in South Africa, 1899–1900* (1902), vol.2. Magersfontein, chapter 11, pp.383–420, Colenso, chapter 12, pp.421–67.

22. MELVILLE, C.H. *Life of General Sir Redvers Buller* (1923), vol.2 p.14.

23. H. Wake, Battle of Colenso, 16 December 1899, Joan Wake Papers.

24. H. Wake to Lady Catherine Wake, 27 December 1899, ibid.

25. CHURCHILL, R.S. *Winston S. Churchill. Youth: 1874–1900* (1966), vol.1, p.510.

26. H. Wake to Ida Wake, 27 January 1900, Courteenhall Papers. On coming down from Spion Kop, Hereward was told by a soldier that he was reported dead on top of the hill 'as he'd seen me shot, and would I take Mr. Wake's bloodstained helmet which he'd brought down? It was my helmet which I was pleased to see again'. H. Wake to Lady Catherine Wake, 1 April 1900, Joan Wake Papers.

27. Ibid., 4 February 1900.

28. H. Wake to Ida Wake, 9 February 1900, Courteenhall Papers.

29. PAKENHAM, T. *The Boer War* (1979), p.307.

30. H. Wake to Ida Wake, 26 February 1900. Hereward's action is described in MAURICE, SIR J.F. and GRANT, M.H. *History of the War in South Africa, 1899–1902* (1907), vol.2, pp.481–2.

31. H. Wake to Lady Catherine Wake, 24 July 1899, Joan Wake Papers.

32. Edwina Roberts to Lady Catherine Wake, 9 March 1900, ibid.

33. H. Wake to Ida Wake, 14 March 1900, Courteenhall Papers.

34. H. Wake to Lady Catherine Wake, 4 April 1900, Joan Wake Papers.

35. Ibid.

36. H. Wake to Ida Wake, 15 May 1900, Courteenhall Papers.

37. Ibid., 18 July 1900.

38. H. Wake to Lady Catherine Wake, 17 August 1900, Courteenhall Papers.

39. Ibid., 9 July 1900.

40. Ibid., 17 August 1900.

41. A full account of the battle is contained in a letter, H. Wake to Ida Wake, 28 August 1900, Courteenhall Papers.

42. H. Wake to Lady Catherine Wake, 1 November 1900, ibid.

43. See *The Times*, 4 January 1901, p.8. The banquet itself was described in WAKE, SIR H. 'Meals I Shall Always Remember', *Wheeler's Review*, Jan-March 1956, pp.14–15.

44. H. Wake to Sir Herewald Wake, 12 September 1900, Courteenhall Papers.

45. H. Wake to Ida Wake, 26 May 1901, ibid.

46. As he added at the time, 'By the mercy of God, I saw the man aiming at me and I dived in time'.

47. H. Wake to Lady Catherine Wake, 28 October 1901, Joan Wake Papers.

48. Ibid., 11 November 1901.

49. Ibid., 16 January 1902.

50. Ibid., 20 January 1902.

51. H. Wake to Sir Herewald Wake, 21 March 1902, Courteenhall Papers.

52. H. Wake to Ida Wake, 29 March 1902, ibid. For full citation, see Royal Humane Society Annual Report for 1902, Case 31, 819, p.66.

53. H. Wake to Sir Herewald Wake, 29 April 1902, ibid.

54. H. Wake to Ida Wake, 30 May 1902, ibid.

55. G.A. Sprigg, formerly Hereward's orderly, to Sir H. Wake, 28 January 1948, ibid.

56. H. Wake to Ida Wake, July 1902, ibid.

57. Ibid., 19 April 1903.

58. Ibid., 1 October 1903.

59. Ibid., 2 January 1904. One novelty which Hereward brought back from South Africa was a meerkat, named Jenny. It became a great favourite of the family and got on well with the dogs and cats. Jenny died in December 1905 and was buried in the Dogs' Graveyard in the Plantation at Courteenhall.

60. Major H. Wilson to H. Wake, 8 April 1904, Courteenhall Papers.

61. BOND, B. *The Victorian Army and the Staff College, 1854–1914* (1972), p.248.

62. H. Wake to Ida Wake, 1 May 1908, Courteenhall Papers.

63. In July 1910, Sir Ian Hamilton, Commander-in-Chief, Mediterranean, offered Hereward a post on his personal staff. After consideration, he turned it down. Lord Roberts to H. Wake, 22 July 1910, ibid.

64. H. Wake to Lady Catherine Wake, 2 July 1912, ibid.

65. Robert's grandfather, also called Robert (1785–1846), had begun in business as an agent for the East India Company with the Rathbones in Liverpool. He later moved down to London. MARRINER, S. *Rathbones of Liverpool, 1845–73* (1961), p.48.

66. ELLIOTT, SIR I. (ed.) *Balliol Register, 1833–1933* (1934), p.60.

67. The collection of 114 Italian paintings, representing all the major schools, were gathered over a period of thirty years in London, Paris and Italy. *Catalogue of Italian Pictures at 16 South Street, Park Lane, London and Buckhurst, Sussex, Collected by Robert and Evelyn Benson* (1914), p.v.

68. He had voted against the disestablishment of the Irish Church in 1869, believing that 'the connection of Church and State is one of the greatest blessings which we possess'. STENTON, M. *Who's Who of British Members of Parliament* (1976), vol.1, p.196.

69. SUTTON, REVD. C.N. *Historical Notes of Withyham, Hartfield and Ashdown Forest* (1902), pp.99–101.

70. *Lutyens Exhibition Catalogue, Hayward Gallery* (1981), p.193.

71. Daisy Benson to Robert Benson, 13 November 1907, Northamptonshire Record Ofice, X46.

72. Daisy Wake to H. Wake, 15 September 1916, Courteenhall Papers. White served in the War as Brigadier-General, commanding the 184th Infantry Brigade. He died, unmarried, on 19 November 1936.

73. H. Wake to Daisy Benson, 22 June 1912, ibid.

74. H. Wake to Lady Catherine Wake, 29 June 1912, Joan Wake Papers.

75. H. Wake to Daisy Benson, 3 June 1912, ibid.

76. H. Wake to Daisy Wake, 7 November 1915, ibid.

77. H. Wake to Daisy Benson, 23 October 1912, ibid.

78. The procession consisted of three little pages, wearing Kate Greenaway costumes and carrying the bride's train, six small bridesmaids wearing mob caps, with blue velvet dresses, and two older bridesmaids. *Daily Sketch*, 30 October 1912.

79. *Northampton Herald*, 1 November 1912.

80. *The Standard*, 23 November 1912.

81. WAKE, REVD. A. *Courteenhall Parish Magazine*, December 1912.

82. CASSAR, G.H. *The Tragedy of Sir John French* (1985), p.81.

83. Recalling their South African campaign days, Hereward stated, 'Lord French shook me by the hand and said it was

quite like old times'. Sir H. Wake to Daisy Wake, 10 October 1916, Courteenhall Papers.

84. FRENCH, FIELD MARSHAL VISCOUNT. *1914* (1919), p.33.

85. H. Wake to Daisy Wake, 16 August 1914, Courteenhall Papers.

86. Ibid., 17 August 1914.

87. Ibid., 9 September 1914.

88. Ibid., 19 September 1914.

89. MAURICE, SIR J.F. (ed.) *The Life of General Lord Rawlinson of Trent* (1928), p.106.

90. H. Wake to Daisy Wake, 29 October 1914, Courteenhall Papers.

91. Ibid., 12 November 1914.

92. Daisy Wake to H. Wake, 1 November 1914, ibid.

93. JAMES, D. P. *Lord Roberts* (1954), p.484.

94. H. Wake to Daisy Wake, 13 November 1914, Courteenhall Papers.

95. CALLWELL, SIR C.E. *Field Marshal Sir Henry Wilson. His Life and Diaries* (1927), vol.1, p.187.

96. ASHWORTH, T. *Trench Warfare 1914–1918. The Live and Let Live System* (1980), p.4.

97. H. Wake to Daisy Wake, 28 March 1915, Courteenhall Papers.

98. Ibid., 3 September 1917.

99. Ibid., 7 June 1916.

100. See CALLWELL, op.cit., vol.1, p.131 and p.134.

101. H. Wake to Daisy Wake, 20 February 1915, Courteenhall Papers.

102. HART, SIR B.H. LIDDELL *History of the First World War* (1930, 1972 edition), p.14.

103. H. Wake to Daisy Wake, 19 March 1913, Courteenhall Papers.

104. Ibid., 27 March 1915.

105. Ibid., 17 April 1915.

106. Ibid., 11 November 1915.

107. 'I am tremendously busy trying to get Daisy's house ready for her', Evelyn Benson told her sister Alice in December 1915. 'She can't come up till it is absolutely in working order as she is nursing and she doesn't want to make more than one move. The vans of furniture began to come yesterday and the last two arrive tomorrow, and I have found a cook and a parlour maid and a charwoman and her housemaid returns to her, so she will have three servants ready to walk in on Tuesday. [4 January 1916]. Hereward is in a tremendous hurry, but he does not realize that after a year and a half of being stored, no mattress is safe to use until it has been well cooked in front of a large fire, and that entails a lot of work and time'. Evelyn Benson to Alice, Lady Grey, 30 December 1915, Grey Papers (4th Earl), Durham University Library.

108. Hereward wrote to his sister, 'I think it is a splendid idea offering Courteenhall as a hospital if Mama would like it. They could pay a nominal rent (say £400 a year), put in electric light and undertake to do it up from top to bottom afterwards, and have it till three months until after the war'. Sir H. Wake to Ida Wake, 5 August 1916, Courteenhall Papers.

109. Sir H. Wake to Daisy Wake, 31 August 1916, ibid.

110. Ibid., 10 April 1915.

111. Ibid., 8 November 1916.

112. Ibid., 22 May 1916.

113. Ibid., 2 July 1916.

114. CRUTWELL, C.R.M.F. *A History of the Great War, 1914–1918* (1934), pp.265–6.

115. Asquith was a frequent visitor to Buckhurst. He particularly admired Daisy's two brothers, Guy and Rex, whom he described as 'manly, good looking, with charming manners and plenty of intelligence – in fact, ideal sons-in-law'. H.H. Asquith to Venetia Stanley, 24 May 1914, BROCK, M. and E. (eds.) *H.H. Asquith. Letters to Venetia Stanley* (1982), p.74.

116. Daisy Wake to Sir H. Wake, 22 July 1916, Courteenhall Papers. After the weekend she told Hereward, 'The P.M. looks horribly seedy'. Courteenhall Papers, 24 July 1916.

117. Sir H. Wake to Daisy Wake, 21 August 1916, ibid.

118. Ibid., 30 August 1916.

119. Ibid., 8 September 1916.

120. Quoted in WILSON, T. *The Myriad Faces of War. Britain and the Great War, 1914–1918* (1986), p.348.

121. Sir H. Wake to Daisy Wake, 28 November 1916, Courteenhall Papers.

122. Ibid., 10 November 1916.

123. Ibid., 23 December 1916.

124. Ibid., 13 December 1916. Wells wrote of his book, 'I think I have contrived to give not only the astonishment and the sense of tragic disillusionment in a civilized mind as the cruel facts of war rose steadily to dominate everything in life, but also the passionate desire to find some immediate reassurance amidst that whirlwind of disaster'. WELLS, H.G. *Experiment in Autobiography* (1934), vol.2, pp.670–1.

125. Sir H. Wake to Daisy Wake, 26 February 1917, Courteenhall Papers.

126. Ibid., 28 December 1916.

127. CORNWALL, SIR J.H.M. *Haig as Military Commander* (1973), p.239.

128. Sir H. Wake to Daisy Wake, 25 August 1917, Courteenhall Papers. The Germans first used gas on 22 April 1915 at the second Battle of Ypres. The British employed it on 25 September that year at the Battle of Loos. HARE, SIR S.W. *The Annals of the King's Royal Rifle Corps: The Great War* (1932), vol.5, pp.75 and 104.

129. Ibid., 8 October 1917.

130. WOOLLCOMBE, R. *The First Tank Battle: Cambrai 1917* (1967), pp.192–202.

131. Sir H. Wake to Daisy Wake, 6 December 1917, Courteenhall Papers.

132. WOODWARD, D.R. *Lloyd George and the Generals* (1983), pp.231–3.

133. Sir H. Wake to Daisy Wake, 31 March 1918, Courteenhall Papers.

134. CALLWELL, op.cit., vol.2, p.42.

135. Sir H. Wake to Daisy Wake, 15 December 1917, Courteenhall Papers.

136. Ibid., 17 January 1918.

137. CALLWELL, op.cit., vol.2, p.53.

138. For an account of the proceedings of the Council see HANKEY, LORD *The Supreme Command, 1914–1918* (1961), vol.2, pp.762–73.

139. Sir H. Wake to Daisy Wake, 29 January 1918, Courteenhall Papers.

140. BARNES, J. and NICHOLSON, D. (eds.) *The Leo Amery Diaries* (1980), vol.1, 1896–1929, pp.202–3.

141. Sir H. Wake to Daisy Wake, 31 March 1918, Courteenhall Papers.

142. AMERY, L.S. *My Political Life* (1953), pp.138–9.

143. *The Times*, 10 April 1918, p.8.

144. Amery recorded on 3 April, 'Hereward Wake and Ollivant [Lt-Colonel A.H. Ollivant, General Staff Officer] both came back from the battle. O. puts the collapse of the Vth. Army down to undue extension and bad placing of reserves, as also does Hereward. Both agree that there is no one at GHQ who has any brains or approves of brains in anyone else. Hereward, in a moment of bitterness, summed it up by asking what was to be expected with a fool like Haig and a liar like Pétain'. *The Leo Amery Diaries*, op.cit., p.213.

145. Sir H. Wake to Daisy Wake, 1 February 1918, Courteenhall Papers.

146. Ibid., 30 January 1918. Lloyd's exploits with Lawrence against the Turks were recounted in LAWRENCE, T.E. *Seven Pillars of Wisdom* (1935 edition), pp.400–10. Three days before, Amery had suggested to Lloyd George that he should meet Lloyd to hear at first hand his experiences in Palestine. L.S. Amery to Lloyd George, 27 January 1918, Lloyd George Papers, F/2/1/14.

147. Sir H. Wake to Daisy Wake, 14 April 1918, Courteenhall Papers.

148. Ibid., 15 April 1918.

149. For the conditions prevailing in this theatre of war, see PRICE, G. WARD *The Story of the Salonica Army* (1917), pp.65–72.

150. Sir H. Wake to Daisy Wake, 10 June 1918, Courteenhall Papers.

151. Ibid., 26 June 1918.

152. Sir H. Wake to General G. Cory, 5 July 1918 (copy); and Cory to Sir H. Wake, 28 July 1918, Northamptonshire Record Office, V222.

153. Sir H. Wakes 'Strategy without Policy', Northamptonshire Record Office, V222, p.3.

154. J.E. Drummond to Sir H. Wake, 9 July 1918, Northamptonshire Record Office, V222.

155. Hereward had discussed this as a matter of urgency with Sir Henry Wilson, now CIGS. Sir H. Wake to L.S. Amery, 13 August 1918, Northamptonshire Record Office, V222.

156. Sir H. Wake to J.E. Drummond, 11 July 1918 (copy), Northamptonshire Record Office, V222.

157. L.S. Amery to Sir H. Wake, 9 August 1918, Northamptonshire Record Office, V222.

158. Sir H. Wake to L.S. Amery, 13 August 1918, Northamptonshire Record Office.

159. Sir H. Wake to Daisy Wake, 22 August 1918, Courteenhall Papers.

160. Sir H. Wake, 'British Interests at the Peace Conference', 29 October 1918, Northamptonshire Record Office, V222.

161. Sir H. Wake to Daisy Wake, 15 July 1918, Courteenhall Papers.

162. Ibid., 31 August 1918.

163. That same day, Hereward produced a document, *'The Principles of Allied Strategy'*, which argued the merits of concentrating resources on the Western rather than the Eastern front. He stated, 'When the German armies are so weakened by defeat that Germany's future appears hopeless, her allies will hasten to make peace and desert the sinking ship before it sinks with them'. Milner Papers, dep., 359, f.157, Bodleian Library, Oxford.

164. Sir H. Wake to Daisy Wake, 9 September 1918, Courteenhall Papers.

Chapter 16
MAJOR-GENERAL SIR HEREWARD WAKE, THIRTEENTH BARONET
II. COURTEENHALL AND THE SECOND WORLD WAR

1. Sir H. Wake, Jungle Diary, 19 December 1921, Courteenhall Papers.

2. On 1 October 1919, Hereward's pay was £850 per annum.

3. Henry Bolton to Hereward Wake 23 August 1912, Courteenhall Papers.

4. At the same time he paid a large sum of money to Waltham Abbey Church, of which he was Lay Rector, thus freeing him and his descendants from paying for the upkeep of the Norman Church.

5. Sir H. Wake to Daisy Wake, 2 April 1925, Courteenhall Papers. Robert Benson, Daisy's father, had, under the terms of the marriage settlement, made over a sum of £25,000 which was settled on her and her children. This was in the form of investments from which Daisy received an annual income.

6. Sir H. Wake to Daisy Wake, 24 May 1917, ibid.

7. Ibid., 3 July 1917.

8. The School proved to be very popular. On 15 June, a 'great cricket match' was played between the School and the Courteenhall Estate, after which the teams were entertained with an 'excellent war-time tea' at the Hall. Shortly before the school left for Essex the headmaster, Mr T.R. Wilcox, invited the parish to the Hall for scenes from *The Merchant of Venice* and *Pirates of Penzance*. As Archie Wake wrote at the time, 'Everyone will be sorry at their departure'. *Preston Deanery Parish Magazine*, January 1919.

9. Sir H. Wake to Ida Wake, 10 April 1918, ibid. See also Ida Wake's *Courteenhall Farm Accounts Book, 1916–1918*, Northamptonshire Record Office, X8918.

10. Sir H. Wake to Ida Wake, 6 September 1921, Courteenhall Papers.

11. Sir H. Wake to Daisy Wake, 2 May 1922, ibid.

12. Ibid., 31 August and 5 September 1922.

13. Ibid., 25 January 1928.

14. Ibid., 16 February 1922.

15. Ibid., 22 April 1922.

16. Edward Raynell, Account, 30 April 1922, ibid.

17. Sir H. Wake to Daisy Wake, 5 September 1922, ibid.

18. Ibid., 10 December 1922.

19. In October, Hereward noted that besides having difficulties with his herd of cows, 'I've got a lot of work on just now as it's Michaelmas, collecting rents, paying wages, closing farm accounts, bills etc'. Sir H. Wake to Daisy Wake, 1 October 1924, ibid.

20. Joan Wake, 'Notes written 10 June 1924', Northamptonshire Record Office, X2386. The official opening took place on 3 June 1924. See 'After 25 years', *Northampton Daily Echo*, 4 June 1924.

21. Courteenhall School Log Book, 1923–50, 17 September 1923, Northamptonshire Record Office, SLB/31.

22. Sir H. Wake to Daisy Wake, 15 November 1927, Courteenhall Papers.

23. On 25 January 1928, the seventh Earl Spencer wrote to Hereward, 'I am sure you will make a very strong candidate', ibid.

24. *The Times*, 12 July 1927, p.12; and see BEHRMAN, S.N., *Duveen* (1952), p.18.

25. Sir H. Wake to Daisy Wake, 12 July 1927, Courteenhall Papers.

26. Ibid., 2 September 1930.

27. *The Times*, 20 September 1932, p.6.

28. *Chatham News*, 29 April 1932.

29. Sir Hereward Wake, fourteenth baronet, to author, 3 June 1987.

30. Earlier, from Buckingham Palace, an official had written to Hereward, 'I do not think they could have found a better man for the post'. W.G. Lindsell to Sir H. Wake, 20 August 1933, Courteenhall Papers.

31. Sir H. Wake to Dowager Lady Catherine Wake, 31 October 1933, Joan Wake Papers.

32. Ibid., 12 November 1933.

33. Gort had taken command of the British Expeditionary Force on 3 September. COLVILLE, SIR J.R. *Man of Valour. Life of Field Marshal the Viscount Gort* (1972), p.146.

34. Sir H. Wake, War Diary, 4 October 1939, Courteenhall Papers. Lloyd, now a Baron, became Colonial Secretary in Churchill's Government in 1940. A promising career was cut short by his death in February 1941. Marshal of the Royal Air Force, Viscount Trenchard, who had built up the RAF into a

fighting force, was sixty six when war was declared. On 23 May 1940, Churchill offered him the post of Commander-in-Chief, Home Forces, but Trenchard refused because of the conditions attached to it. He became an unofficial Inspector-General, visiting RAF squadrons in Europe and Africa. BOYLE, A. *Trenchard* (1962), pp.719–20.

35. In London, Hereward invariably stayed at 16 Sussex Place, home of his brother-in-law, then Major Rex Benson.

36. Sir H. Wake, War Diary, 15 October 1939, Courteenhall Papers.

37. The other person was Lieutenant-Colonel A.V. Jenner. See MAUROIS, A. *Memoirs 1885–1967* (1970), p.106.

38. The first English edition, with translation by Ida, was published as *The Silence of Colonel Bramble* by John Lane in 1919.

39. Sir H. Wake, War Diary, 21 December 1939, Courteenhall Papers.

40. Ibid., 11 January 1940. See MACLEOD, R. (ed.) *The Ironside Diaries, 1937–1940* (1962), pp.167–8, and MINNEY, R.J. (ed.) *The Private Papers of Hore-Belisha* (1960), pp.263–4.

41. Sir H. Wake, War Diary, 29 January 1940, Courteenhall Papers.

42. Ibid, 13 March 1940.

43. Ibid., 15 April 1940.

44. Sir H. Wake to Dowager Lady Catherine Wake, 21 September 1939, Joan Wake Papers.

45. McCOMBE, F.W. (ed.) *Register of St. Lawrence College, 1879 to 1953* (1955, fourth edition), p.xii.

46. Reverend Canon R. Perfect to Sir H. Wake, 30 May 1957, Northamptonshire Record Office, V219.

47. Sir H. Wake to Dowager Lady Catherine Wake, 18 September 1939, Joan Wake Papers.

48. Dowager Lady Catherine Wake, Diary, 23 June 1940, ibid.

49. Ibid., 31 July 1940.

50. Ibid., 7 August 1943.

51. Mary Wake, Air Raid at Courteenhall, 23 August 1940, Northamptonshire Record

Office, X2387.

52. *Hansard*, 5, 361, cols.787–8, 4 June 1940.

53. GILBERT, M. *Winston S. Churchill: Finest Hour 1939–1941* (1983), vol.6, pp.526–7.

54. Courteenhall Papers.

55. Roger Wake, 'Dunkirk 30 May to 4 June 1940', *King's Royal Rifle Chronicle*, (1940), p.31.

56. Sir H. Wake to Marquess of Exeter, 22 June 1940 (copy), ibid.

57. See GRAVES, C. *The Home Guard of Britain* (1943), pp.84–5.

58. Captain N. Arnold to Sir H. Wake, 26 June 1940, and Wake to Arnold 27 June 1940 (copy), Courteenhall Papers.

59. Cleared, in the first instance, by the Censorship Division of the Ministry of Information.

60. *Northampton Chronicle and Echo*, 22 July 1940.

61. Northamptonshire Home Guard, Intelligence Report No.5, 9 September 1940. It emerged later that the spy had been dropped by parachute at 3.0 a.m. that day. In landing, he had hit his head on the wireless set he was carrying. He was discovered later by a farm employee at The Elms, Denton. *Northamptonshire at War 1939–45* (1979), p.44.

62. Sir H. Wake, The Role of the Home Guard, 3 December 1940, Courteenhall Papers.

63. Exeter reported to Hereward, 'I was told from the beginning that the Zone Commander would be merely a figure-head... I must say I am disgusted with the whole procedure'. Marquess of Exeter to Sir H. Wake, 13 February 1941, Courteenhall Papers.

64. Sir H. Wake, Statement to the County Territorial Army Association, 5 March 1941, ibid.

65. Sir H. Wake to Lord Brooke, 2 August 1942 (copy), Northamptonshire Record Office, YZ 9434.

66. Courteenhall Invasion Committee Meeting and Minutes, 16 August 1942, ibid.

67. Ibid., 30 August and 18 October 1942.

68. HMS *Hereward*, Summary of Service, 1939–41, Ministry of Defence, S.7702.

69. THOMAS, D. A. *Crete, 1941: the battle at sea* (1972), p.190.

70. Munn wrote an account of the sinking of the destroyer to Hereward after his release from Italian captivity. W.J. Munn to Sir H. Wake, 28 August 1947, Northamptonshire Record Office, V223.

71. WAKE, Sir H. 'Rooks and Farming', *Northampton Independent*, 30 April 1943.

72. Joan Wake, Diary, 17 August 1944, Joan Wake Papers.

73. Ibid., 5 October 1944.

74. Sir H. Wake, Notes of Speech at Ruridecanal Conference, Preston Deanery, 1 October 1943, ibid.

75. Joan Wake, Diary, 21 October 1944, ibid.

76. Lord Henley to Sir H. Wake, 30 January 1946, Northamptonshire Record Office, V223.

77. Ministry of Health, Report of the Committee on the Restoration of Land Affected by Iron Ore Working (1939), p.85.

78. Ministry of Town and Country Planning, Report of the Committee on Land Utilisation (1942), p.94.

79. See White Paper, Report on the Restoration Problem in the Ironstone Industry in the Midlands. Summary of Findings and Recommendations, Cmd.6906, Sept 1946, p.5.

80. *Northampton Mercury and Herald*, 27 February 1942.

81. *Northampton Chronicle and Echo*, 29 March 1943.

82. Sir H. Wake to R. Manningham-Buller, MP, 21 March 1944 (copy), Courteenhall Papers.

83. Sir H. Wake, Memorandum, Restoration of Iron Ore Workings, 24 January 1943, ibid.

84. Duke of Buccleuch to Sir H. Wake, 1 February 1944, ibid.

85. C.V. Davidge to Sir H. Wake, 31 August 1944, ibid.

86. Northampton Branch, Central Landowners' Association, *Iron-Ore Workings in Northamptonshire* (1944), pp.3–4.

87. Sir H. Wake, Memorandum, January 1954, Northamptonshire Record Office, YZ677.

88. *Kettering Evening Telegraph*, 9 February 1949.

89. *Northampton Chronicle and Echo*, 5 July 1946.

90. IRESON, T. *Northamptonshire* (1954), pp. 305–6.

91. WAKE, Joan, 'Major-General Sir Hereward Wake', *Northamptonshire Past and Present*, vol.3, no.4, 1963, p.168.

92. Joan Wake to Sir H. Wake, 25 September 1961, Northamptonshire Record Office, V221.

93. *Northampton Mercury and Herald*, 18 July 1958.

94. *Daily Telegraph*, 22 December 1947.

95. Information kindly supplied by Lord Deedes to author, 19 June 1990.

96. BRERETON, J.M. *A Guide to the Regiments of the British Army* (1985), p.259.

97. WAKE, SIR H. and DEEDES, W.F. *Swift and Bold. The Story of the King's Royal Rifle Corps in the Second World War* (1949), p.xiv.

98. Sir H. Wake to Colonel Rex Benson, Military attaché, Washington, 1 July 1942, Northamptonshire Record Office, V222.

99. EDEN, A. *Another World, 1897–1917*, (1976), pp.63–5.

100. Sir Anthony Eden to C.G. Bolté, 1 June 1960, Northamptonshire Record Office, V222.

101. This number included ten out of the twelve surviving American officers who had volunteered for the Regiment during the war. MILLS, G.H. *The Annals of the King's Royal Rifle Corps, 1943–1965* (1979), vol. 7, p.244.

102. John Waterfield to Peter Wake, 16 June 1960 (copy), Northamptonshire Record Office, V222.

103. *Daily Telegraph*, 18 June 1960.

104. Programme of Visit to Governor's Island, New York, 16 June 1960, Northamptonshire Record Office, V222.

105. John Waterfield to Peter Wake, 16 June 1960 (copy), ibid.

106. *Northampton Mercury and Herald*, 9 August 1963.

107. Sir H. Wake to Daisy Wake, 29 October 1915, Courteenhall Papers.

108. Cazalet was Conservative MP for Chippenham from 1924 until 4 July 1943, when he was killed in an aeroplane crash whilst travelling with the Polish leader, General Sikorski. See JAMES, R.R. (ed.) *Chips: The Diaries of Sir Henry Channon* (1970), pp.451–2.

109. V. Cazalet to Sir H. Wake, 30 September 1918, Courteenhall Papers.

Chapter 17
JOAN WAKE, HISTORIAN

1. Joan Wake Papers. Unless otherwise stated, all references in the chapter are drawn from this collection.

2. Joan Wake, Notes on Great Uncles and Aunts, Oxford, 7 January 1965.

3. Joan Wake, Courteenhall A Hundred Years Ago, 25 June 1940.

4. She told Christopher Brooke, the historian, in her later years, 'The two most exciting things I've done in my life are finding twelfth century charters and hunting. I don't know which was the most exciting. Hunting, I think'. BROOKE, C. 'Miss Joan Wake',

Northamptonshire Past and Present, vol.5, no. 3, 1975, p.291.

5. Joan Wake to Emily Surridge, 29 January 1970.

6. Joan Wake to Phyllis Wake, 10 July 1897.

7. Joan Wake to Sir Hereward Wake, 22 February 1950.

8. Joan Wake, Speech at the Jubilee Concert of the Northampton School of Music, 24 October 1946. When she was a child, Joan once left lying around a programme of one of the Pupils' Concerts, which her father, Sir

Herewald, who was no musician, had attended. He had scribbled the following lines on it:

The ear for music I have not the least,
I fear Miss Beasley's feelings this
will ravage,
Though music hath charms to soothe
the savage beast,
It only makes yours truly beastly
savage.

9. Joan Wake, Sundays at Courteenhall, n.d.

10. *Northampton Herald*, 16 July 1908.

11. In 1942, Joan published an account of Northamptonshire clergy and their wives and families, extracted from her Preface to vol.14 of the Reverend H.I. Longden's *Northamptonshire and Rutland Clergy*. Joan ended with Uncle Archie and, somewhat incongruously, in view of his lifelong bachelorhood, she entitled the pamphlet *St.Peter . . . Himself a Married Man*.

12. Sundays at Courteenhall, ibid.

13. WAKE, JOAN. 'Cromwell's Head', *Northamptonshire Past and Present*, vol.3, no.1, 1960, p.3.

14. Collins (1848–1908), a leading Shakespearian scholar and essayist on English poets, had campaigned vigorously for the recognition of literature, as distinct from philology, as an academic discipline. In 1904, he was appointed to the first chair in English Literature at the University of Birmingham. Joan probably met him in connection with the University Extension movement, of which he was a fervent advocate. Betweeen 1880 and 1907, Collins gave 3,000 lectures in various centres. COLLINS, L.C. *Life and Memoirs of John Churton Collins* (1912), p.60.

15. Edith Sitwell to Joan Wake, n.d. but 1915, MS. Facs.b.57, f.88, Bodleian Library, Oxford.

16. These included *The Two Archers, Song* and *Lullaby*. Some of the poems were written on Courteenhall-headed paper.

17. Joan Wake to Hope Allen, 29 July 1938.

18. Looking back on these days, Joan wrote in 1938, 'I am idyllically happy at Cosgrove [her home] – happier than I have ever been in my life, except possibly those few pre-war months when I was living on about 25 shillings a week in London as a student at the London School of Economics'. Joan Wake to Hope Allen, 29 July 1938.

19. Alice Raven to Joan Wake, 15 July 1915. Joan never forgot the difficulties which faced educated women of her generation in obtaining suitable employment. Many years later, she reflected: 'After seeing all these sad, bereft, middle-aged, untrained, lonely spinsters, it brings one up against this English problem, and I do hope parents will learn the lesson and educate and train their daughters to some profession'. Joan Wake to Hope Allen, 28 January 1941.

20. WAKE, JOAN. 'Northamptonshire Records', *Speculum*, vol.33, no.2, 1958, p.231.

21. Reverend R.M. Serjeantson to Joan Wake, 5 September 1915.

22. WAKE, JOAN 'Professor Sir Frank Stenton: Some Recollections', *Northamptonshire Past and Present*, vol.4, no.3, 1968, p.181. Stenton (1880–1967), was Research Fellow at the College, 1908–12, Professor of Modern History, 1912–46, Vice-Chancellor, 1946–50. Knight, 1948.

23. KING, P.I. 'Dr. Joan Wake', *Journal of the Society of Archivists*, vol.5, no.2, October 1974, p.149.

24. Joan Wake to Ruth Easterbury, 21 January 1920. Piggott (1852–1925), a Chief Justice of the Supreme Court of Hong Kong, was editor and part author of a six-volume *Law of the Sea Series of Historical and Legal Works*. The first volume was published in 1919. See *The Times*, 13 March 1925, p.7.

25. In January 1919, Joan wrote a poem entitled 'A Student's Aspiration' whilst she was still honorary secretary of the District Nursing Association. In it she expressed her longing to return to work on ancient records:

And when from District Nursing I
With cheerful heart can turn my face,
The institutions, laws and acts,
And thoughts, may it be mine to trace.

For the complete poem, see *Northamptonshire*

Past and Present, vol.5, no.1, 1973, p.17.

26. Frank Stenton to Joan Wake, 1 September 1915.

27. WAKE, JOAN. 'Professor Sir Frank Stenton', op.cit., p.181. Canon Charles Foster had founded the Lincoln Record Society in 1910, which proved an excellent model for Joan to follow; see MAJOR, K. 'Canon Charles Wilmer Foster: A Pioneer Archivist and Editor of Records', *Archives*, vol.18, no.77, 1987, pp.43–9. The Lincoln Society covered both the county and the diocese; the latter included Northamptonshire up to 1536. STENTON, D.M. 'Frank Merry Stenton, 1880–1967', *Proceedings of the British Academy*, vol.54, 1968, p.383.

28. HOLTHOUSE, E. 'A Northamptonshire Record Society', *Northamptonshire Notes and Queries*, vol.2, 1886–7, p.196. Edwin H. Holthouse, FSA, FRCS,was one of the earliest members of the Record Society. In 1949, he bequeathed the Society a generous sum in his will. Joan Wake to Edwin Holthouse, 6 September 1946, Northamptonshire Record Office, Holthouse Papers, 573.

29. *Northampton Herald*, 22 October 1920.

30. Northamptonshire Record Society (hereafter NRS), First Annual Report for year ending 31 December 1921, p.3.

31. NRS, Fourth Annual Report for year ending 31 December 1924, p.5.

32. Joan Wake, Diary, 22 October 1932.

33. Joan Wake to Hope Allen, 13 May 1933.

34. Joan Wake, Visit to Winchilsea at Buckfield, Basingstoke, Hampshire, 1 December 1930.

35. In May 1935, Joan visited Drayton where Nigel Stopford-Sackville offered her literally thousands of deeds, dating from the twelfth century onwards. 'It is funny how used one gets to good luck', she wrote. 'A few years ago I should hardly have slept for excitement over this'. Joan Wake to Hope Allen, 28 May 1935.

36. Joan Wake to A. Brooks, 18 February 1964. She had also attended the court of the Manor of Waltham Holy Cross in 1921. 'The tenants were summoned to the site of the old market-house at Waltham Abbey, long since demolished, and there in the open market-place we stood, the Bailiff with a pile of Testaments on the ground before him, while he proclaimed the court, and afterwards swore in the jury. We then adjourned according to custom to the Inn'. WAKE, JOAN 'Manorial Records'. Proceedings no.2, *British Records Association*, 1937, p.4.

37. Emily Surridge to Joan Wake, 3 September 1972.

38. Joan Wake, Courteenhall and Wakefield, 4 February 1947, Northamptonshire Record Office, X2386.

39. Joan Wake, Mrs. Smith of Oundle, 30 April 1933.

40. See, for example, WARWICK, L. '"I'm expecting a Celestial Postcard". A tribute to Joan Wake', *Northampton Independent*, March 1974, p.63.

41. I am indebted to Mrs E. Lewis, Joan Wake's assistant for many years, for her reminiscences. It should be mentioned that Joan was by no means a strong feminist. In old age, she told Frank Stenton, 'My own secret opinion is that the vote has made my sex altogether too uppish and think a little wife-beating would do no harm – but then I am a spinster'. Joan Wake to Sir Frank Stenton, 8 January 1957, Stenton Papers, University of Reading.

42. Joan Wake, A Day in Peterborough, 22 February 1933. In later years, she reckoned to make at least one 'progress' to the northern end of the County each year.

43. See *Northamptonshire Past and Present*, vol.4, no.6, 1971, p.377. In the Record Society's Annual Reports for 1920 and 1921, Joan gave her address as The Manor House, Weston Turville and from 1923 to 1928, The Ladies' Club, Northampton.

44. HATLEY, V.A. 'Mr. Philip Cox', *Northamptonshire Past and Present*, vol.6, no.6, 1982–3, p.352.

45. WAKE, JOAN 'Collaboration in Historical Research', *Library Association Record*, vol.24, no.8, 1922.

46. *Women's Employment*, 5 January 1923.

47. *The Times*, 22 August 1925, p.11.

48. See Preface to the second edition, October 1925, p.4.

49. Peyton was Librarian at Reading University from 1926 to 1941 and a lecturer in the Department of Modern History, where he taught economic history. HOLT, J.C. *The University of Reading: the first fifty years* (1977) p.49. He had helped Joan with her booklet, *Northampton Vindicated* (see p. 000 of this chapter). Peyton also wrote the introduction to the first volume of the Record Society's publication, Joan's *Quarter Sessions Records of the County of Northampton* and was the editor of Volume 6, *Kettering Vestry Minutes, 1797–1893* (1933).

50. *Northampton Independent*, 25 July and 8 August 1925.

51. Joan Wake to Sidney Peyton, 2 June 1934.

52. For a complete list of her writings, see EADY, R. 'The Published Works of Joan Wake', *Northamptonshire Past and Present*, vol.5, no.3, 1975, pp.162–5.

53. Joan Wake to Hope Allen, 13 May 1935.

54. NRS, Ninth Annual Report for year ending 31 December 1929, p.4.

55. NRS, Diary, 1930–46, 6 June 1930, Northamptonshire Record Society.

56. Joan Wake to Frank Stenton, 25 October 1932.

57. p.vi.

58. NRS, Fourteenth Annual Report for year ending 31 December 1934, p.5.

59. NRS, Seventeenth Annual Report for year ending 31 December 1937, p.5. Joan's ambitions were insatiable. After a private visit to the unique topographical collection of Sir Thomas Phillipps at Thirlestaine House, Cheltenham, which included a large group of Northamptonshire documents, she offered to buy George Baker's manuscript notes for his *History of Northamptonshire*. The bid was unsuccessful. Joan Wake to T. Fitzroy Fenwick, 12 June 1936, Phillipps-Robinson Papers, c.706, f.120, Bodleian Library, Oxford.

60. NRS, Diary, 1930–46, 5 October 1937, Northamptonshire Record Society.

61. NRS, Eighteenth Annual Report for year ending 31 December 1938, pp.4–5. Joan was an early advocate of the preservation of old photographs as an historical record. For a fascinating example of her work in this field, see WAKE, JOAN 'Country Portrait Gallery', *Country Life*, 13 August 1942, p.282.

62. Of Cosgrove, Joan wrote, 'It is damp and not central enough for my work, but as long as Mama is here [Courteenhall] I shall stay if I can'. Joan Wake to Hope Allen, 13 May 1940.

63. NRS, Diary, 1930–46, 12 December 1939, Northamptonshire Record Society.

64. NRS, Twenty First Annual Report for year ending 31 December 1941, p.3.

65. For instance, Joan had seen the vast and organized destruction of Poor Law records which occurred towards the end of the First World War. In rural Unions which she had visited, this destruction ran to anything from two to five tons of 'waste paper' for each Union. WAKE, JOAN, and PEYTON, S. *Memorandum of the British Record Society. Records of Board of Guardians, 1834–1934. Suggestions for the Selection of those which should be Preserved*, October 1931, p.1.

66. NRS, Twentieth Annual Report for year ending 31 December 1940, p.3. Joan had addressed the annual meeting of the Northampton Law Society in July 1939. This was followed up with a letter to 180 individual solicitors in or just over the borders of Northamptonshire. Joan noted, 'Three replies were received. I started personal visits'. Proceedings no.6, *British Records Association*, 12 November 1940, p.7.

67. Joan Wake, Visit to Messrs. Hunnybun and Sykes, Solicitors, Thrapston, 9 July 1940.

68. WAKE, JOAN. 'Lady Etheldreda Wickham', *Northamptonshire Past and Present*, vol.3, no.2, 1961, p.51.

69. Joan Wake, Diary, 9 July 1940.

70. Joan Wake, Business Archives: Loveday and Son, Islip, 9 July 1940. In fact only a few account books of the firm were transfer-

red and are now in the Northamptonshire Record Office.

71. *Northampton Independent*, 20 June 1941.

72. WAKE, JOAN 'Thomas Bell, Schoolmaster and Poet', *Northampton County Magazine*, vol.3, October 1930, p.296. For details of Bell's life and works, see HOLD, T. (ed.) *A Northamptonshire Garland. An Anthology of Northamptonshire Poets* (1989), pp.33–5.

73. Joan Wake to Alice, Duchess of Gloucester, 15 April 1943.

74. Ibid., 12 November 1973.

75. Joan Wake to Hope Allen, 13 June 1948.

76. Also published separately as *A Northamptonshire Rector. The Life of Henry Isham Longden, 1859–1942* (1943). In discussing Longden's work for the Society, Joan recalled the Council meetings which they had attended together and 'the very enjoyable little tea-parties held after the business was done at Franklin's Hotel in the Guildhall Road', ibid., p.36.

77. Joan Wake to Doris Stenton, 9 January 1944.

78. A full account of the ceremony appears in her Diary, 22 March 1944.

79. In October 1950, when Baldwin was ill and alone at Weston Turville, Joan moved there and worked on her book, *The Brudenells of Deene*. Joan Wake to Hope Allen, 1 October 1950.

80. KING, P.I. 'Joan Wake', *Northamptonshire Past and Present*, vol.5, no.3, 1975, p.161. After ten years, the car had covered 55,000 miles 'and now that the engine has been rebored it seems as good as new'. Joan Wake to Godwin Wake, 10 September 1946.

81. Joan Wake, Diary, 22 May 1944.

82. The notorious German V2 rockets, launched from sites near The Hague and in the Scheldt estuary, were aimed exclusively at London. Within two months of their first use in September 1944, 456 people had been killed. After a brief respite, the attacks continued to increase in volume during the early part of 1945. GILBERT, M. *Winston S. Churchill: Road to Victory 1941–1945* (1986),

vol.7, pp.746, 1147.

83. Joan Wake, Diary, 10 February 1945.

84. Ibid., 27 May 1945.

85. NRS, Twenty Sixth Annual Report for year ending 31 December 1946, p.3.

86. NRS, Diary, 1946–49, 3 and 4 November 1946, Northamptonshire Record Society. 'I am working under great pressure', she had written a few weeks earlier, 'with all the Record Society work, the move to Lamport, securing grants from the Local Authorities, training the new staff, making a new inventory, etc. etc., besides lecturing to Women's Institutes and London meetings'. Joan Wake to Edwin Holthouse, 6 September 1946, Northamptonshire Record Office. Holthouse Papers, 573.

87. Information kindly supplied by P.I. King.

88. Joan Wake to Hope Allen, 1 October 1950.

89. Joan Wake to Godwin Wake, 7 April 1947.

90. 'It won't be very comfortable', she wrote, 'but better than those awful long drives in the dark in the winter'. Joan Wake to Hope Allen, 13 June 1948.

91. Ibid., 26 December 1948.

92. NRS, Twenty Sixth Annual Report for year ending 31 December 1946, p.6. Joan told Frank Stenton in the following year, 'I wish I could underpin the Society with £20,000'. Joan Wake to Frank Stenton, 18 October 1947, Stenton Papers, University of Reading.

93. Joan Wake to Godwin Wake, 13 February 1948.

94. NRS, Twenty Eighth Annual Report for year ending 31 December 1948, p.4. The idea of a 'County Magazine' appears to have come from Charles Linnell, a master at Bedford School and a devoted Record Society member, in November 1947. See NRS, Diary, 1946–9, 28 November 1947, Northamptonshire Record Society, and WAKE, JOAN 'Charles Darby Linnell', *Northamptonshire Past and Present*, vol.3, no.5, 1964, p.237. The birth of the journal stemmed from necessity. Joan wrote at the time, 'I am editing a sort of journal

as a means of raising money for the Record Society . . . without it the whole show would have gone bankrupt'. Joan Wake to Godwin Wake, 11 August 1948.

95. Joan Wake to Hope Allen, 25 March 1949.

96. They had established a friendship over many years. Joan described the Society's annual meetings, where 'He and I always do a sort of "knock-about turn" to start with which amuses people. He chaffs me from the chair and it goes down very well'. Joan Wake to Hope Allen, 13 June 1950. See WAKE, JOAN 'William Thomas Brownlow Cecil, Fifth Marquess of Exeter, 1876–1956', *Northamptonshire Past and Present*, vol.2, no.3, 1956, p.120.

97. NRS, Thirtieth Annual Report for year ending 31 December 1950, p.6. Joan expressed her approval of the new arrangement to Frank Stenton. 'I suppose it happens very rarely', she wrote, 'for people to reach the promised land, as we have been allowed to do'. Joan Wake to Frank Stenton, 30 October 1951, Stenton Papers, University of Reading.

98. *The Times*, 17 August 1962, p.12.

99. See WAKE, JOAN 'Mrs. George Brudenell', *Northamptonshire Past and Present*, vol.5, no. 1, 1973, pp.64–5.

100. Joan Wake to Hope Allen, 20 October 1933.

101. Ibid., 16 June 1940.

102. Ibid., 20 October 1940.

103. Joan Wake, Diary, 6 and 9 June 1944.

104. Joan Wake to Hope Allen, 30 November 1946.

105. WAKE, JOAN *The Brudenells of Deene* (1953), p.446.

106. Ibid., pp.448–56 and pp.460–1.

107. Ibid., p.xi.

108. *Punch*, 7 October 1953, pp.442–3.

109. Joan Wake, Travel Talk to Castlethorpe Women's Institute, 9 September 1953.

110. See WAKE, JOAN 'Northamptonshire in Southern Rhodesia', *Northamptonshire Past and Present*, vol.3, no.5, 1964, p.236.

111. WAKE, JOAN. 'A Rhodesian Settler's Home', *Country Life*, 21 November 1947, p.1023.

112. Joan Wake to Ada ?, 21 March 1948.

113. Journal of the Council of Policy of the Dutch East India Company, 27 January-8 February 1751, Cape Archives, South Africa, C.620.

114. R.J. Koke, New York Historical Society, to Major H. Wake, 31 July 1962, Courteenhall Papers.

115. *Northampton Chronicle and Echo*, 16 January 1974.

116. Joan Wake to Ada ?, 21 March 1948.

117. WAKE, JOAN 'Hope Emily Allen', *Northamptonshire Past and Present*, vol.3, no.1, 1960, p.16. Miss Allen had been staying with Joan at Cosgrove when the Second World War broke out. They had not met since. Miss Allen died on 30 June 1960.

118. WAKE, JOAN 'Links with the United States', *Northamptonshire Past and Present*, vol.1, no.1, 1948, p.41.

119. C.R.D. Miller to Hope Allen, 21 May 1957.

120. *Evening Telegraph*, 8 July 1957.

121. *Oneida (New York) Daily Dispatch*, 10 June 1957.

122. *Northampton Chronicle and Echo*, 8 July 1957.

123. WAKE, JOAN 'Traveller's Tale', *Northamptonshire Past and Present*, vol.2, no.4, 1957, p.187.

124. Joan Wake to Sir Hereward Wake, 22 October 1949. For an account of the proceedings, see *Northamptonshire Countryside*, Autumn 1949.

125. 'I am wondering if we should not do better to try and get out to Delapre Abbey', Joan Wake to Frank Stenton, 10 April 1944.

126. Joan Wake, Diary, 26 September 1944.

127. In fact, Miss Bouverie had left Delapre in 1940, but two years later sent for her bailiff and told him that she wished to die at Delapre. Rooms in the stables were prepared for her; she died there on 20 January 1943. WAKE, JOAN and PANTIN, W.A. *Delapre Abbey, Northampton. Its History and Architecture*, 1959, revised edition, 1975, p.11.

128. Joan Wake, Diary, 5 October 1944.

129. Ibid., 12 October 1944.

130. Ibid., 23 November 1944.

131. NRS, Twenty Fourth Annual Report ending 31 December 1944, p.3. On Joan's briefing, see Joan Wake to Frank Stenton, 15 January 1945. Stenton Papers, University of Reading. When she received the news from Lord Exeter, Joan wrote, 'Hurrah! A great relief!' Diary, 19 February 1945.

132. NRS, Thirty Third Annual Report for the year ending 31 December 1953, p.4.

133. Lee, a knowledgeable student of Northampton history and a member of the Record Society, was Leader of the Labour Party on the Council and was Mayor, 1951–2. In 1952, he became the first Chairman of the Northamptonshire Archives Committee. WAKE, JOAN 'Mr Frank Lee', *Northamptonshire Past and Present*, vol.2, no.2, 1955, p.44. As far back as 1945, Joan was priming him with information about Delapre. Diary, 23 February 1945.

134. Lee's plan was lost by 27 votes to 16. *Northampton Chronicle and Echo*, 24 June 1954.

135. *Northampton Mercury and Herald*, 9 April 1954.

136. Ibid., 23 July 1954.

137. NRS, Thirty Fifth Annual Report for the year ending 31 December 1955, pp.3–4.

138. *Northampton Chronicle and Echo*, 5 January 1956.

139. Leaflet, 'Delapre Must Be Saved', 26 April 1956, Northamptonshire Record Office, V223.

140. File: Delapre Abbey, 27 April 1956.

141. 'Northamptonshire Records', *The Times*, 24 May 1956, p.11.

142. *Peterborough Standard*, 21 September 1956. Joan had many difficulties to contend with in raising the money: they included a national credit squeeze, a £100,000 appeal for Peterborough Cathedral started just before the Delapre appeal, the recent great loss of the Society's President, Lord Exeter, and the hostility or apathy of several leading Town Councillors. Joan Wake to Sir Frank Stenton, 17 December 1956, Stenton Papers, Univer-sity of Reading.

143. *Northampton Chronicle and Echo*, 23 November 1956.

144. *Evening Telegraph*, 31 December 1956.

145. *Northampton Chronicle and Echo*, 2 February 1957.

146. Ibid., 5 February 1957.

147. The removal of documents and books to Delapre from Lamport took place between 7 and 22 October 1958.

148. Sir Frank Stenton to Joan Wake, 18 March 1959.

149. Extracts from the speeches are reproduced in *Northamptonshire Past and Present*, vol.2, no.6, 1959.

150. Ibid., pp.269, 271.

151. 'A Home for History', *The Times*, 11 May 1959, p.11.

152. Information kindly supplied by P.I. King.

153. Joan Wake to P.A. Kennedy, 1 December 1959.

154. *Sir Christopher Hatton's Book of Seals*, edited by Lewis C. Loyd and Doris Stenton in honour of Sir Frank Stenton, was published as the Record Society's volume 15, 1950, jointly with the Clarendon Press.

155. Joan Wake to Hope Allen, 19 July 1948. However, she took steps to repair the damage with the Stentons. To Frank she wrote, 'I am so distressed at what I have done ... Do if you can forgive me for being so tiresome and such a consummate fool'. Joan wrote to Doris the same day, 'What devil possessed me on that unlucky 13th. July I can't say, but I know this: that I went full of enthusiasm and the intention to co-operate. I ended up by being haggling and horrible, magnified every difficulty and was very unhelpful. I had a sleepless night after it'. Joan Wake to Frank and Doris Stenton, 30 July 1948, Stenton Papers, University of Reading.

156. Ibid., 18 January 1947.

157. Joan Wake to Roneo Ltd., 31 December 1938.

158. Joan Wake to Sir Hereward Wake, 3 November 1949, Northamptonshire Record Office, YZ 677.

159. MAJOR, K. 'Joan Wake', *Archives*, vol.12, no.53, 1975, p.29.

160. KING, P.I. 'Dr. Joan Wake', *Journal of the Society of Archivists*, vol.5, no.2, 1974, p.148.

161. KING, P.I. 'Joan Wake', *Northamptonshire Past and Present*, vol.5, no.3, 1975, p.161.

162. Joan Wake to Sir Hereward and Daisy Wake, 27 June 1954.

163. Joan started on this project, but after her death the tapes were accidentally wiped out.

164. NRS, Fortieth Annual Report for year ending 31 December 1960, p.3.

165. *Northampton Chronicle and Echo*, 30 May 1960.

166. NRS, Forty First Annual Report for year ending 31 December 1961, p.3.

167. I am grateful to Mrs E. Lewis for this information.

168. Joan Wake. Notebook, 'My Complaints'. This covers the years 1961 to 1969.

169. *Evening Telegraph*, 27 May 1963.

170. A fifth volume of texts which she edited for the Record Society *Northamptonshire Lieutenancy and other Documents, 1580–1614*, was revised and prepared by a joint editor, Jeremy Goring. The volume was published in 1975.

171. *Northampton Independent*, 30 January, 1953.

172. Sir Hereward Wake to Joan Wake, 18 November 1952.

173. Joan Wake to Hope Allen, 12 February 1953.

174. Leicester University College received its charter in 1957.

175. *Northampton Chronicle and Echo*, 7 November 1959.

176. Joan was now entitled to attend University lectures. Her 'Oxford Lecture Notes', which she carefully kept, show that she was a regular attender, particularly at those given by Lawrence Stone, on the rise of the gentry, and by Lord David Cecil.

177. Information kindly supplied by Victor A. Hatley.

178. SLADDEN, D.M. 'Fiftieth Anniversary Celebrations', *Northamptonshire Past and Present*, vol.4, no.6, 1971, p.331.

179. WAKE, JOAN 'Local Sources of History', *Bulletin of the Institute of Historical Research*, vol.1, 1924, p.88.

180. ISHAM, SIR G. 'Joan Wake', *Northamptonshire Past and Present*, vol.5, no.3, 1975, p.160.

Chapter 18

COURTEENHALL TODAY

1. MILLS, G.H. and NIXON, R.F. *The Annals of the King's Royal Rifle Corps, 1921–1943* (1971), vol.6, p.51.

2. Gott's detailed plans for the defence of Egypt were later adopted by his successor, Montgomery. BARNETT, C. D. *The Desert Generals* (1960), p.246.

3. KERSAUDY, F. *Norway 1940* (1990), pp.35–6.

4. Montgomery wrote of Alam Halfa, 'I think that this battle has never received the interest or attention it deserves. It was a vital action, because had we lost it, we might well have lost Egypt. In winning it we paved the way for success at El Alamein and the subsequent advance into Tunisia'. MONTGOMERY, FIELD MARSHAL VISCOUNT *El Alamein to the River Sangro, Normandy to the Baltic* (1973), p.16.

5. WAKE, SIR H. and DEEDES, W.F. *Swift and Bold. The Story of the King's Royal Rifle Corps in the Second World War* (1949), p.96.

6. For Major Wake's own account of this battle, see MILLS and NIXON, op.cit., pp.363–6.

7. HASTINGS, M. *Overlord. D-Day and the Battle for Normandy* (1984), pp.301–2.

8. Joan Wake to Godwin Wake, 1 January 1948, Joan Wake Papers.

9. Ibid., 15 November 1949.

10. WORSLEY, G. 'Carr at Courteenhall', *Country Life*, 30 October 1986, p.1389.

11. *Northampton Mercury and Herald*, 27 October 1984.

12. The London end of the M1 was completed with the opening of the Watford bypass on 21 December 1959.

13. PEVSNER, N. *The Buildings of England. Northamptonshire* (1973, second edition), pp.69–70.

14. *Northampton Chronicle and Echo*, 11 October 1959.

15. Ibid., 2 November 1959.

16. *The Times*, 4 November 1959, p.9.

17. BARTY-KING, H. *Expanding Northampton* (1985), p.20.

18. GREENALL, R. *A History of Northamptonshire* (1979), pp.119–20.

19. *Northampton Chronicle and Echo*, 25 April 1979.

Bibliography

A. MANUSCRIPT SOURCES

Bedford Estate Office, London
5th Duke of Bedford Papers

Bedfordshire Record Office
Whitbread Papers

Bodleian Library, Oxford
Brooke Papers
Milner Papers
Phillipps-Robinson Papers
Willis Papers

British Library
Beauvoir Papers
Cole Papers
Egerton Papers
Harleian Papers
Lansdowne Papers
2nd Earl Spencer Papers
3rd Earl Spencer Papers
5th Earl Spencer Papers
Stowe Papers
Charles Stuart, 3rd Duke of Richmond
   Papers
Sir Isaac Wake Papers

Buckinghamshire Record Office
Dayrell Papers

Christ Church, Oxford
Archbishop Wake Papers

Courteenhall House
Wake Family Papers

Durham University Library
4th Earl Grey Papers

Elton Hall, Cambridgeshire
Proby Papers

Essex Record Office
Arkwright Papers

*Hereford and Worcester Record
Office*
Pakington Papers

Centre for Kentish Studies
Sackville Papers

Lambeth Palace Library
Tait Papers
Archbishop Wake Papers

Lincolnshire Archives Office
Monson Papers

House of Lords
Lloyd George Papers

National Army Museum, Department of Records
Major Charles St. Aubyn Wake Papers

Norfolk Record Office
Humphry Repton Papers

Northamptonshire Record Office
Freke Evans (Laxton) Papers (copy)
Holthouse Papers
Knightley Papers
H.P. Markham Papers
Markham Solicitors Papers
Blanche Sitwell Papers
6th Earl Spencer Papers
Sir Hereward Wake, 13th Baronet Papers

Joan Wake Papers
Wake (Courteenhall) Papers
Wills, 5th Series

Northamptonshire Record Society
Diaries, 1931–49

Principal Probate Registry
Wills of 9th and 10th Wake Baronets

Public Record Office
Admiralty Papers
Education Papers

University of Reading Library
Stenton Papers

Sheffield Record Office
Fenton of Bank Top Papers

Shropshire Record Office
Kyre Park Papers

Somerset Record Office
Clevedon Court Papers

Staffordshire Record Office
Lane Papers

Suffolk Record Office
Drurys of Riddlesworth Papers

B. BOOKS

Unless otherwise stated the place of publication is London.

ABBEY, C.J. *The English Church and Its Bishops, 1700–1800* (Longmans, 1887), 2 vols.

ADAM OF USK *Chronicon Adae de Usk, A.D. 1377–1421* (ed. THOMPSON, SIR. E.M.), (Henry Frowde, 1904).

ADAMS, L (ed.). *William Wake's Gallican Correspondence and Related Documents, 1716–1731* (Peter Lang, New York, 1988–9), 3 vols.

ADDISON, SIR W. *Portrait of Epping Forest* (Robert Hale, 1977).

AKRIGG, G.P.V. *Jacobean Pageant or, The Court of King James I* (Hamish Hamilton, 1962).

ALMON, J. *The Parliamentary Register or, History of the Proceedings and Debates of the House of Commons* (J. Almon, 1775).

AMERY, L.S. *The Times History of the War in South Africa, 1899–1900* (Sampson Low, 1900–09), 7 vols.

AMERY, L.S. *My Political Life* (Hutchinson, 1953).

ANON. *Letters From and To Sir Dudley Carleton, Knt., during his Embassy in Holland from January 1616 to December 1620* (1757).

ANON. *A New and Complete History of Essex by A Gentleman* (1771).

ANON. *Some Account of Clifton Reynes in the County of Buckinghamshire* (Eyres and Son, Brighton, 1821, reprinted 1883).

ANON. *A Complete Parochial History of the County of Cornwall* (William Lake, Truro, 1870), vol.3.

ANON. *Letters of Lord Althorp* (Privately printed, 1879).

ANON. *Records of the Services of the Northamptonshire and Rutland Militia from 1756 to 1889* (Cordeux and Sons, Northampton, 1890).

ANON. *Northamptonshire at War, 1939–45* (Northamptonshire Libraries, 1979).

ARMITAGE-SMITH, S. *John of Gaunt* (Constable, 1904).

ARNSTEIN, W.L. *The Bradlaugh Case: A study in late Victorian opinion and politics* (Clarendon Press, Oxford, 1965).

ARROWSMITH, R.L. (ed.) *Charterhouse Register, 1769–1872* (Charterhouse, Godalming, 1964).

ASHWORTH, T. *Trench Warfare 1914–1918. The Live and Let Live System* (Macmillan, 1980).

ASKWITH, B. *Two Victorian Families* (Chatto and Windus, 1971).

AUBREY, J. *Brief Lives* (ed. CLARK, A.) (Clarendon Press, Oxford, 1898), 2 vols.

AUSTEN, J. *Mansfield Park* (1814, reprinted Oxford University Press, Oxford, 1972).

AUSTEN-LEIGH, R.A. *The Eton College Register, 1753–90* (Spottiswoode,

Ballantyne and Co., Eton, 1921).

AYLING, K. *My Mother's Family* (Privately printed, 1974).

BAILEY, B. *English Manor Houses* (Robert Hale, 1983).

BAKER, G. *The History and Antiquities of the County of Northamptonshire* (J.B. Nicholls and Son, 1822–41), 2 vols.

BALD, R.C. *Donne and the Drurys* (Cambridge University Press, Cambridge, 1959).

BARBER, R. *Edward Prince of Wales and Aquitaine* (Allen Lane, 1978).

BARNES, J. and NICHOLSON, D. (eds.) *The Leo Amery Diaries* (Hutchinson, 1980), vol.1, 1896–1929.

BARNETT, C.D. *The Desert Generals* (William Kimber, 1960).

BARRACLOUGH, G. (ed.) *The Charters of the Anglo-Norman Earls of Chester, c.1071–1237* (Record Society of Lancashire and Cheshire, 1988).

BARTY-KING, H. *Expanding Northampton* (Secker and Warburg, 1985).

BATEMAN, J. *The Great Landowners of Great Britain and Ireland* (Harrison and Sons, 1883 edition).

BAYLEY, A.R. *The Great Civil War in Dorset, 1642–1660* (Barnicott and Pearce, Wessex Press, Taunton, 1910).

BEHRMAN, S.N. *Duveen* (Hamish Hamilton, 1952).

BELL, G.K.A. *Randall Davidson, Archbishop of Canterbury* (Oxford University Press, Oxford, 1935), 2 vols.

BELL, G.M. *A Handlist of British Diplomatic Representatives, 1509–1688* (Royal Historical Society, 1990).

BENHAM REVD. W. (ed.) *Catharine and Craufurd Tait, wife and son of Archibald Campbell, Archbishop of Canterbury. A Memoir* (Macmillan, 1879).

BENNETT, G.V. *The Tory crisis in Church and State, 1688–1730: the career of Francis Atterbury, Bishop of Rochester* (Clarendon Press, Oxford, 1975).

BENSON, R.H. (ed.) *The Holford Collection, Dorchester House* (Oxford University Press, Oxford, 1927), 2 vols.

BEVIS, T.A. (ed.) *De Gestis Herewardi Saxonis* (Westrydale Press, March, Cambridgeshire, 1981).

BILL, E.G.W. and MASON, J.F.A. *Christ Church and reform, 1850–1867* (Clarendon Press, Oxford, 1970).

BIRCH, T. *The Court and Times of James the First* (ed. R.F. WILLIAMS) (Henry Colburn, 1848), 2 vols.

BIRCH, T. *The Court and Times of Charles the First* (ed. R.F. WILLIAMS) (Henry Colburn, 1848), 2 vols.

BLOMFIELD, F. *An Essay Towards a Topographical History of the County of Norfolk* (William Miller, 1805), 11 vols.

BOND, B.J. *The Victorian Army and the Staff College, 1854–1914* (Eyre Methuen, 1972).

BOYLE, A. *Trenchard* (Collins, 1962).

BRERETON, J.M. *A Guide to the Regiments of the British Army* (Bodley Head, 1985).

BRIDGES, J. (ed. WHALLEY, REVD. P.) *The History and Antiquities of Northamptonshire* (T. Payne, 1791), 2 vols.

BROCK, M. *The Great Reform Act* (Hutchinson, 1973).

BROCK, M. and E. (eds.) *H H Asquith. Letters to Venetia Stanley* (Oxford University Press, Oxford, 1982).

BROOKE-LITTLE, J.P. (ed.) *Boutell's Heraldry* (Warne, 1950, 1983 edition).

BROOS, B. *Meesterwerken in het Mauritshuis* (Staatsuitgeverij, The Hague, 1987).

BUCKLAND, E.A. *The Rainsford Family* (Phillips and Probert, Worcester, 1932).

BURKE, J.B. *Dictionary of Landed Gentry of Great Britain and Ireland* (Henry Colburn, 1850).

BUTLER, L. and GIVEN-WILSON, C. *Medieval Monasteries of Great Britain* (Joseph, 1979).

CALLWELL, SIR C.E. *Field Marshal Sir Henry Wilson. His Life and Diaries* (Cassell, 1927), 2 vols.

CAMPLING, A. *The History of the family of Drury in the Counties of Suffolk and Norfolk from the Conquest* (Mitchell, Hughes and Clarke, 1937).

CARTER, G. GOODE, P. and LAURIE, K.

Humphry Repton, landscape gardener, 1752–1818 (Sainsbury Centre for Visual Arts, Norwich, 1982).

CASSAR, G.H. *The Tragedy of Sir John French* (University of Delaware Press, 1985).

CAVE, K. (ed.) *The Diary of Joseph Farington* (Yale University Press, 1982), vol.8, July 1806-Dec 1807.

CAZENOVE, H. de L. *Northamptonshire Yeomanry, 1794–1964* (n.p., 1964).

CHAPMAN, H.F. *St. Mary's Deanery Church, Bocking, Essex* (Tindall Press, Chelmsford, 1954).

CHARLTON, J. *The Banqueting House, Whitehall* (HMSO, 1964).

CHITTY, S. *The Beast and the Monk. A Life of Charles Kingsley* (Hodder and Stoughton, 1974).

CHURCHILL, R.S. *Winston S. Churchill: Youth, 1874–1900* (Heinemann, 1966), vol.1.

CLACY, E. (ed. THOMPSON, P.) *A Lady's Visit to the Gold Diggings of Australia in 1852–53. Written on the Spot* (Hurst and Blackett, 1853).

CLARENDON, EARL OF *The History of the Rebellion* (1702–4, ed. MACKAY, W.D. 1888), vol.2.

CLARK, C.M.H (ed.). *Select Documents in Australian History, 1851–1900* (Angus and Robertson, Sydney, 1955).

CLARK, C.M.H. *A History of Australia. The Earth Abideth For Ever, 1851–1888* (Melbourne University Press, Melbourne, 1978), vol.4.

CLEALL, A. *Waltham Abbey Church Guide* (1948, second edition).

CLIFFORD-SMITH, H. *The Waltham Abbey Room,* Victoria and Albert Department of Woodwork (Board of Education, 1924).

CLINCH, M.C. *The Story of Blisworth, Northamptonshire* (J. Smart, Brackley, 1939).

COBBETT, W. and WRIGHT, J. (eds.) *Cobbett's Parliamentary History of England from the Norman Conquest in 1066 to the year 1803* (Longmans, 1806–12), 12 vols.

COCKAYNE, G.E. *The Complete Peerage* (new edition, GIBBS, V., DOUBLEDAY, H.A. et al.) (St. Catherine Press, 1910–59), 14 vols.

COCKBURN, HENRY, LORD *Memorials of His Time* (A. and C. Black, Edinburgh, 1856).

COLEMAN, T. *The Railway Navvies. A History of the men who made the Railways* (Hutchinson, 1965).

COLLINS, L.C. *Life and Memoirs of John Churton Collins* (John Lane, The Bodley Head, 1912).

COLLINSON, J. *History of Antiquities of the County of Somerset* (R. Crutwell, Bath, 1791), 3 vols.

COLLOMS, B. *Charles Kingsley: the lion of Eversley* (Constable, 1975).

COLVILLE, SIR J.R. *Man of Valour. The Life of Field Marshal the Viscount Gort* (Collins, 1972).

COLVIN, H.M. *A Biographical Dictionary of British Architects, 1600–1840* (Murray, 1978).

COOKE, R. *West Country Houses* (The author, Bristol, 1957).

CORNWALL, SIR J.H.M. *Haig as Military Commander* (Batsford, 1973).

CORYN, M.J. *The Black Prince, 1330–1376* (Arthur Barker, 1934).

COSSONS, N. and TRINDER, B. *The Iron Bridge. Symbol of the Industrial Revolution* (Moonraker Press, Bradford-on-Avon, Wiltshire, 1979).

COTTRELL-DORMER, F. *Reminiscences and Wanderings at Home and Abroad, 1837–1900. Provided for her dear children* (Privately printed, 1906), 3 vols.

CROOK, J.M. and PORT, M.H. *The History of the King's Works* (HMSO, 1973), vol.6.

CROSS, F.L. and LIVINGSTONE, E.A. (eds.) *The Oxford Dictionary of the Christian Church* (Oxford University Press, Oxford, 1957, second edition, 1974).

CRUTWELL, C.R.M.F. *A History of the Great War, 1914–1918* (Clarendon Press, Oxford, 1934).

CUST, L.H. *Anthony Van Dyck* (Hodder and Stoughton, 1911).

DANVERS, F.C. et al. *Memorials of Old Haileybury College* (Constable, 1894).

DAUGLISH, M.G. and STEPHENSON, P.K. (eds.) *The Harrow School Register, 1800–1911* (Longmans Green, 1884, third edition, 1911).

DAVIDSON, R.T. *Life of Archibald Campbell Tait, Archbishop of Canterbury* (Macmillan, 1891), 2 vols.

DAVIES, G. *The Early Stuarts, 1603–1660* (Clarendon Press, Oxford, 1937, second edition, 1959).

DAVIES, L. and GRAY, J.B. *Ashby St. Ledgers, Northamptonshire. A Visitor's Guide* (n.d.)

DEAN, D. *Waltham Abbey Church, Essex* (Bookends, Waltham Abbey, 1984).

DEBRETT, J. *The Parliamentary Register* (J. Debrett, 1784).

DISNEY, J. (ed.) *The Works of John Jebb, with memoirs of the life of the author by J.D.* (n.p., 1787).

DOUBLE, G.H. *The Saints of Cornwall. Part 2. Saints of the Lizard District* (Holywell Press, Oxford, 1962).

DUNN-PATTISON, R.P. *The Black Prince* (Methuen, 1910).

EDEN, A. *Another World, 1897–1917* (Allen Lane, 1976).

EDWARDS, R. and RAMSAY, L.G.C. *The Late Georgian Period, 1760–1810* (Reynal, New York, 1957).

ELLIOTT, SIR I. (ed.) *Balliol Register, 1833–1933* (Oxford University Press, Oxford, 1934).

ELLIOTT, J.M.K. (ed. ELLIOTT, E.K.) *Fifty Years' Fox-Hunting with the Grafton and other packs of hounds* (Horace Cox, 1900).

ELTON, SIR A. and M.A.E. *Clevedon Court* (The National Trust, tenth edition, 1990).

EMERSON, B. *The Black Prince* (Weidenfeld and Nicolson, 1976).

ENSOR, R.C.K. *England, 1870–1914* (Clarendon Press, Oxford, 1936).

EVERS, C.R. *Rugby* (Blackie and Son, 1939).

FARMER, J. *The History of the ancient town, and once famous abbey of Waltham* (1735).

FERRAND, M. *Charles Kingsley* (Princeton University Press, Princeton, 1937).

FINLAYSON, G.B.A.M. *The Seventh Earl of Shaftesbury, 1801–1885* (Eyre Methuen, 1981).

FITZMAURICE, LORD *Life of William, Earl of Shelburne, afterwards first Marquis of Lansdowne* (Macmillan, 1912), 2 vols.

FOISTER, S. *Cardinal Newman, 1801–90* (National Portrait Gallery Publications, 1990).

FORD, E. and HODSON, G.H. *A History of Enfield* (Enfield, 1873).

FORRESTER, E.G. *Northamptonshire County Elections and Electioneering, 1695–1832* (Oxford University Press, Oxford, 1941).

FOSTER, C.W. and LONGLEY, T. (eds.) *The Lincolnshire Domesday and the Lindsey Survey* (Lincoln Record Society, 1924), vol.19.

FOSTER, J. *Alumni Oxonienses: the members of the University of Oxford, 1500–1714* (Parker and Co., Oxford, 1891–2), 4 vols.

FREEMAN, E.A. *The History of the Norman Conquest in England* (Clarendon Press, Oxford, second edition, 1870–5), 6 vols.

FRENCH, FIELD MARSHAL VISCOUNT *1914* (Constable, 1919).

FRYDE, N. *The Tyranny and Fall of Edward II, 1321–1326* (Cambridge University Press, Cambridge, 1979).

FULFORD, R. *Samuel Whitbread, 1764–1815. A study in opposition* (Macmillan, 1967).

FULLER, T. *The History of the Worthies of England* (ed. NUTTALL, P.A.) (Thomas Tegg, 1662, new edition, 1840), 3 vols.

GARDINER, S.R. *Letters and Other Documents Illustrating the Relations between England and Germany at the Commencement of the Thirty Years War* (Camden Society, 1865), vol.90.

GARDINER, S.R. *History of England from the accession of James I to the outbreak of the Civil War 1603–42* (Longmans, Green, 1883–4, 1895 edition) 10 vols.

THE GEORGIAN SOCIETY *The Works in Architecture of John Carr* (Sessions, York, 1973).

GILBERT, M. *Winston S. Churchill: Finest*

Hour, 1939–41 (Heinemann, 1983), vol.6.

GILBERT, M. *Winston S. Churchill: Road to Victory, 1941–1945* (Heinemann, 1986), vol.7.

GILL, C. *History of Birmingham Manor and Borough to 1865* (Oxford University Press, Oxford, 1952), vol.1.

GODBER, J. *History of Bedfordshire, 1066–1888* (Bedfordshire County Council, 1969).

GODBER, J. *The Story of Bedford. An Outline History* (White Crescent Press, Luton, 1978).

GODDARD, H. *Memoirs of a Bow Street Runner* (Museum Press, 1956).

GOLLANCZ, M. (ed.) *Rolls of Northamptonshire Sessions of the Peace* (Northamptonshire Record Society, 1940), vol.11.

GORDON, P. *The Red Earl. The Papers of the fifth Earl Spencer, 1835–1910* (Northamptonshire Record Society, 1981 and 1986), vols. 31 and 34.

GOTCH, J.A. *The Old Halls and Manor Houses of Northamptonshire* (Batsford, 1936).

GOVER, J.E.B., MAWER, A. and STENTON, F.M. *The Place-Names of Northamptonshire* (Cambridge University Press, Cambridge, 1933), vol.10.

GRANT, J. and SEARLE, G. *The Melbourne Scene, 1803–1956* (Melbourne University Press, Melbourne, 1957).

GRAVES, A. *The Royal Academy of Arts. A Complete Dictionary of Contributors and their work from its foundation in 1769 to 1904* (Henry Graves and George Bell, 1906), vol.7.

GRAVES, C. *The Home Guard of Britain* (Hutchinson, 1943).

GRAY, W. *Diary of the late William Gray, Esq. of Courteenhall, Northamptonshire* (Mark Dorman, The Drapery, Northampton, 1875).

GREAVES, R. *The Grafton Hunt* (Reid-Hamilton, 1949).

GREEN, E. *Portbury Priory* (n.p., 1905).

GREENALL, R. *A History of Northamptonshire* (Phillimore, Chichester, 1979).

GRIMES, C.H.D. *A History of Hitcham* (Fisher and Sons, Woburn, Beds., 1926).

HANKEY, LORD *The Supreme Command, 1914–1918* (Allen and Unwin, 1961), 2 vols.

HANSARD, T.C. *The Parliamentary History of England from the earliest period to the year 1803* (T.C. Hansard, 1783).

HARDMAN, SISTER ANNE *English Carmelites in Penal Times* (Burns, Oates and Washbourne, 1936).

HARDMAN, SISTER ANNE *Mother Margaret Mostyn, Discalced Carmelite, 1625–1679* (Burns, Oates and Washbourne, 1937).

HARDMAN, SISTER ANNE *Two English Carmelites: Mother Mary Xaveria Burton and Mother Mary Margaret Wake* (Burns, Oates and Washbourne, 1939).

HARE, MAJ.-GEN. SIR S.W. *The Annals of the King's Royal Rifle Corps: The Great War* (John Murray, 1932) vol.5.

HARRIS, J. *Sir William Chambers, Knight of the Polar Star* (Zwemmer, 1970).

HARRIS, J. *The Palladians* (Trefoil Books, 1981).

HART, SIR B.H. LIDDELL *History of the First World War* (Pan Books, 1972).

HARVEY, J. *The Black Prince and his Age* (Batsford, 1976).

HARWARD, T.N. *Hereward, the Saxon patriot: a history of his life and character, with a record of his ancestors and descendants, A.D.445 to A.D.1896* (Elliot Stock, 1896).

HASTINGS, M. *Overlord. D-Day and the Battle for Normandy* (Joseph, 1984).

HENDERSON, B.W. *Merton College* (F.E. Robinson, Oxford 1899).

HENNING, B.D. (ed.) *The House of Commons, 1660–1690*, The History of Parliament, (History of Parliament Trust/Secker and Warburg, 1983), vol.2.

HERVEY, M.F.S. *The Life, Correspondence and Collections of Thomas Howard, Earl of Arundel* (Cambridge University Press, Cambridge, 1921).

HIGGS, E. *Waltham Abbey* (Pitkin Pictorials, 1979).

HILLCOURT, W. with OLIVE, LADY BADEN-POWELL *Baden-Powell. The Two Lives of a Hero* (Heinemann, 1964).

BIBLIOGRAPHY

HOFFMAN, A. *Bocking Deanery. The Story* (Phillimore, Chichester, 1976).

HOLD, T. (ed.) *A Northamptonshire Garland. An Anthology of Northamptonshire Poets* (Northamptonshire Libraries, Northampton, 1989).

HOLMES, G. *The Good Parliament* (Clarendon Press, Oxford, 1975).

HOLT, J.C. *The University of Reading: the first fifty years* (Reading University Press, Reading, 1977).

HOPE SIMPSON, J.B. *Rugby Since Arnold. A History of Rugby School from 1842* (Macmillan, 1967).

HORN, P. *Joseph Arch (1826–1919): the farm workers' leader* (Roundwood Press, Kineton, Warwickshire, 1971).

HOSKINS, W.G. *The Making of the English Landscape* (Hodder and Stoughton, 1955).

HOWARD, J.J. (ed.) *Miscellanea Genealogica et Heraldica* (Mitchell and Hughes, 1898), vol.2., 3rd series.

HUDLESTON, C.R. and BOUMPHREY, R.S. *Cumberland Families and their Heraldry* (Transactions of the Cumberland and Westmorland Antiquarian Society, 1978), vol.23, extra series.

HUNTER, FATHER THOMAS *An English Carmelite. The life of Catharine Burton* (Burns and Oates, 1876).

HUTCHINS, REVD. J. *The History and Antiquities of the County of Dorset* (W. Bowyer and J. Nichols, Westminster, 1774, third edition, 1874) 2 vols.

HUXLEY, G. *Endymion Porter, the life of a courtier, 1587–1649* (Chatto and Windus, 1959).

IRESON, T. *Northamptonshire* (Robert Hale, 1954).

ITZKOWITZ, D. *Peculiar privilege. A social history of English foxhunting, 1753–1885* (Harvester Press, Hassocks, Sussex, 1977).

JAMES, D.P. *Lord Roberts* (Hollis and Carter, 1954).

JAMES, M.R. *Letters of H.E. Luxmoore* (Cambridge University Press, Cambridge, 1929).

JAMES, R.R. (ed.) *Chips: The Diaries of Sir Henry Channon* (Penguin Books, Harmondsworth, 1970).

JOHNSON, T.H. *The Oxford Companion to American History* (Oxford University Press, New York, 1966).

JONES, M.G. *The Charity School Movement. A Study of Eighteenth Century Puritanism* (Cambridge University Press, Cambridge, 1938, reprinted Frank Cass, 1964).

JUDD, G.P. IV *Members of Parliament, 1734–1832* (Yale University Press, 1955).

KAYE, SIR J.W. *A History of the Sepoy war in India, 1857–1858* (W.H. Allen, 1864–1876), 3 vols.

KEEN, M.H. *The Outlaws of Medieval Legend* (Routledge and Kegan Paul, 1961).

KENWORTHY-BROWNE, J., REID, P., SAYER, M. and WATKIN, D. (eds.) *Burke's and Savill's Guide to Country Houses: East Anglia* (Burke's Peerages, 1981), vol.3.

KERSAUDY, F. *Norway 1940* (Collins, 1990).

KETTON-CREMER, R.W. *Norfolk in the Civil War* (Faber and Faber, 1969).

KINGSLEY, C. *Hereward the Wake, 'the last of the English'* (Macmillan, reprinted from *Good Words*, 1886), 2 vols.

KINGSLEY, F.E. (ed.) *Charles Kingsley, His Letters and Memories of his Life* (H.S. King, 1877), 2 vols.

KIRBY, J.L. *Henry IV of England* (Constable, 1970).

LABORDE, E.D. *Harrow School, Yesterday and Today* (Winchester Publications, 1948).

LAWRENCE, C.H. *Medieval Monasticism. Forms of Religious Life in Western Europe in the Middle Ages* (Longman, 1984).

LAWRENCE, T.E. *Seven Pillars of Wisdom, a triumph* (Cape, 1926, 1935 edition).

LE MARCHANT, SIR D. (ed.) *Memoir of John Charles, Viscount Althorp, third Earl Spencer* (Richard Bentley and Son, 1876).

LE NEVE, P. *Le Neve's Pedigrees of Knights* (ed. MARSHALL, G.W.) (Harleian Society, 1873), vol.8.

LILFORD, LORD *Notes on the Birds of Northamptonshire and Neighbourhood* (R.H. Porter, 1895), 2 vols.

LIPSCOMB, G. *The history and antiquities of the County of Buckinghamshire* (J. and W. Robins, 1847), 4 vols.

LLANOVER, LADY (ed.) *The Autobiography and Correspondence of Mary Granville, Mrs Delany* (Richard Bentley, 1862), vol.3.

LLOYD, D. *State Worthies, or the Statesmen and Favourites of England, from the Reformation to the Revolution* (ed. WHITWORTH, C., 1766), (J. Robson, 1665), 2 vols.

LLOYD, T. *The General Election of 1880* (Oxford University Press, Oxford, 1968).

LOCKYER, R. *Buckingham: the life and political career of George Villiers, 1st Duke of Buckingham, 1592–1628* (Longman, 1981).

LONGDEN, REVD. H.I. *Northamptonshire and Rutland Clergy from 1500* (Archer and Goodman, Northampton, 1938–43), 15 vols.

LONGMAN, W. *The History of the Life and Times of Edward the Third* (Longmans, Green, 1869), 2 vols.

LOWELL, A. LAWRENCE *Colonial Civil Service. The selection and training of colonial officials in England, Holland and France with an account of the East India College at Haileybury, 1806–1857* by STEPHENS, H.M. (Macmillan, 1900).

LUPTON, J.H. *Archbishop Wake and the Project of Union, 1717–1720, between the Gallican and Anglican Churches* (Bell, 1896).

1937–1940 (Constable, 1962).

LYSONS, D. *The Environs of London* (T. Cadell and W. Davies, 1792-6), 4 vols.

McCLURE, N.E. (ed.) *The Letters of John Chamberlain* (The American Philosophical Society, Philadelphia, 1939), 2 vols.

McCOMBE, F.W. (ed.) *Register of St. Lawrence College, 1879 to 1953* (Old Lawrentian Society, Ramsgate, fourth edition, 1955).

McKISACK, M. *The Fourteenth Century* (Clarendon Press, Oxford, 1959).

MACLEOD, R. (ed.) *The Ironside Diaries 1937–1940* (Constable, 1962).

MACNAUGHTEN, SIR M. *Sketchy Memories of Eton* (Thomas Spink and Co., Calcutta), 1904.

MADDICOTT, J.R. *Thomas of Lancaster, 1307–1322. A Study in the Reign of Edward II* (Oxford University Press, Oxford, 1970).

MALONE, E. (ed.) *The Plays and Poems of William Shakespeare* (Rivington and Sons, 1790), vol.4.

MANCHESTER, DUKE OF (ed.) *Court and Society from Elizabeth to Anne* (Hurst and Blackett, 1864), 2 vols.

MARKHAM, MAJOR C.A. *The History of the Northamptonshire and Rutland Militia: now the 3rd Battalion, Militia, of the Northamptonshire Regiment, from 1756 to 1919* (Reeves and Turner, 1924).

MARRINER, S. *Rathbones of Liverpool, 1845–1873* (Liverpool University Press, 1961).

MATHEW, D. *James I* (Eyre and Spottiswoode, 1967).

MAURICE, MAJ.-GEN. SIR J.F. and GRANT, M.H. *History of the War in South Africa, 1899–1902* (Hurst and Blackett, 1906–10), 4 vols.

MAURICE, MAJ.-GEN. SIR J.F. (ed.) *The Life of General Lord Rawlinson of Trent from his Journals and Letters* (Cassell, 1928).

MAUROIS, A. *Memoirs, 1885–1967*, translated by LINDEY, D. (The Bodley Head, 1970).

MAXWELL, SIR H. *The Life and Letters of George William Frederick, fourth Earl of Clarendon* (Edward Arnold, 1913), 2 vols.

MAYO, C.H. (ed.) *The Minute Books of the Dorset Standing Committee, 23rd. Sept. 1646 to 8th. May 1650* (William Pollard, Exeter, 1902).

MELLOWS, W.T. (ed.) *Henry of Pytchley's Book of Fees* (Northamptonshire Record Society, 1923), vol.2.

MELVILLE, C.H. *Life of General the Rt. Hon. Sir Redvers Buller* (Edward Arnold, 1923), 2 vols.

METCALFE, W.C. (ed.) *The Visitations of Northamptonshire made in 1564 and 1618–19* (Mitchell and Hughes, 1887).

MILLAR, O. *The Age of Charles I. Painting in England, 1620–1649* (Tate Gallery, 1972).

BIBLIOGRAPHY

MILLER, E. *Portrait of a College. A History of the College of St. John the Evangelist, Cambridge* (Cambridge University Press, Cambridge, 1961).

MILLS, G.H. and NIXON, R.F. *The Annals of the King's Royal Rifle Corps, 1921–1943* (Leo Cooper, 1971), vol.6.

MILLS, G.H. *The Annals of the King's Royal Rifle Corps, 1943–1965* (Celer et Audax Club, Winchester, 1979), vol.7.

MINCHIN, J.G.C. *Our Public Schools. Their influence on English history* (Swann Sonnenschein, 1901).

MINNEY, R.J. (ed.) *The Private Papers of Hore-Belisha* (Collins, 1960).

MONEYPENNY, W.F. *The Life of Benjamin Disraeli, Earl of Beaconsfield* (John Murray, 1912), vol.2.

MONTGOMERY, FIELD MARSHAL VISCOUNT *El Alamein to the River Sangro, Norway to the Baltic* (Barrie and Jenkins in association with The Arcadia Press, 1973).

MOORMAN, J.R.H. *A History of the Church in England* (A. and C. Black, 1953, third edition, 1973).

MORRAH, P. *Prince Rupert of the Rhine* (Constable, 1976).

MULLINGER, J.B. *St. John's College* (F.E. Robinson, 1901).

MURRAY, B. *The People's Budget, 1909–1910. Lloyd George and Liberal politics* (Clarendon Press, Oxford, 1980).

MYDDELTON, W.M. (ed.) *Chirk Castle Accounts, A.D.1605–1666* (Privately printed, 1908).

MYERS, E. *Lord Althorp* (Richard Bentley and Son, 1890).

NAMIER, SIR L. and BROOKE, J. *The House of Commons, 1754–1790* (HMSO, 1964), 3 vols.

NETHERCOTE, H.O. *The Pytchley Hunt, past and present* (ed. EDMONDS, C.) (Sampson, Low, Marston, Searle and Rivington, 1888).

NEWCOME, T (ed.). *The Life of John Sharp, D.D. Lord Archbishop of York* (C. and J. Rivington, 1825).

NICHOLS, J. *The Progresses, Processions, and magnificent Festivities of King James the First his royal Consort and family* (J.B. Nichols, 1828), 4 vols.

NORMAN, E. *The Victorian Christian Socialists* (Cambridge University Press, Cambridge, 1987).

NOTESTEIN, W. *Four Worthies* (Cape, 1956).

O'BYRNE, R.H. *The Representative History of Great Britain and Ireland: comprising biographical and genealogical notices of the Members of Parliament from Edward VI to Victoria, Part 1. Bedfordshire* (John Ollivier, 1848).

O'BYRNE, W.R. *A Naval Biographical Dictionary; comprising the life and services of every living Officer in Her Majesty's Navy* (1849).

O'GORMAN, F. *Voters, Patrons and Parties. The Unreformed Electoral System of Hanoverian England, 1734–1832* (Clarendon Press, Oxford, 1989).

OLDFIELD, T.H.B. *An Entire and Complete History, Political and Personal, of the Boroughs of Great Britain* (G. Riley, 1792), 3 vols.

PACKE, M. *King Edward III* (ed. SEAMAN, L.C.B.) (Routledge and Kegan Paul, 1983).

PAGE, F.G. *The Church of St. Mary the Virgin, Cottingham* (Cottingham Parochial Church Council, 1951).

PAGET, T.G.F. *The History of the Althorp and Pytchley Hunt, 1634–1920* (Collins, 1937).

PAKENHAM, T. *The Boer War* (Weidenfeld and Nicolson, 1979).

PARIS, MATTHEW *Historia Anglorum, 1189–1245* (ed. MADDEN, SIR F.), (Longmans, Green, Reader and Dyer, 1866), vol.2.

PETERSSON, R.T. *Sir Kenelm Digby, the Ornament of England, 1603–1655* (Cape, 1956).

PETTIT, P.A.J. *The Royal Forests of Northamptonshire: a study of their economy, 1558–1714* (Northamptonshire Record Society, 1968), vol.23.

PEVSNER, N. *The Buildings of England: Cornwall* (Penguin Books, Harmondsworth, Middlesex, 1951).

PEVSNER, N. *The Buildings of England: North-amptonshire* (1961, second edition, 1973).

PEVSNER, N. *The Buildings of England: Oxfordshire* (1974).

PEVSNER, N. *The Buildings of England: Shropshire* (1958).

PINE, L.G. *They Came With the Conqueror. A study of the modern descendants of the Normans* (Evans Brothers, 1954).

PLATTS, G. *Land and People in Medieval Lincolnshire* (History of Lincolnshire Committee for the Society for Lincolnshire History and Archaeology, Lincoln, 1985).

PLAYFAIR, W. *British Family Antiquity* (T. Reynolds and W. Playfair, 1809–11), 9 vols.

POLLOCK, J. *Shaftesbury. The Poor Man's Earl* (Hodder and Stoughton, 1985).

POPE, M.K. and LODGE, E.C. (eds.) *Life of the Black Prince by the Herald of Sir John Chandos* (Clarendon Press, Oxford, 1910).

PRESTWICH, M. *Cranfield. Politics Under the Early Stuarts. The Career of Lionel Cranfield, Earl of Middlesex* (Clarendon Press, Oxford, 1966).

PRICE, G. WARD *The Story of the Salonica Army* (Hodder and Stoughton, 1917).

REX, M.B. *University Representation in England, 1604–1690* (Allen and Unwin, 1954).

RICHARDSON, A.E. *An Introduction to Georgian Architecture* (Art and Technics, 1949).

RIDEN, P. and BLAIR, J. *History of Chesterfield. Records of the Borough of Chesterfield, 1204–1835* (Borough of Chesterfield, 1980), vol.5.

ROBINSON, W.C. *Antwerp. An Historical Sketch* (R. and T. Washbourne, 1904).

ROSS, C. *Richard III* (Eyre Methuen, 1981).

ROWLAND, P. *Lloyd George* (Barrie and Jenkins, 1975).

ROYAL COMMISSION ON HISTORICAL MONUMENTS (ENGLAND) *East Dorset* (HMSO, 1975), vol.5.

ROYAL COMMISSION ON HISTORIC MONUMENTS (ENGLAND) *An Inventory of Archaeological Sites in South-West Northamptonshire* (HMSO, 1982), vol.4.

RUIGH, R.A. *The Parliament of 1624: Politics and Foreign Policy* (Harvard University Press, Cambridge, Mass., 1971).

RUNCIMAN, S. *A History of the Crusades. The Kingdom of Acre and the Later Crusades* (Cambridge University Press, Cambridge, 1954), vol.3.

RUSSELL, P.E. *The English Intervention in Spain and Portugal in the Time of Edward II and Richard II* (Clarendon Press, Oxford, 1955).

SAINSBURY, W.N. *Original Unpublished Papers of Sir Peter Paul Rubens* (Bradbury and Evans, 1859).

SARGEAUNT, J. *Annals of Westminster School* (Methuen, 1898).

SCHREIBER, R.E. *The political career of Sir Robert Naunton, 1589–1635.* Studies in History Series, No.24, (Royal Historical Society, 1981).

SCOFIELD, C.L. *The Life and Reign of Edward the Fourth* (Longmans, Green, 1923), 2 vols.

SENIOR, M. *The Life and Times of Richard II* (Weidenfeld and Nicolson, 1981).

SERJEANTSON, REVD. R.M. *A History of the Hospital of St John in Northampton* (Northampton, 1913).

SHARPE, K. *Sir Robert Cotton, 1586–1631: history and politics in early modern England* (Oxford University Press, Oxford, 1979).

SHEAHAN, J.J. *History and Topography of Buckinghamshire* (Longman, Green, Longman and Roberts, 1862).

SHEILS, W.J. *The Puritans in the Diocese of Peterborough, 1558–1610* (Northamptonshire Record Society, 1979), vol.30.

SITWELL, O. (ed.) *Two Generations* (Macmillan, 1940).

SITWELL, O. *Left Hand, Right Hand!* (Macmillan, 1945).

SITWELL, SIR R. *Renishaw Hall and the Sitwells* (Privately printed, 1985).

SMILES, S. *The Story of the Life of George*

Stephenson (John Murray, 1859, 1873 edition).

SMITH, L.P. *The Life and Letters of Sir Henry Wotton* (Clarendon Press, Oxford, 1907), 2 vols.

SOLLY, G.A. *Rugby School Register. From April 1675 to October 1857* (George Over, Rugby, 1933), vol.1.

STEANE, J.M. *The Northamptonshire Landscape* (Hodder and Stoughton, 1974).

STENTON, M. *Facsimiles of Seals and Charters from Northamptonshire Collections* (Northamptonshire Record Society, 1930), vol.4.

STILLMAN, D. *English Neo-Classical Architecture* (Zwemmer, 1988), 2 vols.

STONE, L. and STONE, J.C.F. *An Open Elite? England, 1540–1880* (Clarendon Press, Oxford, 1984).

STOYE, J.W. *English Travellers Abroad, 1604–1667. Their influence in English society and politics* (Cape, 1952).

STROUD, D. *Humphry Repton* (Country Life, 1962).

SUMMERS, P (ed.). *Hatchments in Britain: Northamptonshire, Warwickshire and Worcestershire* (Phillimore, Chichester, 1974).

SUMMERSON, J. *Architecture in Britain, 1530–1830* (Penguin Books, Harmondsworth, Middlesex, 1953, 1970 edition).

SUTHERLAND, D.W. *The Eyre of Northamptonshire, 3–4 Edward III, A.D. 1329–1330* (Selden Society, 1983).

SUTTON, C.N. REVD. *Historical Notes of Withyham, Hartfield and Ashdown Forest* (A.K. Baldwin, Tunbridge Wells, 1902).

SYKES, N. *William Wake, Archbishop of Canterbury, 1657–1737* (Cambridge University Press, Cambridge, 1957), 2 vols.

THOMAS, D.A. *Crete, 1941: the battle at sea* (Deutsch, 1972).

THOMPSON, F.M.L. *Hampstead, building a borough, 1650–1964* (Routledge and Kegan Paul, 1974).

THORNE, R.G. *The History of Parliament: The House of Commons, 1790–1820* (History of Parliament Trust/Secker and Warburg, 1986), vol.5.

THORNTON, P.M. *Harrow School and Its Surroundings* (W.H. Allen, 1885).

TILBY, A. W. *The English People Overseas. Australia, 1688–1911* (Constable, 1912), vol.5.

TRENT, C. *The Russells* (Muller, 1966).

TUCKER, N.R.F. *Denbighshire Officers in the Civil War* (Colwyn Bay, 1964).

TYSON, D.B. *La Vie du Prince Noir by Chandos Herald* (Max Niemeyer Verlag, Tubingen, 1975).

VAUGHAN, R. *Matthew Paris* (Cambridge University Press, Cambridge, 1958).

VENN, J.A. *Alumni Cantabrigienses* (Cambridge University Press, Cambridge, 1922–54), 6 vols.

VICTORIA COUNTY HISTORY *Bedfordshire* (Constable, 1908), vol.2.

VICTORIA COUNTY HISTORY *Buckinghamshire* (St. Catherine Press, 1927), vol.4.

VICTORIA COUNTY HISTORY *Essex* (University of London Institute of Historical Research, 1966), vol.5.

VICTORIA COUNTY HISTORY *Middlesex. Hampstead and Paddington Parishes* (Oxford University Press, Oxford, 1989), vol.9.

VICTORIA COUNTY HISTORY *Northamptonshire* (Constable, 1902), vol.1.

VICTORIA COUNTY HISTORY *Northamptonshire* (University of London Institute of Historical Research, 1937), vol.4.

VICTORIA COUNTY HISTORY *Oxfordshire* (University of London Institute of Historical Research, 1959), vol.7.

VICTORIA COUNTY HISTORY *Shropshire* (University of London Institute of Historical Research, 1979), vol.3.

VICTORIA COUNTY HISTORY *Somerset* (University of London Institute of Historical Research, 1978), vol.4.

VULLIAMY, C.E. *Royal George. A Study of George III* (Cape, 1937).

WADDY, F.F. *A History of the Northampton General Hospital* (Guildhall Press, Northampton, 1974).

WAKE, LADY CHARLOTTE *The Beaver and the Elephant. Stories in Natural History for Children* (William Blackwood, Edinburgh, 1929).

WAKE, SIR HEREWALD *The Parting of the Ways* (William Mark, Northampton, 1894).

WAKE, SIR HEREWALD *Fiat Justitia!* (Royal Society for the Protection of Birds, Leaflet no.53, 1905).

WAKE, SIR HEREWARD and DEEDES, W.F. *Swift and Bold. The Story of the King's Royal Rifle Corps in the Second World War* (Gale and Polden, Aldershot, 1949).

WAKE, SIR ISAAC *An Essay on Friendship. Written by a Noble Gentleman, Deceased. And now Revised and Illustrated* (Printed by T. Badger for Humfrey Mosley, St. Paul's Churchyard, 1640).

WAKE, SIR ISAAC *Divine Meditations by an Honourable Person. Whereto is adjoyned a Determination of the Question, Whether Men ought to Kneele at the Receipt of the Holy Communion* (Printed by T. Badger for Humfrey Mosley, 1641).

WAKE, SIR ISAAC *A Threefold Help to Political Observations contained in three Discourses* (1655).

WAKE, JOAN *How To Compile a History and Present Day Record of Village Life* (Northamptonshire and Soke of Peterborough Federation of Women's Institutes, Northampton, 1925, third edition, 1935).

WAKE, JOAN *Northampton Vindicated, or Why the Main Line Missed the Town* (Privately printed, Northampton, 1935).

WAKE, JOAN *St. Peter…himself a Married Man* (Archer and Goodman, Northampton, 1942).

WAKE, JOAN *A Northamptonshire Rector. The Life of Henry Isham Longden, 1859–1942* (Archer and Goodman, Northampton, 1943).

WAKE, JOAN *Guide to St. Michael's Mount* (Privately printed, Northampton, 1934, third edition, 1945).

WAKE, JOAN *The Brudenells of Deene* (Cassell, 1953).

WAKE, JOAN and PANTIN, W.A. *Delapre Abbey, Northampton. Its History and Architecture* (Northamptonshire Record Society, 1959, revised edition, 1975).

WAKE, JOAN and PEYTON, S. *Memorandum of the British Record Society. Records of Board of Guardians, 1834–1934. Suggestions for the Selection of those which should be Preserved* (October 1931).

WAKE, LINA *Lord Archbishop William Wake, Archbishop of Canterbury and Family* (Privately printed, 1982).

WAKE, LUCY (ed.) *The Reminiscences of Charlotte, Lady Wake* (William Blackwood, 1909).

WAKE, WILLIAM *A Brief Enquiry into the Antiquity, Honour and Estate of the Name and Family of Wake, written 1694* (ed. BENETT, E.) (J.L. Varley, Warminster, 1833).

WEBBER, R. *The Peasants Revolt, the uprising in Kent, Essex, East Anglia and London in 1381* (T. Dalton, Lavenham, 1980).

WEBSTER, F.A.M. *Our Great Public Schools. Their traditions, customs and games* (Ward, Lock, 1937).

WEIR, Y.E. *A Guide to the Heraldry in York Minster* (Dean and Chapter of York, 1986).

WELLS, H.G. *Experiment in Autobiography* (Gollancz, 1934), 2 vols.

WHINNEY, M.D. *Sculpture in Britain, 1530–1830* (1964, revised edition, ed. PHYSIC, J. 1988, Penguin Books, Harmondsworth, Middlesex).

WHITEHOUSE, J. *A Short History of Cottingham* (St. Mary's Church, Cottingham, 1974).

WHITELOCK, D (ed.). *The Anglo-Saxon Chronicle. A Revised Translation* (Eyre and Spottiswoode, 1961).

WILKINSON, J. *Worsborough: its Historical Associations and Rural Attractions* (T. Lingard, Barnsley, 1879).

WILLIS, B. *A history of the mitred parliamentary Abbies and Conventual Cathedral Churches* (1718–19), 2 vols.

WILSON, T. *The Myriad Faces of War. Britain and the Great War, 1914-1918* Polity Press, Cambridge, 1986).

WINSTANLEY, D.A. *Unreformed Cambridge. A Study of Certain Aspects of the University in the Eighteenth Century* (Cambridge University Press, Cambridge, 1935).

WINTERS, W. *The History of the Ancient Parish of Waltham Abbey or Holy Cross* (W. Winters, Waltham Abbey, 1888).

WOOD, A. *Athenae Oxonienses. An exact history of all the Writers and Bishops who have had their education at the most ancient and famous University of Oxford from 1500 to 1690* (Thomas Bennet, 1691–2), 2 vols.

WOOD, M. *The English Medieval House* (Phoenix House, 1965).

WOODWARD, D.R. *Lloyd George and the Generals* (Associated University Presses, London and Toronto, 1983).

WOOLLCOMBE, R. *The First Tank Battle: Cambrai, 1917* (Arthur Baker, 1967).

WORKMAN, H.B. *John Wyclif, A Study of the English Medieval Church* (Clarendon Press, Oxford, 1926), 2 vols.

WRIGHT, T. *The History and Topography of the County of Essex* (G. Virtue, 1835–6), 2 vols.

WRIGHT, T. *Essays on subjects connected with literature, popular superstitions and history of England in the Middle Ages* (John Russell Smith, 1846), 2 vols.

YONGE, C.M. *Cameos From English History 1. From Rollo to Edward II* (Macmillan, 1868, second edition, 1869).

ZIMMERMANN, FATHER B. *Carmel in England: A History of the English Mission of the Discalced Carmelites, 1615 to 1849* (Burns and Oates, 1899).

C. ARTICLES

ADCOCK, A. 'Notes on the George Hotel, Northampton', *Journal of the Northamptonshire Natural History Society and Field Club*, vol.20, 1919.

ANON 'Tudor Panels from Waltham', *Country Life*, 17 July 1909.

BARBER, R. 'Jean Froissart and Edward the Black Prince', in PALMER, J.J.N. (ed.) *Froissart: Historian*, Boydell Press: Rowman and Littlefield, 1981.

BARKER, G.F.R. 'John Howard', *Dictionary of National Biography*, vol.28, 1891.

BARRETT-LENNARD, T. 'Some Account of the Manor or Castle of Horsford', *Norfolk Archaeology*, vol.15, 1904.

BASCOMBE, K.N. 'Sir Anthony Denny' and 'Sir Edward Denny, Earl of Norwich', in DEAN, D. *The Worthies of Waltham* – Part 2, Waltham Abbey Historical Society, 1978.

BOULGER, G.S. 'Robert Uvedale', *Dictionary of National Biography*, vol.58, 1899.

BROOKE, C. 'Miss Joan Wake', *Northamptonshire Past and Present*, vol.5, no.3, 1975.

CLERKE, A.M. 'Thomas Catton', *Dictionary of National Biography*, vol.9, 1887.

COLDHAM, J.D. 'Early Northamptonshire Cricket', *Northamptonshire Past and Present*, vol.2, no.3, 1956.

COLLINGWOOD, R.G. 'Liddel Strength', *Transactions of the Cumberland and Westmorland Antiquarian Society*, vol.26, 1926.

COURTNEY, W.P. 'Sir John St Aubyn', *Dictionary of National Biography*, vol.50, 1897.

CURWEN, J.F. 'Liddel Mote', *Transactions of the Cumberland and Westmorland Antiquarian Society*, vol.10, 1910.

EADY, R. 'The Published Works of Joan Wake', *Northamptonshire Past and Present*, vol.5, no.3, 1975.

ELTON, SIR A.H. 'Clevedon Court', *Proceedings of the Somersetshire Archaeological and Natural History Society*, vol. 27, 1881.

ELWES, D. REVD. 'Sir Herewald Wake, Bart.', *Journal of the Northamptonshire Natural History Society and Field Club*, vol.18, 1916.

EVANS, J. 'The Wilton Diptych Reconsidered', *Archaeological Journal*, vol. 105, 1950.

GAIRDNER, J. 'William Catesby', *Dictionary of National Biography*, vol.9, 1887.

GALWAY, M. 'Joan of Kent and the Order of the Garter', *University of Birmingham Historical Journal*, vol.1, 1947.

GOMME, A. 'William and David Hiorn', in BROWN, R. (ed.) *The Architectural Outsiders*, Waterstone, 1985.

GORDON, P. '"A County Parliament": The First Northamptonshire County Council', *Northamptonshire Past and Present*, vol.7, no.3, 1985–86.

GREEN, E. 'The Descent of the Manor of Clevedon', *Proceedings of the Somersetshire Archaeological and Natural History Society*, vol.27, 1881.

HARBIN, S.W.B. 'Members of Parliament for the County of Somerset', *Proceedings of the Somersetshire Archaeological and Natural History Society*, 1939.

HASKELL, F. 'Venetian Sixteenth-Century Painting – The Legacy', in MARTINEAU, J. and HOPE, C. (eds.) *The Genius of Venice, 1500–1600*, Royal Academy of Arts/Weidenfeld and Nicolson, 1983.

HATLEY, V.A. 'Northampton Revindicated. More Light on Why the Main Line Missed the Town', *Northamptonshire Past and Present*, vol.2, no.6, 1959.

HATLEY, V.A. 'Philip Cox', *Northamptonshire Past and Present*, vol.6, no.6, 1982–83.

HATLEY, V.A. 'The Headless Trunk: A Study in Northamptonshire Politics, 1795–6', *Northamptonshire Past and Present*, vol.8, no.2, 1990–1.

HOLTHOUSE, E.H. 'A Northamptonshire Record Society', *Northamptonshire Notes and Queries*, vol.2, 1886–7.

HOWARTH, D. 'Charles I and the Gonzaga Collections', in CHAMBERS, D. and MARTINEAU, J. (eds.) *Splendours of the Gonzaga*, Victoria and Albert Museum, 1981.

HUGGINS, P.J. 'Waltham Abbey Monastic site and prehistoric evidence, 1953–1967', with documentary survey by K.N. Bascombe, *Transactions of the Essex Archaeological Society*, vol.2, 1970.

HUTCHISON, S.C. 'The Royal Academy Schools 1768–1830', *Walpole Society* vol.38, 1962.

ISHAM, SIR G. 'Joan Wake', *Northamptonshire Past and Present*, vol.5, no.3, 1975.

JAMES, R.R. 'Berwick Almshouses: Will of Sir Samuel Jones, Knight, Founder 1673', *Transactions of the Shropshire Archaeological and Natural History Society*, vol.8, 4th series, 1921.

KADISH, A. 'Scholarly Exclusiveness and the Foundation of the *English Historical Review*', *Historical Research*, vol.61, no.145, 1988.

KENNEDY, P.A. 'A Gentleman's Home in the Reign of Henry VII', *Northamptonshire Past and Present*, vol.2, no.1, 1954.

KENYON, R.L.L. 'Manor of Sandford and Woolston', *Transactions of the Shropshire Archaeological and Natural History Society*, vol.4, 3rd series, 1904.

KING, E. 'The Origins of the Wake Family: The Early History of the Barony of Bourne in Lincolnshire', *Northamptonshire Past and Present*, vol.5, no.3, 1975.

KING, P.I. 'Dr. Joan Wake', *Journal of the Society of Archivists*, vol.5, no.2, 1974.

KING, P.I. 'Joan Wake', *Northamptonshire Past and Present*, vol.5, no.3, 1975.

KITSON, S.D. 'Carr of York', *Journal of the Royal Institute of British Architects*, vol.17, 3rd. series, 29 January 1910.

KRIEHN, G. 'Studies in the Social Revolt in 1381', *American Historical Review*, vol.7, 1901–2.

LEONARD, E.M. 'The Inclosure of Common Fields in the Seventeenth Century', *Transactions of the Royal Historical Society*, New Series, vol.19, 1905.

LEWIS, S.M. 'A Family of Stone-Carvers: the Coxes of Northamptonshire', *Northamptonshire Past and Present*, vol.6, 1953.

MAJOR, K. 'Joan Wake', *Archives*, vol.12, no.53, 1975.

MAJOR, K. 'Canon Charles Wilmer Foster: A

Pioneer Archivist and Editor of Records', *Archives*, vol.18, no.77, 1987.

MALINS, E. 'Humphry Repton at Stoneleigh Abbey, Warwickshire', *Garden History*, vol.5, no.1, 1977.

MARLOW, N. 'The Coming of Railways to Northamptonshire', *Northamptonshire Past and Present*, vol.3, no.5, 1964.

MONCREIFFE, SIR I. 'Hereward the Wake', *The Genealogists' Magazine*, vol.15, no.10, 1967.

MUSTY, A.E.S. 'Exploratory Excavation within the Monastic Precinct, Waltham Abbey, 1972', with a documentary Survey by K.N. Bascombe, *Essex Archaeology and History*, vol.10, 1978.

OSWALD, A. 'Courteenhall', *Country Life*, 12 and 19 August 1939.

OSWALD, A. 'Clevedon Court, Somerset – 1', *Country Life*, 30 June 1955.

OWEN EVANS, H.F. 'Blisworth, Northamptonshire', *Transactions of the Monumental Brass Society*, vol.9, no.9, 1961.

PALMER, C.J. 'Remarks on the Monastery of the Dominican Friars at Great Yarmouth', *Norfolk Archaeology*, vol.3, 1852.

PRINCE, A.E. 'A Letter of Edward the Black Prince describing the Battle of Nájera in 1367', *English Historical Review*, vol.41, 1926.

RIGG, J.M. 'Sir Robert Drury', *Dictionary of National Biography*, vol.16, 1888.

SERJEANTSON, REVD. R.M. 'The Castle of Northampton', *Journal of the Northamptonshire Natural History Society and Field Club*, vol.14, 1907.

SHERBORNE, J.W. 'The Battle of La Rochelle and the War at Sea, 1372–5', *Bulletin of the Institute of Historical Research*, vol.42, 1969.

SHORTHOUSE, R.W. 'Justices of the Peace in Northamptonshire, 1830–1845', Part 1, *Northamptonshire Past and Present*, vol.5, no.2, 1974.

SITWELL, S. 'English Pictures at Renishaw', *Country Life*, 29 October 1938.

SLADDEN, D.M. 'Fiftieth Anniversary Celebrations', *Northamptonshire Past and Present*, vol.4, no.6, 1971.

STENTON, D.M. 'Frank Merry Stenton, 1880–1967', *Proceedings of the British Academy*, vol.54, 1968.

SUTHERLAND, C.H.V. 'The Coin Collection of Christ Church, Oxford. A Chapter in the History of Numismatics', *Oxoniensia*, vol.5, 1940.

SYKES, N. 'Archbishop Wake and the Whig Party, 1716–23', *Cambridge Historical Journal*, vol.8, no.2, 1945.

TATE, W.E. 'Inclosure Movements in Northamptonshire', *Northamptonshire Past and Present*, vol.1, no.2, 1949.

TOUT, T.F. 'Hereward', *Dictionary of National Biography*, vol.26, 1891.

TOUT, T.F. 'Thomas Wake', *Dictionary of National Biography*, vol.58, 1899.

TREHARNE, R.F. 'The Battle of Northampton, 5th April 1264', *Northamptonshire Past and Present*, vol.2, no.2, 1955.

TUCKER, T.G. 'Memories of Pitsford a Hundred Years Ago', *Northamptonshire Past and Present*, vol.6, no.1, 1978.

WAKE, SIR HEREWALD 'The Entomology of Northamptonshire, with list of Northamptonshire Butterflies', *Journal of the Northamptonshire Natural History Society and Field Club*, vol.1, 1880.

WAKE, SIR HEREWALD 'On the Wing', *Journal of the Northamptonshire Natural History Society and Field Club*, vol.10, 1898–1900.

WAKE, SIR HEREWALD 'Courteenhall School', *Journal of the Northamptonshire Natural History Society and Field Club*, vol.10, 1898-1900.

WAKE, SIR HEREWARD 13th Baronet 'Rooks and Farming', *Northampton Independent*, 30 April 1943.

WAKE, SIR HEREWARD 13th Baronet 'Meals I Shall Always Remember',

Wheeler's Review, Jan-March 1956.

WAKE, SIR HEREWARD 14th Baronet 'A Short Account of the Founding of St. Andrew's Hospital, Northampton', *Northamptonshire Past and Present*, vol.7, no.2, 1984–5.

WAKE, JOAN 'Collaboration in Historical Research', *Library Association Record*, vol.24, no.8, 1922.

WAKE, JOAN 'Local Sources of History', *Bulletin of the Institute of Historical Research*, vol.1, 1924.

WAKE, JOAN 'Thomas Bell, Schoolmaster and Poet', *Northampton County Magazine*, vol.3, October 1930.

WAKE, JOAN 'Manorial Records', Proceedings no.2, *British Records Association*, 1937.

WAKE, JOAN 'Country Portrait Gallery', *Country Life*, 13 August 1942.

WAKE, JOAN 'A Rhodesian Settler's Home', *Country Life*, 21 November 1947.

WAKE, JOAN 'Links with the United States', *Northamptonshire Past and Present*, vol.1, no.1, 1948.

WAKE, JOAN 'Two Justices Fall Out', *Northamptonshire Past and Present*, vol.1, no.5, 1952.

WAKE, JOAN 'The Early Days of the Northamptonshire Natural History Society', *Northamptonshire Past and Present*, vol.1, no.5, 1952.

WAKE, JOAN 'Mr. Frank Lee', *Northamptonshire Past and Present*, vol.2, no.2, 1955.

WAKE, JOAN 'William Thomas Brownlow Cecil, Fifth Marquess of Exeter, 1876–1956', *Northamptonshire Past and Present*, vol.2, no.3, 1956.

WAKE, JOAN 'Traveller's Tale', *Northamptonshire Past and Present*, vol.2, no.4, 1957.

WAKE, JOAN 'Northamptonshire Records', *Speculum*, vol.33, no.2, 1958.

WAKE, JOAN 'Hope Emily Allen', *Northamptonshire Past and Present*, vol.3, no.1, 1960.

WAKE, JOAN 'Cromwell's Head', *Northamptonshire Past and Present*, vol.3, no.1, 1960.

WAKE, JOAN 'The Justices of the Peace, 1361–1961', *Northamptonshire Past and Present*, vol.3, no.2, 1961.

WAKE, JOAN 'Lady Etheldreda Wickham', *Northamptonshire Past and Present*, vol.3, no.2, 1961.

WAKE, JOAN 'Major-General Sir Hereward Wake', *Northamptonshire Past and Present*, vol.3, no.4, 1963.

WAKE, JOAN 'Charles Darby Linnell', *Northamptonshire Past and Present*, vol.3, no.5, 1964.

WAKE, JOAN 'Northamptonshire in Southern Rhodesia', *Northamptonshire Past and Present*, vol.3, no.5, 1964.

WAKE, JOAN 'Professor Sir Frank Stenton: Some Recollections', *Northamptonshire Past and Present*, vol.4, no.3, 1968–9.

WAKE, JOAN 'Ladies' Cricket Match at Courteenhall, 23 July 1883', *Northamptonshire Past and Present*, vol.4, no.4, 1969–70.

WAKE, JOAN 'Mrs. George Brudenell', *Northamptonshire Past and Present*, vol.5, no.1, 1973.

WARWICK, L. '"I'm expecting a Celestial Postcard." A tribute to Joan Wake', *Northampton Independent*, March 1974.

WILLIAMS, N. 'The Risings in Norfolk, 1569 and 1570', *Norfolk Archaeology*, vol.32, 1961.

WORSLEY, G. 'Carr at Courteenhall', *Country Life*, 30 October 1986.

'W.R.W.' 'John Wilde or Wylde', *Dictionary of National Biography*. vol.61, 1900.

'W.W.' *Middlesex and Hertfordshire Notes and Queries*, vol.4, 1898.

List of Illustrations

COLOURED

BLACK AND WHITE

LIST OF ILLUSTRATIONS

LINE DRAWINGS AND MAPS

APPENDIX B

LIST OF ILLUSTRATIONS

ILLUSTRATION CREDITS

Whilst Northamptonshire Libraries and Information Service and the author have made every effort to acknowledge the source of the illustrations they apologise for any omissions. The author also gratefully acknowledges the following individuals and institutions for the use of their material:

Aerofilms Ltd 156; Archbishop of Canterbury and the Trustees of Lambeth Palace Library 41; The Master and Fellows of Balliol College, Oxford 8; British Architectural Library 50, 53, 54; British Library CP1, LD6; British Museum 7, LD1; Cecil Higgins Art Gallery, Bedford 42; The Governing Body of Christ Church, Oxford CP17; Courtauld Institute Galleries CP16; The Master and Fellows of Corpus Christi College, Cambridge 5; Cumberland and Westmorland Antiquarian Society 3; Domesday County Folios published by Alecto Historical Editions LD5; Lady Elton 20, 21; Epping Forest District Museum 30, 31; George Freeston 59; Dr K.R. Green, from the book *A Brief History of Haltemprice Priory* by A.H. Stamp, published by Cottingham Local History Society 4; Hertford Museum 32; Imperial War Museum 103-109, 114, 118-120; Trustees of Lamport Hall 135; The Mother Superior, Lanherne Convent, Mawgan 34; Mary Evans Picture Library 13-15, 35; National Army Museum 92, CP33; National Gallery CP13; National Portrait Gallery 45; Northamptonshire Libraries and Information Service 9, 36, 50, 52, 60, LD3, LD4, LD9, LD10, and Estate Maps; Northamptonshire Record Office LD2, LD6; Northamptonshire Record Society 136, 138, 159, CP46; *Punch* 71; Redundant Churches Fund 37; John Roan Photography Frontispiece, 24, 161; Royal Collection, St. James's Palace © Her Majesty The Queen CP14; Royal Commission on Historic Monuments of England 1, 17, 18, 23, 32, 33, 46, 133, 137; The Master and Fellows of St. John's College, Cambridge 43; The Dean and Chapter of Westminster Abbey CP5; The Dean and Chapter of York Minster CP2. The remainder of the illustrations are from the personal collection of Sir Hereward Wake, 14th baronet.

The right to reproduce the illustrations in this book, rests either with the owners of the collections listed above, the photographers or organisations for whom photographic work was originally taken.

Index

INDEX

INDEX

INDEX

INDEX

INDEX

INDEX

INDEX

INDEX

INDEX